International Finance

A practical perspective

ADRIAN BUCKLEY

Cranfield School of Management, Cranfield University

PEARSON

Harlow, England • London • New York • Boston • San Francisco • Toronto • Sydney
Auckland • Singapore • Hong Kong • Tokyo • Seoul • Taipei • New Delhi
Cape Town • São Paulo • Mexico City • Madrid • Amsterdam • Munich • Paris • Milan

Pearson Education Limited
Edinburgh Gate
Harlow
Essex CM20 2JE
England

and Associated Companies throughout the world

Visit us on the World Wide Web at:
www.pearson.com/uk

First published 2012

ISBN 978-0-273-73186-3

British Library Cataloguing-in-Publication Data
A catalogue record for this book is available from the British Library

Library of Congress Cataloging-in-Publication Data
Buckley, Adrian.
International finance : a practical perspective / Adrian Buckley.
p. cm.
Includes bibliographical references and index.
ISBN 978-0-273-73186-3 (pbk.)
1. International finance. I. Title.
HG3881.B83 2012
332′.042--dc23

2011040033

10 9 8 7 6 5 4 3 2 1
15 14 13 12

Typeset in 9.5/12.5pt ITC Charter by 35
Printed by Ashford Colour Press Ltd., Gosport

Brief contents

Contents

Supporting resources

Visit **www.pearsoned.co.uk/buckley** to find valuable online resources:

Companion Website for students

- Multiple choice questions to help test your understanding
- A mock exam to put your learning into practice
- Additional chapters and extended topics
- An online glossary to explain key terms
- Flashcards to help you prepare for exams

For instructors

- Complete, downloadable Instructor's Manual
- PowerPoint slides that can be downloaded and used for presentations
- Testbank of practice questions

Also: The Companion Website provides the following features:

- Search tool to help locate specific items of content
- E-mail results and profile tools to send results of quizzes to instructors
- Online help and support to assist with website usage and troubleshooting

For more information please contact your local Pearson Education sales representative or visit **www.pearsoned.co.uk/buckley**

Guided tour

to the CDS. In relation to the financial crisis, if the problem created by
ed 10, that created by credit default swaps and related **toxic assets** just
a rating of 100 or more. In most newspaper articles and radio and te
ies at the time of the financial collapse the central cause of the problem
subprime mortgage market. The CDS was barely mentioned. It seeme
How and why can this be so? Perhaps the commentators at the time fo
to understand. And even if they did understand it, they couldn't expla
ught that the public would find the CDS too complicated. Or, maybe t
s – Buckley.[1] Naturally, your author gives the CDS its rightful position
history of the financial crisis of 2007–8.

Key terms
These are colour-highlighted the first time they are introduced, alerting you to the core concepts in each chapter. A full explanation is contained in the glossary at the end of the book.

Example 3 The exporter in the two previous examples now decides to convert the payment in country Y's currency to his own. He does this through his own clearing bank. Here the bank buys the foreign currency and sells the home currency in exchange. Now the bank in country X has acquired country Y's currency. The bank now has a short-term claim on foreigners. All that happened is that the short-term claim on foreigners has been shuffled from one resident of country X, the exporter, to another, the clearing bank. From a balance of payments standpoint, no entry needs to be made.

Example 4 The clearing bank decides to sell the foreign currency acquired in the previous example to country X's central bank in exchange for home currency. Assume that country Y's currency is freely convertible in the foreign exchange markets. When the central bank acquires gold or freely convertible foreign currency, it increases the official reserves. So in this case the balance of payments entry is:

Dr Official reserves of foreign currency
Cr Short-term claims on foreigners (the amount in Y's currency)

Examples
These examples give you step-by-step workings to follow through to the solution, providing an application of the learning points and techniques included within the topics.

PRESS CUTTING 18.1

Don't blame luck when your models misfire FT

By John Kay

When the financial crisis broke in August 2007, David Viniar, chief financial officer of Goldman Sachs, famously commented that 25 standard deviation events had occurred on several successive days. If you marked your position to market every day for a million years, there would still be a less than one in a million chance of experiencing a 25-standard deviation event. None had occurred. What had happened was that the models Goldman used to manage risk failed to describe the world in which it operated.

If the water in your glass turns to wine, you should consider more prosaic explanations before announcing a miracle. If your coin comes up heads 10 times in a row – a one in a thousand probability – it may be your lucky day. But the more likely reason is that the coin is biased, or the person who flips the penny or reports the result is cheating. The source of most extreme outcomes is not the fulfilment of possible but improbable predictions within models, but events that are outside the scope of these models.

Sixty years ago, a French economist described the Allais paradox, based on the discovery that most people treat very high probabilities quite differently from certainties. Not only do normal people think this way, but they are right to do so. There are no 99 per cent probabilities in the real world. Very high and very low probabilities are artifices of models, and the probability

Yet the use of risk models of this type is one of many areas of finance in which nothing much has changed. The European Union is ploughing ahead with its Solvency II directive for insurers, which – incredibly – is explicitly modelled on the failed Basel II agreements for monitoring bank solvency. Solvency II requires that businesses develop models that show the probability of imminent collapse is below 0.5 per cent.

Insurance companies do fail, but not for the reasons described in such models. They fail because of events that were unanticipated or ignored, such as the long-hidden danger from asbestos exposure, or the House of Lords judgment on Equitable Life. They fail because underwriters misunderstood the risk characteristics of their policies, as at AIG, or because of fraud, as at Equity Fundings.

Multiple sigma outcomes do not happen in real life. When all the Merchant of Venice's ships are lost at sea during the interval, we know that we are watching a play, not an account of history. Shakespeare, no fool, knew that too. In Act V Antonio was able to write back his loss provisions in full even if it was too late to fulfil his banking covenant to Shylock.

But today the modellers are in charge, not the poets. Like practitioners of alchemy and quack medicine, these modellers thrive on our desire to believe impossible things. But the search for objective means of con-

Press cuttings
These topical extracts feature real company examples from the press, including commentary that highlights the practical application of finance in the business environment.

Summary of key points
Each chapter ends with a 'bullet point' summary. This highlights the material covered in the chapter and can be used as a quick reminder of the main issues.

Summary

- Transaction exposure is concerned with how changes in exchange rates affect the home currency value of anticipated foreign-currency-denominated cash flows relating to transactions that have already been entered into.
- Empirically, over long periods, the forward rate is an unbiased predictor of the future spot rate. Hence, failing to take cover but running with the spot rate should yield similar returns – in the long run. However, failing to cover may have disastrous short-term results. Avoiding these potential pitfalls by selective covering is therefore claimed by corporate treasurers to be a logical strategy.
- Economic exposure relates to the possibility that the present value of future cash flows of a firm may change due to foreign currency movements. However, exchange rate changes are related, via purchasing power parity, to differences in relative inflation rates. The firm whose operations experience cost inflation exactly in line with general inflation may be returned to its original position by changes in exchange rate exactly in line with purchasing power parity. In these circumstances, economic exposure may be argued not to matter.
- Most firms, of course, experience specific cost inflations which differ from general inflation. In this situation, which is the most common one, economic exposure does matter.
- One approach to minimising this kind of exposure is to finance an appropriate part of the firm's operations in the currency to which the firm's value is sensitive.
- Translation exposure arises as a result of the process of consolidation of foreign-currency-denominated items into group financial statements denominated in the currency of the parent company. Whether it matters is entirely an empirical question.

End of chapter questions
These short questions encourage you to review and/or critically discuss your understanding of the main topics covered in each chapter.

End of chapter questions

3.1 All other things being equal, assume that US interest rates fall relative to UK interest rates. Again, with all other things being equal, how should this affect the:

(a) US demand for British pounds;
(b) supply of pounds for sale; and
(c) equilibrium value of the pound?

3.2 What is the expected relationship between the relative real interest rates of two countries and the exchange rate of their currencies?

3.3 Some Latin American currencies have depreciated against the US dollar on a daily basis. What is the major factor that places such a severe downward pressure on the value of these currencies? What obvious change in Latin American economic policy would prevent the regular depreciation of these currencies?

Test banks featuring exercises and multiple choice questions
These comprehensive examination-style questions appear at the end of selected chapters in the book. They are designed to assess your knowledge and application of the principles and techniques covered in the chapters. Suggested answers and solutions for selected exercises can be found at the end of the book.

Test bank 1

Exercises

Foreign exchange problems

In these problems assume that all interest rates quoted are per annum rates. Calculate 90 day rates by taking one quarter of the annual rate. Also assume that, where only one rate is quoted, rather than a bid/offer rate, deals may be done at this rate whether they are purchase or sale deals, lend or borrow deals. This is, of course, a simplifying assumption. Also disregard any transaction costs; for substantial deals these are generally taken care of in the bid/offer spread. Take one month as one-twelfth of a year, two months as one sixth, and so on.

1 The spot rate for the Swiss franc (CHF) in New York is USD0.55.

(a) What should the spot price for the US dollar to the Swiss franc be in Zurich?
(b) Should the dollar be quoted at CHF1.85 in Zurich, how would the market react?

2 When the Swiss franc spot rate was quoted at USD0.55 in New York, the US market was quoting sterling at USD1.60.

(a) What should the price of the pound to the Swiss franc be in Zurich?
(b) If sterling were quoted at CHF2.80 to the pound sterling in Zurich, what profit opportunities would exist?

Preface

This book describes the theory and practice of international finance. The increasing internationalisation of business has made the study of multinational finance increasingly important.

Forty years ago the majority of financial executives did not have to appreciate what impelled exchange rates to move, what were the opportunities to raise money outside of the domestic market, what influenced the evaluation of overseas capital investment projects, and so on. Some borrowed in Swiss francs because the interest cost was low. Some failed to cover Deutschmark payables as sterling declined precipitously. Some failed to realise the opportunities created by the demise of exchange controls. And some failed to appreciate the benefits that accrue from currency options.

There are few wide-ranging European texts on international finance. This book is intended to improve practice in this most important area of business.

Readership

This book is aimed primarily at students on courses in international finance, multinational finance or financial aspects of international business. They may be at undergraduate levels or pursuing postgraduate studies at MBA level or on masters courses in finance. This book is also structured to meet the needs of aspiring accountants, bankers and treasurers. The emphasis on a student market is not to say that the book is inappropriate for the business-person who needs to know about finance in the international arena. The intention is that it should be relevant to the requirements of financial managers who want to study this special area of finance as well as to non-financial managers who need to know about international money and its implications. My intention is essentially practical. It is that this book should improve awareness, understanding and performance in this important area of finance.

Reading and learning features are facilitated by the inclusion of questions at the end of all chapters (except Chapter 1) and end-of-part test banks comprising exercises and multiple-choice questions. Suggested answers to the end-of-chapter questions and to a selection of the exercises and all multiple-choice questions are given at the end of the text allowing for self-assessment. Each chapter ends with an extensive summary, signposted with bullet points to ease the revision of key aspects by students. Press cuttings are included and these are meant to add an element of real world exemplification to the text. These are valuable for reading and discussion as they draw from eminent journalists and commentators.

A separately published *Instructor's Manual* includes teaching notes, case study suggestions, visual aid masters, and suggested answers to the exercises not given in the text.

Adrian Buckley

Acknowledgements

I am most grateful to Liz Tribe who, again, coped with my handwriting and cheerfully wove it into the coherent whole that you see before you. Liz's ability to take my piecemeal offerings and create the text is to be applauded. Errors must be debited to my account though.

Thanks are also due to Kate Brewin and Katie Rowland, my editors at Pearson, for encouraging the production of this text and making sure that I almost met deadlines.

Publisher's acknowledgements

We are grateful to the following for permission to reproduce copyright material:

Figures

Press Cutting Figure 6.1 'Renminbl 2009–2011' published in "Renminbi: 'Redback' puts the brakes on", *The Financial Times*, 29/03/2011 (Noble, J.). Reproduced by permission of Thomson Reuters Datastream; Press Cutting Figure 6.2 'Foreign Exchange Reserves', 'Change in foreign exchange reserves', 'Currency changes', and 'Renminbi' published in "Why China hates loving the dollar", *The Financial Times*, 25/01/2011 (Wolf, M.). Reproduced with permission of Thomson Reuters Datastream, IMF, OECD and JP Morgan; Press Cutting Figure 6.3 'Yen' as published in "G7 nations in $25bn yen sell-off", *The Financial Times*, 19/03/2011 (Garnham, P. and Oakley, D.). Reproduced with permission of Thomson Reuters Datastream, Nikkei, FTSE, S&P; Press Cutting Figure 6.4 'Reactor crisis rocks the Nikkei' published in "Investors wrestle with meltdown risk", *The Financial Times*, 18/03/2011 (Mackintosh, J,), copyright © Bloomberg LP; Press Cutting Figure 6.5 'Yen' published in "The G7 Samurai", *The Financial Times*, 18/03/2011, copyright © Bloomberg LP; Press Cutting Figure 13.1 'Airlines' fuel hedging' as published in "Hostess to Fortune", *The Financial Times*, 26/02/2011, copyright © Morgan Stanley & Co. International plc; Press Cutting Figure 15.1 'Fall of the $' as published in "Retailers produce some fancy moves to cover their exposure", *The Financial Times*, 12/04/2005 (Johnson, S.). Reproduced with permission of Thomson Reuters Datastream and Morgan Stanley; Figure 19.1 'Household Indebtedness' published in "The Financial Crisis: Reform and Exit Strategies", 2009. Reproduced with permission of Thomson Reuters Datastream and OECD; Figure 19.4 'The Financial Crisis: Reform and Exit Strategies', copyright © OECD, 2009; Press Cutting Figure 19.5 'Government bond yields', 'Government debt', 'Government debt', and 'Primary balance' published in "The eurozone's journey to defaults", *The Financial Times*, 10/05/2011 (Wolf, M.). Reproduced with permission of Thomson Reuters Datastream and IMF; Press Cutting Figure 19.8 "Credit default swap prices climb despite fears that restructuring may not trigger pay-outs" published in "Greek debt talks cast doubt over sovereign CDS", *The Financial Times*, 18/05/2011 (Oakley, D. and Alloway, T.), original data copyright © Depository Trust & Clearing Corporation, 2011. Reproduced with permission of Thomson Reuters Datastream, Markit and DTCC;

Figure 24.1 "Myths and realities of the global capital market: lessons for financial managers", *Journal of Applied Corporate Finance*, Vol 6 (3), pp. 81–90 (Jacque, L. and Hawawini, G., 1993), copyright © 1993, John Wiley and Sons; Press Cutting Figure 26.1 'Orthopaedic market shares, 2010' as published in "Deal could be cure for Johnson & Johnson", *The Financial Times*, 18/04/2011 (Rappeport, A.), copyright © Bloomberg LP; and 'Synthes' as published in "Publicity-shy guiding light", *The Financial Times*, 19/04/2011 (Simonian, H.). Reproduced with permission of Thomson Reuters Datastream and DTCC; Figure 30.1 "Currency changes and management control: resolving the centralization/decentralization dilemma", *The Accounting Review*, Vol LII, pp. 628–637 (Lessard, D.R. and Lorange, P., 1977), copyright © American Accounting Association.

Tables

Tables 24.2, 24.3 from *Triumph of the Optimists*, Princeton University Press (Dimson, E., Marsh, P. and Staunton, M., 2002), copyright © 2002 Elroy Dimson, Paul Marsh and Mike Staunton. Reprinted by permission of Princeton University Press; Appendix 6 'List of countries and codes' extracted from: *BS ISO 4217:2008 Codes for the representation of currencies and funds*, copyright © British Standards Institution (BSI – www.bsigroup.com). Reproduced with permission.

Text

Extracts in chapter 2 from IMF, 1977, 1978, copyright © IMF; Extract in chapter 24 from *Triumph of the Optimists*, Princeton University Press (Dimson, E. Marsh, P. and Staunton, M., 2002), copyright © 2002 Elroy Dimson, Paul Marsh and Mike Staunton. Reprinted by permission of Princeton University Press.

The Financial Times

Press Cutting 6.1 "'Redback' puts the brakes on", *The Financial Times*, 28/03/2011 (Noble, J.), copyright © The Financial Times Ltd; Press Cutting 6.2 "Why China hates loving the dollar", *The Financial Times*, 25/01/2011 (Wolf, M.), copyright © The Financial Times Ltd; Press Cutting 6.3 "G7 nations in $25bn yen sell-off", *The Financial Times*, 19/03/2011 (Garnham, P. and Oakley, D.), copyright © The Financial Times Ltd; Press Cutting 6.4 "Investors wrestle with meltdown risk", *The Financial Times*, 18/03/2011 (Mackintosh, J.), copyright © The Financial Times Ltd; Press Cutting 6.5 "The G7 Samurai", *The Financial Times*, 18/03/2011, copyright © The Financial Times Ltd; Press Cutting 6.6 "A redeeming argument for the carry trade", *The Financial Times*, 29/01/2011 (Authers, J.), copyright © The Financial Times Ltd; Press Cutting 13.1 "Hostess to Fortune", *The Financial Times*, 26/02/2011, copyright © The Financial Times Ltd; Press Cutting 15.1 "Retailers produce some fancy moves to cover their exposure", *The Financial Times*, 12/04/2005 (Johnson, S.); "Groups suffer a rude awakening", *The Financial Times*, 12/04/2005 (Johnson, S.); and "How Sterling's strength goes against the dollar revenues from ticket sales", *The Financial Times*, 12/04/2005 (Johnson, S.), copyright © The Financial Times Ltd; Press Cutting 18.1 "Don't blame luck when your models misfire", *The Financial Times*, 01/03/2011 (Kay, J.), copyright © The Financial Times Ltd; Press Cutting 18.2 "Tailgaters blight the markets as well as the motorways", *The Financial Times*, 20/01/2010 (Kay, J.), copyright © The

Financial Times Ltd; Press Cutting 19.1 "Valukas report finds few heroes", *The Financial Times*, 12/03/2010 (Baer, J.), copyright © The Financial Times Ltd; Press Cutting 19.2 "Accounting: Fooled again", *The Financial Times*, 19/03/2010 (Hughes, J.), copyright © The Financial Times Ltd; Press Cutting 19.3 "Overpaid CEO award", *The Financial Times*, 22/12/2008, copyright © The Financial Times Ltd; Press Cutting 19.4 "Fantasy causes for credit crisis touted", *The Financial Times*, 29/11/2009 (Triana, P.), copyright © The Financial Times Ltd; Press Cutting 19.5 "The eurozone's journey to defaults", *The Financial Times*, 10/05/2011 (Wolf, M.), copyright © The Financial Times Ltd; Press Cutting 19.6 "Eurozone reprofiling", *The Financial Times*, 18/05/2011, copyright © The Financial Times Ltd; Press Cutting 19.7 "Row within Europe over Greece", *The Financial Times* (Atkins, R., Peel, Q. and Hope, K.), copyright © The Financial Times Ltd; Press Cutting 19.8 "Greek debt talks cast doubt over sovereign CDS", *The Financial Times*, 18/05/2011 (Oakley, D. and Alloway, T.), copyright © The Financial Times Ltd; Press Cutting 19.9 "IMF tells Greece to speed up reforms", *The Financial Times*, 18/05/2011 (Hope, K.), copyright © The Financial Times Ltd; Press Cutting 19.10 "Europe to issue €5bn bail-out bond", *The Financial Times*, 19/05/2011 (Oakley, D.), copyright © The Financial Times Ltd; Press Cutting 19.11 "Watch out for tail risks hanging over Treasuries", *The Financial Times*, 19/05/2011 (Tett G.), copyright © The Financial Times Ltd; Press Cutting 20.1 "Choose the correct path for a viable deal", *The Financial Times*, 25/01/2007 (Politi, J.), copyright © The Financial Times Ltd; Press Cutting 26.1 "Synthes confirms discussions with J&J", *The Financial Times*, 18/04/2011 (Simonian H.); "Deal could be cure for Johnson & Johnson", *The Financial Times*, 18/04/2011 (Rappeport, A.); and "J&J deal to dispel speculation on Synthes", *The Financial Times*, 18/04/2011 (Simonian, H.), copyright © The Financial Times Ltd; Press Cutting 26.2 "J&J/Synthes", *The Financial Times, Lex*, 19/04/2011, copyright © The Financial Times Ltd; Press Cutting 26.3 "J&J to buy Synthes for $21.3bn", *The Financial Times*, 27/04/2011 (Simonian, H.), copyright © The Financial Times Ltd; Extracts in Test Bank 2 from "Dispirited Heineken sounds alarm", *The Financial Times*, 11/03/2004 (Bickerton, I.); "Pound sucks profits from babies' bottles", *The Financial Times*, 11/03/2004 (Marsh, P.); "Engineer has learnt to juggle currencies", *The Financial Times*, 11/03/2004 (Brown-Humes, C.); "Specialist lines help insulate German sales", *The Financial Times*, 11/03/2004 (Marsh, P.); "Luxottica stays cool amid earnings drop", *The Financial Times*, 11/03/2004 (Kapner, F.); and "Euro Exchange rate" in 'Europe's exporters get the greenback blues' *The Financial Times*, 11/03/2004 (Marsh, P., Major, T. and Althaus, S.), copyright © The Financial Times Ltd.

In some instances we have been unable to trace the owners of copyright material, and we would appreciate any information that would enable us to do so.

Part A

ESSENTIAL BACKGROUND

With any topic, there are certain key facts that set the scene and are essential to an understanding of a subject. This is as true of international finance as it is of any other subject. In this first section we present some of these key facts about the international monetary system and its institutions.

1 Introduction

Financial management traditionally focuses upon three key decisions – the acquisition of funds, their investment and the payment of dividends. The former is termed the financing decision and it is concerned with obtaining funds, either internally or externally, at the lowest cost possible. The second key area of finance is the investment decision, which is concerned with the allocation of funds to opportunities in order to earn the greatest value for the firm. The third is concerned with whether dividend decisions affect the value of the firm and, if so, how. The study of financial management is built upon the hypothesis that judicious financing, investment and dividend decisions positively affect the present value of shareholder wealth.

Most writers on financial management arrive at their theories by way of a process of deductive reasoning. They then look at data from empirical tests of these hypotheses and from this base build an armoury of rules and recommendations which help us to analyse opportunities and choose the course of action which maximises shareholder value.

Domestic financial management is concerned with the costs of financing sources and the payoffs from investment and dividend decisions. In the domestic arena, movements in exchange rates are substantially ignored. But when we move outside this purely domestic field, we can only analyse international financing and investment opportunities with an understanding of the impact of **foreign exchange** rates upon the basic model of financial management. We are still concerned with raising funds at minimum cost, but there are clearly complications of analysis if, for example, a UK-based company is raising funds by way of a Swiss franc borrowing. There are equally complications in assessing shareholder value creation when, for example, a UK-based company's investments arise from the United States in dollars? Or from Mexico in pesos? And what if exchange controls place barriers on remittances of some proportion of profit?

Obviously, international finance possesses dimensions that make it far more complicated than domestic financial management. We make no bones about it – multinational finance is a complex area of study. It has been sired by the internationalisation of business. If money is the language of business, foreign exchange is the language of international business. We are concerned in this book with foreign exchange markets throughout the world and with the pressures that impel exchange rates to move upwards and downwards. In addition to evaluating theories of exchange rate movements, international finance is concerned with the risks that flow from holding assets and liabilities denominated in foreign currency. Clearly, the home currency value of such assets and liabilities changes as exchange rates move. Exposure to these changes creates foreign exchange risk. We are concerned not only with defining and classifying foreign exchange risk but also with reporting, managing and controlling this risk. But multinational finance is not only about foreign exchange exposure, it also embraces political risk: that is, the exposure which a firm takes on when it enters into business operations located overseas. Again, a practical orientation towards the study of international finance suggests that we should focus upon managing and controlling this exposure. A systematic study of finance in the international arena requires that we consider the funding of international trade, the evaluation of cross-frontier investment decisions and the financing of overseas associate and subsidiary companies as well as understanding international financial markets, the impact of tax regimes in different countries and the ways in which exchange controls affect multinational businesses. These topics are the subject matter of this book.

International financial management is so riddled with complications that there is a critical need to put the subject over simply. One of the motivations for writing this book is that most other texts which devote themselves to international money fail to present a clear picture to their readers. And if they do clear this hurdle they are invariably excessively wordy. There are also a good many texts on multinational finance which approach the subject at a high level of abstraction and with an emphasis upon mathematics that could easily be daunting to even the best of students.

Given this background, the intention of your author is that this text should be oriented towards the requirements of students who need to understand the theory and practice of international finance. A certain amount of mathematics is necessary but the intention has been to keep it to a minimum.

The author's assumption is that the readership will be drawn not only from students but also from businesspeople. Among student readers, it is anticipated that some will be aspiring accountants, bankers and treasurers, some will be business studies undergraduates, some may be majoring in multinational business and international finance, and some will be postgraduates on MSc courses as well as on MBA programmes. It is considered that this text should also appeal to businesspeople drawn from the ranks of treasurers, accountants, bankers and corporate planners who require a coherent presentation of the theory and practice of international finance. However, inasmuch as there is an increasing need for non-financial managers – line managers and members of a company's top-level decision coalition – to understand finance in the international arena, it is intended that this text should meet their needs too.

It is assumed by the author that readers have a basic knowledge of financial management. This would probably embrace such topics as sources of corporate finance, the investment, financing and dividend decision and the efficient markets hypothesis – but such knowledge is not necessarily expected to be at a high level of competence. The line manager with a general manager's understanding of finance should not be disadvantaged as he or she explores most of the topics in this text. Summarised, it is presumed that readers are familiar with the following foundation stones of corporate finance:

- The central hypothesis of corporate financial theory is that the value of the firm (V) is a function of the investment decision (I), the financing decision (F), the dividend decision (D) and the management of corporate resources (M). In other words:

$$V = f(I, F, D, M)$$

- The financing decision is concerned with the obtaining of funds by the corporation; the investment decision is all about the application of resources so obtained and the management of resources (*M*, above) is all about the efficiency of running the corporate entity. The dividend decision concerns flows of monies back to shareholders and, so the hypothesis goes, since equity investors obtain their remuneration via dividend, then enhanced dividend flows may affect shareholder value. So much for the theory, what about the empirical evidence?

- Empirically, the evidence suggests that shareholder value is affected by the investment decision, the financing decision and the management of resources. Evidence is inconclusive on dividends.
- The investment decision affects shareholder value. Relatively high net present value (NPV) projects create relatively high shareholder value.
- Relatively high NPV projects are generally underpinned by market imperfections (for example, barriers to entry, patent protection, product differentiation and so on). A project in perfect competition circumstances should earn a normal profit which, when discounted, should give rise to a zero NPV.
- Over time, the benefits accruing to a project usually erode as the market imperfections themselves are eroded.
- The successful business gives birth to new products and creates gains from the market imperfection created. It regenerates old products by seeking new market imperfections.
- Executives in the successful business try to transfer market imperfections from the home market to overseas markets.
- The financing decision affects shareholder value. The suggestion is that there is an optimum **capital structure**. Moving towards it creates value for shareholders. Moving beyond it may be destructive of value.

Given the target audience of this book, the mathematics has deliberately been kept at a reasonably unsophisticated level. The author's desire is very much to present a complex subject in the style of a good communicator. And this means that mathematics is our servant, not our god.

It is the intention that this book should be adopted by instructors for class use in teaching international and multinational finance, business and management studies and, also, international business. Having studied the content of this book, the reader should be able:

- to appreciate the historic background and existing institutional framework of international money;
- to understand the history and adoption of the single currency, the **euro**, by various European countries;
- to understand the workings and methods of quotation in the foreign exchange markets;
- to understand the theoretical relationship between spot and forward exchange rates, interest differentials, expected inflation differentials and expectations of future spot rates, and know how well they stand up in the real world;
- to understand the essence of theories for predicting future exchange rates;
- to understand how to use purchasing power **parity** data to forecast the future exchange rate;
- to estimate implied future exchange rates via the international **Fisher effect**;

- to define and distinguish different types of foreign exchange risk and recommend appropriate management action given the existence of these different kinds of exposure;
- to design an information system relevant to a multinational company's need to control, cost-effectively, foreign exchange exposure;
- to appreciate the opportunities which the multinational has to control foreign exchange exposure internally – that is, without the need to enter into contracts with third parties;
- to understand the essence of eliminating foreign exchange risk via forward markets, financial futures and currency options;
- to assess the international capital investment decision in a manner consistent with the parent company's desire to maximise the wealth of its shareholders;
- to obtain a general idea of the mode of working, opportunities and pitfalls created by exchange control regulations in countries in which the multinational corporation operates;
- to understand the sources and nature of country risk and political risk for the international company and, moreover, recommend appropriate management action to mitigate their impact in different circumstances;
- to appreciate the problems in financing an overseas subsidiary and make recommendations on the most appropriate financial structure given different sets of circumstances;
- to measure and compare the true cost of borrowing in the international financial arena;
- to appreciate how **currency swaps** work and how market imperfections create opportunities in these directions for the astute corporate treasurer;
- to understand how corporate tax rules in many countries create opportunities and pitfalls for international financing and cross-frontier operations;
- to understand the opportunities available to finance international trade and minimise **credit risk**;
- to understand how and, more importantly, where market imperfections create profitable opportunities for the astute international financial manager.

It is as well for the reader to remember that analysis of international financial and investment opportunities with a view to maximising shareholder wealth for the multinational investor involves searching out market imperfections and temporary disequilibria. And these are usually far more plentiful in the international arena than in its domestic counterpart. Clearly, avoidance of those that are potentially adverse and exploitation of those from which profitable outturns seem likely is the recommended course of action.

In the remainder of this chapter we describe a few key facts that are pertinent to the study of finance in the international arena. They have been set out here because students of the subject repeatedly find themselves asking about these topics. It will therefore be as well for readers to bear them in mind as they peruse the text. The topics briefly considered here are the products that banks market and how banks are categorised and make money. There follows a look at a range of facts about the size of and participants in the foreign exchange markets and this is followed by a summary.

The reader should be aware that we may denote currencies with their normal abbreviations ($ or €) or their **SWIFT** codes (USD or EUR). We do this deliberately to get students used to these two approaches. A list of world currencies with their SWIFT codes appears in Appendix 6. (Knowing these stands you in good stead for quizzes!) Where we merely use the term dollars or the sign $, it refers to US dollars. For other dollars, like Australian dollars or New Zealand dollars, we tend to use their SWIFT codes, for example AUD and NZD, respectively.

1.1 What do bankers sell?

Banks play a key role in financial management, whether in the domestic or in the international market place. Too often students of finance accept that banks occupy this vital position without asking themselves what kind of services bankers actually sell.

Most firms have a clearly visible product, for example, Ford produces cars and GlaxoSmithKline produces pharmaceuticals. Banks basically produce money in the form of demand and time deposits. Demand deposits are those where the investor places money with the bank but the money is repayable to the investor without notice – that is, on demand. This contrasts with time deposits where the investor places money with the bank but the money is only repayable (except with penalty) after the expiration of a fixed time. Most time deposits involve the bank in paying interest to the investor; some demand deposits also attract interest, but some do not. The receipts from these deposits provide the wherewithal to make loans and buy securities and other assets that yield an interest income for the bank. Banks have numerous activities from which they receive fee income. They advise companies, manage trusts and so on. But the bread and butter activity of banking involves trading in demand and time deposits and loans.

Banks deal with two groups of customers – depositors and borrowers. Most borrowers are also depositors; some depositors are also borrowers. Business firms tend to be predominantly borrowers. Households tend to be primarily depositors. Banks are intermediaries between the depositors, who want a safe, secure and convenient place to store some of their wealth, and the borrowers, who want to expand their current production or consumption more rapidly than they can on the basis of their existing wealth and current income. The spread or mark-up between the interest rates bankers charge borrowers as against the cost of borrowing covers their expenses and is the source of their profits.

1.2 Banks in general

A bank is a financial institution licensed by a government to undertake the borrowing and lending of money as its main activity. The level of government regulation of the banking industry varies widely from country to country. In the United States and the United Kingdom, regulation is relatively light. Regulation is heavier (in terms of stricter rules on the level of reserves – the relationship between deposits, capital and lending) in, for example, China.

The term *bank* derives from the Italian word *banco* meaning 'desk' or 'bench'. The word can be traced back to the ancient Roman Empire. Moneylenders would set up their stalls in courtyards called *marcella* on a long bench called a *bancu* – hence the word banco.

However, money-changing activities are depicted on coins from the fourth century BC from Trapezus on the Black Sea, nowadays Trabzon. The banker's table is called trapeze, a clear reference to the name of the city. And, in Modern Greek, the word *trapeza* means both a table and a bank.

Under English law, a banker is defined as a person who carries on the business of banking, which is specified as:

- conducting current accounts for customers;
- paying cheques drawn on him; and
- collecting cheques for customers.

To reiterate, in most jurisdictions, banks are regulated by government and require a special bank licence to operate.

Banks borrow money by accepting funds placed in current and deposit accounts. Such deposits may be demand deposits (repayable on demand) or term deposits (repayable at a specified time in the future). Banks lend money by making advances to customers, either **short term** or **long term**.

Assume that bankers reckon, on the basis of past experience, that only 10 per cent of its deposits will actually be withdrawn at any time. Then the bank may prudently lend up to 90 per cent of its deposits. As it receives more deposits, more loans are possible on a similar basis. Originally, most deposits with the banker were short-term deposits. If the banker were to lend such funds for exactly similar short terms, risk would be minimised and profit would reside in charging more for loans than paying on deposits. Often, deposits on current account have attracted zero interest.

Assume that deposits from personal customers on current accounts are repayable on demand. Also, assume that the bank lends longer term to businesses to finance longer term requirements, for example to finance working capital. In these circumstances, the bank runs a risk due to the maturity mismatch of the deposit versus the loan. In fact, mismatching of maturities like this is the essence of banking. Banks usually earn more on their longer-term lending than they pay for shorter-term deposits. This strategy is clearly dependent upon depositors not being unhappy about the mismatch. In other words, confidence in the bank, its gap between maturities and the quality of the bank's lending is of utmost importance. Without confidence, depositors' worries about maturity mismatching and the quality of the bank's loan portfolio would lead them to ask for their money back – largely demand deposits, remember. The role of confidence is the critical cornerstone of the business of banking.

Traditionally, banks generate profits from the difference between the level of interest they pay for deposits and other sources of funds and the level of interest they charge for lending. This difference is referred to as the spread between the cost of funds and the loan interest rate. Profitability from lending activities is spiky and dependent upon the susceptibility of loan customers to the business cycle. Aware of this, banks have sought more stable revenue streams and they have placed increasing emphasis on loan fees and service charges for ancillary work (international banking, foreign exchange, insurance, investments, financial advice and so on) and fees for arranging loans. However, lending activities do still provide the backbone of a commercial bank's income.

Banks are always exposed to various forms of risk. These include liquidity risk (where depositors request withdrawals in excess of available funds), credit risk (the probability that those who owe money to the bank will not repay), and interest rate risk (the chance that the bank will become unprofitable as interest rates alter, for example, if rising interest rates force it to pay more on its deposits than it receives on its loans). The actual occurrence of risks may trigger systemic crises, where a large part of the banking system is at risk because many banks become susceptible to a particular risk occurrence.

Banks' activities may be divided into:

- retail banking, dealing directly with individuals and small businesses;
- business banking, providing services to middle size businesses;
- corporate banking, directed at large business entities;
- private banking, providing wealth management services to high net worth individuals and families; and
- **investment banking**, relating to activities in the financial markets.

Most banks are profit-making, private enterprises. In some countries they are owned by governments and may be non-profit organisations. **Central banks** are normally government-owned and given regulatory responsibilities, such as supervising commercial banks and/or controlling interest rates. They often have custody of their country's gold and foreign exchange reserves and may, as directed by their central government, intervene in foreign exchange markets by buying or selling the home currency or the away currency, with the objective of strengthening or weakening the home currency.

We now look at the breakdown of banks into commercial banks, investment banks and central banks in more detail.

1.3 Commercial banks

Given the earlier list of bank's activities, **commercial banking** covers retail banking, business banking and corporate banking. The latter two kinds of category are sometimes clubbed together and termed wholesale banking.

After the Great Depression, US law required that banks engage either in commercial banking activities or in investment banking which was limited to capital market activities – we refer further to investment banking immediately below. This regulation was enacted in the Glass-Steagall Acts. Nowadays, and since the final repeal of Glass-Steagall in 1999, the restriction is not part of the legal requirements in the USA. Other developed countries did not implement a Glass-Steagall type law and did not maintain this separation of commercial and investment banking. Nonetheless, the terms commercial banking and investment banking – as well as wholesale banking and retail banking – are still widely used.

1.4 Investment banks

Top bankers are at the summit of the elite. In his poem, 'Don Juan', Byron observed that Rothschild and Baring 'are the true lords of Europe'. In Philip Auger's excellent overview of investment banking,[1] he recalls a retirement party for an investment banker in which the retiree describes it as 'the best business in the world'. And John Kay[2] observes that 'if you want to understand how the City came to play such a central role in British economic and political life . . . you need to understand . . . the influence of investment banks on modern politics and policy'. So what is their business?

Investment banks are financial institutions that deal with raising capital for clients, brokering and trading in securities – on their own behalf or on behalf of clients – and advising on corporate mergers and acquisitions. Investment banks make their profit from companies and governments by raising money through issuing and selling securities in the equity market and bond markets, buying and selling financial instruments, as well as earning fees from advising on corporate finance transactions, such as mergers and acquisitions, share buybacks and flotations of companies on capital markets. Most investment banks also offer advisory services on divestments, reorganisations and other corporate finance services relating to foreign exchange, commodities and **derivatives**. In most countries, performance of these duties are licensed and regulated.

The final repeal of the Glass-Steagall Act in 1999 was a fillip to the investment banking business. Glass-Steagall is briefly referred to later in this chapter. Suffice it to say here that the Act's provisions, instituted in the Great Depression, had restricted commercial banks from **leveraging** in investment banking activities.

But there were other drivers of investment bank growth in the 1990s. Information technology was a major factor. Banks had developed significant proprietary computer systems allowing each bank to act as a global information network. Flows of money, as well as information, around the system were now accelerated. The effect was to increase short-term information asymmetry in the investment bank's favour. As IT intensified and banks and exchanges became computerised, there was a move away from face-to-face relationships – not completely so, of course. Decision-making in markets became more model-based – but, again, hardly completely so.

Another driving force favouring the recent rise of investment banks was the wave of privatisations racing across the world. Each privatisation was managed by a team of investment banks. From zero in 1980, the total number of privatisations grew globally to 675 which had generated USD700 **billion**. And the 18 biggest initial public offerings (IPOs) had all been state-owned businesses privatised through IPOs. The effect was that many near-dormant stock markets were transformed becoming bigger and more liquid. Investment bankers and their shareholders were gainers too.

Also driving growth was the expansion in foreign exchange (**FX**) markets. This is discussed further in this chapter in section 1.14.

Finally, the emergence, on a massive scale, of derivative markets was another driver of investment banking growth. The market in derivatives grew over a century ago out of farmers using futures markets to secure prices in advance of marketing their produce. Of course, derivatives are now much more complex and the market is worth around 10 times world GDP. These figures are startling. The value of the financial economy is bigger, much bigger than the value of the world economy on which it is based. This has really emerged over the last 20 years.

Derivatives can be used to eliminate risk by taking on a position in the derivative market which is the opposite of the risk to be hedged. Or, they can be used to speculate by entering into a derivatives position without an underlying risk exposure. So the derivative can be used to hedge risk or to create risk. So, do derivatives make the finance system safer? Or, do they make it riskier? In this latter respect, Warren Buffet described derivatives as 'financial weapons of mass destruction, carrying dangers that are potentially lethal'. We will look at this issue as we study international finance in this book.

One of the main activities of investment banks is buying and selling investment products, whether on their own account or for clients. Because they do buy and sell for their own bank's account, this part of operations has, pejoratively, been termed their casino business.

In their activities, investment banks talk about the front office, middle office and back office. The distinctions in these parts of the business are now described.

The front office is concerned with:

- Services for corporate or government clients in the raising of funds in the capital markets and advising on mergers and acquisitions.
- Investment management of clients' securities (for example, shares, bonds and real estate). Such clients may be institutions (insurance companies, pension funds) or private investors.
- Corporate finance work.
- Foreign exchange, equity and fixed interest, commodities and derivatives trading and brokering.
- **Merchant banking** work, which is an old term for investment banking but also embraces international trade work for clients.
- Research involving the valuation of equities or other corporate investments.

Under the last bullet point, there is a clear conflict of interest within the bank because corporate finance work for clients invariably involves inside information. The relationship between the research arm and the rest of the investment bank has become highly regulated requiring a Chinese wall between these functions.

Turning to the middle office, this is concerned with:

- Risk management embracing the analysis and control of market and credit risk that traders in the bank are taking in conducting their daily deals. This involves setting limits on the amount of capital that traders are able to deal and monitoring them.
- Finance which, in this context, refers to the bank's capital management and risk monitoring. This embraces the bank's overall global risk exposure and profitability. The importance of this role cannot be overemphasised. It is complicated and demanding.
- Compliance, which is concerned with the bank's daily operations and the personal investment activities of bank personnel to ensure that they accord with government regulations, market rules and internal regulations.

Moving to the back office, this is concerned with:

- Operations involving checking trades that have been conducted and ensuring that they are accurate and involve the required paperwork. Trades have to be within written bank rules, limits and with approved counterparties. In times of buoyancy, backlogs can become massive.
- Internal audit of operations including those described immediately above.
- Technology. All banks have vast amounts of in-house software and technical support and this role cannot be underestimated.

It is not difficult to guess that the back office has been massively overwhelmed by the growth referred to earlier. Moreover, in the hierarchy of the investment bank, the front office is regarded as the location of the star performers – the elite in the banks. We have been told of conversations in which back office personnel query front office deals and the dealer fobs off the enquiry with the observation that 'yes, everything's alright. It's not a problem. The deal is exactly as stated there. Don't worry. The paperwork is fine and in line with the deal done.' End of conversation. So much for this brief overview.

1.5 Bank holding companies

The term bank **holding company** is applied to those banks which mix commercial and investment banking. In situations where banks only engage in investment banking, they are said to be part of the shadow banking system – see later in this chapter.

1.6 Glass-Steagall Act

Two separate United States laws are known as the Glass-Steagall Act. The first was passed in 1932 and the second in 1933. In the Great Depression, Congress examined the mixing of commercial banks and investment banks that had occurred in the twenties. Hearings revealed conflicts of interest – and even fraud in some banking institutions' securities activities. Barriers to the mixing of these activities were established by the Glass-Steagall Act. This influence has been felt elsewhere around the globe – for example, China separates the activities of commercial banks from the securities industries. The earlier McFadden Act of 1927 had prevented commercial banks' activities from expanding across state boundaries, designed to limit a bank's geographic representation in the USA.

In tandem with successful lobbying to repeal the McFadden Act, achieved via the Riegle-Neal Interstate Banking and Branching Efficiency Act of 1994, the banking industry also sought the phasing out of the Glass-Steagall Act. In 1987, a report was tabled before Congress which explored the pros and cons of the case. In fact, in 1987, The Federal Reserve altered the Glass-Steagall rules, allowing commercial banks to undertake investment banking activities up to 5 per cent of their turnover. This dilution of the Act continued until, in 1996, it reached 25 per cent.

Just before the Act was finally repealed, the USD85 billion merger of Travelers, an insurance company which also owned investment bank Salomon Brothers, and Citicorp was approved in 1998. This created Citigroup, the biggest financial company in the world. The US Treasury Secretary, Robert Rubin, had waived the rules in advance of Glass-Steagall being repealed. Rubin, himself, became Co-CEO of Citigroup in October 1999. Ultimately, after continued bank lobbying, the Act was repealed under the Gramm-Leach-Bliley Act of 1999. The repeal enabled commercial banks to underwrite and trade financial instruments and various derivatives.

1.7 Central banks

The central bank, (sometimes called the Reserve Bank or Monetary Authority) is the body responsible for the monetary policy of a country or of a group of countries or states. Responsibilities vary but usually embrace:

- implementation of monetary policy;
- control of the nation's money supply;
- duties as the government's banker and the bankers' bank (leader of last resort – see later in this chapter);

- managing the country's foreign exchange and gold reserves and the government's bond register;
- regulating and supervising the banking industry;
- setting the official interest rate (with implications for managing both inflation and the country's exchange rate).

Nowadays, many countries have an independent central bank, designed to limit political interference. Examples include the **European Central Bank (ECB)**, and the Bank of England. In these countries (although they are termed independent) central banks are publicly owned. In other countries they may be privately owned. Indeed, although formed in 1694 as a chartered joint stock company, the Bank of England was only taken into public ownership in 1946. In fact, **nationalisation** merely formalised a state of affairs that had existed for years and involved no change in the way the Bank operated.

All banks are required to hold a certain percentage of their assets as capital, a rate established by the central bank or other banking supervisor. For international banks the requirement is 8 per cent of risk-adjusted assets (some assets, such as government bonds are considered to have lower risk than others for purposes of calculating capital adequacy – hence the risk-adjusted process).

In terms of regulating banks, central banks usually establish reserve requirements for other banks. For example, they may require that a percentage of liabilities be held as cash or deposited with the central bank. Such reserve requirements were introduced in the nineteenth century to reduce the risk of banks overextending themselves and suffering bank runs, which could lead to knock-on effects on other banks.

In Britain, UK banking supervision is carried out by the UK Treasury, the Bank of England, a Financial Policy Committee and a Prudential Regulatory Authority (to be renamed). Control and monitoring is achieved by examination of the banks' ongoing balance sheets and their behaviour and policies in the market place.

1.8 Asset-liability mismatch

An asset-liability **mismatch** occurs when the financial terms of the assets and liabilities do not correspond. Asset-liability mismatches may occur in various ways. A bank may have substantial long-term assets, such as long-term loans to business customers, but short-term liabilities, such as demand deposits. This creates a maturity mismatch. Also, a bank could have all of its liabilities at floating interest rates but its assets in fixed rate instruments. Another example is where a bank borrows entirely in US dollars and lends in euros, creating a currency mismatch. If the value of the euro were to fall dramatically, the bank would lose out. Asset-liability mismatches like this may be controlled by **hedging** activities.

Controlled maturity mismatch, with average short-term deposits being less than average longer-term loans and with average higher interest rates accruing in the bank's favour, is of essence to the business model of commercial banks.

Asset-liability mismatches may also occur in insurance and pensions management, where long-term liabilities (promises to pay the insured or pension plan participants) may not exactly correspond to the maturity and value of assets. Appropriately **matching** financial assets and obligations is very important in these businesses.

Business investment on plant, property and equipment generally gives rise to cash generation over a number of future years and this cash flow is usually insufficient to provide loan repayment over merely one year. So, when businesses need to borrow to finance their investments, they prefer loans with a long maturity. By contrast, individual savers, mainly households and small firms may have somewhat unpredictable needs for cash, due to unforeseen expenditures. Consequently, they prefer liquid accounts which permit them immediate access to their deposits, namely short maturity deposit accounts. With this background, banks provide a valuable service by channelling funds from many individual depositors to corporate borrowers. Since banks provide a service to both sides, providing the long-maturity loans to businesses and liquid accounts to depositors, they are in a position to earn profit from such activities.

Under ordinary circumstances, savers' unpredictable needs for cash are unlikely to occur at the same time. In accepting demand deposits from many different sources, the bank expects only a small fraction of withdrawals in the short term, even though depositors have the right to take their deposits back at any time. Thus a bank can make loans over a long horizon, while keeping only relatively small amounts of cash on hand to pay depositors that wish to make withdrawals. Given that individuals' expenditure needs tend to be uncorrelated, banks may expect relatively few major withdrawals on any single day. We now turn to various institutions of international finance.

1.9 Offshore money a.k.a. Eurodollars

The traditional definition of a **Eurodollar** is a dollar deposited in a bank outside the United States. A Euro-yen is a yen deposited in a bank outside Japan. A Eurosterling deposit is created by depositing UK pounds in a bank account outside the United Kingdom. The term '**Eurocurrency**' is used to embrace all forms of Eurodeposits. A certain amount of care needs to be exercised when interpreting information in this field because the term 'Eurodollars' is sometimes used as a generic term for all Eurocurrency deposits. In this book we will use the term offshore dollars to prevent confusion with the euro which is the currency of certain countries within Europe.

In the domestic economy, the capacity of banks to expand their deposits is limited by the monetary authorities. They determine both the reserve base of the banking system (the supply of high-powered money) and reserve requirements. But in the offshore currency market there are no reserve requirements.

The absence of reserve requirements on offshore deposits does not mean that there is the potential for an infinite expansion of deposits and credit. The growth of offshore deposits is limited by the willingness of investors to acquire such deposits in competition with domestic deposits. For investors, the relevant comparison involves the risk and return on offshore deposits and the risk and return on domestic deposits.

Dollar deposits in London differ from New York dollar deposits in terms of political risk. They are subject to the actions of a different set of government authorities. Maybe investors who continue to hold dollars in New York believe that London dollars are too risky, and that the additional interest income is not justified in terms of the possible loss if a move of funds back to New York were somehow restricted, perhaps as a package of exchange controls or an attack on the offshore banking system. The continued growth in external deposits has reflected increasing investor confidence that the additional risks attached to external deposits were small. The risks of holding dollars offshore seemed small, particularly when viewed in the light of the differential in dollar interest rates on offshore deposits relative to domestic deposits.

Depositors contemplating a move of their funds to the offshore currency markets must decide whether to acquire external deposits in London, Zurich, Paris or some other centre. Depositors choose among centres on the basis of their estimates of political risk. This rules out many potential centres where regulation or the threat of regulation is evident. Even though there may be an interest rate that would induce lenders to acquire dollar deposits in Sofia, banks issuing these deposits would not necessarily have the investment opportunities to justify paying such high interest rates. We now turn to some of the institutions of international finance.

1.10 International Monetary Fund (IMF)

The **IMF** was formally set up in July 1944 during the United Nations Monetary and Financial Conference. The representatives of 45 governments met in **Bretton Woods**, New Hampshire, USA, with delegates agreeing on a framework for international economic cooperation. The IMF's influence in the global economy has increased as it has obtained more members.

When created, the IMF's objective was to stabilise exchange rates and assist in the reconstruction of the global payments system. Countries contributed to a pool which was available for borrowing from, on a temporary basis, by countries with payment imbalances. As of 2007, the IMF described itself as an organisation of 185 countries working to foster global monetary co-operation, to secure financial stability, to facilitate international trade, to promote high employment and sustainable economic growth and to reduce poverty. Most IMF member countries are represented by other member states on a twenty-four-member Executive Board but all member countries belong to the IMF's Board of Governors. It offers financial and technical assistance to its members, effectively making itself an international lender of last resort. Its headquarters are located in the USA in Washington DC. Although termed a fund, the IMF is really a bank, whilst the World Bank – see below – is a fund.

1.11 World Bank

The World Bank is an international financial institution that provides financial and technical assistance to developing countries (for example, by inputs to large projects like roads, bridges, ports and schools) with the stated goal of reducing poverty. Its main operating company is the International Bank for Reconstruction and Development (IBRD), a non-profit organisation. The IBRD began operations in 1945 and was initially concerned with the reconstruction of war-devastated Europe. Nowadays, it is chiefly concerned with helping less developed countries in advancing their economies. It makes loans for up to 20 years at rates slightly below commercial interest rate levels with repayment guaranteed by the government of the borrowing country. Most loans are for specific projects in the areas of agriculture, energy and transport. The IBRD obtains its funds from members – the same countries that are members of the IMF – as well as through issuance of international bonds where its high credit rating enables it to raise funds at favourable rates.

There are other institutions that are under the World Bank umbrella. The International Finance Corporation (IFC) was set up in 1956 as an investment bank to provide risk capital, without government guarantee, to private sector enterprises in LDCs, as well as having the goal of encouraging loans from other sources. Second, there is the International Development Association (IDA) set up in 1960 as the soft loan arm of the World Bank. It provides some interest-free loans for up to 50 years to the poorest developing countries and some low interest rate loans and grants to low-income countries with little or no access to capital markets. The IDA's resources come from grants from the richest members of the World Bank, with the US usually subscribing some 25 per cent of funds. The IDA is funded primarily by periodic 'replenishments' (grants) voted to the institution by its more affluent member countries.

The current focus of the World Bank is upon lending primarily to middle-income countries at interest rates which reflect a small mark-up over its own (AAA-rated) borrowing rate from capital markets.

The Bank also distributes grants for the facilitation of development projects through the encouragement of innovation, cooperation between organisations and the participation of local stakeholders in projects. The IDA grants are predominantly used for:

- debt burden relief in the most indebted and poverty stricken countries;
- improvement of sanitation and water supply;
- support of vaccination and immunisation programmes for the reduction of diseases such as malaria;
- combating the HIV/AIDS pandemic;
- creating initiatives for the reduction of greenhouse gases;
- helping maintain rainforests and the people living there.

1.12 Bank for International Settlements

The Bank for International Settlements (BIS) is an organisation of central banks which fosters international money and financial cooperation and serves as a bank for central banks. It is not accountable to any national government and carries out its work through subcommittees, secretariats and through meetings of its members. It also provides banking services, but only to central banks, or to similar international organisations to itself. Based in Basel, Switzerland, the BIS was established in 1930. The BIS provides a valuable service in terms of establishing capital adequacy rules on equity and debt for banks.

1.13 World Trade Organization

The **World Trade Organization** (WTO) is an international organisation designed to supervise and liberalise international trade. It came into being in 1995 as the successor to the General Agreement on Tariffs and Trade (GATT), which was created in 1947.

The World Trade Organization deals with the rules of trade between unions at an almost global level. It is responsible for negotiating and implementing new trade agreements, and is in charge of policing member countries' adherence to WTO agreements, signed by the majority of the world's trading nations and ratified in their parliaments.

The WTO has 153 members, which represents more than 96 per cent of total world trade. It is governed by a Ministerial Conference, which meets every two years. The WTO implements the conference's policy decisions and is responsible for day-to-day administration. It is headquartered in Geneva, Switzerland.

Central to WTO is its rules framework for trade policies. Five principles are of paramount importance in understanding both WTO and GATT strategy. These are:

- **Non-discrimination**. This has two major components – namely, the most favoured nation (MFN) rule, and the national treatment policy. Both are key to WTO rules on goods, services, and intellectual property. The MFN rule requires that a WTO member must apply the same conditions on all trade with other WTO members. This means that a WTO member has to grant the most favourable conditions under which it allows trade in a certain product type to all other WTO members. The second component, national treatment, means that imported and locally-produced goods should be treated equally, at least after the foreign goods have entered the market. It was introduced to tackle non-tariff barriers to trade (such as technical standards, security standards and discrimination against imported goods).
- **Reciprocity**. This follows the MFN rule and is designed to ensure that fairness in international trade prevails.
- **Binding and enforceable commitments**. Tariff conditions of a multilateral trade negotiation are enumerated in a list of concessions. These schedules establish 'ceiling bindings'. A country may change its bindings, but only after negotiating with its trading partners, which could mean compensating them for any loss of trade. If satisfaction is not obtained, the complaining country may appeal to the WTO dispute settlement procedures.
- **Transparency**. WTO members are required to publish their trade regulations, to maintain institutions allowing for the review of administrative decisions affecting trade, to respond to requests for information by other members, and to notify changes in trade policies to the WTO. These requirements are supplemented by periodic country-specific reports through the Trade Policy Review Mechanism (TPRM). The WTO tries to ensure predictability and stability, discouraging the use of quotas and other means to set limits on quantities of imports.
- **Safety valves**. In specific circumstances, governments are able to restrict trade. There are three types of provisions in this area. There are articles allowing for the use of trade measures to attain non-economic objectives, articles aimed at ensuring fair competition and provisions permitting intervention in trade for economic reasons.

Having briefly looked at some institutions of international finance, we now turn to the foreign exchange market.

1.14 Facts about the foreign exchange markets

The foreign exchange market emerged because in any trade involving nations with different currencies and with settlements in money at least one will pay or receive foreign currency. We say 'at least one' because it is possible that both will be involved in a foreign currency. For example, if an Australian exporter and a French importer were trading, but with settlement in US dollars, both would be faced with a foreign currency problem. We also specify 'with settlement in money' because it is perfectly possible that barter might be used.

For the majority of foreign exchange markets, there are no individual, physical market places. The market is made up of banks and dealers carrying out transactions via computers, telephones and other telecommunication devices. The major players in the market are as follows:

- commercial banks, investment banks and merchant banks, which may be dealing foreign currency on behalf of their clients engaged in international trade or which may be investing, speculating or hedging on their own account or for customers;
- central banks, which may be managing their reserves or smoothing fluctuations in their own currency;
- foreign exchange brokers, which act as intermediaries between other participants;
- investment funds, moving from one currency to another;
- corporations, which require foreign currency for trade or which may be hedging or speculating;
- individuals, many with high net worth, who may be investors or speculators.

The high-street bank customer, requiring foreign exchange for travel or holiday purposes, is an utterly insignificant participant in terms of the overall market.

The purpose of the foreign exchange is to assist international trade and investment, by allowing businesses and individuals to convert one currency to another currency. Thus, it enables, for example, a business in the USA to import goods from the UK and pay British pounds, even though the US firm's income may arise in US dollars. The market also enables speculation, including the carry trade (in which investors borrow in low-yielding currencies and deposit in high-yielding currencies), to occur. This is a risky tactic and can lead to losses as well as to profits.

The total world foreign exchange market is the largest of all markets on Earth. Trading around the world is estimated almost to have doubled between 1989 and 1992 and increased by around 50 per cent to $1.21 **trillion**[3] per day in 2001 and, as of 2010, has reached $3.98 trillion[4] per day. This is well over 20 times the turnover of the New York Stock Exchange. The market is a twenty-four hour market which moves from one centre to another – from Tokyo to Hong Kong to Singapore to Bahrain to London to New York to San Francisco to Sydney – as the sun moves round the world.[5] Foreign exchange turnover in 1973 averaged a mere $15 billion per day.

The largest centre of foreign exchange dealing is located in London with an estimated 2010 turnover of $1.36 trillion per day.[6] This compares with $187bn per day in 1989, $291bn per day in 1982, $464bn per day in 1995 and $504bn in 2001. London's turnover represents 34.1 per cent of the world total. New York is next in the league table with a daily turnover in 2010 of $657bn (2001 – $254bn, 1998 – $351bn, 1995 – $244bn) and Tokyo's daily turnover is put at $238bn (2001 – $147bn, 1998 – $149bn, 1995 – $161bn). Other major centres include Singapore, Hong Kong and Australia.

Exports of goods and services account for less than 2 per cent of all foreign exchange deals. The lion's share of turnover in FX markets is made up of capital movements from one centre to another and the taking of positions by bankers in different currencies. That only around 2 per cent of FX turnover is driven by trade may seem a little counterintuitive since the FX market was created to enable traders in goods to convert receipts of foreign currency to home currency – and vice versa. Even earlier, of course, trade was settled by barter. And,

Table 1.1 Most traded currencies

Currency	Symbol	% daily share (April 2010)
United States dollar	USD	84.9%
Euro	EUR	39.1%
Japanese yen	JPY	19.0%
Pound sterling	GBP	12.9%
Australian dollar	AUD	7.6%
Swiss franc	CHF	6.4%
Canadian dollar	CAD	5.3%
Hong Kong dollar	HKD	2.4%
Swedish krona	SEK	2.2%
New Zealand dollar	NZD	1.6%
Other currencies		18.6%
Total		**200%**

still, barter does remain a means of settlement – although only a relatively small amount of international trade is done in this way.

Between 90 and 95 per cent of all foreign exchange transactions involve banks. This high preponderance is reflected by banks taking and unravelling positions in currencies and dealing on behalf of corporate customers. Eighty-five per cent of all trade involves the US dollar. The precise breakdown of trades by currency is shown in Table 1.1. This tabulation totals 200 per cent because there are two currencies in any FX deal.

There is a spot market in which deals are arranged with immediate effect and there is a forward market in which purchase or sale is arranged today at an agreed rate but with delivery some time in the future. Forward markets exist for most, but not all, currencies. For a few currencies the forward market goes out to ten years or more; for many it is up to five years; for others it is out to one or two years and for others again it is only in existence for up to six months. The term '**deep market**' refers to those currencies that are widely dealt – for example US dollars, euros, sterling. At the opposite end of the spectrum, the term 'shallow' or 'thin market' is applied to currencies such as many developing countries' currencies which are only occasionally traded.

The foreign exchange market is the cheapest market in the world in which to deal. If one were to start with $1m, switch this into euros and then immediately reverse the transaction so that one returned to US dollars, the proceeds would be less than $1m by the amount of twice the bid/offer spread (the rate for selling and the rate for buying) for euros against US dollars – after all, two deals have been done. But the total amount by which one would be out of pocket would only be $250 or so. For major currencies, the large banks act as market-makers. This means that they hold stocks of foreign currencies and are prepared to deal in large amounts at stated prices.

Foreign exchange dealers can make or lose a lot of money for the banks which employ them. While they can make a million dollars a day for the bank, they can also lose this sum. Their salaries and bonuses are high too. Some make $1m per annum and more. But their business life is strenuous – watching currency movements for 10 hours per day in the bank (and having a foreign exchange rate screen at home) and dealing on the finest of margins take a toll. Dealers on banks' foreign exchange desks seem to be aged between 20 and just over 30. Perhaps beyond 30 reflexes are slower; perhaps the adrenaline flows more slowly – or maybe dealers have made so much money already that motivation is not quite so great.

1.15 Financial crisis 2007–8

In this Introduction, we feel that we have to mention the recent financial crisis. However to explain in detail the mechanisms of the failure of the system it is necessary to understand how certain instruments, for example, **credit default swaps**, work. And to do this it is better if we first explain how the derivative known as a swap works. This means that we have to defer the fascinating topic of the crisis until later chapters. Chapter 12 is devoted to swaps. Chapter 18 homes in on credit default swaps, and Chapter 19 presents an overview of the financial crisis of 2007/8.

Summary

- An offshore dollar is a dollar deposited in a bank account outside the United States.
- An offshore yen is a yen deposited in a bank account outside Japan.
- Offshore sterling is represented by pounds deposited in a bank account outside the United Kingdom.
- In the domestic banking market, government regulation is exercised through capital adequacy ratios, reserve asset requirements, the 'nod and wink' and other means – usually via the central bank and other monetary authorities.
- In the offshore markets, there is no regulation, therefore no reserve asset requirements and no other controls.
- Dollars deposited in London or in the United States do not differ in terms of exchange rate risk – but they do in terms of political risk. They do in terms of credit risk, if the deposits are with different bankers.
- Significant participants in the foreign exchange market include commercial banks, investment banks, merchant banks, central banks, foreign exchange brokers, investment funds and institutions, corporations and high-net-worth individuals.
- The foreign exchange market is the largest market on Earth.
- Volume as at 2010 was running at an average of $3.98 trillion per day – in excess of 20 times that of the New York Stock Exchange. The 2001 figure was around $1.21 trillion per day.
- The foreign exchange market is a twenty-four hour market.
- The largest trading centre in the foreign exchange market is London with an estimated 2010 turnover of $1.36 trillion per day. Comparable New York figures are of $657bn per day and $238bn per day for Tokyo. Respective figures for 2001 were around $504bn, $254bn and $147bn.
- International trade and services account for less than 2 per cent of all FX turnover.

2 The international monetary system

What do we mean by 'the international monetary system'? Essentially, it encompasses the institutions, instruments, laws, rules and procedures for handling international payments, in particular those in final settlement of intercountry debts. Money has sometimes been defined as whatever is used in final settlement of debt. Internationally, central banks have come to be the institutions that make final settlements, and hence the assets they use may be termed 'international money'. Central banks hold reserves of international money. These have also been termed 'reserve assets'.

Prior to the Second World War there was no international central bank. Usually central banks of individual countries made final settlements through transfers of gold, sterling or US dollars. A transfer of gold, sterling or US dollars from one country (other than the United Kingdom or the United States) to another (again, leaving aside the United Kingdom and the United States) reduced the former's reserve assets and increased the latter's. A transfer of sterling from the United Kingdom to another country could be made by creating sterling deposit liabilities owed to the other country. The same was true for the United States. Thus reserve currency countries (as the United Kingdom and the United States came to be termed) had a different status from that of other countries. They could finance purchases, loans and investments by creating debt. They were effectively bankers to the world. They could create international money. If other countries had deficits in their **balance of payments**, they had to export gold or sterling or US dollars, thus reducing their holdings of international money. But as long as foreign countries accepted dollars or sterling, the United States and the United Kingdom could settle deficits by creating international money.

In this chapter we trace the international monetary system from before the First World War to the present time.

2.1 The gold standard

The international monetary system that operated immediately prior to the 1914–18 war was termed the '**gold standard**'. Then, countries accepted two major assets – gold and sterling – in settlement of international debt. So the term 'gold/sterling standard' might be more appropriate.

Most major countries operated the gold standard system. A unit of a country's currency was defined as a certain weight – a part of an ounce – of gold. It also provided that gold could be obtained from the treasuries of these countries in exchange for money and coin of the country concerned.

The pound sterling could be converted into 113.0015 grains of fine gold, and the US dollar into 23.22 grains. The pound was effectively defined as 113.0015/23.22 times as much gold as the dollar – or 4.8665 times as much gold. Through gold equivalents, the pound was worth $4.8665. This amount of dollars was termed the '**par value**' of the pound.

A country is said to be on the gold standard when its central bank is obliged to give gold in exchange for its currency when presented to it. When the United Kingdom was on the gold standard before 1914, anyone could go to the Bank of England and demand gold in exchange for bank notes. The United Kingdom came off the gold standard in 1914, but in 1925 it returned to a modified version termed the 'gold bullion standard'. Individual bank notes were no longer convertible into gold, but gold bars of 400 ounces were sold and bought by the Bank of England. Other countries adopted either this system or the gold exchange standard, under which their central banks would exchange home currency for the currency of some other country on the gold standard rather than for gold itself. The United Kingdom was forced to abandon the gold standard in 1931.

The gold standard was a keystone in the classical economic theory of equilibrium in international trade. The currency of countries on the gold standard was freely convertible into gold at a **fixed exchange rate** and enabled all international debt settlement to be in gold. A balance of payments surplus caused an inflow of gold into the central bank. This enabled it to expand its domestic money supply without fear of having insufficient gold to meet its liabilities. The increase in the quantity of money tended to raise prices, resulting in a fall in the demand for exports and therefore a reduction in the balance of payments surplus. In the event of a deficit in the balance of payments, the reverse was expected to happen. The outflow of gold would be accompanied by a relative money supply contraction, resulting in exports becoming more competitive and the deficit automatically becoming corrected.

The adoption of the gold standard began in the United Kingdom early in the nineteenth century. An attempt was made in the 1860s by a number of European countries to establish the Latin Monetary Union, involving bimetallism for gold and silver. The intention was that both gold and silver should be used for international debt settlement. But the establishment of the gold standard in Germany in 1871, together with less demand for silver in other areas, led to a diminished use of silver as international money. The United States was forced to abandon **redemption** of paper money in metal during the Civil War, but the redemption of paper money for gold began in 1879.

Key dates for the adoption of the gold standard in selected countries are summarised in Table 2.1.

The First World War had a serious effect on the international monetary system. The United Kingdom was forced to abandon the gold standard because of the wartime deficit on its balance of payments, and its reluctance at that time to provide gold to settle international differences. This was, perhaps, the beginning of a reduction in confidence in sterling as an international reserve asset.

Many other countries abandoned the gold standard temporarily, but none had the same significance as the action of the United Kingdom because sterling had financed 90 per cent of world payments. The UK government, recognising the importance of sterling and of UK institutions in international finance, wished to return to the gold standard as soon as possible. Delay occurred because of the recession in the United States in 1920 and 1921, coupled with the post-First World War inflation, which reversed itself as rapidly as it had occurred. Recovery

Table 2.1 Dates for the adoption of the gold standard

Country	Year
United Kingdom	1816
Germany	1871
Sweden, Norway and Denmark	1873
France, Belgium, Switzerland, Italy and Greece	1874
Holland	1875
Uruguay	1876
United States	1879
Austria	1892
Chile	1895
Japan	1897
Russia	1898
Dominican Republic	1901
Panama	1904
Mexico	1905

came in the United States, and a degree of recovery also occurred in the United Kingdom. After its disastrous hyperinflation, ending with the value of the mark at 4 trillion to the dollar, Germany also experienced stabilisation and returned to the gold standard in 1924.

The gold standard to which major countries returned in the mid-1920s was different from that which had existed before the First World War. The major difference was that instead of two international reserve assets – gold and sterling – there were several. Both the United States and France had become much more important in international finance, and dollar and franc deposits were used for much financing. However, generally speaking, countries other than the United Kingdom had only small amounts of gold. When some countries, including France, accumulated sterling balances, they sometimes attempted to convert these into gold, drawing upon the United Kingdom's gold reserves. When sterling had been the only international currency apart from gold, operating the international monetary system had not been difficult, but when there were a number of countries whose bank deposits constituted international money, and when confidence in different currencies varied, the system became more difficult to operate.

A second important difference was that flexibility in costs and prices no longer existed as it had before the First World War. This was especially important in the United Kingdom which had returned to the gold standard based on pre-war par values. But only with a decline in relative costs and prices could the former par value of the pound have been maintained in the long run. Given that flexibility in costs and prices was lacking, confidence in sterling deteriorated, culminating in the United Kingdom abandoning the gold standard in 1931. Most other countries followed the UK example in quitting the gold standard.

But there were other forces impinging on the United Kingdom in the early 1930s which also had a significant effect on its decision to discard the gold standard. Two of these were the Great Depression of the late 1920s and early 1930s and the international financial crisis of 1931.

As explained, the early 1930s saw the international monetary system then in use begin to disintegrate. By the beginning of 1933 the major economies of the world could be categorised as those of the gold bloc (France, Switzerland, the Netherlands and Belgium) which maintained the value of their currencies in terms of gold; those that maintained their

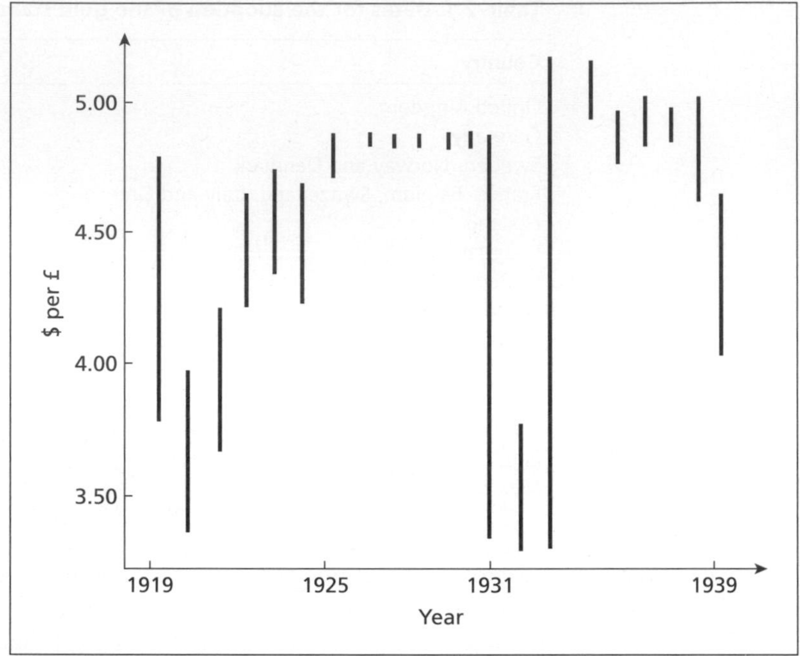

Figure 2.1 The sterling/dollar exchange rate, 1919–39 (range based on monthly earnings)

currencies' values by strict exchange controls (such as Germany) enforced under a dictatorship; and those that permitted their currencies to depreciate. Many currencies depreciated by as much as 35 to 50 per cent during the first half of the decade. Those countries that did not permit their currencies to depreciate – for example, the United States, France, Belgium, Switzerland and the Netherlands – resorted to strong deflationary pressures. A frequent complaint was that some countries deliberately encouraged currency depreciation, engaging in a beggar-my-neighbour policy. International trade was at a low level, and international capital flows virtually stopped.

The depreciation of key currencies in the 1930s – especially that of the pound (see Figure 2.1) – meant a decline in the foreign exchange component of international reserves relative to the gold component. With limited production of gold and with strong flows thereof to the United States, most countries found their gold holdings reduced. Large fluctuations in exchange rates, accompanied by low levels of international trade and world depression, led to influential calls in the late 1930s and early 1940s in favour of a return to a stable exchange rate environment.

However, the Second World War led to more extensive and tighter controls on international trade and investment. Transactions with enemy countries became illegal, and much of the trade between friendly nations consisted of munitions and warfare supplies. Private markets (as opposed to intergovernmental ones) for most currencies almost ceased to exist. Much of the trade that continued was under various intergovernmental agreements. But even the intergovernmental transactions that took place then were generally either barter transactions or grants made to carry on hostilities against the enemy. There was virtually no role for international finance. Foreign exchange markets, exchange rates and other institutional mechanisms were effectively suspended during the war and were not re-established until the war ended. Trade controls and exchange controls frequently meant that the usual methods of financing could not be used. So the financing of trade was not an urgent problem during the war.

By the end of the Second World War, many commentators, bankers and economists were agreed upon the need for a new monetary system. Sterling's dominance of international trade had gone; the era of the gold standard was passed. Governments might have waited for a new international monetary order to evolve to replace the system that had worked well before 1914 but which had failed in the period from 1914 to 1944. However, this would have meant uncertainty. Action was urgently needed. The action taken stemmed from the Bretton Woods agreement and saw the creation of a new international institution, the International Monetary Fund. The monetary system that emerged from Bretton Woods occupied the international stage for the immediate post-1945 period through to 1971.

2.2 The Bretton Woods system

The framework for a new international monetary system was created in July 1944 in the United States at Bretton Woods, New Hampshire. The prime movers were John Maynard Keynes and Harry Dexter White, the respective UK and US representatives. The key innovations of the Bretton Woods agreement were as follows:

- A new permanent institution, the International Monetary Fund (IMF), was to be established to promote consultation and collaboration on international monetary problems and to lend to member countries in need due to recurring balance of payments deficits.
- Each fund member would establish, with the approval of the IMF, a par value for its currency and would undertake to maintain exchange rates for its currency within 1 per cent of the declared par value. Countries that freely bought and sold gold in settlement of international transactions were deemed to be adhering to the requirement that they maintain exchange rates within 1 per cent margins. Hence, the United States, the only country that met this condition, was not expected to intervene in the foreign exchange markets. Other countries would intervene by buying or selling dollars against their own currencies, to keep their rates within 1 per cent of their parities with the dollar.
- Members would change their par values only after having secured IMF approval. This approval would be granted only if there were evidence that the country was suffering from a fundamental disequilibrium in its balance of payments. It was generally agreed that a long and continuing large loss of reserve assets in support of an exchange rate would be evidence of this fundamental disequilibrium.
- Each IMF member country would pay into the IMF pool a quota, one-quarter being in gold with the remainder in its own currency. The size of the quota was a function of each member's size in the world economy.
- The IMF would be in a position, from the subscription to quotas, to lend to countries in ongoing deficit.

A new monetary framework was thus established which created fixed exchange rates subject to alteration should fundamental disequilibria emerge. Since there was a mechanism for discontinuous adjustment to exchange rates, the system became known as the adjustable peg system.

During its early years, the Bretton Woods system played a positive part in a rapid expansion in world trade. However, its success obscured one of its basic shortcomings – there was no provision for expanding the supply of international reserves necessary to support growing trade flows. The unmet demand for international reserves eventually led to increased holdings of national currencies and in particular it strengthened the US dollar's position as an international reserve currency.

The dollar's expanding role in international trade and finance raised new problems in monetary relations. This difficulty has been referred to as the Triffin dilemma after Triffin[1] who focused attention upon it. Because the US dollar played the part of a reserve currency, US balance of payments deficits were necessary in order to increase international liquidity. But as US liabilities to foreign central banks grew, so confidence in the convertibility of dollars into gold wavered. US gold reserves were becoming a decreasing fraction of foreign liabilities. This method of providing international liquidity could continue only as long as no central bank attempted a run on the US gold reserves. Concern over this dilemma led to the introduction of a new international reserve asset administered by the IMF. This asset, the **special drawing right (SDR)**, was proposed and ratified in 1969.

SDRs were allocated to individual countries by the IMF through the deliberate decision of IMF members to accept them as a new form of international reserve. These credits were allocated to IMF members in proportion to their quotas – rather like a bonus issue of shares in a company. A country holding SDRs may use them to acquire foreign currency by transferring them, via the IMF special drawing account, to another country in exchange for foreign currency. Only member states of the IMF and certain designated official institutions may legally hold SDRs.

2.3 International reserves

The IMF provides its members with international reserves through the SDR. Changes in the calculation of the value and interest rate earned on excess holdings of SDRs have increased their attractiveness as a reserve asset. The value of the SDR is no longer fixed in terms of the US dollar. Its value is now calculated using a currency basket.

The dollar value of the SDR is computed daily using the average of the buying and selling rates at midday on the London foreign exchange markets. The amounts of currency making up the SDR are fixed for longish periods. The composition of SDR1 from the beginning of 2011 was:

USD0.6600	(41.9%)
EUR0.4230	(37.4%)
JPY12.1000	(9.41%)
GBP0.1110	(11.3%)

The interest rate paid to members holding more than their allocation of SDRs and owed to members holding less than their allocation is determined quarterly as a weighted average of market interest rates. The attractiveness of the SDR has also been increased by expanding the types of transaction in which it can be used. In addition to financing outright purchases of foreign currencies, members can now use SDRs in forward and swap transactions and they can donate SDRs and make SDR-denominated loans to other members and authorised non-member institutions.

2.4 The role of gold up to 1971

Gold has long existed as a medium of international exchange. But in its role as a reserve asset it has significant shortcomings. First, it is wasteful to use a commodity with a significant positive cost of production to perform a function that could equally well be performed by a financial instrument with a zero cost of production. Secondly, the use of gold gives benefits to the country where the gold is produced and which may not necessarily benefit the world economy. And there have been objections to the political nature of the world's largest gold producer, South Africa. Thirdly, the increase in the supply of gold may not reflect the world's increasing need for extra international liquidity. Indeed increases in gold supplies may be unrelated to the world's needs. They may be influenced, though, by the need for foreign exchange on the part, for example of South Africa.

The price of gold was fixed in 1933 at $35 an ounce and this fixed value held up to the early 1970s. Since the currencies were fixed in relation to the dollar, central banks could exchange their currencies for dollars and with their dollars they could obtain gold. The US Federal Reserve Bank was willing to buy and sell gold at this rate. This willingness of the United States to back the world monetary system is understandable given that the United States, at the end of the Second World War, had a gold stock valued at $20bn or 60 per cent of the total of official gold reserves. As long as the dollar and its gold backing was considered invulnerable, foreign central banks had an incentive to hold currencies, which earned interest, rather than gold, which earned nothing.

In 1954 a gold market was opened in London in which private buyers and sellers could operate. A central bank gold pool of $80m was set up in 1962. The gold pool was an arrangement among eight countries, including the United States, to sell or buy gold in the free market to keep the price close to the official price of $35 an ounce. France left the gold pool in 1967.

By the late 1960s there existed a situation whereby the dollar had become convertible into gold not only by foreign central banks but also by private speculators all over the world. Until 1968, under the gold pool arrangement, major central banks clubbed together to hold the gold price at $35 an ounce. As there was no prospect of the gold price going down, but a good prospect of it going up, this gave speculators a one-way option. In 1968 central banks were forced to set the gold price free for commercial transactions. However, for settlements between themselves, they agreed to stick to the old price and not to sell gold on the free market. The central banks expected that under this two-tier gold system, the free-market gold price would stay within easy reach of the official price. It did not do so for long.

Increasingly, fixed exchange rates were becoming more and more difficult to defend and various governments around the world were very reluctant to devalue and revalue despite what many would have described as fundamental disequilibria. In other words, national governments were abusing the system.

In 1971 the system was clearly under pressure on two fronts – the fixed gold price and fixed exchange rates made little sense. Matters were brought to a head when President Nixon, as a preparation to the 1972 election, sought to expand demand in the United States. Speculation against the dollar mounted and many central banks in continental Europe and Japan were forced to buy dollars to keep their currencies within the narrow bands required by Bretton Woods – rather than rising, which economic and speculative pressures were favouring. The free-market gold price rose sharply. This led several countries to demand conversion of their surplus dollars into gold at the official price of $35 per ounce. The United

States, with $10bn in gold reserves versus liabilities of $50bn in other countries' reserves, decided to suspend convertibility in August 1971 and the US dollar was set free to float.

There being considerable anxiety about the international monetary system, a conference of finance ministers was summoned in December 1971 at the Smithsonian Institute in the United States. The so-called Smithsonian Agreement resulted. This increased the fixed exchange rate band spread to 4.5 per cent, allowing central banks more room for manoeuvre before intervention became necessary. At the same time upward revaluations of various currencies against the US dollar were agreed, with the dollar formally devaluing against gold. The price of the metal was increased from $35 per ounce to $38 per ounce – an effective dollar devaluation of 9 per cent.

The dollar-based international monetary system continued to function for just over another year, when the failure of the US balance of payments to respond to the dollar's initial devaluation led to a second realignment. The dollar was devalued again in February 1973; this raised the official gold price to $41.22 per ounce. But this realignment was almost immediately brought under excessive strain when a new exchange crisis emerged in March 1973 and European central banks refused to buy dollars. In mid-March the Bretton Woods era finally crumbled when 14 major industrial nations abandoned the adjustable peg and allowed their currencies to float against the dollar. But we are not universally in a **floating exchange rate** world now, as we shall see shortly.

2.5 The Second Amendment

Following abandonment of pegged exchange rates in March 1973, floating exchange rates were introduced for many countries. In Europe, the opinion was widespread that floating should be only temporary, a view most forcibly expressed by the French. In the United States, opinion favoured a continuing float.

Discussions at summit level moved from Rambouillet in France in November 1975 to Jamaica in January 1976 and culminated in a new IMF article on exchange rate practices. This amendment, the second in the history of the IMF, was ratified by the required majority and became effective on 1 April 1978.

The Second Amendment provided for the reform of three key aspects of international monetary relations. First, it allowed substantially more flexibility in the management of exchange rates and expanded the IMF's responsibility for supervising the international monetary system. Secondly, it altered the nature of the SDR to increase its attractiveness as an international reserve asset. And finally, it simplified and expanded the IMF's ability to assist members in financing short-term imbalances in their international payments accounts.

Under the first innovation, IMF members are expected to 'collaborate with the fund and other members to assure orderly exchange arrangements and to promote a stable system of exchange rates' (IMF, 1978). Their method of collaboration is left to members' discretion.

Members' obligations regarding their exchange practices are specified under Article IV of the fund's Articles of Agreement. Under this amended article (IMF, 1978), each member shall:

- endeavour to direct its economic and financial policies towards the objective of fostering orderly economic growth with reasonable price stability, with due regard to its circumstances;
- seek to promote stability by fostering orderly underlying economic and financial conditions and a monetary system that does not tend to produce erratic disruptions;

- avoid manipulating exchange rates or the international monetary system in order to prevent effective balance of payments adjustment or to gain an unfair competitive advantage over other members.

In April 1977, the IMF adopted principles (IMF, 1977) to provide additional guidance in the choice of an exchange policy. These principles of exchange rate management state that:

- a member shall avoid manipulating exchange rates or the international monetary system to prevent effective balance of payments adjustment or to gain an unfair competitive advantage over other members;
- a member should intervene in the exchange market if necessary to counter disorderly conditions, which may be characterised *inter alia* by disruptive short-term movements in the exchange value of its currency;
- members should take into account in their intervention policies the interests of other members, including those of countries in whose currencies they intervene.

The above principles give members a great deal of latitude in the choice of an exchange rate policy. Members may peg, float or manage their currencies to whatever degree they feel is consistent with their own domestic economic policies. The Second Amendment restricts the role of gold in the international monetary system. Par values may not be set in terms of gold and an official price for gold has been abolished. Members are expected to co-operate in reducing the role of gold with the intention that the SDR should become the primary reserve asset of the international monetary system. The IMF abolished requirements that members make some payments in terms of gold and began to dispose of its gold reserve.

Through its surveillance, the IMF identifies members causing disruptive variations in exchange rates through their domestic economic policies. The IMF may then suggest alternative domestic policies which would have less of an effect on the exchange market.

Providing members with assistance in overcoming payments imbalances continues to be one of the IMF's prime objectives. A member in need of foreign exchange to finance short-term exchange rate intervention may apply to the IMF for borrowing assistance.

2.6 Exchange rate arrangements

Exchange rate practices around the world span the range of alternatives from pegging to floating. Pegged exchange rates are generally managed on a day-to-day basis through official intervention in the foreign exchange markets and by internal regulations limiting exchange market transactions. Exchange rate parities are set in terms of a foreign currency or group of currencies, and fluctuations in the exchange rate around this parity are managed by official intervention.

Countries that peg their exchange rate may select from a wide range of alternatives. Many nations peg to a single currency, but it has become increasingly common to peg against a group of currencies. Pegging is attractive because it helps reduce the variability of prices in the domestic economy. However, pegging has its costs. These flow from the need to regulate international transactions and intervene in foreign exchange markets.

Generally speaking, floating exchange rates are managed less closely, although practices vary. Some members refrain altogether from intervention, while others intervene strongly. In most cases, nations with developed financial markets prefer floating exchange rates.

In truth, countries that allow their currency to float do not commit themselves not to intervene. Indeed they either manage exchange rates informally, or use some set of economic indicators or rely on a co-operative exchange rate agreement. Informal managed floats are the most frequently used. Many of these floaters follow strategies of leaning against the wind. This approach involves official intervention to smooth short-term fluctuations in exchange rates without unduly restricting long-term trends. Other nations with informally managed floats set target exchange rates and intervene to move market rates towards these levels.

Some countries rely on objective indicators to provide signals rather than either using targets or leaning against the wind. These indicators are used to show the economic need for a devaluation or a revaluation. Parities are adjusted frequently, in small amounts, as dictated by the indicators. Exchange market intervention is used to limit exchange rate fluctuations around these central rates.

When a country chooses to peg or float its currency, it is not obliged to co-operate with the IMF or any other nation in the day-to-day management of exchange rates. Although most members value this independence, some nations wish to maintain closer economic ties with their trading partners. The IMF does not prohibit these nations from co-operating with each other in the management of their bilateral exchange rates. This practice, classified by the IMF as a co-operative exchange arrangement, has become known as group floating, of which the **European Monetary System**, a forerunner of the euro, was the most well known.

In Table 2.2, we summarise these exchange rate arrangements.

Table 2.2 Exchange rate pegging around the world

Exchange rate regime	Description
Exchange arrangements with no separate currency specific only to the country concerned	The currency of another country circulates as the sole legal tender or the member belongs to a monetary or currency union in which the same legal tender is shared by the members of the union. The eurozone provides the most obvious example
Currency board arrangements	A monetary regime based on an explicit legislative commitment to exchange domestic currency for a specified foreign currency at a fixed exchange rate
Other conventional fixed peg arrangements	The country pegs its currency (formally or de facto) at a fixed rate to a major currency or a basket of currencies where the exchange rate fluctuates within a narrow margin of less than ±1 per cent around a central rate
Pegged exchange rates within horizontal bands	The value of the currency is maintained within margins of fluctuation around a formal or de facto fixed peg that are wider than at least ±1 per cent around a central rate
Crawling pegs	The currency is adjusted periodically in small amounts at a fixed, preannounced rate or in response to changes in certain quantitative indicators
Exchange rates within crawling bands	The currency is maintained within certain fluctuation margins around a central rate that is adjusted periodically at a fixed preannounced rate or in response to changes in certain quantitative indicators
Managed floating with no preannounced path for exchange rates	The monetary authority influences the movement of the exchange rate through active intervention in the foreign exchange market without specifying, or precommitting to, a preannounced path for the exchange rate
Independent floating	The exchange rate is market determined, with any foreign exchange intervention aimed at moderating the rate of change and preventing undue fluctuations in the exchange rate, rather than at establishing a level for it. Examples include the USA and the UK

2.7 The European single currency – the euro

On 1 January 1999, a single European currency (the euro) was introduced in eleven EU countries. New entrants have arrived bringing the number of **eurozone** countries, at the time of writing – April 2011 – to 17. These countries include Austria, Belgium, Cyprus, Estonia, Finland, France, Germany, Greece, Ireland, Italy, Luxembourg, Malta, the Netherlands, Portugal, Slovakia, Slovenia and Spain. Major countries of the EU that remain outside the eurozone include the United Kingdom, Denmark and Sweden.

The 17 EU countries form an economic and monetary union (EMU) and use the single currency – the euro. These countries locked the exchange rates of their national currencies to the euro and share the new currency.

The 17 countries share a single interest rate, set by the European Central Bank (ECB), and a single foreign exchange rate. The ECB is responsible for the monetary policy of these eurozone countries, but there is no common representation, governance or fiscal policy for the currency union.

Ever since the European Economic Community (EEC) started in 1957, there were suggestions of more economic co-operation between countries – including a single currency. The creation of the Single Market in 1992 brought the economies of different EU regions closer together, created lower inflation and experienced increased EU income. Economic convergence between participating countries is the primary condition for a single currency.

There are convergence criteria for new members of the eurozone. These are that individual countries should confirm the following requirements, known as the Maastricht criteria. They are that:

- The inflation rate must be within 1.5 percentage points of the average rate of the three EU states with the lowest inflation.
- The long-term interest rates must be within 2 percentage points of the average rate of the three EU states with the lowest interest rates (now, of course, there is only a single interest rate).
- The annual government deficit to GDP must be below 3 per cent (save for exceptional circumstances).
- The rate of gross government debt to GDP must not exceed 60 per cent.

In fact, these criteria seem to have been treated rather lightly with respect to new entrants to the eurozone, for example, Greece was profligate in its use of financial engineering to ensure that it met the entry criteria.

EU countries that have decided not to join yet will be able to join when they are ready, provided that they meet the conditions for entry set out in the convergence criteria.

It is claimed that the euro has brought big changes for business both within eurozone countries and throughout Europe. For example, there are cheaper transaction costs, exchange rate certainty and transparent price differences. We look at these in turn.

- **Cheaper transaction costs**. The single currency allows firms in countries in the eurozone to trade with each other without changing currencies. This reduces transaction costs. It now costs less for companies to make payments between countries within the eurozone.

- **Stable exchange rates**. The single currency removes exchange rates between countries in the euro zone. This leads to better decision making for its companies.
- **Transparent price differences**. The single currency makes price differences in different countries in the euro zone more obvious. This may affect companies who charge different prices for their products in countries within the euro zone. Also, companies buying from the euro zone will be able to compare prices more easily. Either way, this should sharpen competition.

Even though the United Kingdom has not joined the single currency, the euro zone has had an effect on many UK businesses, especially those that buy and sell products throughout Europe. Some UK companies are using the euro for buying and selling goods and services within the United Kingdom itself. This is the case in supply chains which substantially involve euro inputs and receipts. However the ability of eurozone countries to conform to a common inflation rate has been honoured in the breach. And, as we shall see, a common currency is helped if similar inflations by participants are exhibited. Failure on this score can sow the seeds of destruction for the common currency – see the sections on purchasing power parity and an optimum currency area. These appear, respectively in Chapters 3 and 19.

Summary

- Immediately prior to 1914 most major countries operated the gold standard system – two major assets, gold and sterling, were accepted in settlement of international debt. A country's central bank was obliged to give gold in exchange for its currency when presented to it.
- In 1914 the United Kingdom, in common with many other countries, left the gold standard.
- In 1925, the United Kingdom adopted the gold bullion standard. Individual bank notes were not convertible into gold but gold bars were sold and bought by the Bank of England. Many other countries adopted this system on the gold exchange standard under which their central banks exchanged home currency for the currency of some other country on the gold standard rather than gold itself.
- The United Kingdom abandoned the gold standard in 1931. Until the Second World War, most countries moved to a system of fluctuating exchange rates while others adopted strict exchange controls.
- The post-war monetary system was created in 1944 at Bretton Woods, New Hampshire.
- The Bretton Woods agreement created the International Monetary Fund (IMF), a world central bank. It established a fixed exchange rate system with countries maintaining their exchange rates within 1 per cent of a declared par value against the US dollar. The United States itself would buy and sell gold in settlement for international transactions. Other countries would intervene in the FX market to keep their currency value within 1 per cent of the declared parity, against the dollar. This parity, the par value, would only be changed with IMF approval. All IMF member countries would pay a quota into the IMF pool and this would be available for loan to countries in need of the wherewithal to intervene in FX markets to keep rates at their par value.

- The US dollar became the reserve asset of the new monetary order. But with world trade growing, the need for international liquidity grew. To meet this need for international currency, continuing US balance of payments deficits were necessary to put dollars into the system. This shortage of international liquidity reached a head in the late 1960s. The IMF countered in 1969 by creating a new international reserve asset, the SDR (special drawing right).
- Originally the SDR was equal to a fixed number of dollars, it is now a basket currency consisting of 41.9 per cent dollars, 37.4 per cent euros, 9.4 per cent Japanese yen and 11.3 per cent sterling.
- In 1969, SDRs were allocated to IMF members rather like a bonus issue of shares in a company.
- Strains on the system came to a further head in the early 1970s. The official price of gold had remained fixed at $35 an ounce since 1933. The US Federal Reserve Bank was willing to buy and sell gold at this rate. In 1954 a gold market had been opened in London. As of the early 1970s many countries which should have revalued their currencies had failed to do so – Germany and Japan were two.
- The fixed exchange rate system and the fixed gold price made little economic sense.
- With the US president seeking to expand demand prior to the 1972 presidential elections, expectations of dollar devaluation began to materialise.
- The free-market gold price rose sharply and in August 1971 the United States suspended convertibility and set the dollar free to float. At the Smithsonian Institute in the United States in December 1971, the fixed exchange rate spread was widened from 1 per cent to $4^1/_2$ per cent and the dollar was devalued against gold – from $35 an ounce to $38.
- This was not enough. In February 1973 the dollar was again devalued to $41.22 per ounce of gold and in March 1973 the Bretton Woods era formally crumbled when 14 major nations decided to float their currencies.
- Nowadays, most major currencies around the world have floating exchange rate regimes while many maintain fixed rate systems. Some are fixed against the dollar, some against the euro, some against the SDR. In Europe, 12 countries have adopted the euro as their currency.
- On 1 January 1999, a single European currency (the euro) was introduced in 11 EU countries. The original 11 countries of the eurozone are Austria, Belgium, Finland, France, Germany, Ireland, Italy, Luxembourg, Netherlands, Portugal and Spain. Greece has subsequently joined the eurozone as have Cyprus, Estonia, Malta, Slovakia and Slovenia.
- The 17 countries share a single interest rate, set by the European Central Bank (ECB), and a single foreign exchange rate. The ECB is responsible for the monetary policy of these eurozone countries.
- Countries whose economies were not ready to join the euro system, and countries that have decided not to join yet, will be able to join when they are ready, provided that they meet the conditions for entry set out in the Maastricht Treaty.
- The euro is the legal currency in the eurozone.
- Euro banknotes and coins were introduced in the eurozone on 1 January 2002 and old national banknotes and coins were withdrawn from circulation.

- Even though the United Kingdom has not joined the single currency, the eurozone has had an effect on many UK businesses, especially those that buy and sell products throughout Europe.

End of chapter questions

2.1 Compare and contrast the fixed exchange rate, free floating, and managed floating systems.

2.2 How can central banks use direct intervention to move the value of a currency?

2.3 List and discuss the advantages and disadvantages of a freely floating exchange rate system versus a fixed exchange rate system?

Part B

FOREIGN EXCHANGE

International financial management involves manipulation of more than one currency. Its understanding necessarily involves confronting such questions as how foreign exchange markets work and what makes exchange rates move. Making sense of the complexities of international finance has no magic answer – but this section presents in Chapter 3 the single most important theorem of foreign exchange. Without understanding it, the student will always flounder in the dark when confronted with exchange rates and interest rates, but if it is understood, light begins to appear.

3

Exchange rates: the basic equations

International corporate finance and domestic corporate finance have much in common, but there are also many ways in which they differ. International financial management usually involves manipulation with more than one currency. So its understanding necessarily involves questions about how foreign exchange markets work, why exchange rates change, how one can protect oneself against foreign exchange risk and so on.

But before we can begin to approach these topics, there are a number of basic relationships that must be examined. This chapter focuses upon one series of approaches to the determination of foreign exchange rates – but it is by no means the only explanation and we briefly examine some others in Chapter 6.

3.1 Foreign exchange markets

A US company importing goods from Germany with their price denominated in euros may buy euros to pay for the goods. A US company exporting goods to Germany, again with the price denominated in euros, receives euros which it may then sell in exchange for dollars. The currency aspects of these transactions involve use of the foreign exchange markets.

In most centres, the foreign exchange market has no central, physical market place. Business is conducted by screen trading or by telephone or a number of other telecommunications mechanisms. The main dealers are commercial banks and central banks. Most companies wishing to buy or sell currency usually do so through a commercial bank.

In the United Kingdom, exchange rates are usually quoted in terms of the number of units of foreign currency bought for one unit of home currency, that is £1. This method of quotation is termed the indirect quote. By contrast, exchange rates may be quoted in terms of the number of units of home currency necessary to buy one unit of foreign currency. This is the direct quotation method. In the United States, the convention is to use the direct quote when dealing internally with residents of the United States and the indirect quote when dealing with foreigners. The exception to this latter rule is that the direct US quote is used when dealing with British-based banks or UK businesses. This practice means that New York uses the same figure when talking to foreign dealers as such foreign dealers use for their own transactions and quotations. A quote of $1.6050 per British pound in New York means that each pound costs $1.6050. In other words, to put it in indirect New York terms, there are £0.6231 to the dollar given by 1/1.6050. On the face of it, buying or selling a currency at the **spot rate** of exchange implies immediate delivery and payment. The practice of the foreign exchange market is for delivery to be at two working days after the deal – but this applies only to spot transactions.

There is also the forward market where deals are for future delivery – usually one, three, six or 12 months' time, although a whole host of other durations, including odd periods (such as 12 days, for example) can be dealt. The forward market enables companies and others to insure themselves against foreign exchange losses (or, of course, to speculate on future movements in exchange rates). If you are going to need CHF100,000 (CHF is the symbol for Swiss francs) in six months' time, you can enter into a six-month **forward contract**. The forward rate on this contract is the price agreed now to be paid in six months when the CHF100,000 are delivered.

If the six-month forward rate for the pound against the dollar is quoted at \$1.6100 per GBP as opposed to the spot rate of \$1.6050, the implication is that you pay more dollars if you buy forward than if you buy pounds spot. In this case the dollar is said to trade at a forward discount on the pound. Put another way, the pound trades at a forward premium on the dollar. Expressed as an annual rate, the forward premium is:

$$\frac{1.6100 - 1.6050}{1.6050} \times \frac{12 \text{ months}}{6 \text{ months}} \times 100 = 0.62\% \text{ p.a.}$$

Assuming that forward markets and interest rates are in equilibrium, the currency of the country with the higher interest rate is said to be at a discount on the other currency. At the same time, looking at things from the opposite side of the fence, the currency of the country with lower interest rates will be at a premium on the other currency.

3.2 Some basic relationships

Why should one currency be quoted at a different rate in the forward market versus the **spot market**? The hypothesis – the whys and wherefores of which will be examined later in this chapter – is that, in the absence of barriers to international capital movements, there is a relationship between spot exchange rates, forward exchange rates, interest rates and

Table 3.1 Notation used in this chapter

s_0 = spot \$/£ exchange rate now (direct New York quote)
f_0 = forward \$/£ exchange rate now (direct New York quote)
$i_\$$ = Offshore dollar interest rate
$i_£$ = Offshore sterling interest rate
r = real return
$\tilde{p}_\$$ = expected US inflation
$\tilde{p}_£$ = expected UK inflation
$p_\$$ = US price level now
$p_£$ = UK price level now
$\tilde{s}_t$ = expected spot \$/£ exchange rate at time t (direct New York quote)

inflation rates. This relationship can be summarised as shown in Figure 3.1. For definitions of all notations used in this chapter, see Table 3.1. The theoretical underpinning to the hypothesised link between variables is now examined.

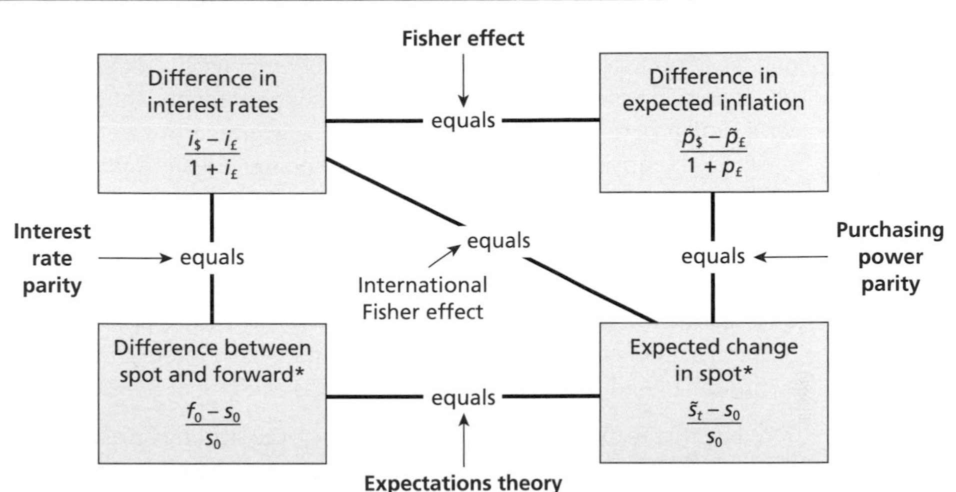

* *Important note*: Using the notation here, f_0, $\tilde{s}_0$ and $\tilde{s}_t$ must be stated in terms of \$/£: that is, the number of dollars to the pound. If the rate is quoted as £/\$ – that is, the number of pounds to the dollar – the expectations theory boxes should read:

$$\frac{s_0 - f_0}{f_0} \text{ and } \frac{s_0 - \tilde{s}_t}{\tilde{s}_t}$$

This should be self-evident.

If it is not, consider the following situation. The £/\$ quotation is equal to 1/(\$/£). $(f - s)/s$ can be shown to be equal to $[(1/s) - (1/f)]/(1/f)$. This is demonstrated below.

$$\frac{(1/s) - (1/f)}{(1/f)} = \left(\frac{1}{s} - \frac{1}{f}\right)f$$

$$= \frac{f}{s} - 1$$

$$= \frac{f - s}{s}$$

Great care must be taken on this point on all occasions when using the above formulations. It is recommended that readers use the four-way model as set out above but always use the direct New York quote. When the dollar is not involved in a problem, be careful to get the substitution consistent with the formulations above. To get approximate results, the number of months may be used. In practice, the actual number of days, rather than months, has to be used in calculations. Further modification is necessary inasmuch as bankers and the financial institutions quote all Eurocurrency notes on the basis of a 360-day year. Domestic sterling and most Commonwealth country currencies are based on a 365-day year – all others are quoted by reference to a 360-day year, including domestic US dollars. For purposes of quick approximation, the four-way model relationships may be written as:

$$i_\$ - i_£ = \tilde{p}_\$ - \tilde{p}_£ = \frac{f_0 - s_0}{s_0} = \frac{\tilde{s}_t - s_0}{s_0}$$

But this is very much an approximation.

Figure 3.1 The four-way equivalence in the foreign exchange market

3.3 Interest rates and exchange rates

Assume that an investor has £1m to invest for a period of 12 months. He has a whole spectrum of investment opportunities: he could put the money into sterling or dollar investments, or into yen, or whatever. But for simplicity, suppose we look at only two of these opportunities. The currency markets are quoting the dollar against sterling at $1.6800 spot and $1.6066 for 12 months forward. Offshore market fixed interest rates are 13 per cent per annum for twelve months sterling and $8^1/_{16}$ per cent per annum fixed rate for US dollars for a similar period. These are deliberately exaggerated to greater than those prevailing in the markets currently because they make the point here more clearly. Given the information on interest rates and FX rates, the investor may:

- either invest £1m in offshore sterling at a 13 per cent per annum fixed interest rate for 12 months;
- or convert £1m into US dollars at $1.6800; invest the proceeds in the offshore dollar interest market at an $8^1/_{16}$ per cent per annum fixed interest rate for one year and sell the pre-calculated proceeds forward 12 months at a rate of $1.6066.

What are the expected proceeds? Obviously, the sterling investment yields £1,130,000 at the end of 12 months. The dollar investment yields, to all intents and purposes, the same amount. The proceeds from the spot transaction are $1,680,000. Investing at $8^1/_{16}$ per cent per annum, the proceeds in 12 months' time will total $1,815,450, and selling this forward at $1.6066 yields £1,129,995. This is, more or less, the same outcome as from the sterling investment opportunity. If one thinks about it, this is what one would expect. After all, each investment opportunity is of equal risk (the investor carries the credit risk associated with the bank with which he invests, but if he invests with the same bank, the credit risk associated with each opportunity is equal). To the UK company, investment in sterling carries no foreign exchange risk. Neither does the dollar investment when covered via the forward markets. The two investments carry equal risk and should, according to financial theory, promise equal returns.

Were this not the case, **arbitrageurs** in the foreign exchange and interest rate markets would borrow currency in one centre, convert it to the other, invest there and sell the proceeds forward. Such proceeds would, if equilibrium did not hold, exceed the amount repayable in terms of the borrowing plus accrued interest and thereby yield a virtually riskless profit to the operator. This mechanism is referred to as **covered interest arbitrage**. The actions of dealers ensure that profitable opportunities of this kind do not last for more than fleeting instants. Exploitation of these brief opportunities creates movements in spot and forward exchange rates and in interest rates – and such movements ensure that the tendency in the currency and interest rate markets is towards equilibrium.

Covered interest arbitrage involves borrowing in centre A for a specified period at a fixed interest rate and shipping the proceeds borrowed to centre B. The sum shipped is deposited there for the same period as the borrowing in centre A, again at a fixed interest rate. The total proceeds of investment in centre B that will accrue at the end of the investment period can be calculated, since the interest rate is fixed. Such proceeds are sold via the forward market for the period of the borrowing and lending, and the sum received in centre A from this forward transaction will more than repay the borrowing in centre A plus accrued interest. This profit is said to be a covered interest arbitrage profit.

By contrast, **uncovered interest arbitrage** involves a borrowing in centre A for a specified period at a fixed interest rate and shipping the proceeds borrowed to centre B via the spot market. The sum is again placed on deposit for the same period as that for which the borrowing was arranged in centre A and again it is at a fixed rate. This time the investor speculates that the proceeds from lending in centre B, when shipped to centre A at the spot rate prevailing at the end of the investment period, will exceed the borrowing plus accrued interest in centre A. Note that, under uncovered interest arbitrage, the operator speculates on the future spot rate. Any profit earned is a risky profit. Under covered interest arbitrage, the operator is not speculating but making a risk-free profit based on momentary disequilibria in interest differentials and forward and spot rates.

It should be noted in the numerical example above that we have used single (presumably middle) rates for quotations of interest and spot and forward rates. In reality the investor needs to look at buy and sell rates in the spot and forward markets and at borrow and lend rates in interest markets.

It should also be noted that the **interest rate differential** is termed the 'interest agio'.[1] In the numerical example above it would be given by:

$$\frac{i_\$ - i_£}{1 + i_£} = \frac{8\frac{1}{16}\% - 13\%}{1.13}$$
$$= -0.0437$$
$$= -4.37\%$$

Note that calculating the interest differential in this manner – which is the precisely correct way – differs from taking a straight difference between interest rates: that is, $i_\$ - i_£$. The rationale for using the precise calculation rather than the approximation is demonstrated algebraically at the end of this section.

The annual forward discount is termed the 'exchange agio'. In the numerical example it would be equal to:

$$\frac{f_0 - s_0}{s_0} = \frac{1.6066 - 1.6800}{1.6800}$$
$$= -0.0437$$
$$= -4.37\%$$

If arbitrageurs' actions ensure that opportunities for profitable covered interest arbitrage are eliminated, then the interest agio will equal the exchange agio. This is the essence of interest rate parity theory (see Figure 3.2).

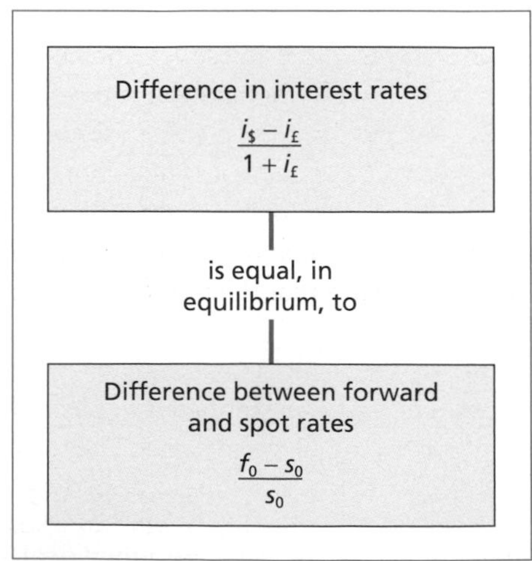

Figure 3.2 The interest rate parity theorem

The whole of the above theory is, of course, built upon the assumption that we are looking at markets in which money is internationally mobile. Many governments restrict the mobility of money. But that does not invalidate the hypothesis. Furthermore, governments also frequently place restrictions on lending and borrowing rates charged in domestic interest rate markets. To avoid the effects of this market imperfection we should look at free markets, and these are available in the form of Eurocurrency markets. Clearly, then, in applying the interest rate parity theorem, our attention should focus upon the comparative term structure of interest rates in the Eurocurrency markets.

We now consider the whys and wherefores of using the precise calculation rather than the approximation. Assume that a US exporter is due to receive £*A* in one year (or at time t where $t = 1$ year), and assume the notation in Table 3.1 (earlier).

The US exporter might avoid foreign exchange risk by using the forward market. His proceeds in US dollars at time t would be $\$f_0A$. Alternatively, he might avoid the risk by **covering** in the **money markets**. He could borrow:

$$\frac{£A}{1+i_£}$$

in sterling at time $t = 0$. At time $t = 1$, £*A* will be due to the lender and this will be obtained via payment of the receivable. Meanwhile, the US exporter would convert

$$\frac{£A}{1+i_£}$$

to dollars at time 0 to give:

$$\frac{\$A}{1+i_£}s_0$$

Investing this in the Eurodollar market would yield, at time t:

$$\frac{\$A}{(1+i_£)}s_0(1+i_\$)$$

Assuming equilibrium between money markets and forward markets, each formula of cover will yield the same amount. So we can say that:

$$f_0A = \frac{A}{(1+i_£)}s_0(1+i_\$)$$

Rearranging this expression, we get:

$$f_0 = s_0\frac{1+i_\$}{1+i_£}$$

and dividing through by s_0 and then taking 1 from each side gives:

$$\frac{f_0}{s_0} - 1 = \frac{1+i_\$}{1+i_£} - 1$$

This yields the exact interest rate parity[2] formula of:

$$\frac{f_0 - s_0}{s_0} = \frac{i_\$ + i_£}{1+i_£}$$

This precise formulation, rather than the approximate one, is used by traders when dealing or making calculations for foreign exchange purposes. We now turn our attention to the second leg of the theoretical four-way equivalence in the foreign exchange markets.

3.4 Exchange rates and inflation rates

Just like the above relationship between interest rates and exchange rates, there exists a similar hypothesis – again underpinned to some extent by the actions of arbitrageurs – relating inflation rates and exchange rates. This relationship is also best approached by a numerical example. If a commodity sells in the United States at $400 per kg, and in the United Kingdom for £250 per kg, and the exchange rate is $1.70 to the pound sterling, then a profitable opportunity exists to buy the commodity in the United States, ship to the United Kingdom and sell there – always assuming, that is, that the gross profit of $25 per kg, given by (250 × 1.70) – 400, exceeds shipping and insurance costs from the United States to the United Kingdom.

Were this profitable opportunity to exist, so the theory goes, arbitrageurs buying in New York and selling in London would increase the price in the United States and depress it in the United Kingdom, and this would go on until the profit potential was eliminated. Arbitrage ensures that, in the absence of market imperfections, the prices of a commodity in two centres should not differ. When talking about prices of a particular good in this way, economists are invoking the law of one price.[3] Applied to the case in point, one could say that:

$$\text{£ price of a commodity} \times \text{price of £} = \text{\$ price of the commodity}$$

That is:

$$\text{Price of £} = \frac{\text{\$ price of the commodity}}{\text{£ price of the commodity}}$$

This kind of relationship should tend to hold for all internationally traded goods. That is:

$$\text{Price of £} = \frac{\text{\$ price of an internationally traded commodity}}{\text{£ price of the internationally traded commodity}}$$

Changes in the ratio of domestic prices of internationally traded goods in two centres should be reflected in changes in the price of currencies – the exchange rate.

In order to take the argument to the next stage, we should, strictly speaking, limit our focus to relative prices of internationally traded goods. But we approximate. **Purchasing power parity (PPP)** theory uses relative general price changes as a proxy for prices of internationally traded goods. And, applying it to the previous equation, we would obtain:

$$\text{Change in \$ price of £} = \frac{\text{change in \$ price level}}{\text{change in £ price level}}$$

Thus if inflation is 8 per cent p.a. in the United States and 12 per cent p.a. in the United Kingdom, then applying purchasing power parity theory we would expect the pound sterling to fall against the dollar by:

$$\frac{0.08 - 0.12}{1.12}$$

that is, 3.6 per cent p.a. Again this calculation is precise. A quick approximation based merely on straight inflation differentials would suggest a **devaluation** of 4 per cent p.a. The justification for using the precise formulation, rather than the approximate one, is considered in the algebraic formulation below.

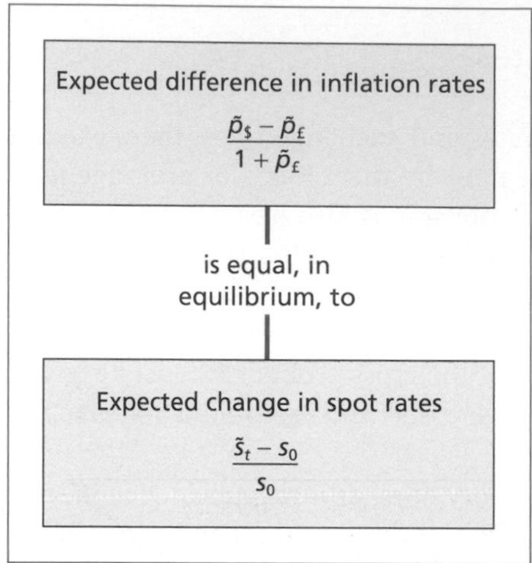

Figure 3.3 The purchasing power parity theorem

PPP theory, itself an approximation since it uses the general price level as a proxy for the price level of internationally traded goods, suggests that changes in the spot rate of exchange may be estimated by reference to expected inflation differentials. When looking at past exchange rate movements, the hypothesis might be tested by reference to actual price level changes. When making *ex-ante* estimates of spot changes we should look at the expected change in inflation rates. Figure 3.3 summarises the PPP hypothesis.

The precise formulation of the PPP theory, illustrated diagrammatically in Figure 3.3, can be easily substantiated by relatively simple algebra. Using the notation in Table 3.1 (earlier) and given that the spot rate of exchange at any date is underpinned by relative price levels, it follows that the values of the respective spot rates of exchange at time 0 and those expected for time t are given by:

$$s_0 = \frac{p_\$}{p_£}$$

$$\tilde{s}_t = \frac{p_\$(1 + \tilde{p}_\$)}{p_£(1 + \tilde{p}_£)}$$

Substituting, we can obtain:

$$\frac{\tilde{s}_t - s_0}{s_0} = \frac{p_\$}{p_£}\left[\frac{1 + \tilde{p}_\$}{1 + \tilde{p}_£} - 1\right]\frac{p_£}{p_\$}$$

from which it follows that:

$$\frac{\tilde{s}_t - s_0}{s_0} = \frac{\tilde{p}_\$ + \tilde{p}_£}{1 + \tilde{p}_£}$$

At its simplest, then, PPP predicts that the exchange rate changes to compensate for differences in inflation between two countries. Thus, if country A has a higher inflation rate than its trading partners, the exchange rate of the former should weaken to compensate for this relativity. If country A's **nominal exchange rate** falls and if that fall is an exact compensation for inflation differentials, its real **effective exchange rate** is said to remain constant. PPP predicts that real effective exchange rates will remain constant through time.

In terms of using purchasing power parity to forecast exchange rates, it should be clear that the predicted equilibrium rate will vary according to which year is chosen as a base date.

Thus, referring to Figure 3.4, if 2007 were used as the base year with trade-weighted, inflation-adjusted exchange rates of currencies A, B and C fixed at 100 as of that date, then, as of 2012 currency A would appear overvalued, currency B would appear correctly valued and currency C would appear undervalued. But if 2010 were taken as the base year, currency A would appear undervalued by 2012; at this time currency B would look overvalued and currency C would look correctly valued. So how does one get over this problem?

The answer is that one should start the analysis at a time when the exchange rate of the country being analysed is in equilibrium. And what is meant by the exchange rate being

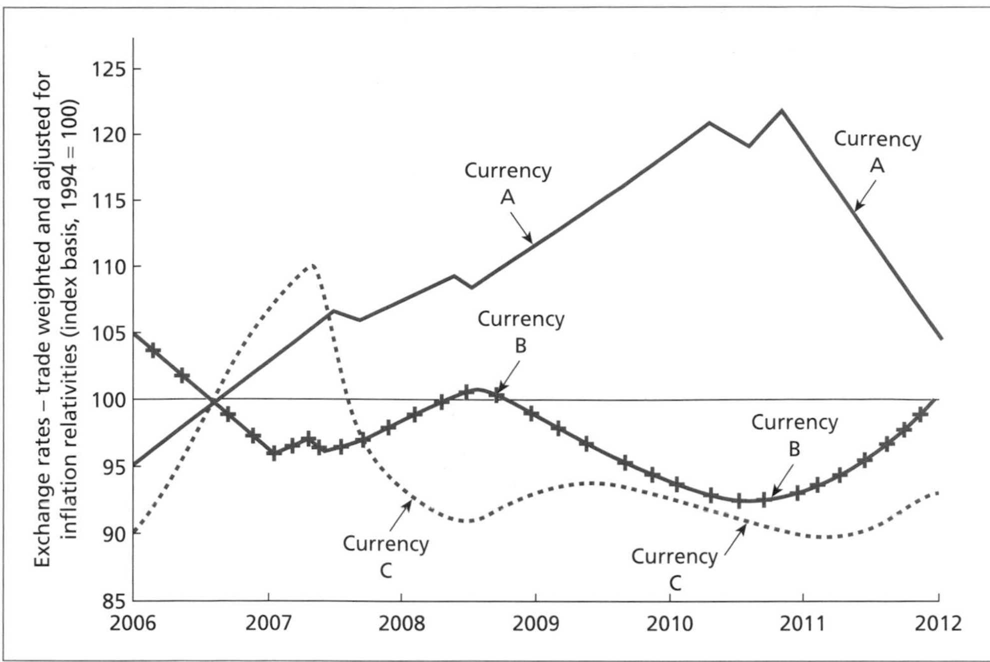

Figure 3.4 Real effective exchange rates

in equilibrium? We believe that the best approach in this area is to commence at a time when the exchange rate is such that the overall balance of trade plus invisibles is equal (or approximately equal) to zero. In one sense, exchange rate equilibrium may be defined as that level at which its impact results in the balance on trade and invisibles coming out at zero overall. This is the approach that we adopt in Section 3.9 headed 'Purchasing power parity applied'. But there are other approaches. For example, Williamson[4] views the equilibrium exchange rate as that rate which is consistent with overall external balance given underlying capital flows.

One of the biggest problems with PPP is that most applications of it use retail price indices, wholesale price indices or gross domestic product (GDP) deflators. Some international economists have suggested that the use of indices based upon traded goods would better reflect the nature or sentiment of the underpinning theory. They argue that a price index that embraces both traded and non-traded goods can impart a bias into the purchasing power parity calculations, and this is particularly marked when there are significant productivity differences between countries; this is known as the Balassa–Samuelson thesis (see Balassa[5] and Samuelson[6]). As an example, consider two countries producing similar export goods. Country X experiences substantial productivity gains in the export sector, while country Y achieves higher productivity advances in home-consumed goods and services. If productivity increments were of similar proportions as a percentage of their respective economies, both countries would have similar advances in their price indices. But, of course, if exchange rates were to remain constant, country X would, all other things being equal, gain in the export market at the expense of country Y. More probably, the exchange rate of country X would strengthen to reflect its lower export input costs per unit following the productivity gain; clearly, though, PPP calculations based on total data for all output would not pick up this effect. Evidently, care has to be exercised when using purchasing power parity as a model for calculating equilibrium exchange rates. Towards the end of this chapter, PPP is applied to arrive at estimations of where exchange rates should be using macroeconomic data of major world economies. Now let us turn to the theoretical relationship between interest rates and expected inflation rates.

3.5 Interest rates and inflation rates

According to the 'Fisher effect', a term coined because it was observed by US economist, Irving Fisher, nominal interest rates in a country reflect anticipated **real returns** adjusted for local inflation expectations. In a world where investors are internationally mobile, expected real rates of return should tend towards equality, reflecting the fact that in search of higher real returns, investors' arbitraging actions will force these returns towards each other. At least this should hold with respect to the free-market offshore currency interest rates. Constraints on international capital mobility create imperfections which, among other things, prevent this relationship from holding in domestic interest rate markets. So nominal offshore currency interest rates may differ for different currencies, but according to the Fisher effect only by virtue of different inflation expectations. And these inflation differentials should underpin expected changes in the spot rates of exchange. In other words, we would expect US and UK free-market interest investments to yield equal real returns. Differences in nominal returns would reflect expected inflation differentials. This would give us the theoretical relationship summarised in Figure 3.5.

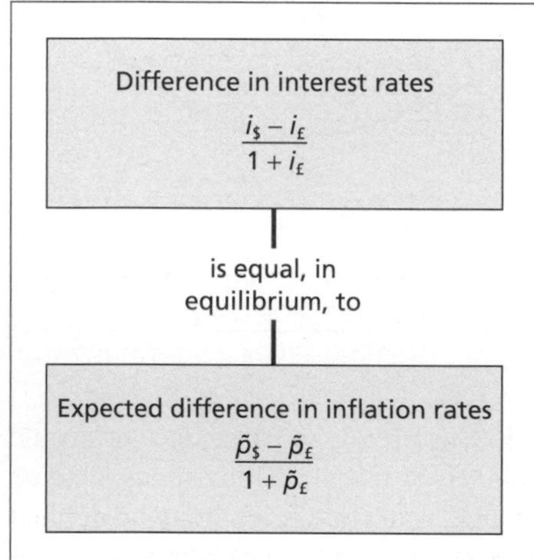

Figure 3.5 The Fisher effect

Again, the implications of the Fisher effect (sometimes termed 'Fisher's closed hypothesis') can be followed through algebraically towards the formulation shown in Figure 3.5. Since the Fisher theorem suggests that local interest rates reflect a real expected return adjusted for inflationary expectations, when money is internationally mobile and market imperfections are eliminated, local interest rates will be equal to the international real return adjusted for domestic inflationary expectations. Put algebraically, the following two equivalences are implied:

$$1 + i_\$ = (1 + r)(1 + \tilde{p}_\$)$$

and

$$1 + i_£ = (1 + r)(1 + \tilde{p}_£)$$

Subtracting the latter from the former gives:

$$i_\$ - i_£ = (1 + r)(\tilde{p}_\$ - \tilde{p}_£)$$

And this leads to:

$$\frac{i_\$ - i_£}{1+r} = \tilde{p}_\$ - \tilde{p}_£$$

Now multiplying through by $1/(1+\tilde{p}_£)$ we get:

$$\frac{i_\$ - i_£}{1+i_£} = \frac{\tilde{p}_\$ - \tilde{p}_£}{1+\tilde{p}_£}$$

Before we turn to the relationship between expected changes in the spot rate and the forward discount or premium on a currency we briefly refer to the Taylor Rule.

3.6 Taylor Rule

John Taylor, professor of economics at Stanford, created the Taylor Rule. It uses three variables, namely the target inflation rate, the target GDP growth and the existing inflation rate, to suggest logical levels of interest to be set by the central bank. The Taylor Rule is often summarised in the following manner:

$$i_t = \pi_t + r_t^* + \alpha_\pi(\pi_t - \pi_t^*) + \alpha_y(y_t - \bar{y}_t)$$

In the above equation, i_t is the target short-term nominal interest rate (in the USA, the Federal Funds rate), π_t is the rate of inflation as measured by the GDP deflator, π_t^* is the desired rate of inflation, r_t^* is the assumed equilibrium real interest rate, y_t is a measure of real GDP, and $\bar{y}_t$ is a measure of potential output.

In Taylor's original paper[7] α_π and α_y were suggested to be 0.5 each implying that equal policy weightings are given to inflation and to output targets.

The Rule suggests a relatively high interest rate when inflation is above target or when output is above potential – and vice versa. It can be seen that if the desire is to eliminate a 1 per cent excess inflation rate then, all other things being equal and with an α_π and are both equal to 0.5, the interest rate should rise by 1.5 per cent.

Presumably, immediately following the recent financial crisis, economic decision-makers have given a higher weighting to α_y at the expense of α_π. But before the crisis using the rule indicates that the Federal Funds rate dropped significantly below the rate predicted by the rule from the end of 2001 and remained significantly below it until 2006. This deviation from the rule was larger than at any time since the 1970s. Taylor calls this 'clear evidence of monetary excesses during the period leading up to the housing boom'.

3.7 Changes in the spot rate and the forward discount

This is the fourth side of the quadrilateral and must logically give rise to equality because of the hypothesised equality of the other three sides. This is the expectations theory of exchange rates and its implications are summarised diagrammatically in Figure 3.6.

This hypothesised relationship can be proved by *a priori* reasoning. If users of the foreign exchange market were not interested in risk, then the forward rate of exchange would depend solely on what people expected the future spot rate to be. A twelve-month forward rate on sterling of \$1.7635 to the pound would exist only because traders expected the spot rate in 12 months to be \$1.7635 to the pound. If they anticipated that it would be

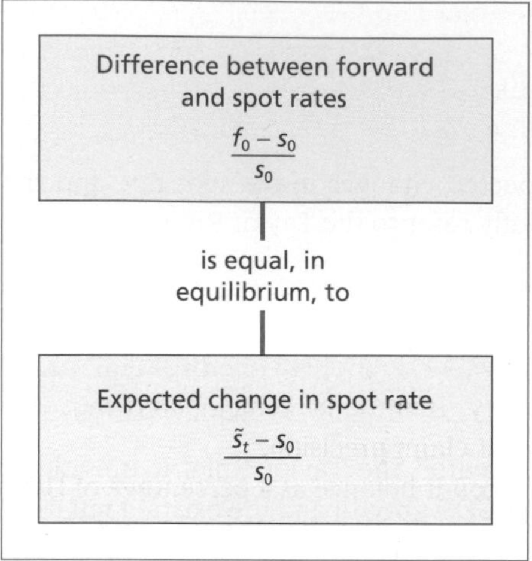

Figure 3.6 The expectations theory of exchange rates

higher than this, nobody would sell sterling at the forward rate. By the same token if they expected it to be lower, nobody would buy at the forward rate.

As traders do care about risk, the forward rate might be higher or lower than the expected spot rate. Suppose that a US exporter is certain to receive £1 million in six months' time. It might wait until six months have elapsed and then convert to dollars, or it might sell the pound forward. The first action involves exchange risk; the latter does not. To avoid foreign exchange risk, the trader may be willing to pay something slightly different from the expected spot price.

On the other side of the equation, there may be traders who wish to buy sterling six months away. To avoid the risk associated with movements in foreign exchange rates, they may be prepared to pay a forward price a little higher than the expected spot price.

Some traders find it safer to sell sterling forward; some traders find it safer to buy sterling forward. If the former group predominates, the forward price of sterling is likely to be less than the expected spot price. If the latter group predominates, the forward price is likely to be greater than the expected spot price. However, the actions of the predominant group are likely to adjust rates until they arrive at the hypothesised position in Figure 3.6.

3.8 Interest rate differentials and changes in the spot exchange rate

The hypothesis that differences in interest rate should underpin the expected movement in the spot rate of exchange is termed the 'international Fisher effect'; it is sometimes also called Fisher's open hypothesis. Referring back to Figure 3.1, international Fisher appears as one of the diagonals in the quadrilateral. What international Fisher predicts is summarised in Figure 3.7.

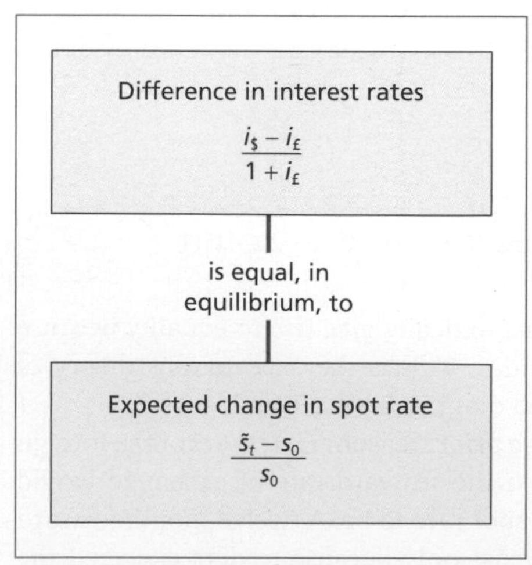

Figure 3.7 The international Fisher effect

When discussing the interest rate parity theorem, we referred to covered and uncovered interest arbitrage. Effectively, the actions of arbitrageurs eliminate continuing opportunities to make riskless profits by covered interest arbitrage. Their operations bring into equilibrium interest differentials and spot and forward exchange rates.

A similar line of reasoning underpins the international Fisher effect, but this time it is uncovered interest arbitrage that is at the heart of the argument. Rational investors may make estimates of future spot rates of exchange. If their views are such as to justify expectations of profit (in excess of that commensurate with the risk involved) from uncovered interest arbitrage, then their actions in purchasing one currency spot and selling another would move exchange rates so as to eliminate excess returns from the uncovered speculation. In a world of **efficient markets**, investors would use all available information to arrive at fair estimates of spot and future exchange rates, such that the relationship between them would eliminate consistently profitable opportunities of uncovered interest arbitrage. The effect of this would, of course, be to bring interest rate differentials into line with spot exchange rates and expectations of future spot rates.

3.9 Purchasing power parity applied

In this section we show how current account data may be used to help identify equilibrium exchange rates according to purchasing power parity. It must be remembered that the exercise which follows is approximate only; it does not claim precision.

Table 3.2 presents a matrix showing the **current account** balance as a percentage of GDP for a number of world economies for the period from 1985 onwards. Data have been presented as a percentage because relative values are far more meaningful than absolute figures. If a current account balance is shown as zero, this may be interpreted as being indicative of exchange rate equilibrium. This was the case for country N in 2008. For Country M, no year in the tabulation has a nil balance, but between 2007 and 2008, the current account appears to have flipped from surplus to deficit – it would, for the purposes of this exercise, be acceptable to take 2007 as being as near to equilibrium as is feasible. The format of data in Table 3.2 appear in the fashion shown in IMF published statistics.

Of course, there are a number of problem factors affecting current account data. First of all, they include some items that are not really to do with selling and buying goods and services internationally. Data includes interest and dividends earned and paid overseas; it also includes unilateral transfers. Strictly speaking, these items should be excluded in arriving at our estimate of equilibrium for the exchange rate. If great sophistication is required in the exercise, data may be modified to correct these potential distortions.

Table 3.2 Current account balance as a percentage of GDP for countries from 1995

Country	1995	1996	1997	1998	1999	2000	2001	2002	2003	2004	2005	2006	2007	2008	2009	2010	2011
A	–3.0	–3.3	–3.4	–2.4	–1.8	–1.4	.1	–.8	–1.2	–1.7	–1.5	–1.5	–1.7	–2.5	–3.5	–4.5	–4.1
B	–1.6	–3.1	–3.2	–3.0	–4.0	–3.4	–3.7	–3.6	–3.9	–2.3	–.7	.5	–1.3	–1.3	.2	2.6	2.8
C	3.7	4.2	3.4	2.7	2.1	1.4	2.0	3.0	3.0	2.7	2.1	1.4	2.2	3.1	2.4	2.5	2.2
D	–.2	.2	–.2	–.2	.2	.7	–	–.4	–.6	–1.5	–2.3	–2.1	–2.5	–2.5			
E	.8	2.5	1.9	2.2	2.2	1.7	2.2	2.8	4.9	5.0	4.8	4.8	5.3	4.5			
F	–1.5	–1.0	–1.9	–2.5	–5.0	–5.1	–5.5	–4.7	–1.3	1.1	4.0	3.9	5.4	5.7			
G	–	.3	–.5	–.5	–.5	–.8	–.5	.3	.7	.5	.7	1.3	2.7	2.6			
H	2.8	4.6	4.2	4.2	4.8	3.2	–1.0	–.9	–.7	–1.0	–.8	–.3	–.1	–.3			
I	–3.9	–3.2	–.2	–.1	–1.6	–.8	.6	1.1	3.5	2.9	2.6	2.8	2.3	1.2			
J	–1.0	.4	–.3	–.9	–1.5	–1.5	–2.1	–2.4	.8	1.3	2.3	3.2	2.8	1.7			
K	3.2	2.3	1.8	3.0	4.2	2.7	2.5	2.0	4.1	4.9	6.2	5.2	6.7	3.4			
L	1.7	1.7	–.1	–1.1	–2.9	–3.7	–3.7	–3.7	–1.2	–1.3	.1	.1	.5	–.6			
M	–4.6	–5.3	–2.8	–1.2	–1.0	1.0	1.5	2.9	3.5	2.1	1.0	1.7	.5	–1.2	1.7	1.6	2.6
N	4.8	–6.0	–4.5	–4.0	.2	3.5	4.3	3.5	3.0	3.1	3.6	7.0	6.5	–	5.5	15.6	15.9
O	–1.0	–	–	–0.3	–1.6	–2.8	–1.9	–3.6	–2.2	.4	2.1	2.2	3.1	1.9	2.5	2.9	3.2
P	6.3	3.4	3.6	4.7	4.5	3.0	4.5	5.9	7.6	6.7	7.1	7.1	10.4	10.2	10.9	13.6	
Q	.7	–.2	–1.8	–4.2	–5.1	–3.9	–1.8	–2.2	–1.9	–1.0	–1.3	–1.1	–.2	–.6	–2.2	–2.0	–2.1

Table 3.3 Real effective exchange rate indexes based on relative consumer prices

Country	1997	1998	1999	2000	2001	2002	2003	2004	2005	2006	2007	2008	2009	2010	2011	Mid-2012
A	112.4	105.9	109.3	104.7	103.5	101.2	104.7	103.4	100.0	104.3	112.0	120.0	119.3	125.2	134.5	131.1
B	114.7	121.0	129.5	128.0	131.9	121.1	113.6	103.3	100.0	101.7	103.2	98.6	97.6	99.5	98.7	96.6
C	82.5	88.1	80.7	71.6	76.8	79.2	93.6	98.3	100.0	84.5	80.2	78.9	89.3	95.5	85.5	81.9
D	92.6	92.1	90.8	92.4	91.6	93.3	95.7	96.4	100.0	98.0	94.6	94.6	92.8	90.3	91.1	92.5
E	94.8	92.2	90.9	94.8	94.1	95.0	95.0	96.5	100.0	98.2	93.6	93.4	91.8	88.7	89.3	90.6
F	110.3	112.8	119.3	122.4	116.9	101.1	86.2	91.7	100.0	96.0	93.0	93.1	90.7	87.1	89.1	90.8
G	99.1	96.9	94.8	98.1	95.1	96.6	97.7	97.4	100.0	99.9	95.6	96.0	93.2	88.4	88.4	90.2
H	92.5	90.1	88.1	90.8	87.2	91.5	95.4	95.7	100.0	96.8	92.0	92.5	89.5	84.6	85.6	87.1
I	108.4	104.7	102.4	107.1	104.1	106.9	99.1	99.4	100.0	101.9	101.6	97.1	94.2	91.2	94.5	100.7
J	124.0	122.9	125.6	131.5	132.5	130.6	110.5	107.2	100.0	111.6	112.3	113.1	110.9	106.3	107.7	111.0
K	97.9	95.6	91.8	93.7	92.1	93.7	95.3	96.0	100.0	98.2	93.6	94.4	93.7	89.9	92.7	96.6
L	97.5	102.1	108.1	114.8	116.2	115.7	103.1	98.3	100.0	102.2	97.4	97.4	96.7	94.2	95.9	98.4
M	96.2	95.7	93.9	98.1	94.9	96.0	96.4	95.9	100.0	99.3	96.5	98.3	97.5	93.5	94.9	97.4
N	105.7	108.3	107.6	106.5	103.2	103.5	99.3	97.2	100.0	99.8	101.1	98.2	97.9	96.1	99.6	109.7
O	108.2	110.9	113.7	118.2	123.9	123.9	101.7	100.2	100.0	108.4	103.0	100.1	97.0	95.1	87.6	89.3
P	90.0	88.5	83.0	89.2	89.3	87.7	89.7	93.9	100.0	97.3	90.0	91.1	89.4	87.3	89.8	93.3
Q	104.5	112.8	113.3	117.1	119.8	115.6	103.5	103.7	100.0	102.4	120.5	128.0	127.6	131.9	129.5	129.3

Secondly, using current account data as an indicator of equilibrium presents problems for economies that are very substantially affected by earnings from one commodity – for example, sterling was frequently referred to as a petro-currency in the early 1980s, reflecting the large role of oil in the United Kingdom's balance of payments figures. Zambia's balance of payments ebbs and flows in line with copper prices, this mineral being its major export by a very long way. Movements towards equilibrium on Zambia's balance of payments will have more to do with world demand for copper than with exchange rates.

We now move on to Tables 3.3 and 3.4. These show real effective exchange rate indices for a disguised sample of industrialised countries from 1997. Table 3.3 involves a computation of the index on the basis of consumer prices; Table 3.4 is based upon unit labour costs normalised to iron out cyclical effects. For these tables, the 2005 figure is set at 100. Real effective exchange rates have been arrived at in the following manner:

- The nominal exchange rate for a particular country – say country X – against its trading partners has been tracked.
- The weighting of trade and services of country X with its trading partners has been extracted from published data.
- Inflation for country X compared with its trading partners has been extracted from published statistics – duly weighted according to aggregate trade and services transactions.
- Nominal exchange rates have been adjusted to a trade-weighted figure by applying weightings in accordance with amounts of trade and services transacted with international partners.
- Such figures have been adjusted to allow for comparative inflation rates of country X and its trading partners.

Notice the dramatic difference obtained by using the different measures in Tables 3.3 and 3.4. This is particularly sharp in the case of the country Q. From 2005 to mid-2012, country Q figures have moved from 100 to 129.3 according to consumer prices and from

Table 3.4 Real effective exchange rate indexes based on normalised unit labour costs

Country	1997	1998	1999	2000	2001	2002	2003	2004	2005	2006	2007	2008	2009	2010	2011	Mid-2012
A	130.9	122.9	124.5	115.8	111.6	109.0	111.1	108.5	100.0	103.6	109.5	116.6	114.8	123.5	135.1	130.6
B	94.6	101.4	110.6	113.6	118.8	113.6	107.4	100.8	100.0	100.8	103.5	97.0	95.9	96.0	92.2	91.3
C	74.3	79.1	75.7	68.4	73.3	75.6	89.5	95.1	100.0	85.6	81.7	76.3	86.9	93.3	82.6	77.3
D	121.5	116.4	111.7	108.8	104.7	105.6	106.2	103.8	100.0	95.2	90.5	89.2	87.4	85.7	85.4	86.1
E	98.7	94.9	94.3	96.4	97.0	96.6	98.0	97.1	100.0	95.8	92.4	91.9	88.4	85.6	86.5	85.9
F	126.9	129.7	133.6	134.6	123.7	102.0	86.4	90.6	100.0	92.5	87.2	86.0	82.9	79.0	79.7	79.3
G	108.2	104.5	101.5	102.7	98.4	99.3	100.1	99.0	100.0	96.9	92.9	92.5	91.8	88.2	87.2	88.3
H	75.6	76.7	76.8	81.9	81.3	84.9	90.5	93.2	100.0	98.7	92.9	90.5	87.8	82.7	82.0	82.4
I	163.5	155.6	145.3	142.8	129.4	126.0	115.2	107.1	100.0	95.0	89.0	80.5	75.2	68.0	67.4	68.0
J	126.8	125.4	131.4	135.8	138.1	134.7	114.9	108.7	100.0	114.6	117.1	114.8	114.3	110.4	109.7	111.9
K	108.1	102.6	96.5	95.4	92.3	94.6	96.7	97.7	100.0	97.1	92.7	93.9	93.3	91.3	93.1	96.7
L	89.7	93.3	100.6	106.5	110.3	115.4	107.5	100.9	100.0	102.6	100.1	102.0	102.3	101.1	103.4	106.7
M	96.3	94.8	93.3	97.7	94.2	95.3	97.9	97.1	100.0	98.2	95.8	97.4	97.2	94.2	95.5	97.6
N	96.6	98.4	97.6	97.1	96.5	96.8	94.9	94.7	100.0	102.5	106.9	108.1	113.3	115.5	122.0	139.1
O	115.7	120.0	125.7	124.4	122.4	123.8	100.3	99.4	100.0	112.8	110.0	108.2	104.9	104.2	94.7	96.5
P	88.1	89.6	85.2	89.7	90.8	86.3	86.8	94.1	100.0	100.2	97.2	102.8	102.5	102.2	107.4	114.1
Q	104.6	109.7	107.2	107.9	113.0	110.1	101.4	103.6	100.0	103.6	123.5	131.3	133.6	141.0	140.6	142.6

100 to 142.6 if data is based on unit labour costs. In other words, as at 2011, on the basis of the latter figure, country Q seems more overvalued than on the former criterion.

We now show how the figures can be used to assess whether a currency is overvalued or undervalued. Take the example of country Q. According to Table 3.2, the current account for country Q moved, most recently, into approximate balance in 2007 and 2008. With a J-curve effect of 12 months, it is assumed that the 2006 and 2007 exchange rates are around the equilibrium rate. In essence, the J-curve effect assumes that the equilibrium exchange rate takes some 12 months to work its way through to exports and imports. Turning to Table 3.3 – the consumer price tabulation – the real effective index averaged 111.5 for these two years. According to the mid-2012 figure (remember that real effective rates in the tables are based upon weighted averages for the year) the currency of country Q index was 129.3. Obviously, the conclusion is that the 2012 value of the currency was overvalued on purchasing power criteria, using consumer prices, against the currencies of its trading partners. By how much is it overvalued? The figure given by 129.3 divided by 111.5 suggests a 16 per cent overvaluation. But if we wish to know whether country Q currency is too strong against currency A, we need to do another calculation. This involves assessing whether the currency of country A is too strong on PPP criteria. Currency A's current account was near to zero in 2001, and with a twelve-month lag, this suggests that the figure for consumer prices in 2000 might be taken as a starting point. The appropriate index, according to Table 3.3, is 104.7. This suggests an overvaluation of the currency A by around 25 per cent in mid 2012. This is given by the mid-2012 figure of 131.1 divided by the 2000 figure of 104.7. The combined effect on the basis of consumer prices is that currency A is overvalued by around 9 per cent against currency Q.

Remember that the estimate is approximate only. We should really question which is the more appropriate index. Certainly if we use unit labour costs, we get a different answer to that based on consumer prices. Would some index based on import and export prices be better? The answer is, in all probability, yes. But there is also a further problem because data are continually being altered and updated. So maybe an approximation is the best we can expect.

As a check, it is useful to run the numbers beginning from two or three current account equilibrium dates. On the same kind of criteria, students are encouraged to do a similar exercise for their own home currency. What do you find? Clearly, the tables of real effective exchange rate indices, especially if kept regularly up-to-date, are of great value to companies, investors, speculators and others.

In passing, it should be mentioned that one of the major causes of the Asian financial crisis in 1997 was the fact that so many countries in South East Asia were pegging their currencies to the US dollar at a time of substantial local inflation and when PPP was suggesting significant devaluations. Needless to say, a freely floating currency regime is recommended for most, if not all, currencies.

South American countries have frequently created problems for themselves by failing to adjust their currencies in a devaluation to the figure implied by PPP. They seem to prefer to maintain too strong a rate for their currency, compounding the problems for their economy. Their Ministers of Finance might well be advised to study this book.

3.10 Big Mac purchasing power parity

We now turn to *The Economist's* **Big Mac Index**. Invented in 1986 as a light-hearted guide to whether currencies are at their right level, the index is based upon the price of a McDonald's Big Mac burger around the world. The Big Mac is produced locally to roughly the same recipe in 118 countries. The Big Mac purchasing power parity methodology aims to calculate the exchange rate that would leave non-USA burgers costing the same as in the United States. *The Economist's* burgernomics compares the Big Mac exchange rate with the actual exchange rate as a test of whether a currency is over- or undervalued. Take an example. It uses prices in July 2010. The price of the Big Mac averaged over New York and Chicago was USD3.73. The price in Britain was £2.99, giving an implied Big Mac PPP rate of £1 = USD1.63. At the time, the actual exchange rate was £1 = USD1.52. If the Big Mac were the only item in your shopping basket, this would imply an undervaluation of the £ against the USD of 7 per cent.

Light-hearted burgernomics has become a matter of increasing academic interest and has spawned many articles and even a whole book by Ong[8] of the International Monetary Fund. Little did McDonald's and *The Economist* know what they were starting with the Big Mac as the assumed sole constituent of the basket for PPP calculations. Continuing the good humour of this section, may we suggest that your shopping basket should be slightly more diversified. A shopping basket solely consisting of burgers is not recommended if longevity is one of your goals.

It is interesting to note that the Economist did give us a Starbucks Tall Latte Index one year. And there is an iPod index and also one based on Ikea's Billy bookshelf. By the time this book is published will we have a Kindle index? Probably.

Summary

- The direct quotation method means a rate of exchange quoted in terms of *X* units of home currency to one unit of foreign currency.

- The indirect quotation method means a rate of exchange quoted in terms of *Y* units of foreign currency per unit of home currency.
- The United Kingdom generally uses the indirect quotation method; most others usually employ direct quotation.
- The foreign exchange spot market is a currency market for immediate delivery. In practice, payment and delivery are usually two working days after the **transaction date**.
- The forward market involves rates quoted today for delivery and payment at a future fixed date of a specified amount of one currency against another.
- Forward markets go out to ten years and more for major currencies, but not for all. Some currencies do not even have a forward market.
- The forward market enables companies and others to insure themselves against foreign exchange loss.
- In the absence of barriers to international capital movements, there is a theoretical relationship between exchange rates, inflation and fixed interest rates.
- Note how bankers quote interest rates. If the banker wants a 2 per cent return over three months, he or she quotes an annual rate of 8 per cent. In reality, based on compounding every quarter, 2 per cent every three months means an interest rate over a year of 8.24 per cent. But the banker does not quote 8.24 per cent; he or she quotes 8 per cent. Note too that bankers always quote annual rates – even though lending for a week or a month or whatever.
- Figure 3.1 is most important. Note that dollars and pounds are used in the figure. It can be used for any pair of currencies – simply substitute in the formulae. But remember that the formulae are based on a logic that uses New York direct quotations – that is London indirect. So when you substitute, remember to ensure consistency. Use the direct quote for both currencies as if you were in the centre substituted for dollars in the equations.
- Interest rate parity concludes that there is a relationship between spot and forward exchange rates which is underpinned by Eurocurrency interest rate differentials. These interest rate differentials are based on fixed – not floating – interest rates for the period concerned. With the notation of Table 3.1 in the text:

$$\frac{f_0 - s_0}{s_0} = \frac{i_\$ - i_£}{1 + i_£}$$

- Note that in the above formulation, the left-hand side is termed the forward premium or forward discount. The right-hand side is termed the interest differential.
- Note in the above formula, and indeed all formulae used in this section, that we are using precise relationships based on correct deductive reasoning. In the formulae above, we do not use $(i_\$ - i_£)$ as the interest differential. We actually use this as the numerator in our calculation. There is an essential denominator – and this is given by $(1 + i_£)$.
- Remember also that if we do calculations connected with a three-month forward rate, we have to use corresponding interest rates – that is for three months. Thus, an 8 per cent rate as quoted by the banker becomes 2 per cent over three months.

- In reality, in the market place, forward rates are based on numbers of days. In this text, we approximate by using months.
- The logical proof of interest rate parity is based upon covered interest arbitrage. Note what is entailed in this process – see the text.
- Some courses on international financial management require you to be able to prove the four-way equivalence model; some do not require this facility. As a matter of information, courses that the author teaches do not demand such proof.
- Purchasing power parity is concerned with the relationship between movements in spot exchange rates and relative inflation rates. With the notation in the text:

$$\frac{\tilde{s}_t - s_0}{s_0} = \frac{\tilde{p}_\$ - \tilde{p}_£}{1 + \tilde{p}_£}$$

- This formula is clearly forward-looking since it uses expected movements in exchange rate and inflation rates.
- A currency whose value moved exactly in line with purchasing power parity would have a real effective exchange rate of 100 throughout the period concerned.
- If the exchange rate for a currency over time were exactly to reflect inflation differentials as defined above, one would say that its real effective exchange rate (sometimes abbreviated to real exchange rate) was constant.
- A formulation which is backward-looking (that is, based on historic data) would take the form:

$$\frac{s_t - s_0}{s_0} = \frac{p_\$ - p_£}{1 + p_£}$$

  In this form, rather than using expected data, past rates would be used.
- A currency would be overvalued if it were too strong compared with its purchasing power parity value. It would be undervalued if it were too weak compared with its purchasing power parity values.
- If purchasing power parity calculations are to reflect a currency's strength against all of its trading partners, it is necessary to weight exchange rate movements and relative inflation rates in accordance with its trade patterns.
- Note that different purchasing power parity values will be obtained as different base years for calculation are used.
- The above difficulty may be overcome by using a base date when the exchange rate is in equilibrium. This is perhaps best taken as a time when the country's current account in its balance of payments is zero.
- A real exchange rate of 100 implies correct valuation. A real effective exchange rate of 100 plus implies overvaluation and a real effective rate of less than 100 implies undervaluation.
- Note that inflation may be based on consumer prices, wholesale prices, the GDP deflator or export prices. The last of the above four gives the best purchasing power parity valuation. After all, this is the best definition of inflation for international trade purposes.

- The Fisher effect is concerned with the relationship between interest rates and inflation. With the notation of Table 3.1 it suggests that:

$$\frac{i_\$ - i_£}{1 + i_£} = \frac{\tilde{p}_\$ - \tilde{p}_£}{1 + \tilde{p}_£}$$

- Expectations theory relates the forward discount and changes in spot rate. It suggests that:

$$\frac{f_0 - s_0}{s_0} = \frac{\tilde{s}_t - s_0}{s_0}$$

- The international Fisher effect links interest rate differentials with expected changes in spot rates. It suggests that:

$$\frac{i_\$ - i_£}{1 + i_£} = \frac{\tilde{s}_t - s_0}{s_0}$$

- The four-way equivalence model developed in this chapter is a deductive model. In terms of using it in the real world, we have to ask how will it stand up empirically. Findings are summarised in Chapter 6. In a nutshell, at the level of most corporate users of foreign exchange rate markets it is only interest rate parity that holds in the short term. The other relationships are found to stand up fairly well long term. But more of that later.

End of chapter questions

3.1 All other things being equal, assume that US interest rates fall relative to UK interest rates. Again, with all other things being equal, how should this affect the:

(a) US demand for British pounds;
(b) supply of pounds for sale; and
(c) equilibrium value of the pound?

3.2 What is the expected relationship between the relative real interest rates of two countries and the exchange rate of their currencies?

3.3 Some Latin American currencies have depreciated against the US dollar on a daily basis. What is the major factor that places such a severe downward pressure on the value of these currencies? What obvious change in Latin American economic policy would prevent the regular depreciation of these currencies?

4 Foreign exchange markets

The foreign exchange market is the framework of individuals, firms, banks and brokers who buy and sell foreign currencies. The foreign exchange market for any one currency, for example the US dollar, consists of all the locations such as Paris, London, New York, Zurich, Frankfurt and so on, in which the US dollar is bought and sold for other currencies. Foreign exchange markets tend to be located in national financial centres near the local financial markets. The most important foreign exchange markets are found in London, New York, Tokyo, Frankfurt, Amsterdam, Paris, Zurich, Toronto, Brussels, Milan, Singapore and Hong Kong.

There are four main types of transaction undertaken in these foreign exchange markets: spot transaction, forward deals, futures transactions and **currency options**.

In the spot market, currencies are bought and sold for immediate delivery. In practice, this means that settlement is made two working days after the spot date. The intervention of these two days allows for necessary paperwork to be completed. In the forward market, currencies are bought and sold at prices agreed now but for future delivery at an agreed date. Not only is delivery made in the future, but payment is also made at the future date.

4.1 The players

The main participants in the market are companies and individuals, commercial banks, central banks and brokers. Companies and individuals need foreign currency for business or travel reasons. Commercial banks are the source from which companies and individuals obtain their foreign currency. Through their extensive network of dealing rooms, information systems and arbitrage operations (buying in one centre and selling in another), banks ensure that quotations in different centres tend towards the same price. There are also foreign exchange brokers who bring buyers, sellers and banks together and receive commissions on deals arranged. The other main player operating in the market is the central bank, the main part of whose foreign exchange activities involves the buying and selling of the home currency or foreign currencies with a view to ensuring that the exchange rate moves in line with established targets set for it by the government.

Not only are there numerous foreign exchange market centres around the world, but dealers in different locations can communicate with one another via the telephone, telex and computers. The overlapping of time zones means that, apart from weekends, there is always one centre that is open.

4.2 Methods of quotation

A foreign exchange rate is the price of one currency in terms of another. Foreign exchange dealers quote two prices, one for selling, one for buying. The first area of mystique in foreign exchange quotations arises from the fact that there are two ways of quoting rates: the **direct quote** and the **indirect quote**. The former gives the quotation in terms of the number of units of home currency necessary to buy one unit of foreign currency. The latter gives the quotation in terms of the number of units of foreign currency bought with one unit of home currency.

Continental European dealers normally quote via the direct method for their centre. In London dealers generally use the indirect London method. In the United States, both quotation methods are used. When a bank is dealing with a customer within the United States a direct quotation is given, but when dealing with other banks in Europe (except the United Kingdom), the indirect quotation is generally used.

Foreign exchange dealers quote two prices: the rate at which they are prepared to sell a currency and that at which they are prepared to buy. The difference between the bid rate and the offer is the dealer's **spread** which is one of the potential sources of profit for dealers. Whether using the direct quotation method or the indirect quote, the smaller rate is always termed the bid rate and the higher is called the offer, or ask, rate.

If we assume that the middle quote (that is, halfway between the sell and buy price) for Swiss francs to the US dollar is CHF1.3753 = USD1, then the New York direct quote for this rate would be $0.7271 and the Zurich direct quote is CHF1.3753. Where both centres use the same method of quotation (that is, they both use the direct quote or they both use the indirect method) and when they are both in effect quoting the same price (in other words there are no arbitrage opportunities) the quote in one centre is the reciprocal of the other. Thus the two quotes multiplied together will equal 1.0. To the extent that this condition fails to hold, possibilities for profitable arbitrage (selling in one centre and buying in the other) exist. Of course, operators need to look at the buy rate in one centre and the sell rate in the other in terms of assessing arbitrage opportunities. In carrying out a profitable arbitrage, dealers force the prices in various centres towards equality.

If, in terms of the middle quote, the US dollar/sterling rate is $1.6015 equals £1, then the New York quote (using the local direct method) will be $1.6015 and the London quote (using the indirect method) will also be $1.6015. Where one centre uses the direct quotation method and the other uses the indirect method, the two quotations will, assuming no profitable arbitrage opportunities exist, be exactly the same.

The size of the bid/offer spread varies according to the depth of the market and its stability at any particular time. Depth of a market refers to the volume of transactions in a particular currency. Deep markets have many deals; shallow markets have few. High percentage spreads are associated with high uncertainty (perhaps owing to impending devaluation) and low volumes of transactions in a currency. Lower spreads are associated with stable, high-volume markets. Deep markets usually have narrower spreads than shallow ones.

If US dollars are quoted in terms of sterling as $1.6050 to $1.6060, it means that the dealer is prepared to sell dollars at $1.6050 to the pound, or buy dollars at $1.6060. Conversely, the dealer is prepared to buy pounds at the rate of $1.6050 or sell pounds at $1.6060. In the above example, the spread is equal to $0.0010, or 10 points. A point (or pip, as it is widely referred to) is the last significant figure in the quotation.

Next, it is necessary to consider the meaning of **cross-rates**. A cross-rate may be defined as an exchange rate that is calculated from two (or more) other rates. Thus the rate for the Swiss franc to the Swedish krona will, most likely, be derived as the cross-rate from the US dollar to the Swiss franc and the US dollar to the krona.

The practice in world foreign exchange markets is that currencies are quoted against the US dollar. If one bank asks another for its Swiss franc rate, that rate will be quoted against the US dollar unless otherwise specified. Most dealing is done against the US dollar, hence it follows that the market rate for a currency at any moment is most accurately reflected in its exchange rate against the US dollar. A bank that was asked to quote sterling against the Swiss franc would normally do so by calculating this rate from the £/$ rate and the $/Sfr rate. It would therefore be using cross-rates to arrive at its quotation.

Let us suppose that we require a quote for the euro against the Swiss franc. The quotation that we would receive would articulate with the quote of both currencies against the US dollar. If these rates against the dollar were $1 = €1.1326/1.1336 and $1 = CHF1.3750 /1.3755, it would be possible to derive the cross-rate for the euro against the Swiss franc. Our goal is to derive the selling and buying rates for euros in terms of Swiss francs. If we are selling euros we will be buying Swiss francs. So we begin with the rate for selling euros and buying dollars; we then move to selling dollars and buying Swiss francs. The amalgamation of these two rates gives us the rate for selling euros and buying Swiss francs. The rate for selling euros to the dealer and buying dollars is €1.1336; the rate for selling dollars and buying Swiss francs is CHF1.3750. So selling €1 gives $0.8822. Selling $0.8822 gives CHF1.2130. The rate for selling euros and buying Swiss francs is a1 = CHF1.2130, or CHF1 = €0.8244.

Similarly, in our example, if we are buying euros we will be selling Swiss francs. This time we begin with the rate for buying euros from the dealer and selling dollars, and then we move to buying dollars and selling Swiss francs. Amalgamating these two rates gives us the rate for buying euros and selling Swiss francs. The rate for buying euros and selling dollars is €1.1326; the rate for buying dollars and selling Swiss francs is CHF1.3755. Selling CHF1 gives $0.7270. Selling $0.7270 gives €0.8234. The rate for buying euros and selling Swiss francs is CHF1 = €0.8234, or €1 = CHF1.2145. The cross-rate quotation using direct euro figures would be €0.8234/0.8244 = CHF1, and the direct Zurich quote would be CHF1.2130/1.2145.

It is also worth mentioning the manner of quotation when the market or financial commentators use a slash between two currencies. Take the following example:

EUR/JPY 128.56 ↑ 0.32

This means that you get (or, more precisely it is the middle price of buy and sell prices) JPY128.56 for €1. So the slash means that the currency before the slash should be equated to one and you get the number of units quoted (128.56) of the currency after the slash. Imagine that our quotation is a mid-morning quote in London. The figure of 0.32 with the upward arrow implies that the quote has moved upwards by 0.32 since the opening of the London trading session. So, the opening price was therefore 128.24. The upward arrow means that at mid-morning, in our example, you get more JPY for your € than at the opening. So the upward arrow implies that the currency before the slash (€ in the example) has strengthened in the trading session versus the JPY.

Take another example. Check it out yourself before going on to the explanatory note below it. Can you understand this quotation? How many Swiss francs are there to one

US dollar? How many US dollars are there to one Swiss franc? Which currency has strengthened during the trading session? The quotation is:

US$/CHF 1.3785 ↓ 0.0026

This means that US$1 equals CHF1.3785. And, during the trading session since the opening, the US$ has weakened against the CHF. The opening price was 1.3811 and the dollar has moved down against the Swiss franc to 1.3785. The downward percentage movement is therefore 0.0026 divided by 1.3811 (the opening price) with the result multiplied by 100 – that is 0.19 per cent. Looked at from a reverse position, CHF1 equals US$0.7254. Try working out the quotation with CHF before the slash. Do it without looking at the figures below. The answer should be:

CHF/US$ 0.7254 ↑ 0.0013

Note that the movement upwards is from 1.0 divided by 1.3811, that is 0.7241 at the opening, giving a Swiss franc rise of 0.0013.

4.3 Forward contracts and quotations

It is necessary to consider next how **forward rates** are quoted by foreign exchange dealers. A forward foreign exchange contract is an agreement between two parties to exchange one currency for another at some future date. The rate at which the exchange is to be made, the delivery date and the amounts involved are fixed at the time of the agreement.

One of the major problems that newcomers to foreign exchange markets have is understanding how the forward **premium** and discount works and how foreign exchange dealers quote for forward delivery. Assume that a quoted currency is more expensive in the future than it is now in terms of the base currency. The quoted currency is then said to stand at a premium in the forward market relative to the base currency. Conversely, the base currency is said to stand at a discount relative to the quoted currency.

Consider an example in which the US dollar is the base currency and the Swiss franc is the quoted currency. Assume that the spot rate is $1 = CHF1.3753. The rate quoted by a bank today for delivery in three months' time (today's three-month forward rate) is $1 = CHF1.3748. In this example, the dollar buys fewer Swiss francs in three months' time than it does today. So the Swiss franc is more expensive in the forward market. Thus the dollar stands at a discount relative to the Swiss franc; conversely, the Swiss franc stands at a premium relative to the dollar. The size of the dollar discount or Swiss franc premium is the difference between 1.3753 and 1.3748, that is, 0.05 centimes. The convention in the foreign exchange market is frequently to quote in terms of points, or hundredths of a unit. Hence 0.05 centimes is frequently quoted as 5 points.

In order to arrive at the forward prices, the Swiss franc premium or dollar discount must be subtracted from the spot rate. Were there a Swiss franc discount or dollar premium, this would be added to the spot rate. But care has to be taken: in our example we used a New York indirect quote. Had we used a New York direct quote, the reverse would apply: in other words, the Swiss franc premium or dollar discount would have to be added to the spot quotation. An easier way to deal with this little problem is always to remember (and this has never, in practice, been found to be otherwise) that the bid/offer spread on the forward quote is always wider than the spread on the spot figure. If this is remembered it is an easy process to compare the two spreads and if the forward spread is narrower than the spot spread, the sums have been done incorrectly and recomputation is necessary.

Just as in the spot market, dealers quote selling and buying rates in the forward market, too. As in the spot market the convention, whether using direct or indirect quotation methods, is that the smaller rate is quoted first. In the above example the spot rate for Swiss francs to US dollar might be quoted as CHF1.3748/1.3758 and the three-month Swiss franc premium (or dollar discount) might be 6/3. Thus, if the foreign exchange dealer is buying dollars forward, there will be a Swiss franc premium of 6 points, or 0.06 centimes. But if he is buying the Swiss franc, the premium will only be 3 points or 0.03 centimes. Using the convention that the forward spread is wider than the spot spread, the full three-month forward quotation comes out at CHF1.3742/1.3755.

	Bid rate	**Offer rate**	**Spread in points**
Spot quotation	1.3748	1.3758	10
Forward spread	6	3	3
Subtract to make forward spread 13 points	1.3742	1.3755	13

Sometimes forward quotes are given as –10/+10 or 10P10. In this situation the forward market is said to be 'round par'. Thus, to get the forward rate, 10 points have to be added to either the bid or offer and 10 points have to be subtracted so that the forward spread widens on the spot spread. For example, take the quotations of:

1.3748/1.3758 –10/+10

The forward rate could be construed as 1.3738/1.3768, i.e. it may be quoted in full rather than as points distance from spot. This is called the outright forward price. It would be computed as:

	Bid rate	**Offer rate**	**Spread in points**
Spot quotation	1.3748	1.3758	10
Forward spread	(10)	10	20
	1.3738	1.3768	30

Sometimes this kind of situation is quoted in terms of the spread from the spot rate as 10 centimes discount, 10 centimes premium.

It is important to bear in mind that the currency quoted at a discount in the forward market relative to another currency will have higher Eurocurrency interest rates than the currency which is at the premium. The rationale for this was discussed in the previous chapter.

As an adjunct to the above methods of quoting forward foreign exchange rates, we sometimes see the percentage per annum cost of forward cover. What does this mean and how is it calculated? The annualised forward premium may be expressed as a percentage by reference to the formula:

$$\frac{\text{Forward rate} - \text{spot rate}}{\text{Spot rate}} \times \frac{12}{n} \times 100$$

where n is the number of months in the forward contract.[1] It should be noted that small differences in the annual percentage cost of forward cover arise when using the direct quotation method as opposed to using the indirect quote. Slightly different results arise too from using the buying rate as opposed to the selling rate or the middle price. The problem of differing costs of forward cover for buying and selling is easily resolved. While different figures are achieved using mathematics, the relevant figure for a company executive using the forward market is the percentage cost of doing the transaction that he or she wishes to undertake.

Let us look at an example. Suppose again that we have a spot rate of USD1 = CHF1.3748/1.3758 and that the three-month forward quote is 6/3. The forward rate came out (see above) as CHF1.3742/1.3755. If we were a buyer of Swiss francs forward, the forward premium would be obtained by comparing the rates for buying Swiss francs (that is CHF1.3748 spot and CHF1.3742 three months forward). The annualised forward premium for buying Swiss francs would therefore amount to:

$$\frac{1.3742 - 1.3748}{1.3748} \times \frac{12}{3} \times 100 = -0.17\% \text{ p.a.}$$

The Swiss franc is said to be at an annualised premium of 0.17 per cent in the three-month forward market against the US dollar based on rates for buying marks.

4.4 Spot settlement

A spot foreign exchange deal is made for settlement in two working days' time. So, in normal circumstances, a deal done on Monday is settled on Wednesday. The **value date** is the date of Wednesday.

A working day is defined as one in which banks for currencies on either side of the deal are open for business in both settlement countries – with one exception. If the deal is done against the US dollar and if the first of the two days is a holiday in the United States but not in the other settlement country, then that day is also counted as a working day.

In the case of a US dollar/Swiss franc deal done on Monday, settlement would normally be on Wednesday. This would not be affected by a US holiday on the Tuesday. But it would be affected by a Swiss holiday on the Tuesday. In the latter case, the spot date would be postponed until Thursday, provided that both centres were open on Thursday. If Tuesday were a normal working day, but Wednesday were a holiday in either the United States or Switzerland, then the spot day would be Thursday, assuming that both centres were open that day.

In the case of a US dollar/Swiss franc deal done, say, in London, the occurrence of UK bank holidays during the spot period is entirely irrelevant. This is because all bank account transfers are made in the settlement country rather than the dealing centre.

In certain countries, such as the United States or Switzerland, bank holidays may affect only part of the country – depending on whether it is a local state holiday, or, if religious, whether the area is mainly Catholic or Protestant. In this case, the date for settlement could vary according to the regional location of the bank accounts involved. This complication is ignored in this book, but it is clearly relevant in the real world.

Settlement of both sides of a foreign exchange deal ought to be made on the same working day. Given time zone differences, settlement on any given working day will take place earlier in the Far East, later in Europe, and later still in the United States. This implies a risk. Using the US dollar/Swiss franc example, a bank selling Swiss francs may deliver them in Zurich before receiving the dollars in New York. Should the recipient in Switzerland go bankrupt before delivering the dollars, losses may arise. Hence the worry about limits and the section devoted to this in Chapter 11. The notion that the two sides of the deal should be completed on the same day is referred to as the principle of *valeur compensée* or compensated value.

The only exception to compensated value arises in deals in Middle Eastern currencies for settlement on Friday. This is a holiday in most Middle East countries. When this happens, the person buying the Middle Eastern currency – for example, Saudi riyals – makes payment, say in US dollars, on Friday. Delivery of the riyals takes place on Saturday, which is a normal business day in the Middle East.

4.5 Forward value dates

The first step in finding the normal forward value date for periods of one, two, three months, and so on, is to fix the spot value date. The normal forward value date will be the same date in the relevant month. So, if spot is 8 October, one month is 8 November, two months is 8 December and so on.

If the date so calculated is a holiday, then the date is rolled onward to the next day on which banks are open for business in both centres. Assume that we were dealing US dollars/ Swiss francs for one month and 8 November is on a weekend or a holiday in New York or Zurich. Then we roll the date onward to the 9th, if that day is a business day in both centres. If it is not, then we keep rolling the date onward until a business day is reached.

Exceptions to this rule arise in the case of month-ends. A month-end date is the last day of a month where banks are open for business in the two settlement countries. In the US dollar/Swiss franc deal, if 30 September is a US holiday, then month-end would be 29 September, provided that day is a business day in both centres.

There are two further exceptions to the standard rule set out in the first paragraph of this section. Both of these concern month-ends. The first is the so-called 'end–end rule'. This says that if the spot value date is a month-end, then all forward value dates are also month-ends. Suppose that the October month-end is 28 October, and the 29th and 30th are on a weekend and 31 October is a public holiday. Then if spot is 28 October (that is, the month-end) the 'end–end rule' makes the one-month date 30 November if that is the November month-end, not 28 November.

The second exception is that forward value dates must not be rolled on beyond the month-end. Suppose the one-month date would normally be 31 March but that is a holiday. We do not roll the one-month date on to 1 April, but roll it back to 30 March.

However, we would also stress that pricing contracts for foreign exchange and interest rates actually depend upon day counts.

4.6 Main purpose of the forward market

By entering into a forward foreign exchange contract, a UK importer or exporter is able to fix, at the time of the contract, a price for the purchase or sale of a fixed amount of foreign currency for delivery and payment at a specified future time. By so doing, the importer or exporter may eliminate foreign exchange risk due to future exchange rate fluctuations. This enables the exact sterling value of an international commercial contract to be calculated despite the fact that payment is to be made in the future in a foreign currency.

If a foreign currency stands at premium in the forward market, it shows that the currency is 'stronger' than the home currency in that forward market. By contrast, if a foreign currency stands at a discount in the forward market, it shows that the currency is 'weaker' than the home currency in that forward market. The words 'stronger' and 'weaker' are put in inverted commas because, in the context of forward markets, strength and weakness merely take account of interest rate differentials as suggested by the interest rate parity part of the four-way equivalence model encountered in Chapter 3.

Summary

- Foreign exchange market transactions may involve spot, forward, futures and options deals and deposit and borrowing market transactions. This chapter does not deal with futures or options.
- In all of these markets, dealers quote bid and offer rates – one for buying, one for selling.
- So, in the spot market, dealers quote bid/offer rates.
- In the forward market, dealers quote the spot bid/offer rate and then quote, as a bid/offer rate, the forward points. The forward points give the distance from spot to forward.
- To obtain the outright forward rate, if the bid and offer on the forward points have the same sign – positive or negative – then, assuming the bid points exceeds the offer points, deduct both from the spot. If both have the same sign but the offer points exceed the bid points, then add both to the spot.
- If the forward points have the opposite sign, a bid that is positive and an offer that is negative or vice versa, one is added and the other deducted from the corresponding bid/offer rate for spot to get the outright forward. In this circumstance, the bid forward points are deducted from the spot bid quote; the offer forward points are added to the spot offer quote. This gives the respective bid/offer quotation for the outright forward rate.
- The forward premium or discount is always calculated as the annualised percentage difference between the spot and forward rates as a proportion of the spot rate, that is:

$$\frac{f_0 - s_0}{s_0} \times \frac{12}{n} \times 100\%$$

- When spot and forward rates are compared, one currency will usually bc more expensive forward than spot. The currency that is more expensive in the forward market is said to be at a premium. This currency can be said to be 'strengthening' in the forward market. The term 'strengthening' is in inverted commas because it is not really strengthening as such – its relative strength merely reflects interest differentials.
- If interest rate parity is holding – and at the level that most company treasurers deal, it always holds – then the currency that is 'strengthening' is said to be at a premium and this currency will have lower fixed interest rates. Here is a mnemonic: SPIL means strengthening, premium, interest rates, lower.

- Or how about Spain and Portugal form the Iberian landmass?
- Or here is another: SLIP means strengthening, lower interest rates, premium.

End of chapter questions

4.1 Assume the following information:

	Bank X	Bank Y
Bid price of Swiss francs	$.401	$.398
Ask price of Swiss francs	$.404	$.400

Given this information, is arbitrage possible? If so, explain the steps that would create the arbitrage. Compute the profit from this arbitrage if you had $1,000,000 to use.

4.2 Based on the information in the previous question, what market forces would occur to eliminate any further possibilities of the locational arbitrage described in your answer to Question 4.1.

4.3 Assume the following information for a particular bank:

	Quoted price	
Value of Batavian drac (BTD) in US dollars	USD	.90
Value of Ulerican crown (ULC) in US dollars	USD	.30
Value of Batavian drac in Ulerican crown	ULC	3.02

Given this information, is triangular arbitrage possible? If so, explain the steps that would reflect triangular arbitrage, and calculate the profit from this strategy if you had $1,000,000 to use.

5 The balance of payments

The balance of payments position of a country is often claimed to be an important piece of information for anyone wishing to predict the future of a currency's strength in exchange rate terms. A recurring current account surplus is often associated with a strengthening of a country's exchange rate; a continual deficit on current account is frequently associated with a fall in a country's exchange rate. A surplus on current account is underpinned by an excess of exports over imports. Suppose that exports from a country are denominated in the home currency. Payment for them involves a foreigner in buying home currency and selling foreign currency. This tends to strengthen the home currency. Hence surpluses and the strengthening of the exchange rate tend to go hand in hand. Conversely, deficits on the current account are associated with an excess of imports over exports. Recurring current account deficits and weakening of the exchange rate are generally related.

There are a good many frailties in a forecasting model based solely on current account outturns. The current account is only part of the balance of payments picture: the **capital account** has to be considered as well. Before we can truly discuss the problems of using balance of payments data to forecast foreign exchange rates, we need to consider a number of concepts associated with the balance of payments. This chapter attempts to describe these concepts and draws conclusions about foreign exchange rate forecasting using balance of payments information.

5.1 The essence of international trade

The basis of international trade has been explained in terms of the principle of comparative advantage. This presumes that, for a number of reasons, some individuals and some countries produce some goods and services more efficiently than others. It is conceivable that one particular country might produce every product more efficiently than any other. Even if this were so, it might be to this country's advantage to apply all of its skills and resources towards the production of only those goods or services that gave it the greatest payoff and to buy in other products and services which gave a lower payoff. It is, of course, extremely unlikely that one particular country would produce all goods and services more efficiently than its international competitors. However, as long as one country has an greater advantage, a comparative advantage, in producing certain goods and services, it benefits by specialising in those lines, exporting those goods and services and importing other goods and services from other countries. A country gains then by specialising in products in which it has the greatest comparative advantage because any shift of resources to other products reduces output. Naturally, a country must produce enough of the goods and services in which it possesses a comparative advantage not only to meet its own needs but also to export in exchange for imports of goods and services needed to meet demand.

International trade usually involves the cross-frontier payment of money to pay for goods and services. The word 'usually' is deliberately employed because a significant volume of international trade is by barter. Indeed, in dealing with certain countries that are short of foreign exchange, trade is largely via barter. But for most transactions, barter is as awkward internationally as it is domestically. Unless international trade is by barter alone, it must be financed.

One of the most valuable services rendered by the foreign exchange markets is the provision of a mechanism for transferring the money of one country into the money of another. As long as different currencies exist and as long as international trade embraces payment other than by barter, foreign exchange will be a necessary dimension of international trade.

5.2 The balance of payments and foreign exchange rates

A foreign exchange rate is the price of one currency in terms of another. The balance of payments summarises the flow of economic transactions between the residents of a given country and the residents of other countries during a certain period of time.

The balance of payments measures flows rather than stocks. These flows represent payments and receipts. Balance of payments data record only changes in asset holdings and liabilities; they do not present the absolute levels of these items. So the balance of payments of a country is rather like the statement of sources and use of funds of a firm. For a country, sources of funds are acquisitions of external purchasing power, rights a country has to claim goods and services or to invest in another country. For a country, uses of funds, in the context of the balance of payments, means a decrease in its external purchasing power. For balance of payments purposes, a resident is any person, individual, business firm, government agency or other institution legally domiciled in the given country.

The balance of payments measures transactions among countries. Transactions that affect only local residents and involve only the national currency (in contrast to foreign exchange) are not recorded in the balance of payments.

The balance of payments comprises three distinct types of account, namely:

- the current account;
- the capital account;
- the **official reserves**.

Table 5.1 shows a simplified balance of payments format for Ruritania in 2011. It is simplified because it contains merely 23 lines of figures whereas the full balance of payments as published by the IMF in International Financial Statistics contains over 50 lines. In terms of putting this rather complex presentation of data into a more manageable design for purposes of forecasting exchange rates, the model used in Table 5.1 is recommended.

Balance of payments information is compiled by government statisticians from questionnaires completed by companies, banks, export agencies and others. The overall balance of

Table 5.1 Simplified balance of payments in Ruritania, 2011 ($m)

CURRENT ACCOUNT			
Trade account			
Exports of goods	2,500		
Imports of goods	−1,500		
Balance of trade		1,000	
Invisibles account			
Receipts from interest and dividends, travel and services such as shipping, property, banking and financial charges	1,000		
Payments for interest and dividends, and services such as shipping, travel, property, banking and financial charges	−500		
Balance of invisibles (services)		500	
Unilateral transfers			
Gifts received from abroad	200		
Grants to foreign countries	−600		
Balance on unilateral transfers		−400	
Current account balance			1,100
CAPITAL ACCOUNT			
Long-term capital flows			
Direct investment			
Sale of financial assets	1,000		
Purchase of financial assets	−2,000	−1,000	
Portfolio investments			
Sale of financial assets	3,000		
Purchase of financial assets	−1,500	1,500	
Balance on long-term capital		500	
Private short-term capital flows			
Sale of financial assets	5,000		
Purchase of financial assets	−2,000		
Balance on short-term private capital		3,000	
Capital account balance			3,500
OVERALL BALANCE			4,600
OFFICIAL RESERVES ACCOUNT			
Gold decrease (+) or gold increase (−)			−2,400
Decrease (+) or increase (−) in foreign exchange			−2,200
TOTAL OFFICIAL FINANCING			−4,600

Note: Sources of funds are given by +; use of funds is given by −.

payments is, by definition, equal – the sum of the current and capital accounts equals the official financing. If the aggregate of data obtained by government statisticians does not balance, a heading called 'net errors and omissions' is introduced. This item is a permanent feature of balance of payments figures. We now consider, in turn, the content of the current account, the capital account and the official financing parts of the balance of payments. In this description we constantly refer to data in Table 5.1 by way of illustration.

The current account records trade in goods and services and the exchange of gifts among countries. Trade in goods comprises exports and imports. A country increases its exports when it sells goods to foreigners; this is a source of funds. It increases imports when it buys goods from foreigners; this is a use of funds. The difference between exports and imports is called the 'trade balance'. According to Table 5.1, Ruritania has a positive trade balance of $1,000m in 2011. Sources of external purchasing power exceed uses thereof through trade by $1,000m.

The difference on services is called the 'balance of invisibles'. In balance of payments terminology, services include interest, dividends, travel expenses, shipping, property, banking, financial and other consultancy services. The rendering of these services to foreigners is a source of funds and their receipt from foreigners is a use of funds. Respectively, they increase or reduce external purchasing power. From Table 5.1 it is seen that Ruritania has a positive balance on invisibles of $500m. In other words, sources of external purchasing power exceed uses by $500m in respect of transactions in invisibles.

Gifts are recorded in the unilateral transfers account. This account is frequently called 'remittances' or 'unrequited transfers'. It embraces money that migrants send home, and gifts and aid that one country makes to another. A gift represents a use of external purchasing power. Ruritania has a negative balance on unilateral transfers amounting to $400m. Uses of funds exceed sources by this amount.

The overall current account of Ruritania shows a positive balance of $1.1bn, made up of positive balances in trade and invisibles and a negative balance on unilateral transfers.

Turning now to the capital account, this details international movements of financial assets and liabilities. These are classified in the balance of payments according to their maturity and according to the involvement of the owner of the asset or liability. There are a number of sub-divisions such as direct investment, **portfolio investment** and private short-term capital flows. Direct investment and portfolio investment involve financial assets with an initial maturity of more than a year when issued. Short-term capital movements consist of claims with an original maturity of less than one year. The distinction between direct investment and portfolio investment is made on the basis of the degree of management involvement. In the case of direct investment, considerable management involvement is presumed to exist; this is interpreted as a minimum of 10 per cent ownership in a firm. No management involvement is presumed to exist for portfolio investment.

Ruritania has a deficit on direct investment to the extent of $1,000m. While foreigners invested $1,000m in the country, Ruritania invested $2,000m out of the country in respect of situations when in excess of 10 per cent ownership was acquired.

Under the heading of portfolio investment, Ruritania has an inflow of $3,000m compared with an outflow of $1,500m. Together with the balance on direct investment, this gives a positive balance on long-term capital account of $500m.

In the private short-term capital account, Ruritania increased its liabilities to foreigners – a source of funds for the country – by $5,000m, while Ruritania increased its claims on foreigners (a use of funds for Ruritania) by $2,000m. These two items gave rise to a positive net balance on the short-term capital account of $3,000m.

Summing long-term and short-term capital flows gives the balance on capital account. For Ruritania there is a positive capital account balance of $3,500m.

When the current account and capital account are added up, we get a total that is frequently called the 'overall balance'. For Ruritania, this amounts to $4,600m. In other words, Ruritania has acquired a net source of external purchasing power of this amount.

The official reserves account rounds off the balance of payments. It shows the means of international payment that the monetary authorities of a country have acquired or lost during a particular period. The term 'means of international payment' includes gold and convertible foreign currency. It must be borne in mind that only foreign currency holdings that are freely convertible are included in the official reserves. Really this means that only a handful of currencies find their way into official reserves. Currencies such as the US dollar and sterling qualify as they are freely convertible at the present time. Most governments do not allow their country's currency to be freely converted to others, so holdings of Brazilian reals, Indian rupees, Chinese renminbi yuan and so on would not be classified as official reserves.

If there is a surplus at the overall balance level on a country's balance of payments, the effect will be for there to be an inflow of official reserves. But we must bear in mind the notation used in balance of payments accounting. As we shall see later in this chapter, balance of payments accounting is just a variant of double-entry bookkeeping. For every debit there is a credit; for every plus entry on the balance of payments, there will be a compensating minus entry. So, in the official reserves part of the balance of payments, a negative entry implies an increase in reserves. In Table 5.1, Ruritania has expanded its gold reserves by $2,400m and its foreign exchange reserves by $2,200m. Care must be taken to interpret the sign in front of official reserves data correctly because of the counter-intuitive nature of the way of recording information.

Movements in the official reserves may be interpreted as an indicator of the extent of direct intervention in the foreign exchange markets by the central bank. When the monetary authorities support the home currency (or associated currencies where there is a joint float), they do so by selling reserves and buying the home currency – this would reduce official reserves. Conversely, when they depress the home currency, they do so by buying in convertible currency and selling home currency – this would increase official reserves.

5.3 Balance of payments accounting

The balance of payments always balances. The sum of the debits and credits on the current account, the capital account and the official financing is always equal. This arises because balance of payments tabulations are built on double-entry bookkeeping principles. Table 5.2 summarises the accounts used in balance of payments accounting. These accounts are numbered so that such numbers can be used as a form of shorthand in subsequent examples. The accounts are classified according to whether they are typically debit or credit – or both.

Through a series of simple examples the essence of balance of payments accounting may be understood.

Example 1

A resident of country X exports goods to a resident of country Y, who signs a bill of exchange, denominated in country Y's currency, which matures in 90 days. In country X's balance of payments, an export has occurred and a short-term claim on a foreigner has been acquired. The debit and credit position is therefore:

Dr Short-term claims on foreigners (the bill of exchange)
Cr Export of goods

Example 2

The exporter in Example 1 holds the bill to maturity when he receives payment in country Y's currency. The exporter now has a claim (the payment in Y's currency) on a bank in country Y. Effectively, the debit and credit are therefore in the same account.

Dr Short-term claims on foreigners (the amount in Y's currency)
Cr Short-term claims on foreigners (the bill of exchange)

Table 5.2 Balance of payments accounting

Debit (–)	Credit (+)
1. Import of goods	
	2. Export of goods
3. Purchase of services from foreigners	
	4. Sale of services to foreigners
5. Interest, dividends, rents and royalties to foreigners	
	6. Interest, dividends, rents and royalties from foreigners
7. Gifts to foreigners	
	8. Gifts from foreigners
9. Direct investment	
• by residents in foreign countries	• by foreigners in home country
10. Portfolio investment	
• by residents in foreign country	• by foreigners in home country
11. Long-term claims on foreigners	
• increase	• decrease
12. Long-term liabilities to foreigners	
• decrease	• increase
13. Short-term claims on foreigners	
• increase	• decrease
14. Short-term liabilities to foreigners	
• decrease	• increase
15. Official reserves of gold	
• increase	• decrease
16. Official reserves of foreign exchange	
• increase	

Example 3

The exporter in the two previous examples now decides to convert the payment in country Y's currency to his own. He does this through his own clearing bank. Here the bank buys the foreign currency and sells the home currency in exchange. Now the bank in country X has acquired country Y's currency. The bank now has a short-term claim on foreigners. All that happened is that the short-term claim on foreigners has been shuffled from one resident of country X, the exporter, to another, the clearing bank. From a balance of payments standpoint, no entry needs to be made.

Example 4

The clearing bank decides to sell the foreign currency acquired in the previous example to country X's central bank in exchange for home currency. Assume that country Y's currency is freely convertible in the foreign exchange markets. When the central bank acquires gold or freely convertible foreign currency, it increases the official reserves. So in this case the balance of payments entry is:

Dr Official reserves of foreign currency
Cr Short-term claims on foreigners (the amount in Y's currency)

Example 5

If the previous example had differed in only one respect, namely that country Y's currency had not been freely convertible, then there would have been no increment to the official reserves. In this case there would be no balance of payments entry – the short-term claim on foreigners would merely have been shuffled from the clearing bank to the central bank, and since the short-term claim was not convertible foreign currency it would not count as part of the official reserves. It would, in fact, remain as a short-term claim on foreigners, but the claim would be held by the central bank rather than the clearing bank.

Example 6

A US resident on holiday in country X changes dollar travellers' cheques for country X's currency at an airport bank. All of this is spent on her vacation. In this case the balance of payments entry would be:

Dr Short-term claims on foreigners (the holding of US dollars)
Cr Travel services to foreigners (part of account number 4 in Table 5.2)

Example 7

Had the airport bank in the previous example then sold the US dollars to the central bank, this would have increased the official reserves. The balance of payments entry would be:

Dr Official reserves of foreign currency
Cr Short-term claims on foreigners (the holding of US dollars)

The acquisition of convertible foreign currency within a country does not lead to an entry in the official reserves until that foreign currency finds its way to the central bank. This is a very important feature of balance of payments accounting which needs to be clearly understood.

Example 8

A resident of country X sends a cheque to a relative in Australia. In country X's balance of payments the above transaction is shown as:

Dr Gifts to foreigners
Cr Short-term liabilities to foreigners (the cheque)

Example 9

A foreign bank uses a deposit in country X's currency to buy country X's treasury bills. This transaction is classified as a reduction in short-term liabilities to foreigners (the deposit in country X's currency) matched by an increase in short-term liabilities to foreigners (the treasury bills). Note that since treasury bills have a maturity of less than twelve months, they do not constitute portfolio investment. So the transaction is:

Dr Short-term liabilities to foreigners – decrease (the currency deposit)
Cr Short-term liabilities to foreigners – increase (the treasury bills)

It is worth pointing out that current account and capital account movements are termed *autonomous* in balance of payments parlance. These movements can be considered as a barometer of pressures on the exchange rate of the home currency. Official reserves movements are termed 'compensating' or 'accommodating' items. Sometimes this distinction is expressed in 'above the line' and 'below the line' terms respectively. Accounts 'above the line' embrace autonomous accounts whose balance determines whether the balance of payments is in surplus or deficit. Accounts 'below the line' represent compensating accounts that show how the balance of payments surplus or deficit was financed.

When the balance of payments is in surplus, international purchasing power of the country has increased during the period in question – that is, autonomous receipts exceed autonomous payments. When the balance of payments is in deficit, international purchasing power of the country has decreased during the period in question – thus autonomous payments exceed autonomous receipts. A surplus in the autonomous account is accompanied by an increase in foreign reserves or a decrease in official liabilities in the compensating accounts. This puts an upward pressure on the external value of the home currency. A deficit in the autonomous accounts is associated with a decrease in foreign reserves or an increase in liabilities to foreigners. This tends to put a downward pressure on the external value of the home currency. Countries with continuous deficits in the balance of payments experience international currency depreciation.

In practice, balance of payments statistics are not compiled on an entry-by-entry basis. Only aggregates of transactions are measured for a period. The customs and excise authorities provide the main source for figures on exports and imports; financial institutions, government agencies and industry report the changes in foreign financial assets and in liabilities to foreigners. Hence the almost perennial item in balance of payments accounting – net errors and omissions – arises because sources and uses fail to balance.

5.4 Forecasting exchange rates and the balance of payments

The use of balance of payments data to forecast foreign exchange rates is predicated upon the assumption that when a country's currency is in equilibrium, that country will display a break-even position in respect of trade and those invisibles that reflect the rendering of services (as opposed to the remuneration of capital: that is, interest and dividends). Although not exactly in accordance with the above formula, this is frequently interpreted as being equivalent to an even current account outturn. The other key assumptions in forecasting foreign exchange rates from the balance of payments are that currencies that are undervalued will have the effect of creating positive current account outturns, while currencies that are overvalued will have the effect of creating negative current account results.

These key underpinnings also assume that no market imperfections exist, such as the absence of any significant valuable raw materials or a trained labour force which typifies so many Third World countries. Often one concludes that, on the basis of balance of payments data, there is no way to identify the exchange rate at which many Third World countries will break even on current account.

There are also frailties of the forecasting model which need to be borne in mind. These concern three key areas.

The first relates to situations when exports are denominated in a third currency and where the exporter continues to hold the proceeds of an export sale in the said currency. Consider an example. Many raw materials are priced in US dollars. This is true of oil. A UK oil exporter will sell petroleum to Europe, for example with the price denominated in US dollars. When the European importer pays the UK oil company it will pay dollars. The export will show as a positive increment to the British balance of payments current account. But if the exporter continues to hold the proceeds of the sale in a US dollar bank account, it will not strengthen the pound sterling. As far as the balance of payments is concerned, the dollar deposit will show as a short-term claim on foreigners. Now if the UK oil company were to sell its dollars for pounds via its clearing bank, then this deal would tend to strengthen sterling. But even if the UK oil company sells its dollars to a clearing bank, the transaction will still show as a short-term claim on foreigners from a balance of payments viewpoint. But the claim is now held by the bank rather than the oil exporter. Clearly, from the standpoint of using balance of payments data to forecast exchange rates with great confidence, we have inadequate information based on the normal package of published figures.

The second frailty involves a country's capital account. While it may experience substantial deficits on current account, a country may have substantial capital inflows from multinationals. These capital flows may exceed the current account deficit, resulting in an overall tendency for a country's currency to strengthen despite its negative current account balance. This situation underpinned the strength of the Mexican peso and the Indonesian rupiah in the early 1970s when inflows from oil companies undertaking exploration activities propped up deficits on current accounts and allowed the governments of both countries to postpone devaluations which were indicated by purchasing power parity.

The third frailty also arises in the area of the capital account. Among other things the capital account includes borrowings from bankers or from the IMF. These would show as long-term liabilities to foreigners. The conversion of such borrowings from, say, US dollars to the home currency would tend to strengthen the home currency in the short term but would not, in the very short term, affect the current account of the country.

Evidently, using current account data as indicators of potential foreign exchange movements is fraught with pitfalls. Forecasters need to tread very warily but, with care, have a useful tool at their disposal.

Summary

- The balance of payments summarises economic transactions between the residents of a given country and the residents of other countries during a given period of time.
- The balance of payments measures flows; these flows represent payments and receipts.
- Balance of payments data do not embrace absolute levels of assets and liabilities – but they do include changes in these items, rather like a source and use of funds statement as opposed to a balance sheet.
- The balance of payments comprises three distinct types of account, namely the current account, the capital account and the official reserves.
- The current account records trade in goods and services and gifts between countries. Trade comprises exports and imports. Services include interest, dividends, travel, shipping, insurance and consulting fees for banking, property and financial matters.
- The difference on trade is called the balance of trade or visibles. The difference on services is called the balance of invisibles.
- The capital account details international movements of financial assets and liabilities.
- Direct investment and portfolio investment relate to situations where investment overseas occurs in respect of assets with a maturity of over one year. Short-term capital movements refer to situations were assets and liabilities have maturities of less than one year.

- The degree of management involvement activity distinguishes direct and portfolio investment. Direct investment implies considerable management involvement, and is interpreted as a minimum of 10 per cent ownership in a venture or firm. No management involvement is presumed for portfolio investment.
- The total of long- and short-term capital movements gives the balance on capital account.
- The capital account would include payables and receivables outstanding on trade or services. It will also include inflows from multinationals and borrowings from bankers or from the IMF.
- There is also the official reserves. It shows changes in the means of international payment held by the monetary authorities of a country during a particular period. The term 'means of international payment' includes gold and convertible foreign currency.
- Movements in official reserves indicate the extent of direct intervention in foreign exchange markets by the central bank. When the home currency is supported, there will be an outflow of official reserves. By a reverse token, pushing down the home currency is reflected by an increase in official reserves.
- The three accounts constituting the balance of payments sum to zero.
- The nearest we have to the idea of a country's currency being in equilibrium is to interpret this as meaning a level at which the country displays a break-even portion on trade and services – which is not exactly the current account balance since interest and dividends should be excluded from invisibles for this purpose.

End of chapter questions

5.1 How would a relatively high home inflation rate affect the home country's current account, all other thing being equal?

5.2 How would you expect a weakening home currency to affect the home country's current account, all other things being equal?

5.3 It is sometimes suggested that a floating exchange rate will adjust to reduce or eliminate any current account deficit. Explain why this adjustment would occur. Why does the exchange rate not always adjust to correct a current account deficit?

6

Theories and empiricism on exchange rate movements

Explanations of economic phenomena often conflict. Hypotheses are advanced and tested. For a while it looks as if one particular series of explanatory variables is accounting for changes in the dependent variable, then the relationship breaks down. As social scientists we should not be surprised at the infuriatingly unpredictable way in which our world seems to work.

Multinational finance is no exception. The key question to which we seek a solution is: what makes foreign exchange rates move and can these movements be predicted? We are looking for the typical kind of regression equation in which the future spot rate is the dependent variable and there may be one or more independent variables whose coefficients can be estimated, hopefully with acceptably high levels of significance, and the equation has a high R^2.

Unfortunately, the models that have been developed do not necessarily hold for anything but quite short periods. So we do not have the kind of model upon which we can rely with high degrees of certainty in terms of predicting movements in spot rates.

Summarising the position about our ability to explain exchange rate movements after the fact, or to forecast them before the event, Meese[1] highlighted the forecasting superiority of the random walk model versus structural models and argued that:

> Economists do not yet understand the determination of short- to medium-run movements in exchange rates. Neither models of exchange rates based on macroeconomic fundamentals nor the forecasts of market participants as embodied in the forward rate or survey data can explain exchange rate movement better than a naïve alternative such as a random walk model. Worse yet, exchange rate changes are hard to explain after the fact, even with the knowledge of actual fundamental variables. It remains an enigma why the current exchange rate regime has engendered a time series database where macroeconomic variables and exchange rates appear to be independent of one another.

This view was reiterated by Frenkel and Froot[2] who observed that:

> It is now widely accepted that standard observable macroeconomic variables are not capable of explaining, much less predicting ex ante, the majority of short-term changes in the exchange rate.

But note Frankel and Froot's reference to the majority of short-term exchange rate changes – they do not say all changes. So what is the evidence? What are the competing hypotheses? And can we do anything at all about predicting movements in foreign exchange rates?

6.1 Inflation and interest rate differentials

As outlined in Chapter 3, one of the major deductive hypotheses about expected movements in the spot exchange rate is underpinned by the following:

- expected inflation differentials;
- interest rate differentials (and here we should be looking at free-market interest rates such as offshore rates);
- spot and forward rate differentials.

The rationale for the hypothesised relationships was dealt with at length in Chapter 3. The four-way equivalence model developed there is extremely important. It is essential that readers understand the theoretical relationships among inflation differences, interest rate differences, the forward premium/discount and expected spot movements.

However, remember that the existence of non-traded goods logically gives rise to deviations from the purchasing power parity theory of exchange rates. Also systematic deviations from PPP theory are to be expected due to short-term capital flows and current account imbalances.

As we will discuss later in this chapter, the PPP theory of exchange rate movements holds up fairly well in the long term. The fact that short-term deviations abound has stimulated the search for a better model. One such model is the balance of payments approach.

6.2 The balance of payments approach

There are different balance of payments explanations of exchange rate movements. The emphasis has tended to change through time as the international financial scene has itself undergone change.

In its original form, this explanation tended to ignore capital flows. Prior to the 1960s, this was excusable since most major currencies were not convertible, with the consequence that there were minimal private capital flows. The current account theory can best be explained by approaching it under the two distinct systems of exchange rate regime – namely, fixed and floating.

Assume a fixed exchange rate regime first. The national income model suggests that the current account gets worse as national income rises. The basic tendency is then for the domestic currency to weaken (to pay for the increased imports), and the fixed exchange rate system requires that, should this fall beyond certain narrow limits, this should be countered by support from the domestic government. This might take the form of selling reserves of foreign currency in the foreign exchange markets. Usually this would be accompanied by domestic severity to dampen home demand, evidenced by lower relative money supply growth with consequent lower relative inflation, leading to an improvement in exports and a lowering of imports. According to this formula – which looks fine on paper – the current account deficit is automatically corrected.

So, too, is a surplus. Here, rather than selling foreign exchange reserves, the foreign currency is bought. To pay for this, borrowings are increased – probably by the issue of treasury bills. As treasury bills are a reserve asset, this results in an increase in money supply,

Table 6.1 Murenbeeld's devaluation/revaluation hypotheses

Devaluation		Revaluation
High	Inflation	Low
Up	Trend in unemployment	Down
Low	Ratio of reserves to imports	High
Down	Change in level of reserves	Up

which in turn leads, all other things being equal, to higher inflation. Remember we are looking at a fixed parity regime: this means that exports become less competitive and hence the surplus reduces. Again this is an automatic corrective mechanism.

On paper, then, the Bretton Woods system should avoid permanent disequilibria – after all, there are automatically correcting means of achieving current account stability. But empirically, things did not turn out this way as anyone who has examined the evidence of the United Kingdom in the 1950s and 1960s knows.

Of course, devaluation or revaluation was an option designed to counter recurrent disequilibria. Predicting changes in exchange rates in these circumstances became a potentially fruitful area of investigation. An interesting study carried out in the 1970s by Murenbeeld[3] is worth mentioning. Using discriminant analysis, Murenbeeld studied a series of devaluations and revaluations from the late 1950s to early 1970s and came up with a discriminating equation. His original hypotheses may be summarised in the format shown in Table 6.1.

Having obtained data on a number of currency realignments, the researcher arrives at a Z-score predictor of foreign exchange parity change using respective quarterly and monthly data as follows:

$$Z = -0.487 + 0.732\text{RI} + 0.058\Delta\text{R} - 0.123\Delta\text{WP} - 0.145\text{UNEM} - 0.25\text{M} + 0.167\text{G}$$

$$Z = 0.33 + 0.69\text{RI} + 0.17\Delta\text{R} - 2.29\Delta\text{WP} - 0.45\text{UNEM} - 0.66\text{M} + 15.35\text{G}$$

where the quarterly and monthly independent variables are:

RI = ratio of reserves to imports,
ΔR = % change in reserves,
ΔWP = % change in wholesale price index,
UNEM = change in trend of number becoming unemployed as % of total number unemployed,
M = change in trend of money supply as % of total money supply,
G = change in trend of government budgetary surplus/deficit as % of GNP.

According to Murenbeeld, quarterly Z-scores in excess of 2.0 are indicative of an upward valuation of the currency concerned and scores below –1.5 are indicative of a devaluation. And for monthly data, discriminating scores are respectively 1.0 and –1.5. Interested readers are referred to the original.[4] In pursuit of an economic and political model which would provide a leading indicator of devaluations, Bilson[5] examined a monetary model of the exchange rate and an international liquidity variable (measured by the stock of international reserves divided by the monetary base – that is the money supply, specifically high powered money). He found that his methodology, using these variables, provided a good proxy for the extent of the currency depreciation and a good lead indicator of the timing of the devaluation. When the international liquidity indicator fell substantially relative to its historical norm, the actual exchange rate depreciated thereafter within one to two years. The technique is not guaranteed, but Bilson suggested that these indicators offered exchange rate forecasters useful information and insights. Clearly, it is most readily applied to fixed or pegged exchange rate systems.

The economics departments in numerous international banks have similar proprietary models which they use internally and offer to favoured clients. The developers of models nowadays prefer to market them to banks rather than publish them in reputable journals.

Having deviated slightly from the mainstream of this chapter, let us now return to it by examining the current account theory of the exchange rate under a floating currency regime.

Again, in terms of illustrating the mechanism, let us begin from an increase in national income and a worsening of the current account balance. If we leave the capital account out of the equation for now, paying for the increased imports results in demand for foreign currency at the expense of the home currency. Buying foreign exchange for domestic currency weakens the local currency, which then makes exports more competitive and (assuming that the Marshall–Lerner[6] conditions on elasticities are met) consequently improves the current account. By a reverse route in the argument, current account surpluses lessen, with a strengthening exchange rate as the corrective mechanism.

So far, of course, our models have been simplistic to the extent that the capital account and the interest rate have been left out of the equation. Extending the argument now to make good this omission, we come up with the essence of the Mundell[7] and Fleming[8] models. The overall balance of payments is the current account plus the capital account. Using a simple example to illustrate the workings of the model, let us begin by assuming an increase in national income with an accompanying deterioration in the current account balance. If overall balance of payments equilibrium is to be maintained at zero as national income increases, the domestic rate of interest must also rise – this improves capital flows to compensate for the initial deterioration on the current account. This increase in the interest rate dampens domestic demand, which, in its turn, has the effect of reducing imports and consequently improves the current account. The mechanism of this version of the balance of payments model involves the interest rate increase as a means of avoiding a weakening in the domestic currency. This is in line with conventional wisdom, but does not accord with the monetary approach.

6.3 The monetary approach

In the world of classical economics, trade deficits were associated directly with money supply changes. In its more modern form, the monetary approach predicts that an excess supply of money domestically will be reflected in an outflow across the foreign exchanges.

Beginning with a growth in national income, under the monetary approach, this will be associated with a growing demand for money for transaction purposes. An excess demand for money can be met in one of two ways: either through domestic credit creation or through a balance of payments surplus. This rationale explains the apparent paradox (remember that the Keynesian model predicts that an increase in national income will be associated with a weakening current account balance) of fast growing countries such as Germany which have had almost perpetual balance of payments current surpluses. Fast real growth causes a growth in transactions demand for money: the economy induces an inflow of money via the foreign balance to the extent that this money is not created by the central bank.

Assuming that two countries have equal real growth but one increases its money supply more than the other (or there is no money supply growth in either but different real growth rates), rational expectations would suggest that relative interest rates and expected relative inflations would alter. Either through the purchasing power parity theorem or via the mechanism referred to in the previous paragraph, the economy with the high relative money supply growth will have a weakening exchange rate. According to the monetary approach, high nominal interest rates and weakening currencies both flow from high relative money supply growth.

The discussion of the monetary approach so far has been simplistic. It can be made more sophisticated by bringing together purchasing power parity and the quantity theory of money. In this description of exchange rate determination drawing on the above two theories, the usual quantity theory notation is used. That is:

M = money stock,
V = velocity of circulation of money,
P = price of goods,
T = number of transactions per year.

Setting the supply of money equal to its demand, the key quantity theory of money equation suggests that:

$$MV = PT \tag{6.1}$$

If transactions, T, are a function of real income, Y, then:

$$T = aY$$

and, where k is equal to a/V, it follows that:

$$M = kPY \tag{6.2}$$

Equation (6.2) is, of course, a slight reformulation of the key quantity theory expression set out in equation (6.1). Letting * refer to foreign currency variables, as is the practice in the literature, obviously:

$$M^* = k^*P^*Y^* \tag{6.3}$$

Rearranging terms in the last two equations, clearly:

$$P = \frac{M}{kY} \quad \text{and} \quad P^* = \frac{M^*}{k^*Y^*} \tag{6.4}$$

Purchasing power parity is now brought into the discussion. It will be recalled from Chapter 3 that:

$$\frac{\tilde{p}_\$ - \tilde{p}_£}{1 + \tilde{p}_£} = \frac{\tilde{s}_t - s_0}{s_0} \tag{6.5}$$

As an approximation, we can rewrite equation (6.5) as shown below, where we let a dot over a variable represent a percentage change:

$$\dot{s} = \dot{P} - \dot{P}^* \tag{6.6}$$

Remember that we are always using the New York direct quotation when talking about exchange rates. If, therefore, foreign price levels are inflating at a rate in excess of US prices, the direct New York exchange rate in dollars goes down – in other words, the dollar hardens.

Substituting the expression for P and P^* from equation (6.4) in the last equation, we obtain:

$$\dot{s} = (k^* - k) + (\dot{M} - \dot{M}^*) + (\dot{Y}^* - \dot{Y}) \tag{6.7}$$

Equation (6.7) suggests that the rate of change of the exchange rate is a function of three terms, each of which compares the rate of change of a variable in the home country with the rate of change of the same variable in the foreign country. The first term compares the velocities of money, the second compares the money supplies and the third term compares incomes.

Now we will, for illustrative purposes, change the parameters of the model – while maintaining the relationships in equation (6.4) – and observe how they affect the rate of change of the exchange rate, $\dot{s}$. Thus:

- If $\dot{k}$ rises, this means that the velocity of money is decreasing at home so the rate of inflation is falling. If $\dot{P}^*$ is constant throughout, the home currency should appreciate, or at least not depreciate as fast.
- If $\dot{M}$ rises, the rate of growth of the domestic money supply is increasing, so inflation at home will increase and the currency will depreciate.
- If $\dot{Y}$ rises, the rate of growth of real income has increased, which means, with the rate of growth of the money supply fixed, inflation will decrease and the currency will appreciate.

No one would argue that purchasing power parity holds in the short run – indeed, the empirical evidence suggests that purchasing power parity is anything but a short-run phenomenon. It is essentially a long-run tendency. It is not a complete theory of exchange rate determination. The money supply and prices tend to move slowly whereas exchange rates change rapidly – like share price movements. And, again like share prices, movements overshoot the theoretical equilibrium rate. How can we explain this tendency for foreign exchange rates to exaggerate on their path towards equilibrium?

6.4 Overshooting – the Dornbusch model

A modern version of the Keynesian model – associated with Dornbusch[9] and endorsed by Driskill[10], Papell[11] and Levin[12] – can be invoked to explain the empirically observed reality of overshooting. Frequently, spot exchange rates seem to move too much given some economic disturbance. And they seem to move contrarily too. For example, country A may have a higher inflation rate than country B, yet the currency of country A may appreciate relative to that of B. Such anomalies may be explained in the context of an overshooting exchange rate model. Our knowledge and experience suggest that financial markets adjust instantaneously to an exogenous shock, whereas goods markets adjust slowly over time. With this background, let us analyse what happens when country A increases its money supply.

For equilibrium to hold in the money market, money demand must equal money supply. If the money supply increases, something must happen to increase money demand. It is assumed that people hold money for transactions purposes and that they also hold **bonds** that pay an interest rate, i. This assumption allows us to write a money demand equation of the form:

$$M_d = aY + bi \tag{6.8}$$

where M_d is the real stock of money demanded – the nominal stock of money divided by the price level – Y is income and i is the interest rate. Money demand is found positively to relate to income: in other words, the coefficient, a, exceeds zero. As Y increases, people tend to demand more of everything, including money. Since the interest rate is the opportunity cost of holding money, there is an inverse relation between money demand and i: in other words, b in equation (6.8) is negative. It is generally found that in the short run, following an increase in the money supply, both income and the price level are relatively constant. As a result, interest rates must drop to equate money demand to money supply. We now consider the effect given a second country.

The interest rate parity relation for countries A and B may be written as:

$$\frac{i_A - i_B}{1 + i_B} = \frac{f - s}{s} \tag{6.9}$$

Here we use the same notation as in Chapter 3 and quotations for f and s, the forward and spot exchange rates, are in terms of the direct quote in country A. Now, if i_A falls, given the foreign interest rate i_B, then it follows that $(f - s)/s$, that is the forward premium/discount, must fall too. When the money supply in country A increases, we would expect that eventually prices in A will rise because we have more A currency chasing the limited quantity of goods available for purchase. This higher future price level in country A will imply that its currency should weaken to achieve purchasing power parity. This long-run change in the exchange rate, Δs, if it is to be consistent with purchasing power parity, will be given by the approximation:

$$\Delta s = p_A - p_B \tag{6.10}$$

Since p_A is expected to rise over time, given p_B, s will tend to weaken. This weaker expected future spot rate will be reflected in a weaker forward rate now. But if f, the forward rate for country A, weakens while, at the same time, $f - s$ falls to maintain interest rate parity, the current value of s will have to weaken more than f. Subsequently, once prices start rising, real money balances should fall so that the domestic interest rate rises. Over time, as the interest rate increases, s will alter to maintain equilibrium. Therefore, the initial fall in the spot rate of country A will be in excess of the long-run spot rate for country A. In other words, s will overshoot its long-run value.

To summarise the discussion, Figure 6.1 shows the passage of price levels, interest rates and the exchange rate for currency A over time. The initial equilibrium position at time t_0, is given by variables with subscripts 0. When the money supply increases at time t_0, the domestic interest rate falls and the exchange rate weakens, while the price level remains fixed. The eventual long-run equilibrium price ρ_{LR} and exchange rate s_{LR} will move in proportion to the increase in the money supply. Although the forward rate should move immediately to its new equilibrium f_1, the spot rate will weaken below the eventual equilibrium s_{LR} owing to the need to maintain interest parity – remember that i_A has fallen in the short run. Over time, as prices start to rise, the interest rate increases and the exchange rate converges to the new equilibrium level s_{LR}.

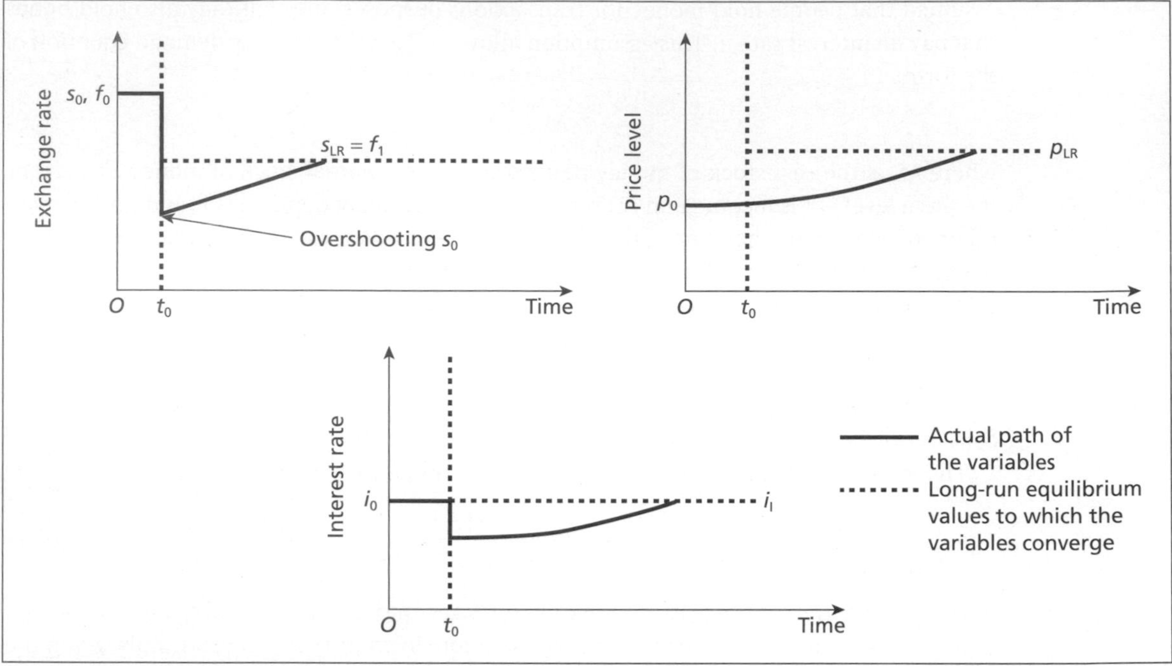

Figure 6.1 Forward and spot exchange rates, interest rate and price level path following increase in domestic money supply

6.5 The portfolio balance theory

An extension of the monetary model is the portfolio balance theory. In the monetary model, exchange rates are determined by the relative supply and demand for money at home. The portfolio balance model uses this idea but introduces foreign money and foreign bonds as potential substitutes for bonds and money at home. If foreign and domestic bonds are perfect substitutes and assuming that conditions of interest arbitrage hold, the portfolio balance model reduces to the monetary model and exchange rates are determined solely by activities in the money markets. In the portfolio balance theory, they are not perfect substitutes in the short term. Thus, exchange rates are determined in part by the relative demand and supply of money and in part by the relative demand and supply of other assets.

In the monetary approach, the determinants of exchange rates are specified by the long-run steady-state situation. In the portfolio balance model, agents may hold international portfolios of assets denominated in different currencies. This makes the demand for money a more complex function than in the monetary model and an additional determinant of exchange rates is the presence of imperfect substitution between assets. Also, in the portfolio balance approach there is a wealth effect – changes in exchange rates impact upon the wealth of holders of assets denominated in foreign currency.

The key assumptions of the portfolio balance model are as follows:

- Members of the public use their domestic wealth, W, to hold a combination of the following assets – domestic money, M, foreign money, M_F, domestic bonds, B, and foreign bonds, B_F. Residents of the home country can hold assets denominated in foreign currencies, while overseas residents can hold assets denominated in home currency. The exchange rate equation, in these circumstances, can be written as:

$$s = f(M, M_F, B, B_F)$$

- The domestic economy is a price taker in all markets including the international financial markets.
- Foreign interest rates are assumed to be kept constant by the foreign monetary authorities.
- Expectations about forward rates and inflation are assumed to be formed in accordance with rational expectations.

The portfolio balance theory has implications, as shown in Figure 6.2, for interest rates and currency depreciation. In the figure, the vertical axis shows the nominal interest rate, i, and the horizontal axis denotes home exchange rate depreciation.

Curve b in Figure 6.2 shows the combinations of interest rates and exchange rates for which the bond market is in equilibrium. Its negative slope is obtained via the following reasoning. If interest rates at home rise, investors will wish to hold more domestic bonds in their portfolios. If the supply of such bonds is fixed, then an excess demand for domestic bonds emerges and the only way to eliminate this excess demand is by a fall in the domestic currency value of foreign bonds. So the home currency appreciates in value, reducing the real wealth of the portfolio holders, since their foreign bond holdings are now worth less. Through this income effect, so the argument goes, the excess demand for domestic bonds is eliminated. Therefore, with a fixed supply of domestic bonds, equilibrium is maintained by the relation between the exchange rate and the domestic interest rate or via the relationship between the value of the home currency and the interest rate.

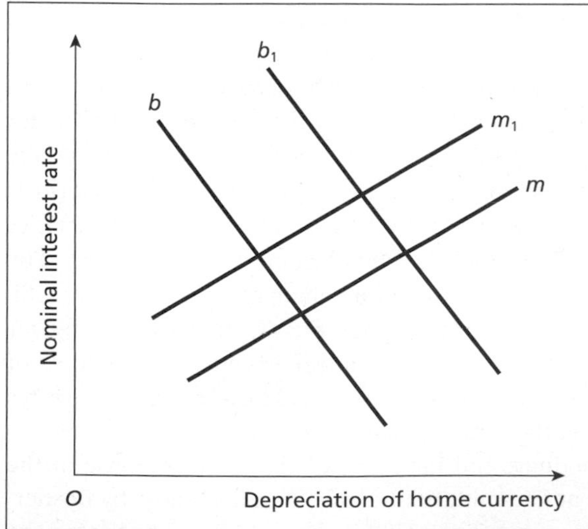

Figure 6.2 The portfolio balance model of exchange rate determination

Curve m in Figure 6.2 indicates the combination of interest rate and exchange rate for which the domestic money market is in equilibrium. It has a positive slope indicating that as interest rates rise the exchange rate depreciates in order to maintain money market equilibrium assuming, of course, that the money supply is held constant. An increase in interest rates reduces the demand for money, but with a constant money supply, the only way to eliminate the implied excess supply of money is to make people feel wealthier through the income effect which raises the demand for money. This is achieved through depreciation of the home currency which increases the domestic currency value of foreign bonds.

Figure 6.2 shows the effects of an increase in the supply of domestic bonds. The b curve moves to b_1, as domestic residents require higher interest rates if they are to be persuaded to hold more domestic bonds, less money, and fewer foreign bonds. The *m* curve shifts to the left to m_1. This is because the stock of bonds is increased and, assuming that the government is engaging in open market operations, the money supply falls.

The combined effect of these movements is to raise the interest rate in the home country. The effect on the exchange rate is ambiguous and depends on which curve shifts by more and on the relative gradients of the curves. In Figure 6.2, curve *b* shifts by more, resulting in a depreciation of the home currency. In this case, domestic bonds and money are closer substitutes than domestic and foreign bonds, and hence the drop in the demand for foreign assets is less than the drop in the demand for money. If the *m* curve had shifted by more, the domestic currency would have appreciated. In such a case domestic and foreign bonds are closer substitutes than domestic bonds and money. Hence the decline in the demand for foreign bonds is greater than the decline in the demand for money.

Referring to Figure 6.2, an increase in the overall money supply causes the *m* curve to shift to the right. Individuals find that they are holding an excess of money balances and the resulting readjustment in their portfolios is reflected in an excess demand for foreign and domestic bonds. Thus the domestic rate of interest declines – the price of bonds rises – resulting in a depreciation of the home currency. An increase in the volume of foreign bonds held by home investors is generated by a current account surplus in the home country and this raises wealth at any given exchange rate. With domestic money and bond supplies fixed, wealth must be reduced towards the original level to restore equilibrium. This is achieved by an appreciation of the domestic currency.

6.6 The role of news

Before we round off this section on theories of exchange rate determination, we must consider the role of news, which has received substantial focus in the literature. Our coverage of exchange rate theories, so far, might lead the reader to conclude that experts should be adept at forecasting future spot exchange rates. In reality, the prediction of future currency paths is very difficult. Research has shown that the theories we have covered are relevant in explaining systematic patterns of exchange rate behaviour. But the value of these theories for predicting exchange rates is limited, first by the fact that some of our theories actually conflict, and secondly by the propensity for the unexpected to occur. The real world is characterised by unpredictable shocks and surprises. When an unexpected event takes place, it is often referred to as news. Interest rates, prices and incomes are often affected by news, and the same is true of exchange rates. Exchange rate changes linked to news will, by definition, be unexpected. Errors in predicting future spot ratios are often excused by our inability to forecast sudden shocks. Periods dominated by unexpected announcements of economic policy changes will result in great fluctuations in spot and forward exchange rates as expectations are revised resultant upon these unexpected pieces of news.

An interesting study by Almeida, Goodhart and Payne[13] examined the response of the DEM/US$ rate to macroeconomic news at five-minute intervals. Another study, by Bosner-Neal, Roley and Sellon[14], looked at the response of the US$ exchange rate to changes in the interest rate of the US Federal funds target. Both studies found a significant relationship between these news events and unanticipated exchange rate movements.

News also has implications for purchasing power parity. Because exchange rates are financial asset prices that respond quickly to new information, news on prices will have an immediate impact on exchange rates. But exchange rates change much more rapidly than do goods prices, which make up typical price indices. Consequently, during periods dominated by news, we observe exchange rates varying a great deal relative to prices so that large deviations from purchasing power parity are realised. Periods, such as the 1970s, the 1980s and the early 1990s, where many unexpected economic events occurred – oil price rises, international debt problems and so on – are periods of large unexpected exchange rate changes with substantial deviations from purchasing power parity. Volatile exchange rates reflect turbulent times. While world political events remain unpredictable, so exchange rates will remain volatile.

Given the discussion so far in this chapter, it is clear that different economic models may predict different directions of movement in exchange rates consequent, for example, upon a change in interest rates. Invariably, when the student is confronted with a plethora of different explanations for a phenomenon, it is a fair conclusion that we are not sure of what causes what. This is very true of exchange rates in the short run – as we will learn later in this chapter. Indeed it becomes clear then that empirical tests indicate that we would not be well advised to risk large amounts of money on the forecasts produced by econometric models. So what about relying on charts? There seem to be plenty of forecasters of exchange rates who produce charts. And how do charts work anyway?

6.7 Chartism

Applied to share price movements, commodity price movements and currencies, this technique involves the study of past price movements to seek out potential future trends. Implicit in this possibility is the assumption that past price patterns provide a guide to future movements.

Just in case readers are not familiar with what **chartism** – sometimes called 'technical analysis' – does, this section attempts to give a very brief description. If readers want a more detailed review, especially of the point and figure approach which is most frequently used, they are referred to other specialist works on chart techniques such as Beckman[15] and a host of others. Chartists attempt to predict share price movements by assuming that past price patterns will be repeated. There is no real theoretical justification for this. Chartists do not attempt to predict every price change. They are deeply interested in trends and trend reversals – that is, when the price of a share or commodity has been rising for several months but suddenly starts to fall. Features of chartism that are considered important for predicting trend reversals include the following:

- the observance of resistance levels;
- head-and-shoulders patterns;
- double-bottom or double-top patterns.

But there is a great deal more too. All that can be done in a general section of this sort is to give a flavour. So the main features referred to can best be illustrated by examples.

Consider Figure 6.3. In this, the broken line represents the lower resistance level on a rising trend. It will be noted that many of the troughs lie on this line, but only at the end

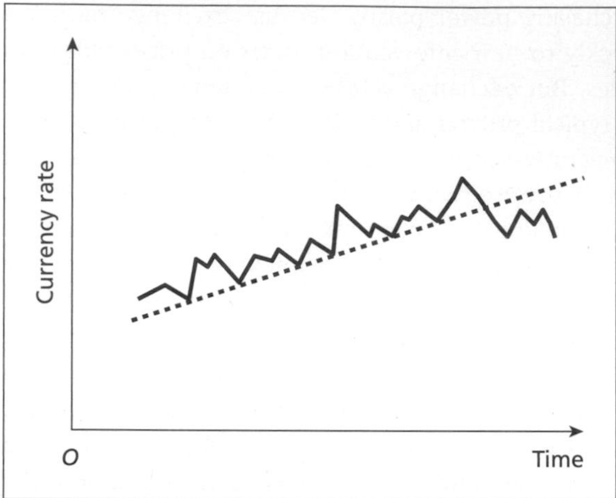

Figure 6.3 Breach of a rising trend

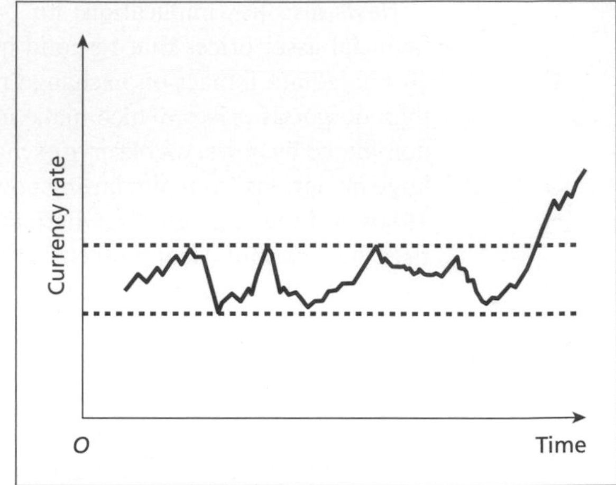

Figure 6.4 Movement out of a channel

is it breached. The chartist would tend to view this breach as an indication that the trend had been reversed.

In Figure 6.4 the basic trend has been flat with oscillations within a channel. There are upper and lower resistance levels which bound this channel and, according to chartists, the breach of either of these will indicate a new trend. This sort of pattern arises from market indecision, as does the triangular pattern in Figure 6.5. In this figure the breach of the resistance lines is said to indicate a change of trend.

Let us now look at a resistance level on a double top. Suppose that the price of a share has been rising steadily for some time. Recently the price fell as some investors sold to realise profits and it then rose to its maximum level for a second time before starting to fall again. This is known as a double top and, based on experience, the chartist would predict that the trend has reversed. A typical double top might appear as shown in Figure 6.6. Double bottoms are interpreted in a similar – but reverse – way.

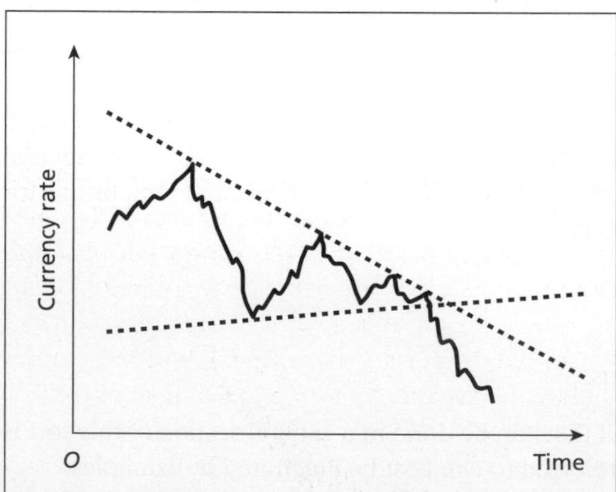

Figure 6.5 Breach of a triangular pattern

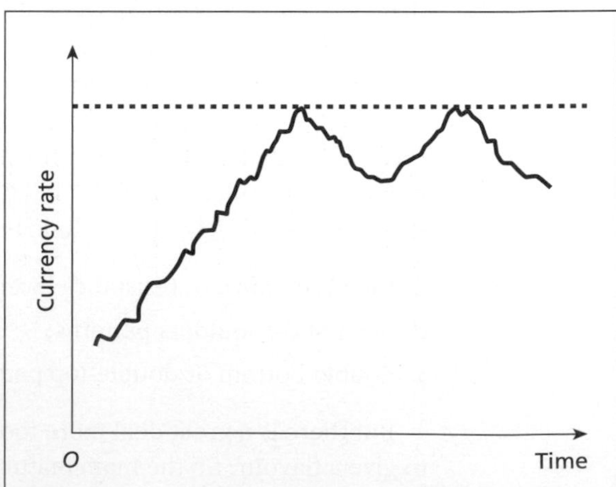

Figure 6.6 Double-top formation

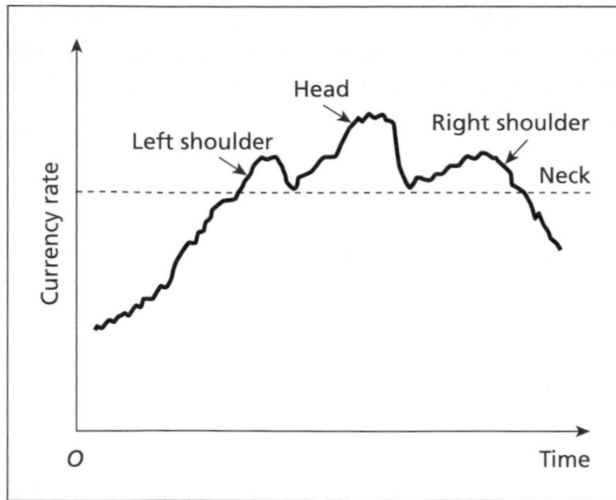

Figure 6.7 Head and shoulders formation

Another indication of a trend reversal is the head-and-shoulders formation of the type shown in Figure 6.7. In this kind of situation the chart might be interpreted as follows. The price has been rising for some time. At the peak of the left shoulder, profit taking has caused the price to drop. The price has then risen steeply again to the head before more profit taking causes the price to drop to around the same level as before – the neck. Although the price rises again, the gains are not as great as at the head. The level of the right shoulder together with the frequent dips down to the neck suggest to the chartist that the upward trend previously observed is over and that a fall is imminent. The breach of the neckline is the indication to sell. An inverse head and shoulders is interpreted using a reverse, but similar, argument.

In preparing charts of movements, the technical analyst usually employs one of two types of chart. These are the line and bar chart and the point and figure chart. We consider the line and bar chart first.

In this kind of chart, each day's trading is represented by one vertical line with a horizontal bar. The length and position of the vertical line represents the day's trading range in a particular market, and the horizontal bar represents the closing price in that market. There will thus be a different chart plotted in each time zone of a globally trading foreign exchange market. Consecutive days' lines and bars are plotted consecutively on a time axis as shown in Figure 6.8.

The point and figure chart is different. It is composed of a matrix of boxes in rows and columns. The vertical axis represents the exchange rate, as in the line and bar chart. Each box represents a particular exchange rate movement, say 10 points. Unlike the line and bar chart, a new column is not started each new day, but only when the exchange rate changes direction.

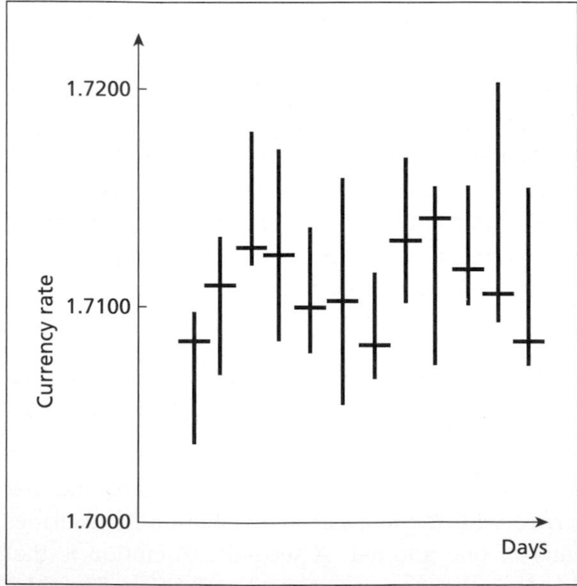

Figure 6.8 Line and bar chart

The point and figure chart is therefore composed of a series of columns representing rising and falling sequences of exchange rate movements. Sequences of a rising exchange rate are usually represented by columns of Xs; sequences of falling rates by columns of 0s. As the exchange rate rises, the chartist will add new Xs to the top of the existing column of Xs. Once the rate begins to fall, the chart analyst will abandon the column of Xs and begin a new column of 0s to represent the falling sequence. This new column will be started diagonally down from the last X. A point and figure chart might look like that in Figure 6.9.

The technical analyst has other techniques. Besides charts, oscillators, moving averages and momentum analysis can be used to forecast exchange rates. How do these methods work?

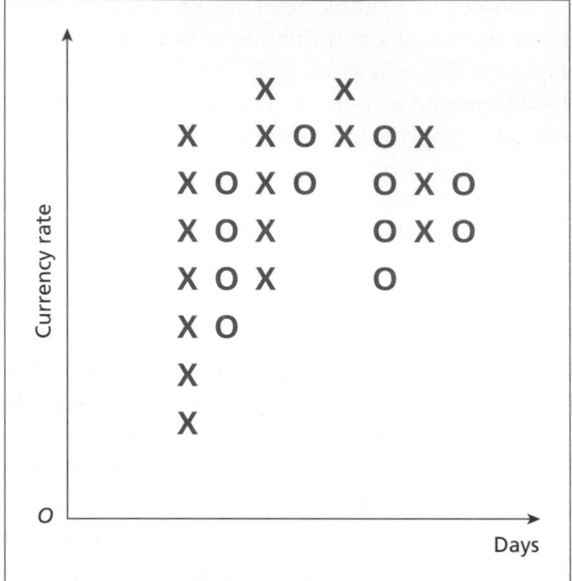

Figure 6.9 Point and figure chart

An oscillator is usually taken to mean the difference between the latest closing exchange rate and the closing exchange rate a specified number of days earlier. So, a three-day oscillator may be constructed by plotting the difference between the latest closing rate and the closing rate three days earlier. When plotted, oscillators frequently exhibit familiar chart patterns – like those already referred to – and the identification of these patterns can assist the technical analyst in detecting trend reversals.

A moving average is usually taken to mean the average of the closing exchange rates over a specified number of previous days. A ten-day moving average can be constructed by plotting for each day the average of the ten previous closing exchange rates. Moving averages are often plotted against the current spot exchange rate. A moving average tends to lag behind the current spot rate, so the two rates will not cross while a trend remains intact. However, once a trend begins to reverse, the two rates will tend to cross. This indicates a buy or sell signal to the technical analyst, depending upon the direction of cross-over.

Momentum refers to the underlying strength of a particular trend and may be calculated in a number of different ways. One simple way of measuring momentum is to track the difference between two different moving averages. For example, this may involve the difference between the five-day and the ten-day moving averages. While a trend remains intact, both moving averages will lag behind the current spot rate, the ten-day more than the five-day, but the difference between the two will remain relatively constant. When the trend shows signs of tiring, the five-day average will react more quickly than the ten-day. Consequently, the difference between the two moving averages will change, indicating a fall in momentum to the technical analyst. Such falls in momentum provide the technical analyst with the wherewithal to make a buy or sell recommendation.

Modern financial theory based upon efficient markets has little time for chartist techniques in deep markets. But there is some evidence (see later in this chapter) that in foreign exchange markets, at least in the short term, chartism pays greater dividends than does reliance upon econometric models for forecasting exchange rates. Perhaps it is worth reminding readers of the essence of the efficient markets hypothesis.

6.8 The efficient markets hypothesis

An initial, and very important, premise of an efficient market is that there are a large number of profit-maximising participants concerned with the analysis and valuation of securities and they are all operating independently of one another. A second assumption is that new information regarding securities comes to the market in a random fashion. The third assumption of an efficient market is especially crucial. Investors adjust security prices rapidly to reflect new information. While the price adjustments made are not always perfect, they are unbiased – sometimes there is an overadjustment; sometimes there is an underadjustment. But one does not know which it will be. Adjustment of security prices takes place rapidly because the market is dominated by profit-maximising investors. The combined effect of new information being obtained by market participants in a random, independent fashion plus the presence of numerous investors who adjust stock prices rapidly to reflect this new information means, according to efficient market theorists, that price changes are likely to be independent and random. According to chartism, of course, price changes are not independent – they are to some extent a function of past price movements. It is evident why efficient market proponents utterly reject the claims of chartists.

Also, in our brief overview of efficient markets, it should be mentioned that, because security prices adjust to all new information and, therefore, supposedly reflect all public information at any point in time, the security prices that prevail at any point in time should be an unbiased reflection of all currently available information.

Based on this brief description, an efficient market is evidently one in which security prices adjust rapidly to the infusion of new information, and current stock prices fully reflect all available information, including the risk involved. Therefore, the returns implicit in a security's price reflect merely the risk involved, so the expected return on a security is consistent with risk – nothing more. There are three gradations of efficient market: the weak form, the semi-strong form and the strong form.

The weak form of the efficient market hypothesis assumes that current stock prices fully reflect all stock market information, including the historical sequence of prices, price changes and any volume information. Because current prices already reflect all past price changes and any other stock market information, this implies that there should be no relationship between past price changes and future price changes. That is, price changes are independent. In other words, past market data cannot be of any use in predicting future prices.

The semi-strong efficient markets hypothesis asserts that security prices adjust rapidly to the release of all new public information. In short, stock prices fully reflect all publicly available data. Obviously, the semi-strong hypothesis encompasses the weak form hypothesis because all public information includes all market information such as past stock prices, trends and so on, plus all non-market information such as earnings, stock splits, economic news and political news. A direct implication of this hypothesis is that investors acting on important new information after it is public cannot derive above-average profits from the transaction, allowing for the cost of trading, because the security price already reflects this new public information.

The strong form of the efficient markets hypothesis contends that stock prices fully reflect all information whether public or otherwise. Hence, it implies that no group of investors has a monopolistic access to information relevant to the formation of prices. Therefore, no group of investors should be able to derive above-average profits consistently. The strong form hypothesis encompasses both the weak and the semi-strong forms. Further, the strong form hypothesis requires not only efficient markets, where prices adjust rapidly to the release of new public information, but also perfect markets in which all information is available to everyone at the same time. This form of the efficient markets hypothesis contends that, because all information is immediately available to everyone and is rapidly discounted by everyone, no group has monopolistic access to important new information and, therefore, no individual trader can consistently derive anything more than the average profit for all traders. Continuing scandals of insider trading are evidence that information is not automatically and evenly distributed between all players.

The notion that shares and other assets are fairly priced given their expected risks and returns, is appealing. In a world where thousands of investors, including professional fund managers and risk arbitrageurs are continuously searching for marginally better returns, it would be difficult to see how overvalued or undervalued securities could exist for more than a few seconds. Furthermore, it should be the case that new information would be required to move markets – especially if movements are really dramatic. Evidence of big market movements without accompanying new information, together with other anomalies that are referred to later in this chapter, has cast doubts upon market efficiency. October 19, 1987 has acquired the moniker 'Black Monday' because leading stocks fell 23 per cent in one day. When one asked oneself what new information caused such a setback, it was not clear that there were any substantive new things happening since Friday's close. No new information but a massive market movement. This is clearly not what efficient market theory suggests. And this is not the only occasion that dramatic falls have taken place without apparent new information. To quote Triana[16] in his argument that market movements resemble fat tail distributions rather than bell shaped normal distributions, 'events in the credit, equity, and interest markets implacably bear witness, but there is also plenty of historical precedent. During the European Exchange Rate Mechanism debacle in 1992 (whereby Europe's system of officially managed currency rates collapsed), 50 standard deviation moves in interest rates were witnessed, while 1987's Black Monday was a 20-standard deviation (or 20-sigma) event. During the summer 1998 convolutions that eventually brought down Long Term Capital Management, 15-plus sigma deviations were occurring. Plenty of smaller (yet still sensationally non-normal) similar gyrations have been observed in finance. So-called 'one in a million years' events have been experienced, several times, by people whose age is way below one million years. Which one is wrong, the real world or the model?' Such happenings are nails in the coffin of the efficient markets hypothesis. Paraphrasing the television show *Monty Python's Flying Circus*, this looks like a dead parrot.

It will be recalled that at the beginning of the discussion of the efficient markets hypothesis the basic premise of an efficient market was that there were a large number of profit-maximising participants. So there are in the foreign exchange markets. But there are also very large non-profit-maximisers – central banks. Their intervention is designed not to make profits but to ease currency price movements in order to achieve a multiplicity of political objectives. The question is: does this intervention stop currency markets from exhibiting market efficiency? This is entirely an empirical question and it is looked at later in this chapter. We now turn to evidence as it relates to purchasing power parity.

6.9 Empiricism and purchasing power parity

Purchasing power parity (PPP), in its absolute form, maintains that, in competitive markets free of transportation costs and official barriers to trade, such as tariffs, identical goods sold in different countries must sell for the same price where their prices are expressed in terms of the same currency – this is the law of one price. Various studies show that the law of one price is widely and strikingly violated by empirical data. Purchasing power parity, in its

PRESS CUTTING 6.1

'Redback' puts the brakes on

By Josh Noble

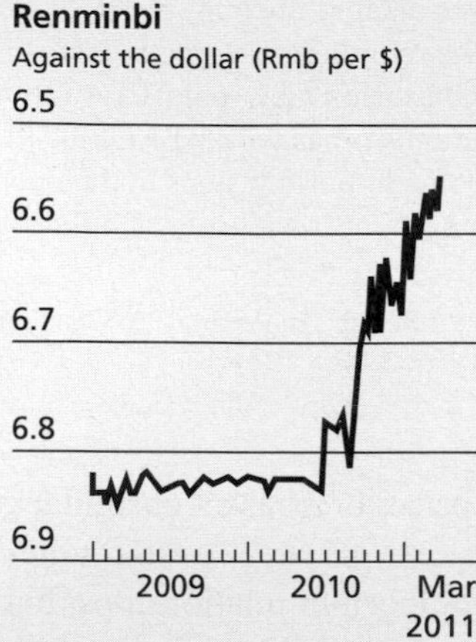

Source: Thomson Reuters Datastream.

The rise of the renminbi appears inexorable. The Chinese currency hits fresh record highs on a regular basis, making the appeal of the 'redback' as an investment clear.

China's economy is in the ascendancy, and its currency will go with it.

Hong Kong is where China's currency meets international investors – permanent residents in the city can open renminbi bank accounts, and buy up to HK$20,000 ($2,565) worth every day. Appetite looks robust – renminbi as a share of Hong Kong's retail deposit base grew from 0.1 to about 5 per cent during 2010, according to the Monetary Authority, the city's de facto central bank.

Because of the Chinese currency's lack of convertibility, the main reason to hold it remains for speculation. HSBC offered a payroll facility for clients wanting to pay staff in renminbi, but so far there have been no takers.

'The average Hong Kong resident views the renminbi itself as a half-decent investment opportunity', says Mark McCombe, chief executive of HSBC's Hong Kong operations. 'It may not be long before taxi drivers and restaurants start accepting it. But for most people –they are paid in Hong Kong dollars, they buy things with Hong Kong dollars, their lives are in Hong Kong dollars.'

For all the hype about the rise of the redback, those banking on even modest gains may be disappointed.

At the start of March, Yi Gang, deputy governor at the Chinese central bank, said the renminbi exchange rate was at its closest yet to 'equilibrium'. The powerful manufacturing lobby is also worried about further appreciation, putting pressure on the government to keep the redback's rise in first gear.

Since the People's Bank of China announced it was moving to a slightly more flexible exchange-rate regime last June, the renminbi has returned to its path of gradual appreciation. But in that time it has risen just 4.3 per cent, outperforming only a handful of currencies in the region, including the Pakistani rupee and the Vietnamese dong.

Only four currencies in Asia have moved less in any direction. Meanwhile, the Japanese yen has leapt 13 per cent, the Singapore dollar 10 per cent and the Korean Won 9.5 per cent.

The action in the forward market suggests continued plodding gains. Non-deliverable forwards – or NDFs – are essentially a derivatives contract pricing future values. Over the next 12 months, the market points to less than 2 per cent of further appreciation.

While the more bullish forecasts point to a rise of anything up to 6 per cent, consensus is for 4.1 per cent by year end, according to a recent poll of economists by Bloomberg. Many analysts remain doubtful.

'Over the next year or so, investors may be disappointed. It's not undervalued by as much as some would hope', says Ashley Davies, senior FX strategist at Commerzbank in Singapore.

Inflation is also a factor. China's prices surged at the end of 2010, prompting a round of monetary tightening from the central bank.

China has used a stronger currency to help damp the effects of imported inflation – principally caused by rising commodity prices. So long as China is battling inflation, there is potential for faster appreciation. But that may be a temporary phenomenon.

'Once China gets a grip on inflation, there could be a reduced need for appreciation', says Albert Leung, FX strategist at Citi. 'The [renminbi] is no longer as undervalued as a few years ago. It will still appreciate, but it's not going to be exciting. Over the longer term, we're likely to see more modest appreciation, and more two-way risk.'

Some analysts go even further. TJ Bond, chief Asia economist at Bank of America Merrill Lynch – though

Press cutting 6.1 (*continued*)

bullish on the currency – says the renminbi 'is not significantly undervalued', and will even become overvalued during the next few months.

'On a risk/reward basis, it has exceeded any other currency in the region', says Daniel Hui, senior FX strategist at HSBC.

One thing that might facilitate a more rapid rise of the redback is a faster opening up of the Chinese capital account. Beijing maintains strict controls on money flowing in or out of the mainland for investment. Pilot projects to allow residents in Wenzhou and Shanghai to invest overseas suggest that authorities are looking at new ways to liberalise some of those restrictions.

'Historically, economies have either had an open or a closed capital account. Once you choose to open it, it feeds itself, making it very difficult to open the capital account gradually in practice', says Mr Davies.

He believes a rapid opening of the capital account could push the renminbi to strengthen faster.

But the consensus view points to a slow pace of reform. 'Gradualism has worked well for the Chinese. We've seen some important steps in the opening of the capital account, but it's a journey of a thousand miles', says Mr Bond.

Source: *Financial Times* Special Report on Foreign Exchange, 29 March 2011.

relative forms, maintains that changes in relative prices of a basket of similar goods among countries determine changes in exchange rates.

Many economic theories are concerned with equilibrium relationships, but equilibrium relationships rarely hold at all times. The distinction is made between the short run and the long run. The most general statement that emerges from the empirical work on PPP is that it shows regular and consistent deviations from equilibrium in the short run but, in general, the equilibrium relationship is found to hold in the long run.

Evidence of the long run mean reverting behaviour of the real exchange rate is extensive. And this is consistent with PPP working well in the longer term. So, it seems that PPP offers a reasonably good guide to long run exchange rate movements. Plotting real exchange rates of sixteen leading currencies against the US dollar, over the last one hundred years, Dimson, Marsh and Staunton[17] show remarkable stability. The substantial deviations that they do note are in respect of the German mark in its colossal inflation period in the early 1920s and also for the same currency following the Second World War. The latter period was one in which the inflation calculations were dubious and subject to extensive government manipulation.

In a review of the literature, Rogoff[18] suggested that, for a broad sample of countries, the half-life of deviations from PPP are around three to five years, implying that deviations from PPP dampen out at a rate of about 15 per cent per year. More recently, Taylor and Peel[19] have suggested that the speed of return to PPP increases when the deviation is larger. These findings on the tempo of mean reversion are valuable in forecasting exchange rate returns to an equilibrium path.

For a much more extensive overview of research work in this area and in the areas that follow in this chapter, see Buckley,[20] MacDonald,[21] Copeland,[22] Pilbeam[23] and Feenstra and Taylor.[24]

In practical terms, note how China has allowed its currency to creep up marginally out of a pegged system (see Table 2.2). Press Cuttings 6.1 and 6.2, interestingly, show the movement. Purchasing power parity data show the rationale with low Chinese inflation on the basis of costs of exports (not CPI inflation) where productivity gains and efficiencies have been highly influential. Note also the massive growth of China's foreign reserves resulting from the country's balance of payments current account surpluses.

PRESS CUTTING 6.2

Why China hates loving the dollar

By Martin Wolf

FT

'The current international currency system is the product of the past.' Thus did Hu Jintao, China's president, raise doubts about the role of the US dollar in the global monetary system on the eve of last week's state visit to Washington. Moreover, he added, 'the monetary policy of the United States has a major impact on global liquidity and capital flows and therefore, the liquidity of the US dollar should be kept at a reasonable and stable level.' He is right on both points.

In criticising US fiscal and monetary policies and, in particular, the Federal Reserve's policy of 'quantitative easing', Mr Hu was following a well-trodden path. In the 1960s, Valéry Giscard d'Estaing, then French finance minister, complained about the dollar's 'exorbitant

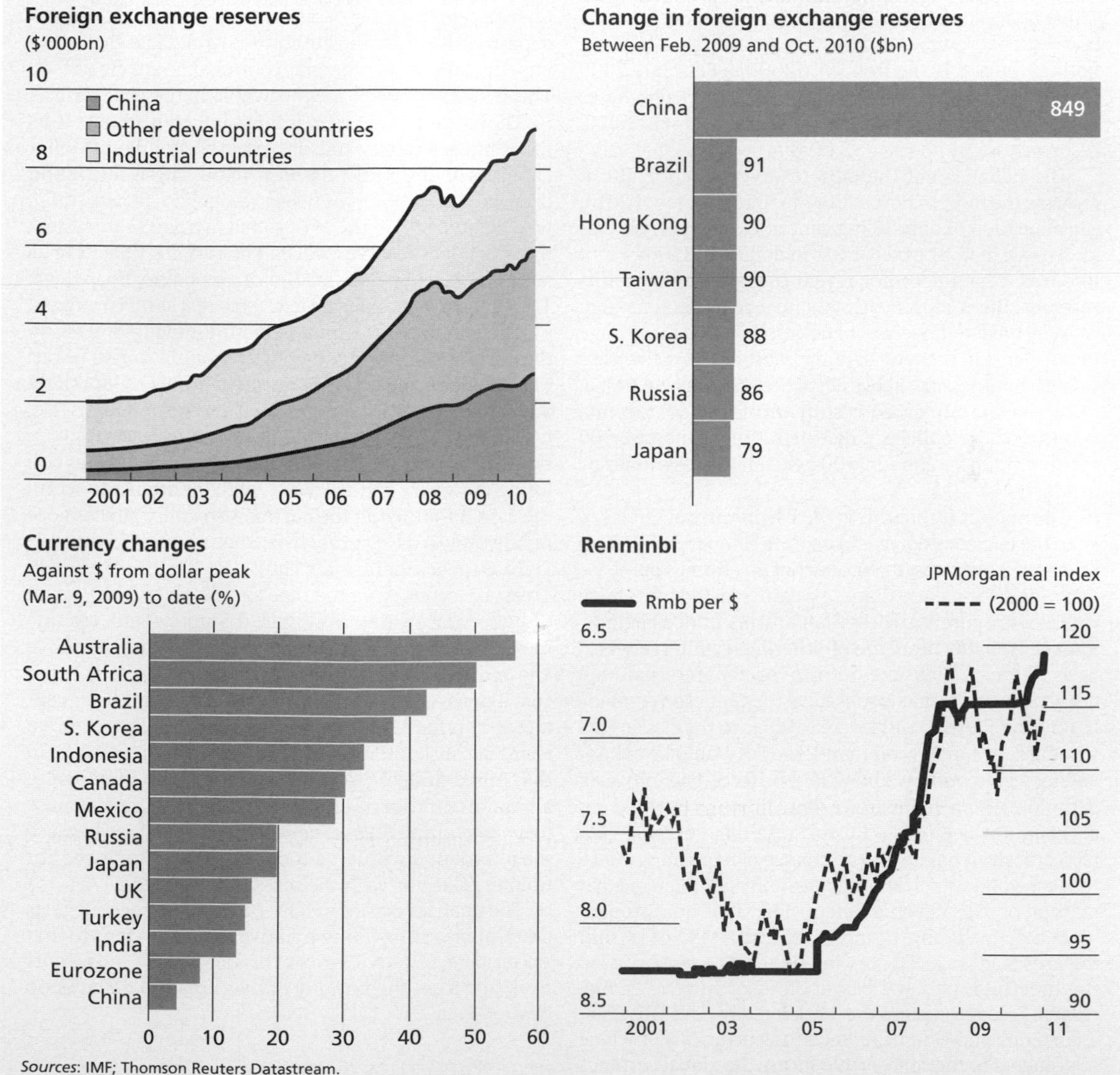

Sources: IMF; Thomson Reuters Datastream.

Press cutting 6.2 (*continued*)

privilege'. John Connally, US Treasury secretary under Richard Nixon, answered when he described the dollar as 'our currency, but your problem'. The French and now the Chinese desire exchange rate stability but detest the inevitable result: an open-ended commitment to buying as many dollars as the US creates. Both want to discipline US policies. Both have failed. Are things likely to be different this time? No.

The Chinese and other heavy interveners have a peculiar way of showing their distrust of the dollar. Between January 1999, just after the Asian financial crisis, and October 2010, the global stock of foreign currency reserves increased by the staggering total of $7,450bn. China alone added $2,616bn. During the recent financial crisis, global reserves did provide a cushion to holders, falling by just $473bn from July 2008 to February 2009 (6 per cent of the initial stock). But then purchases restarted: between February 2009 and October 2010, reserves rose by another $2,004bn.

The dollar is not the only reserve currency. But it remains the most important. In the third quarter of 2010, the allocation of only 56 per cent of global reserves was known. Of that, 61 per cent was in dollars and 27 per cent in euros. China does not reveal the composition of its reserves. But it must be heavily invested in dollars, too.

Why have relatively poor countries made these huge investments in the low-yielding liabilities of the world's richest countries and, above all, of the US? Why has China, in particular, purchased vast quantities of debt from a country whose policies it distrusts – more than $2,000 for every Chinese and some 50 per cent of gross domestic product?

The answer is that this is the by-product of efforts to keep the currency down and exports competitive. It is no longer, if it ever was, the product of an effort to purchase insurance: the risks to Chinese wealth created by its huge reserves are surely greater than any insurance benefits. That is probably now true of other heavy interveners.

Is there a plausible reform of the international monetary system that would solve the Chinese dilemma? If, for example, the world were to go on to the classic gold standard, as some recommend, the US would be experiencing a gold outflow and would be forced to adjust via deflation. China might prefer that, although it would not be good for its exports. But to state this outcome is to indicate why it has next to no chance of happening. Since the first world war no important country has tolerated that method of external adjustment. The US is not Estonia.

Some, including Chinese officials, talk of a shift towards SDRs (special drawing rights) as a reserve asset. But the SDR is merely a basket of major currencies. Any reserve holder can grasp that basket today. The SDR is not a currency and cannot replace the currencies of which it is made. For the conceivable future the global currency regime will depend on national fiat (man-made) currencies. SDR issuance may be a supplement; it will not be a replacement. The Chinese do not seem to disagree.

What about turning the renminbi itself into a global reserve currency? In the very long run, this must happen. But any swift move in that direction would raise two difficulties for China. First, it would only make sense if the currency were to be unpegged from the dollar, in which case the mercantilist strategy would collapse. Second, for a currency to become global it must be freely convertible and traded in deep and liquid financial markets. China would have to abandon exchange controls and liberalise its financial system. It would become impossible to force Chinese people to hold vast quantities of low-yielding bank deposits. Above all, the authorities would lose their most important source of economic control: the banking system. This is surely close to inconceivable in the near term.

The big point, however, is that China cannot pursue its mercantilist strategy and also avoid accumulating dollar liabilities of doubtful long-term value. This is the 'Triffin dilemma', named after the Belgian economist, Robert Triffin, who pointed out, in the 1960s, that in a fixed-rate system the supplier of reserves will end up running deficits in its basic balance of payments (before monetary financing). These must threaten the system's stability, as Mr Hu argues.

The solution for China is to stop buying dollars on the current scale and allow the renminbi to rise faster. That would surely create adjustment problems. But those adjustments are in China's own interests. Otherwise, it will end up accumulating vastly more reserves, continue distorting its own financial system and even risk losing monetary control. Now, with inflation a concern, the case for allowing the currency to adjust much more rapidly upwards is surely overwhelmingly strong.

In a speech before Mr Hu's visit, Tim Geithner, US Treasury secretary, noted that 'since June of 2010, when Chinese authorities announced they would resume moving toward a more flexible exchange rate, they have allowed the currency to appreciate only about 3 per cent against the dollar. This is a pace of about 6 per cent a year in nominal terms, but significantly faster in real terms because inflation in China is much higher than in the United States. We believe it is in China's interest to allow the currency to appreciate more rapidly in response to market forces. And we believe China will do so because the alternative would be too costly – for China and for China's relations with the rest of the world.'

The analysis is surely right. But the evidence suggests that China is still willing to move only very slowly. That is a mistake. My advice to Mr Hu is simple: if China wants to escape from the tyranny of that dreadful dollar, stop buying. Please.

Source: *Financial Times*, 26 January 2011.

6.10 Empiricism and the Fisher effect

It will be recalled that the Fisher effect attributes differences in nominal interest rate in different countries to different inflation expectations for those countries. But the impact of the Taylor rule way of thinking would be likely to result in deviations from Fisher. And, the majority of recent empirical work on the Fisher effect indicates a Taylor rule influence. It should be borne in mind, however, that most tests of the Fisher effect have been carried out in conjunction with tests of the associated international Fisher effect which suggests that differences in interest rates between countries are related to expected changes in the spot exchange rate.

Again, for a full summary of research in this area, see the three references at the conclusion of section 6.9.

6.11 Empiricism and the international Fisher effect

If the international Fisher effect were to hold over the medium to long term, investment in interest-bearing monetary assets held for the medium to long term should not be subject to exchange rate risk in the sense that the higher rate of interest would compensate for currency depreciation. Thus, an investor may achieve a higher interest return by placing his money in sterling than by putting it into euros. But this should be evened out over the medium to long term by the fact that the euro should, according to international Fisher, appreciate versus the pound sterling. If we superimpose upon this some of the ideas associated with efficient markets, it should not be possible to formulate a **filter rule** for investment policy which would consistently outperform the average rate of return achieved from investing in international interest-bearing securities of comparable quality. International Fisher, linked with the efficient markets hypothesis, suggests that the average return over all currencies – taking into account relative interest rates and appreciation/depreciation – should be equal and filter rules should not yield abnormal returns when taking into account associated risk.

Various investigators have undertaken empirical tests to establish whether this was so. For example, one such study by Robinson and Warburton[25] devised four investment rules for placing and switching money in three-month treasury bills or three-month offshore currency deposits. The four filter rules were as follows:

- Invest for the highest nominal rate of interest.
- Invest for the highest real rate of interest with inflation expectations based on consumer prices over the preceding six months.
- Invest for the highest real rate of interest with inflation expectations based on wholesale prices over the preceding six months.
- Invest for the highest real rate of interest with a 'correction' factor built in to allow for exchange rates being out of equilibrium.

The investigators' findings are thought-provoking since their filter rules seemed to yield substantial excess returns. These findings seem to cast some doubt about the received wisdom on two fronts. Can they be reconciled with the international Fisher effect? Are foreign exchange markets efficient? Of course, it may just be a quirk that the filter rules produced the kinds of results shown; efficient markets advocates would suggest that finding *ex-post* rules that yield superior returns is not difficult. Also Robinson and Warburton's methodology might be improved. They use a single period of analysis running from 1972 to 1979 and this would have been improved had they used a number of investment periods covering different spans and terminating at varying dates. Given the comment above about ease of finding *ex-post* decision rules which yield superior returns, Bell and Kettell[26] sought to replicate the Robinson–Warburton experiment for the two further years after their filter rules were published. Their results were not dissimilar; the filter rules continued to yield excess returns. It is possible that the excess returns simply reflected higher risk.

More replications of this work were carried out by Madura and Nosari.[27] They simulated a speculative strategy in which the currency with the lowest quoted interest rate was borrowed by a US-based speculator and converted and invested in the currency with the highest nominal interest rate. At the end of the speculation period, the funds were repatriated and the loan repaid. Substantial profits were found to result from this policy. This filter rule was repeated for investment with the speculation located in seven other major Western economies and similarly large profits resulted. Various other studies have ended up with similar findings. Theorists of efficient markets would suggest that reactions by rational players in the market place to the dissemination of the information would close the profit opportunity, again suggesting, perhaps, that the profits simply reflect risk taken on. Clearly we have a problem seeking a solution.

That the international Fisher effect seems not to hold in the short-term substantially underpins the substantial strategy of investment banks and hedge funds in pursuit of profit for the carry trade. The carry trade is risky and big profits and losses have occurred in the past. The frequently quoted recent strategy has involved borrowing Japanese yen and investing in Australian dollars. Careful readers will observe that the carry trade is, effectively, an uncovered interest arbitrage strategy. The topic is considered further in section 6.15 of this chapter.

As financial economists, we should hardly be surprised that our models do not hold immutably for all periods. But there seem to be legitimate questions to be asked about efficient markets in foreign exchange. A discussion on this topic follows in section 6.14 of this chapter.

6.12 Empiricism and interest rate parity

It will be recalled that interest rate parity theory equates the forward premium or discount with interest differentials. Empirical studies have generally confirmed that the covered interest differential is not significantly different from zero except when there are market imperfections such as those created by government controls on capital flows, exchange restrictions, prohibitions on profit remittances and capital repatriations, and so on.

There is a host of studies that support the covered interest differential as being zero. Many texts have used short-term data. But markets in long-term forwards have emerged strongly over the recent past. With the emergence of long-term forwards, what is the evidence? Many studies have examined five-, seven- and ten-year securities and found deviations from long-term IRP. Some of these have even implied profit opportunities after allowing for transaction costs. Deviations of this sort create a window of opportunity for firms and may partly explain the rapid growth in long-term currency swaps. Again, the three texts referred to at the end of section 6.9 summarise research in this area.

6.13 Empiricism and expectations theory

Although we would not expect the forward rate today always to equal the future spot rate, expectations theory suggests that, on average, this will tend to be so. In other words, the forward rate will exceed the future spot rate as often as it is below it. This means that, the forward rate will be an unbiased predictor of the future spot rate. Empirical evidence casts some doubt upon this.

The general findings of empirical studies can best be summarised by an example. If one were to look at movements of the US dollar against sterling one would tend to find that during periods of pound strength, forecasts based on the forward rate would undervalue sterling, whereas during phases of pound weakness, the forward rate would overvalue the UK currency.

As Hodrick[28] states, in summarising the 'evidence against the unbiasedness hypothesis [it] appears to be very strong and consistent across currencies, maturities and time periods'. Studies indicate that the formulation of a forecasting model capable of beating the forward rate can be devised – something of a challenge to the idea of the efficient nature of foreign exchange markets. But we must take great care. This is a risky tactic. Some researchers have found that evidence shows a reversal in the sign of the future spot rate versus that implied in the forward rate. Put mathematically, this evidence would accord to a model based on:

$$(s_{t+1} - s_t) = a_i + a_2(f_t - s_t) + u_{t+1}$$

Once again, see the references in the last paragraph of section 6.9 for further detail on research studies.

6.14 Empiricism and foreign exchange market efficiency

A market is said to be efficient if current prices quoted therein approximately reflect all currently available information and there are no opportunities for making extraordinary profits by further exploiting such information. In the context of foreign exchange markets, the hypothesis would presumably suggest that profit-seeking market participants act upon information available to them in such a way that the spot exchange rate always reflects all available information that could potentially be useful in earning excess profits. Absolutely definitive empirical evidence about efficiency in the foreign exchange markets is unavailable because of the inadequacy of a comprehensive testing model. However, there has been no lack of empirical work in this complex area – and findings differ. Some find evidence favouring efficiency. But there is, a wealth of studies which conclude that foreign exchange markets do not necessarily behave in a manner altogether consistent with an efficient market. We have already discussed Robinson and Warburton's work and there have been numerous other studies. Much of this work suggests that filter rules may yield substantial profits; this supports the essence of the carry-trade – see section 6.15.

If there is some evidence suggesting less than complete market efficiency, can we explain it? The answer may lie with the behaviour of central banks. One of the key assumptions about efficient markets is that they comprise profit-maximising participants all acting independently of one another. Central bank intervention, either directly by dealing in the foreign exchange markets or indirectly by influencing interest rates, is rarely directed towards profit maximisation and the banks' behaviour is frequently a function of the effects that other participants are having on the market – for example, if the concerted actions of profit-maximising market operators were to push the exchange rate towards a sensitive level, sustained central bank intervention might follow. That central banks' operations in foreign exchange markets are not profit oriented is well substantiated by Taylor[29] who tabulates profits and losses – mainly the latter – accruing to nine major central banks through official intervention in the foreign exchange market during the bulk of the floating period in the 1970s.

Perhaps the conflicting evidence on market efficiency is nothing more than we should expect. Central banks do not intervene all of the time in the market. At times when they are not intervening, we would expect the foreign exchange markets to show all of the features associated with efficiency; at times when central banks are intervening it would be doubtful whether markets would display efficiency. According to this explanation then, foreign exchange markets in some currencies, for some periods, would be seen to be efficient, but for other periods – that is, when the central bank is intervening – they would not.

As an example of bank intervention, Press Cuttings 6.3, 6.4 and 6.5 tell the story of the 2011 co-ordinated move by central banks to weaken the yen in the wake of a destruction following a tsunami and a nuclear power plant explosion. Shortly following these tragedies, the yen strengthened as traders worldwide expected inflows of cash to Japan in order to rebuild properties. The intervention of the central banks was designed to counter this strengthening. The press cuttings speak for themselves.

PRESS CUTTING 6.3

G7 nations in $25bn yen sell-off

By Peter Garnham and David Oakley

The world's most powerful central banks joined forces to sell billions of dollars worth of yen, battling speculators – described as 'sneaky thieves' by one Japanese official – who have driven the currency to record highs.

The intervention by banks including the Federal Reserve, European Central Bank, Bank of Japan and Bank of England began in the early hours of Friday morning, after ministers from the Group of Seven most industrialised nations approved the first such co-ordinated action in more than a decade.

Traders estimate more than $25bn was spent by the world's richest nations, a great deal of it by Japan, in an effort to drive the Japanese currency sharply lower against the dollar after it soared to a post-war high of ¥76.25.

The rise in the yen was the result of dealers betting that Japanese insurers and other big companies would have to repatriate funds to meet claims and pay for reconstruction. Its strength threatens to inflict further pain on Japan as it struggles with the aftermath of last week's earthquake, tsunami and the risk of a nuclear meltdown.

Costs to the insurance industry could yet reach the levels of the record $40bn-plus claims from Hurricane Katrina. RMS, the only leading catastrophe loss forecaster to publish an estimate, told clients it expected total economic losses to be between $200bn and $300bn.

Fumihiko Igarashi, Japan's deputy finance minister, warned foreign exchange markets they should not assume Friday's intervention was a one-off move.

'G7 countries agreed that if we caved in to such speculators that took advantage of people's misfortunes, the Japanese economy would be ruined and the whole world economy would be harmed,' he told Reuters.

'Our stance remains un-changed that we will take decisive steps against speculators who act like sneaky thieves at a scene of a fire.'

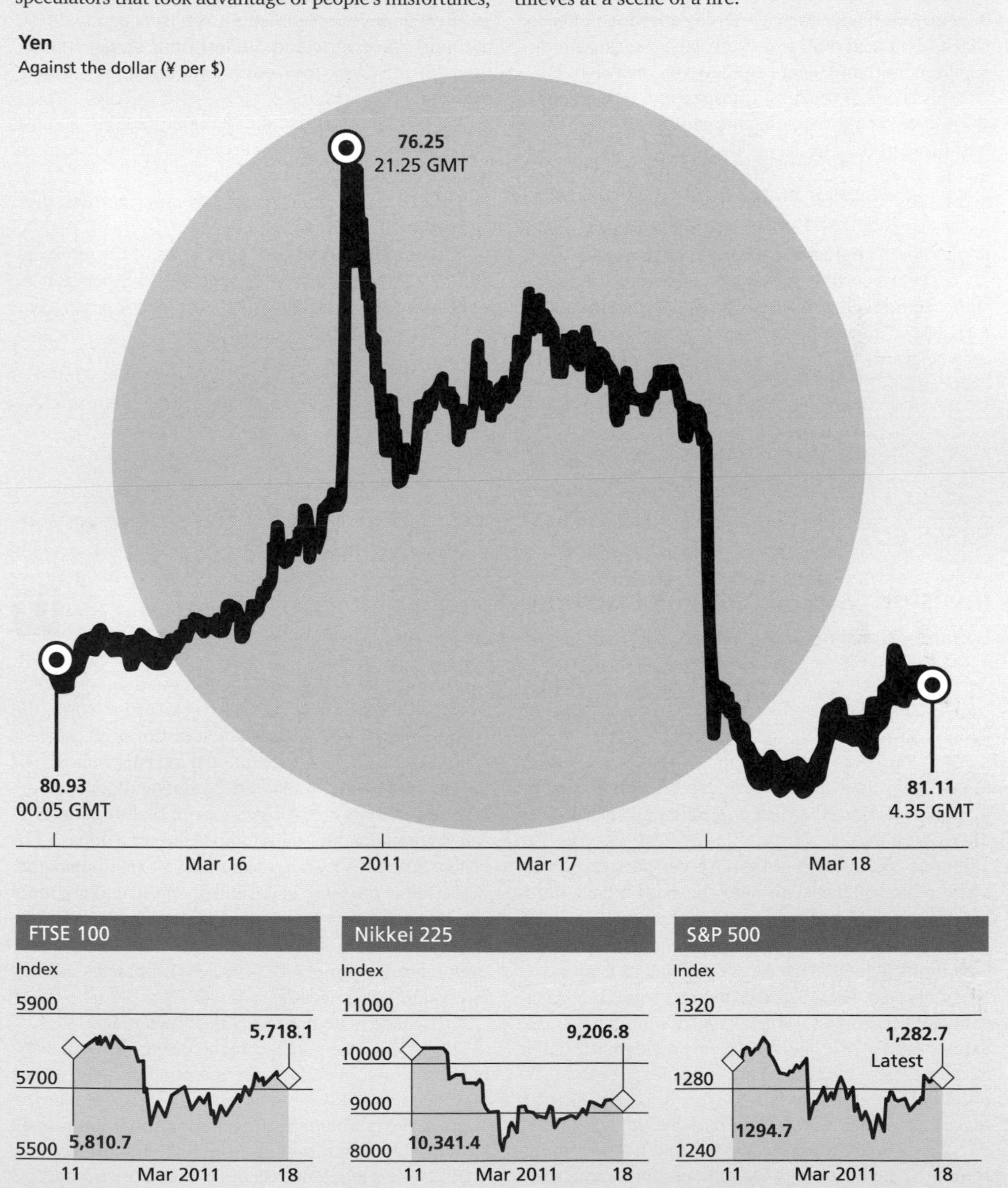

Source: Thomson Reuters.

Source: Bloomberg News. Times are GMT.

Press cutting 6.3 (*continued*)

News of the G7 action sent the yen tumbling, to ¥81, and triggered a rebound in Japanese stocks that rippled across Europe and the US. The S&P 500 was trading 0.7 per cent higher early yesterday afternoon after the Nikkei bounced 2.7 per cent. Japanese shares still ended more than 10 per cent down on the week.

'This is one of the most transparent interventions of size I have seen. No beating around the bush, no hush-hush', said a senior trader at Citigroup. 'This is sanctioned by the G7 to save Japan and, indirectly, global growth momentum. It will continue all day and all week.'

The yen is a powerful influence on Japan's economy and its sharp appreciation represented a threat.

'Excessive currency volatility negatively affects consumer sentiment', said Kaoru Yosano, Japan's economy minister. 'The significance of the intervention is to limit share price and currency moves within market expectations.'

The central banks' move capped a frenetic week for the world's financial markets, during which Japanese stocks suffered their biggest two-day fall since the 1987 crash. Investors pulled $8.2bn from equity funds, the most since July, and $4.3bn from money market funds in the week to Wednesday, said EPFR, a data provider.

Traders said the BoJ sold ¥2,000bn ($25bn) against the dollar, similar to the record ¥2,125bn it sold to weaken its currency last September.

The Fed and the Bank of Canada confirmed that they had been selling the yen too.

The yen fell 2.6 per cent after news of the intervention to ¥81.14 against the dollar, lost 3.5 per cent to ¥114.58 against the euro and dropped 2.8 per cent to ¥131.15 against the pound.

Source: Financial Times, 19/20 March 2011.

PRESS CUTTING 6.4

Investors wrestle with meltdown risk

By James Mackintosh, Investment Editor

As Japan's nuclear crisis escalated this week, financial traders around the world scrambled to become instant experts on the risks of atomic power.

GLG Partners, the hedge fund owned by London's Man Group, had an in-house expert: Simon Savage, head of risk, started at Britain's National Nuclear Corp after Chernobyl.

'I was able to offer a sense of perspective at what we're really dealing with here', he says. 'When words like "meltdown" and "going critical" are being thrown around people think "bloody hell, it could blow a major hole in the planet". That's just not going to happen.'

Traders elsewhere relied on industry sources or hastily contacted academics. What all had in common was that expert views on the likely outcome provided little guide to the direction of the market. As one Japanese minister observed, every time smoke rose from the stricken reactor, share prices fell, even though it meant little.

'Clearly we're trading an event that nobody understands the implications of', admits one prominent hedge fund manager.

The outcome of that lack of understanding was shown in the wild market swings all week. At its worst, the Japanese stock market was down just over 20 per cent – a full-on crash. It then leapt, making back almost half its loss in two days, to end Friday down 10.2 per cent.

The country's credit risk shot up; Markit data show Japan credit default swaps jumped almost a third to 115 basis points, ranking it as riskier than Mexico or Panama.

To add to the sense of crisis in financial markets, there was also an extraordinary spike in the yen on Thursday. In 20 minutes, it shot through its record high against the dollar, prompting the first co-ordinated currency intervention in a decade.

These effects do not just come down to fear.

Financial markets are terrible at pricing highly unlikely, but disastrous events. Even reasonably likely events may be ignored if they do not fit the quarterly reporting cycle or the mathematical risk models that limit many traders – as was shown by the 2007 subprime crisis. Then, models relied on recent US house price data, and so ignored the possibility of price falls.

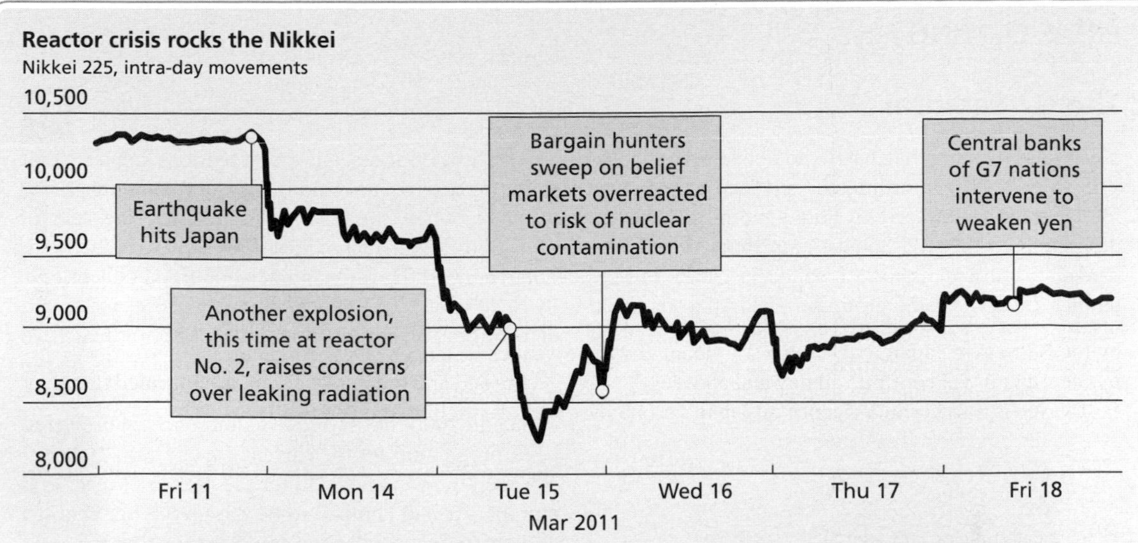

Source: Bloomberg.

Even in Japan, a very seismically active region, equities could not be prepared for a quake and tsunami on a scale barely known in living memory.

'The markets don't do a good job because by definition these are events that are highly unlikely to happen', says Jack Bogle, founder of Vanguard, the fund manager.

It took investors days to figure out the economic ramifications of the quake, while nuclear catastrophe loomed. That left an information gap that markets were not equipped to fill.

'Human nature causes you to exaggerate this kind of thing, typically by many multiples', says Jeremy Grantham, chief investment strategist at fund manager GMO. 'If you list things where the psychological effect is far greater than the expected value you would put nuclear at the top. Not that it isn't a disaster, but the world is particularly sensitive to Three Mile Island-type events. Even the dreadful consequences of Chernobyl were only a tiny fraction of what was feared.'

For Mr Grantham, shares overreacted. 'It may knock 2 per cent off [Japan's] GDP', he estimates. 'And you saw 20 per cent knocked off the market.'

Market panic is really no different to other panics. Reports of a surge in American orders for potassium iodide tablets, designed to protect against certain radiation-induced cancers, fit a well-known pattern: sales of earthquake insurance can be relied on to boom just after a quake.

Financially this effect appears most clearly in options, which investors can use to protect against share price falls.

The cost of protection against shares dropping soared in Japan as the market tumbled. Implied volatility on the Nikkei 225, indicating the cost of options, leapt from 21 to 70, though still some way off the 92 reached after Lehman Brothers collapsed. On Friday it fell back to 50.

But just because the market initially overreacted does not mean the quake and nuclear calamity will not hurt the economy.

Japan faces a heavy clean-up bill, power shortages, and the continued risk of a major radiation leak.

Longer term, the world faces renewed constraints on nuclear power, meaning more demand and higher prices for fossil fuels, and possibly alternative energy (as the markets woke up to midweek). This comes as investors try to grasp the implications of another very serious but unlikely event: the possibility that rising tensions between Iran and Saudi Arabia disrupt oil supplies.

The markets took a long time to understand the importance of the Arab revolutions. They are still struggling to work out how far revolt will spread. As one large London hedge fund manager put it when asked how to assess the risks of Saudi shares (cheap on many measures): 'You just don't. You close your eyes, and you buy. Saudi must be where the US love of democracy runs out.'

Extreme risks will always be with us, and almost impossible to predict. One prediction: most investors will continue to find it easier to ignore them.

Source: *Financial Times*, 19/20 March 2011.

PRESS CUTTING 6.5

The G7 Samurai

FT

It was hard to argue that Japan did not deserve a break. The world's first co-ordinated currency intervention for 11 years, announced on Friday morning, has been described by the G7 finance ministers and central bankers as an expression of 'solidarity'. Back in September 2000, the same group propped up a weak and volatile euro out of a 'shared concern . . . for the world economy'. Friday's campaign is all about Japan, and what it needs to get back on its feet.

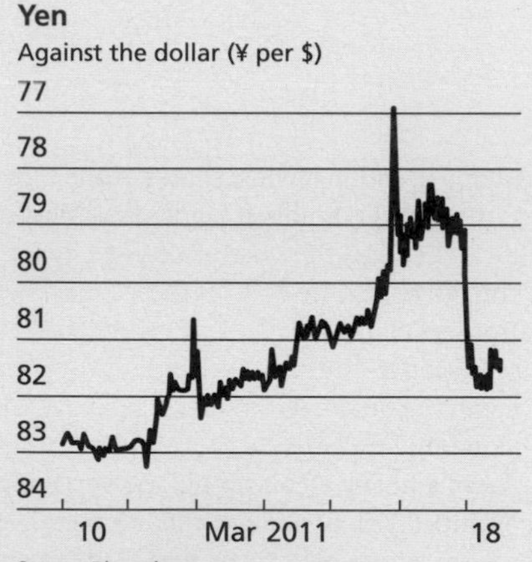

Source: Bloomberg.

The history of currency interventions suggests that solitary action is not enough. In mid-September, for example, when the BoJ went it alone, the sale of ¥2,125bn ($26bn) (the biggest-ever one-day intervention) reversed the yen's appreciation trend only briefly. By November 1, as the Fed announced a second round of quantitative easing, the yen had strengthened to 80.22 to the dollar, from 82.08 at the time of the intervention. But there is strength in numbers. Between 1985 and 2000 there were five; four of them proved to be turning-points for the currency in question. If the G7 can keep the yen above 80 for the next few weeks and months – it had climbed to 81.80, up 3.5 per cent, by 4.30pm in Tokyo – this too could change the trend.

But there are a few things to note. One is global risk aversion. The conflicts in the Middle East, and the possible need to bring reconstruction funds back into Japan, are not conducive to yen weakness. Neither are ultra-low interest rates elsewhere, diminishing the appeal of the dollar and euro. Then, of course, there is China, which may not entirely welcome a weaker yen, if that implies dollar strength. The international community, via the G7 and G20, has spent years lecturing Beijing on the virtues of market-determined exchange rates. Friday's abandonment of that principle, however well-intentioned, may have unintended consequences.

Source: *Financial Times* Lex Column, 19/20 March 2011.

6.15 The carry trade a.k.a. uncovered interest arbitrage

In recent years, the main low-interest rate currency in the world economy has been the Japanese yen. Carry traders have often borrowed in low-interest currencies and made an investment in higher interest-rate currencies such as the Australian dollar and New Zealand dollar, but also others. The profits from these trades have been regular and high. This is the essence of the carry trade, also known as uncovered interest arbitrage. It is a risky strategy though. If the yen were to appreciate significantly, returns could easily become negative. Losses would result.

Critical to the carry trade is regular review of open positions and immediate action to close such deals if markets look like moving sharply against the trader. The carry trade strategy is subject to **volatility** because the players are all trying to exploit a disequilibrium.

Many players in this market are highly leveraged too. This magnifies risks but could magnify profits. Clearly with the business risk inherent in the trade itself plus the financial risk resulting from leverage, minute by minute monitoring is justified. Imagine that you have put up EUR10,000 of your own money and that you borrow the equivalent of EUR190,000 in Japanese yen. This gives vast leverage but it is not uncommon in the carry trade. Imagine that you then invest the EUR200,000 in Australian dollars. A 5 per cent loss on this trade will wipe out all of your equity. A 10 per cent loss will put you in a position where you have lost your investment and you are EUR10,000 in the red.

History tells us that, in the carry trade, big profits have accrued but big reversals do happen. In downturns, all players rush for the exit, they all unwind their positions at the same time; the market bombs; blood on the street. If you're last out of the exit, don't expect too much sympathy.

However, the truth of the carry trade is that it has yielded fairly persistent profits with occasional meltdowns. You have been warned. In Press Cutting 6.6, John Authers reports some virtues but is also somewhat cautious.

Bringing things together, it is fair to say that foreign exchange movements seem to be driven by four key factors. These are yield differentials, relative inflation rates, trade flows and growth prospects. Yield has probably been a short term dominant influence of the past decade, particularly in the form of the carry trade.

PRESS CUTTING 6.6

A redeeming argument for the carry trade

FT

By John Authers

The carry trade gets a bad press. It created one of the biggest bubbles of the last decade. But, handled differently, could it help bring the world's deep economic imbalances back into kilter?

Simply defined, a carry trade involves borrowing at cheap rates and parking it somewhere with higher rates. In the jargon, this gives a positive 'carry'.

In the 2000s, the most popular carry trade involved the yen, as Japanese interest rates were virtually zero. Investors could borrow in yen and put the money in a currency with higher rates, notably the Australian dollar. This was a great, low-risk trade; unless the currencies went into reverse. If the yen suddenly gained on the Aussie dollar, you could soon lose a lot of money.

This did not happen for many years because the carry trade tends to be self-fulfilling. Selling the yen tended to weaken it; buying into the Aussie dollar tended to strengthen it. As the carry trade's profits are quite small, it was only worthwhile if investors used borrowed money to do it. So the trade carried on making money until disaster struck in the wake of the Lehman Brothers bankruptcy. Carry traders suffered losses of as much as 30 per cent in a matter of weeks and the chaos of sharply shifting exchange rates contributed to the calamitous fall in global trade.

Financial commentators (this one included) therefore attacked carry trading as a dangerous form of speculation that destabilised financial markets and economies.

But there is an alternative argument. Neil Record, who runs Record Currency Management in London, suggests that the carry trade can be regarded as an asset class and as an ongoing investment for regular retail investors. He even suggests that it can help resolve the world's long-term economic imbalances.

How? Countries running a deficit need to raise funds but they are also riskier than those running a surplus. Their risk is encapsulated by the exchange rate – if the government's fiscal management breaks down, that will show up in a weaker currency.

If there is extra risk, investors need to be offered an extra premium in order to take that risk. That is the extra interest rate on offer in the carry trade. This extra interest rate then becomes the key to working out how to treat currencies like other investment assets. Currency trades have equal and opposite winners and losers; it is not always at all clear which of two currencies is more risky.

If this theory works, over the very long term carry trade currencies should outperform others, just as stocks

Press cutting 6.6 (*continued*)

outperform bonds, thanks to the risk premium investors demand before investing in them.

To test the theory, Mr Record had FTSE set up an index that took a range of currency pairs (the different permutations available between dollar, the euro, the pound sterling, the Japanese yen and the Swiss franc, such as the dollar-sterling, the euro-yen and so on) and systematically bought whichever currency in these pairs had the higher nominal interest rate. It reviews these pairs once a month and switches currencies if the country with the higher interest rate has changed – although this generally happens only once every few years for most pairs.

The results are shown in the chart – as theory predicted, the carry trade performed nicely over time, with less volatility than stocks. It has worked less well since the crash of 2008 but still has decent returns combined with lower volatility. An index with more currencies did better.

A strategy of buying into this strategy and waiting, therefore, does make sense. If investors worked this way en masse, the currency market would become a mechanism for easing world imbalances.

Now for the caveats. Mr Record suggests patient 'buy and hold' investing with real money, rather than with borrowed funds. That is different from the opportunistic, leveraged approach to carry trading today. His research does not back the increasingly popular practice of retail trading in foreign exchange using leverage.

To grasp how extreme that activity is, note that in 2007–10 the Bank of International Settlements found that total daily foreign exchange trading volume was $3,980bn (or, as people not subject to the Financial Times's style book would say, almost $4 trillion). Annual volume is about a quadrillion dollars ($1,000,000,000,000,000). Daily forex trading volume in London, the centre for such activity, is 140 times that of the London Stock Exchange. That is evidence of speculative, leveraged investing. Rather than exploit a recognisable anomaly as Mr Record's strategy does, it distorts markets and makes it harder for economies to function.

Treated in the way, Mr Record suggests, foreign exchange has some of the facets of an asset class, and might be an interesting addition to a portfolio. But is it an argument to lever up and try to play the forex market? No. A quadrillion times no.

Source: *Financial Times*, 29/30 January 2011.

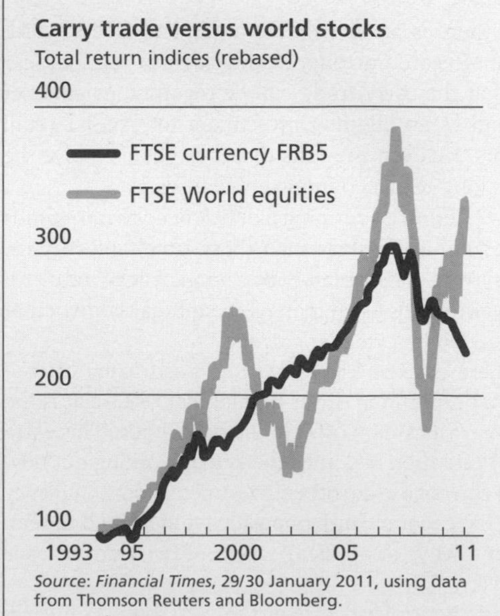

Source: Financial Times, 29/30 January 2011, using data from Thomson Reuters and Bloomberg.

- The FRB5 Indices represent the return generated from investing, on an equally weighted basis, in all 10 currency pairs that can be derived from the following five currencies: CHF, EUR, GBP, JPY and USD.
- Each month, the higher interest rate currency of each pair is bought against the lower using one-month forward contracts. Contracts are rolled at maturity or reversed if the direction of the rate differential has reversed. Interest rate differentials are indicated by forward contract pricing.
- All 10 positions are re-balanced monthly to maintain equal weighting.
- FX deals are fully costed, so the index is investable.
- Excess return and total return index values are calculated daily.
- The FRB5 indices are denominated in CHF, EUR, GBP, JPY and USD and a product file is available in each currency. Those shown on the chart are in USD terms as is the FTSE world equities index.
- An index methodology and calculation example are freely available to the public for all FTSE forex indices.

In the longer term, a country with a relatively high inflation rate ought to see its currency depreciate so that its real exchange rate is roughly stable over time. This does tend to happen, especially when inflation rates are very high.

A country with a persistent current account deficit might expect to see its currency fall. That has indeed been the experience of the USA over recent years. But markets tend to overlook a trade deficit when they are excited by an economy's growth prospects. The dollar's strength in the late 1990s owed much to a belief that productivity gains, driven by the internet, would increase the growth rate of the USA. At the time, investors clamoured to get hold of dot com stocks resulting in portfolio flows pushing the dollar higher.

Summary

- We are seeking a model that explains exchange rate movements. The goal is a regression model that works, in which the spot rate is the dependent variable and coefficients can be estimated for a series of independent variables and which has a high statistical significance. The search has been no more successful than the hunt for El Dorado, the fabled South American city rich in gold and treasure sought by Spanish explorers of the sixteenth century.
- We have, nonetheless, a number of competing theories of exchange rate movements including purchasing power parity theory, balance of payments theories, monetary theories and portfolio balance theory. How do these work?
- Purchasing power parity was summarised in Chapter 3. It is found to be a poor predictor of exchange rates in the short term. But when developed from an equilibrium base year and used as a long-term forecasting device, it seems to work well.
- The balance of payments theory of exchange rate determination has gone through many forms. The original form ignored capital flows and was applied to a fixed exchange rate mechanism. The way it works – simplistically – is as follows. Assume an increase in national income. This results in a pressure for imports to rise. To pay for them, the exchange rate weakens as funds flow out to buy foreign currency. Support for the home currency is necessary – remember we are talking about a fixed rate regime. And worries about the balance of payments current account deficit lead to severity in the home market. This may be manifest in lower money supply growth and lower inflation. The effect should be to dampen demand for imports and force resources into export production, improving the current account – and strengthening the exchange rate.
- The above version of the balance of payments theory has been overtaken by events. Remember that it is based on a fixed exchange rate regime. Balance of payments theory may be approached in a floating exchange rate environment either ignoring capital flows or with them. Let us do the former first. Under such an environment, improvements in national income tend to worsen the current account and weaken the exchange rate. The lower currency rate should, *ceteris paribus*, improve exports and dampen imports with the attendant force to improve the current account and strengthen the currency.
- In the version of balance of payments theory which takes cognisance of floating exchange rates and allows for capital flows, the reasoning is as follows. As national income increases, the current account deteriorates. If official reserve movements are to be avoided, there

must be an improvement in capital account. This may be achieved via higher interest rates (assuming underlying inflation remains unchanged this implies higher real interest rates) which has the effect of damping demand – and hence imports. Thus the current account swings back into an improved position. Note that though interest rates increase under this version of balance of payments theory, the exchange rate tends to remain constant.

- This is not so with the monetary theory of exchange rates. Using the route outlined above, improvements to national income result in increased transactions demand for money. To the extent that this is not created by the domestic banking system, it is imported from abroad. The increased money supply tends to push up inflation and interest rates and the exchange rate consequently worsens. The driving force in this model is relative money supplies between the home country and trading partners.
- The portfolio balance theory suggests that the exchange rate is a function of the relative supply of domestic and foreign bonds. Simplistically, the effect can be seen in an example. Assume that the supply of bonds in a country increases. Its bond prices would then fall but bond yields to redemption should increase. All other things being equal, money flows into the country and forces up the exchange rate. Note that in this model interest rates move up without any effect on inflation – in other words, real interest rates rise. If, of course, expected inflation were to rise too, then the exchange rate should not be enhanced.
- Empirically, we observe a tendency for exchange rates to overshoot the level implied by economic models.
- The news explanation of exchange rates is different. It suggests that as unexpected news occurs, these unanticipated pieces of information affect rates appropriately. But remember it is unexpected news that moves markets – expected news should be discounted in present levels.
- Note how chartist models work. This is explained fairly straightforwardly in the text.
- The efficient market hypothesis is an important proposition. It is based upon markets for securities being composed of players out to maximise profit. Their pursuit of profit moves security prices rapidly to reflect the effect of new information. Prices achieved are not always perfect – but they are unbiased. Security prices adjust to all new information. The efficient market hypothesis comes in three gradations.
- The weak form of efficient market is one in which current security prices reflect all market information including the historic sequence of past prices, changes and returns. Thus there should be no relationship between past prices and future prices because past price movements should be impounded in today's security price. This form of efficient market clearly has no time for chartism which predicts on the basis of past prices.
- The semi-strong efficient market asserts that security prices move in sympathy with all new public information. So stock prices reflect all published available data. The semi-strong form embraces also the weak form.
- The strong form efficient market implies, by definition, that no group of investors has monopolistic access to information relevant to the formation of security prices and that security prices reflect all information – whether publicly or privately available.
- By and large, stock markets in advanced Western economies exhibit semi-strong form efficiency for major stocks traded. However, evidence is emerging to challenge this notion.

- But currency markets are different. They seem to exhibit efficiency some of the time – but not all the time. Chartism seems to work quite well when efficiency is less than perfect. Why might this be so? Why might this biggest market in the world exhibit less than perfect efficiency? Perhaps the answer lies in the fact that the biggest player in the market is not a profit maximiser. And who is the biggest player? Not the big commercial banks. It is, of course, the central banks – they are not profit maximisers. They are more concerned, as a rule, with achieving political, as opposed to economic, goals in their intervention in foreign currency markets.
- Hardly surprisingly, chartism seems to perform better than econometric models in terms of forecasting exchange rates over the short term. Chartist models should be most superior when foreign exchange market intervention is rife.
- The four-way equivalence model is an equilibrium model arrived at by deductive reasoning. It should not be surprising if, for lengthy periods, parts of the model do not hold in the real world. Markets move towards equilibrium and the same is true of foreign exchange markets.
- The test of a good theory is how well it stands up in the real world. Evidence suggests that interest rate parity holds virtually all the time at the level of quotations by banks to companies, but the remaining parts of the model are found to have more of a long-run nature.
- Purchasing power parity is found to hold up well in the medium to longer term but there are very substantial deviations from it in the short run – so much so that using it as a short-run predictor of exchange rate movements is utterly unjustified by the evidence.
- Evidence on the international Fisher effect is more conflicting than on purchasing power parity. Some have found international Fisher to work well in the medium to long term while others have found evidence to challenge this conclusion. Tests of international Fisher have found substantial short-term deviations.
- The same kinds of finding apply in respect of the Fisher effect too.
- Evidence on interest rate parity suggests that it works really well in the real world in terms of explaining spot versus forward exchange rates by Eurocurrency interest differences. It works outstandingly well for short-term forwards.
- The forward exchange rate is generally found to be an unbiased predictor of the future spot rate. But, empirically, a bias is found when looking at very short-term movements. Thus the forward rate itself has been found consistently to undervalue the future spot rate when the spot rate is rising strongly, and vice versa.
- We also have evidence on foreign exchange market efficiency – and this is conflicting too.
- If foreign exchange markets are efficient, we should not be able to use mechanical dealing rules which consistently yield excess profits. Profits that are achieved should be commensurate with the level of risk undertaken. The empirical evidence is somewhat unclear. Some investigators have found results consistent with market efficiency; others appear to have identified filter rules which consistently yield excess profits over lengthy periods.
- At first sight, the above evidence may be conflicting. But it is possible that there are periods when the substantial presence of central banks, operating in a non-profit-maximising way in the foreign exchange markets, may create the environment where operators may beat the market.

End of chapter questions

6.1 Explain the theory of purchasing power parity (PPP). Based on this theory, what is a general forecast of the values of currencies in highly inflated countries?

6.2 Explain how you could determine whether purchasing power parity exists.

6.3 For each of the following six scenarios, say whether the value of the dollar will appreciate, depreciate, or remain the same relative to the Japanese yen. Explain each answer. Assume that exchange rates are freely floating and that all other factors are held constant.

(a) The growth rate of national income is higher in the United States than in Japan.
(b) Inflation is higher in the United States than in Japan.
(c) Prices in Japan and the United States are rising at the same rate.
(d) Real interest rates become higher in the United States than in Japan.
(e) The United States imposes new restrictions on the ability of foreigners to buy American companies and real estate.
(f) US wages rise relative to Japanese wages, and American productivity falls behind Japanese productivity.

7

Definitions of foreign exchange risk

Foreign exchange risk management begins by identifying what items and amounts a firm has exposed to risk associated with changes in exchange rates. An asset, liability, profit or expected future cash flow stream (whether certain or not) is said to be exposed to exchange risk when a currency movement would change, for better or for worse, its parent or home currency value. The term 'exposure' used in the context of foreign exchange means that a firm has assets, liabilities, profits or expected future cash flow streams such that the home currency value of assets, liabilities, profits or the present value in home currency terms of expected future cash flows changes as exchange rates change. Risk arises because currency movements may alter home currency values.

In this sense, assets, liabilities and expected future cash flow streams denominated in foreign currencies are clearly exposed to foreign exchange risk. But some expected future cash flows denominated in home currency terms may also be exposed. For example, a UK company selling in its home market may be competing with firms based in Germany. In such circumstances changes in the euro/sterling exchange rate will almost certainly affect the present value of the UK company's expected cash flows by strengthening or weakening its competitive position against its German rivals.

Foreign exchange exposure is usually classified according to whether it falls into one or more of the following categories:

- **transaction exposure**;
- **translation exposure**;
- **economic exposure**.

Transaction exposure arises because a payable or receivable is denominated in a foreign currency. Translation exposure arises on the consolidation of foreign-currency-denominated assets and liabilities in the process of preparing consolidated accounts. This concept is essentially concerned, then, with what might be called **accounting exposure**. Economic exposure arises because the present value of a stream of expected future operating cash flows denominated in the home currency or in a foreign currency may vary because of changed exchange rates. Transaction and economic exposure are both **cash flow exposures**. Transaction exposure is a comparatively straightforward concept but translation and economic exposure are more complex. Each of the three categories of exposure is now examined and defined in more detail.

7.1 Transaction exposure

Transaction exposure arises because the cost or proceeds (in home currency) of settlement of a future payment or receipt denominated in a currency other than the home currency may vary because of changes in exchange rates. Clearly, transaction exposure is a cash flow exposure. It may be associated with trading flows (such as foreign-currency-denominated trade debtors and trade creditors), dividend flows or capital flows (such as foreign-currency-denominated dividends or loan repayments).

7.2 Translation exposure

Consolidation of financial statements that involve foreign-currency-denominated assets and liabilities automatically gives rise to translation exposure, sometimes termed accounting exposure. Consolidation of foreign subsidiaries' accounts into group financial statements denominated in home currency requires the application of a rate or rates of exchange to foreign subsidiaries' accounts, in order that they may be translated into the parent currency. Both balance sheets and income statements must be consolidated and they both give rise to translation exposure. Translating foreign currency profit and loss accounts at either the average exchange rate during the accounting year or at the exchange rate at the end of the accounting year (both methods are currently permissible UK accounting procedures) will mean that expected consolidated profit will vary as the average or the expected closing rate changes. So the whole amount of profit earned in foreign currency is exposed to translation risk in the sense that the home currency consolidated profit may vary as exchange rates vary.

Balance sheet exposure is somewhat more complex. Some items in a foreign subsidiary's balance sheet may be translated at their **historical exchange rates** (the rate prevailing at the date of acquisition or any subsequent revaluation). Thus their home currency translated value cannot alter as exchange rates alter; such assets and liabilities are not exposed in the accounting sense. Other items may be translated at the **closing exchange rate** – the rate prevailing at the balance sheet date at the end of the accounting period. While the value of such items is fixed in the foreign subsidiary's currency, the amount translated into the parent currency will alter as the exchange rate alters. Hence, all foreign currency items that are consolidated at current rates are exposed in the accounting sense.

Accounting exposure, therefore, reflects the possibility that foreign-currency-denominated items which are consolidated into group published financial statements at current or average rates will show a translation loss or gain as a result. This kind of exposure does not give an indication of the true effects of currency fluctuations on a company's foreign operations.

Economic exposure, to be discussed later, is a far better measure of true value exposure. Translation exposure, as will become clear later, is really a function of the system of accounting for foreign assets and liabilities on consolidation which a group of companies uses. Clearly it has little to do with true value in an economic sense.

There are four basic translation methods. These are the **current/non-current method** (sometimes called the traditional or working capital method), the **all-current** (or closing rate) **method**, the **monetary/non-monetary method**, and the **temporal method**. These differing means of translation are considered in detail below. It is worth mentioning that the all-current method is now the most frequently used in the United Kingdom, the United States and many other countries.

The current/non-current method

This approach uses the traditional accounting distinction between current and long-term items and translates the former at the closing rate and the latter at the historical rate. Accounting exposure for a foreign subsidiary at a particular point in time is given by the net figure of assets less liabilities that are exposed to potential change should exchange rates alter. Evidently, according to the current/non-current method, the sum exposed is net current assets.

One of the implications of this method of translation is that inventory is exposed to foreign exchange risk but long-term debt is not. The logic of such an assumption is by no means apparent. Indeed it should be clear that long-term debt is very much exposed to exchange risk. In home currency terms, the cash amount of a foreign-currency-denominated loan (whether a payable or receivable loan) will change as exchange rates change. This lack of logic underpins the move away from the current/non-current method which has been witnessed over recent years.

The all-current (closing rate) method

This method merely translates all foreign-currency-denominated items at the closing rate of exchange. Accounting exposure is given simply by net assets or shareholders' funds (sometimes called equity). This method has become increasingly popular over time and is now the major worldwide method of translating foreign subsidiaries' balance sheets.

The monetary/non-monetary method

Monetary items are assets, liabilities or capital, the amounts of which are fixed by contract in terms of the number of currency units regardless of changes in the value of money. Translation via the monetary/non-monetary method involves monetary assets and monetary liabilities being translated at the closing rate while non-monetary items are translated at their historical rate. Accounting exposure under this method is given by net monetary assets.

In terms of development of accounting reporting, this method of translating foreign subsidiaries' accounts seems to have been a halfway house between the current/non-current method and the all-current method.

The temporal method

The temporal method of translation uses the closing rate method for all items stated at replacement cost, realisable value, market value or expected future value, and uses the historical rate for all items stated at **historic cost**.

The rationale for the temporal approach is that the translation rate used should preserve the accounting principles used to value assets and liabilities in the original financial statements. According to the temporal method, the translation rate for each asset or liability depends upon the measurement basis used in the foreign subsidiary's original account.

Applied to traditional historic cost accounts, the temporal and monetary/non-monetary methods give almost the same results. The main difference arises in the case of certain items of inventory. Where stock is stated in the original accounts at market value (where it is below historic cost) the temporal method would translate it at the current rate while the monetary/non-monetary approach would use the historic rate of exchange. But it should be emphasised that the temporal method is by no means synonymous with the monetary/non-monetary approach.

Example 1

A numerical example

It should be clear that identical firms with identical assets, liabilities, capital structures and trading results may show different translation gains and losses and different translated balance sheets depending upon the method used for converting foreign currency items to home currency values. This can be demonstrated by a simple numerical example.

Assume that a UK company sets up a subsidiary in Australia on 1 March and that the opening transactions are booked in the Australian company's accounts according to the prevailing exchange rate of £1 = AUD3. The opening balance sheet is shown in Table 7.1.

Assume, further, that no additional business or transactions go through the Australian company during March and consequently the Australian dollar balance sheet at the end of the month remains as at the beginning. But assume that during March sterling fell against the Australian dollar and the exchange rate at the end of the month was £1 = AUD2.5. This means that the sterling-translated balance sheet of the subsidiary will alter, the extent of the change differing according to whether the current/non-current, all-current, or monetary/non-monetary method of translation is used. Table 7.1 shows the results.

From the table it will be noted that the translation gain or loss is equal to 16.67 per cent of the accounting exposure. This is, of course, consistent with the movement in sterling value versus the Australian dollar from 3 to 2.5. But it will further be noted from the table that translation outturns range from a gain of over £491,000 to a loss of over £349,000. These differences arise merely because of varying accounting methods.

Table 7.1 Example illustrating translation exposure

			Subsidiary's balance sheet as at 31 March translated according to:		
	Subsidiary's balance sheet as at 1 March AUD000	Subsidiary's balance sheet as at 1 March £000	All-current rate £000	Current/ non-current £000	Monetary/ non-monetary £000
Fixed assets	8,400	2,800	3,360*	2,800	2,800
Inventory	4,200	1,400	1,680*	1,680*	1,400
Cash	1,065	355	426*	426*	426*
Total assets	13,665	4,555	5,466	4,906	4,626
Current payables	2,100	700	840*	840*	840*
Long-term debt	4,200	1,400	1,680*	1,400	1,680*
Equity	7,365	2,455	2,946	2,666	2,106
Translation gain/(loss)			491	211	(349)
Accounting exposure as at 31 March exchange rate			2,946	1,266	(2,094)
But accounting exposure is better measured in foreign currency as AUD000			7,365	3,166	(5,234)

* Assets and liabilities exposed, as of 31 March, to translation exposure under different translation conventions.

Example 2

Moving towards a consensus

Internationally, the accounting profession has been concerned about the position on translation of foreign-currency-accounting statements. Indeed, major accounting professions around the world have now almost identical rules for accounting for foreign currency translation in published accounts. Generally speaking, translation of foreign balance sheets uses the current rate method. Transaction gains, whether realised or not, are usually accounted for through the income statement. But there is a major exception. Where a transaction profit or loss arises from taking on a foreign currency borrowing in a situation in which the borrowing can be designated as a hedge for a net investment denominated in the same foreign currency as the borrowing, then the gain or loss on the borrowing, if it is less than the net investment hedged, would be accounted for by movements in reserves rather than through the income statement. If this kind of transaction gain or loss exceeds the amount of the loss or gain respectively on the net investment hedged, the excess gain or loss is to be reported in the income statement. Non-transaction gains and losses are to be dealt with by reserve accounting direct to the balance sheet rather than through the income statement.

While translation methods affect group balance sheet values, the key point is that they have nothing to do with economic value. The value of the Australian subsidiary in the example should not be affected by adopting a different method of accounting. Its worth will be the same whether the all-current, current/non-current or monetary/non-monetary method is used. In all probability its discounted net present value will have changed as a result of the strengthened dollar. But this changed present value is hardly what we pick up by using different methods of translating balance sheets. Clearly, changes in value resulting from changed exchange rates show in terms of different present values. If we are concerned with how true value has changed because of exchange rate movements, we should be looking at economic value and how it changes in sympathy with moving exchange rates. This is what true exposure to exchange rate movements is all about.

7.3 Economic exposure

Economic exposure is concerned with the present value of future operating cash flows to be generated by a company's activities and how this present value, expressed in parent currency, changes following exchange rate movement. The concept of economic exposure is most frequently applied to a company's expected future operating cash flows (unhedged) from sales in foreign currency and from foreign operations. But it can equally well be applied to a firm's home territory operations and the extent to which the present value of those operations alters resultant upon changed exchange rates. For the purpose of convenience, the exposition that follows is based on a firm's foreign operations, although an uncovered foreign-currency-denominated receivable or payable will vary as exchange rates vary.

The value of an overseas operation can be expressed as the present value of expected future operating cash flows which are incremental to that overseas activity discounted at the appropriate discount rate. Expressing this present value in terms of the parent currency can be achieved via equation (7.1) – but remember that incremental cash flows to the whole group of companies include management fees, royalties and similar kinds of flow as well as direct cash flows from trading operations. The present value of the foreign subsidiary may be expressed as:

$$PV = \sum_{t=0}^{n} \frac{(CI_t - CO_t)e_t}{(1+r)^t} \qquad (7.1)$$

where PV is the parent currency present value of the foreign business, CI represents estimated future incremental net cash inflows associated with the foreign business expressed in foreign currency, CO is the estimated future incremental net cash outflows associated with the foreign business expressed in foreign currency, e is the expected future exchange rate (expressed in terms of the direct quote in the home territory), r is the appropriate discount rate, namely the rate of return that the parent requires from an investment in the risk class of the overseas business, t is the period for which cash flows are expected and n is the final period for which all flows are expected. Equation (7.1) assumes that all net incremental cash flows accruing to the overseas operation are distributable to the parent company in the home country.

At first sight the reader might conclude that quantifying economic exposure and the impact of changing exchange rates is fairly straightforward. For example, assume that a UK company has a wholly owned Danish subsidiary with a net present value of DKK120m. If the exchange rate is £1 = DKK8 and subsequently moves to £1 = DKK10, presumably the value of the subsidiary has moved from £15m to £12m. Such a conclusion would, in all probability, be incorrect. It is necessary to be far more analytical to reach a worthwhile conclusion on valuation.

Devaluation will affect cash inflows and cash outflows as well as the exchange rate. Consider a company competing in export markets. While devaluation will not affect the total market size, it should have a favourable market share effect. The company in the devaluing country should increase sales or profit margins – in short, it should benefit. Similarly, companies competing with imports in the domestic market should also gain since a devaluation will tend to make imported products more expensive in local currency terms. However, this benefit may be offset to some extent by domestic deflation which frequently accompanies devaluation. So, in the import competing sector of the domestic market there will be beneficial and negative impacts. Next, in the purely domestic market, devaluation may lead to reduced company performance in the short term as a result of deflationary measures at home which so often accompany currency depreciation.

All of the above factors affect cash inflows. Devaluations also affect cash outflows. Imported inputs become more expensive. If devaluation is accompanied by domestic deflation it will probably be the case that suppliers' prices will rise as their financing costs move up. An inverse line of reasoning applies with respect to revaluation of a currency.

Getting to grips with economic exposure involves us in analysing the effects of changing exchange rates on the following items:

- Export sales, where margins and cash flows should change because devaluation should make exports more competitive.
- Domestic sales, where margins and cash flows should alter substantially in the import competing sector.
- Pure domestic sales, where margins and cash flows should change in response to deflationary measures which frequently accompany devaluations.
- Costs of imported inputs, which should rise in response to a devaluation.
- Cost of domestic inputs, which may vary with exchange rate changes.

The analysis is clearly complex, but it is necessary in order to assess fully how the home currency present value of overseas operations is likely to alter in response to movements in foreign exchange rates. We look further at a practical example of measuring economic exposure in Chapter 29.

So far it has been assumed that the parent's present value of its foreign subsidiary is a function of that subsidiary's estimated future net cash flows. In other words, there is an assumption that all cash flows are distributable to the parent. In fact, host governments frequently restrict distribution to foreign parents by exchange controls. Suffice here to say that where distribution of cash flows to the parent is limited, the present value formula needs to be adjusted a little:

$$PV = \sum_{t=0}^{n} \frac{(\text{Div}_t + \text{OPF}_t)e_t}{(1+r)^t} + \frac{\text{TV}e_n}{(1+r)^n} \tag{7.2}$$

The notation is as before except that Div represents the expected net dividend inflow in a particular year, OPF represents other parent flows such as royalties and management fees in a particular period, and TV represents the terminal value remittable over the foreign exchanges at the end of the project's life.

The reader should always bear in mind that economic exposure is equally applicable to the home operations of a firm inasmuch as a change in exchange rates is likely to affect the present value of its home operations; this may arise for all of the reasons which would impinge upon foreign businesses.

There is another, related dimension to economic exposure. A UK firm exporting goods to the United States, denominated in dollars, in competition with a German manufacturer will be facing a transaction exposure against the dollar and an economic exposure against the euro. Clearly, as the exchange rate between the pound and the euro changes, so the UK manufacturer is in a stronger or weaker position and this will filter through to sales levels, profit and cash generation. As such, the present value of the UK company's export business will alter as exchange rates change. Just like the previous kind of economic exposure, this subset is difficult to quantify for reasons similar to those mentioned before.

It can be seen that assessing economic exposure necessarily involves us in a substantial amount of work on elasticities of demand and behaviour of costs in response to changes in exchange rates. But the critical question that we would ask is whether economic exposure (or transaction exposure or translation exposure for that matter) is of any relevance to the financial manager of an international company. This question is addressed in Chapter 8.

7.4 Accounting for financial market derivatives

There are specific accounting rules relating to financial derivatives. We defer consideration of this because we have not yet encountered the whole area of derivatives. Hence we present a brief overview of this topic in Chapter 30.

Summary

- Foreign exchange risk concerns risks created by changes in foreign currency levels.
- An asset, liability or profit or cash flow stream, whether certain or not, is said to be exposed to exchange risk when a currency movement would change, for better or worse, its parent, or home, currency value.

- Exposure arises because currency movements may alter home currency values.
- Categorisations of foreign currency exposure vary from text to text. This chapter distinguishes three forms of currency risk. These are transaction exposure, translation exposure and economic exposure. Later, in Chapter 9, a further classification, macroeconomic exposure, is highlighted. But we shall leave this to one side for the moment. In any case it is really more than foreign exchange exposure.
- Transaction exposure arises because a payable or receivable is denominated in a foreign currency.
- Translation exposure (sometimes also called accounting exposure) arises on the consolidation of foreign-currency-denominated assets, liabilities and profits in the process of preparing accounts.
- Economic exposure arises because the present value of a stream of expected future operating cash flows denominated in the home currency or in a foreign currency may vary because of changed exchange rates.
- Note that transaction and economic exposure are both cash flow exposures. Pure translation exposure is not cash flow based.
- A particular item may be classified under more than one heading. For example, a long-term foreign-denominated borrowing is both a transaction exposure (because the home currency equivalent to repay the loan varies as exchange rates change) and a translation exposure.
- The magnitude of a translation exposure varies according to the accounting convention used for translation of foreign-denominated items. There are four basic translation methods. These are the current/non-current method, the all-current (sometimes called closing rate) method, the monetary/non-monetary method, and the temporal method. The exact mechanisms by which each method works are summarised in the main text.
- It is worth noting that, nowadays, most advanced economies, consolidate foreign-denominated balance sheet items according to the all-current method. These countries tend to use either the closing rate or the average rate during an accounting period for the purpose of translating foreign-denominated profit and loss accounts.
- The relevance of classifying foreign exchange risk according to its transaction, translation or economic nature is that we would advocate that some categories of exposure should be actively managed by the headquarters treasury while our prescription for other categories is that since some of them do not matter, there is little point in applying treasury time in taking action to avoid the risk concerned – more of this later.

End of chapter questions

7.1 Compare and contrast transaction exposure and economic exposure.

7.2 Why might the cash flows of purely domestic firms be exposed to exchange rate fluctuations?

7.3 How do most companies deal with economic exposure?

Test bank 1

Exercises

Foreign exchange problems

In these problems assume that all interest rates quoted are per annum rates. Calculate 90 day rates by taking one quarter of the annual rate. Also assume that, where only one rate is quoted, rather than a bid/offer rate, deals may be done at this rate whether they are purchase or sale deals, lend or borrow deals. This is, of course, a simplifying assumption. Also disregard any transaction costs; for substantial deals these are generally taken care of in the bid/offer spread. Take one month as one-twelfth of a year, two months as one sixth, and so on.

1 The spot rate for the Swiss franc (CHF) in New York is USD0.55.

(a) What should the spot price for the US dollar to the Swiss franc be in Zurich?
(b) Should the dollar be quoted at CHF1.85 in Zurich, how would the market react?

2 When the Swiss franc spot rate was quoted at USD0.55 in New York, the US market was quoting sterling at USD1.60.

(a) What should the price of the pound to the Swiss franc be in Zurich?
(b) If sterling were quoted at CHF2.80 to the pound sterling in Zurich, what profit opportunities would exist?

3 Your company has to make a USD1m payment in three months' time. The dollars are available now. You decide to invest them for three months and you are given the following information:

– the US dollar deposit rate is 8 per cent p.a.;
– the sterling deposit rate is 10 per cent p.a.;
– the spot exchange rate is GBP1 = USD1.80;
– the three-month forward rate is GBP1 = USD1.78.

(a) Where should your company invest for the better return?
(b) Assuming that interest rates and the spot exchange rate remain as above, what forward rate would yield an equilibrium situation?
(c) Assuming that the US dollar interest rate and the spot and forward rates remain as in the original question, where would you invest if the sterling deposit rate were 14 per cent per annum?
(d) With the originally stated spot and forward rates and the same dollar deposit rate, what is the equilibrium sterling deposit rate?

4 The spot rate for the Danish krone is USD0.1500 and the three-month forward rate is USD0.1505. Your company is prepared to speculate that the Danish krone will move to USD0.1650 by the end of three months.

(a) Are the quotations given direct or indirect Copenhagen quotations?
(b) How would the speculation be undertaken using the spot market only?
(c) How would the speculation be arranged using forward markets?

(d) If your company were prepared to put USD1m at risk on the deal, what would the profit outturns be if expectations were met? Ignore all interest rate implications.
(e) How would your answer to (d) above differ were you to take into account interest rate implications?

5 A foreign exchange trader gives the following quotes for the Ruritanian doppel spot, one-month, three-month and six-month to a US-based treasurer.

USD0.02478/80 4/6 9/8 14/11

(a) Calculate the outright quotes for one, three and six months forward.
(b) If the treasurer wished to buy Ruritanian doppels three months forward, how much would he or she pay in dollars?
(c) If he or she wished to purchase US dollars one month forward, how much would the treasurer have to pay in Ruritanian doppels?
(d) Assuming that Ruritanian doppels are being bought, what is the premium or discount, for the one-, three- and six-month forward rates in annual percentage terms?
(e) What do the above quotations imply in respect of the term structure of interest rates for US dollars and Ruritanian doppels?

6 You are given the following spot quotations in London:

USD1 = CHF1.5485/95
USD1 = AUD1.7935/45
GBP1 = USD1.6325/35

Calculate the following bid/offer quotations, also in London:

(a) CHF against AUD.
(b) GBP against AUD.

Foreign exchange rates

Consider the tabulation below which is given by a bank to a customer. For questions 1 to 16, the required rate is against the home currency, which is sterling. The word 'premium' or 'discount' implies that the foreign currency quoted at the head of each column is at the premium or discount respectively. For questions 1 to 16, do the calculation against the home currency, that is sterling.

Spot	**USD1.6325–35** **Premium**	**AUD2.30–2.30$^3/_4$** **Premium**	**JPY263.15–25**
1 month forward	0.75–0.73 cents	$^5/_8$–$^1/_2$ cents	0.15 yen premium 0.10 yen discount
2 months forward	1.35–1.32 cents	1$^1/_8$–1 cents	0.17 yen premium 0.08 yen discount
3 months forward	2.03–2.00 cents	1$^5/_8$–1$^1/_2$ cents	0.19 yen premium 0.06 yen discount

1 At what rate will the bank buy spot USD?
2 At what rate will the customer buy JPY three months forward?
3 At what rate will the customer sell USD one month forward?
4 At what rate will the bank sell spot yen?
5 At what rate will the customer buy AUD spot?

6 At what rate will the bank buy JPY two months forward?
7 At what rate will the customer buy USD two months forward?
8 At what rate will the bank sell USD two months forward?
9 At what rate will the bank buy AUD three months forward?
10 At what rate will the customer sell JPY one month forward?
11 At what rate will the bank buy USD three months forward?
12 At what rate will the customer sell JPY three months forward?
13 At what rate will the customer sell USD three months forward?
14 At what rate will the bank sell JPY one month forward?
15 At what rate will the bank buy AUD one month forward?
16 At what rate will the bank sell AUD three months forward?

For questions 17 to 22, calculate the annual percentage forward premium/discount, state which currency is at the premium, and indicate where interest rates should be higher if interest rate parity holds.

17 Home currency versus USD, 1 month. Assume you are a buyer of USD.
18 Home currency versus USD, 3 months. Assume you are a buyer of home currency.
19 Home currency versus USD, 3 months. Assume you are a seller of USD.
20 Home currency versus JPY, 3 months. Do the calculation on middle prices.
21 Home currency versus JPY, 3 months. Assume you are a seller of home currency.
22 Home currency versus AUD, 2 months. Assume you are a buyer of home currency.

Multiple choice questions

There is one right answer only to each question.

1 If a firm based in the Netherlands wishes to avoid the risk of exchange rate movements, and is due to receive USD100,000 in 90 days, it could:

(a) enter into a 90-day forward purchase of US dollars for euros;
(b) enter into a 90-day forward sale of US dollars for euros;
(c) purchase US dollars 90 days from now at the spot rate;
(d) sell US dollars 90 days from now at the spot rate.

2 Under a fixed exchange rate system:

(a) a forward foreign exchange market does not exist as it would be pointless since rates do not move;
(b) central bank intervention in the foreign exchange market is not necessary since rates do not move;
(c) central bank intervention in the foreign exchange market is often necessary;
(d) central bank intervention in the foreign exchange market is not permitted.

3 Given a home country and a foreign country, purchasing power parity suggests that:

(a) the home currency will depreciate if the current home inflation rate exceeds the current foreign interest rate;

(b) the home currency will depreciate if the current home interest rate exceeds the current foreign interest rate;
(c) the home currency will appreciate if the current home inflation rate exceeds the current foreign inflation rate;
(d) the home currency will depreciate if the current home inflation rate exceeds the current foreign inflation rate.

4 If purchasing power parity were to hold even in the short run, then:

(a) real exchange rates should tend to increase over time;
(b) real exchange rates should tend to decrease over time;
(c) real exchange rates should be stable over time;
(d) quoted nominal exchange rates should be stable over time.

5 If Euro-sterling interest rates were consistently below Eurodollar interest rates, then for the international Fisher effect to hold:

(a) the value of the British pound would tend to appreciate against the dollar;
(b) the value of the British pound would tend to depreciate against the dollar;
(c) the real value of the British pound would remain constant most of the time;
(d) the value of the British pound against the dollar would appreciate in some periods and depreciate in others, but on average, there would be a zero rate of appreciation.

6 The following information is available:

\$ deposit rate for 1 year	= 11 per cent
\$ borrowing rate for 1 year	= 12 per cent
Ruritanian doppel deposit rate for 1 year	= 8 per cent
Ruritanian doppel borrowing rate for 1 year	= 10 per cent
Ruritanian doppel forward rate for 1 year	= \$0.40
Ruritanian doppel spot rate	= \$0.39

A US exporter denominates its Ruritanian exports in Ruritanian doppels (RUD) and expects to receive RUD600,000 in one year. What will be the approximate value of these exports in 1 year in US dollars if the firm executes a forward hedge?

(a) \$234,000
(b) \$238,584
(c) \$240,000
(d) \$236,127

7 If direct spot quotations in New York and London were \$1.5995–1.6000 and £0.6250–0.6254 respectively, arbitrage profits per \$1m would be:

(a) 0
(b) \$313
(c) \$327
(d) \$640

8 Calculate the forward per annum premium or discount given the following quotes. Spot £1 = \$1.4000; 3 months forward £1 = \$1.4200.

(a) The \$ is at a premium of 1.43 per cent.
(b) The \$ is at a discount of 1.43 per cent.
(c) The \$ is at a premium of 5.71 per cent.
(d) The \$ is at a discount of 5.71 per cent.

9 The international Fisher effect suggests that should pound interest rates exceed US dollar interest rates:

(a) the pound's value will remain constant;
(b) the pound will be at a discount on the dollar;
(c) the pound will depreciate against the dollar;
(d) UK inflation rate will decrease.

10 Inflation in the United States and Sweden is expected to be 4 and 9 per cent, respectively, in the forthcoming year and 6 and 7 per cent, respectively, in the year following. The current spot rate for the Swedish krona is \$0.1050. Based on purchasing power parity, the expected spot value for the Swedish krona in two years would be:

(a) \$0.1111
(b) \$0.1024
(c) \$0.0992
(d) \$0.1074

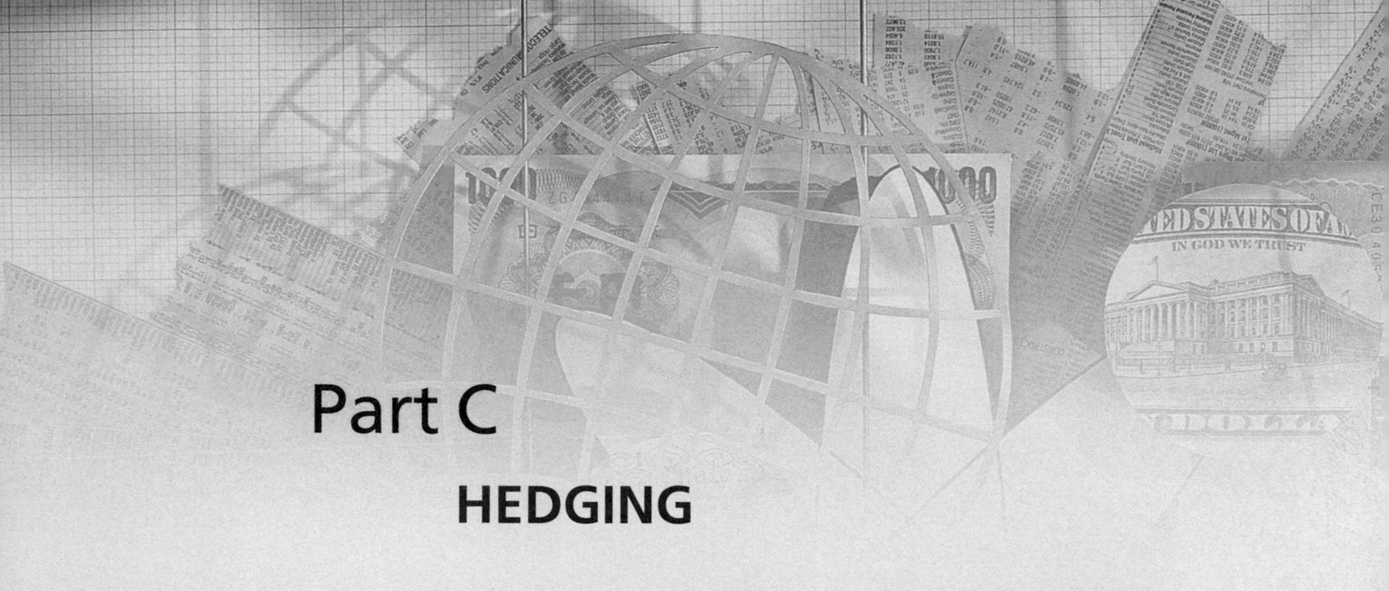

Part C

HEDGING

There is a wide range of methods available to minimise foreign exchange risk. This section is devoted to examining whether currency risk should, logically, be managed and then focuses upon internal and the third-party contract (external) means of managing foreign exchange risk.

8

Does foreign exchange exposure matter?

Most of the arguments about whether or not foreign exchange exposure matters draw on material summarised in the earlier chapters on the four-way equivalence model, definitions of foreign exchange exposure and the empirical work on the four-way model. Foreign exchange exposure can be looked at under three separate headings: transaction exposure, economic exposure and translation exposure. Chapter 7 provided a discussion on these different perspectives of foreign exchange exposure. In this chapter we consider the extent to which each should be a relevant factor for the corporate treasurer in the maximisation of the present value of the firm.

8.1 Transaction exposure

Transaction exposure is concerned with how changes in exchange rates affect the value, in home currency terms, of anticipated cash flows denominated in foreign currency relating to transactions already entered into.

According to the bulk of empirical work on the expectations theory part of the four-way equivalence model, the current forward rate is, at least in the longer run, an unbiased predictor of the future spot rate. If in the long term using the forward rate to approximate the future spot rate results in being on the high side as often as on the low side – which is what the term 'unbiased predictor' means – then it follows that covering forward will be of little worth to the firm that has a large number of transactions denominated in foreign currency. It might as well not cover forward but take the spot rate at the time the payable or receivable matures, since the results from adopting the strategy of covering forward will, in the long run, equal the results achieved from running the debt to maturity and taking the spot rate. Indeed, given that foreign exchange dealers charge their customers a wider bid/offer spread on forward contracts compared with spot transactions, it follows that avoiding cover should be more profitable in the long run.

But it can also be an extremely dangerous policy. By failing to cover transaction exposure, a firm may incur a vast loss on a single very large receivable or payable denominated in a foreign currency. This may result in an overall loss for the firm in a particular financial period, which could, in its turn, lead to all sorts of financial distress. It is not much comfort to the finance director of a company which has just failed as a direct result of not covering transaction exposure that it would have been all right in the long run because at some time in the future it could hope to win on another contract the amount that it has just lost on this one. There is little consolation in the company being all right in the long run if it is dead in the short run. Bearing this in mind, the prudent finance director will argue that covering forward reduces potential variability in home currency cash flows as well as in profits. Thus covering forward reduces some of the threat of short-term financial problems. In the longer term, the cost of such insurance against foreign exchange risk is small, since it effectively amounts to the dealer's spread on forward transactions less the spread on spot deals. It may not be the case that this policy maximises profits in the long run but from the standpoint of a risk-averse satisfier it has clear appeal.

Remember that all of the above argument about expectations theory is based upon the forward rate being an unbiased predictor of the future spot rate in the long run. It needs to be emphasised, and reiterated, that the empirical evidence on this part of the four-way model (see Chapter 6) indicates that, especially, for short periods when a currency can be identified as being in a phase of strength against other currencies, the forward rate tends, on average, to underestimate the strength of the currency being analysed in terms of its future spot rate. And the reverse seems to apply in respect of phases of weakness in the short term.

It is understandable that the firm that enters into very few transactions denominated in foreign currency may cover all of them. It is also understandable that risk-averse managers in companies with a vast number of transactions denominated in foreign currency would make a habit of covering them. However, treasurers in such firms usually adopt policies of selective covering. The rationale of this tactic and its frequent mode of operation are considered further in Chapters 9 and 11.

The same kind of argument, but with some essential differences, applies with respect to lending and borrowing denominated in foreign currencies. Most lending or borrowing involves respective receipt or payment of interest at regular intervals with capital repayment at a specified date. According to the **international Fisher effect**, the penalty for borrowing in a hard currency will be exactly offset by the benefit of a low interest rate. Perhaps this can best be illustrated by an example. Assume that the expected inflation in the United Kingdom is higher than that in Switzerland. If we begin from a base year in which exchange rates between sterling and the Swiss franc are in equilibrium, then we would anticipate, via purchasing power parity, that the Swiss franc would strengthen against sterling. And, via the Fisher effect, we would expect interest rates in Switzerland to be lower than sterling interest rates. Thus the international Fisher effect would be suggesting a weakening of sterling against the Swiss franc compensated for by lower Swiss franc interest rates. So a company considering raising £5m might do so in sterling and it might expect then to pay a higher interest rate than would be the case were that same company to raise the money in Swiss francs. But raising the money in Swiss francs would have the drawback that when repayment was due the company would probably have to find in excess of £5m sterling because of the strengthening of the Swiss franc during the period that the loan was outstanding. Leaving aside imperfections in the market created by taxation treatment of foreign exchange losses on loans (but note that in the real world these market imperfections created by non-symmetrical tax treatment are far too important to be left aside), the international Fisher effect would predict that the gain resulting from the lower interest rate on the Swiss franc borrowing would be exactly offset by the loss on capital repayment at maturity.

The above kind of situation is illustrative of how the international Fisher effect underpins the argument that foreign exchange exposure on borrowings does not matter. But, of course, we have seen in our overview of empirical investigations of the four-way equivalence relationship that our deductive, theoretical model does not hold too often in the real world. Some studies suggest that international Fisher holds in the **medium** to long **term**, but there is other work that suggests that we can wait an awfully long time for international Fisher to assert itself. For the international company these findings are crucial. In the long run our company borrowing in hard currencies might expect to come out even and thus be indifferent about the currency denomination of its borrowings, but in the short run its Swiss borrowing might wipe it out.

This kind of problem has dramatically affected more than a few UK companies. Laker Airways arranged lease finance denominated in US dollars for the bulk of its aircraft. When the dollar strengthened, the company's balance sheet and cash flow ability to service debt came under excessive strain. J. Lyons, another UK company, had a wealth of Swiss franc borrowings on its balance sheet. As sterling weakened against the Swiss franc, its plight became similar to Laker's. Laker went out of business partly, but by no means solely, due to its unhedged dollar borrowings; Lyons was rescued when it was taken over by Allied Breweries but its problems stemmed from uncovered **hard currency** debt.

The problem that treasurers of international companies have is not just that international Fisher is often found empirically to be a long-run phenomenon, but also that when they undertake a borrowing denominated in foreign currency the exchange rates between the home currency and the foreign one may not be in equilibrium. Subsequent correction of the disequilibrium can incur a vast loss (or profit) for the international borrower.

Perhaps it is fair to conclude that, were the four-way equivalence model to hold in the real world immutably and with no time lags, and if tax is ignored, then transaction exposure should not matter. That the real world is not so convenient as the theoretical one, that the four-way equivalence model does involve time lags, and very big ones, and that tax treatment of interest and currency gains and losses are not entirely symmetrical mean that transaction exposure is very important to international financial executives. In short, it needs to be managed.

8.2 Economic exposure

Economic exposure refers to the possibility that the present value of future operating cash flows of a business, expressed in the **parent currency**, may change because of a change in foreign exchange rates. According to purchasing power parity theory, exchange rate changes are associated with different relative rates of inflation. The argument that economic exposure does not matter draws on the PPP theorem.

Devaluation of the home currency tends to favour companies competing in export markets. It also has a favourable impact on import-competing areas. And it creates advantages for firms that are domestically sourced (imports become relatively more expensive) and domestically financed. Revaluations have precisely opposite effects.

A relatively high home-country inflation rate, if not accompanied by devaluation, has an adverse effect on companies competing in export markets and those competing domestically with imported goods. It adversely affects firms that are domestically sourced and (because the tendency will be for the home interest rate to rise) domestically financed.

Devaluation creates advantages that correct disadvantages flowing from high relative inflation rates. The benefits created for some firms by devaluation should offset earlier adverse effects created by inflation. If relative inflation rates are being accompanied by appropriate exchange rate adjustments, as predicted by PPP, it may be argued that we have a situation where the overall effect is neutral. The benefits of devaluation exactly offset the earlier penalties of inflation. But should this be universally true? Maybe the above argument would be applicable to the firm all of whose costs were inflating at the same rate as the general level of inflation in the country in which it was based. The devaluation or revaluation would then be exactly offsetting movements in the firm's specific costs. In these circumstances economic exposure would not matter to the firm.

Of course, it is most unusual for the firm's individual costs to move exactly in line with general inflation. And where they do not, economic exposure will matter to the firm. Indeed, multinationals consider relocating or switching manufacture from one country to another, or altering the sourcing of cost inputs, to correct for local costs having inflated in excess of general inflation levels or, more specifically, in excess of competitor nations' costs.

If, then, economic exposure does matter to the international company, should it endeavour to hedge this exposure through forward market purchases or sales of currency? The author believes that the answer to this question veers towards the negative. This is not because economic exposure is based on uncertain cash flows or because it is difficult to quantify since it involves detailed analysis of elasticities of demand, but because there are easier ways to deal with the fact that the present value of expected cash flows accruing from operations may alter in response to changes in exchange rates. This simple way involves financing operations, either partially or wholly, in the foreign currency (or currencies) which is judged as having a significant impact upon the present value of operations. It should be mentioned that this approach does not provide an exact cover for economic exposure. This arises because the hedge via financing is a function of relative inflation rates, with differences corrected via PPP; the changing value of operating cash flows is affected by relative specific price and cost increases and these are only partially corrected by changing exchange rates based on general inflation levels.

It should be mentioned that the author has come across anecdotal evidence of international companies actively managing economic exposure via forward markets and via currency options. This involves the calculation of exposed net present values based on anticipated operating cash flows, deducting from them the hedge effect achieved by financing and then using forward and/or option markets to hedge net exposure should this be deemed the advantageous course of action.

It should be mentioned that there is a strong case for monitoring and managing economic exposure by entering into forward or option markets to protect the present value of expected future cash flows where the tenor of the firm's involvement in a particular overseas environment has a finite time horizon, such as a joint venture which will terminate after, say, three years of operation. Since the firm's involvement does not span sufficient time to ensure a cycle running through to equilibrium, economic exposure can be material. However, this kind of situation has more of a transaction exposure dimension (although the residual cash flow is not yet certain or contracted), since the residual value of the project will, presumably, be remitted to headquarters at the end of the period of overseas involvement.

8.3 Translation exposure

Translation exposure arises as a result of the process of consolidation of foreign currency items into group financial statements denominated in the currency of the parent company. This was discussed in Chapter 7. Some items frequently viewed as being solely translation exposure are essentially transaction exposure items. This is the case with respect to borrowings or lendings denominated in foreign currency. Repayment of the loan requires cash to pass from borrower to lender, and this creates a cash flow exposure. With respect to the question of whether foreign exchange exposure matters for these kinds of item, which may be classified as both transaction exposure and translation exposure, the answer should flow from viewing them as transaction, rather than as translation, items.

As we saw in Chapter 7, different translation methods may have different impacts upon a firm's reported earnings per share. But do these different accounting methods affect the valuation of the firm? Clearly, from a theoretical standpoint, the accounting methods of reporting for overseas subsidiaries' results should not impact on their own upon valuation of a subsidiary. Its valuation to the parent company should be a function of expected future cash flows which are distributable to the parent. Admittedly, this may alter as exchange rates alter. It can be argued from a theoretical point of view that, should subsidiaries' values change in response to movements in exchange rates, then it is logically a result of their present value, in home currency terms, being perceived by investors to have altered. Note that this theoretical argument has nothing to do with accounting reporting for foreign operations.

But the key question is: how does the investment community interpret changing subsidiary results based on changed translation methods? In other words, whether translation exposure matters is essentially an empirical question. Our answer therefore draws on empirical investigations. Since the relevant studies have not yet been referred to elsewhere in this book, it is necessary to spend some time discussing them.

Under a now-deceased accounting standard in the USA, FASB 8, translation gains and losses were included in the group consolidated profit and loss account and caused wide fluctuations in reported corporate profits and earnings per share. The effect of the US standard brought forth such comments as 'nothing is surer to upset a chief executive than an accounting provision that disturbs the smooth year-to-year earnings gains so cherished by securities analysts'. This kind of reasoning on the part of some large multinationals has undoubtedly led to some questionable decisions designed to hedge translation exposure by incurring transaction exposure. Srinivasula[1] describes a situation where ITT, the US-based multinational, sold forward \$600m worth of foreign currencies with a view partially to hedging its balance sheet exposure. The dollar fell relative to most foreign currencies and this resulted in a translation gain and an offsetting loss on forward cover. This gain was unrealised but the forward loss involved a cash loss in the order of \$48m. Although ITT achieved its objective of partially hedging balance sheet exposure, it could be argued that such transactions make little or no economic sense. Of course, more modern accounting rules obviate the need for any company to take this illogical action. It is worth mentioning that ITT was by no means alone in its response to accounting exposure under FASB 8. A number of studies reported similar actions by US-based multinationals designed to counter translation exposure by incurring transaction exposure. A paper by Griffin[2] summarises a number of studies by other researchers into the effects FASB 8 had on corporate financial policy. It should be noted, though, that it was a minority of US multinationals which responded to exposure under FASB 8 by taking on transaction exposure in the opposite direction.

But did the reporting requirements of FASB 8 affect the stock market performance of companies reporting translation gains and losses? Clearly, this is entirely an empirical question. There have been at least three major investigations in this area. These have been undertaken by Makin,[3] Dukes[4] and Garlicki, Fabozzi and Fonfeder;[5] their results are by no means identical. Makin assessed share price performance for three sample groups comprising typical multinational companies, comparable domestic companies and, thirdly, a group of multinationals which were considered to be particularly sensitive to FASB 8 reporting requirements. He found that the accounting standard requirements did not affect share price performance for the typical multinational group, but he did find a downgrading in share price for the sensitive group. While he interprets this as implying that FASB 8 reporting requirements may affect share prices, Giddy[6] has challenged this interpretation on the basis that the sensitive group of multinationals would be affected not only in terms of income statement reporting but also in terms of dollar remittances from dividends declared by overseas subsidiaries – an area to which Makin's study failed to address itself.

Dukes sought to investigate the stock market effect of FASB 8 reporting requirements in a study in which he compared security returns from a sample of 479 multinational companies with a control sample of domestic firms. The empirical results are that the security return behaviour of portfolios of multinational firms, despite the impact of FASB 8 on reported earnings, is not significantly different from the return behaviour of comparable portfolios of domestic firms. Although Dukes' methodology can be challenged, his conclusions are that the US stock market is not fooled by pure translation gains and losses.

His findings are reinforced by Garlicki, Fabozzi and Fonfeder study. Their work was concerned with estimating shareholder effects pursuant to the announcement of the change in translation guidelines away from FASB 8. The researchers focused their attention in particular upon two announcement dates: the initial exposure draft date, 28 August 1980, and the date of the subsequent statement by the Financial Accounting Standards Board that FASB 8 was to be replaced. In respect of neither of these significant dates could the researchers identify any abnormal gain or loss accruing to shares of companies affected by the revised standard. They conclude that this is consistent with shareholders having the sophistication not to be moved by revised accounting translation guidelines. Moreover, the actions of some multinationals in hedging translation exposure with transaction exposure is seen not only to be illogical from a deductive standpoint but also to be unjustified empirically, since stock market analysts seem not to be interested in pure translation gains and losses.

Generally speaking, our interpretation of the available evidence accords with the findings of Dukes and of Garlicki, Fabozzi and Fonfeder, which in turn underlines the theoretical view that pure translation exposure does not matter. But notice the rider at the beginning of the previous sentence – generally speaking. Why such a caveat?

The answer is best given by way of an example. Consider the company in Table 8.1. It is a UK-based corporation with a subsidiary in the United States. Initially, the group appears to have as large an operation, in asset terms, in the United States as in the United Kingdom – £100m in each country – and the US operation's dollar assets are matched by dollar debt. In the base case situation – that is, with an exchange rate of $1.8 to £1 – the group has a consolidated debt to equity ratio of 1 to 1. Imagine further that loan covenants place a figure

Table 8.1 Gearing can make pure translation exposure relevant

	Base case	Subsequent movement to
Exchange rate $ to £	1.80	1.40
Assets (£m)		
In UK	100	100
In USA ($180m)	100	128.6
	200	228.6
Financed by (£m):		
Shareholders' funds	100	100
US$ debt ($180m)	100	128.6
	200	228.6
Debt to equity ratio	1 to 1	1.3 to 1

of 1 to 1 as the maximum gearing allowed, calculated according to the consolidated accounts. It can readily be seen that, should the dollar strengthen against the pound, there is a problem for the company in terms of its loan covenant on gearing. Certainly, as Table 8.1 shows, dollar assets and liabilities are matched, but nonetheless the debt to equity constraint is breached at any time when the dollar is stronger than $1.8 to the pound. A company in this kind of situation will certainly have something to worry about when it is near to its specified debt limitations; it will, quite rightly, be concerned with translation exposure. This topic is considered again in Chapter 29 on practical problems in corporate hedging.

We also have the situation where a firm's overseas subsidiaries' profit and loss account results may change in home currency terms as exchange rates move. Table 8.2 illustrates how an international company's consolidated results may show a drop in reported earnings even though, in all local currencies, trading results have improved. Does this kind of exposure constitute a pure translation exposure? Probably not, because profit after tax, when adjusted for depreciation, fixed and working capital inputs and so on, represents one of the most significant aspects of cash generation. For this reason, profit and loss account exposure must be more than pure translation exposure. If it were not, it would not be suggested that it merited exposure management time and attention. Interpreted as more than just translation exposure, managing foreign subsidiaries' bottom-line profit and loss results (and certainly

Table 8.2 Income statement translation exposure

	Last year (million)			Budget (million)			Actual (million)		
	Local currency	Rate	£	Local currency	Rate	£	Local currency	Rate	£
Home country results									
UK	43		43	48		48	44		44
Overseas results									
USA	32	1.6	20	36	1.5	24	32.4	1.8	18
Switzerland	105	2.1	50	112	2.15	52	114	2.5	45.6
Australia	116	2.9	40	127.6	2.9	44	119	3	39.7
			153			168			147.3
Shares in issue		250m			250m			250m	
Earnings per share		61.2p			67.2p			58.9p	

dividends payable from a foreign subsidiary) is warranted. One **instrument** to achieve this is the average rate option. But since currency options have not yet been discussed in this book, examination of how to achieve cover for this kind of exposure is deferred until later (see Chapter 15).

There is clearly an accounting communications problem since earnings per share appear to have fallen in home currency terms when, in reality, this is not the case in local currency terms. A fairer picture may be given by detailing financial results assuming constant exchange rates. Where used in published accounts, details usually appear as a note to the accounts rather than being within the double entry bookkeeping underpinning the income statement.

Remember too that the empirical evidence that has led us to the view that pure translation exposure is usually of relatively little importance to the corporate treasurer derives from the United States. To conclude that such evidence is applicable, for example, to the United Kingdom or the Netherlands implies that capital markets are of similar sophistication in London and Amsterdam as in New York. Whether this is so is a moot point. Clearly, there is a need for some caution.

8.4 Forecasting exchange rates

With the word of warning sounded in the last paragraph, the general conclusion of the foregoing discussion in this chapter is that pure translation exposure can, except in respect of its gearing implications, be ignored for all practical purposes. In the long run, taking on transaction exposure should result in gains equalling losses, but in the short term gains or losses may accrue. From a practical point of view the author recommends selective cover of transaction exposure for the large international company and (perhaps) blanket cover for the very occasional exporter/importer or company which is only casually into cross-frontier financial exposure. Economic exposure is best countered by financing in those currencies that materially create the exposure.

The conclusion in favour of selective covering of transaction exposure begs the question of whether or not buying professional forecasts of exchange rates might be helpful. The rationales of selective cover and of buying forecasts of foreign exchange rates are really interrelated. We now examine the evidence. If forecasts consistently achieve better results than using forward rates, we may wish to buy them to help us to take selective action on transaction exposure. And we may wish to use them to make speculative profits or to undertake leading and lagging operations (which will be discussed in Chapter 10 in advance of devaluations and revaluations of currencies. Aliber's cynical comments[7] epitomise the negative point of view on buying foreign exchange forecasts. He observes that 'since 1973, about 20 firms have been established to sell forecasts of exchange rate movements. One inference is that they can make more money selling forecasts than using them.' This view may have a lot of substance during those periods when foreign exchange markets are displaying the characteristics associated with market efficiency. The contrary view, namely that forecasting foreign exchange rates can lead to consistently profitable results, is based on evidence to the effect that the foreign exchange market does not always display the typical features associated with efficient markets. Chapter 6 summarised the findings of available evidence.

Summary

- Transaction exposure is concerned with how changes in exchange rates affect the home currency value of anticipated foreign-currency-denominated cash flows relating to transactions that have already been entered into.
- Empirically, over long periods, the forward rate is an unbiased predictor of the future spot rate. Hence, failing to take cover but running with the spot rate should yield similar returns – in the long run. However, failing to cover may have disastrous short-term results. Avoiding these potential pitfalls by selective covering is therefore claimed by corporate treasurers to be a logical strategy.
- Economic exposure relates to the possibility that the present value of future cash flows of a firm may change due to foreign currency movements. However, exchange rate changes are related, via purchasing power parity, to differences in relative inflation rates. The firm whose operations experience cost inflation exactly in line with general inflation may be returned to its original position by changes in exchange rate exactly in line with purchasing power parity. In these circumstances, economic exposure may be argued not to matter.
- Most firms, of course, experience specific cost inflations which differ from general inflation. In this situation, which is the most common one, economic exposure does matter.
- One approach to minimising this kind of exposure is to finance an appropriate part of the firm's operations in the currency to which the firm's value is sensitive.
- Translation exposure arises as a result of the process of consolidation of foreign-currency-denominated items into group financial statements denominated in the currency of the parent company. Whether it matters is entirely an empirical question.
- US-based research has tended to indicate that pure translation exposure does not affect share prices. As such, it seems that pure translation exposure should not matter most of the time. However, when a company is near to its gearing constraints it needs to be actively vigilant about translation exposure lest exchange rate movements precipitate breach of a borrowing covenant.
- There are financial instruments available to enable the company that is concerned with the adverse effects of translation exposure upon its consolidated profit and loss account to insure against the adverse impact on reported earnings per share – one such method involves the average rate option, which is considered in a later chapter.

End of chapter questions

8.1 (a) Present an argument for why translation exposure is relevant to an MNC.
(b) Present an argument for why translation exposure is not relevant to an MNC.

8.2 Disney Inc built the EuroDisney theme park in France that opened in 1992. How do you suppose this project affected its overall economic exposure to exchange rate movements? Why?

9

Principles of exposure management

In this chapter we focus upon a number of key issues in the management of exposure in general and of foreign exchange exposures in particular. The structure of the chapter involves us, first of all, in looking at the question of why a firm might wish to hedge. This is followed by focusing upon information necessary for foreign exchange management and the chapter ends with a re-examination of economic exposure.

9.1 The essence of hedging

Essentially, hedging a foreign currency exposure involves the firm dealing with an exposed item, perhaps acquired in its operations, by taking on a reverse exposure. Thus a US firm may have a euro receivable based on exports to France. The receivable is, say, for EUR5 million and is payable in three months' time. By this sale, the US firm has acquired a foreign currency asset. It hedges this by selling EUR5 million versus US dollars for delivery in three months' time at the three-month forward rate. Thus, through its operations it acquired a EUR asset which it has hedged in the financial markets by acquiring a EUR liability (to pay the EUR5 million to its bank in three months' time with the bank paying a USD amount based on the forward rate). All hedging works in this, essentially, simple way. A foreign currency asset is matched by a foreign currency liability. However, it is worth mentioning that the firm may already have a matching position in euros through its operations elsewhere in its businesses. Things may get more complicated when **options** are used or a package of future sales is hedged but the underpinning idea remains essentially simple.

9.2 Why hedge anyway?

An attempt is first made to summarise the arguments against and in favour of covering corporate exposures to risk. The reader might reasonably raise the point that it is a little bit late in the day to discuss these points – why was such a fundamental issue not raised in Chapter 1?

In defence of the positioning of such a key topic as 'why hedge?' as late as Chapter 9, the author is prepared to advance an argument. But first of all, let it be said that the objection that this chapter could easily have occurred at the very beginning of the book is a valid one.

In the end it was felt that because this book is intended as an essentially practical guide to the theory and practice of international financial management, it made more sense to keep the early sections on the practical side. In short, the author did not wish to put the reader off by raising a series of arguments that, to a large extent, derive from the academic literature on financial management. So the defence rests its case on a somewhat pragmatic point, but concedes that an equally strong argument may be advanced to say that the fundamental question – why hedge? – should be addressed immediately and on page 1 of a book on international finance. So much for this discussion; let us now turn to answering the poser.

9.3 What does exposure management aim to achieve?

Hedging exposures, sometimes called risk management or exposure management, is widely resorted to by finance directors, corporate treasurers and portfolio managers. The practice of covering exposure is designed to reduce the volatility of a firm's profits and/or cash generation, and it presumably follows that this will reduce the volatility of the value of the firm. Figure 9.1 shows graphically what such efforts aim to achieve.

Certainly, among practitioners at least, the overriding view of the virtue of exposure management is as a device to reduce the variability of the firm's profits, cash flow or valuation caused by changes in interest rates and exchange rates. But there is a countervailing argument advanced by a number of financial academics. Its essence is as follows. Reducing the variability of the firm's returns, while leaving their expected level unchanged, should have little or no effect on the value of the firm. This view derives from the **capital asset pricing model**. The firm's operations are viewed as being risky in the sense that they move or fail to move in tandem with the market as a whole. The proposition continues with the idea that well-diversified international investors should not be willing to pay a premium for corporate hedging activities which they can readily duplicate for themselves simply by adjusting their portfolios. This line of argument leads to the view that hedging to reduce overall variability of profits, cash flow or firm value may be important to managers compensated on the basis of short-term results; however, it is a matter of irrelevance to

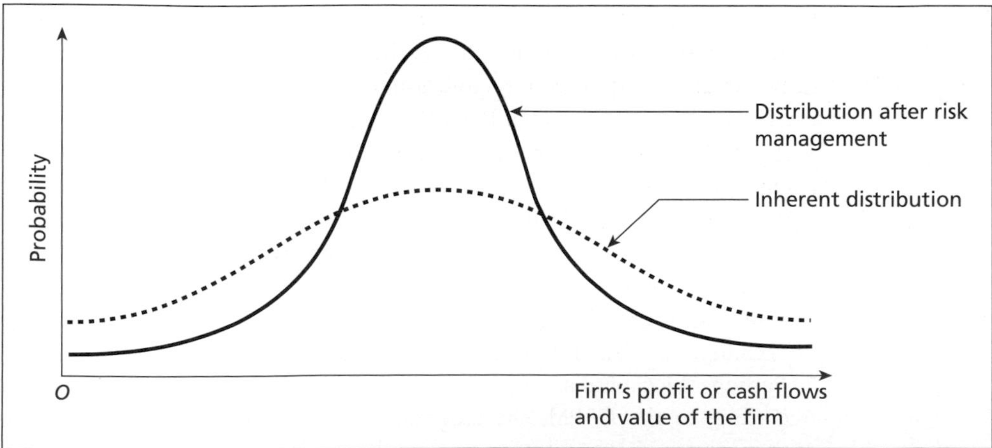

Figure 9.1 The goal of risk management

diversified shareholders. They even out the ups and downs of individual corporate investments by holding well-diversified portfolios. Rather than being interested in how particular corporations hedge their own outturns, what is important is how the portfolio manager diversifies his or her investments.

9.4 The arguments against corporate hedging

Really, the above argument is but one of a battery of attacks drawing their pedigree from the heavyweights of corporate finance. The range arrayed against hedging represents not only the capital asset pricing model but also purchasing power parity and the disciples of Modigliani and Miller. With such artillery in place, can hedging be remotely justified? As we will show, some arguments are more valid than others. So let us look at the map of the battlefield more closely.

According to purchasing power parity (PPP), movements in exchange rate offset price level changes. If PPP were to hold immutably and with no time lags, there would, so the argument goes, be no such thing as exposure to exchange rate risk and consequently no need to hedge. If the annual rate of inflation in the United Kingdom is 10 per cent higher than that in the United States, the pound will depreciate against the US dollar by an appropriate percentage rate. As a result, it follows that there is no relative price risk. If two units of US wheat exchanged for one unit of UK beef at the beginning of the year, that same exchange ratio would hold at the end of the year. The mere fact that the pound has depreciated is of no concern. The effect on the US exporter of wheat and the UK exporter of beef is of no significance, since the change in nominal prices in their national currencies has been compensated for by the exchange rate change.

There are numerous problems with this highly simplified version of PPP. Empirical tests have confirmed that the adjustment between changes in price levels and exchange rates is anything but immediate – there are long lags in the PPP relationship working in the real world. Even if, over the long-term horizon, PPP seems to have greater empirical validity, there are substantial short-term deviations. If a firm's planning horizon is shorter than that required for PPP to hold, then the firm is exposed to exchange risk – and this is probably the case for most firms.

Furthermore, even if PPP holds in the aggregate with respect to the price level indices of two countries, it need not – and usually does not – hold for every commodity. In short, the law of one price does not hold. If the increase in the price levels of wheat in the United States and beef in the United Kingdom do not correspond to the increases in the inflation levels in their respective countries, there will be a relative price risk. Even if PPP and the law of one price were to hold, prices of a firm's specific inputs and outputs might change relative to each other, and thus expose the firm to risk, which – if caused by unexpected exchange rate changes – must be viewed as exchange rate risk. That there are deviations from PPP and that there are relative price risks for at least some goods imply the presence of exchange risk. The PPP-based argument against hedging is not a substantial one.

Perhaps the capital asset pricing model (CAPM) has more guns arrayed against hedging. According to the CAPM, the essential aspect of risk that matters is **systematic risk**. If exchange rate risk and interest rate risk are considered to be **unsystematic**, they can be diversified away by investors in the process of constructing their own portfolios. On the other hand, if currency risk and interest rate risk are systematic and if forward exchange and interest hedge contracts are priced according to the CAPM, all that a firm does by entering into these kinds of contract is to move along the security market line. If this is so, then there is no addition to the value of the firm. As Adler[1] puts it, 'in the absence of imperfections like transaction costs and default risks, the value of a forward contract would be zero at the instant at which it was initiated'. In reality, there are transaction costs – the **bid/offer spread** for one. So in the real world, according to this argument, companies could be said to destroy value by entering into forward contracts.

But inevitably there is another point of view. This concerns companies' motivations to avoid financial distress. Greater variability of net cash flow implies a higher probability of bankruptcy. In turn, this affects the firm's cost of funds and its ability to raise finance. To quote Makin,[2] 'costs of capital in the short run can be influenced by the perceived riskiness of claims on multinationals and that perceived riskiness, relative to other multinationals, could be altered in the short run by heavy exposure in foreign currencies'. His view is reinforced by Logue and Oldfield[3] who observe:

> creditors may be concerned with total variability of cash flows where default is possible . . . gains and losses that a firm experiences due to random currency fluctuations may influence valuation through the effect on debt capacity. Where total variability is important, hedging in the foreign exchange markets may add to the firm's debt capacity.

And Adler[4] argues that the evidence of default is the most justifiable goal for hedging. He observes:

> on the dimension of default risk, stockholders' and management's interests largely coincide. Stockholders are averse to bankruptcy risk on the grounds that the associated costs can permanently deplete their equity. When the market perceives a rise in default risk, share prices drop. Managers prefer to reduce the probability of default or of cash inadequacy so as to avoid abdicating control in favour of creditors. Jobs may then also be in jeopardy. Large exchange losses can affect the adequacy of reference currency cash flows. Consequently, bankruptcy-risk reduction can partly be achieved by a policy of hedging.

In short, despite countervailing CAPM arguments, there is a strong case that avoidance of default risk justifies minimising variations in cash flows through hedging.

Turning next to arguments against hedging which derive from the Modigliani–Miller (MM) propositions,[5] it will be recalled that in relation to corporate gearing they advance the argument that what the firm can do, so can the investor. Extending this argument to the foreign exchange or interest rate domain, the same could be said to apply. Modigliani and Miller's argument suggested that a shareholder could obtain 'home-made leverage' by borrowing on his or her own account. In a similar way, why should the shareholder not obtain 'home-made hedging'? And, like MM's argument that home-made leverage would make corporate gearing irrelevant, so would home-made hedging make corporate hedging irrelevant.

Of course, if for any reason hedging by investors is not as effective as corporate hedging, then it will be in the interest of the shareholders to let the firm manage exchange and interest rate risk. As we have seen in this book heretofore, the main hedging instruments are forward markets, options markets, Eurocurrency markets and foreign money markets. Their nature is wholesale and they deal in minimum amounts that tend to be too large for individual investors. Commercial banks tend to limit access to forward and options markets. True, markets for currency futures exist which are readily accessible to individual investors, so some of the arguments about barriers to entry based on size applying to individual investors disappear. But remember that on financial futures exchanges there is a minimum contract size and the individual investor may be seeking cover at below this level.

Furthermore, there are techniques of currency management which are truly only available at the company, rather than the shareholder, level. For example, intercompany invoicing, leading and lagging of intercompany and third-party payments and judicious transfer pricing of both financial and real resources – to name but a few – are techniques for moving funds across borders and thus altering exposure. And there are opportunities for hedging which are often open only to corporations and not to individual investors – for example, subsidies are sometimes available to hedgers in some countries in the form of special credit facilities, subsidised exchange risk insurance, or special forward rates offered by central banks.

The argument in favour of corporate hedging does not stop here. There is an information-based argument too. For the individual investor to hedge, he or she needs to be aware of the level and timing of currency and interest rate exposure for all the companies in the portfolio. Such information is required not only for today but also for future dates. This information may already have been collected by the firm for planning purposes. For the company, information gathering for hedging purposes may involve no additional opportunity cost. In contrast, an individual may have to incur very large costs to obtain similar information – and it is not just for one company either, but for a whole portfolio of investments.

Even though, in an ideal world, shareholders should be able to manufacture home-made hedging, it is extremely doubtful whether, in the real world, this would be either feasible or economic. And this militates in favour of corporate hedging.

There are other propositions which begin as arguments against corporate hedging and end up pointing in the opposite direction. One of these is the self-insurance and market efficiency argument (see Aliber[6] and Feizer and Jacquillat[7]). It goes as follows. Currency and interest rate markets do not provide bargains – only fair gambles based on fair prices.In other words, by leaving foreign exchange positions uncovered, the firm may gain or it may lose. Such gains and losses will tend to average out, so the argument goes, over the long run. Hence, an **open position** is essentially the same as a hedged position. 'The implication', to quote Dufey and Srinivasulu,[8] 'is that one should aim to maximize the expected value without undue concern for the variance of returns'.

Similarly, it is argued that, since foreign exchange and interest rate markets are efficient in the sense that contracts are priced on the basis of all currently available information, one cannot earn any excess returns in such markets, and hence hedging is of no value. As Shapiro and Rutenberg[9] observe, 'unless capital market imperfections exist and persist, a treasurer . . . engaged in selective hedging . . . will not be able to earn consistent foreign exchange profits . . . in excess of those due to risk taking'.

But what is the treasurer trying to do by hedging? Surely, even if pursuing a selective hedging policy, the treasurer is not necessarily seeking excess returns, but merely trying to establish a risk/return profile with which the management feels comfortable. Furthermore, several others with interests in the firm are surely interested in reducing the variance of its returns flowing from currency and interest rate risk exposure. These groups include managers, other employees, financial regulators and creditors.

Managers and employees do not have a diversified portfolio of jobs. Their income stream from employment flows from their single job. By definition, investing in their career with one firm implies an undiversified portfolio. Clearly, managers and employees have a strong interest in reducing the variability of profit and cash flows and, in so doing, reducing the risk of financial distress. Another group concerned with reducing the variability of earnings is financial regulators. Governments around the world have increased their regulatory activity related to banks and other financial institutions' foreign exchange exposure policies. And creditors too have an obvious interest in their customers reducing their risk of incurring financial distress.

There is another argument that may be offered against corporate hedging. This concerns the desire of the shareholder for corporate risk. Take a company such as BP. Although a UK quoted company with a substantial sterling base of shareholders (and also US shareholders too), BP's income flows are essentially in dollars since oil is priced in dollars. If the shareholders' consumption patterns were dollar-based or if shareholders wanted to take on dollar risk, it might make sense for BP not to hedge its dollar exposure at all. Of course, companies are unable to know intimately their shareholders' consumption patterns or desires for risk and this line of reasoning leads to the conclusion that the company might hedge its exposures. But the obverse of this argument contends that, should companies leave themselves unhedged and communicate the nature of their exposures to shareholders, it would then be up to investors to make their own decisions about whether they wished to take on the company's risk by investing. In short, the argument is essentially one to the effect that shareholders may actually prefer that a portion of their income stream be exposed to foreign currency risk. In particular, this might be so when exchange controls prevent an investor from diversifying internationally. In any case, if the individual shareholder then wished to do so, he or she would be at liberty to hedge the exposure.

9.5 The arguments for corporate hedging

If risk management is to be logically justified in financial terms, there has to be a positive answer to the question 'will exposure management increase the value of the firm?' And, furthermore, it is necessary to specify the route by which such value is created.

The fact that a firm is confronted with interest rate, exchange rate and/or commodity price risk is only a necessary condition for the firm to manage that risk. The sufficient condition is that exposure management increases the value of the firm.

The equation that is the cornerstone of finance suggests that the value of the firm (V) is a function of expected future net cash flows – $E(\text{NCF})$ – discounted at the firm's cost of capital, k. It can be written as:

$$V = \sum_{t=0}^{n} \frac{E(\text{NCF}_t)}{(1+k)^t}$$

From this equation it is immediately apparent that, if the firm's value is to increase, it must do so as a result of either an increase in expected net cash flows or a decrease in the discount rate.

How might hedging affect the firm's discount rate? If we look at the risks that are usually hedged in an exposure management policy – currency risk, interest rate risk and commodity price risk – we can see that all of these may be interpreted, from the standpoint of modern portfolio theory, as diversifiable risks. Shareholders can manage these risks by holding a diversified portfolio. It follows that active management of these risks should have no effect on the firm's cost of capital. Unless the company is held by undiversified owners, risk management should not increase the expected value of the firm through a reduction in the discount rate.

In the case of a company held by well-diversified investors, exposure management can only be expected to increase the value of the firm through an increase in expected net cash flows. A logical question follows: how can hedging affect the value of the firm's expected net cash flows, as opposed to their variability? We would argue that avoidance of financial distress and a reduction in the present value of taxes paid are both potential sources of such value creation via hedging.

In Figure 9.1 it was noted that risk management can reduce the volatility of profit, cash flows and the value of the firm. Figure 9.2 goes a step further. It indicates that, by reducing cash flow volatility, hedging reduces the probability of the firm getting into financial difficulty and bearing the consequent costs of such distress.

Where V_{FD} is the value of the firm below which financial distress is encountered, it can be seen that hedging reduces the probability of financial distress from point p to point q. Hedging can reduce the costs of financial distress by:

- reducing the probability of financial distress;
- reducing the costs imposed by financial problems.

Clearly, as Figure 9.3 shows, the probability of financial distress may be lowered by hedging.

We can also use the subsequent diagram, Figure 9.3, to point out the virtue of hedging in terms of enabling the firm to achieve its desired corporate strategy, presumably the key to the firm's value. Assume that the cash flow level, CF, on the horizontal axis of Figure 9.3 is that level of cash generation that the firm needs to undertake to pursue its desired investment plans. Clearly, by hedging, the firm reduces the probability that its cash throw-off will be insufficient to enable it to pursue its planned strategy. As can be seen from Figure 9.3, the probability of its being able to pursue the desired policy from self-generated funds increases greatly from level a to level b as a result of exposure management techniques.

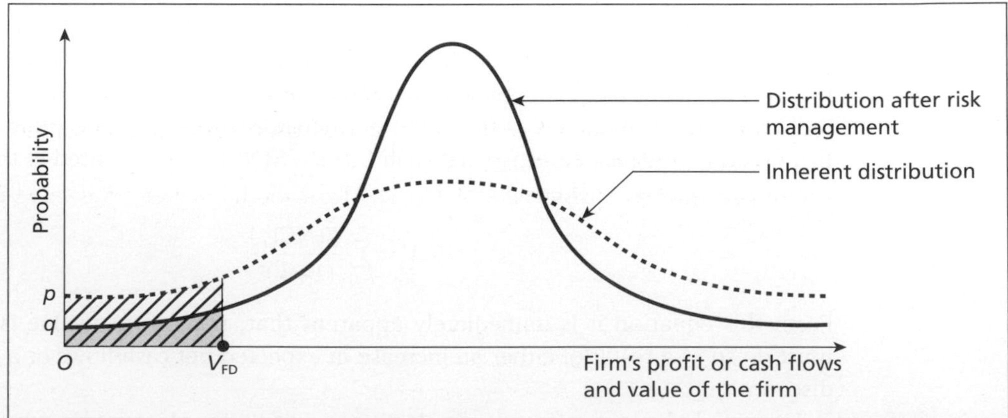

Figure 9.2 Hedging reduces the probability of financial distress

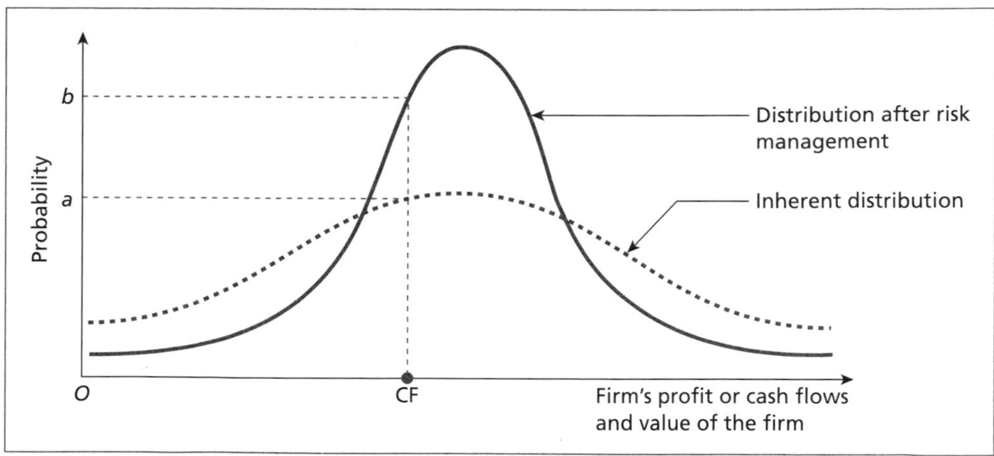

Figure 9.3 Hedging better enables the firm to pursue its desired strategy

Returning to hedging as a device to lower risk of financial distress, even short of bankruptcy, the possibility of financial distress can impose substantial costs on the firm. These involve higher contracting costs with customers, employees and suppliers. Companies that provide service agreements or warranties make a long-term commitment to their customers. The value customers place on these agreements and warranties depends on their perception of the financial viability of the firm. If the future of the firm is in doubt, customers will place less value on the service back-up and warranties and may turn to a competitor or demand a lower price to compensate. Either way, there is an evident impact upon profit and cash generation of the firm.

The essential argument may be summarised as follows. The marketing of a firm's product may be eased by a stable corporate track record since buyers want some assurance that the firm will stay in business to service the product and to supply parts. By a similar line of argument, potential employees may be scared off by a volatile earnings record which could suggest less job security. To compensate for this, employees may demand higher salaries and perks.

With the probability of financial distress increased by an absence of hedging, suppliers of debt capital might demand higher returns to compensate for higher expected bankruptcy costs and/or they might negotiate tighter debt covenants. Either way, the tendency would be for the cost of debt to increase. In parallel, it could be argued that, *ceteris paribus*, a reduction in the probability of financial distress or default would lower the cost of debt and increase the firm's debt capacity.

The reader might believe that a more realistic model of corporate valuation conforms to that following:

$$V_F = \Sigma V_i - P(\sigma)$$

where V_F is the value of the firm, V_i is the net present value of each of the firm's parts and $P(\sigma)$ is a penalty factor that reflects the impact on after-tax cash flows of the total risk of the firm. Note that this formula, which has some guru support, is not consistent with CAPM ideas – the penalty factor is a function of total risk, not just systematic risk. And, if you think about it, firms are usually bankrupted because of total risk rather than systematic risk.

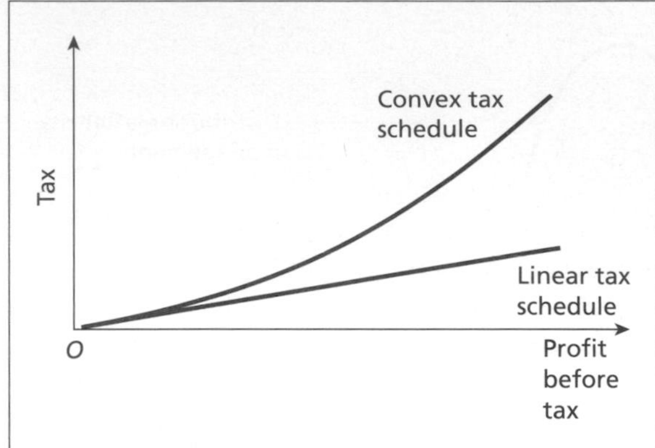

Figure 9.4 A convex tax function

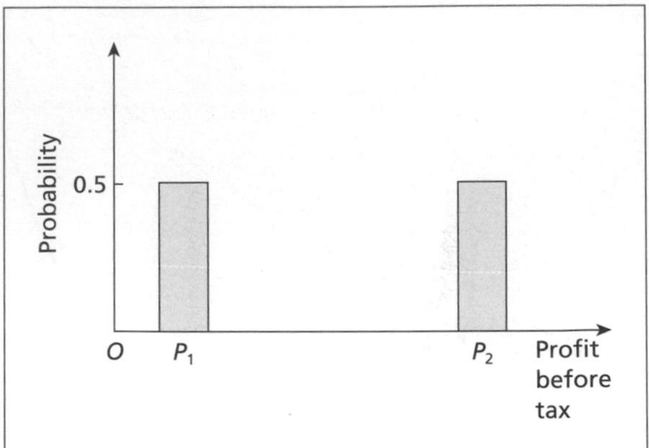

Figure 9.5 Unhedged profit expected outturns

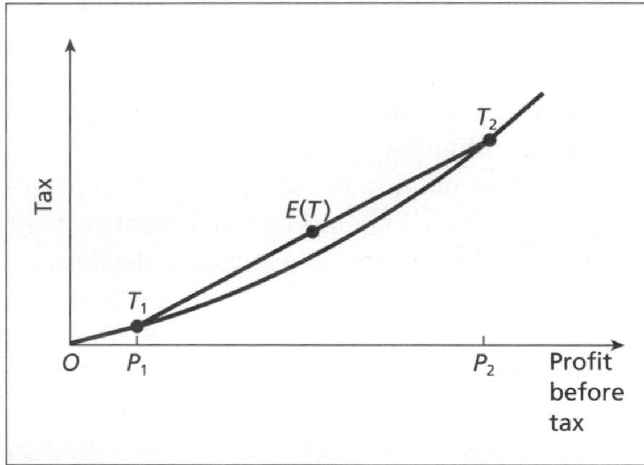

Figure 9.6 Tax payable in unhedged case

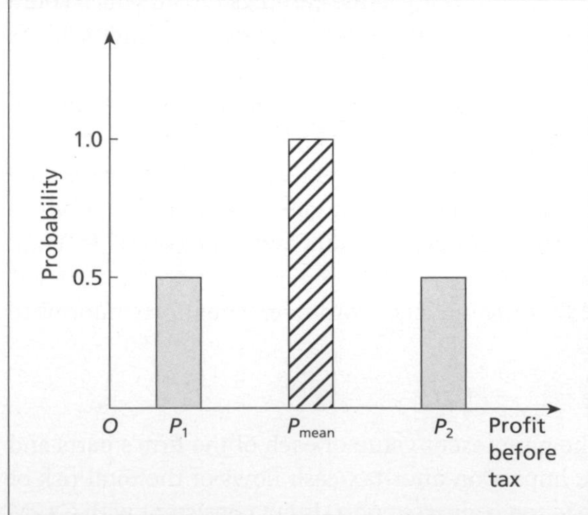

Figure 9.7 Hedged profit versus profit expected outturns

Anyway, the above proposition of corporate value would obviously suggest that hedging is a good thing for shareholders because, in lowering the penalty factor, corporate value is enhanced.

It was stated earlier that hedging and the tax system interrelate to impact upon the level of net cash flows of the firm. How does this work? If a company is facing an effective tax schedule which is convex, then a reduction in the volatility of profit through hedging can reduce corporate taxes payable. What is meant by a convex tax schedule? Figure 9.4 gives an example – clearly the firm's average effective tax rate rises as pre-tax profit rises.

So how does this give lower total taxes with risk management? Let us assume that, with no hedging at all, the firm faces a distribution of pre-tax income as shown in Figure 9.5. A low profit of P_1 or a high profit of P_2 each has an equal probability of occurrence of 50 per cent. With a profit of P_1 the firm would pay taxes of T_1, and with a profit of P_2 the firm would pay taxes of T_2. Clearly, the expected value of the tax payment $E(T)$ will be equal to:

$$\frac{T_1 + T_2}{2}$$

The position is summarised in Figure 9.6.

If the firm were to hedge, the volatility of its pre-tax income would decline – both P_1 and P_2 would move towards their mean profit level. Suppose that hedging were so successful that the distribution of profit outturns became simply P_{mean}, as shown in Figure 9.7. Then, with profit at this level, taxes

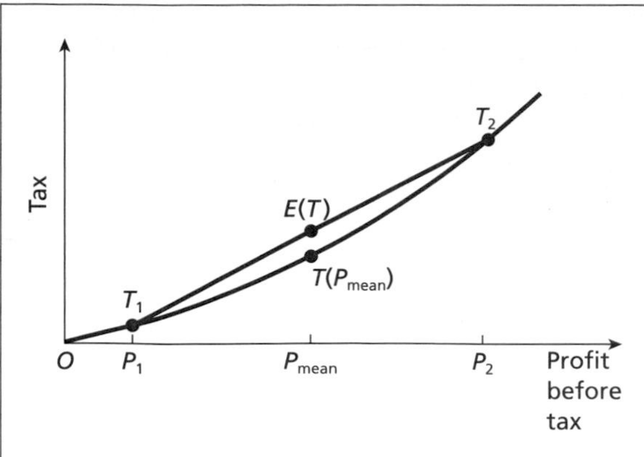

Figure 9.8 Tax payable in hedged case versus tax payable in unhedged case

payable would become $T(P_{mean})$, as indicated in Figure 9.8. Clearly, with the convex nature of the effective tax schedule, the tax on the hedged income is less than the expected tax if the firm were not to hedge.

The implication of all of the above is that if the tax schedule is convex, hedging can lead to a reduction in the firm's expected taxes. The more convex the tax schedule and the more volatile the firm's pre-tax profits, the greater are the tax benefits that accrue to the company. Corporate tax schedules in the United Kingdom and the United States currently give the firm only minimal, if any, benefits on this front. Nonetheless the principle should be clear.

The line of argument advanced in this section is similar to that of Dufey and Srinivasulu,[10] Abuaf[11] and Rawls and Smithson.[12] We now turn to the topic of relevant information for hedging purposes.

9.6 Information for exposure management

Management of foreign exchange exposure is an integral part of the treasury function in the multinational company. Rational decision taking presupposes that relevant information pertinent to the decision is available. This generalisation is no less true of treasury management than it is of any other aspect of business. To make logical decisions on foreign exchange exposure, relevant information is required. This part of the chapter is devoted to the topic of an information system for exposure management.

But what is the problem? Maybe an example would help. Suppose that one wholly owned subsidiary of a US-based group has a receivable of €5m due in three months' time, while another wholly owned subsidiary has a payable of €5m three months away. It would make no sense for the two subsidiaries each to cover their exposure by respectively selling and buying €5m three months forward. Obviously, these two exposures cancel out when viewed on a group basis. Perhaps the boards of directors of the two wholly owned subsidiaries would each reach a decision to the effect that they would want to cover their exposure. It is no problem to ensure that for internal management accounting purposes or for performance appraisal a notional hedge is done. Most multinationals achieve this by requiring that divisions wishing to cover foreign exchange exposures do so by buying or selling forward with the group treasury. But reverting to our numerical example, the point is that from a group standpoint there is no need to cover the receivable and payable referred to because setting the **long position** in one wholly owned subsidiary against the short position in the other wholly owned company provides an exact cancelling out. The difficulty for the multinational in this area is that it needs continuous flows of information from all subsidiaries on their foreign exchange exposure. And this is costly. As in any centralised system, the question needs to be asked when it is initially instituted and regularly reiterated: do the benefits of centralisation outweigh its costs?

In this context, savings are likely to accrue in terms of saved bid/offer spreads on deals eliminated – in the numerical example, by not hedging the €5m receivable in one subsidiary and the €5m payable in the other, the effective cash saving is the bid/offer spread because one subsidiary would be dealing at the market rate to buy and the other at the market rate to sell. Benefits will also accrue to a centralised treasury through greater financial control, matching, **netting** and **leading** and **lagging** opportunities (see Chapter 10), better ability to optimise group cash management, tax bills, movement of funds to avoid exchange controls and an ability to raise funds worldwide at lower rates than through a piecemeal approach. To justify a centralised system the value of such benefits has to exceed their costs in terms of expensive manpower such as treasury personnel, dealers, information systems and so on. It should not be taken for granted that the centralised treasury is always superior to the decentralised operation – indeed it rarely is for the small business. Centralisation may be difficult to justify when there are many partly owned subsidiaries, since different shareholders may have different attitudes in terms, for example, of risk aversion and so on. Even were centralisation justified, as it might have been five years ago, a regular post-audit is really needed to ensure that benefits have accrued and outstripped costs and that it continues to be the rational, cost-effective policy.

However, before getting fully to grips with information for exposure management, we need to ask ourselves with which definition of exposure the firm is concerned. It is to this topic that we now turn.

9.7 What kind of foreign exchange exposure is significant?

We have classified foreign exchange exposure under three headings: transaction exposure, translation exposure and economic exposure. Earlier in this book we argued that the firm should be crucially concerned with transaction exposure and economic exposure, since these two classifications of exposure are essentially underpinned by cash flows. This contrasts with pure translation exposure where differences arise due to accounting conventions in the process of consolidating the financial accounts of companies within a group. Of course, pure translation gains and losses are now dealt with by way of reserve accounting under the consolidation procedures, most countries, including the USA and the UK. This means that distortions to earnings per share and profit trends which were brought about by the requirements of the US accounting standard **FASB 8** have been eliminated. Furthermore the indications of most serious empirical studies – admittedly US-based – are that security analysts are sufficiently sophisticated not to be fooled by the inclusion of these translation gains and losses in income statements, and since they do not seem to affect security prices, the conclusion follows that translation exposure should not matter to the multinational company. And if companies need not worry about translation exposure – except in respect of gearing (see Chapter 8) – it follows that collecting information on it is not a worthwhile process. Furthermore, companies should not enter into transactions to hedge pure translation exposures. As Ross, Clark and Taiyeb[13] state, 'as a very general . . . first principle, it is uncommercial to hedge a non-cash item with a cash one'. In this connection, it should be reiterated that gains and losses arising from converting borrowings and lendings denominated in foreign currency are classified by this author as transaction gains and losses and are therefore left outside of the definition of pure translation exposure used here. Should information be required on pure translation exposure, the normal rolling budgets which most large companies prepare ought to be sufficient to meet any needs of users.

Having argued against the inclusion of pure translation exposure within the exposure information system, we now turn to economic exposure and transaction exposure. The computation of economic exposure is a complex process, requiring as it does detailed analysis of elasticities of demand, competitor appraisals and other aspects discussed in Chapter 8 and exemplified later in Chapter 29. Identifying economic exposure presupposes that corporate executives are able to specify how the value of the firm will respond to exchange rate changes. Since we have argued elsewhere in this book that economic exposure matters, presumably treasurers in multinational companies will wish to manage it. The sort of information necessary to manage economic exposure concerns the impact of exchange rate changes upon the value of the firm. With rapidly changing exchange rates and a competitive world, economic exposure may also change regularly. But keeping track of this class of foreign exchange exposure is difficult. It clearly requires the input of very skilled executive time and as such is not easily amenable to being systematised. Given this background we would argue that, if economic exposure is being actively managed, it is regularly necessary to update information about it. But, given that identification of economic exposure should be based upon the sensitivity of the present value of the firm to changes in exchange rates, we believe that this is so complex an issue that we would not recommend that it becomes the subject of a routine, simple information system. However, if a firm is actually managing economic and transaction exposure, it needs to equip itself with current figures on both kinds of exposure. For economic exposure, this would mean that regular net present value details of operating cash flows would be necessary for all of a multinational company's operations, plus details of the extent to which they are hedged by local and other financing. A later part of this chapter is devoted to a more advanced consideration of the difficulties involved in analysing and controlling economic exposure.

The other class of exposure that is also based on cash flows is, of course, transaction exposure. We have argued in Chapter 8 that transaction exposure matters to the firm. Identification of transaction exposure is not difficult, unlike economic exposure. Unmanaged transaction exposure may result in loans denominated in foreign currency being left exposed while the foreign currency strengthens dramatically. This may have very far-reaching effects on the firm, as we pointed out in Chapter 8. And passively managed transaction exposure may result in subsidiary companies in a group pursuing policies which are optimal from their own viewpoint as subsidiaries but which result in sub-optimisation from a group standpoint. The example of the €5m exposure is a case (see section 9.6) which would cost the group two bid/offer spreads to cover exposures when an internal cover was already available. Managing transaction exposure presupposes that the group treasury has information on its magnitude and maturity. We shall now attempt to outline an information system for transaction exposure that is relatively easy and inexpensive to operate. It might be implemented even though a fully fledged, centralised treasury is not in existence.

9.8 The transaction exposure information system

Although no single transaction exposure information system will be universally applicable to every business, there are certain features that should be present in all. First, the information system should be forward looking. Given that we are concerned with taking decisions about future events, it follows that we need information about anticipated outturns. Secondly, the frequency of reporting needs to be adequate. What constitutes sufficient frequency is entirely a practical question but we have found that for most companies, with significant international operations, monthly reports bolstered by computer communication to the centre on additional exposures taken on is adequate. But clearly very large groups or those with vast items denominated in foreign currency may wish to shorten this reporting time-scale. Thirdly, the flow of information should be direct to the treasury rather than being routed via other departments, such as accounting departments, which can create delays. Finally, the need for information must be sold to management in subsidiary companies. It is essential that such managers comprehend the rationale for data on foreign currency commitments and it is essential that subsidiary company performance should not be distorted. Failure in these areas usually results in reduced motivation on the part of subsidiary management and a weak and tardy system of control.

Information systems should be timely, succinct and oriented to decision and control. There is no place for irrelevant information. Thus the routine exposure information system

Table 9.1 Transaction cash flow exposure schedule (£000)

Company: US Sub Inc. Country: USA	Currency: £ Forecast period: 6 mths to 30.6.12	Prepared by: AB Date prepared: 24.12.11	Rate: $ v. £ as at 24.12.11 Spot: 1.7200 1 mth 1.7300 3 mths 1.7500

	Jan.	Feb.	Mar.	Apr.	May	June	Beyond June	
Receipts								
Third party	2,000	3,000	1,000	1,000				Due Sept. 11
Intercompany Swedish sub		2,000						
______								
______								
______								
Total receipts	2,000	5,000	1,000	1,000			1,000	
Payments								
Third party	3,000	3,000					2,000	Due Oct. 11
Intercompany German sub			2,000					
______								
______								
______								
Total payments	3,000	3,000	2,000				2,000	
Net receipts/(payments)	(1,000)	2,000	(1,000)	1,000			1,000	Sept. 11
Cover against receipts		1,000					(2,000)	Oct. 11
Cover against payments	1,000		1,000				2,000	
Net exposure	–	1,000	–	1,000			1,000	
Details of forward cover*	1.8.11	1.9.11	30.9.11				16.10.11	
(specify contract date;	Jan.	Feb.	Mar.				Oct.	
settlement date;	1.7350	1.7450	1.7550				1.7580	
rate; amount)	1,000	1,000	1,000				2,000	

* Details of forward cover frequently appear on a separate schedule.

should home in solely upon transaction exposure. McRae and Walker[14] extend the currency exposure information system to translation exposure. For reasons set out above, the author believes this to be unnecessary and unjustified – except when gearing constraints loom.

Our concern is with transaction exposure, using a minimum monthly reporting frequency. Reports are essentially forecasts specifying receipts and payments to be made in foreign currency. They should focus upon currency of denomination, maturity and cover already taken. It is recommended that reports should distinguish four key data. These embrace intercompany versus third-party flows, capital versus trading items, firm contractual flows versus probable flows and, finally, details of covered and uncovered flows.

Table 9.1 is an example of such an exposure forecast. Although it does not split out capital and trading items or firm and probable flows as such, this can easily be achieved by entering the respective initials C or T and F or P. Thus the treasury at the UK holding company level would require from the US subsidiary a form like the table showing all non-US$ exposures which had been taken on by that subsidiary. Similar schedules would also be required from all other subsidiaries showing transaction exposures in currencies other than the local currency. In addition to these schedules, material changes would be immediately communicated by telex to the group treasury. This enables the group treasury to co-ordinate covering activities in response to the overall transaction exposure position.

Receipt of transaction exposure schedules from all around the world enables the central treasury to prepare a group exposure statement. Like the previous schedule this is usually prepared monthly; an example of such a summary report appears in Table 9.2. In the table, it will be noted that currencies are categorised according to whether a forward market exists or not. This is a useful distinction since ease of action to obtain cover is more readily available when a forward foreign exchange market exists. However, where forward markets do not exist, cover may be synthesised by borrowing or lending in the local currency, assuming that financial markets have sufficient depth for this strategy to be pursued. It is also useful to categorise currencies according to their membership of joint

Table 9.2 Group cash flow exposure schedule (£000)

Prepared by: .... **Date prepared:** .... **Forecast period:** ....

	Jan.	Feb.	Mar.	Apr.	May	June	Beyond June
Currencies with forward market							
Euros							
Canadian $							
Japanese yen							
Swedish krone							
Swiss franc							
US$							
Others (specify)							
Total							
No forward market							
Currency (specify)							
Currency (specify)							
Currency (specify)							
Total							

floats. The value of this kind of device lies in the fact that, sometimes, large companies cover against the net cash flow exposure having netted out positions with respect to all currencies in a joint float.

9.9 Histogramming

Having estimated a company's transaction exposure on a group basis, the question for the group treasurer is what to do about it. Action is clearly a function of the management's view on the directions in which exchange rates are likely to move. Here the histogramming technique is frequently used. This involves obtaining and giving weight to estimates of exchange rate movements from well-informed parties inside and outside the company. Sources inside the company might include the group treasury, the economics department, local management and various others. Sources outside the company would include bankers and forecasting groups. The technique involves each forecaster assigning probabilities to a range of estimated future exchange rates over various periods. It should be noted that ranges, rather than single point estimates, are usually used. Table 9.3 shows a format that might be used for this process. As can be seen, Table 9.3 contains a weighting factor in addition to the actual forecast. Weightings are built into the process by reference to individual forecasters' previous track records. The sum of the weightings for all forecasters must equal 1.00. With reference to Table 9.3, the probability assigned by the forecaster is multiplied by the forecaster's weighting to give a final weighted probability. These weighted probabilities are brought together in a summary histogram (see Table 9.4) and they may then be compared with the forward rate for the purpose of decision taking.

Reverting to Table 9.3, this shows a format for individual forecasts – in this case it is for the treasury. Forecasts of this kind will be prepared by each of the forecasting participants for one month, two months, three months forward and so on. These forecasts are weighted according to each forecaster's past record – this has been done in Table 9.4 over three months – and histograms as shown at the foot of the table can readily be prepared for one month, two months, three months forward and so on. In the example, the forecasting participants are group treasury, group economics, local treasurer, group financial planning, the company's bankers and a consultant foreign exchange forecasting company. The respective weights given to each party are 20, 15, 15, 20, 15 and 15 per cent.

Table 9.3 Currency forecast (£000)

Forecaster:	Group treasurer		Current spot rate:	$1.7750 = £1
Currency:	£/$		Forward rate:	$1.7800 = £1
Forecast period:	3 months		Date prepared:	....

Expected range	Mid-point	Probability	Forecaster weighting	Weighted probability
1.7400 to 1.7699	1.7550	0.05	0.20	0.0100
1.7700 to 1.7999	1.7850	0.3	0.20	0.0600
1.8000 to 1.8299	1.8150	0.35	0.20	0.0700
1.8300 to 1.8599	1.8450	0.25	0.20	0.0500
1.8600 to 1.8899	1.8750	0.05	0.20	0.0100
		1.00	1.00	0.2000

Table 9.4 Summary histogram (£/$)

Currency: £/$				**Date prepared:**	
Forecast period: 3 months				**Forward rate:** $1.7800 = £1	
	Forecast range				
	1.7400 to 1.7699	1.7700 to 1.7999	1.8000 to 1.8299	1.8300 to 1.8599	1.8600 to 1.8899
Grp treasurer	0.01	0.06	0.07	0.05	0.01
Grp economics	0.01	0.08	0.05	0.01	0
Local treasurer	0	0.08	0.07	0	0
Financial planning	0.01	0.09	0.07	0.02	0.01
Banker	0.01	0.07	0.07	0	0
Forecaster	0.01	0.06	0.07	0.01	0
Total	**0.05**	**0.44**	**0.40**	**0.09**	**0.02**
Summary Confidence level (50% / 25% / 0%)	5%	44%	40%	9%	2%
	1.7400 to 1.7699	1.7700 to 1.7999	1.8000 to 1.8299	1.8300 to 1.8599	1.8600 to 1.8899

From Table 9.4 it can be seen that the weighted forecast suggests a very high probability that the exchange rate in three months' time will be within the range 1.77 to 1.83. If the forward rate for three-month dollars is $1.78 to £1 (see Tables 9.3 and 9.4), then if the company expected to be short of dollars against the pound three months away (that is, it has to buy in dollars for pounds in three months' time), it would most probably benefit by waiting and buying dollars through the spot market in three months' time, since, according to the histogram, there is a good chance that the dollar will have weakened in three months' time and the histogram promises a better payoff by using the spot rate in three months' time rather than the forward rate. Remember that the rationale for the use of selective hedging is that, at least in the short term, the forward rate has been found to be a biased predictor of the future spot rate. Evidence was summarised in Chapter 6.

In the example above, were our company long of dollars three months away, it might decide, logically according to the implications of the histogram, to sell dollars forward. Thus, the histogramming technique facilitates rational selective hedging. If selective hedging of this kind is undertaken, it is most important to monitor its effectiveness. The recommended post-audit procedure should compare the outturns achieved from selective hedging with those that would have resulted from a policy of hedging everything in the forward market, and it should also compare selective hedging achievements with results based on hedging nothing at all in the forward market. Clearly, one needs to do this kind of post-audit over a fairly lengthy time-span, including periods when the home currency was rising and falling. If selective hedging is to be pursued, the results of post-audits must justify choice of this strategy. Such post-audits need to be undertaken regularly. Individual forecaster weightings may also be changed as a result of this process. It cannot be stressed too much that the post-audit is an essential part of a selective hedging policy.

9.10 Reinvoicing vehicles

Many multinational companies have turned their treasury department into a separate company. All intergroup trade is then invoiced through this central company. Such companies are known as '**reinvoicing vehicles**' or 'netting vehicles' or 'multi-currency management centres'. Practice varies from company to company, but the general outline set out below is reasonably typical.

Group companies invoice exports to other group companies through the reinvoicing company in the currency of the exporter. The reinvoicing company in its turn invoices the importing company in its home currency. This means that neither exporter nor importer has any exchange risk; this is borne by the reinvoicing company, which ultimately takes all covering decisions on a basis which it views as reflecting a balance of future outturns and the extent of its risk aversion.

Exports outside the group are either invoiced in the exporter's currency or, if the importer requires a different currency of sale, the exporter bills the invoicing centre in its own currency and the reinvoicing company bills the customer in the currency agreed between seller and purchaser. Again, all currency risk is concentrated into the reinvoicing centre. Imports are handled in the same manner, enabling all currency risk to be borne by the invoicing company. Of course, the reinvoicing centre does become the legal owner of the goods in these transactions and should therefore have little difficulty in obtaining exchange control permissions to cover its exposure in countries where exchange controls are in place.

This technique concentrates all currency exposure into the reinvoicing centre. It therefore becomes an ideal vehicle for controlling and monitoring the group's foreign exchange exposure. In addition, the reinvoicing centre frequently acts as the banker to the group. In such circumstances cash management is centred in the reinvoicing company as are group borrowings. Such fully fledged, sophisticated and (frequently) costly vehicles are appropriate to large international groups with substantial cross-frontier trade, international borrowings and cash flows – but earlier comments in this chapter about cost effectiveness and its regular review still hold.

Some companies have used reinvoicing centres less than scrupulously in order to lower worldwide tax bills and in cost-plus pricing. However, reinvoicing vehicles need not be part of a less than ethical operation. Indeed, the practice of using the reinvoicing centre for dubious purposes has receded somewhat in recent years because host governments have become suspicious when they are used.

9.11 Strategies for exposure management

It has been argued that firms should take management action in the foreign exchange markets to counter cash flow exposure. But there is another basic question that top management needs to answer: is its posture one of making as much profit as it can through changes in foreign currency rates? Or is it basically in the business of making and selling goods or services, with a foreign exchange stance designed to minimise losses through changing rates? Is the treasury a profit or a cost centre? There is no universal, clear-cut response to these questions. Different firms will adopt different postures because of their varying degrees of risk aversion. Maybe their postures on foreign exchange risk will vary from time to time. The firm that seeks to maximise profits in the foreign exchange markets is termed an 'aggressive' firm; its counterpart that aims merely to minimise potential losses resulting from changed exchange rates is termed a 'defensive' firm. In reality, judged by their overall strategies and tactics, firms rarely fall neatly into one category or the other but rather lie on a continuum of foreign currency risk between aggressive and defensive – sometimes a particular firm adopts an aggressive policy; at other times the same firm will pursue a defensive policy.

The aggressive posture will involve the firm in deliberately seeking and leaving open foreign exchange positions in currencies in which it expects to make profits. The defensive posture involves the avoidance of foreign exchange exposure by the techniques referred to in the next few chapters. In countries without foreign exchange controls, it is easy for the aggressive firm to back its judgement on future currency movements by opening up exposure unrelated to trade via the forward or swaps markets or the futures or options markets. In countries with exchange controls, the only substantial opportunity open to the firm legally to take currency positions is based on trade transactions. As an example of the aggressive stance in an environment with exchange controls, an exporter might endeavour to invoice a sale in the currency that it expects to be **hard** relative to its own currency. An aggressive posture would also involve only covering a foreign currency receivable when the forward rate of exchange was more favourable than the expected spot rate on the **settlement date**. By contrast to these examples, the defensive firm would seek to invoice in its own currency and, where it had a foreign currency receivable or payable, it would cover automatically in the forward market. It should be reiterated that when there are no exchange controls it is far more logical for the firm to take open positions via the forward, swaps, futures or options markets rather than through trade transactions.

With respect to decisions of a long-term nature, the aggressive firm would similarly seek to obtain debt denominated in a **soft currency** relative to its own, having due regard to interest costs taken together with expected currency depreciation/appreciation. The defensive firm might endeavour to match the currency denomination of cash inflows and outflows, thereby minimising cash flow exposure, or to match the currency denomination of assets and liabilities.

A firm's posture on foreign exchange risk is usually a function of two key factors. The first is the aggregate risk aversion of the key members of the organisation's decision coalition. The second relates to the firm's ability to forecast exchange rates and its ability to beat the forward market. This latter factor takes us back to the whole range of questions concerned with efficiency of foreign exchange markets and the ability of forecasts consistently to yield excess returns.

Were foreign exchange markets efficient and subject to no imperfections, then there would be no systematic biases in rates and management's currency expectations would be synonymous with those of the market as embodied in forward rates. According to this scenario, consistent profit opportunities would not exist. But in a world in which governments create market imperfections by intervening in foreign exchange markets – this is termed 'dirty floating' under the current floating exchange rate regime – and interest rate markets, these actions are likely to create systematic deviations between realised rates and expectations of future rates as embodied in forward rates. Certainly, as we saw in Chapter 6, there have been consistent and persistent biases which have continued for short periods and for substantial periods too, suggesting that recurring profit opportunities do accrue to investors in foreign exchange markets. So the aggressive stance may be justified by two factors. First, market imperfections, such as government intervention in foreign exchange markets, may result in sustained periods when markets fail to demonstrate the features of efficiency. Secondly, and somewhat more doubtful, it may be the case that forecasters have special abilities based on access to information not available to most other participants in the market, or the firm or forecaster may have special expertise in interpreting available information. As pointed out earlier, firms adopting aggressive exposure policies need carefully to monitor the results of pursuing such tactics.

The essence of the defensive strategy varies according to the nature of the company concerned. For the basically domestic company, which occasionally exports or imports, the low-risk policy involves consistent use of the forward markets. For the significant exporter, the defensive policy most frequently used involves forward markets or currency of financing policy. This latter approach is best illustrated with an example. If a firm's operations generate exposed assets or cash inflows, these exposures may be countered by taking on financial liabilities or cash outflows in the same currencies. According to this formula, a company with significant exports denominated in foreign currencies would try to match these by holding part of its liabilities in these currencies.

For the truly multinational company which has interrelated operations in many countries, the defensive financial strategy involves use of forward, swaps and options markets, but it also has a significant further policy at its disposal. This involves protection of expected profit and cash flow levels against changes in foreign exchange markets and financial markets by adjusting operating and financial variables. Operating responses consist of alteration to sourcing, product, plant location, market selection, credit, pricing and currency of invoicing policies – these will be considered in Chapter 10. In passing, we would point out that Jenkins,[15] on the basis of case study evidence, views the first three of the above to be more effective than financial markets in combating competitive disadvantages created by exchange rate disequilibria – although care must be exercised lest long-term operational changes are entered into in order to attack short-term disequilibria. Adjustments of financial variables to protect profit and cash flows generally occur on the liabilities side. A company may finance itself in those currencies with which its operating cash flows are positively correlated. For example, consider a US holding company with a UK subsidiary exporting in euros to Germany. Operating returns of the UK subsidiary are positively correlated with movements in the euro and the subsidiary might therefore decide to raise finance in euros. A movement in the euro against sterling would affect not only operating returns but also financing costs. The change in the one would be countered by changes in the other, thereby reducing foreign exchange risk.

9.12 Economic exposure revisited

So far in this text, the view has been taken that economic exposure is concerned with the present value of future operating cash flows to be generated by a company's activities and how this present value, expressed in parent currency terms, changes following exchange rate movements. Ideas about hedging economic exposure have been based upon this definition. But nowadays another view of economic exposure is emerging and it is one that may be more useful and powerful from the standpoint of providing information upon which the risk-averse firm may plan a hedging strategy. The term 'macroeconomic exposure' has been coined for it and – as its name implies – it goes far beyond mere exposure to exchange rate changes. Work on this topic is in its infancy; however, the author is firmly of the opinion that the potential for using macroeconomic exposure techniques is not to be underrated. Perhaps in ten or 20 years' time it will be this kind of exposure that is the main focus of the corporate treasurer's job.

9.13 Macroeconomic exposure

Macroeconomic exposure is concerned with how a firm's cash flows, profit and hence value change as a result of developments in the economic environment as a whole – that is, within the total framework of exchange rates, interest rates, inflation rates, wage levels, commodity price levels and other shocks to the system. All firms are clearly vulnerable to this kind of exposure. The economic shocks may originally emanate from the home economy or abroad – the idea behind managing macroeconomic exposure is first of all to identify the nature of the exposure and then to manage it by hedging techniques. The methodology outlined in this section draws on the work of Oxelheim and Wihlborg.[16]

The identification of a firm's sensitivity to macroeconomic variables may be established by determining the way in which cash flow, profits and value vary in response to changes in key economic variables, such as interest rates, price levels, exchange rates, commodity prices and so on. The relevant variables would first of all be put forward as a result of deductive reasoning. They would then be fed into a statistical model and recent values would be set against them with the objective of establishing the coefficients of sensitivity using regression analysis techniques. Data must be available for a sufficiently long period of time and it is usual to begin this analysis by breaking down data by product, strategic business unit, country of operations and so on.

Let us assume that an analysis has been undertaken for a UK-based company in terms of estimating, by regression techniques, the percentage rate of change in the firm's real cash flows from unanticipated changes in prices levels abroad and at home, the exchange rate, domestic and foreign interest rates and relative prices of significant inputs. Let us assume that this analysis produces the results, in terms of the exposure coefficients, noted in Table 9.5.

The figures in the second column of the table indicate, for example, that a 1 per cent unanticipated increase in UK price levels will lead to a fall of 0.6 per cent in real cash flows. The table shows that real UK cash flows are insensitive to changes in foreign price levels. But the table goes on to indicate that, for a 1 per cent unanticipated rise in the exchange rate, real cash flows drop by 0.5 per cent, holding other variables constant. As the table shows, the reference in this case is to the sterling/dollar exchange rate. Depending upon the reality of macroeconomic relationships for the firm concerned, it might be the case that the critical exchange rate to be included in the analysis turned out to be sterling/yen movements or sterling/euro fluctuations. The next exposure coefficient which is highlighted is the domestic interest rate. Here, the indication is that, for a 1 per cent unanticipated rise in

Table 9.5 Effect of a 1 per cent unanticipated change in macroeconomic variables on the firm's real cash flows

Variable	Exposure coefficient	Real effect (£m)	Example of 1% change
Domestic price level	–0.6	–0.45	Retail prices move from 100 to 101
Foreign price level	0	0	
Exchange rate	–0.5	–0.375	$/£ rate moves from 1.80 to 1.7820
Domestic interest rate	–0.8	–0.6	Interest rates move from 10% to 10.1%
Foreign interest rate	0.2	+0.15	US interest rates move from 10% to 10.1%
Commodity prices	–0.2	–0.15	Copper prices move from £1,500 per tonne to £1,515 per tonne
Relative prices	0.6	+0.45	Output price index relative to RPI increases from 1 to 1.01

interest rates, real cash flow falls by 0.8 per cent. The effect that the domestic interest rate has upon cash flow may ripple through other lead indicators. For example, one of the key lead indicators in the building materials industry is housing starts, but this is predicated, in turn, upon interest rate levels. The next exposure coefficient shown in the table, foreign interest rates, indicates that, for a 1 per cent unanticipated change in their level, real cash flow of the firm rises by 0.2 per cent. Again, it may be the case that only the euro or US interest rate is of any relevance, since it may impinge upon competitors or consumers located in these respective countries. The table goes on to indicate that a 1 per cent unanticipated rise in commodity prices results in a 0.2 per cent fall in real cash flow of the firm. Clearly, what constitutes relevant commodity prices will vary from industry to industry. Cement prices may be critical for one industry but not for another. Steel prices may be significant in one business and not another. And it may be the case that one would wish to allow for more than one critical commodity for a particular strategic business unit. Finally, there is reference in the table to relative prices. This measures the firm's output and/or input prices relative to the general price level. A 1 per cent increase in this ratio results in an increase of 0.6 per cent in the firm's real cash flows.

If the firm's expected real cash flows in the base case are £75m, then by multiplying the exposure coefficient by this amount, we obtain the real effect of changes in the macroeconomic variable detailed in the third column of Table 9.5. We have assumed that the exposure coefficients are partial. This means that they refer to the sensitivity of real cash flows to changes in each variable while other variables are held constant. Thus the domestic interest rate coefficient indicates the effect of a change in domestic interest rates with all other variables held constant.

Once sensitivity measures have been established, financial instruments may be used to hedge exposures. For example, assume that the firm for which data are given in Table 9.5 were concerned only with hedging its dollar/sterling currency exposure. The firm would then deal in the forward market for such an amount that, should there be a 1 per cent strengthening in the dollar against sterling, then the firm would make a profit of £375,000. This would offset the lost £375,000 shown in the table. On the basis of the exchange rate data set out in Table 9.5, the firm would buy 12-month forward dollars of approximately $67m. Buying this amount of dollars for delivery in 12 months implies that, should there be a depreciation of sterling equivalent to 1 per cent against the dollar, the firm obtains a cash gain of £375,000, which offsets the cash flow loss resulting from the trading depreciation of sterling. Through this means, then, the firm might hedge itself against changes in the sterling/dollar exchange rate.

Other financial contracts, such as interest rate futures, may be used to hedge interest rate exposures. The same can be done in respect of commodity futures. So if the firm wished to hedge exchange rate, interest rate and commodity exposure, it would use foreign exchange forwards, interest rate futures and commodity futures. However, some extra care has to be taken. This arises because of the fact that the value of the forward contract is sensitive to interest rate changes and the value of the interest rate and commodity futures depends upon the exchange rate. The effect of this is that the size of each hedge contract depends upon the size of other hedge contracts.

In connection with the effect upon corporate cash flow of interest rate and exchange rate changes, Oxelheim and Wihlborg[17] point out that, on the basis of their practical experience with measures of macroeconomic exposure, they have found that the effects of changes in world interest rate levels have been more statistically pronounced than the effects of exchange rate changes. This evidence would suggest that the traditional method of looking at economic exposure – that is, by focusing upon foreign exchange rate changes – is likely to achieve less good results than the methodology that focuses upon macroeconomic exposure.

Analysis of macroeconomic exposure is very much the leading edge of hedging techniques. Readers interested in pursuing the literature are referred to Oxelheim and Wihlborg's work, of which the content of this chapter so far is a very brief summary. It should be pointed out that they suggest that, in making an analysis of macroeconomic exposure, the analyst should disaggregate cash flows in terms of products, subsidiaries and types of cash flow. While the author would agree that such an analysis would produce a better understanding of the operations of the total corporate entity, it is not necessarily clear why such a breakdown would give us better information with which to undertake a hedging policy. After all, if we are concerned with undertaking a covered strategy designed to eliminate macroeconomic exposure at the group level, it would seem that it is group exposures that are critical rather than exposures at the level of the individual operating companies. Admittedly, if the group has a large number of subsidiary or associated companies which may or may not be wholly owned, then there may be some value in undertaking hedges at the level of the individual companies. However, if this is not so, then there would seem to be no great advantage, beyond that of greater informational content and understanding, to be obtained from carrying out the analysis to the disaggregated level.

Experiments with macroeconomic exposure

It is easy to argue that future developments in corporate hedging policy will take place in the macroeconomic exposure arena. Clearly, assuming that the statistical analysis is undertaken correctly, macroeconomic exposure analysis provides a tool that gets to the very heart of cash flow and profit uncertainty. At the present point in time, there is a widening number of companies using this technique.

9.14 Value at risk

Value at risk (VAR) is a single number estimate of how much a company can lose due to the price volatility of the instrument it holds for example, a fixed-rate bond or an unhedged currency payable/receivable. More precisely, it defines the likelihood of potential loss not exceeding a particular level, given certain assumptions. These assumptions may involve time horizon, holding period, confidence limits, distribution of probabilities, correlation and the potential for shocks to the system. It has to be said that it was found to have failed at the time of the recent financial crisis where the **normal distribution** upon which it is based morphed to a **fat tail distribution** – a feature which is typical at times of financial upheaval. Nonetheless, it is reported here because it remains in use and we have learned much about the sources of its shortcomings.

The development of VAR owes much to bankers JP Morgan whose past chairman demanded a one-page report at the end of business each day summarising the bank's exposures to losses because of possible market movements in the coming day. JP Morgan's 'Riskmetrics' (a system of measuring VAR) evolved from this request.

VAR promised the possibility of aggregating risks across a range of diverse activities and fits well with the banking industry's interest in installing group risk management systems. Corporates, concerned about group risk, seized on VAR as a risk measurement tool. VAR is conceptually and practically a powerful tool and needs to be understood – but there are caveats, see section 9.15. Besides these, VAR falls far short of providing a complete panacea for group risk measurement, particularly for corporates. It does, however, provide a useful estimate of possible losses over a short period under normal market conditions for investments and other instruments which are liquid.

To explain the concept, assume that a financial institution holds a portfolio of fixed interest bonds. The portfolio is unhedged and its value today is therefore based on the current **term structure** of interest rates – the yield curve today. If we have comparable historic yield data, then we can calculate the value of the portfolio under a wide range of past interest rate scenarios in order to get a distribution of values and of potential changes in value. Most VAR models assume that changes in the value of the portfolio are, on average, random and that their frequency distribution can be estimated using a normal curve – see Figure 9.9. For a normal curve, the standard deviation (σ) is the measure of volatility and data points will be distributed as follows:

$$68.3\% \text{ within } \pm 1\ \sigma$$
$$95.5\% \text{ within } \pm 2\ \sigma$$
$$99.7\% \text{ within } \pm 3\ \sigma$$

If the standard deviation in Figure 9.9 is £10,000, then 95.5 per cent of the time the change in value of the portfolio will be within ± £20,000 (that means, in loss 47.75 per cent of the time and in gain 47.75 per cent of the time). So, the VAR at a 95.5 per cent confidence level is £20,000. If the data are at daily intervals, then this would give the 24-hour VAR. This is what the chairman of JP Morgan wanted.

It is easy to see how the concept can be applied to exchange rate exposure or interest rate exposures that banks may hold. Indeed, bank capital adequacy regulations required measurement of market risk on bank open currency positions as the VAR at 95 per cent confidence limits based on five years' daily data or at 99 per cent confidence limits based on three years' daily data. The bank would then be obliged to support that VAR by a specific amount of capital. (However, this needs to be reinforced by stress tests of possible adverse outturns.)

Like most management techniques, there are problems with VAR too. The following are some of the caveats concerning VAR:

- Changes in value may not be normally distributed. For outturns from some instruments they are definitely not normally distributed – especially at times of crisis.

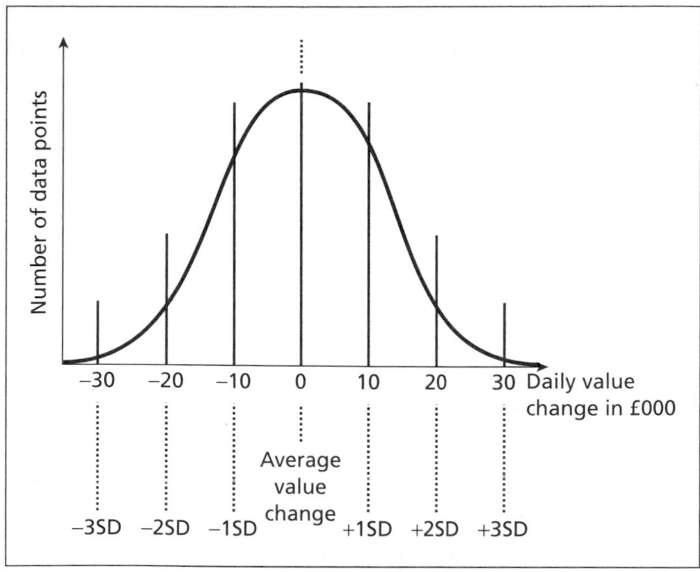

Figure 9.9 The normal curve applied to changes in portfolio value

- Shocks to the system may occur with greater frequency than the normal curve implies. So VAR is typically used for normal market conditions and supplemented by stress testing and scenario analysis as modelling devices to allow for the impact of large shocks.
- For portfolios of risks, some may be correlated, for example, exposures to groups of currencies. Thus, for other than very simple portfolios, one of three calculation methods is normally used. These include:
  (i) the variance/covariance method, involving statistically adjusting data for historic correlation and correlation arrived at using deductive logic
  (ii) simulation using historic portfolio returns and expected outturns
  (iii) Monte Carlo analysis, which involves a large run of scenarios, say 10,000, to generate a distribution, using one's own assumptions about volatility and correlation. Future volatilities implied by option prices (see Chapters 14 and 15) are sometimes used.
- The holding period used in the example was 24 hours. An appropriate holding period for each risk type needs to be established and corresponding data captured. One key factor is the degree of **liquidity** – that is, how fast can the position be liquidated? For holding periods exceeding one month, VAR may not be appropriate because reliability tails off. And, in the light of the recent financial crisis this holding period may be contracted dramatically.
- Indeed, evidence provided by the recent financial crisis casts doubt on VAR as anything more than a moderately useful risk management device. It falls short of erstwhile claims made for it.

It has to be stated that VAR was found to be totally inadequate as an early warning system at the time of the financial crisis of 2007–8. We now discuss this issue in the context of normal distribution models.

9.15 Risk management models and the normal distribution

One of the great questions in the theory and practice of financial economics is whether the widespread use of the normal distribution is justified. Its elegance has been accepted and applied in terms of securities movements and in terms of options pricing, to name but two important cases.

In the normal distribution, often called the bell curve, the first and second standard deviations together cover 95.4 per cent of outturns. The two ends of a normal distribution curve are called the tails – see Figure 9.10. The two tails cover the remaining 4.6 per cent. They may include really disastrous outcomes with very low probabilities. Terrorist attacks may only have a 2 per cent chance of occurrence, but the results may be awful in the extreme.

In truth, most of us tend to underestimate the likelihood of occurrence of tail events in the financial markets. Benoit Mandelbrot[18] showed that if the Dow Jones industrial average moved in accordance with a normal distribution, it would have moved by 4.5 per cent or more on only six days between 1996 and 2003. In reality, it moved by at least that amount 366 times during the period.

Clearly, the normal curve may not be entirely applicable to many financial situations. The probability of future financial events may be better captured by a distribution with fat tails. Figure 9.10 shows both the normal distribution and one with fat tails. In the former, the two tails cover 4.6 per cent of possible outturns. In the latter, they cover 10 per cent. With other fat tail shapes, it could be more.

In support of the fat tails description, Triana[19] has observed that 'during the European Exchange Rate Mechanism debacle in 1992 (whereby Europe's system of officially managed currency rates collapsed), 50-standard deviation moves in interest rates were witnessed, while 1987's Black Monday was a 20-standard deviation (or 20-sigma) event. During the summer 1998 convolutions that eventually brought down Long Term Capital Management, 15-plus sigma deviations were occurring.' As we mentioned earlier in Chapter 6, he goes on to say that 'so-called "one in a million years" events have been experienced, several times, by people whose age is way below one million years. Which one is wrong, the real world or the model?'

And to reproduce the quotable quote by Lanchester,[20] that in financial markets 'the last decades have seen numerous five-, six- and seven-sigma events. Those are supposed

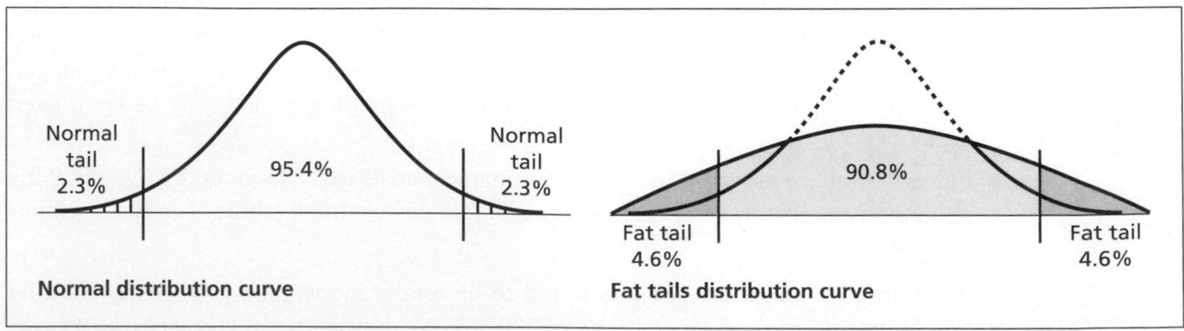

Figure 9.10 Normal distribution versus fat tails

to happen, respectively, one day in every 13,932 years, one day in every 4,039,906 years, and one day in every 3,105,395,365 years. And yet no one concluded from this that the statistical models in use were wrong. The mathematical models simply didn't work in a crisis. They worked when they worked, which was most of the time; but then the whole point of them was to assess risks, and some risks by definition happen at the edge of known likelihoods.' Precisely.

Generally, in the world of earthquakes and hurricanes, the low probability events in the fat tails are independent of each other. In the financial world, by contrast, apparently independent events may be linked, multiplying their likelihood of occurrence. For example, assume that there is a 2 per cent chance of the housing market falling by over 20 per cent sometime during next year in the absence of problems in the bond market. However, housing prices could also fall if the market for bonds froze over for reasons unrelated to the housing market. If this problem spread from the bond market to the mortgage market and reduced the financing available for houses, then the chances of housing prices falling by over 20 per cent would surely be far higher than 2 per cent. The need to identify low probability events that could put one out of business over the next several years, especially those involving linked events is clear. And the advice to hedge or insure against them then follows.

Many risk management models are based upon the following dubious assumptions:

- that financial returns and risks follow normal (Gaussian) distributions, ignoring the fat tails which on some occasions can be so destructive;
- that a single statistic, the standard deviation (which tells us much about normal distributions), captures potential outturns in capital markets;
- that correlations are constant, although they tend to change in crises and can make perfect diversification and hedging more complicated;
- that liquid funds will always be available even though, in extreme conditions, they may not be.

Risk management models often focus too much on routine market conditions and tend to ignore the abnormal conditions typical of a crisis. As a result, they may give managers a false sense of security.

Summary

- Covering exposures is designed to reduce the volatility of a firm's profits and/or cash generation. Presumably, from this it might be deduced that the idea is to reduce the volatility of the value of the firm. And this should lead to enhanced shareholder value. But such a deduction needs to be challenged. While practitioners might accept the virtue of the foregoing argument, financial academics might not. So what is their argument?
- According to the capital asset pricing model (CAPM), well-diversified international investors should not be willing to pay a premium for corporate hedging activities that they, themselves, can readily replicate by adjusting their own portfolios. Hedging to reduce overall variability of cash flow and profits may be important to managers, compensated

according to short-term results, but it is irrelevant to diversified shareholders. The ups and downs of individual investments are compensated by holding a well-diversified portfolio.

- CAPM suggests that what matters in share pricing is systematic risk. If exchange risk and interest rate risk are considered to be unsystematic, then their effect can be diversified away by holding a balanced portfolio. On the other hand, if they are systematic and if forward and interest rate instruments are priced according to CAPM, then all that the firm does by entering into hedging contracts is to move along the security market line. And this adds no value to the firm. In reality, it is arguable that, at the margin, transaction costs in forward contracts actually destroy value.
- The armoury of Modigliani and Miller (MM) may be arrayed against hedging. MM argue, in respect of gearing, that the investor can manufacture home-made leverage which achieves the same result as corporate gearing. The same kind of argument applies in respect of individual hedging versus corporate hedging. In other words, home-made hedging would make corporate hedging irrelevant. But there are counter-arguments here too. Hedging markets are wholesale markets and corporate hedging may, therefore, be cheaper. Furthermore, some hedging techniques are only available to the company – leading and lagging and transfer pricing to name but two. But that is not all. Hedging requires information about current and future exposures and contingent exposures too and it is doubtful whether investors have anything like the wherewithal on this front to achieve optimal hedging – remember that information would be needed for the total portfolio, not just for an individual share. Remember also that data on economic exposure would be embraced by an optimal requirement for information.
- Hedging may be argued to be a good thing from the standpoint of employees and managers who, clearly, do not have a diversified portfolio of jobs.
- If the model of corporate valuation is of the form:

$$V_F = \sum \frac{E(\text{NCF}_t)}{(1+k)^t}$$

  reflecting that the value of the firm (V_F) is a function of expected net cash flows, E(NCF), discounted at the firm's cost of capital, k, then value can be created by increasing expected net cash flows or lowering the discount rate. If currency risk, interest rate risk and commodity price risk are viewed as diversifiable risks, their hedging cannot lower k – at least, at first sight. But hedging can lower the risk of corporate financial distress – see Figure 9.2. Lowering the risk of bankruptcy enables the firm better to deal with suppliers, customers and employees, to say nothing of bankers. Reducing the risk of financial distress may, from this standpoint, provide significant wherewithal to enhance E(NCF). And it is possible that by lowering the risk of financial distress, debt capacity may be increased with a lowering of the value of k in the above model (assuming an NPV model is used for valuation) or an increase in the value of the tax shield due to debt (should an APV approach be preferred).
- The reader may believe that a more realistic model of valuation conforms to that referred to in the chapter, namely:

$$V_F = \sum V_i - P(\sigma)$$

where V_F is the value of the firm, V_i is the net present value of each of the firm's parts and $P(\sigma)$ is a penalty factor that reflects the impact on after tax cash flows of the total risk of the firm. Note that this formula, associated with Adler and Dumas and also Lessard and Shapiro, is not consistent with CAPM ideas – the penalty factor is a function of total risk, not just systematic risk. Anyway, the above proposition of corporate value would obviously suggest that hedging is a good thing for shareholders because, in lowering the penalty factor, corporate value is enhanced.

- Furthermore, this chapter shows that under a tax regime with a convex tax schedule, the firm's net-of-tax cash generation may be increased under an exposure management policy. Again, this is good news for managers, employees, customers, financiers and, in particular, shareholders. Even under a pure CAPM approach, this factor alone would tend to enhance shareholder value.
- The rationale for the centralisation of exposure management information can best be seen by virtue of an example. One subsidiary of a UK-based international company may have a C$5m receivable due in six months' time, while another subsidiary has C$5m payable in six months' time. The nature of these two exposures will, at a group level, cancel out. Without an information system that reveals the existence of this kind of internal hedge, divisions may both find themselves covering this kind of exposure.
- To highlight the existence of internal hedges, the chapter suggests a framework for an information system to communicate transaction exposures to head office.
- Like all information systems, it is essential that it should be regularly reviewed to ensure that it is cost effective.
- This chapter makes suggestions as to how a cost-effective system might work. This involves all foreign and home subsidiaries reporting all foreign-currency-denominated transaction exposures and anticipated transaction exposures to the group treasury. The central treasury function then has the information necessary to take decisions designed to optimise at the level of the overall group.
- So far in the text, we have focused upon economic exposure in its guise as the present value of future cash flows expressed in home currency terms and how this present value changes as a result of changed exchange rates. But macroeconomic exposure is broader than this.
- Macroeconomics is concerned with how the firm's cash flows, profits and value change as a result of developments in the economic environment as a whole – that is within the total framework of exchange rates, interest rates, inflation rates, wage levels, key commodity prices and other unexpected shocks to the system.
- The sensitivity of a firm's cash flows, profits, and/or value to changed macroeconomic variables may be estimated deductively and measured statistically using regression analysis techniques. The coefficients so obtained can provide the wherewithal for a firm to undertake a logical hedging strategy.
- Macroeconomic exposure management promises to be one of the most powerful tools available to the corporate treasurer. Such techniques are at the leading edge of treasury management.
- The normal distribution provides insights into returns from financial markets – at normal times. But, in crisis conditions its validity has been found to be wanting.

End of chapter questions

9.1 Why would an MNC consider examining only its 'net' cash flows in each currency when assessing its transaction exposure?

9.2 A US-headquartered MNC is assessing its transaction exposures. Its projected cash flows are as follows for the next year:

Currency	Total inflow	Total outflow	Current exchange rate in US$
Ruritanian doppels (RUD)	RUD 4 million	RUD 2 million	$.15
British pounds (GBP)	GBP 2 million	GBP 1 million	$1.50
Batavian dracs (BTD)	BTD 3 million	BTD 4 million	$.30

What is your assessment as to the firm's degree of economic exposure? Assume that the RUD and the BTD move in tandem against the US$.

9.3 Are currency correlations perfectly stable over time? What does your answer imply about using past data on correlations as an indicator for the future?

10

Internal techniques of exposure management

There are many methods available to minimise foreign exchange risk. This chapter and Chapter 11 focus respectively upon internal and external techniques. Internal techniques use methods of exposure management which are part of a firm's regulatory financial management and do not resort to special contractual relationships outside the group of companies concerned. External techniques use contractual means to insure against potential foreign exchange losses.

Internal techniques of exposure management aim at reducing exposed positions or preventing them from arising. External techniques insure against the possibility that exchange losses will result from an exposed position which internal measures have not been able to eliminate.

Internal techniques embrace netting, matching, leading and lagging, pricing policies and asset/liability management. External techniques include forward contracts, borrowing short term, **discounting**, **factoring**, government exchange risk guarantees and currency options. Frequently, some of the above methods are unavailable to the multinational company – netting, matching and leading and lagging are illegal in some countries and restricted in others. It should also be borne in mind that for many less developed countries there is no forward market in their currencies. We now examine, in turn, netting, matching, leading and lagging, pricing policies and asset/liability management.

10.1 Netting

Netting involves associated companies which trade with each other. The technique is simple. Group companies merely settle inter-affiliate indebtedness for the net amount owing. Gross intragroup trade receivables and payables are netted out. The simplest scheme is known as bilateral netting. Each pair of associates nets out their own positions with each other and cash flows are reduced by the lower of each company's purchases from or sales to its netting partner. Bilateral netting involves no attempt to bring in the net positions of other group companies.

Bilateral netting is easily illustrated by an example. Assume that the UK subsidiary in a group owes the French subsidiary of the same group the euro equivalent of $6m and at the same time the French company owes the UK company the sterling equivalent of $4m.

The actual remittance to clear the intercompany accounts would be netted down to the equivalent of $2m (in an agreed currency which may be dollars, sterling, euros or any other currency) to be paid by the UK subsidiary to the French counterpart. Between them, the two companies have saved the transfer and exchange costs on the equivalent of $8m. Netting basically reduces the amount of intercompany payments and receipts that pass over the foreign exchanges. Bilateral netting is fairly straightforward to operate, and the main practical problem is usually the decision about what currency to use for settlement.

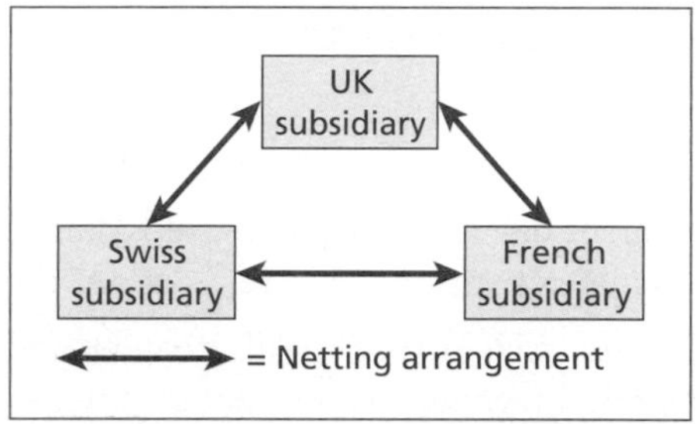

Figure 10.1 Scheme for bilateral netting

Multilateral netting is more complicated but in principle is no different from bilateral netting. Multilateral netting involves more than two associated companies' intergroup debt and virtually always involves the services of the group treasury. Bilateral netting involves only two sides and is usually undertaken without the involvement of the corporate centre. Of course, it is true that many subsidiaries may involve themselves in bilateral netting. Figure 10.1 shows how three subsidiaries in a group might be involved in bilateral netting with each other by netting off balances due between pairs of subsidiaries. This scheme involves three lots of bilateral nettings.

Multilateral netting is easily exemplified. Consider a group of companies in which the UK subsidiary buys (during the monthly netting period) $6m worth of goods and services from the Swiss subsidiary and the UK company sells $2m worth of goods to the French subsidiary. During the same month, assume that the Swiss company buys $2m worth of goods and services from the French subsidiary. The potential for multilateral netting is shown in the matrix in Table 10.1. It can be seen that settlement of the intercompany debt within the three subsidiaries ends up involving a payment of the equivalent of $4m from the UK company to the Swiss subsidiary.

Unlike the instance referred to in Table 10.1, where bilateral netting could be achieved by a number of subsidiaries netting off balances between each other in pairs, multilateral netting always involves the group treasury as the centre of netting operations (see Figure 10.2). Participating subsidiaries report all intercompany balances to the group treasury on an agreed date and the treasury subsequently advises all subsidiaries of amounts to be paid to and received from other subsidiaries on a specified date. Multilateral netting yields

Table 10.1 Multilateral netting matrix ($m)

	Paying subsidiary			Total receipts	Net receipts	Eliminated
	Swiss	UK	French			
Receiving subsidiary						
Swiss	–	6	0	6	4	2
UK	0	–	2	2		2
French	2	0	–	2		2
Total payments	2	6	2	10		
Net payments		4			4	
Eliminated	2	2	2			6
	Netting potential:		Gross flows	$10m		
			Net flows	$4m		
			Eliminated flows	$6m		

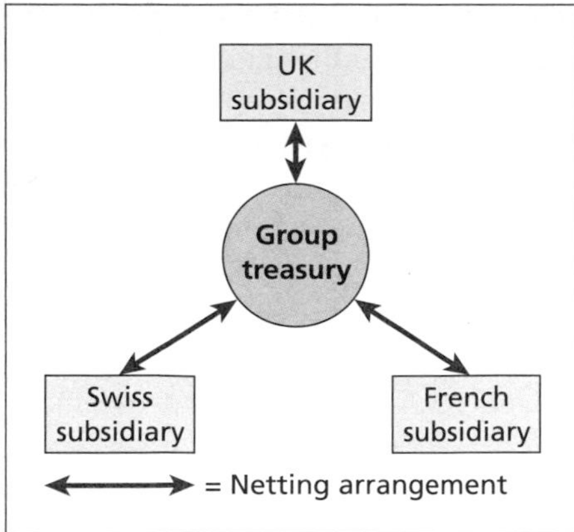

Figure 10.2 Scheme for multilateral netting

considerable savings in exchange and transfer costs but it requires a centralised communications system and discipline on the part of subsidiary companies. It should be noted that many countries' exchange controls put restrictions on bilateral and multilateral netting. Exchange control regulations need to be investigated carefully before embarking on a policy of netting.

Systems of netting used by international groups of companies involve fairly tight timetables in the period immediately prior to settlement. They usually vary around the following kind of basic schedule:

- Fix settlement day (e.g. the sixth of every month).
- Five days before settlement day all participating subsidiaries telex intercompany balances to the centre, stating the currencies of the debt and translating them into a common currency at specified exchange rates.
- Four days before settlement day intercompany balances are reconciled.
- Three days before settlement day the group treasury calculates the extent of netting to be used. The centre then issues instructions on payment to subsidiaries.
- Two days before settlement day subsidiaries instruct their banks to make payments two days hence.
- Settlement day is when payments and receipts occur.

Netting reduces banking costs and increases central control of intercompany settlements. The reduced number and amount of payments yields savings in terms of buy/sell spreads in the spot and forward markets and reduced bank charges. It is difficult to estimate total benefits but as a guide to the extent of gains flowing from netting techniques McRae and Walker[1] estimate that savings approximate to one-sixth of 1 per cent of the flows eliminated.

10.2 Matching

Although netting and matching are terms that are frequently used interchangeably, there are distinctions. Strictly speaking, netting is a term applied to potential flows within a group of companies, whereas matching can be applied to both intragroup and third-party balancing.

Matching is a mechanism whereby a company matches its foreign currency inflows with its foreign currency outflows in respect of amount and approximate timing. Receipts in a particular currency are used to make payments in that currency, thereby reducing the need for a group of companies to go through the foreign exchange markets to the unmatched portion of foreign currency cash flows.

The prerequisite for a matching operation is a two-way cash flow in the same foreign currency within a group of companies; this gives rise to a potential for natural matching. This should be distinguished from parallel matching, in which the matching is achieved with receipt and payment in different currencies but these currencies are expected to move closely together, near enough in parallel. An example would be currencies that adhere to a joint currency float. Of course, there is always the chance with parallel matching that the currencies concerned may move away from their previously parallel paths. In this case the expected match fails to be realised.

The practical mechanics of matching are rather like multilateral netting, since it involves the group treasury and gives rise to the need for information centralisation with the group finance function just before settlement. Practical problems may arise because of the uncertain timing of third-party receipts and payments. Unexpected delays can create problems for the multinational treasury in its endeavours to match receipts and payments. There are obvious difficulties in the possibility that receipt of a sum due on a certain settlement day is postponed, but payment is nonetheless made on that same date as originally anticipated.

For this reason, success in matching is very much a function of the quality of information coming to the corporate financial centre, including realistic and accurate predictions of settlement dates. Like netting, the extent of matching is constrained by the exchange controls of some countries.

10.3 Leading and lagging

Leading and lagging refer to the adjustment of credit terms between companies. They are most usually applied with respect to payments between associate companies within a group. Leading means paying an obligation in advance of the due date. Lagging means delaying payment of an obligation beyond its due date. Leading and lagging are aggressive foreign exchange management tactics designed to take advantage of expected devaluations and **revaluations** of currencies.

An example may help to indicate the processes involved. Suppose that subsidiary b in country B owes money to subsidiary a in country A with payment due in three months' time and with the debt denominated in US$. Suppose further that country B's currency is expected to devalue within three months relative to the US$ and also *vis-à-vis* country A's currency. Obviously, if company B leads – that is, if it pays early – it will have to part with less of country B's currency to buy US$ in order to make payment to company A. So the temptation to lead is attractive.

However, decision takers need to look a little further than this. Should the international Fisher effect be holding in the short term, then the interest rate on deposits in country B's currency should exceed the interest rate on US$ deposits by the amount of the expected devaluation. Decisions on leading and lagging need to take account of relative interest rates as well as expected currency movements. And there is a third relevant dimension, namely the effective tax rates on interest in differing countries. So reverting to our example, we need to compare the net-of-tax cash flow effects after allowing for interest from a group standpoint. Thus, should company b lead, it will save in terms of country B's currency by beating the impending devaluation. But the group will then receive a US$ interest rate rather than an interest rate based on the currency of country B – and this US$ interest rate should be lower than that of country B's currency. All of this has to be taken into account on a net-of-tax basis over the period of the lead.

A similar example could be devised which would suggest lagging. Should country B's currency be expected to revalue or harden against the US$, then lagging would, on the face of things, be suggested. But once again, as is always the case with leading and lagging decisions, we need to consider from a group standpoint the combined impacts of:

- the expected currency change and its timing;
- relative interest rates;
- after-tax effects.

As with matching, the group treasury is usually involved to ensure that the timing of intercompany settlement is functional from a group standpoint rather than merely from a local one. It is also worth mentioning that performance measurement may be affected if some subsidiaries are asked to lead and some to lag. Clearly, the subsidiary that does the leading loses interest receivable and incurs interest charges on the funds led. To overcome this problem, evaluation of performance is frequently done on a pre-interest, pre-tax basis.

The existence of local minority interests gives rise to complications on leading and lagging decisions. Significant local shareholders in the 'losing' subsidiary always raise strong objections because of the added interest costs and lower profitability resulting from the consequent local borrowing. In such cases, the interests of the minority shareholders appear to be subordinated to those of the majority shareholder, the parent company. The existence of strong local minorities frequently results in companies refraining from lead and lag techniques.

Leading and lagging may also be constrained by exchange control regulations. Leading and lagging affect balance of payments figures as well as exchange rates. Because of this, host governments frequently impose allowable bands on credit terms which must be followed in all international trading.

The application of leading and lagging techniques extends beyond the realm of pure risk minimisation in exposure management. Opportunities are created for taking aggressive stances on financing. It should be understood that this aggressive strategy is based upon the view, borne out by empirical evidence, that the international Fisher effect does not hold in the short term. Thus an expected devaluation in a host country would probably cause an international company to consider raising local finance to repay borrowings denominated in foreign currency.

10.4 Pricing policy

In exposure management terms, pricing policy embraces two strategies: price variation and currency of invoicing. Under these headings there are two subsets which are functions of whether trading is with third parties or inside a group of companies. Each of these is now considered.

Price variation

Price variation involves increasing selling prices to counter the adverse effects of exchange rate changes. This tactic raises the question as to why the company has not already raised prices if it is able to do so. In some countries, price increases are the only legally available tactic of exposure management. In most South American countries, for example most other methods are illegal, there is no forward market and local financial markets are so shallow as to make borrowing with the objective of achieving exposure management impossible.

We now turn to price variation on intercompany trade. Transfer pricing is the term used to refer to the pricing of goods and services that change hands within a group of companies. As an exposure management technique, transfer price variation refers to the arbitrary pricing of intercompany sales of goods and services at a higher or lower price than the fair, **arm's-length price**. This fair price would be the market price if there were an existing market or, if there is not, the price which would be charged to a third-party customer. Taxation authorities, customs and excise departments and exchange control regulations in most countries require that arm's length pricing be used. In virtually all countries in the world, tax authorities have the power to impute a price where transfer price manipulation is suspected, and customs and excise departments base excise duty on an imputed price when the transfer price is not considered to be a fair one.

Having said all this, many multinationals nonetheless attempt to maximise after-tax group cash flows by transfer pricing to minimise tax payable.

Invoicing in foreign currency

Companies engaged in exporting and importing, whether of goods or services, are concerned with decisions relating to the currency in which goods and services are to be invoiced. Trading in a foreign currency gives rise to transaction exposure with its attendant risks and opportunities. Although trading purely in a company's home currency has the advantage of simplicity, it fails to take account of the fact that the currency in which goods are invoiced has become an essential aspect of the overall marketing package given to the customer.

A seller will usually wish to sell in its own currency or the currency in which it incurs cost; this avoids foreign exchange exposure. But buyers' preferences might be for other currencies. Many markets, such as oil or aluminium, effectively require that sales be made in the same currency as that quoted by major competitors, which may not be the seller's own currency. In a buyers' market, sellers increasingly tend to invoice in the buyer's ideal currency. The closer the seller can approximate the buyer's aims, the greater chance it has to make the sale.

Should the seller elect to invoice in foreign currency, perhaps because its prospective customer prefers it that way, or because sellers tend to follow the market leader, then the seller should only choose a major currency in which there is an active forward market for maturities at least as long as the payment period. Currencies that are of limited **convertibility**, are chronically weak, or have only a limited forward market in London should not be considered.

Where there is the prospect of a major export to a country with a small economy, such that the value of the contract is likely to be a significant factor in that country's balance of payments, then further considerations apply. The seller is advised to avoid the buyer's currency. Where the government or one of its agencies is the customer, it behoves the seller to bear in mind that the customer itself is able to devalue the currency prior to payment, effectively reducing proceeds in the currency of the exporter.

The seller's ideal currency is either its own or one that is stable relative to its own. Often the seller is forced to choose the market leader's currency. Anyway the chosen currency should certainly be one with a deep forward market.

But for the buyer, the ideal currency is usually its own or one that is stable relative to its own, or it may be a currency of which it has reserves or a currency in which it earns reserves.

Strong buyers may be in a position to insist on their own currency being used for pricing; it is often a condition of any deal and quotes in other currencies are simply ignored. An advantage to the seller when selling in the purchaser's currency is that payment is rendered simpler for the buyer; all it must do is make a payment in its own currency. In these circumstances payment is usually much more rapid, and this may constitute good reason for invoicing in the buyer's currency.

Of course, many international traders seek to buy in the same currencies as those in which they receive income, in order to net out exposure at source. This will not necessarily be their home currency. Furthermore, many markets are economically structured in such a way that competitors follow the market leader. In such circumstances it is often the practice of participants to quote in the same currency as that in which the market leader quotes – and this may be the home currency of neither the buyer nor the seller.

Occasionally, it happens that the invoice currency becomes a bone of contention between seller and buyer. Often a proxy currency – that is, one that moves similarly to the buyer's currency – is resorted to as a way of resolving the impasse. Another technique, which was popular in the past although it is less frequently used now, is a currency clause whereby payment is made in one currency but the amount due is fixed by reference to another.

Usually in export contracts at least one party enters into a foreign exchange transaction. It may be the exporter if it is selling in a foreign currency; it may be the importer if it is buying in a currency other than its own. If the currency of the contract is not the home currency of either the importer or the exporter, then both will have to undertake a foreign exchange transaction. Given this background it is eminently sensible to arrange matters such that the cost of doing the foreign exchange contract is minimised. Foreign currency markets within Europe vary widely in their competitiveness and spread or commission structure. For example, French exchange controls used to require that a French company did its foreign exchange deals with a bank in France where costs were high by London standards. The same was true in Scandinavian countries. For those who are able to access it, the London market is the cheapest foreign exchange market to deal in throughout the world. If one of the parties to a trade is based in a country where exchange controls make it relatively expensive to use local foreign exchange markets, it may be wise to structure the deal such that the cheaper London market may be accessed. This is pertinent for intergroup trading. For example, assume that Ruritania (or another fictitious country) has exchange controls. For an Anglo-Ruritanian trade it may be worthwhile to invoice in the Ruritanian currency so that no foreign exchange transaction arises in Ruritania and the foreign exchange deal takes place in London.

The arguments set out above relate to marketing aspects of the question of invoicing in foreign currency. None relates to aspects such as seeking to invoice in strong currencies, which is an issue that seems to concern a great number of companies. Our view is that, in countries without exchange controls, devoting time to seeking to invoice in strong currencies is a waste of effort, since if the company wishes to be long in particular currencies it is free to buy these whether or not there is any underlying trade. Forward markets, futures, currency swaps and currency options all provide scope for the aggressive company to take positions in currencies if its top management so desires. This would seem to be a more direct method of backing one's judgement on currencies without involving directly the basic business operations of the company.

Having said this, there are commercial reasons why a company in a country with or without exchange controls might prefer to use a strong currency as the medium in which it invoices in international trade. The most frequently quoted reason is to enable the firm to maintain stable price lists in circumstances where price lists are expensive to alter. In countries with exchange controls, it is usually the case that trade represents the only mechanism by which a company is able, legally, to take positions in foreign currencies.

Many companies with strong positions in markets where they are under short-term pressure from competitors may decide to invoice in a currency expected to be weak. Thus, as the currency of invoicing depreciates, so the customer receives an increasing discount on the goods without the company formally announcing a price cut. This tactic enables the company to protect market share while market conditions are poor. Conversely, a company in a strong market position in a sellers' market might, in the short term, specify a strong currency for invoicing, thus obtaining the benefit of a continuously rising price in the home currency without formally changing its prices.

In countries where exchange controls limit the taking of positions in foreign currencies, international companies use cross-frontier trade as one of the very few mechanisms available to back their commercial judgement on future exchange rate movements. In these circumstances, and with respect to third-party trade, the defensive strategy is to attempt to invoice all exports and to have all imports invoiced in the home currency irrespective of the strength and weakness of other currencies. By contrast, the aggressive tactic is to seek to invoice export sales in hard currencies and seek to obtain purchases invoiced in relatively soft currencies. When exchange controls are in place and forward markets are expensive to use, the currency of invoicing technique becomes pertinent. Customers frequently seek to buy goods in weak currencies, while the selling company may prefer to invoice in strong currencies. So there is a clear conflict of interests. Marketing executives may prefer to close a sale by whatever means possible and may be functionally influenced to choose the weak currency, while this policy is dysfunctional from a total company standpoint. Evidently, there should be some marketing systems control mechanism which prevents this dysfunctional tactic.

We now turn to currency of invoicing in the context of intercompany trade. Analysed from a pre-tax point of view, the distinction between aggressive and defensive currency of invoicing disappears when looking at intercompany trade between subsidiaries of equal ownership status, but this is not so where there are minority interests. Currency of invoicing is a **zero-sum game** and therefore the potential benefit to one subsidiary from currency of invoicing equals the potential loss to the other. However, after-tax effects must never be left out of our decision-making criteria and in this context there may be gains to be achieved from currency of invoicing techniques. Consider two subsidiaries, A and B (both in different countries), which trade with each other. Suppose that A pays a higher marginal tax rate than B. In these circumstances, and with all other things being equal, A might logically invoice B in a weak currency while B invoices A in a strong currency. This policy concentrates exchange profits in B and puts losses into A, hence increasing overall after-tax income and cash flow.

10.5 Asset and liability management

We now consider the final internal technique of exposure management: asset and liability management. This technique can be used to manage balance sheet, income statement or cash flow exposures. As stated earlier, we believe that concentration on cash flow exposure makes economic sense but emphasis on pure translation exposure is misplaced. Hence, our focus here is on asset/liability management as a cash flow exposure management technique. However, there are many other texts that take the other and, in our opinion, ill-conceived view that asset/liability management should be applied to non-cash flow exposure management.

In essence, asset/liability management can involve aggressive or defensive postures. In the aggressive attitude, the firm simply increases exposed cash inflows denominated in currencies expected to be stronger and increases exposed cash outflows denominated in weak currencies. By contrast, the defensive approach involves matching cash inflows and outflows according to their currency of denomination, irrespective of whether they are in strong or weak currencies.

Commentators frequently distinguish between operating variables and financing variables. This distinction is useful from an asset/liability standpoint. Manipulation of operating variables to manage cash flow exposure can best be illustrated by an example. Suppose that a UK exporter with an ongoing inflow from sales in US dollars wishes to avoid the dollar exposure. It will most probably use the forward market to do this. However, it might decide to source a significant volume of purchases from the United States, or, at least, denominated in US dollars. By adopting this policy there is a partial match of currency denomination of inflow with currency denomination of outflow.

With respect to financing variables, the international company has considerable discretion in terms of asset/liability management. The aggressive stance will be to increase exposed cash, debtors and loans receivable in strong currencies (taking due consideration of interest impact, potential currency movements and tax effects) and to increase borrowings and trade creditors in weak currencies (again allowing for interest effects, potential currency depreciation and tax impacts). At the same time, policy will involve reducing exposed borrowings and trade creditors in strong currencies and reducing cash, debtors and loans receivable in weak currencies. In the multinational company operating in a country with a weak currency, the aim will be to acquire local debt and remit cash balances as quickly as possible to the hard currency parent either as dividend remittances or as parent loan repayments. The capital structure of subsidiaries based in countries with a weak currency may be organised to facilitate transfer of funds. For example, retained earnings may not be capitalised so that dividend flexibility is maintained by keeping up revenue reserves. Also a high ratio of intercompany debt to parent equity in the subsidiary company's capital structure might help the repatriation of money in circumstances where a high dividend payment might be restricted or discriminated against tax-wise.

However, some of these financial strategies are constrained in many countries by a paucity of local financial sources. Furthermore, host governments often impose limits for debt to equity ratios and restrict dividend repatriation to certain percentages of capital raised outside of the host country. Host governments frequently also penalise, with heavy taxes, dividends in excess of certain stipulated levels.

Summary

- Internal techniques of exposure management are those that do not resort to special contractual relationships outside the group of companies concerned. Such techniques include netting, matching, leading and lagging, pricing policies and asset/liability management.

- Netting involves associated companies with debts, possibly as a result of trade with each other. Associate companies simply cancel out amounts owed with amounts due and settle for the difference. At its simplest level, there is bilateral netting; at a more sophisticated level, we have multilateral netting. Either way, the group treasury plays an active part in co-ordinating settlement payments between associated companies. Netting reduces banking costs. It has been estimated that savings of approximately one-sixth of 1 per cent of the flows eliminated are likely to accrue from netting.
- Matching is a term applied to a similar technique which involves not just affiliates but also third parties.
- Leading and lagging are techniques that are resorted to in the light of expected devaluations or revaluations. These mechanisms simply involve making an advance payment or delaying payment on amounts due and denominated in foreign currency. The basic idea is to reduce the amount of local currency needed to settle a debt. It should be noted that it is necessary to take into account the effects of interest payments and receipts when considering the implementation of a leading or lagging tactic.
- Pricing policy, used as an exposure management technique, simply involves increasing prices to allow for expected changes in exchange rates or invoicing in a particular currency to reduce the risk associated with invoicing in the host currency when a devaluation is expected.
- Asset and liability management, used in the context of exposure management, involves manipulation of operating or financial variables to balance the currency of payments with the currency of inflows. Thus, a UK subsidiary may raise Canadian dollar finance with a view to offsetting, partially, the fact that its sales are denominated in Canadian dollars. It takes on a Canadian dollar liability to balance the Canadian dollar asset.

End of chapter questions

10.1 What is netting and how can it improve an MNC's performance?

10.2 How can an MNC implement leading and lagging techniques to help subsidiaries in need of funds?

11 External techniques of exposure management

External techniques of exposure management resort to contractual relationships outside a group of companies to reduce the risk of foreign exchange losses. External techniques include forward exchange contracts, short-term borrowing, financial **futures contracts**, currency options, discounting bills receivable, factoring receivables, currency overdrafts, currency swaps and government exchange risk guarantees. Each of these, bar currency swaps, financial futures and currency options, is briefly considered in this chapter.

11.1 Forward markets

Forward markets are available in most, but not all, major currencies of the world. Although in some markets very large sums may be difficult to deal, forward markets for periods out to 10 years are available for popular currencies such as the US dollar against sterling, Swiss francs, yen, guilders, Canadian dollars, euros and so on. Generally speaking, the larger the deal, the longer the settlement date is away and the more exotic the currencies involved, the less is the likelihood that a forward contract is obtainable.

A forward foreign exchange contract is an agreement between two parties to exchange one currency for another at some future date. The rate at which the exchange is to be made, the delivery date and the amounts involved are fixed at the time of the agreement. Such a contract must be distinguished from a foreign exchange futures contract and a brief definition is given here. A futures foreign exchange contract is a contract between two parties for the exchange of a standardised amount of foreign currency at a standard future date. On most financial futures exchanges, the sterling/US dollar contract is for £62,500 with delivery dates in most markets fixed for a specified day in the contract month, which may be either March, June, September or December. A forward contract is usually completed by actual delivery of the currency involved. Futures contracts are more usually closed out by completing a deal in the reverse direction before the **maturity date** – rather than actually taking delivery on the delivery date.

Reference was made in Chapter 4 to the methods by which bankers quote forward rates. It may be worthwhile briefly revising the content of that chapter.

11.2 Trading purpose of the forward market

By entering into a forward foreign exchange contract, a UK importer or exporter is able to fix, at the time of the contract, a price for the purchase or sale of a fixed amount of foreign currency for delivery and payment at a specified future time. By so doing they may eliminate foreign exchange risk through future exchange rate fluctuations. This enables the exact sterling value of an international commercial contract to be calculated despite the fact that payment is to be made in the future in a foreign currency. Table 11.1 indicates the mechanism of forward cover.

If a foreign currency stands at premium in the forward market, it shows that the currency is 'stronger' than the home currency in that forward market. By contrast, if a foreign currency stands at a discount in the forward market, it shows that the currency is 'weaker' than the home currency in that forward market. The words stronger and weaker are put in inverted commas because, in the context of forward markets, strength and weakness merely take account of interest rate differentials as suggested by **interest rate parity.**

Of course, the reality of the business world is such that one cannot be certain when a customer will pay a bill. He or she may pay before the due date or may pay afterwards. In the example in Table 11.1 it was assumed that the customer in Jansland (a fictitious non-eurozone country) would pay on 31 July 2012, that is three months after invoice date.

Table 11.1 Forward cover example

Contract data	
Seller	UK exporter
Buyer	Importer in Jansland
Contract date	1 May 2012
Credit term	3 months
Expected payment date	31 July 2012
Invoice value	Geld 5m (the geld is the currency of Jansland)
Exchange rates quotes at 1 May 2012	
Spot	$7.92^3/_4$–$7.93^1/_2$ (geld $7.92^3/_4$–$7.93^1/_2$ to the £)
1 month forward	$3^7/_8$–$3^1/_2$ cpm (100 cents = 1 geld)
2 months forward	$6^3/_4$–$6^1/_8$ cpm
3 months forward	$9^5/_8$–$8^7/_8$ cpm
4 months forward	$12^1/_2$–$11^5/_8$ cpm
Outright exchange rate quotes at 1 May 2012	
Spot	$7.92^3/_4$–$7.93^1/_2$
1 month forward	$7.88^7/_8$–7.90
2 months forward	7.86–$7.87^3/_8$
3 months forward	$7.83^1/_8$–$7.84^5/_8$
4 months forward	$7.80^1/_4$–$7.81^7/_8$
Mechanism of forward contract	
1 May 2012	UK exporter sells geld 5m forward 3 months at $7.84^5/_8$
31 July 2012	UK exporter receives geld 5m from Jansland importer
	UK exporter delivers geld 5m and receives sterling at the rate of geld $7.84^5/_8$ equals £1
	For geld 5m he receives £637,755

Let us suppose now that the Jansland purchaser is expected to pay on some uncertain date between 30 June and 31 August 2012.

Forward options

The UK exporter may decide to cover despite an uncertain payment date via a forward option. How does the forward option work? Like all forward contracts, the exchange rate is irrevocably fixed when the contract is made, but with a **forward option contract** the precise maturity date is left open – it is for the company to decide subsequently. There is a caveat though; the maturity date must fall within a specified option period. Reverting to our numerical example, assume that the UK exporter expects payment between 30 June and 31 August 2012 – that is between two and four months from invoice date. Since the bank giving the option as to timing does not know exactly when exercise of the option will occur, it charges the premium or discount for the most costly of the settlement dates within the customer's option period. In other words, the bank charges its customer the worst rate during the option period. In our example, the forward option is over the third and fourth months. In Table 11.1 it will be seen that the rate is therefore geld $7.87^{3}/_{8}$; in this case (but not always) the rate to the seller of geld is the full two months' discount. This is the worst rate between month 2 and month 4 for selling geld.

It should be clearly understood that the forward option contract, or optional date forward contract as it is sometimes called, is not a currency option. The forward option is optional in terms of the date of delivery – currency must be delivered under the contract. However, under a currency option, currency need not be delivered.

Swap deals

Another method of dealing with unspecified settlement dates is by a swap deal. This method is virtually always cheaper than covering by way of forward options. A **swap** involves the simultaneous buying and selling of a currency for different maturities. Swap deals used for forward cover are of two basic types: forward/forward and spot/forward. In either case, the exporter begins by covering the foreign currency transaction forward to an arbitrarily selected but fixed date, just as in an ordinary fixed-date forward contract. Then, if the precise settlement date is subsequently agreed before the initial forward contract matures, the original settlement date may be extended to the exact date by a **forward/forward swap**. Alternatively, if an exact settlement date is not agreed by the date when the initial forward contract matures, the forward cover may be extended by a **spot/forward swap**. This may sound quite complicated; a closer look shows that it is not all that difficult.

A forward/forward swap, or forward swap as it is sometimes called, is merely a pair of forward exchange contracts involving a forward purchase and a forward sale of a currency, simultaneously entered into but for different maturities. A numerical example may help describe how the forward/forward swap works.

Assume that the details of an export contract from the United Kingdom to Jansland are as set out in Table 11.1 except that the expected settlement date is uncertain (maybe because delivery date is equally uncertain). The UK exporter takes out a forward contract on 1 May 2012 (the date of the sale contract with the Jansland importer). This forward contract is for an arbitrary period, say two months. So he or she sells geld 5m forward for delivery on 30 June 2012. Now let us suppose that on 20 June 2012, the UK exporter and the Jansland purchaser agree that settlement will take place on 31 July 2012. What the UK exporter needs to do now is to counter the original forward sale of geld for settlement on 30 June and replace it with a contract for delivery on 31 July. This he or she does by buying geld 5m forward for delivery on 30 June (thereby creating a contra to the original forward sale of geld) and simultaneously selling geld 5m forward 41 days, thereby extending delivery to 31 July. Let us further assume that on 20 June 2012, the bank gives the UK exporter the following quotes:

Spot	7.94–7.95
10 days forward	$^1/_4$c–$^1/_2$c discount
1 month forward	$^1/_2$c–$^3/_4$c discount
41 days forward	$^3/_4$c–1c discount

Turning these quotes into full forward data, remembering that the bid/offer spread is wider in the forward market than in the spot market, we obtain:

Spot	7.94–7.95
10 days forward	7.9425–7.9550
1 month forward	7.9450–7.9575
41 days forward	7.9475–7.9600

Thus the overall covering mechanism can be seen to involve the following:

1 May 2012	Sell geld 5m for £ forward 2 months at 7.87$^3/_8$ (delivery 30 June 2012)	£635,021
20 June 2012	Buy geld 5m for £ forward 10 days at 7.9425 (delivery 30 June 2012)	(629,525)
20 June 2012	Sell geld 5m for £ forward 41 days at 7.96 (delivery 31 July 2012)	628,141
	Net sterling proceeds	£633,637

As can be seen from the above, leg two of the total mechanism reverses leg one. Legs two and three are the opposite sides of the forward swap.

The effect of the above forward swap deal is that the UK exporter has locked in as of 1 May 2012 at the forward rate for two months' cover adjusted for the premium/discount for a further month given by the bid/offer spread incurred on the forward/forward swap. Of course, as at May 2012 the exporter does not know what the premium/discount will be on extending the contract, neither will he or she know what the bid/offer spread will be on the swap. The unknown premium/discount is a function of interest rate differentials prevailing on Eurosterling and Euro-geld at the date when the forward swap is done.

This forward swap deal will mean that on the first two legs the UK exporter makes a profit which will be received from the bank on 30 June 2012. The UK exporter's cash flow on the foreign exchange cover becomes:

30 June 2012	Profit received from bank	£ 5,496
31 July 2012	Sale of receivable at 7.96	628,141
		£633,637

Rather than doing a forward/forward deal the bank would be prepared to roll the contract for their customer. Rolling this old contract forward would work as follows. The market rate for rolling the contract forward by one month is 1.75 centimes (7.96 less

7.9425). So the bank will adjust the original forward deal by 1.75 centimes. For settlement on 31 July 2012, the bank would charge 7.89¹/₈ and the sterling proceeds, payable on 31 July 2012 would be:

$$\frac{5,000,000}{7.89125} = £633,613$$

This amount is approximately the same as from the forward/forward swap. Differences are frequently much greater than the small variation in our example. However, the rolling process illustrated above is approximate and it can cost the bank's customer dear at times. The swap mechanism is always cheaper for the customer.

A spot/forward swap is similar to a forward swap. It again involves a simultaneous pair of foreign exchange contracts, one of which is a spot contract while the other is a forward contract. Reverting to our numerical example, the original forward deal would be for the arbitrarily set two-month period. But the exporter would wait until 30 June 2012 to reverse this deal and to extend maturity to the expected settlement date, namely 31 July 2012. The mechanism might then be summarised as:

1 May 2012	Sell geld 5m for £ forward 2 months at $7.87^3/_8$ (delivery 30 June)	£635,021
30 June 2012	Buy geld 5m for £ spot at (say) 8.05	(621,118)
30 June 2012	Sell geld 5m for £ forward 31 days at (say) 8.0725 (delivery 31 July 2012)	619,387
	Net sterling proceeds	£633,290

The above figuring assumes the spot rate to buy geld as of 30 June 2012 had moved to 8.0500 and the one-month forward rate as of that date had become 8.0725 to sell geld for sterling. Had the customer rolled the old contract forward on 30 June 2012, the proceeds as of 31 July would have been:

$$\frac{5,000,000}{7.89625} = £633,212$$

Again, this is not far out compared with the spot/forward method.

In practice, the forward/forward or spot/forward swap is the preferred method of dealing with uncertain settlement dates. But the option forward contract is a useful mechanism for dealing with a continuing stream of foreign currency payments or receipts. Where a firm's sales include a large number of small transactions denominated in foreign currency terms, it is expensive both in transaction and administrative costs to cover each individual deal. This problem may be overcome by taking out a single, large forward option contract to cover the approximate expected total cash value of the large number of different receivables or payables. Although the large number of small exports would normally have different settlement dates, forward options are ideally suited to this kind of situation. The amount of the forward contract is usually rounded off. Because of this, it is usually necessary to close out bulk forward contracts of this sort by a spot purchase or sale to balance amounts due from or to the bank.

As an example, assume that a UK exporter is sending goods to Koudland (a fictitious non-euro zone country). The exporter is expecting a series of Koudland kas receipts during the course of the six months from 10 January to 10 July. This rough total is estimated at kas 10m. To cover this, the exporter sells kas 10m on a six-month forward option with the option over the whole period. Assume that the rate is kas 15.61 to the pound and that the Koudland kas receipts delivered from proceeds of sales are as follows:

Feb 16	kas 2.4m @ 15.61 = £153,748
Mar 21	kas 2.6m @ 15.61 = 166,560
June 16	kas 3.1m @ 15.61 = 198,591
June 21	kas 1.5m @ 15.61 = 96,092
Sterling proceeds from	kas 9.6m @ 15.61 = £614,991

Thus the exporter has delivered kas 9.6m. If no more kas receipts come in from sales up to 10 July, the exporter must close out the deal by buying in kas 400,000 in the spot market on that date and delivering this against the balance of the forward option contract. If the spot rate on 10 July is kas 15.25, then the receipts for the forward option come out at:

Sterling proceeds from sale of kas 9.6m (as above)	£614,991
Cost of buying in kas 0.4m on 10 July at spot rate of kas 15.25	(26,230)
Sterling proceeds from sale of kas 0.4m at kas 15.61	25,625
Net sterling proceeds	£614,386

Had our exporter actually received in excess of the kas 10m during the forward option period, the excess would be sold spot for sterling.

11.3 Short-term borrowing

Short-term borrowing provides an alternative way of covering a receivable or payable denominated in a foreign currency. The availability of this technique as a practical tool of exposure management is subject to local credit availability and transactions must conform to **exchange controls**, which may restrict its use.

The mechanism is best illustrated by a numerical example and for this purpose we return to the data in Table 11.1. Our UK exporter had a three-month exposure of geld 5m from the contract date of 1 May 2012, through to settlement date on 31 July 2012. Assume that the exporter decides to use short-term borrowing to cover the transaction exposure. Simultaneously with the signing of the contract, he should borrow a sum in Jansland geld such that with interest the expected receipt of geld 5m in three months' time will repay the principal and accrued interest. This geld sum should be switched immediately to sterling via the spot market. With Jansland geld three-month interest rates equal to $5^3/_{32}$ per cent p.a., the sum to borrow would be geld 4,937,129 since this would mean that geld 5m would be payable to clear the loan and interest in three months' time. Converting the borrowing to sterling at the spot rate of geld 7.935 = £1 would yield £622,196 and if this were immediately put on deposit at the UK investment rate of 10 per cent p.a., this would grow to £637,751 (given by £622,196 × 1.025) at the end of three months. This is approximately the same as the yield on the forward transaction (see Table 11.1).

In practice, it might be the case that our exporter decided to borrow geld 5m on the signing of the contract and at the same date to buy geld 63,672 forward (made up as geld 5m × $5^3/_{32}$ × $^3/_{12}$). He would simultaneously sell the geld 5m for sterling via the spot market. Thus the UK exporter is completely covered against exchange risk. On 31 July 2012 the UK company receives geld 5m from its Jansland customer and this is used to repay principal of the Jansland geld borrowing. The exporter simultaneously receives geld 63,672 from the forward contract and this amount is used to cover accrued interest. All these transactions can be tied in at rates determined on 1 May 2012. Then rates are unaffected by subsequent currency and/or interest rate movements over the exposure period. If the proceeds of the geld 5m borrowing are switched to sterling at the spot rate on 1 May 2012, the overall proceeds of the deal are as follows:

1 May 2012	Borrow geld 5m at $5^3/_{32}$% p.a. Buy geld 63,672 forward 3 months at $7.83^1/_8$ Sell geld 5m spot to give £630,120 at $7.93^1/_2$ Invest £630,120 for 3 months at 10% p.a.	
31 July 2012	Receive geld 5m from customer; use this to repay principal of loan Deliver geld 63,672 to cover loan interest	
	This comes from forward contract	(£8,131)
	Receive proceeds of sterling loan given by £630,120 at 10% p.a. for 3 months	645,873
	Net sterling proceeds	£637,742

The slightly different proceeds from this transaction arise because the amount borrowed is geld 5m as opposed to geld 4.937m.

By this kind of mechanism, any receivable or payable which can be covered by a forward contract may be covered by short-term borrowing, assuming credit is available and that exchange controls do not prohibit any leg of the transaction.

Just as we looked at imprecise settlement dates and how to cover these via a forward option, so we can cover this eventuality by taking an overdraft type of loan. Rather than doing a forward option for, say, between three and six months, we could arrange an overdraft borrowing for the amount of a receivable for a period of up to six months and remit the proceeds of the borrowing via the spot market to the home country. A complication arises because interest rates on overdraft loans float up and down. Consequently, interest payable cannot be tied in for certain. Interest is usually catered for by a spot transaction, after the event, namely at the date when the borrowing is repaid. But by the same token, the proceeds of the borrowing remitted to the home country via the spot market will earn interest and this will vary according to market conditions in the home country. The interest payable and receivable may both be left to market conditions at floating rates.

Earlier in this chapter we considered briefly how a continuing stream of foreign currency exposures could be covered using the forward market. This kind of situation can also be covered via short-term borrowing. The company in the home country arranges a borrowing facility in the currency of invoicing. This technique can be used simultaneously to handle the problems of continuing foreign currency exposures and uncertain settlement dates. Assume that we have a UK exporter with a continuing stream of Koudland kas export receipts. These can be covered by arranging a fixed rate kas borrowing. When each export contract is finalised, the exporter immediately draws down the kas loan by the amount of the sale and converts the proceeds into sterling. As the receivables are settled, the kas are paid into the exporter's kas account so that the borrowing is reduced. As long as the kas borrowing rate is fixed over the exposure term, the receivable is fully covered against exchange risk.

11.4 Discounting foreign-currency-denominated bills receivable

Discounting can be used to cover export receivables. Where an export receivable is to be settled by a bill of exchange, the exporter may discount the bill and thereby receive payment before the settlement date. The bill may either be discounted with a bank in the customer's country, in which case the foreign currency proceeds can be repatriated immediately at the current spot rate, or it can be discounted with a bank in the exporter's country so that the exporter may receive settlement direct in home currency. Either way, the exporter is covered against exchange risk, the cost being the discount rate charged by the bank.

11.5 Factoring foreign-currency-denominated receivables

Like discounting, factoring can be used for covering export receivables. When the export receivable is to be settled on open account, rather than by a bill of exchange, the receivable can be assigned as collateral for bank financing. Normally such a service gives protection against exchange rate changes, though during unsettled periods in the foreign exchange markets appropriate variations in the factoring agreement are usual. Commercial banks and specialised factoring institutions offer factoring services. For the exporter the technique is very straightforward: he simply sells his export receivables to the factor and receives home currency in return. The costs involved include credit risks, the cost of financing, and the cost of covering exchange risk. For these reasons, factoring tends to be an expensive means of covering exposure, although there may be offsetting benefits such as obtaining export finance and reducing sales accounting and credit collection costs.

11.6 Currency overdrafts

Overdrafts in Eurocurrencies are available in the London money markets in all of the major currencies although banks tend to specialise by currency. The US dollar and the euro are the currencies in which the greatest amounts are advanced.

In terms of avoidance of exposure, all that a company needs to do is to maintain the amount of its foreign currency receivables in a particular currency equal to the balance on the overdraft in that currency. However, if the company uses the proceeds of the receivables to run down the overdraft, then it also needs to draw down the foreign currency loan as sales denominated in foreign currency are made. Some companies find it more convenient to sell the proceeds of foreign-denominated receivables spot rather than to be perpetually adjusting the level of the overdraft. However, if the level of the currency overdraft remains constant, there is an assumption that new sales denominated in foreign currency are exactly offsetting incoming foreign receipts. This may not be realistic. If this is the case then, even with this method, it becomes necessary to refer to the level of foreign currency receivables and increase or run down the overdraft to ensure that exposure is being covered.

The currency overdraft is a particularly useful and economical technique of exposure management where a company carries a large number of small items denominated in foreign currency, all with uncertain payment dates.

In some countries, use of the currency overdraft exposure management technique may be limited by exchange controls which prevent residents from using foreign-currency-denominated bank accounts.

Another similar technique is the currency bank account. This is particularly useful where a company engaged in international trade has receivables in excess of payables in the same currency. The company opens a foreign-currency-denominated deposit account into which receivables in a particular currency are paid and out of which foreign-denominated payments in that currency are made. For example, should a UK company have a US dollar receivable of $2m due on 31 October and should it also have a payment to be made on 30 November of $1.5m, the company might open a dollar-denominated deposit account into which it pays the $2m. Of this, $\$^1/_2$m would be remitted via a previously arranged forward deal for delivery on 31 October and $\$1^1/_2$m would remain in the account to meet the payment due on 30 November. In addition, at the end of November some interest would have accrued on the US dollar bank account.

This kind of exercise is designed to save making a large number of forward deals which are priced to the bank's customer on the basis of the worst rate during a future period. In the above example, the trader received US dollar interest on the deposit left in the currency account. Had he or she remitted all proceeds from the initial receivable to the UK, he or she could have obtained a UK interest rate on the proceeds. It can be seen that the essential net saving for the company arises from eliminating the bid/offer spread on amounts left in the currency account to meet future payables. However, a careful comparison should be made of the expected proceeds from the currency account technique with both the outturns from doing a large number of forward deals and the payoff from a forward option since the currency account may not always be the best choice. Remember that the pricing of forward deals is based on interbank Eurocurrency interest differentials, and using markets based on these differentials may give a superior result to the reliance on bank deposit accounts.

11.7 Exchange risk guarantees

As part of a series of encouragements to exporters, government agencies in many countries offer their businesses insurance against export credit risks and certain export financing schemes. Many of these agencies offer exchange risk insurance to their exporters as well as the usual export credit guarantees. The exporter pays a small premium and in return the government agency absorbs exchange risk, thereby taking profits and absorbing losses.

The precise details vary from one export finance agency to another and the exact offerings should be checked with various local exchange risk guarantee organisations in the appropriate country concerned, for example Eximbank in the United States, ECGD in Britain and so on. Nowadays, most countries have export credit and other similar government agencies offering to absorb foreign exchange exposure risk on export and import transactions in return for a fee.

11.8 Counterparty risk

In providing forward cover for customers, banks take on risk. And just as they do for loans, they evaluate this risk and set credit limits. In this section we consider how a bank might go about this process of risk evaluation. The risk that the bank runs arises from two areas; the risk on unmatured forward contracts and settlement risk. We consider the risk on unmatured contracts first.

When a bank contracts a forward foreign exchange deal with its customer, it will wish at the same time to enter into an opposite transaction so that the net effect is for the bank to have a square position or balanced book.

If the bank's customer should go bankrupt prior to the maturity of the contract, then the bank knows that it will not receive the funds from the customer to satisfy the matching deal done in the market. The bank will enter the market again to buy in the necessary funds to meet the deal at current exchange rates. This will probably be at a different rate from that at which the original deal was done. This difference will cause the bank to incur either a loss or perhaps a profit resulting from the financial failure of its customer.

Because of this, banks set limits on the extent of the risk they are prepared to run on each customer on their books. This credit assessment is done in the normal manner by reference to the company's balance sheet and other indicators of financial health. Setting a limit for foreign exchange deals is exactly similar to setting a limit for the amount and period of an unsecured loan. But it is less easy to establish the extent of the risk represented by an unmatured forward contract. One might set a limit on the total deals outstanding to each counterparty as a gross total. But clearly this implies that all unmatured deals carry an equal degree of risk. An improvement would be an acceptance that deals with a short maturity involve less risk than longer ones and to allow for that in calculating exposure. In fact, banks have computer programs designed to estimate their exposure to each customer allowing for such factors as past exchange rate volatility as between currencies, period to run to maturity and whether the existing contracts would show a profit or a loss if the customer failed and it became necessary to replace them at ruling market rates.

We now turn to settlement risk. This may arise should the customer fail to deliver the currency concerned to the bank on settlement day and then go bankrupt. The bank's problem is that settlement of a foreign exchange contract is simultaneous – the bank pays away the currency due to the customer or its supplier in expectation of simultaneous receipt from the customer of countervalue. Banks are not usually in a position to ensure that countervalue has been received prior to paying away the currency amount. So if the customer fails just after the bank has paid away currency without receipt of countervalue from the customer, the bank has lost this amount. This kind of risk is only present on and immediately after settlement day up to when settlement is made. Most banks operate a system of settlement limits fixing a maximum amount for the settlement to be made on one date for each customer prior to receipt of countervalue.

Having calculated a limit for a customer, the essence of what banks do in terms of estimating whether a limit is breached is to weight contracts that are near to maturity by a small amount and those far from maturity by a larger figure. Thus a bank might adopt a policy of weighting contracts with one month or less to run to maturity by 0.10, contracts with up to three months to run by 0.15, contracts with up to six months to run by 0.20 and contracts with over six months to run by 0.25.

Summary

- External techniques of exposure management resort to contractual relationships outside a group of companies to reduce the risk of foreign exchange losses.
- External techniques include forward exchange contracts, short-term borrowing and depositing, financial futures contracts, currency options, discounting bills receivable, factoring receivables, currency overdrafts and currency hold accounts, currency swaps and government exchange risk guarantees. Most of these are considered in this chapter, but swaps, financial futures and currency options are considered in Chapters 12, 13, 14 and 15.
- The most well-known external method of exposure management involves the forward contract. This may be used to cover receivables and payables, but it also enables a company or high-net-worth individual to speculate on foreign currency movements.
- Forward markets are available in most major currencies of the world – but by no means all.
- Forward markets are available for periods beyond five years for such currencies as US dollars, sterling, euros, Swiss francs, yen, Canadian dollars, Danish kroner, Swedish kronor and so on. Ten-year forwards are quoted by some banks for many of the above. The forward market may be used to cover a receipt or payment denominated in a foreign currency when the date of receipt for payment is known. But it can be readily adapted to allow for situations when the exact payment date is not known.
- Techniques available to deal with imprecise payments dates include the forward option, the forward/forward swap and the spot/forward swap.
- Note how these three techniques work; a fair amount of space is devoted to them in the main text.
- Note that it is always cheaper to extend the maturity of a forward contract with a forward/forward swap or a spot/forward swap rather than undertaking a forward option in the first place.
- Note that a forward option, or option forward, or option dated forward contract, as it is sometimes called, is not a currency option. A forward option involves a right and an obligation to deal in foreign currency – the option is merely as to timing. In the case of a currency option, the holder has a right but not an obligation to deal at a particular price.
- Short-term, fixed rate borrowing or depositing is another technique for covering foreign-currency-denominated receivables and payables respectively.
- Currency overdrafts and currency hold accounts simply use floating rate borrowing and depositing, respectively, to achieve the same ends as under short-term borrowing or depositing with a fixed rate. The difference is clearly one of interest rate exposure. Floating rate borrowing or depositing clearly gives rise to an interest rate exposure; fixed rate finance does not.
- Note that when a forward contract is extended by a forward/forward swap or a spot/forward swap, the overall effect is to lock in the original forward rate plus or minus the effect of interest rate differences for the period by which the original maturity of the forward contract was extended. If this is not clear, check it out with the numerical example in the main text.

End of chapter questions

11.1 Assume that US Co Inc has net receivables of CHF100,000 in 90 days. The spot rate of the franc is \$.50, and the Swiss interest rate is 2 per cent over 90 days (not 2 per cent per annum). Suggest how US Co Inc could implement a money market hedge.

11.2 Assume that US Co Inc has net payables of 200,000 Ballarian watsits (BLW) in 180 days. The BLW interest rate on deposits is 7 per cent over 180 days (not a per annum rate) and the spot rate of the BLW is \$.10. Suggest how US Co Inc could implement a money market hedge.

11.3 If interest rate parity were to prevail, would a forward hedge be more favourable, equally favourable, or less favourable than a money market hedge on BLW payables in the last question?

Test bank 2

Exercises

1 Manana SA is the Coluvian subsidiary of a US manufacturer. Its local currency balance sheet is shown below. The current exchange rate is 20 pesos to the US dollar.

Figures in million pesos

Shareholders' funds	42	Fixed assets	36
Long-term debt	9	Debtors	12
Current liabilities	3	Cash	6
	54		54

(a) Translate the peso balance sheet of Manana SA into dollars at the existing exchange rate of 20 pesos to the dollar. All monetary items in Manana's balance sheet are denominated in pesos.

(b) If Manana's balance sheet remained as above but the peso moved to 25 pesos per dollar, what would be the translation gain or loss if translated by the monetary/non-monetary method? By the current/non-current method? By the all-current rate method?

(c) If the peso moved to $0.06, what would be the translation gain or loss according to the three accounting translation methods referred to under (b)?

(d) What is Manana's translation exposure under the three accounting methods?

2 Imagine that you have just been appointed treasurer of a consumer goods company. It manufactures only in the United Kingdom, but exports over 50 per cent of its sales. As the market is an international one, you face the same competitors in each national market, including your domestic market. Your major competitors are Japanese and German.

(a) How does your foreign exchange exposure arise?

(b) How would you measure it?

(c) Could your exposure be reduced by investing in manufacturing facilities abroad?

3 Imagine that you work for a company wishing to deal in the foreign exchange markets in Norwegian kroner and US dollars against the pound. The *Financial Times* gives the following quotation $ and NKr against the £:

	US$	**NKr**
Spot	1.2775–1.2785	11.25–11.26
Forward		
1 month	0.56–0.53 cent pm	1/4 ore pm–3/8 dis
2 months	1.03–0.99 pm	1/2–1 1/4 dis
3 months	1.50–1.45 pm	7/8–1 3/4 dis

You notice that Eurocurrency interest rates are as following according to the *FT*:

	Sterling	US$
Short-term	$12^7/_8$–$12^5/_8$	$7^7/_8$–$7^1/_4$
1 month	$12^3/_4$–$12^5/_8$	$7^7/_{16}$–$7^5/_{16}$
3 months	$12^1/_2$–$12^3/_8$	$7^9/_{16}$–$7^7/_{16}$

Assuming that your company's bank gives the same quotation as all of those tabulated above, answer the following:

(a) At what rate would your company sell NKr for sterling three months forward, option over the second and third months?

(b) At what rate would the bank sell NKr for sterling three months forward, option running from day 30 to day 90?

(c) At what rate would the bank sell $ for sterling three months forward, option over the third month?

(d) At what rate would your company sell $ for sterling three months forward, option over the third month?

(e) At what rate would the bank buy NKr one month forward?

(f) At what rate would the bank sell NKr one month forward?

Note: There are 100 ore in 1 krone.

4 Imagine that you work for a company wishing to deal in the foreign exchange markets in Danish krone and US dollars against the pound. The *Financial Times* gives the following quotations $ and DKr against the £:

	US$	DKr
Spot	1.3820–1.2830	$13.85^3/_4$–$13.86^3/_4$
Forward		
1 month	0.26–0.29 dis	0.40 ore pm–0.40 ore dis
2 months	0.50–0.54 dis	0.45 ore pm–0.60 ore dis
3 months	0.80–0.85 dis	0.55 ore pm–0.55 ore dis

You notice that Eurocurrency interest rates are as follows according to the *FT*:

	Sterling	US$
Short-term	9–$8^3/_4$	$10^7/_8$–$10^3/_4$
1 month	$9^1/_4$–$9^1/_8$	$11^1/_4$–$11^1/_8$
3 months	$9^1/_2$–$9^3/_8$	$11^{11}/_{16}$–$11^9/_{16}$

Assuming that your company's bank gives the same quotations as all of those tabulated above, answer the following:

(a) At what rate would your company sell DKr three months forward, option over the second and third months?

(b) At what rate would the bank sell $ three months forward?

(c) At what rate would the bank sell $ three months forward, option over the third month?

(d) At what rate would your company sell $ three months forward, option over the third month?

(e) At what rate would the bank buy DKr two months forward?

(f) At what rate would the bank sell DKr spot?

Note: There are 100 ore in 1 krone.

5 A service company with 100 per cent owned subsidiaries in four countries experiences major cash flows between these subsidiaries. The subsidiaries are in Alphaland, Betaland, Gammaland and Deltaland. The respective countries currencies are the ax, the bon, the cop and the drac. The monthly cash flows are as follows:

Alphaland pays	bon 500,000 to Betaland
	drac 40,000,000 to Deltaland
Betaland pays	ax 250,000 to Alphaland
	drac 60,000,000 to Deltaland
	cop 400,000 to Gammaland
Gammaland pays	bon 600,000 to Betaland
	drac 50,000,000 to Deltaland
Deltaland pays	ax 200,000 to Alphaland
	bon 400,000 to Betaland
	cop 500,000 to Gammaland

where ax 1 = cop 4 = bon 4 = drac 200.

How might this system be improved, and what would be the benefits?

Questions relating to Press Cutting TB

Questions 1 to 10 inclusive draw from the Press Cutting TB (below). Read this before answering the questions. The Press Cutting comes from the *Financial Times* of 11 March 2004 when sterling, and much more so, the euro were experiencing ongoing strength against the US dollar and, indeed, most other currencies.

1. In the column devoted to Heiniken, para 5 states that 'its policy merely deferred the currency impact'. Why should this be so?
2. In the Heineken column, para 8, do you think that Heineken will be pleased with its decision to hedge about 88 per cent of its 2004 net dollar revenues? Why?
3. In the Cannon Avent column, given that the firm has 40 per cent of its sales in the USA (presumably in USD) and two-fifths of its sales to the eurozone (presumably in EUR), why should Edward Atkin, Cannon's managing director and main owner, be worried by foreign exchange risk?
4. In the Cannon Avent column, para 3, is the indication that the USD was stronger against sterling in 2003 versus 2002? Why?
5. In the Cannon Avent column, last para, reference is made to the possibility of setting up a plant in the USA, partially driven by currency considerations. Do you think this is Mr Atkin's best alternative? Why? Why not?
6. In the Atlas Copco column, refer to paras 5 and 6. Do you think Mr Meyer, CFO of Atlas Copco, is correct to view hedging to three or four months as truly hedging but covering beyond four months as speculation? Why?
7. In the Atlas Copco column, last paragraph, it is stated that the firm tries to balance the currency basket of receipts and payments. Do you think that Atlas Copco is currently successful on this score? Why?
8. In the Mittelstand column, para 3, why should quality be a factor in foreign exchange policy?
9. According to the Mittelstand column, how has Süss Microtec managed and acquired flexibility in respect of its foreign exchange exposures? How and why is this important for the profitability of Süss Microtec?
10. In the Luxottica column, in para 4, it is stated that the firm keeps most of its manufacturing in Italy. How does the firm appear to be managing its foreign exchange exposure? Why?

PRESS CUTTING TB

Dispirited Heineken sounds alarm

Ian Bickerton, Amsterdam

The profit warning by Heineken, the world's third-biggest brewer by volume, last month was the clearest indication yet of the impact US dollar exposure is having on Dutch company earnings.

Het Financieele Dagblad, the Dutch financial daily, has calculated that, of 15 blue-chip Netherlands-listed companies to have reported 2003 earnings, exchange rate movements pruned a combined 7 per cent from turnover.

In building a defence against dollar exposure, companies have turned primarily to hedging and restructuring.

ABN Amro, the biggest Dutch bank, where currencies stripped €561m ($685m, £381m) from record operational earnings of €6.2bn and €377m from pre-tax profit of €4.9bn in 2003, has fully hedged expected dollar profits for 2004 and 2005.

While hedging shielded Heineken's earnings to some extent last year, the company noted that its policy merely deferred the currency impact.

Dollar weakness vis-a-vis the euro will wipe out profit gains this year, Heineken said. One third of operating profit comes from North and South America.

Exchange rate movements trimmed €88m from the company's operating earnings of €1.2bn, €42m thanks to the dollar. The dollar impact will be more than four times greater, at the operational level, this year and nearly double last year's hit in 2005.

In 2004 net dollar revenues are estimated at $800m, of which $709m has been hedged at an average of $1.12 to the euro. On that basis the dollar will reduce operating income by €129m and net profit by €84m in 2004 compared with 2003, assuming a spot-rate of $1.28 to the euro for the unhedged portion of Heineken's dollar cash flow.

While it might seem sensible to reduce euro production costs for beer bought in dollars, Heineken says it is cheaper to ship its beer from the Netherlands to the US than produce it locally.

Source: *Financial Times*, 11 March 2004.

Pound sucks profits from babies' bottles

FT

Peter Marsh, London

Babies' bottles might seem unlikely products for a high-technology success story, but this is the way it has turned out for Cannon Avent.

The British-based company makes a range of feeding products for infants and last year converted a fifth of its sales into pre-tax profits, an unusually high ratio for a European manufacturer.

But now the strength of sterling against the dollar is causing a few headaches for Edward Atkin, Cannon's managing director and main owner. With 40 per cent of Cannon's sales last year of £106m (€157m, $193m) sold in the US or other dollar-denominated countries – and all the company's production based in Britain – Mr Atkin says its earnings would have been £1.5m higher in 2003 had currencies stayed level.

Although Cannon can hedge against currency movements to some degree, he is resigned to the dollar remaining weak for at least a few more months, which is likely eat into the company's bottom line a little more.

But in general Mr Atkin – whose company is a big spender on product development and bases its production in a modern factory in rural Suffolk, eastern England – is fairly sanguine about the direction of the US currency.

'I believe it would not take much for the dollar to start strengthening considerably – perhaps some more encouraging news on the US economy, or the capture of Osama bin Laden. In an election year I think [US] President [George W.] Bush will want a stronger currency and this will help.'

Diminishing the impact of the weak dollar is that the euro has been strengthening against the pound. This helps Cannon's exports to continental Europe – which accounts for nearly two-fifths of its sales. As to strategic changes, Mr Atkin is considering setting up a plant in the US, a move that makes sense in the light of the dollar's weakness.

Source: *Financial Times*, 11 March 2004.

Engineer has learnt to juggle currencies

Christopher Brown-Humes, Stockholm

As a large multinational based in a small country, Sweden's Atlas Copco has got used to juggling different currencies over the years.

A weak dollar and strong euro hits the company particularly hard: last year pre-tax profit would have been SKr1bn ($133m, €109m, £74m) higher without adverse currency movements.

The engineering group has more than 40 per cent of its sales in US dollars, and if you add dollar-linked currencies such as the Hong Kong dollar and the Chinese renminbi, the figure rises above 50 per cent. But less than 20 per cent of its manufacturing costs are in dollars, while around 50 per cent are in euros and 20 per cent in Swedish kronor.

On the positive side, the weak dollar has helped the group reduce its dollar debt after a series of acquisitions in the US. 'Our interest-bearing debt shrank by SKr2.5bn last year, purely as an effect of the weakening of the dollar against the krona', says Hans Ola Meyer, chief financial officer.

The company's operating units hedge their currency flows – but on rolling basis and only over the duration from order to payment. That means the group as a whole is only hedging its currency flows over an average of three to four months ahead.

'If we lock in rates further than that, we would be taking a speculative view', says Mr Meyer.

He stresses that the group would not relocate any core manufacturing operation purely because of currency factors. Other considerations – such as closeness to customers and suppliers, or availability of good personnel – weigh more heavily in its thinking. But it does have an impact on sourcing.

'We strive all the time to ensure that the currency basket in which we source is as similar to the revenue basket as possible', he says.

Source: *Financial Times*, 11 March 2004.

Specialist lines help insulate German sales

Peter Marsh, London

Germany is the global home of specialist machinery companies – with Mittelstand (mid-sized) businesses dotted around the country that produce and sell on a global basis machines for doing the most esoteric jobs imaginable in a range of production industries.

It is this characteristic, according to Hans-Günther Vieweg, an engineering expert at the Ifo economics institute in Munich, that has reduced the impact of the dollar's weakness on these companies when they are exporting from Germany.

'Even with their companies' costs being mainly in euros, they are not necessarily all that much affected [by the euro's strength] because they are selling not so much on price but on factors such as quality.'

An example is Süss Microtec, one of a handful of companies globally that make specialist machines for semiconductor production. The Bavarian company focuses on developing high-technology equipment that prepares semiconductor chips for 'packaging' with other items of electronic hardware – a vital field that is important in integrating chips with other computer systems.

Franz Richter, chief executive, says the specialist nature of the products has helped to mitigate the impact of the currency shift in recent months: only 35 per cent of Süss's sales are from the eurozone, with the rest mostly in the US and Asia. 'To some degree this insulates us from currency swings', he says.

The main problem in the past three years has been the weakness of demand from the semiconductor industry – which is just coming out of a prolonged downturn – that has shrunk Süss's sales by half to €93m ($114m, £63m) last year.

While Mr Richter says he 'can see more activity now among our customers' that should push up sales this year, he can also counter the impact of the dollar's weakness by making more use of the company's US-based plant.

Source: *Financial Times*, 11 March 2004.

Press cutting TB (*continued*)

Luxottica stays cool amid earnings drop

Fred Kapner, Milan

US demand for trendy eyewear has made Leonardo Del Vecchio, founder of the Luxottica eyewear empire, one of the world's wealthiest men, and Italy's second richest after Silvio Berlusconi.

The dollar's weakness, however, last year gave a black eye to the owner of Ray-Ban and Persol glasses and the Sunglass Hut and LensCrafters chains. Two-thirds of Luxottica's €2.85bn (£1.92bn) in sales are in dollars, and the currency's plunge, coupled with a fragile US economy for much of last year, caused its first drop in annual earnings since it was quoted on the New York Stock Exchange in 1990.

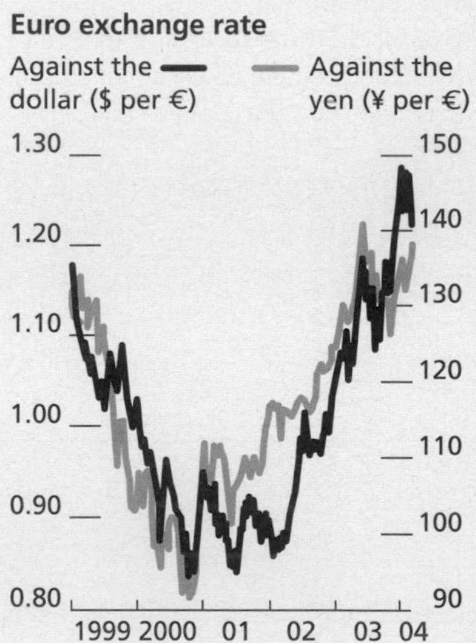

Still, as with many Italian fashion companies, currency troubles are less of a worry than weak economies, analysts say. Helped by the nascent US rebound, Luxottica estimates its earnings per share this year will rise 5 per cent even if the dollar this year will be 10 per cent lower on average than in 2003, when the euro fetched an average of $1.13.

Like other mid-level fashion groups, Luxottica keeps most of its manufacturing in Italy and cannot easily lower its production costs. The company has also steadily built up production facilities in China and expects to boost production there faster than in Italy over the next few years.

Other luxury groups such as Prada and Gucci have also boosted their store presence in the US and Asia to reach consumers who in recent years have not been travelling and shopping as heavily in airport stores or in Italy. Margins might be lower, company executives admit, but sales in dollar terms have been picking up strongly for the past six months.

Said one fashion executive recently: 'The US will be our biggest market for years but the dollar risk only accentuates the attraction of a market like China for production but especially for sales.'

Source: *Financial Times*, 11 March 2004.

Multiple choice questions

There is one right answer only to each question.

1 Assume the following information is applicable to the $ and the Swiss franc (CHF) in a particular situation:

Current spot rate of Swiss francs to the US dollar is USD/CHF = 1.70.
Forecast spot rate of Swiss franc one year from now USD/CHF = 1.80.
One year forward rate USD/CHF = 1.76.
Annual interest rate for Swiss franc deposit = 10 per cent.
Annual interest rate for USD = 6 per cent.

Given the above information, the return from covered interest arbitrage by US investors with $500,000 to invest is _____ per cent.

(a) about 3.89 per cent;
(b) about 5.31 per cent;
(c) about 10.62 per cent;
(d) about 6.00 per cent;
(e) about 6.25 per cent.

2 Assume that Eurosterling interest rates are higher than Eurodollar rates. Assume also that the sterling/dollar spot rate is equal to the forward rate. Covered interest arbitrage puts ______ pressure on the pound's spot rate, and _______ pressure on the pound's forward rate.

(a) downward; downward;
(b) downward; upward;
(c) upward; downward;
(d) upward; upward.

3 Assume that both US and UK investors require a real return of 3 per cent. If the nominal Eurodollar interest rate is 11 per cent and the nominal Eurosterling rate is 9 per cent, then according to the Fisher effect, UK inflation is expected to be about _______ US inflation, and the UK pound is expected to _______.

(a) 2 percentage points above; depreciate by about 2 per cent;
(b) 3 percentage points above; depreciate by about 3 per cent;
(c) 3 percentage points below; appreciate by about 3 per cent;
(d) 3 percentage points below; depreciate by about 3 per cent;
(e) 2 percentage points below; appreciate by about 2 per cent.

4 Translation exposure reflects the exposure of a firm's:

(a) ongoing international transactions to exchange rate fluctuations;
(b) local currency value to transactions between foreign exchange traders;
(c) financial statements to exchange rate fluctuations;
(d) cash flows to exchange rate fluctuations.

5 The US$ five-year interest rate is 5 per cent annualised, and the Danish krone (DKK) five-year rate is 8 per cent annualised. Today's spot rate is USD/DKK = 5.00. If the international Fisher effect holds, what is the best estimate of the Danish krone spot rate against the US dollar spot rate in five years' time?

(a) USD0.131;
(b) USD0.226;
(c) USD0.262;
(d) USD0.140;
(e) USD0.174.

6 Suppose the spot New York indirect quotes for the Batavian drac and Swedish krona are 1249.25–75 and 5.9925–75, respectively. What is the direct quote for the Swedish krona in Batavia?

(a) 0.0047969–0.0048008;
(b) 208.30–47;
(c) 208.30–55;
(d) 208.47–55;
(e) none of the above.

7 If inflation is expected to be 5 per cent higher in the United Kingdom than in Switzerland:

(a) the theory of purchasing power parity would predict a drop in nominal interest rates in the United Kingdom of approximately 5 per cent;
(b) purchasing power parity would predict that the UK spot rate should decline by about 5 per cent;
(c) expectations theory would suggest that the spot exchange rates between the two countries should remain unchanged over the long run;
(d) the efficient market hypothesis suggests that no predictions can be made under a system of freely floating rates.

8 If inflation in the United States is expected to be 5 per cent annually and the Danish krone is expected to depreciate by 3 per cent per annum relative to the US dollar, Danish krone prices of raw materials imported by a Danish company from the United States and priced in dollars can be expected (*ceteris paribus*) to:

(a) increase by about 8 per cent per annum;
(b) increase by about 2 per cent per annum;
(c) increase by 5 per cent per annum;
(d) increase by 3 per cent per annum.

9 A strong pound sterling places ______ pressure on UK inflation, which in turn places ______ pressure on the pound:

(a) upward; upward;
(b) downward; upward;
(c) upward; downward;
(d) downward; downward.

10 What would be the amount of the exchange gain or loss in the following situation? The exchange rate changes from 1 peso = $1.00 to 1 peso = 75c. Translate using the temporal approach. Inventory is valued at cost, this being lower than market value.

	'000 pesos		**'000 pesos**
Owners' equity	1,000	Fixed assets	1,000
Non-current debt	600	Inventory	200
Current payables	400	Cash	800
	2,000		2,000

(a) $50,000 gain;
(b) $150,000 gain;
(c) $150,000 loss;
(d) $50,000 loss;
(e) none of the above.

Part D

DERIVATIVES

Derivative instruments comprise financial products that have grown up around securities, currency and commodity trading and whose price is a function of some other underlying security, currency rate or other commodity. The term is usually used to embrace swaps, financial futures, options and a wide range of financially engineered instruments which are hybrids of other financial products. But it also includes, of course, forwards – which have already been discussed in Parts B and C.

12 Swaps

Bankers are in the business of taking deposits in various currencies on the basis of a **fixed** or **floating interest rate**. At the same time, banks offer to make loans in various currencies on a fixed or on a floating interest rate basis. The fact that banks are prepared to take deposits on a floating basis and to lend on a fixed basis – and vice versa – in a particular currency gives the essential rationale for the **interest rate swap** market. The fact that banks will take deposits in one currency on a fixed or floating basis and also make loans to customers in a different currency on a fixed or floating basis provides an underpinning to the currency swap market.

Take a simple example. A real estate company has funded itself with floating rate debt. This is likely to increase its risk profile. When interest rates rise, demand for new homes generally falls. The housing company faces a double whammy. Its income statement will be hit by lower sales and increased interest cost. The reverse will occur in boom times. This effect makes its income statement volatile. To reduce this volatility, the real estate firm should have funded itself with fixed rate debt. And it can achieve this by means of an interest rate swap.

Assume that the amount of the floating rate finance involved was EUR100 million borrowed for five years from now. The housing firm could deposit EUR100 million at a floating rate with its bank and, at the same time, borrow EUR100 million at a fixed rate from the same bank each transaction being for five years. But, better still, it could enter into an interest rate swap in which it pays fixed rate interest on EUR100 million for five years and receives a floating rate on EUR100 million for a similar period. Clearly, by such a mechanism, the real estate firm has transformed its floating rate liability into fixed rate liability. Through the swap it has acquired a floating rate asset to set against its original floating rate liability. And, furthermore it has taken on a fixed rate liability. Quite simple, really.

12.1 Swaps – the basics

In an interest rate swap a company may deposit, for example, €100m with the bank for a five-year period at a floating rate of interest (based, for example on six-month **LIBOR**) and, at the same time, borrow €100m from the same bank for a five-year period at a fixed rate of interest. Why might the firm wish to do this? Perhaps, as in our example, because it already has a floating rate borrowing with five years to run to repayment, which it wished to convert to a fixed rate loan. The reader may well ask why did the firm not raise fixed rate funds initially? It is banking practice only to lend at floating rates in a particular set of circumstances – for example in most management buyouts. The reader might also ask why does the firm not repay the first loan which has been contracted at a floating rate and replace it by a new loan at a fixed rate? It is possible that there would be a penalty for early repayment and the interest rate swap is cheaper than incurring this penalty – this is usually the case.

Note that the interest rate swap exemplified, the amount (€100m) and the term (five years) are the same for each side of the swap. This makes sense and is a key characteristic of an interest rate swap. Note also that since the amount of the swap is the same on each side of the equation (€100m), no money need change hands at the instigation of the swap. The same is true at the end of the interest swap period. The two amounts involved at the end of five years are the same (€100m) so in an interest rate, at maturity no principal changes hands. Each year, though, the two parties to the swap settle interest amounts due (fixed versus floating) usually on a difference basis. The documentation to a swap is standardised and very short. But it incorporates general clauses such that, should the credit standing of the non-bank party deteriorate significantly, the bank may terminate the swap early. Of course, the same thing applies if the non-bank party is in **default** on an interest payment (or difference) due.

The same kind of logic applies in cross-currency swaps. The interest rate swap described was in one single currency, the euro. What about when two currencies are involved? The underpinning idea remains. Banks are in the business of taking deposits in one currency (A) and lending in another (currency B). Naturally the bank sets interest rates appropriate to currencies A and B for lending or borrowing as the case may be. Such interest rates would be market based and would approximately take account of inflation in the different countries involved plus a real rate of return (usually between 2 and 4 per cent) plus a premium for the credit risk of the borrower (and maybe a premium for political risk in one, or both of the currencies, if appropriate). So, a bank would be happy to take a twelve-month deposit of USD1.6m from a customer, for a twelve-month period, GBP1m. We assume that the exchange rate is GBP1 = USD1.6. Interest rates set as above would apply. It is this possibility that provides the essence of a cross-currency swap.

Let us assume that the company, headquartered in London, in our example has, this time, a borrowing outstanding of USD160m and the loan is at a fixed interest rate. The loan has five years to run to maturity. The reason that the British firm negotiated the loan initially was to hedge a US business that it had bought for USD160m. Now, just for the purpose of our example, assume that the British firm has just sold on this US-based business for exactly GBP100m and that the GBP/USD exchange rate is 1.6. The proceeds of GBP100m are to be used to finance expansion in operations in Britain. Of course, the UK firm no longer needs the dollar loan to hedge the dollar exposure on the US-based business. But the loan has five years still to run to final maturity – payable in one shot (a **bullet** repayment, as it is termed). The British firm might repay the loan early – although to do so would incur a penalty – or it might consider a cross-country swap, which would convert the borrowing liability out of dollars and into sterling (or any other currency that the firm desired). How would this work?

Remember that the firm has a USD160m borrowing at a fixed rate with five years to run, but it no longer needs this dollar loan in its books. It wishes to replace it with a sterling borrowing because the proceeds of the US sale have been invested in the UK operations. So, it arranges a cross-currency swap.

Via the swap, the firm effectively borrows GBP100m from the bank and deposits USD160m with the bank, both deposit and borrowing are at a fixed rate and both for a five-year period. At the prevailing exchange rate of GBP/USD = 1.60, these two amounts are equal when the swap is arranged. Year by year, the balance of interest difference will be paid between the bank and the firm. Effectively, and for balance sheet reporting purposes, the British company now has a sterling liability. At the end of the five-year swap period the company must pay to the bank GBP100m and the bank must pay to the company USD160m. Of course, the company will then use this USD160m to repay the original dollar borrowing. But note that under the swap, at the exchange rate prevailing five years hence the GBP100m that the company pays to the bank will not necessarily equal the USD160m the bank pays to the company. Indeed, at any exchange rate other than 1.60, there will be a balancing payment either from the bank to the company or vice versa, at year 5 to square the books. Note that this was not the case with the one-currency interest rate swap. In five years' time, €100m will equal €100m; but GBP100m will not necessarily equal USD160m. Hence there will be a balancing payment at the end of the cross-currency swap, but not at the end of an interest rate swap.

Once again, the documentation on a cross-currency swap is very short and focused but again there are rules to the effect that the significant deterioration of the credit quality of the non-bank party may result in early termination of the swap. In the cross-currency swap that we have described, we have referred to one involving fixed interest rates on both sides – USD and GBP interest were both at fixed rates. This need not be the case, one side of the equation could be fixed while the other was floating. Or, both sides could be floating but using a different floating formula, for example LIBOR versus a specified floating interest base rate.

Before going any further, we would remind readers that in Chapter 11 we introduced forward/forward swaps and spot/forward swaps. It is a little confusing but these are altogether different from currency and interest rate swaps. Basically, swaps involve the exchange of interest or foreign currency exposures or a combination of both by two or more borrowers. They do not necessarily involve the legal swapping of actual debts but an agreement is made to meet certain cash flows under loan or lease agreements. This sounds rather complicated, so what, in practical terms, does it mean? We will approach the problem by focusing upon interest rate swaps first and then moving on to currency swaps.

12.2 Interest rate swaps

As indicated above, a swap – whether an interest rate swap or a currency swap – can simply be described as the transformation of one stream of future cash flows into another stream of future cash flows with different features. An interest rate swap is an exchange between two counterparties of interest obligations (payments of interest) or receipts (investment income) in the same currency on an agreed amount of notional principal for an agreed period of time. The agreed amount is called notional principal because, since it is not a loan or investment, the principal amount is not initially exchanged or repaid at maturity. An exchange of interest obligations is called a liability swap; an exchange of interest receipts is called an asset swap. Interest streams are exchanged according to predetermined rules and are based upon the underlying notional principal amount.

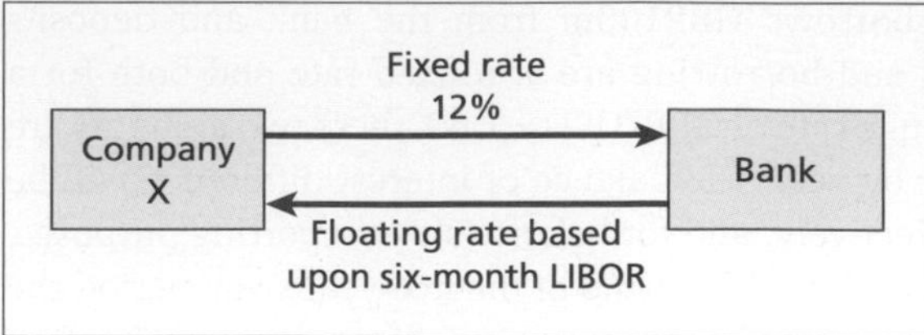

Figure 12.1 Coupon swap

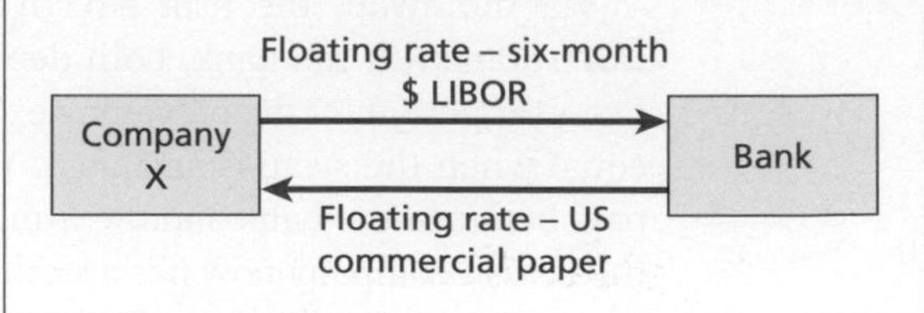

Figure 12.2 Basis swap

There are two main types of interest rate swap: the **coupon** swap and the **basis swap**. Coupon swaps convert interest flows from a fixed rate to a floating rate basis, or the reverse, in the same currency. A simple example is shown in Figure 12.1. In the figure the arrows refer to interest payment flows.

Basis swaps convert interest flows from a floating rate calculated according to one formula to a floating rate calculated according to another. For example, one set of interest flows might be set against six-month dollar LIBOR (London interbank offered rate), while the other set of flows might be based upon another floating rate such as US **Commercial Paper**, US **Treasury Bill** Rate or LIBOR based upon one- or three-month maturities. Figure 12.2 gives an example of a basis swap.

To reiterate then, interest rate swaps involve the exchange between two counterparties of interest obligations in the same currency on an agreed amount of notional principal for an agreed period of time. The principal amount applies only for the purpose of calculating the interest to be exchanged under an interest rate swap. At no time is any principal amount physically passed between the parties. The exchange of fixed or floating interest payments is made by reference to prevailing fixed and floating rates available in the market place, due account being taken of credit standing. The counterparties are thus able to convert a fixed rate asset or liability into a floating rate asset or liability and vice versa. Costs savings may be obtained by each party.

When the swap market took off during the early 1980s, these cost savings arose from differentials in the credit standing of the counterparties and other market imperfections. To be more specific, usually investors in fixed rate instruments were more sensitive to credit quality than floating rate lenders. Thus a larger premium was demanded of issuers of lower credit quality in the fixed rate debt market than in the floating rate market. The counterparties to an interest rate swap effectively obtained an arbitrage advantage by drawing down funds in the market where they had the greatest relative cost advantage, subsequently entering into an interest rate swap to convert the cost of the funds so raised from a fixed rate to a floating rate or vice versa.

The methodology of the arbitrage and its cost-saving potential can be seen by reference to an example involving two companies, X and Y. The former has a higher credit rating, as can be seen by the data in Table 12.1. Its superior credit standing gives it a 110 basis point advantage in the fixed rate funding market and a 50 basis point advantage in the floating rate market. Despite the fact that company X can raise funds more cheaply than company Y in both markets, a potential for interest rate arbitrage exists. Company X draws down funds in the fixed rate market, while company Y borrows on a floating basis. Each then enters into an interest rate swap, requiring the payments from one to the other as shown under the heading 'Swap payments' in Table 12.1. It can be seen by comparing the 'All-in cost of funding' line in the table with the 'Cost of direct funding' line that each party has saved

Table 12.1 Example of an interest rate swap

	Company X	Company Y
Credit rating	AAA	BBB
Cost of direct fixed rate funding	10.40%	11.50%
Cost of direct floating rate funding	Six-month LIBOR + 0.25%	Six-month LIBOR + 0.75%
Funds raised directly		
Fixed rate by company X	(10.40%)	
Floating rate by company Y		(Six-month LIBOR + 0.75%)
Swap payments		
Company X pays company Y	(Six-month LIBOR) 10.45%	
Company Y pays company X		Six-month LIBOR (10.45%)
All-in cost of funding	Six-month LIBOR – 0.05%	11.20%
Comparable cost of direct funding	Six-month LIBOR + 0.25%	11.50%
Saving	30 basis points	30 basis points

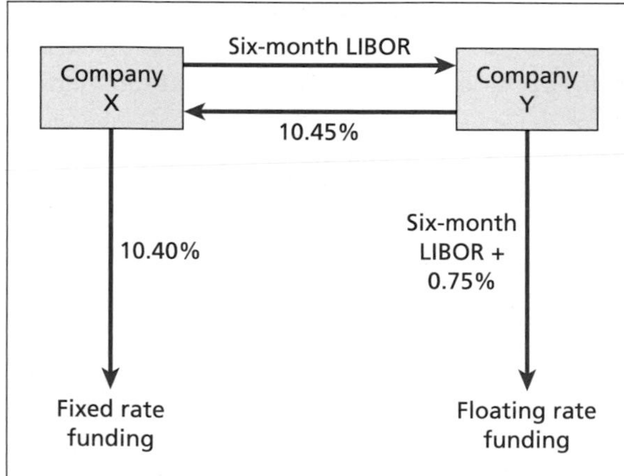

Figure 12.3 Direction of interest flows

30 basis points on the swap. The interest rate flows are summarised in Figure 12.3, in which the direction of the arrows represents the direction of interest rate flows. Such interest rate arbitrages are much less apparent nowadays.

The ability to transfer relative cost advantages in the manner shown in Table 12.1 and Figure 12.3 has led to many highly creditworthy companies issuing fixed rate bonds solely with the purpose of swapping and frequently obtaining funding at an effective sub-LIBOR cost. In the early phase of the interest rate swap market, a triple A issuer could expect to achieve between 75 and 100 basis points below LIBOR on a swap. Nowadays, gains for a comparable borrower might bring the cost of funding down to 25 or 30 basis points below LIBOR.

Note carefully that the potential for such big arbitrage gains as exemplified in Table 12.1 has now disappeared as more and more corporates have accessed the market. The effect has been that the disparity between different credit loadings in fixed and floating markets has narrowed very substantially.

Besides providing cost advantages, interest rate swaps enable borrowers effectively to access markets which might otherwise be closed to them – for example, by virtue of credit quality, lack of a familiar name or because of excessive use of a particular capital market segment. Even private companies are able to tap particular markets without the need to comply with disclosure requirements, credit ratings and other formal requirements. Swaps based upon commercial paper as the underlying floating rate instrument are a significant part of the interest rate swap market.

Interest rate swaps may be used as a means of reducing interest rate exposure or as a pure financing tool. They may also be used to enable a corporate treasurer to back his or her judgement on future trends in interest rates. For example, consider a company with fixed

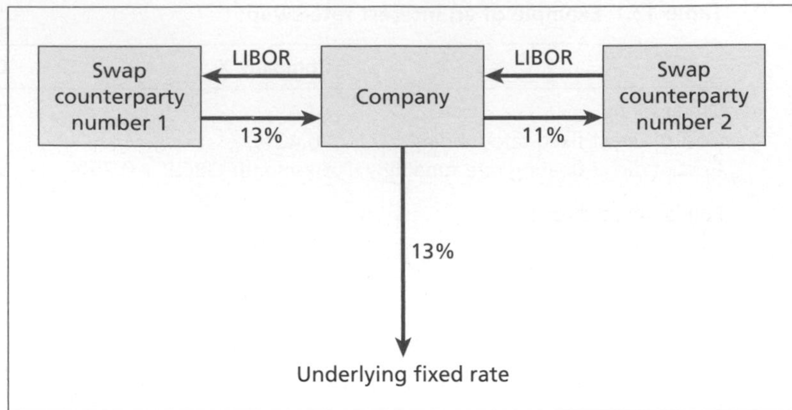

Figure 12.4 Position of company following two swaps

rate debt costing 13 per cent per annum at a time when the treasurer expects a decline in interest rates to occur. The company might enter into a swap to obtain LIBOR-based funding and leave this swap in place during the period when interest rates were falling. At the end of the decline, the company might enter into a second swap to lock into the new lower fixed rate of, say, 11 per cent per annum. The company's position would then be like that summarised in Figure 12.4.

The interest rate swap process has the advantage of utter simplicity. It is often conducted by telephone and confirmed by telex subject to agreement on documentation, which usually incorporates the minimum of restrictive covenants and is now in a standard format. There are both primary and secondary interest rate markets. Many new bond issues are swap driven. Bonds are issued with the express intention of swapping the fixed interest rate obligations into floating interest rate debt at highly competitive rates.

During 1982 the volume of interest rate swaps transacted was estimated to be in the order of \$3bn. Nowadays, the amount of such swaps outstanding is around \$342 trillion as of mid-2009. Netting off hedged portions, the figure is still around \$14 trillion.

We have so far used the terms 'fixed', 'floating' and 'LIBOR' without exactly defining our meaning. It is proposed to do this now. The term 'fixed' or 'fixed rate' refers to an interest rate which is set at the beginning of a loan or an investment and which holds for the entire life of the loan or investment. For example, a five-year £10m loan with interest rate of 10 per cent requires an annual interest payment of £1m for five years, at the end of which the total principal amount – £10m – would be repayable. By contrast, the term 'floating' or 'floating rate' refers to an interest rate on a loan or an investment which is reset on a regular basis. For example, a three-year £10m loan with a six-month floating rate of interest would have the interest rate reset every six months at the then prevailing interest rate for six months. The six-month reference rate used is normally LIBOR.

The term 'LIBOR' is an acronym for London interbank offered rate. It is the interest rate at which major banks offer to lend funds to other major banks in the London interbank market. The rate at which they bid to borrow funds from other banks is known as '**LIBID**', the London interbank bid rate. Another rate, known as '**LIMEAN**', is simply the midpoint between LIBOR and LIBID. Both LIBOR and LIBID are frequently used as marker rates against which floating payments of interest are calculated. A bank will quote its own LIBOR and LIBID; sometimes interest rate payments under a swap use LIBOR based on an average of several banks' rates. The way in which LIBOR is determined will be clearly stated in the swap agreement.

Also worthy of mention here is the term **EURIBOR**. This refers to the reference rate for euros. Quotations are posted at 11 a.m. Brussels time on an actual/360 day basis (see later in this chapter). It is proving to be a widely used reference rate in financial circles.

Why, then, should a company use interest rate swaps? They can be employed for a number of reasons – these are the main ones:

- to achieve funding at rates below those otherwise available in bond markets or from banks;
- to obtain fixed rate financing when it is impossible to access the bond markets directly;
- to restructure a debt profile without raising new finance;
- to restructure the profile of interest receipts or investments;
- to hedge against, or speculate upon, the direction of movement of interest rates.

The first point referred to above is fairly straightforward; it formed the basis of Table 12.1. The second point is more complicated. International bond markets are usually open to companies of the highest quality – well-known and large borrowers. Smaller, top-quality companies may be able to borrow at fixed rates in their domestic markets where they are well known, but the opportunity to do so may arise only infrequently. Companies that cannot raise funds in the bond markets, but which are sufficiently creditworthy for banks to be willing to lend to them, may borrow at a floating rate and swap the proceeds into a fixed rate, thus locking in a fixed rate liability. The third, fourth and fifth points are self-explanatory.

Interest rate swap markets are used by various players – the major ones are set out below:

- supra-nationals, such as the World Bank;
- sovereign and public sector institutions, such as the Kingdom of Sweden;
- multinational corporations;
- smaller companies;
- banks, either as an intermediary between the two counterparties or as an end counterparty itself to manage its own funding or investment requirements.

It is now necessary to consider a small amount of swap jargon so that the ways in which participants deal can be better understood. The terms 'payer' and 'receiver' are frequently used and their meaning is straightforward (see Figure 12.5).

The market 'talks the fixed rate'. This piece of jargon can best be illustrated by an example. If a swap **dealer** says that he wants payers in the five years, he means that he wants counterparties who will pay fixed rate on five-year funds. Swap dealers maintain what they call a swap book, which will have positions – that is, exposures to interest, currency and other risks.

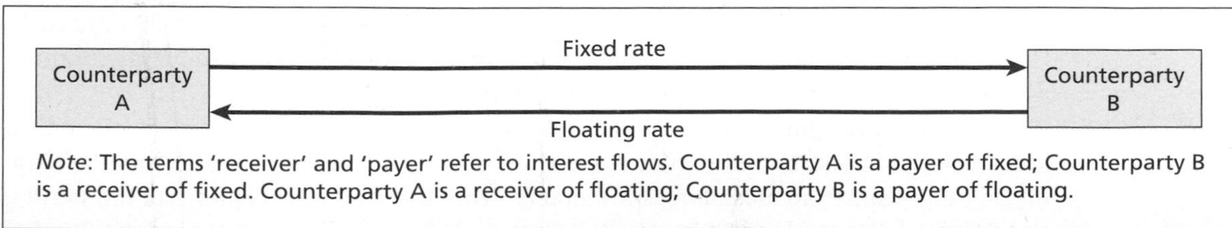
Counterparty A
Fixed rate
Floating rate
Counterparty B
Note: The terms 'receiver' and 'payer' refer to interest flows. Counterparty A is a payer of fixed; Counterparty B is a receiver of fixed. Counterparty A is a receiver of floating; Counterparty B is a payer of floating.

Figure 12.5 Swap payers and receivers

These positions may be covered or left open. One way to cover a position is to match it with an offsetting swap. This is known as 'squaring the book' or 'running a matched book'.

As market-makers in the swap market, banks quote rates to clients on a regular basis. Like straight interest markets, banks will typically quote two fixed rates on a swap – a rate where the bank is willing to pay the fixed rate and a rate where the bank is willing to receive the fixed rate. In the sterling swap market, the fixed rate is always considered to be quoted against six-month LIBOR as the floating rate – unless specified otherwise. If, therefore, a bank is quoting a five-year **swap rate** as 10.70–10.85 per cent, then this means that at 10.70 per cent the bank is willing to pay a fixed rate and to receive six-month LIBOR and at 10.85 per cent the bank is willing to receive the fixed rate and to pay six-month LIBOR. Clearly, on the basis set out, the bank stands to make 0.15 per cent on the deal. However, negotiations and competitive pressures may enable the customer to get a better rate from the bank.

Although the sterling market uses six-month LIBOR as its benchmark against which rates are quoted, in the USD interest rate swap market, the fixed rate is quoted as an amount, or spread, above the equivalent maturity US treasury bond. For example, five-year US treasury swap spreads could be given by a bank as 82–88. This means that the bank is willing to pay the fixed rate in a five-year swap at a rate that is 0.82 per cent, or 82 basis points, above the five-year US Treasury bond rate. If the current US treasury bond rate is 8.08 per cent, then this bank is willing to pay 8.9 per cent (8.08 + 0.82 per cent) on a semi-annual **bond basis** – both the US treasury bond and the swap spread are considered to have interest calculated on a semi-annual bond basis. The above bank is also willing to receive the fixed rate in a five-year swap at 8.96 per cent (8.08 + 0.88 per cent) on a semi-annual bond basis. Having referred, in the last few sentences, to the semi-annual bond basis, it is perhaps worth while considering methods of calculation of interest. The next section is devoted to this topic.

12.3 Calculation of interest

There are several ways of calculating interest flows for swaps, especially on the fixed rate. Care has to be taken to ensure that all parties to a transaction are using the same calculation method. The floating rate is usually six-month LIBOR, unless otherwise stated. The fixed rate in a US dollar swap is usually quoted as a semi-annual interest rate, and is calculated on a bond basis. 'Semi-annual' means that interest payments are made twice a year. Thus, if the fixed rate is 10 per cent semi-annual, then every six months 5 per cent would be payable. The term 'bond basis' refers to the manner in which the number of days in a year is treated. In the non-financial world, every year has 365 days – except for leap years. However, financial calculations frequently use a different number of days in a year. The 'bond basis' means that, in calculating interest payments, a year is considered to have 12 months of 30 days each. Hence, calculations would be made on the basis of 360 days in a year – sometimes written as: 360/360. This convention is used in the **Eurobond** market.

Each currency or interest rate market may have a different approach to calculation, so it is crucial to check that all parties agree the interest calculation basis. Euromarkets use the 360-day year, as do most domestic markets – with the notable exceptions of the sterling and Belgian franc markets. Some bank customers may wish to have the fixed rate quoted on an annual basis – that is, as if interest were paid only once a year at the end of the year.

This is frequently required for swaps associated with bonds where the bond pays interest once a year.

There are simple formulae for converting fixed rates from a semi-annual to an annual interest rate basis and vice versa. Two such key formulae are set out below:

- To convert semi-annual to an annual basis:

$$\left[\left(1+\frac{\text{semi-annual}}{200}\right)^2-1\right]\times 100=\text{annual interest}$$

- To convert annual to a semi-annual basis:

$$\left[\left(1+\frac{\text{annual}}{100}\right)^{1/2}-1\right]\times 200=\text{semi-annual interest}$$

In the above formulae, one should input the known interest rate and convert as required – for example, 10.4 per cent payable as 5.2 per cent every six months is input to the first equation as 10.4 to arrive at 10.67 per cent if paid annually. Many market professionals notate semi-annual as s.a. and quote annual interest as p.a. It must be borne in mind that an interest rate may look cheaper if quoted on a different basis. So it pays always to check with the counterparty as to the basis being used.

Note that, in swaps, the floating rate will usually be paid or received every six months, while the fixed interest will be received or paid either semi-annually or annually. These payments will generally be netted out when they occur on the same day, so that only one payment between the parties is made.

Bond basis versus money-market basis

The bond basis of calculating interest refers to a year assumed to consist of 360 days (360/360). Another method, the **money-market basis**, calculates interest on an actual number of days in a year, but by reference to each year being 360 days (365/360). Some swap counterparties may wish to have the fixed rate on the swap quoted on a money-market basis. It is worth mentioning that LIBOR is always quoted and calculated on a money-market basis. Anyway, it may be necessary to convert the standard bond basis swap quote to a money-market basis.

The following formulae allow for bond and money-market conversions. The need to make the conversions for swaps is to ensure that the actual interest basis flow amounts will be equivalent no matter which way the swap is quoted.

- To convert from a bond to a money-market basis:

$$\text{bond rate}\times\frac{360}{365}=\text{money market rate}$$

- To convert from a money market to a bond basis:

$$\text{money-market rate}\times\frac{365}{360}=\text{bond rate}$$

An example will help to illustrate the difference in interest amounts using the two methods:

- 10 per cent interest on a bond basis on $1m for one year:

$$0.10 \times 1{,}000{,}000 \times \frac{360}{360} = \$100{,}000$$

- 10 per cent interest on a money-market basis on $1m for one year:

$$0.10 \times 1{,}000{,}000 \times \frac{365}{360} = \$101{,}389$$

Clearly, since different interest amounts result from using these interest bases, care must be taken to utilise the correct one.

Swap termination

Once an interest rate swap has been transacted, it will normally run to maturity. However, circumstances can arise where a swap counterparty needs to change the nature of existing cash flows or to get out of the swap. There are typically three ways of eliminating an already existing swap: reversal, termination and buy-out. In a reversal, a swap counterparty simply transacts another swap with the opposite flows to the original swap. The net effect is to reverse out the original position. Of course, since interest rates may have changed since the inception, the swap counterparty may have losses to make up or it may be able to realise gains. The swap counterparty need not deal with the same bank on the second swap. In a termination, a swap counterparty can approach the other counterparty to assess whether a termination of an existing swap is possible. Generally, the remaining cash flows are valued at current rates and any gains or losses between the two parties are settled. The swap is then considered terminated. In a buy-out, also sometimes known as a swap sale or assignment, a swap counterparty approaches another bank to buy out the existing swap and take over the swap counterparty's position. The new bank will either pay the swap counterparty if the remaining life of the swap has value, or be paid by the swap counterparty if the swap position is at a loss. The new bank will take over the swap counterparty's position *vis-à-vis* the original bank. Clearly, the original bank must agree to the new counterparty and must be willing to accept its **counterparty risk**.

Documentation

Interest rate swaps are generally agreed over the telephone by the parties involved. Before the end of the day, written communications are exchanged which detail all aspects of the transaction so that there is no misunderstanding or confusion. After this, an interest rate swap agreement is signed by the counterparties. The International Swap Dealer's Association (ISDA) has co-operated with various other associations to produce standard documentation for swaps. It runs to about 12 pages and includes sections relating to:

- *Payments* – the basis of calculation, amounts and timing.
- *Representations* – the swap counterparties represent that they are authorised to enter into the swap.
- *Events of default* – the conditions under which a party to a swap will be considered to be in default.

- *Termination* – the conditions under which the swap can be terminated. These are normally limited and include taxation or a material change in the circumstances of one of the parties to the swap, for example substantial deterioration of credit quality.
- *Damages* – how these are to be calculated under early termination.
- *Assignability* – swaps are not usually assignable to a new counterparty without the other party's consent.
- *Credit support documents* – these may be required due to the lower credit quality of one counterparty; guarantees and security agreements can then be utilised.
- *Simple boiler plating* – the bank effectively has a material adverse clause enabling settlement (in whole or in part) if the counterparty's financial condition deteriorates significantly. Also, if the swap itself (excluding the item being hedged) shows a loss to the client above a specified level, recompense may be called for by the swap bank. This feature cannot be stressed too strongly.

Swaps versus other financial instruments

Although we have not yet considered, in detail, the hedging of interest rate exposure (this is looked at in Chapters 13 and 14, we now compare the use of interest rate swaps with such other mechanisms as **caps**, **floors**, **collars**, swap options and futures. Since these instruments have not yet been covered, we will define them briefly.

We first of all look at the cap. A cap is, in essence, an insurance policy for a company wishing to protect itself against a rise in short-term interest rates (six-month LIBOR, for example) above a certain capped level, but at the same time hoping to take advantage of any future drop in rates. A cap, like an interest rate swap, is independent of a company's underlying floating rate borrowing. But, unlike in the case of a swap, the financial institution writing the cap agrees, in consideration for the payment by the company of a one-off premium, to compensate the company to the extent to which LIBOR on the predetermined roll-over dates exceeds the cap rate. Thus the company continues to pay LIBOR plus any margin on its underlying loan, but with the comfort that it will be reimbursed should LIBOR exceed the capped level, as illustrated in Figure 12.6.

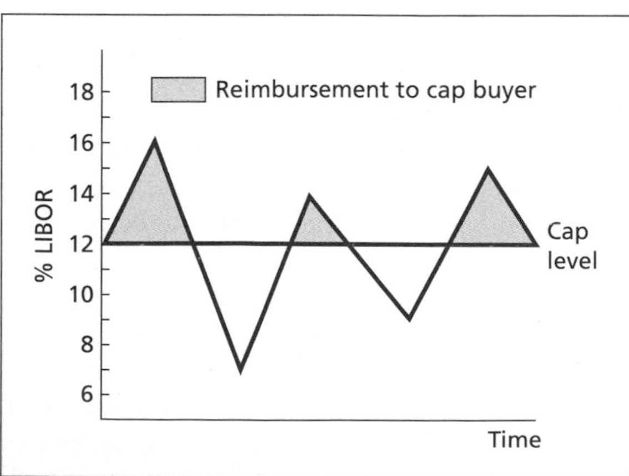

Figure 12.6 Example of a cap

We now examine floors. A floor is similar to a cap, but has the reverse effect. It achieves, for the investor or lender who is receiving floating rate interest, what a cap does for the borrower who pays it. While protecting the investor from a fall in interest rates below the floor, it allows the investor to benefit from any rise, as illustrated in Figure 12.7.

A collar is a cap and floor combined. It gives a company protection against rates rising above a certain level – the cap – and the ability to take advantage of a fall in rates, but only down to a certain level – the floor. Thus a company buying a collar will have a band of tolerance across a minimum and maximum cost of borrowing, as illustrated in Figure 12.8. If rates rise above the cap rate, it is compensated by the counterparty. If rates fall through the floor, it will

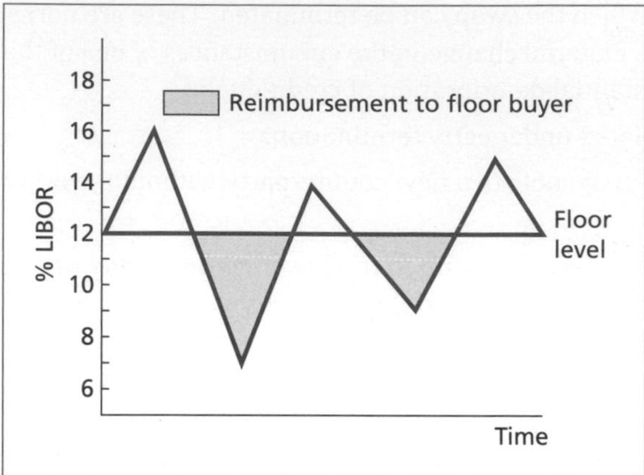

Figure 12.7 **Example of a floor**

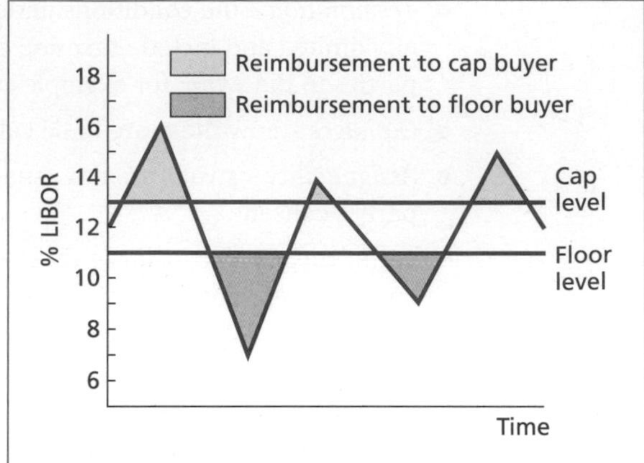

Figure 12.8 **Example of a collar**

compensate the counterparty. Deals may be structured such that the premium for buying the cap equals the premium at which the writer will buy the floor from the company; in such cases, no up-front payment will be made by either party. Variations in this cap/floor rate will produce a net payment one way or the other.

We now look briefly at swap options or, as they are sometimes called, options on swaps or even swaptions. An option on a swap is an agreement between a company and a financial institution that gives one of the parties the right, but not the obligation, to call upon the other, either on a specified date or during a pre-agreed period, to enter into a swap at a pre-arranged rate. A premium for this facility is paid by the party buying the option.

Financial futures are examined in Chapter 13, but here is a brief definition. A financial futures contract is a legally binding contract to deliver or take delivery on a specified day of a given quality and quantity of a financial commodity at an agreed price and the contract is traded on an organised financial futures exchange.

All the above instruments provide hedging facilities which are widely used in asset and liability management; the suitability of one approach compared with another depends on a company's particular requirements.

Swaps, however, do have several advantages. For example, whenever an up-front payment is required, it appears on a company's accounts. A swap does not normally involve an up-front payment. The avoidance of an up-front cash payment is also a positive advantage for companies with restraints on liquidity. A classic example would be a company that has completed a leveraged buy-out: an interest rate swap is a way for it to switch its debt burden out of floating rate and into fixed rate interest with no cash penalties and no detrimental effect on what might be an already poor gearing ratio.

Swaps do have pitfalls, as any treasurer who has swapped into paying fixed rate interest just before rates began to fall will testify. However, carefully monitored, they can usually be reversed with minimal adverse effect. The substantial depth of the swap market relative to the competing instruments listed above is another advantage. Swaps can be reversed easily because they are generally more widely understood and traded than caps, floors, collars and options. Furthermore, global standardised documentation is now in place for swaps, while documentation for caps, floors and collars tends to be custom-made.

Swaps also have the edge in terms of volume and maturity. Interest rate swaps can last for maturities sometimes in excess of 10 years and are commonly transacted for sums in excess of $100m. Caps, floors and collars, by contrast, are typically not written for much beyond five years and cap contracts for amounts of $100m are relatively rare.

12.4 Currency swaps

We now turn to currency swaps. The most frequently encountered currency swaps have floating rates on both sides, so it might be $ LIBOR against £ LIBOR. However, we begin with fixed rate currency swaps. They are slightly easier to understand. A fixed rate currency swap involves counterparty A exchanging fixed rate interest in one currency with counterparty B in return for fixed rate interest in another currency. Currency swaps usually involve three basic steps:

- initial exchange of principal;
- ongoing exchange of interest;
- re-exchange of principal amounts on maturity.

The initial exchange of principal works as follows. At the outset, the counterparties exchange the principal amounts of the swap at an agreed rate of exchange. This rate is usually based on the spot exchange rate, but a forward rate set in advance of the swap commencement date may also be used. This initial exchange can be on a notional basis – that is, with no physical exchange of principal amounts – or, alternatively, on a physical exchange basis. Whether the initial exchange is on a physical or notional basis, its importance is solely to establish the reference point of the principal amounts for the purpose of calculating, first, the ongoing payments of interest and, secondly, the re-exchange of principal amounts under the swap. The ongoing exchange of interest is the second key step in the currency swap. Having established the principal amounts, the counterparties exchange interest payments on agreed dates based on the outstanding principal amounts at fixed interest rates agreed at the outset of the transaction. The third step in the currency swap involves the ultimate re-exchange of principal amounts at maturity.

This three-step process is standard practice in the currency swap market and it effectively transforms a fixed rate debt raised in one currency into a fixed rate liability in another currency, which may be valuable for hedging purposes. Indeed, the currency swap is similar to a conventional long-date forward foreign exchange contract. Like interest rate swaps, currency swaps are advantageous because they enable borrowers to reduce the cost of borrowing by accessing markets that might otherwise be closed to them. For example, a strong borrower in the Swiss franc market may obtain a finer fixed US dollar rate by raising funds directly in fixed Swiss francs and then swapping them into US dollars. Besides having cost advantages, the currency swap market enables borrowers effectively to access foreign capital markets and obtain funds in currencies that might otherwise be unobtainable except at relatively high cost. The most important currencies in the currency swap market are the US dollar, the Swiss franc, the euro, sterling, the yen and the Canadian dollar. The market is dominated by the US dollar on one side but direct swaps have been frequent in yen/Swiss francs, yen/euro and sterling/euro. The currency swap is one further tool that enables corporate treasurers to manage currency exposure and reap cost benefits at the same time.

We now turn very briefly to the currency coupon swap. Essentially, this is a combination of interest rate swap and fixed rate currency swap. The transaction follows the three basic steps described for the fixed rate currency swap except that fixed rate interest in one currency is exchanged for floating rate interest in another currency.

Imagine a borrower that is in a relatively favourable position, for example, to raise long-term fixed rate US dollar funding but in fact wants floating rate yen. The currency swap market enables it to marry its requirements with another borrower of relatively high standing in the yen market but which does not have similar access to long-term fixed rate dollars. The gain accrues by each corporation swapping liabilities raised in those markets which each can readily access; the effect is to broaden the access of borrowers to international lending markets. Clearly, the currency swap enables the treasurer to alter the denomination of his or her liabilities and assets.

Swap transactions may be set up with great speed, and their documentation and formalities are generally much less detailed than in other large financial deals – swap documentation is normally shorter and simpler than that relating to term loan agreements. Transaction costs are relatively low too. And swaps can be unwound easily.

At the beginning of the 1980s, the currency swap market was extremely small; by 1990, the amount of new business being done was in excess of $100bn during the year. A swap has already been defined as the exchange of one stream of future cash flows for another stream of future cash flows with different characteristics. In the currency swap, two currencies are being utilised. The market standard is to quote a fixed rate of interest – an interest rate set for the entire life of the transaction – in one currency against a floating rate of interest, generally reset every six months, for the US dollar.

A rate of exchange between the two currencies must be established at the outset. This will produce principal amounts in the two currencies upon which payments of interest are to be made. At the final maturity of the transaction, along with the final periodic payment of interest, the principal amounts of the two currencies which were fixed at the outset must be exchanged by the swap counterparties. It is possible to have an exchange of the two principal amounts at the beginning of the swap, but this is not a requirement. For example, if the sterling/US dollar exchange rate is 1.80 at the outset of a five-year currency swap, the bank could lend to the corporate customer $18m in exchange for the customer lending the bank £10m – this would create an initial exchange of principal. However, there could be merely a notional exchange. The corporate customer wants $18m and it could get this amount merely by doing a spot deal to sell £10m and buy $18m. If the swap were for fixed rate sterling versus six-month floating rate US dollars, the interest flows would be as in Figure 12.9(a). But there would be a principal payment at maturity – in five years' time – as in Figure 12.9 (b). Thus, at final maturity, in addition to the interest

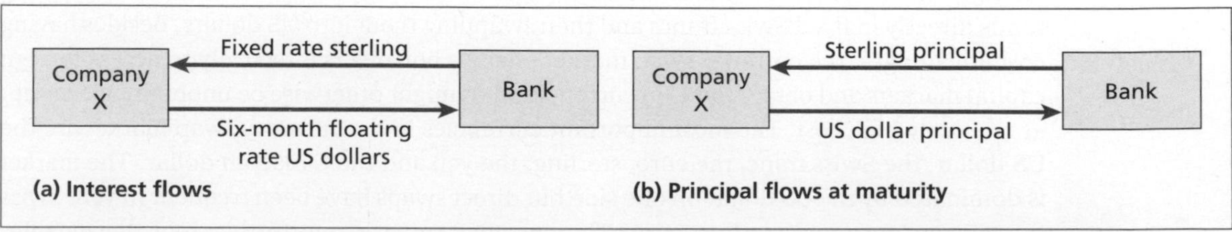

Figure 12.9 Currency swap example: fixed rate sterling versus six-month floating rate US dollars

flows, each swap counterparty pays the principal amount of that currency on which it had been paying interest over the life of the swap, as one would repay the principal amount of a maturing loan.

Currency swaps are typically arranged for periods ranging from two to ten years, with maturities of five years being most usual. For long maturities, the currency swap market has far greater depth and offers better prices than the forward market and is widely used for covering lengthy exposures. Currency swaps can be executed in most major currencies (fixed rate) against the US dollar (floating rate). Currency swaps between two currencies other than the US dollar are possible, but two separate swaps may be needed to achieve the desired result. The minimum size for a currency swap is approximately USD3m, or the equivalent in other currencies. Currency swaps attached to bond issues may be as large as $350m. It is possible to have currency swaps where both currencies are calculated on a floating rate basis, but these are rarer than fixed against floating. Generally, banks do not like to arrange only one side of a currency swap, thereby creating a mismatch. Instead they prefer to match their positions by arranging deals with counterparties that have opposite requirements. This matched position reduces the bank's risk. An example of such a matched position is set out in Figure 12.10.

In Figure 12.10, company A is the payer of fixed rate sterling and the receiver of six-month dollar LIBOR. The swap dealer might, using market jargon, say that 'company A is a payer of fixed sterling against USD LIBOR'. Company B is the receiver of fixed rate sterling and the payer of US dollar six-month LIBOR. The swap dealer might shorten this to 'company B is a receiver of fixed rate sterling against USD LIBOR'. In dealing in swaps, one must be careful to specify whether interest is to be calculated on an annual or a semi-annual basis and whether it will be calculated on a bond basis or a money-market basis. This has already been referred to earlier in the chapter.

Currency swaps are typically used to achieve one of the following objectives:

- hedging a currency exposure, or speculating;
- obtaining funds at lower costs;
- obtaining access to a restricted market;
- altering the currency of a payments stream or investment income.

Each of these objectives is now considered in turn.

Many companies around the world generate cash flows, either receipts or payments, in currencies other than the home currency. One way to minimise the long-term risk of one currency being worth more or less in the future is to offset a particular cash flow stream with an opposite flow in that currency created by a swap against the home currency. The swap also enables the corporate treasurer to transform the currency profile of a company's

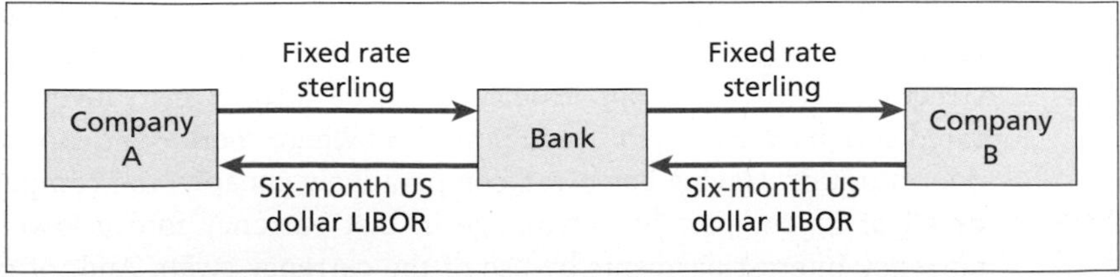

Figure 12.10 Matched currency swap

liabilities relatively quickly. In this respect, the currency swap can easily be used to hedge liabilities or deliberately to take positions in currencies that the treasurer anticipates will soften.

In terms of obtaining lower-cost funds, by raising new borrowings in capital markets in one currency and executing a currency swap into the desired currency, a borrower may reduce the cost of raising funds. This type of swap-driven new issue has been utilised extensively in the Eurobond market. Borrowers have been able to get competitively priced funds by issuing Eurobonds in those segments in which investors' demand is not being met. These funds, when swapped back to the borrower's desired currency, may produce a lower cost of funds than a direct borrowing in the desired currency.

Direct access to a particular segment of the international capital market may be somewhat restricted. In certain countries there are restrictions on the type of borrower that can raise new funds in the bond markets. The currency swap can be used to transform borrowings in one currency into a liability in the desired currency. For example, to issue a yen bond the borrower must qualify for at least a single A credit rating. If a company does not qualify in this respect, it can raise new funds elsewhere – for example, in the US dollar market. And to obtain a yen-denominated liability it might arrange a swap into yen (so long as the bank is willing to accept the company's credit quality).

In terms of altering the currency of investment income for investors, the currency swap can be used to change the currency of cash inflows too. For investors the objective is clearly to change investment receipts from one currency to a more desired currency. This type of currency swap is frequently called an 'asset swap'.

As in the interest rate swap market, the main participants in the currency swap market are supra-nationals, sovereign and public-sector institutions, multinational companies, smaller companies and banks. For currency swaps, the documentation and the closing of a deal by reversal, termination or buy-out are exactly as described in the section relating to interest rate swaps.

Currency swaps – general points

We have referred to the fact that companies may be able, through the currency swap, to raise money cheaply. How can this be achieved if interest rate parity always holds? First of all, windows of opportunity appear only fleetingly, often reflecting a brief arbitrage opportunity between domestic and international markets. The fleet-of-foot company may exploit such arbitrage opportunities by raising currency in foreign debt markets where funds are available at below market rates and then swapping the proceeds into the desired currency at a cost lower than might be achieved by accessing the desired denomination money market directly. There are many reasons – psychological as well as technical – why a company can borrow more cheaply in one currency than another. For instance, a company may well need to provide inducements to domestic investors who are over-familiar with its paper, while in a foreign capital market the novelty of its name – or an unusually structured investment opportunity – can be attractive to investors. Similarly, a highly rated company can exploit capital markets where there is a dearth of low-risk investment opportunities. Having borrowed comparatively cheaply, the company can translate some or all of its comparative advantage in that currency into a lower cost on its domestic currency interest payments by use of the currency swap. And, of course, funds at below market rates may be available linked to the purchase, for example of assets from a particular supplier. Yen finance at less than market rates for yen may be on offer to the purchaser of Japanese machinery.

Players in the swap market are aware of each other's prices. So a corporate treasurer shopping around for the cheapest price is likely to receive quotes within a spread of five basis points per annum. Variations within that spread will usually be a measure of how far the market has moved in the direction of each financial institution's swap book. However, differences in price between two rival bids can sometimes be more apparent than real, largely as a result of how they are expressed. So the treasurer comparing two or more prices has to bear a number of factors in mind. These include the following:

- days basis;
- payment schedule;
- delayed start;
- benchmarks;
- payment dates;
- transaction size.

In respect of a day's basis, the two main day-count conventions for interest rate calculations under a swap are the 30-day month/360-day year basis ('Eurobond') and the actual days elapsed/360-day year basis ('money market'). Swaps in sterling are quoted on an actual days elapsed/365-day basis. Another variation is the actual days elapsed/365–6 basis (actual/actual). When comparing prices, it is incumbent upon the treasurer to check that both quotes are expressed using the same basis. A financial institution's quote to receive a fixed rate under a swap expressed using a money-market basis will appear cheaper than the same price expressed using the bond basis. For a proper comparison of two swap prices, they must also be based on the same frequency of payment. Because of the **time value** of money, a swap price based on quarterly fixed interest payments will appear cheaper than a price based on the semi-annual equivalent of the quarterly interest rate quoted. If there is a delayed start to a swap, there may be value in the 'stub' period for one of the parties, determined by the funding cost of the bank's underlying hedge for the period of carry. This value may represent the apparent difference between two quotes if it is included in one and not the other.

Swap prices for maturities in excess of two to three years are typically quoted as a spread over the semi-annual yield to redemption of an underlying government security or parallel instrument. For a proper comparison of two apparently identical quotes on a spread basis, a corporate treasurer must ensure that both banks are using the same underlying bonds as benchmarks and are pricing them at the same level. The absolute rate is critical to any comparison. In some cases, particularly where a swap is for an odd maturity – say, four and a half years – one financial institution may be quoting a spread over the five-year bond, whereas another could be taking an interpolation of the four- and five-year bond which will produce a different result.

Unless asked to quote on a swap with specific interest payment dates, a financial institution will assume a 'straight run' – that is, equal, semi-annual interest periods from the contract date. Any variation may affect the quotes. Potential corporate users of the swap market also need to bear in mind that there may be a premium for transacting unusually large or small swaps, reflecting the degree of difficulty of placing such a swap in the market place.

12.5 Assessing risk in swaps

First of all, we consider how one would assess risk in an interest rate swap. Risk in interest rate swaps can be divided into two main types: credit risk and market risk. Credit risk is that the opposite counterparty might default before the end of the swap. If it does, the other counterparty will be thrown back, with little or no warning, into paying an interest rate structure on its liabilities which it deliberately set out to avoid by transacting the swap in the first place. In reality, this scenario rarely happens because the vast majority of swaps are conducted with solid financial institutions acting as principals to the swap and, secondly, the boiler plating referred to under Documentation in Section 12.3 should prevent this.

Market risk can be defined as the cost of reversing a swap before maturity. There are at least two ways to do this. One is to transact an equal but opposite swap. This is perfectly satisfactory but doubles the credit risk exposure. Another way is to request the original counterparty to cancel the initial agreement in consideration for a payment from or to them. This is easily done, especially where the counterparty is a financial institution. The cancellation payment represents the cost to the financial institution of hedging its resulting interest rate exposure by transacting a replacement swap. Its size will depend on how far interest rates have moved since the first swap began. Whether the payment is positive or negative is determined by whether rates have moved up or down.

How it works is shown in Figures 12.11 and 12.12. The shipping corporation is a weak credit and borrows at six-month US dollar LIBOR – say, 9 per cent p.a. – plus a 2 per cent premium. Believing rates are set to rise, it fixes its interest cost by transacting the swap illustrated in Figure 12.11 with a bank for five years. After year 3, however, six-month US dollar LIBOR has fallen – say, to 8 per cent p.a. – and expectations are that further falls are imminent. The shipping company is now paying 2 per cent p.a. above what it would have been paying had it not transacted the swap. It therefore wishes to cancel the swap. The bank may agree to do this in return for a cancellation payment which it calculates from the interest flows it can obtain by transacting a replacement swap as shown in Figure 12.12. The bank will receive the current two-year fixed rate, which is, say, 8.5 per cent p.a. So in the second swap, the bank is receiving 1.5 per cent less for two years than it was receiving in the first swap. This rate, calculated in present value terms, will be the compensation paid to the bank by the shipping company for cancelling the swap. If cancellation occurs between interest payment dates, then the bank calculates the difference in present value terms between the interest rates it is now paying and receiving compared with what it would have paid and received.

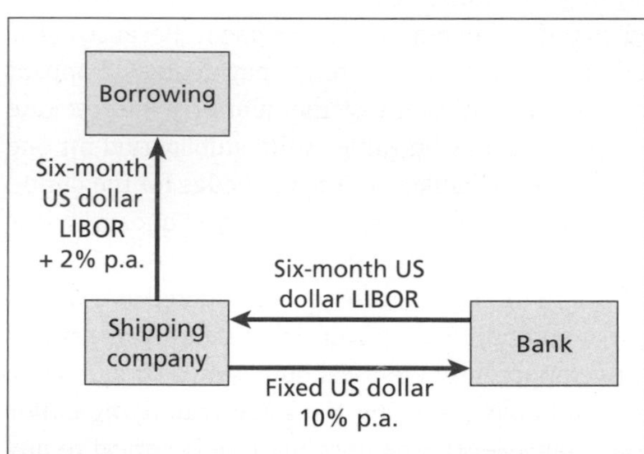

Figure 12.11 Initial swap

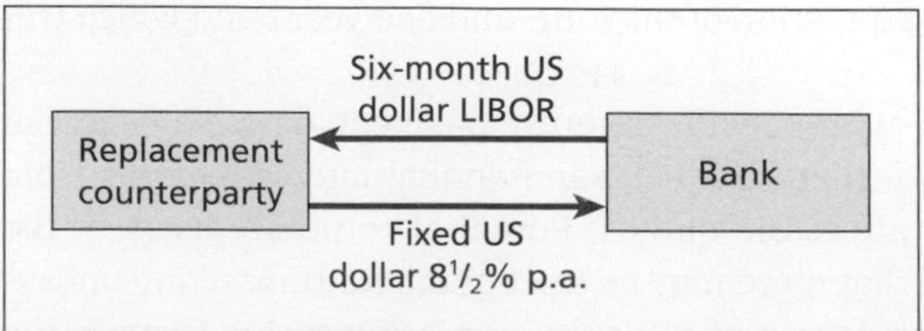

Figure 12.12 Replacement swap

The more exotic the interest rate bases are in swaps, the less liquid they are and so the more difficult they will be to replace. Transacting a swap

Table 12.2 Cost of cancelling an interest rate swap

Years left to run	% of notional principal
9	6.00
7	5.03
5	3.89
3	2.53

with 90-day US dollar commercial paper as the index is more difficult than transacting a swap based on six-month US dollar LIBOR. Swaps with US treasury bills as their base are even more unusual, and are consequently more expensive to reverse.

As an approximate rule of thumb, assuming that a ten-year interest rate swap has an initial coupon of 10 per cent p.a., the cost of cancellation, assuming a 1 per cent shift in prevailing rates to 9 per cent p.a., expressed as a percentage of the notional principal, is shown in Table 12.2.

We now turn to risk assessment for a currency swap. The complexity of currency swaps, compared with interest rate swaps, means that they are virtually never transacted by two companies without a financial institution standing between them and acting as principal with both counterparties. This means that the risk of default by the opposite counterparty is substantially reduced. The risk remains that a company may wish to cancel a currency swap prior to maturity. Doing so will have a cost, either positive or negative, depending on the direction of movements in interest and foreign exchange rates since the swap first began. The method used to calculate that cost is essentially the same as for assessing risk in an interest rate swap – that is, to calculate the cost to the other counterparty of hedging itself by replacing it at current market rates with another currency swap. However, for currency swaps the calculation is made more complicated by the introduction of an additional variable – foreign currency exchange rates.

Here is an example of how the replacement cost can be calculated. Under the terms of a five-year swap there is an initial exchange of the principal amount as shown in Figure 12.13. The US corporation gives the swap bank \$15m in exchange for receiving £10m from the swap bank at the spot foreign exchange rate of \$1.5 = £1. Figure 12.14 shows the periodic payments made by both parties throughout the life of the swap. The US corporation agrees to make fixed payments to the swap bank at 10.50 per cent – or £1,050,000 per year. In return, the swap bank makes fixed payments to the US corporation at 9.75 per cent – or \$1,462,500 per annum. Now, assume that after four years – that is, one year before maturity – the US corporation wishes to cancel the swap. The swap bank agrees to do so, but must hedge its resulting exposure by transacting another currency swap. However, the interest and exchange rate environment will now be different from that prevailing four years before when the original swap was agreed, meaning that it is not possible to transact an identical swap. Assume that the one-year US dollar fixed interest

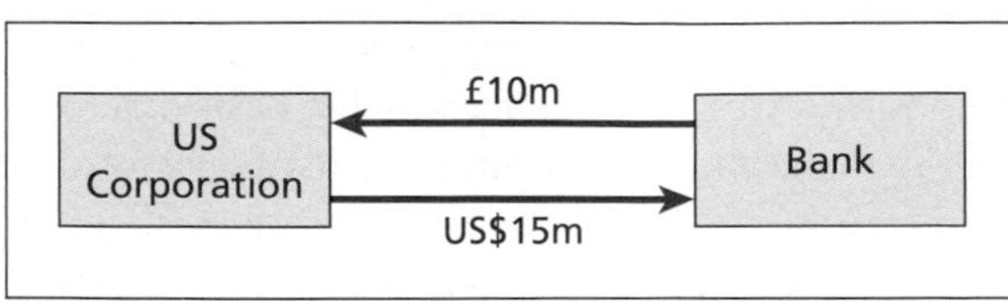

Figure 12.13 Initial exchange of principal

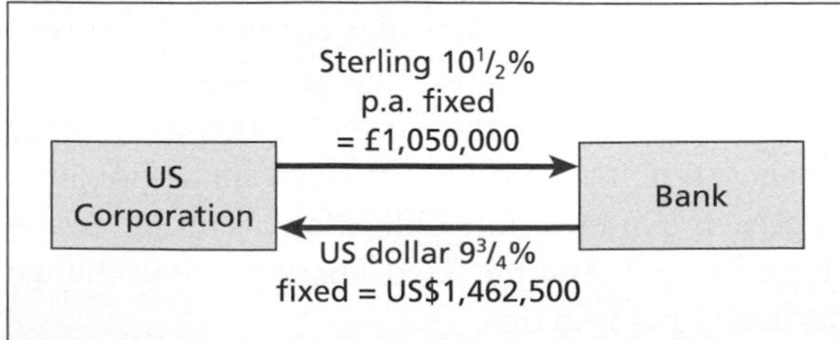

Figure 12.14 Periodic payments

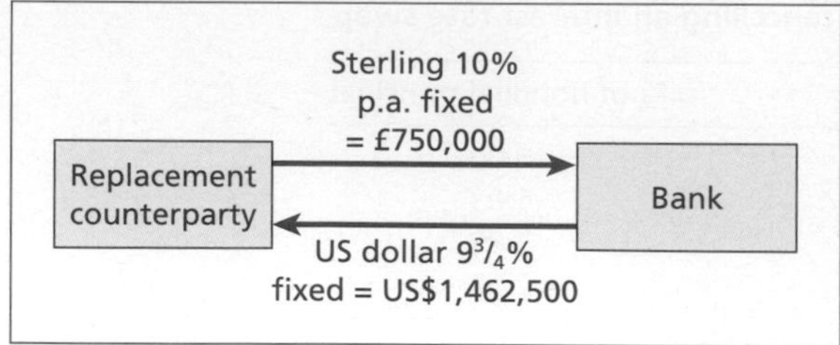

Figure 12.15 Periodic payments in replacement swap

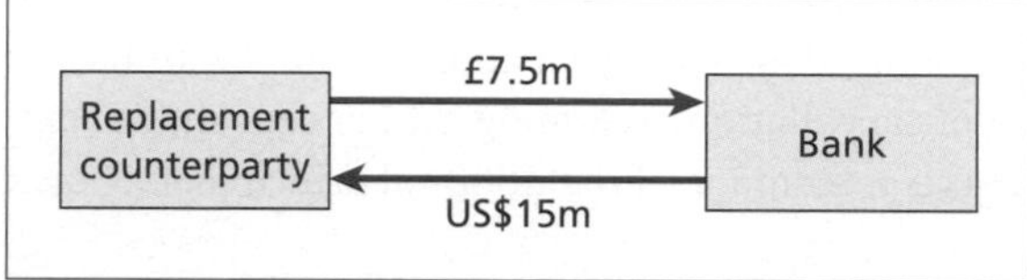

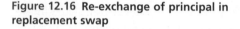

Figure 12.16 Re-exchange of principal in replacement swap

rate is 9.75 per cent p.a. and that the one-year UK sterling fixed interest rate is 10.0 per cent p.a. And the foreign exchange rate has moved to $2.0 = £1. With only one year left until the swap's maturity, the bank expects to make one more interest payment of $1,462,500 and a final exchange of principal of $15,000,000. The one-year US dollar interest rate is 9.75 per cent p.a. – the same as the five-year rate four years ago – so the fixed outflow can remain the same. However, the spot foreign exchange rate has moved. That means the final exchange of principal of $15,000,000 only buys £7,500,000. This, in turn, will yield a fixed inflow of only £750,000 at the new one-year UK sterling swap rate of 10 per cent p.a. as shown in Figure 12.15. Therefore, on the final exchange of interest payments the bank loses £300,000, and on the re-exchange of the principal amount (see Figure 12.16) it loses £2,500,000, a total loss of £2,800,000 discounted for one year at 10.0 per cent p.a. to give a present value of £2,545,454. This loss, expressed in terms of US dollars at the new spot rate of $2.0 = £1, is equivalent to a loss of $5,600,000 (discounted for one year at 10 per cent p.a. to a present value of $5,090,909) – or 37.3 per cent of the original $15m principal amount. This sum is the cost to the US corporation of cancelling the currency swap one year before maturity.

A general issue of risk in swaps arises from the point made in section 12.3 under the sub-head 'Documentation' and contained in the bullet point on 'Simple boiler plating' (see page 205).

Summary

- Bankers are in the business of taking deposits in various currencies on the basis of a fixed or floating interest rate. Also, banks offer to make loans in various currencies on a fixed or on a floating interest rate basis.
- That banks are prepared to take deposits on a floating basis and to lend on a fixed basis (and vice versa) in a particular currency gives the essential rationale for the interest rate swap.
- An interest rate swap involves the banker in lending a particular currency on a fixed interest rate basis and receiving a deposit on a floating interest rate basis – or vice versa. In the swap, of course, the amounts lent and borrowed by the banker are the same. Since they are the same, these capital sums cancel out. The interest rate swap simply involves the servicing by one party of the counterparty's interest rate obligation according to the terms of the swap. No principal sum is exchanged. And the fixed/floating rate exchange reflects market rates prevailing at a particular point in time.

- The fact that banks will take deposits in one currency on a fixed or floating basis and also make loans to customers in a different currency on a fixed or floating basis provides the rationale to the currency swap market.
- The essential logic of the currency swap follows the same kind of thinking that applies to the earlier bullet point on the interest rate swap market. The key difference is that principal sums may be exchanged at the initiation of the currency swap. However, this need not be the case. The point is that if a swap is being done involving UK pounds and euros amounting to the equivalent of £2m, if the exchange rate is euro 1.45 to the pound, then the party wanting to obtain a pound liability might give €2.9m and receive £2m. In this circumstance all that has happened is that a principal sum in one currency is exchanged for a principal sum in another – but the amounts are, of course, equal; this might equally well have been achieved by a spot foreign exchange transaction. In short, the currency swap need not kick off by an exchange of principal. The parties concerned can obtain a capital sum in whatever currency they like simply through the spot market. So, in a currency swap with no exchange of principal, the parties to the agreement agree to pay and receive interest in different specified currencies at fixed or floating interest rates depending upon the agreement in respect of an assumed capital amount and also agree to repay notional principal amounts at maturity. Once again the interest rates (whether fixed or floating) will reflect prevailing market conditions.
- Be sure that you understand how to convert semi-annual to an annual interest rate basis. And also remember how to convert annual interest to a semi-annual basis.
- In terms of covering exposures, the swap market provides an alternative to forward hedging. For most currencies, the forward marker beyond five years is shallow. This is not so in respect of the swap market, where more competitive rates are generally available compared to long-term forwards, and markets go out to maturities of 20 years or more – if required. But care has to be taken in connection with swaps being revalued resulting in calls for the swap bank's customer to post additional margin – see the bullet point on 'Simple boiler plating' (page 205). And this problem can be larger for longer maturity swaps.

End of chapter questions

12.1 Explain both interest rate swaps and currency swaps. Which instrument has a greater credit risk: an interest rate swap or a currency swap?

12.2 How can multinational companies utilise a currency swap to reduce borrowing costs?

12.3 If you expect short-term interest rates to rise more than the yield curve suggests, would you rather pay a fixed long-term rate and receive a floating short-term rate, or receive a fixed long-term rate and pay a floating short-term rate?

13 Financial futures and foreign exchange

A financial futures contract is an agreement to buy or sell a standard quantity of a specific financial instrument at a future date and at a price agreed between the parties through open outcry on the floor of an organised financial futures exchange. With respect to standard quantity, each contract for a given type of financial instrument is for the same standard quantity, for example $100,000. The term 'specific financial instrument' implies that the contract specification lays down the type of financial instrument (for example a twenty-year gilt-edged stock with a stated interest rate, or a foreign currency) with delivery at an explicit maturity. With respect to future date, the delivery of the amounts specified in the contract must take place on one of four specified dates in the forthcoming year. The vast majority of financial futures deals are reversed before delivery date: thus most purchase deals are reversed by matching sale deals, thereby avoiding the need for delivery physically to be effected. Standardisation as to quantity and type of instrument enables easy transferability of futures contracts. Financial futures contracts can be sold via the financial futures exchange.

13.1 Financial futures in general

Someone who buys an interest rate future has the right and obligation to deposit money to the nominal amount contracted for at a specified interest rate for a specified period with the seller. Someone who sells an interest rate future becomes available to take a deposit amounting to the nominal amount contracted at a specific rate of interest for a specific period of time.

Trading in some financial futures markets is still by open outcry but, increasingly, this is being replaced by computers, screen trading, telephones and other telecommunications devices. Under the open outcry system, a principal may give instructions to a broker by telephone but the broker will effect the deal for the client on the financial futures floor (or pit, as it is called). Users, under this system, transact business only through authorised brokers who receive a commission. It is clearly less than ideal, hence its replacement by higher levels of technology.

A **clearing house** exists to ease the funds flow from the execution of contracts. In financial futures trading, the clearing house evolved to assume the credit risk in futures transactions by guaranteeing the performance of buyer and seller to each other.

While all financial futures transactions must have a buyer and seller, their obligation is not to each other but to a clearing house. After a transaction is recorded, the clearing house substitutes itself for the other party and becomes the seller to every buyer and the buyer to every seller. In this way the clearing house achieves its primary objective which is to guarantee the performance of every transaction done on the floor of the financial futures exchange. Trading on margin is a feature of financial futures. Only a small fraction, called the initial margin, of the underlying instrument's value has to be put up initially by the purchaser or seller as security for performance. This amount varies according to the contract which is being dealt in, but it is typically between 1 and 5 per cent of the instrument's value. Clearly, this produces gearing which may be attractive to market operators. Gearing acts to the advantage of the operator in terms of magnifying his or her gains when markets are moving in that person's favour. But the reverse holds when markets move against the operator. Margin positions are revised daily, accounts are debited or credited according to movements and **margin calls** are made to cover accrued losses and to top up subsequent margin to the required percentage level. The essential differences between the mechanics of financial futures and forward foreign exchange transactions are summarised in Table 13.1.

Financial futures provide a means of hedging for those who wish to lock in currency exchange rates on future currency transactions. So foreign currency receivables and payables

Table 13.1 Comparison of forward and futures markets in foreign exchange

	Financial futures	Forward markets
Location	Futures exchanges for some countries. But increasingly banks without a specific physical exchange location.	Banks and other traders – no single location
Trading medium	Screen trading/computers/ telephone/other telecommunications devices. Where futures exchanges have a specific physical location, trading via open outcry.	Screen trading/computers/telephone/ other telecommunications devices
Contract size	Standardised	As required by customer
Maturity/delivery date	Standardised	As required by customer
Counterparty	Clearing house	Known bank or other trader
Credit risk	Clearing house	Individual counterparty
Commissions	Always payable – flat rate for small deals; otherwise negotiable	Negotiable or implied in dealer's spread when no specific commission is payable
Security	Margin required	Counterparty credit risk; banks set this against credit limits according to their own house rules
Liquidity	Provided by margin payments	Provided by credit limits
Leverage	Very high	No formal gearing, but since payment is not required until delivery, although credit limits are used, gearing may in effect be achieved
Settlement	Via clearing house	Via arrangements with banks

may be hedged via financial futures if a market exists in the foreign and home currency. In fact, financial futures markets in foreign currencies exist for only a small spectrum of currencies; these are listed later in this chapter.

Financial futures may be traded by those who are willing to assume risk and wish to profit from the rises or falls they expect to occur in interest rates or exchange rates. This enables users to take a view about trends in rates without actually having to purchase or sell the underlying currency or financial instrument. They may sell a contract which they do not already own (going short) when they feel that it is likely that interest rates will rise or a currency's value will decline. The operator hopes to buy the contract in after a fall in its price prior to the delivery date, thereby making a profit.

Hedgers and speculators each have an important role to play in creating efficient operations in financial futures markets. Traders (or speculators) provide liquidity to the market, enabling hedgers to buy or sell in volume without difficulty. Only a small percentage of futures contracts is held until delivery. The reason for this is that most hedgers have no further need for the hedge once they have traded out of their position in the cash market. Traders usually close their position once they have achieved their profit objectives or decided to cut their losses. A buyer closes his or her position by making an offsetting sale of the same contract; a seller makes an offsetting purchase.

There are two key elements of cost involved in dealing in financial futures. These are direct costs and margin costs. Members charge a negotiated commission for executing orders for a customer. Commission is charged for a round trip. This covers both the opening and the closing of a position and is normally payable either when the position is closed or when delivery takes place. This is the direct cost element.

Margin works differently. When a deal has been done, both buyer and seller have to put up margin to the clearing house (either cash or **collateral**) to provide against adverse price movements of the futures contract. The minimum level of this margin, the initial margin, is set by the clearing house and reflects the volatility of the underlying instrument. Typically, margin may range from 1 to 5 per cent of the face value of the contract. As prices fluctuate daily, the value of outstanding contracts (open positions) will change. The amount of each day's gain or loss (called variation margin) is added to or subtracted from the margin account. Daily profits may be drawn by the investor. However, in order to maintain the initial margin intact, any losses have to be paid to the broker. Because the initial margin is greater than the likely daily movement of the underlying cash instruments, losses on a given day will not generally exceed the amount in a customer's margin account. If a contract is held until delivery, the buyer has to pay the seller the full value of the contract.

13.2 Currency contracts

We are concerned here with currency contracts traded on financial futures exchanges. For purposes of illustration we use as an example contracts for the dollar against sterling, the euro, the Swiss franc and the Japanese yen. Sizes and key data for such currency future contracts, based on the data in Table 13.2.

Financial futures contracts in currencies are priced in terms of the underlying exchange rate. The sterling futures contract (that is, sterling against the US dollar) might be quoted one day at 1.6800 and at 1.6950 on the next day. The pricing system is similar to that in the

Table 13.2 An example of currency futures contracts*

	Currency against US dollar			
	Sterling	**Euros**	**Swiss franc**	**Japanese yen**
Unit of trading	£62,500	€125,000	Sfr 125,000	¥12,500,000
Delivery months	For all contracts, delivery months are March, June, September and December			
Delivery date	For all contracts, delivery is on a specified day of the above delivery months			
Quotation	US$ per £	US$ per €	US$ per Sfr	US$ per ¥100
Minimum price movement	0.01 cent per £	0.01 cent per €	0.01 cent per Sfr	0.01 cent per ¥100
Tick size and value	$6.25	$12.50	$12.50	$12.50
Initial margin	$1,000	$1,000	$1,000	$1,000

* The contract sizes shown are for illustrative purposes only and may not reflect real world contract magnitudes – but they are not too far out. The difficulty for a writer of a textbook is that they do change as time goes on and they are not the same for all exchanges.

foreign exchange market. Other forms of currency contracts in yen, euros and Swiss francs were quoted in terms of the number of dollars per unit of foreign currency, that is, equivalent to the direct quote as in New York. As shown in Table 13.2, the tick value is 0.01 per cent unit of foreign currency. The term 'tick' refers to the minimum price movement in a contract – it is the last decimal place quoted by dealers. With this background, let us consider a simple example. A trader buys three sterling currency contracts at a price of $1.6800; he may find that within a week the position is closable at a price of $1.7300. This would yield a profit of $9,375 as calculated below:

$$3 \text{ contracts} \times 500 \text{ ticks}$$

Or, put another way, profit equals:

$$\$\frac{(1.7300-1.6800)}{0.0001}\times 6.25\ (\$\text{ per tick})\times 3\text{ contracts} = \$9{,}375\ (\text{total profit})$$

The trader calculates the overall profit or loss by multiplying the number of contracts by the number of ticks of price change by the tick value. These three contracts would require initial margin of $3,000 and this would be outstanding for one week.

It should be noted that rates of initial margin quoted in Table 13.2 would only apply between clearing members of the financial futures exchange and the clearing house. Margin arrangements for others may vary. A member may insist on being paid higher initial margins than those stated; the effect of this is to provide a cushion to cover variation margin calls and obviate the need for frequent charges or payments for small price changes on futures contracts. The key factor regarding margin is to know exactly how much cash will be needed to take up the desired futures position, and to relate interest forgone on financing the deal to potential trading profits.

The financial futures markets do not claim to be superior to forward markets in terms of covering foreign exchange risk. However, they may be used to enable a company respectively to cover a receivable or payable by selling or buying the appropriate foreign currency. Clearly, there are disadvantages compared with forward markets. Financial futures markets have only four delivery dates per year; deals are done for standard quantities of currency; and only a small number of currencies are dealt. The problem of specific delivery dates can be overcome by trading a number of contracts for the next delivery date immediately beyond the exposure, and selling on such contracts when the receivable or payable is met.

Arbitraging between financial futures currency quotations and forward markets tends to lead to equality of quotations. So it should be the case that the profit or loss on the financial futures currency contract used to cover an exposure should approximate the profit or loss accruing where cover is achieved through the forward markets. Normally the proceeds from covering via forwards and futures are similar, but forward contracts use up credit lines negotiated with a bank whereas futures contracts do not.

Standardisation of size of financial futures contracts is a problem for the corporate treasurer seeking cover for foreign exchange exposure via financial futures. This is easily overcome by taking that number of contracts which approximates the value of the desired exposed amount – but of course this method cannot yield an exact hedge.

Financial futures exchanges deal with a vast range of currencies against the US dollar: for example, Mexican peso, Swiss franc, sterling, euros, Canadian dollar, Japanese yen, and more. UK-based brokers will readily arrange Chicago contracts for clients wishing to do business in these markets. The range of contracts offered is expanding all the time as new financial futures centres open all around the world.

PRESS CUTTING 13.1

Hostess to fortune

FT

Investors who think the oil price has overshot in the past week might be tempted to buy airline shares. After all, the sector's profits are highly sensitive to changes to the price of jet fuel and the Bloomberg global airlines index has fallen 6 per cent in seven days.

But the potential downside to this strategy is much bigger than the upside. Imagine oil remains near $120 a barrel or even spikes higher. European airlines have only hedged 60 per cent of this year's fuel needs and the rest of the world is even more exposed, Morgan Stanley estimates. Oil at just $100 a barrel last month prompted European low-cost carrier EasyJet to warn that its half-year loss would double.

Even when an airline is hedged, this only buys time to pass on the extra fuel costs to passengers. The trick is to do that without hurting demand. While the economic outlook is better than it was in 2008, the last time airlines faced oil prices this high, many US and European consumers still act like they are in a recession. Business travellers are less price-sensitive but cannot pull all the weight, even if corporate profits remain high.

Imagine instead that the Middle East settles down, and so does the oil price. Even then, airlines have problems. After a year in which passenger ticket prices rose as demand recovered, there are signs that airlines are returning to their self-defeating expansionary ways: capacity is now expanding more quickly than demand on some long-haul routes, according to UBS.

Investing in a sector that struggles even in good times to cover its cost of capital is rarely wise. The International Air Transport Association predicts that the industry will retain just 1.5 per cent of 2011 revenues as net profit – and that forecast assumes oil at $84 a barrel.

Source: *Financial Times* Lex Column, 26/27 February 2011.

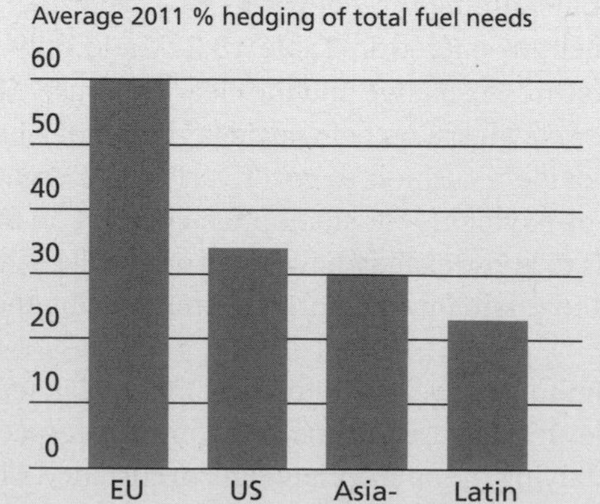

Source: Morgan Stanley.

The financial futures markets are frequently used for currency trading and speculation. Trading may involve taking an uncovered position in a financial futures contract. This occurs when the trader backs his opinion that exchange rates are going to move in a particular direction and when he believes that the general expectations of rates which are reflected in the current level of futures prices do not fully, or even correctly, discount likely events enabling a position to be taken that will show a profit should rates move in the way the trader predicts.

Future exchanges deal in agricultural products – wheat, pig bellies and numerous others. This was the source of such exchanges. And they have grown to include most metals as well as currencies. The good news is that if you understand how futures for one commodity work, you can really relax about all the rest. They basically use the same mechanism – although, clearly, contract sizes and tick sizes vary. Press Cutting 13.1 indicates that airlines use the futures market (in varying degrees) to hedge oil prices. Of course, they may use currency markets to hedge currency risk too.

13.3 Hedging a borrowing

One of the most useful features of hedging via financial futures concerns the rolling over of floating rate borrowings. The financial futures markets enable an investor or borrower to tie in to a fixed rate; the way in which futures may be used to achieve this with respect to a borrowing is best explained with the help of a numerical example. Suppose that it is 1 February. A borrower has a three-month Eurodollar loan of $1m at a rate of 8 per cent per annum, which is due to be rolled over on 31 May. The borrower suspects that by that date rates will have risen. By using a three-month Eurodollar interest rate contract the borrower may cover the risk of higher interest rates. The contract is for a three-month deposit of 1m Eurodollars beginning in March, June, September or December. Since the March contract will have matured before the 31 May roll-over date, the borrower selects the June delivery month for covering. The contract is priced in the normal way by deducting the deposit interest rate from 100. On 1 February the interest rate is 8 per cent, giving a contract price of 92.00. Assume that the contract tick size is 0.01 cents and the value of one tick is $25. Being concerned that interest rates will rise, the borrower sells one June contract at 92.00. By 31 May, when the borrowing is due to be rolled over, assume that Eurodollar interest rates for the month deposits have risen to 10 per cent per annum. The result of the hedge is as follows:

1 February	Sells one June contract at 92.00
31 May	Buys one June contract at 90.00
Profit on deal	= 200 ticks at $25
	= $5,000

The profit on the financial futures deal exactly offsets the extra cost of interest amounting to $5,000, given by:

$$\text{Additional interest paid} = 2\% \times \frac{3 \text{ months}}{12 \text{ months}} \times \$1{,}000{,}000$$

$$= \$5{,}000$$

The hedge has worked perfectly because the cash market interest rates have moved exactly in line with financial futures prices. In practice such perfect matching is rare – futures prices and cash market rates do not move exactly in line.

13.4 Basis risk

Hedging via financial futures is not always exactly achievable. Standardisation of contract size means that precise hedges may not be possible. Remember that it is only possible to deal whole contracts. But the main reason why perfect hedges are not always achievable is the existence of **basis risk**. So what is basis risk? It simply arises because the rates that the cash market (for example, the foreign exchange forward market) and the futures market quote may be different and the amount of the difference varies over time. For example, to cover an interest rate exposure in the futures market, a company will have to buy at one time and to sell before the expiry of the contract concerned. The difference between the futures market price and the cash market interest rate may be 40 **basis points** (0.40 per cent p.a.) at the time of the purchase and 20 basis points at the time of sale. Clearly, the hedge may make a profit or incur a loss as a result of the changing basis risk in the above example. The relationship between yields in the cash and futures markets may arise in part due to the different cash flows required – remember that futures contracts require margin payments whereas currency forward contracts require no up-front payment (except for relatively weak credits – and very poor credits cannot access the forward market). This source of basis risk is termed the 'carrying cost' element.

The second source of basis risk is different expectations in the two markets, largely brought about by the relative risk aversion of the participants in the different markets. Of course, there is a ceiling to the extent of basis risk inasmuch as arbitrageurs will whittle it away should it become excessive. Diagrammatically, the sources of basis risk can be summarised as shown in Figure 13.1.

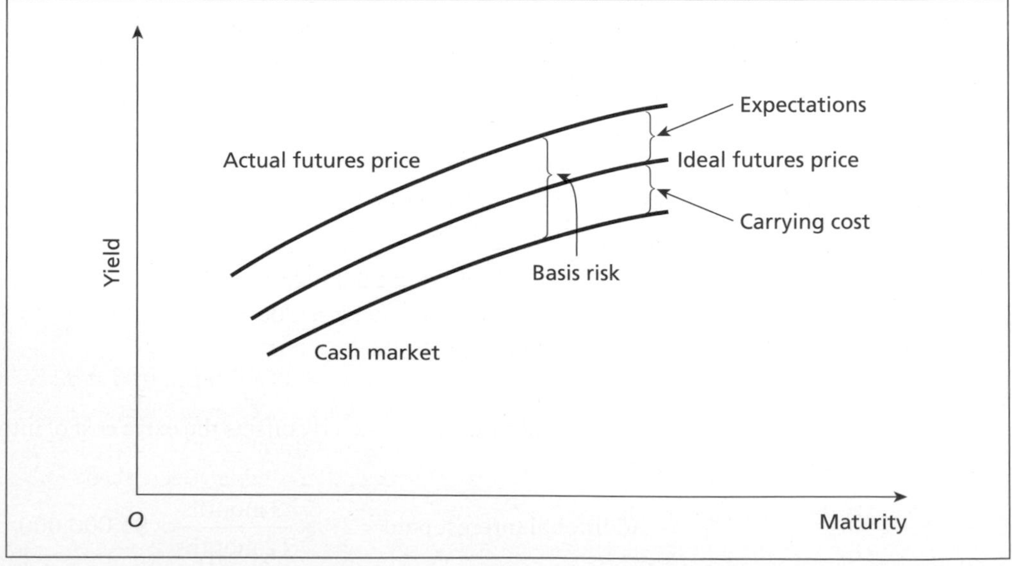

Figure 13.1 Sources of basis risk

13.5 Use of currency futures market

Companies are comparatively small users of the currency futures markets. They can invariably achieve cover more easily, more cheaply and more effectively via the forward market. As we have mentioned earlier, the forward market does not require – for the reasonably strong company – any up-front payment; banks set forward deals against negotiated credit lines. Weak credits may be asked for an up-front payment for forward deals based upon a percentage of the size of the contract. And very weak companies, financially speaking, may be denied access to the forward market because commercial banks may not wish to carry the risk that the firm may default on its obligations under any contract granted. For such companies, the futures market may be an ideal alternative. Their brokers will, remember, require initial and variation margin and, to the extent that this is not forthcoming as requested, the futures contracts will be closed out at the prevailing market price. This mechanism reduces the credit risk attached to the financially weak corporation in its dealings in futures markets. However, some corporate treasurers and many speculators frequently use currency futures.

13.6 Using currency futures in corporate hedging

Most firms prefer to use forwards to hedge exposures because they are customisable – that is, they can be structured to meet specific timing and cash amounts that articulate precisely with a sales or purchase deal. But the use of futures is possible.

Futures are heavily used by banks and other financial institutions. For example, a swap dealer might use futures as a temporary hedge until an offsetting swap can be arranged. Futures are also a popular medium for speculators, who wish to play markets.

If you have purchased a USD future, and the price of the future rises against the other currency, your margin account will be credited with the increment. If you have sold the future and the price of the future rises against the other currency, your margin account will be charged with the increment – you must ensure that funds are credited to the account to cover the loss. Currency futures can be traded on various exchanges such as Euronext (USD/EUR), Chicago Mercantile Exchange (CME), or the Philadelphia Board of Trade (PBOT or PHLX), both of which trade futures on all the major currencies, with the USD as settlement currency. Key features of a Chicago sterling futures contract is as follows:

CME sterling futures	
Trade unit	62,500 GBP
Settlement method	Physical delivery, 3rd Wednesday of the contract month
Tick description	1 tick – 0.0001 per pound sterling, or USD6.25 per contract (Ticks may also be referred to as points)
Contracts listed	Six months in the March quarterly cycle, i.e. March, June, September, December
Trading house (Mid-West time)	7 a.m.–2 p.m.

Futures contract prices are based on the similar terms for a corresponding forward contract, though minor pricing differences may arise and they will always be very minor differences due to the timing of cash flows under futures versus forwards. Futures contracts require up-front margin payments whilst forwards do not.

Treasurers who cannot access the forward market, maybe due to a low credit rating for their company, are likely to use financial futures. But some treasurers prefer futures because they have time flexibility. This typically arises because hedging a foreign currency receivable with a forward, one often enters into the forward according to the expected date of actual payment. With futures cover, the future can be left until the foreign currency receivable is actually paid and then converted to home currency in the spot market. And, at this point in time, the currency future is sold on in the secondary market.

Summary

- Cover against foreign exchange exposures may be obtained through the forward or swap markets. Financial futures on foreign currency provide another means of covering currency exposures. Forward rates, swap rates and financial futures quotations on currency are based upon interest rate differentials.
- The pricing of financial futures contracts on foreign exchanges varies slightly from forward quotations by virtue of the different timing of cash flows. Note that financial futures requires an initial margin; this contrasts to the forward contract which, for corporations with an acceptable credit standing, involves exchange of cash only at maturity. It is this difference in cash flow configuration that gives rise to quotation differences.
- It is worth noting that the forward market provides a far better way of achieving cover than financial futures on foreign currency.
- The futures market may be resorted to by corporations whose inferior credit standing precludes them from access to the forward market. It is a relatively cumbersome market to monitor positions in and is a more expensive market to deal in compared with the forward market. Futures markets are used by individuals for speculative purposes.

End of chapter questions

13.1 Explain how a US corporation could hedge net receivables in British pounds with futures contracts.

13.2 What is basis risk? How does a cross-hedge (where the cash flow exposure being hedged has different characteristics to the future used as a hedge – hence the expression across markets – hence the expression cross-hedge) create basis risk? How does a mismatch in maturities between the asset being hedged and the futures contract in the hedge create basis risk?

13.3 Assume that, on 1 November, the spot rate of the £/US$ was $1.58 and the price on a December futures contract was $1.59. Assume that the pound depreciates over November, so that by 30 November it is worth $1.51.

(a) What do you think would happen to the futures price over the month of November? Why?

(b) If you expected this to occur, would you have purchased or sold a December futures contract on GBP on 1 November? Explain.

14 Options

Many finance students will have come across options already in their studies. This chapter may be skipped by them. They should move on to the next chapter which is on currency options. Other readers who may not have studied options are advised to read it. This chapter focuses upon the general topic of options and the following chapter looks specifically at currency options.

Options are contractual arrangements giving the owner the right to buy or sell an asset at a fixed price anytime on or before a given date. Share options are options to buy and sell shares. Share options are frequently referred to as stock options. Both terms have the same meaning. Share options are traded on stock exchanges. This chapter contains a description of different types of options. We identify and discuss factors that determine option values.

An option is a contract giving its owner the right to buy or sell an asset at a fixed price on or before a given date. For example, an option on a building might give the buyer the right to buy the building for £1m on or any time before the Saturday prior to the third Wednesday in January 2014. Options are a singular type of financial contract because they give the buyer the right, but not the obligation, to do something. The buyer uses the option only if it is a sensible thing to do so. Otherwise, the option can be simply discarded.

There is a vocabulary associated with options. Some of the most important definitions are as follows:

- **Exercising** *the option*. The act of buying or selling the underlying asset via the option contract is referred to as exercising the option.
- **Strike or exercise price**. The fixed price in the option contract at which the holder of the option can buy or sell the underlying asset is called the strike price or exercise price.
- **Expiration date**. The maturity date of the option is termed the expiration date. After this date, the option is dead.
- *American and European options*. An **American option** may be exercised at any time up to the expiration date. A **European option** differs from an American option in that it can only be exercised on the expiration date.

14.1 Call options

The most frequently encountered option is a **call option**. It gives the owner the right to buy an asset at a fixed price during a particular time period. The most common options traded on exchanges are options on shares and bonds. Usually the assets involved are ordinary shares.

For example, call options on XYZ plc shares can be purchased on the London Stock Exchange. XYZ itself does not issue (that is, sell) call options on its ordinary shares. In fact, individual investors or banks are the original sellers and buyers of call options on XYZ ordinary shares. A call option on XYZ enables an investor to buy 1,000 shares of XYZ on or before, say, 15 July 2012, at an exercise price of £12. This is a valuable option if there is some probability that the price of XYZ ordinary shares will exceed £12 on or before 15 July 2012.

Virtually all option contracts on shares specify that the exercise price and the number of shares are adjusted for stock splits and stock dividends. Suppose that XYZ shares were selling for £18 on the day the option was purchased. Suppose that the next day it split 6 for 1. Each share would drop in price to £3, and the probability that the share would rise over £12 per share in the near future becomes very remote. To protect the option holder from such an occurrence, call options are typically adjusted for stock splits and stock dividends. In the case of a 6-for-1 split, the exercise price would become £2 (£12 divided by 6). Furthermore, the option contract would now cover 6,000 shares, rather than the original 1,000 shares. Note that no adjustment is made for the payment by XYZ of cash dividends to shareholders. This failure to adjust clearly hurts holders of call options, though, of course, they should know the terms of option contracts and the proximity of dividends before buying.

The value of a call option at expiration

The value of a call option contract on ordinary shares at expiration depends on the value of the underlying shares at expiration. We use S_T as the market price of the underlying shares on the expiration date, T. This price is not known prior to expiration. Suppose that a particular call option could be exercised one year from now at the exercise price of £50. If the value of the ordinary shares at expiration, S_T, is greater than the exercise price of £50, the option will be worth the difference, $S_T - £50$. When $S_T > £50$, the call is said to be in the money.

Suppose the share price on expiration day is £60. The option holder has the right to buy the share from the option seller[1] for £50. Because the share is selling in the market for £60, the option holder would exercise the option, that is, buy the share for £50. If he were to wish to do so, he could then sell the share for £60 and keep the difference of £10 (£60 – £50) Options are not usually on just one share. More usually the option might be on 1,000 shares or 10,000 shares.

Of course, it is possible that the value of the share will turn out to be less than the exercise price. If $S_T < £50$, the call is said to be out of the money. The holder would not exercise in this case. If the share price at the expiration date were £40, no rational investor would exercise. Why pay £50 (by exercising the option) for a share worth only £40? Since the option holder has no obligation to exercise the call, he can walk away from the option. Thus, if $S_T < £50$ on the expiration date, the value of the call option will be zero. In this case the value of the call option is not $S_T - £50$, as it would be if the holder of the call option had the obligation to exercise the call. The *payoff of a call option at expiration* is:

	if $S_T \leq £50$	if $S_T > £50$
Call-option value:	0	$S_T - £50$

Figure 14.1 plots the value of the call option at expiration against the value of the share. It is often referred to as the hockey-stick diagram of call-option values. If $S_T < £50$,

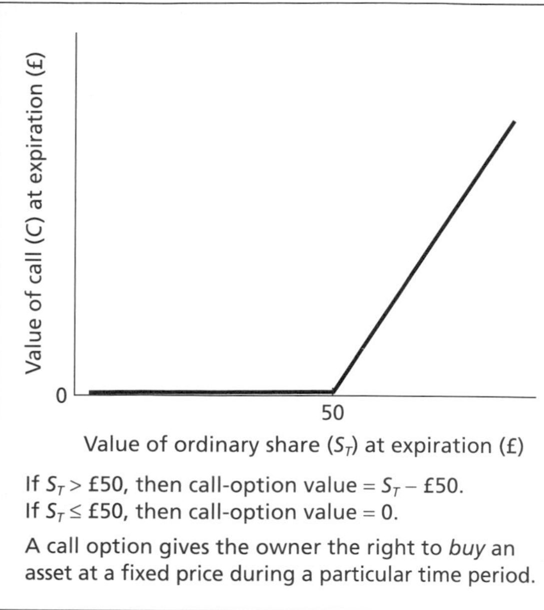

Value of call (C) at expiration (£)
0
50
Value of ordinary share (S_T) at expiration (£)
If $S_T >$ £50, then call-option value = $S_T -$ £50.
If $S_T \leq$ £50, then call-option value = 0.
A call option gives the owner the right to *buy* an asset at a fixed price during a particular time period.

Figure 14.1 The value of a call option on the expiration date

the call is out of the money and worthless. If $S_T >$ £50, the call is in the money and rises one-for-one with increases in share price. Note that the call can never have a negative value. A call is a limited liability instrument; the maximum amount that the holder can lose on a call option is the initial amount he or she paid for it.

Consider an example. Suppose that Henry Hope holds a one year call option for 1,000 shares of ABC plc. It is a European call option and can be exercised at £15 per share. Assume that the expiration date has arrived. What is the value of the ABC call option at the expiration date? If ABC is selling for £20 per share, Henry Hope can exercise the option-purchase 1,000 shares of ABC at £15 per share – and then immediately sell the shares at £20. Henry Hope will have made £5,000 (1,000 shares × £5). Instead, assume that ABC is selling for £10 per share on the expiration date. If Henry Hope were still to hold the call option, he would tear it up. The value of the ABC call on the expiration date would, in this case, be zero.

14.2 Put options

A **put option** is really the opposite of a call option. Just as a call gives the holder the right to buy shares at a fixed price, so a put gives the holder the right to sell shares for a fixed exercise price.

The value of a put option at expiration

Circumstances that determine the value of a put option are the opposite of those for a call option, because a put option gives the holder the right to sell shares. Assume that the exercise price of the put is £50. If the price, S_T, of the underlying ordinary shares at expiration is greater than the exercise price, it would be foolish to exercise the option and sell shares for £50 each. The put option is worthless if $S_T >$ £50. In this case, the put is out-of-the-money. However, if $S_T <$ £50, the put is in-the-money. It will pay to buy shares at S_T and use the option to sell shares at the exercise price of £50. So, if the share price at expiration is £40, the holder should buy the shares in the open market at £40. By immediately exercising, he receives £50 for the sale. His profit is £10 per share (£50 – £40).

The *payoff of a put option at expiration* is given by:

	if $S_T <$ £50	if $S_T \geq$ £50
Put-option value:	£50 – S_T	0

Figure 14.2 plots the values of a put option for all values of the underlying shares. It is instructive to compare Figure 14.2 with Figure 14.1 for the call-option value. The call option

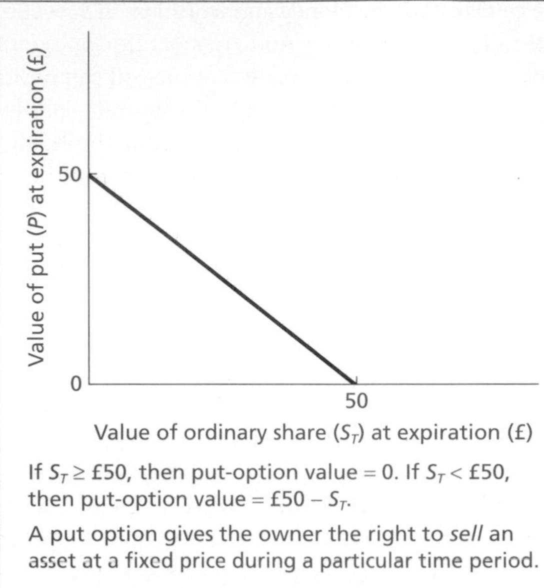
Value of put (P) at expiration (£)
50
0
50
Value of ordinary share (S_T) at expiration (£)
If $S_T \geq$ £50, then put-option value = 0. If $S_T <$ £50, then put-option value = £50 – S_T.
A put option gives the owner the right to *sell* an asset at a fixed price during a particular time period.

Figure 14.2 The value of a put option on the expiration date

is valuable whenever the stock is above the exercise price. The put is valuable when the stock price is below the exercise price.

Take an example. Felicity Fear is quite certain that ABC plc will fall from its current £16 per share price. So she buys a put on 1,000 ABC shares. Her put option contract gives her the right to sell 1,000 shares of ABC at £15 per share one year from now. If the price of ABC is £20 on the expiration date, she will tear up the put option contract because it is worthless. She will not want to sell shares worth £20 for the exercise price of £15. On the other hand, if ABC is selling for £10 on the expiration date, she would exercise the option. Felicity Fear has the right to sell 1,000 shares of ABC for £15 per share. In this case, she could buy 1,000 shares of ABC in the market for £10 per share and turn around and sell the shares at the exercise price of £15 per share. Her profit would be £5,000 (1,000 shares × £5). The value of the put option on the expiration date would be £5,000.

14.3 Writing options

An investor who writes a call on ordinary shares promises to deliver shares of the company concerned if required to do so by the call-option holder. Note that the seller is obligated to do so. The option writer is the original seller of the option. The seller of a call option obtains a cash payment from the holder, or buyer, at the time the option is bought. If, at the expiration date, the price of the ordinary share is below the exercise price, the call option will not be exercised and the seller's liability will be zero.

If, at expiration date, the price of the ordinary share is greater than the exercise price, the holder will exercise the call and the writer or seller must give the holder shares in exchange for the exercise price. The seller loses the difference between the share price and the exercise price. Assume that the share price is £60 and the exercise price is £50. Knowing that exercise is imminent, the option seller buys shares in the open market at £60. Because he is obligated to sell at £50, he loses £10 (£50 – £60) per share.

By a reverse logic, an investor who sells a put option on ordinary shares agrees to purchase shares if the put holder should so request. The seller loses on this deal if the share price falls below the strike price and the holder puts the shares to the seller. For example, assume that the share price is £40 and the exercise price is £50. In this case, the holder of the put will exercise. So he will sell the underlying shares at the exercise price of £50. This means that the seller of the put must buy the underlying shares at the strike price of £50. Because the share is only worth £40, the loss here is £10 (£40 – £50) per share under option.

The 'sell-a-call' and 'sell-a-put' positions are depicted in Figure 14.3. The chart (a) on the left-hand side of the figure shows that the seller of a call loses nothing when the share price

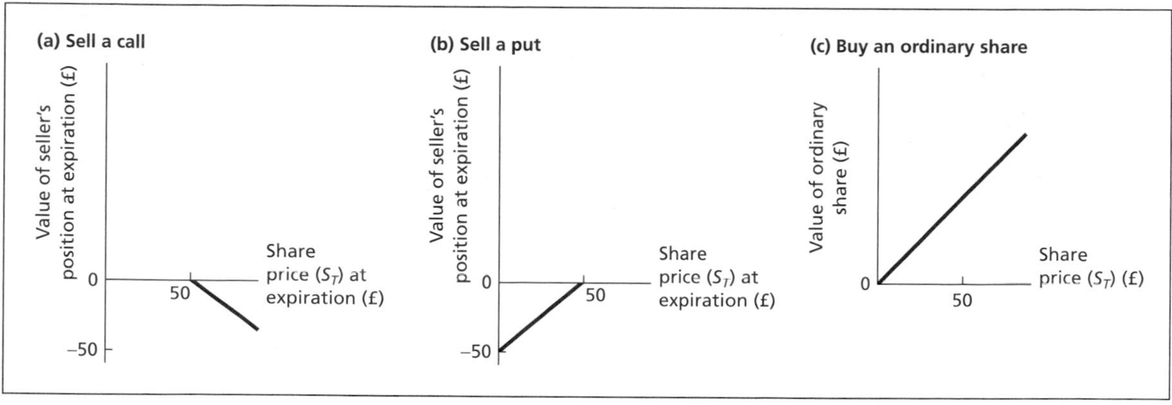

Figure 14.3 The payoffs to sellers of calls, puts, and to buyers of ordinary shares

at expiration date is below £50. However, the seller loses £1 for every £1 that the share price rises above £50. The chart (b) in the centre shows that the seller of a put loses nothing when the share price at expiration date is above £50. However, the seller loses £1 for every £1 that the share falls below £50. The third chart (c) also shows the value at expiration of simply buying ordinary shares.

14.4 Reading the *Financial Times*

Now that we understand the definitions for calls and puts, let us see how options are quoted. Table 14.1 presents information on the options of ABC from a financial newspaper. The options are traded on an option exchange and this would be stated where the words 'Name of options exchange' appears in Table 14.1. The London International Financial Futures Exchange (LIFFE) is one of a number of options exchanges. The first column tells us that the shares of ABC closed at $48^1/_2$ pence per share on the previous day, say 13 February. Now consider the second and third columns. Thursday's closing price for an option maturing at the end of April with a strike price of 45 pence was 6.75 pence. Because the option is sold as a 1,000-share contract, the cost of the contract is £67.50 (1,000 × 6.75p) before commissions. The call maturing in April with an exercise price of 50p closed at 4.00p.

The last three columns display quotes on puts. For example, a put maturing in April with an exercise price of 45p sells at 3.00p.

Table 14.1 Information on the options of ABC

		Name of options exchange					
		Calls			Puts		
Option & London close	Strike price	April	July	Oct.	April	July	Oct.
48.50	45	6.75	9.00	11.00	3.00	5.00	6.50
48.50	50	4.00	6.75	8.75	5.25	7.50	9.00

Source: data from *Financial Times*, 14 February 2003.

14.5 Combinations of options

Puts and calls may serve as building blocks for more complex option contracts. For example, Figure 14.4 illustrates the payoff from buying a put option on a share and simultaneously buying the share.

If the share price is above the exercise price, the put option is worthless and the value of the combined position is equal to the value of the ordinary share. If, instead, the exercise price is above the share price, the decline in the value of the shares will be exactly offset by the rise in value of the put.

The combination of buying a put and buying the underlying share has the same shape in Figure 14.4 as the call purchase in Figure 14.1. Furthermore, the shape of the combination strategy in Figure 14.4 is the mirror image of the shape of the call sale in the upper left-hand corner (a) of Figure 14.3. This suggests that a strategy in the options market may offset another strategy, resulting in a riskless return.

This possibility is in fact true, as shown in the following example. Assume that both the exercise price of the call and the exercise price of the put on Breitner GmbH are €55. Both options are European. Thus, they cannot be exercised prior to expiration. The expiration date is one year from today. The share price is currently €44. At the expiration date, the stock will be priced, say, at either €58 or €34.

The *offsetting strategy*: suppose you pursue the following strategy:

- Buy the stock.
- Buy the put.
- Sell the call.

The *payoffs at expiration* are:

Initial transaction	Share price rises to €58	Share price falls to €34
Buy an ordinary share	€58	€34
Buy a put	0 (You let put expire)	€21 = €55 – €34
Sell a call	–€3 = –(€58 – €55)	0 (Holder lets call expire)
Total	€55	€55

Note that, when the share price falls, the put is in the money and the call expires without being exercised. When the share price rises, the call is in the money and you let the put expire. The major point is that you end up with €55 in either case.

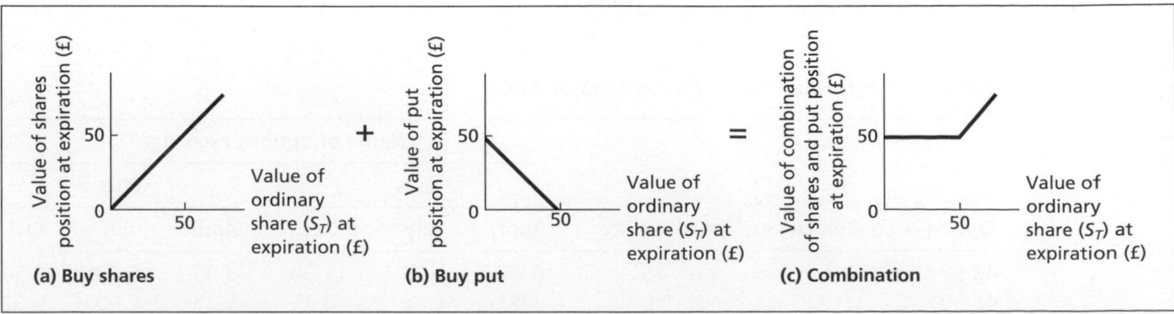

Figure 14.4 Payoffs to the combination of buying puts and buying stock

There is no risk in this strategy. While this result may bother students – or even shock some – it is actually quite intuitive. As pointed out earlier, the graph of the strategy of buying both a put and the underlying shares is the mirror image of the graph from the strategy of selling the call. Thus, combining both strategies, as we did in the example, should eliminate all risk.

The above payoff diagram separately valued each asset at the expiration date. Actually, a discussion of the actual exercise process may simplify things, because here the share is always linked with an option. Consider the following *strategy* tabulation:

Share price rises to €58		**Share price falls to €34**	
You let put expire.	0	Call expires.	0
Call is exercised against you, obligating you to sell the share you own and receive the exercise price of:	€55	You choose to exercise put. That is, you sell the share you own at the exercise price of:	€55
Total	€55	Total	€55

Again, we see the riskless nature of the strategy. Regardless of the price movement of the share, exercise entails surrendering the share for €55.

Though we have specified the payoffs at expiration, we have ignored the earlier investment that you made. To remedy this, suppose that you originally pay €44 for the share and €7 for the put and receive €1 for selling the call.[2] In addition, the riskless interest rate is 10 per cent.

You have paid:

−€50 =	−€44	−€7	+€1
	Share purchase	Purchase of put	Sale of call

Because you pay €50 today and are guaranteed €55 in one year, you are just earning the interest rate of 10 per cent. Thus, the prices in this example allow no possibility of arbitrage or easy money. Conversely, if the put sold for only €6, your initial investment would be €49. You would then have a non-equilibrium return of 12.2 per cent (€55/€49 − 1) over the year.

It can be proved that, in order to prevent arbitrage, the prices at the time you take on your original position must conform to the following fundamental relationship:

$$\begin{array}{ccccccc} \text{Value of share} & + & \text{Value of put} & - & \text{Value of call} & = & \text{Present value of exercise price} \\ €44 & & €7 & & €1 & & = €50 = €55/1.10 \end{array}$$

This result is called *put–call parity*. It shows that the values of a put and a call with the same exercise price and same expiration date are precisely related to each other. It holds generally, not just in the specific example we have chosen.[3]

14.6 Valuing options

In the last section, we determined what options are worth on the expiration date. Now we wish to determine the value of options when we buy them well before expiration. We begin by considering the upper and lower bounds on the value of a call.

Bounding the value of a call

Consider an American call that is in the money prior to expiration. For example, assume that the share price is €60 and the exercise price is €50. In this case, the option cannot sell below €10. To see this, note the simple strategy if the option sells at, say, €9.

Date	Transaction	
Today	(1) Buy call	–€ 9
Today	(2) Exercise call, that is, buy underlying share at exercise price	–€50
Today	(3) Sell stock at current market price	+€60
Arbitrage profit		+€ 1

The type of profit that is described in this transaction is an arbitrage profit. Arbitrage profits come from transactions that have no risk or cost and cannot occur regularly in normal, well-functioning financial markets. The excess demand for these options would quickly force the option price up to[4] at least €10 (€60 – €50).

Of course, the price of the option is likely to sell above €10. Investors will rationally pay more than €10 given the possibility that the share price will rise above €60 before expiration. Is there also an upper boundary for the option price? It turns out that the upper boundary is the price of the underlying share. Thus, an option to buy ordinary shares cannot have a greater value than the ordinary share itself. A call option can be used to buy ordinary shares with a payment of an exercise price. It would not be sensible to buy shares this way if the shares could be purchased directly at a lower price. The upper and lower bounds are represented in Figure 14.5.

The factors determining call-option values

The previous discussion indicated that the price of a call option must fall somewhere in the shaded region of Figure 14.5. Now, we can determine more precisely where in the shaded

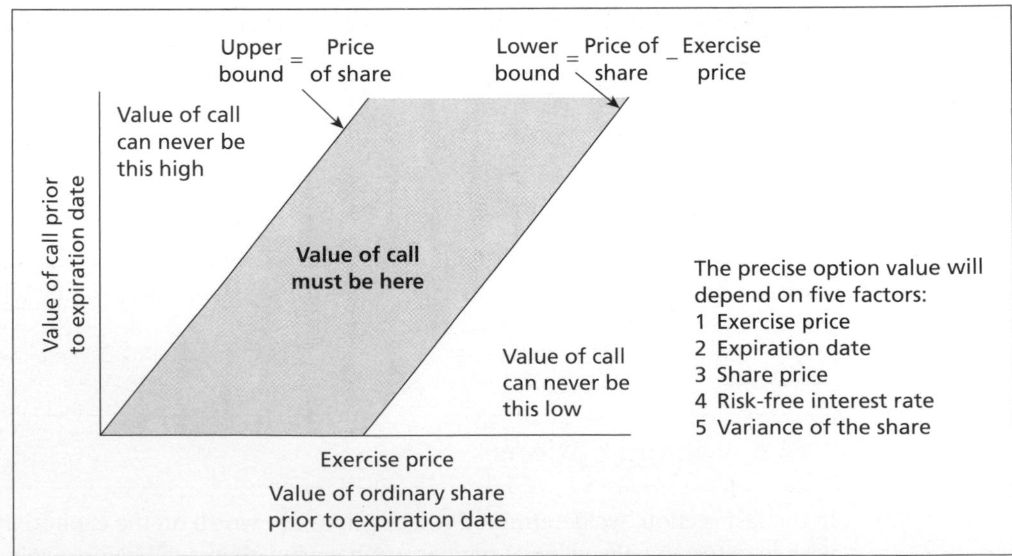

Figure 14.5 The upper and lower boundaries of call-option values

region it should be. The factors that determine a call's value can be broken into two sets. The first set contains the features of the option contract. The two basic contractual features are the expiration price and the exercise date. The second set of factors affecting the call price concerns characteristics of the share and the market.

Exercise price

It should be obvious that if all other things are held constant, the higher the exercise price, the lower the value of a call option. However, the value of a call option cannot be negative, no matter how high we set the exercise price. Furthermore, as long as there is some possibility that the price of the underlying asset will exceed the exercise price before the expiration date, the option will have value.

Expiration date

The value of an American call option must be at least as great as the value of an otherwise identical option with a shorter term to expiration. Consider two American calls. One has a maturity of nine months and the other expires in six months' time. Clearly, the nine-month call has the same rights as the six-month call but it also has an additional three months within which these rights can be exercised. It cannot be worth less and will generally be more valuable.[5]

Share price

Other things being equal, the higher the share price, the more valuable the call option will be. This is obvious and is illustrated in any of the figures that plot the call price against the share price at expiration.

Now consider Figure 14.6, which shows the relationship between the call price and the share price prior to expiration. The curve indicates that the call price increases as the share price increases. Furthermore, it can be shown that the relationship is represented, not by a

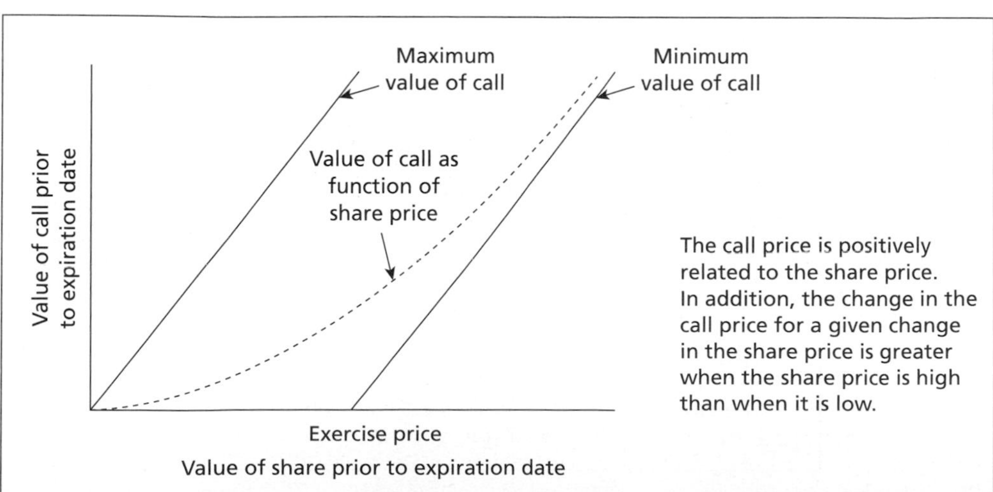

Figure 14.6 Value of a call as a function of share price

straight line, but by a convex curve. That is, the increase in the call price for a given change in the share price is greater when the share price is high than when the share price is low.

The variability of the underlying asset

The greater the variability of the underlying asset, the more valuable the call option will be. Consider the following example. Suppose that just before the call expires, the share price will be either €100 with probability 0.5 or €80 with probability 0.5. What will be the value of a call with an exercise price of €110? Clearly, it will be worthless because no matter what happens to the share, its price will always be below the exercise price.

Now let us see what happens if the share is more variable. Suppose that we add €20 to the best case and take €20 away from the worst case. Now the share has a one-half chance of being worth €60 and a one-half chance of being worth €120. We have spread the share returns, but, of course, the expected value of the share has stayed the same:

$$({}^1/_2 \times €80) + ({}^1/_2 \times €100) = €90 = ({}^1/_2 \times €60) + ({}^1/_2 \times €120)$$

Notice that the call option has value now because there is a one-half chance that the share price will be €120, or €10 above the exercise price of €110. This illustrates an important point. There is a fundamental distinction between holding an option on an underlying asset and holding the underlying asset. If investors in the market place are risk-averse, a rise in the variability of the share will decrease its market value. However, the holder of a call receives payoffs from the positive tail of the probability distribution. As a consequence, a rise in the variability in the underlying share increases the market value of the call.

This result can also be seen from Figure 14.7. Consider two shares, A and B, each of which is distributed differently. For each security, the figure illustrates the probability of

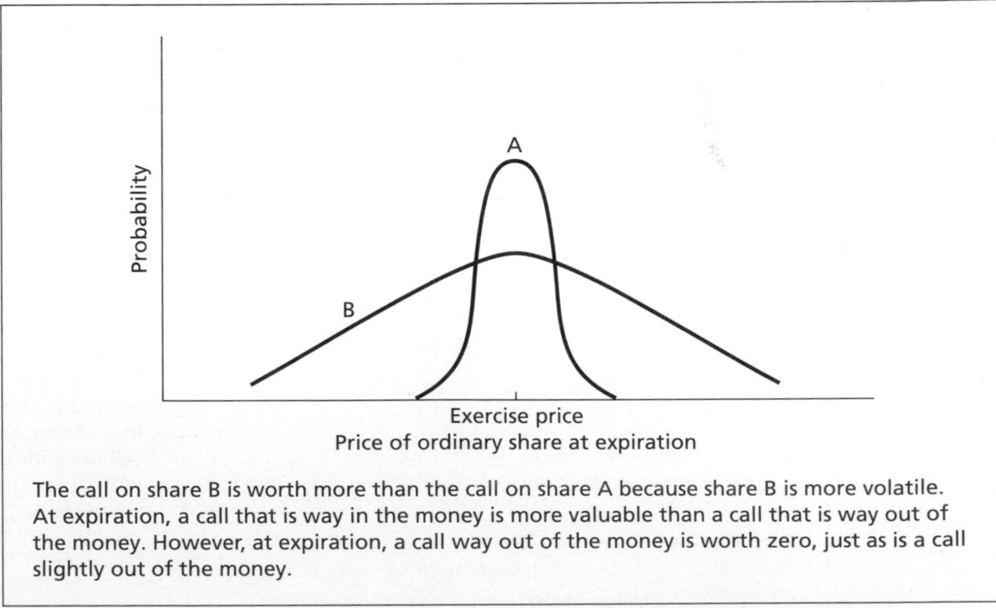

The call on share B is worth more than the call on share A because share B is more volatile. At expiration, a call that is way in the money is more valuable than a call that is way out of the money. However, at expiration, a call way out of the money is worth zero, just as is a call slightly out of the money.

Figure 14.7 Distribution of ordinary share price at expiration for both security A and security B. Options on the two securities have the same exercise price

different share prices on the expiration date.[6] As can be seen from the figures, share B has more volatility than does share A. This means that share B has higher probability of both abnormally high returns and abnormally low returns. Let us assume that options on each of the two securities have the same exercise price. To option holders, a return much below average on stock B is no worse than a return only moderately below average on share A. In either situation, the option expires out of the money. However, to option holders, a return much above average on share B is better than a return only moderately above average on share A. Because a call's price at the expiration date is the difference between the share price and the exercise price, the value of the call on B at expiration will be higher in this case.

The interest rate

Call prices are also a function of the level of interest rates. Buyers of calls do not pay the exercise price until they exercise the option, if they do so at all. The delayed payment is more valuable when interest rates are high and less valuable when interest rates are low. Thus, the value of a call is positively related to interest rates.

Factors determining put-option values

Given our extended discussion of the factors influencing a call's value, we can examine the effect of these factors on puts very easily. Table 14.2 summarises the five factors influencing the prices of both American calls and American puts. The effect of three factors on puts are the opposite of the effect of these three factors on calls:

- The put's market price *decreases* as the share price increases because puts are in the money when the share sells below the exercise price.
- The market value of a put with a high exercise price is *greater* than the value of an otherwise-identical put with a low exercise price for the reason given above.
- A high interest rate *adversely* affects the value of a put. The ability to sell a share at a fixed exercise price sometime in the future is worth less if the present value of the exercise price is diminished by a high interest rate.

The effect of the other two factors on puts is the same as the effect of these factors on calls:

- The value of an American put with a distant expiration date is greater than an otherwise identical put with an earlier expiration. The longer time to maturity gives the put holder more flexibility, just as it did in the case of a call.

Table 14.2 Factors affecting US options values

	Call option	Put option
Value of underlying asset (share price)	+	–
Exercise price	–	+
Share volatility	+	+
Interest rate	+	–
Time to exercise date	+	+

The signs (+, –) indicate the effect of the variables on the value of the option. For example, the two +s for share volatility indicate that an increase in volatility will increase both the value of a call and the value of a put.

- Volatility of the underlying share increases the value of the put. The reasoning is analogous to that for a call. At expiration, a put that is way in the money is more valuable than a put only slightly in the money. However, at expiration, a put way out of the money is worth zero, just as is a put only slightly out of the money.

Of course, it must be remembered that the option pricing ideas related so far refer to options on shares that do not pay a dividend in the period concerned. In fact, the concepts illustrated may be augmented to provide for the wherewithal to deal with dividend paying shares.

14.7 An option pricing formula

We have explained qualitatively that the value of a call option is a function of five variables:

- the current price of the underlying asset, which for share options is the price of the ordinary shares;
- the exercise price;
- the time to expiration date;
- the variance of the underlying asset;
- the risk-free interest rate.

We now replace the qualitative model with a precise option-valuation model. The model we use is the well-known **Black and Scholes**[7,8] **option pricing model**. One can put numbers into the Black and Scholes model and get values back. The Black and Scholes model is represented by a rather imposing formula. A derivation of the formula is not presented in this textbook since it is fairly complicated.

Black and Scholes argue that a strategy of borrowing to finance a share purchase duplicates the risk of a call. Then, knowing the price of a share already, one can determine the price of a call such that its return is identical to that of the share-with-borrowing alternative.

The intuition behind the Black and Scholes approach in illustrated by considering a simple example where a combination of a call and a share eliminates all risk. This example works because we let the future share price be one of only two values. Hence, the example is called a two-state option model. By eliminating the possibility that the share price can take on other values, we are able to duplicate the call exactly.

A two-state option model

To find the option price, we assume a market where an arbitrage possibility can never be created. To see how the model works, consider the following example. Suppose the market price of a share is €50 and it will be either €60 or €40 at the end of the year. Further suppose that there exists a call option for 100 shares with a one-year expiration date and a €50 exercise price. Investors can borrow at 10 per cent.

There are two possible trading strategies that we shall examine. The first is to buy a call on the share, and the second is to buy 50 shares and borrow a duplicating amount. The duplicating amount is the amount of borrowing necessary to make the future payoffs from buying stock and borrowing the same as the future payoffs from buying a call on the stock. In our example, the duplicating amount of borrowing is €1,818. With a 10 per cent interest rate, principal and interest at the end of the year total €2,000 (€1,818 × 1.10). At the end of one year, the *future payoffs* are set out as follows:

Initial transactions	If share price is €60		If share price is €40
1 Buy a call (100-share contract)	100 × (€60 – €50) =	€1,000	0
2 Buy 50 shares	50 × €60 =	€3,000	50 × €40 = €2,000
Borrow €1,818	–(€1,818 × 1.10) =	–€2,000	–€2,000
Total from strategy 2		€1,000	0

Note that the future payoff structure of 'buy a call' is duplicated by the strategy of 'buy shares' and 'borrow'. These two trading strategies are equivalent as far as market traders are concerned. As a consequence, the two strategies must have the same cost. The cost of purchasing 50 shares while borrowing €1,818 is €682, given by:

Buy 50 shares	50 × €50 =	€2,500
Borrow €1,818 at 10%		–€1,818
		€682

Because the call option gives the same return, the call must be priced at €682. This is the value of the call option in a market where arbitrage profits do not exist.

Before leaving this simple example, we should comment on a remarkable feature. We found the exact value of the option without even knowing the probability that the share would go up or down! If an optimist thought the probability of an up move was very high and a pessimist thought it was very low, they would still agree on the option value. How could that be? The answer is that the current €50 share price already balances the views of the optimists and the pessimists. The option reflects that balance because its value depends on the share price.

The Black and Scholes model

The above example illustrates the duplicating strategy. Unfortunately, a strategy such as this will not work in the real world because there are many more than two possibilities for next year's share price. However, the number of possibilities is reduced as the time period is shortened. In fact, the assumption that there are only two possibilities for the share price over the next infinitesimal instant is plausible.

In our opinion, the fundamental insight of Black and Scholes is to shorten the time period. They show that a specific combination of shares and borrowing can indeed duplicate a call over an infinitesimal time horizon. Because the price of the share will change over the first instant, another combination of shares and borrowing is needed to duplicate the call over the second instant and so on. By adjusting the combination from moment to moment, it is possible continually to duplicate the call. It may seem difficult to comprehend but an appropriate formula can, firstly, determine the duplicating combination at any moment and, secondly, value the option based on this duplicating strategy. Suffice to say that the Black and Scholes dynamic strategy allows one to value a call in the real world just as we showed how to value the call in the two-state model.

the gain or loss on the stock-and-put combination. In equilibrium, the return on this strategy must be exactly equal to the riskless rate. From this, the put–call parity relationship was established:

Value of stock + Value of put – Value of call = Present value of exercise price.

- The value of an option depends on five factors:

  (i) the price of the underlying asset;
  (ii) the exercise price;
  (iii) the expiration date;
  (iv) the variability of the underlying asset;
  (v) the interest rate on risk-free bonds.

  The Black and Scholes model can determine the intrinsic price of an option from these five factors. An option-pricing table (Appendix 4) is available to ease calculation.

End of chapter questions

14.1 What are the components of an option premium?

14.2 Why is the price of an option always greater than its intrinsic value?

14.3 What is an in-the-money option? When is a call versus a put in the money?

15 Currency options

Currency options provide the right, but not the obligation, to buy or sell a specific currency at a specific price at any time prior to a specified date. That options provide 'the right but not the obligation' means that commercial users of the market are able to obtain insurance against an adverse movement in the exchange rate while still retaining the opportunity to benefit from favourable exchange movements. At the same time, the maximum risk to the buyer of an option is the actual up-front premium cost of the option. Currency options have not been designed as a substitute for forward markets but as a newer, distinct financial vehicle that offers significant opportunities and advantages to those seeking either protection or profit from changes in exchange rates. One of the most interesting areas argued to favour their use (and indeed, the use of options in general) is where outcomes are expected to have a bimodal result (either very good or very bad) giving jumps in value rather than a continuous movement to prices. Fortunes have been made using this line of reasoning – see, for example, Lewis.[1] Of course, the Black and Scholes model is based upon a continuous development to prices. Hence the potential when prices are expected to reflect bimodal development.

Currency options are now traded on numerous exchanges. For ease of reference, we will look at those traded on the Philadelphia Stock Exchange. Since December 1982, Philadelphia has been trading standardised foreign currency option contracts. Philadelphia offers a competitive market place in which to buy and sell options against US dollars on numerous currencies. Philadelphia was the first trading centre to deal in currency options and it remains a world market leader although it has been joined by other centres in numerous locations. They provide the means to deal currency options for a vast range of currencies.

In this chapter we focus upon Philadelphia options. It begins with a description of how currency option markets work. This is linked with a discussion of currency option terminology and is followed by a discussion relating to currency option pricing. A section is devoted to use of currency options as risk-reducing instruments available to the corporate treasurer.

15.1 How currency option markets work

Philadelphia currency options are similar to options on ordinary shares. The buyer of an option cannot lose more than the cost of the option and is not subject to any margin calls. The Philadelphia Stock Exchange offers investors an organised market place in which to buy and sell options on sterling, euros, Canadian dollars, Swiss francs, Japanese yen,

Australian dollars and others too, all against the US dollar. Options are traded on three-, six- and nine-month cycles.

Currency option markets have a jargon of their own, although this language has much in common with that of traded options on shares. Because we shall frequently use the jargon in this chapter, a short list of currency options terms and definitions follows. Readers of the previous chapter should be familiar with their meanings already, but here we apply them to currency options.

- *American option.* A currency option that can be exercised on any business day within the option period.
- *European option.* A currency option that can only be exercised on the expiry date.
- *A call option.* An option to purchase a stated number of units of the underlying foreign currency at a specific price per unit during a specific period of time. By 'underlying foreign currency' we refer to the currency that is not the US dollar. Thus the term 'underlying foreign currency' could refer to sterling in the context of a US dollar/sterling currency option.
- *A put option.* An option to sell a stated number of units of the underlying foreign currency at a specific price per unit during a specific period of time.
- *Option buyer.* The party who obtains the benefit under a currency option by paying a premium. These benefits are the right, but not the obligation, to buy the currency if the option is a call or to sell the currency if the option is a put. The option buyer is known as the option holder.
- *Option seller.* The party who has the obligation to perform if the currency option is exercised. This person will have to sell the foreign currency at a stated price if a call is exercised or buy the foreign currency at a stated price if a put is exercised. The original option seller is known as the option writer.
- *Exercise price, exercise rate or strike price.* The price at which the currency option holder has the right to purchase or sell the underlying currency. Except for the Japanese yen, exercise prices are stated in US cents. Thus a CHF75 (CHF is the code for Swiss francs) call would be an option to buy Swiss francs at USD0.75 per Swiss franc, that is CHF1.33 = USD1. The Japanese yen option exercise prices are stated in hundredths of a cent, so a JPY67 call entitles the holder to purchase the underlying yen at USD0.0067 per yen.
- *Expiration months.* The expiration months for currency options are usually March, June, September and December. At any given time trading is available in the nearest three of these months.
- *Option premium.* The option premium is the price of a currency option, that is the sum of money that the buyer of an option pays when an option is purchased or the sum that the writer of an option receives when an option is written.
- **Intrinsic value**. The extent to which a currency option would currently be profitable to exercise. In the case of a call, if the spot price of the underlying currency is above the option exercise price, this difference is its intrinsic value. In the case of a put, if the spot price is below the option exercise price, this is its intrinsic value. Options with intrinsic value are said to be **in-the-money**. If the spot Swiss franc price is USD0.75, a CHF72 call would have an intrinsic value of USD0.03 per CHF, but a CHF72 put would have no intrinsic value.
- *Time value.* That part of the premium representing the length of time that the currency option has to run. In other words, the premium less the intrinsic value.

- *Notice of exercise.* Notice given by a currency option holder to the option writer that an option is being exercised. Only an option holder may exercise an option. The option holder may exercise the option and the option writer may be assigned a notice of exercise at any time prior to expiration of the option. But only an American option will result in immediate delivery.
- *Opening transaction.* A purchase or sale transaction that establishes a currency option's position.
- *Closing transaction.* A transaction that liquidates or offsets an existing currency option's position. Option holders may liquidate their positions by an offsetting sale. An option writer may liquidate his or her position by an offsetting purchase.
- **At-the-money**. An option whose exercise price is the same as the spot price or the forward price. To distinguish the two, the jargon used is, respectively, at-the-money and at-the-money forward.
- **Out-of-the-money**. A call whose exercise price is above the current spot price of the underlying currency or a put option whose exercise price is below the current spot price of the underlying currency. Out-of-the-money options have no intrinsic value.
- *In-the-money.* A call whose exercise price is below the current spot price of the underlying currency or a put whose exercise price is above the current spot price of the underlying currency. In-the-money options have intrinsic value.

Traded currency option contracts are standardised. When trading is introduced in an option with a new expiration month, the practice is for one option to be introduced with an exercise price above the current spot price and one to be introduced with an exercise price below the current spot price. As the spot price of a currency changes over time, additional options are introduced with the same expiration month but higher or lower exercise prices. The exercise price intervals are USD0.01 for euros, sterling and Swiss francs; and USD0.0001 for Japanese yen.

If Swiss franc options with a September expiration are introduced when the spot price is USD0.75, exercise prices would normally be established at 74, 75 and 76. If the spot price were to change to USD0.76, a new series of options, having the same expiration date, would be introduced with an exercise price of 77.

Prices, or premia, for foreign exchange options are arrived at through competition between buyers and sellers in stock exchanges or in futures and options exchanges. The premium quoted represents a consensus opinion of the option's current value and will comprise intrinsic value and time value. Option premium quotations have bid and offer rates like most financial exchange contracts. We would expect Philadelphia option prices to be in equilibrium with other markets' option quotations. Otherwise, riskless arbitrage profits would be available. Table 15.1 shows contract sizes for a selection of Philadelphia currency option contracts. Contract sizes on other exchanges vary.

Intrinsic value is the amount, if any, by which an option is currently in the money. Time value is that sum of money which buyers are willing to pay over and above any intrinsic value. Such buyers hope that, before expiration, the option will increase in value and may be sold or exchanged at a profit. If an option has no intrinsic value, its premium will be entirely a reflection of its time value.

The price or premium of an option reflects changes in the spot price of the underlying currency and the length of time remaining until expiration. Thus, with the spot Swiss franc price at US$0.75, a CHF73 call option with three months until expiration may command a premium US$1,600. Of this, US$1,250, given by US$0.02 × CHF62,500, is intrinsic value

Table 15.2 Standard and average rate options compared

	Standard option	Average rate option
Strike	135.00	135.00
Exchange rate at expiry (e)	137.50	137.50
Average exchange rate over period	–	141.21
Payment to option buyer	20m (137.50 – 135)*e*	20m (141.21 – 135.00)*e*
	$363,636	$903,273
Premium (% of US$ principal)	0.61	0.52

An average rate option is an option whose strike price is compared not to the exchange rate at maturity, but to the average exchange rate over the period of the option. This sounds a bit complicated. Let us see whether an example can make things easier. Consider a company with a US dollar/yen exposure. It might have entered into an option giving it the right to buy USD20m against Japanese yen over a three-month period at a rate of JPY135 = USD1. In terms of calculating the payment to the option buyer, assume that the exchange rate at the option's maturity is JPY137.50. But also assume that the average exchange rate during the whole of the term of the option is JPY141.21. Now the payment to the option buyer can be calculated under the standard currency option and under the average rate option – this is shown in Table 15.2.

The example in the table shows the average rate option with a higher return than the standard option. But depending upon the spot price at maturity, the standard option could offer a better return. The average rate option may be 35–50 per cent cheaper than the standard option depending on the frequency of sampling to obtain the average rate. Why this is so has everything to do with volatility. The more volatile an underlying instrument, the greater the cost of the option. Average rates are more stable than the spot rate itself, hence their lower volatility. If the average is computed by taking daily spot rate fixings, then it will turn out to be cheaper than if the average is computed every month. Beyond twenty periodic fixings in one year, the premium does not fall very much.

The average rate option gives the buyer two advantages compared with typical straight options:

- Standard options may be very effective when covering single cash flows at a known future maturity. Standard options and forwards are less effective when hedging a large number of smallish cash flows distributed uncertainly over time. Many firms with foreign exchange exposures have just this type of fluctuating cash flow configuration. Average rate options are ideal instruments to cover this kind of exposure.
- Although only traded over-the-counter (OTC), they are relatively cheap. The hedging institution is concerned about the average exchange rate, not the exchange rate when each separate cash flow comes due. The average rate option costs less than the sum of the separate options for each period – by some 40 per cent or so.

How does a potential user set about hedging with an average rate option? The trader not only decides the principal amount, strike price and period for the option, but also agrees the data source to compute the average and the time period between samples. For example, Reuters daily, weekly or monthly figures might be used.

The option settles net cash. At the end of the option's life, the average exchange rate is computed and compared with the strike price. A cash payment is made to the buyer of the option equal to the face amount of the option multiplied by the difference between these two rates, assuming that the option is in the money. Otherwise, the option expires worthless. For an in-the-money expiry, this approach was set out in the numerical example above.

Finally in this section, we outline its application to hedging on profit and loss account denominated in foreign currency – assuming, of course, that this is deemed to be a valid goal of currency management. A multinational corporation has an exposure in respect of its foreign subsidiaries' budgeted profits. The average rate option may be used to hedge this. Dealing an Asro for the budgeted after-tax foreign profit at a strike rate equivalent to the budgeted average exchange rate effectively locks in such an exchange rate. Take an example. Assume that a UK-based international group expects its US subsidiary to make \$60m after tax and anticipates an average exchange rate of \$1.70, giving sterling-denominated profits of £35.3m. By dealing an average rate sterling call (dollar put) for \$60m at a strike price of \$1.70, this will be achieved – assuming that the budget is also at least achieved. Arranging the deal through a tax haven will avoid problems of tax asymmetry. Should the subsidiary make its budget of \$60m and if the average exchange rate is, say, \$2, then this will give sterling profits of £30m. But the profit on the option will amount to £5.3m. Of course, the company has to achieve – or beat – its budget in dollar terms for the hedge to work. The reporting anomaly referred to in discussing Table 8.2 is avoided by the hedge described here. Of course, if the exchange rate averages 1.50, the option lapses but the sterling value of translated profit comes out at £40m.

By arranging an average rate option with the same frequency of fixings as for the measurement of the average exchange rate for translation purposes, the hedge is readily achieved. Remember that this is possible given the lack of direction under SSAP20 as to how to work out the average exchange rate. Remember also that the hedge achieved will, substantially, cover exchange risk on dividends paid out of profits. Care must be taken on this point to avoid double hedging.

15.4 Hedging a currency option

There are ways in which writers of currency options can cover themselves. The detail of covering strategies is outside the scope of this book but it is worth while spending a little time on the generalities of covering option writing.

Assume that, at the time a call option is written, the pound spot rate is \$1.70, the exercise price of the call option is \$1.70 and the price of the call is 4 cents per dollar. A UK exporter expects to receive \$1,000,000 in six months' time. It can guarantee a minimum rate of exchange by buying a six-month call on sterling. At the maturity of the option, if the spot rate is above \$1.70, the option will logically be exercised and the \$1,000,000 will be converted to sterling at \$1.70 rather than at the spot rate. This guarantees that the net proceeds of the trade will be at least £588,235 minus the £23,529 paid for the call.

In this example, at the time the call is written, sterling is trading at \$1.70 and the value of the call is 4 cents. If sterling were to rise to \$1.72, the call premium might rise to 5 cents; if sterling were to fall to \$1.68, the call premium might fall to 3 cents. So, for every 2 cents move in the spot price there is a 1 cent move in the option value. The call is behaving like a spot position equal to half the currency on which the call is written. The ratio of the move

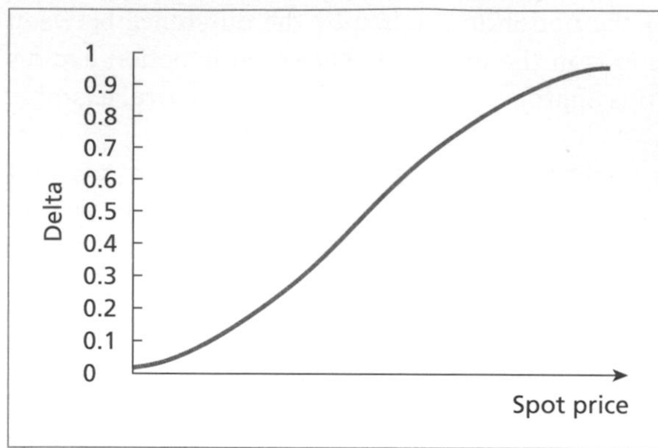

Figure 15.2 Call option delta (30-day option)

in the call value to the move in the spot price is known as the 'hedge ratio' or '**delta**' of the position. In our example, the delta is 0.5.

The importance of the delta is that it tells the writer of the option how much spot currency to hold in order to eliminate the risk of the option. In this example, if the writer of the option had held sterling of an amount equal to £294,117.50, half the face value of the call, the writer would not have been exposed to the change in the value of the currency option. Over a particular period, if the spot rate had risen to $1.72, the call value would have risen in value by $10,000 and the spot sterling position would also have changed by the same amount, offsetting the loss on the written call.

It must be stated that, as the spot price moves, so the delta may change and the spot position that is equivalent to the option changes accordingly. To construct a spot position that is equivalent to the option over its entire life, the amount of spot currency held to hedge the option must therefore change in response to the spot price. As a result, if a call is written and a spot position in delta is taken, and delta is revised frequently enough, the **net position** will be riskless over the entire life of the option. This forms the basis of one approach to covering for banks that write options.

To recapitulate, the hedge ratio, or the delta, is the amount that should be held in the currency in order to hedge the option position. It is the rate of change in the premium given a change in the underlying currency (see Figure 15.2).

Thus, if a call option on sterling with a strike at $1.60 costs 3 cents and has a delta of 0.4, an instantaneous move of 1 cent in the spot rate will result in an immediate increase or decrease in the option premium of 0.4 cents. With the spot at $1.61 the premium will increase to 3.4 cents, and with the spot at $1.59 the premium will fall to 2.6 cents. With a delta of 1, which would apply only to very deep in-the-money options, a 1 cent move in the spot would result in a 1 cent move in the premium. With a delta of 0.1 for far out-of-the-money options, a 1 cent move in the spot would see the premium change by only 0.1 cent.

Delta can never be below zero and never, in normal circumstances, above 1. In other words, an option can move one for one with the underlying currency but, all things being equal, never more than the change in the spot rate. Whereas the delta for an at-the-money option is always about 0.5, the delta for an out- or in-the-money option varies according to the intrinsic value of the option, the time left to expiry, the volatility of the underlying currency, and even the level of interest rate differentials. Another way of using delta is as a probability measure: the higher the delta, the greater the probability of the option being exercised. Delta is important for option traders because it provides a key to the gearing of the option position. Traders who buy far out-of-the-money options because they appear 'cheap' are often disappointed when the anticipated move in the spot market occurs and the option itself hardly moves. Option writers should be aware of the increasing sensitivity of their **short positions** as the delta picks up from 0.25 through 0.35 and eventually moves above 0.5.

The delta, the first derivative of the option-pricing model, is a dynamic concept. It changes as the market changes. The 'gamma', the second derivative of the model, describes the change in the delta given a change in the underlying price. Gamma measures the sensitivity of the delta – it is the delta of the delta. The higher the gamma, the higher the delta sensitivity. Gamma is at its highest for short-dated at-the-money options. This can be explained using the following example.

If the spot sterling rate is at $1.51, the $1.50 sterling call expiring in a few minutes' time has a delta of 1. In the statistical sense, the option will certainly be exercised, which means that the option writer should hold 100 per cent of the currency as a hedge against the short options position. But if the spot rate suddenly falls to $1.49, the option delta falls to zero because the option, statistically, now has a virtually zero chance of being exercised. Therefore no hedge is required. By contrast, consider a one-year at-the-money call on sterling which has a delta of 0.47; an instantaneous move up or down in the spot rate of 1 cent will result in the delta moving up to 0.49 or down to 0.45 respectively. Thus:

At-the-money call deltas expiry	A few minutes' time	One year
Delta	0.5	0.47
Delta as a result of 1 cent increase in spot rate	1	0.49
Delta as a result of 1 cent decrease in spot rate	0	0.45

Option buyers are attracted to high gamma options because of the gearing in such a position. Conversely, writers of high gamma options are taking considerable risks because of the large potential fluctuations in the premium caused by relatively small movements in the spot rate.

The trade-off of high delta sensitivity – gamma – is high time decay. Short-dated, at-the-money options are highly leveraged and subject to sharp premium loss in stable conditions. Low gamma options, such as longer-dated options, are less sensitive to market movement and experience only minor losses in premium on a day-to-day basis. The technical term for the rate of time decay is 'theta'. A theta of 0.01 means that the premium will decline by 0.01 over a one-day period, all other factors remaining the same. High gamma and high theta options go hand in hand with each other. To return to the sterling option expiring in a few minutes, if the strike is at the money, the delta is about 0.5 and the option is worth only time value; in a few minutes' time – that is, on the expiry of the option – the premium will be zero, assuming that the spot rate is at the same level. This is an extreme example of high time decay loss, or high theta. We also know that such an option has a very high gamma. Conversely, a very long-dated option has very little gamma or theta risk. In other words, the delta hardly changes even given comparatively large spot movements and, day to day, the time decay loss on the premium is virtually nil.

If long-dated options are insensitive to spot or time decay effects, they are very vulnerable to shifts in volatility. 'Vega' is the technical term used to describe the effect on the premium of a change in volatility. A vega of 0.1 means that the premium will change by 0.1 per cent given a 1 per cent change in volatility. Whereas the time decay effect (namely theta) and the change in the delta (namely gamma) are low for long-dated options, the volatility sensitivity – vega – is at its highest. This is another example of the trade-off effect in option markets. Currency traders may well decide to buy options rather than spot because their view of the market is that a substantial move is likely, but over a longer time-scale rather than a short **duration**. The trader feels that, because implied volatility is at a relatively high level, the shorter-dated options are too expensive. In other words, the trader is well aware of the possibility of high time decay loss – the high theta effect – in shorter maturity options. Thus, the trader buys a one-year sterling at-the-money call option. But, in high volatility conditions, buying long-dated options may result in larger than expected losses, not through time decay loss, which is negligible day to day, but because of the option's sensitivity to declines in implied volatility – vega.

For example, consider the data shown in Table 15.3 for an at-the-money sterling call at 1.60. Although the absolute loss through a fall in volatility is much higher with the longer-dated option, namely 1.5 cents against only 0.5 cent for the one-month option, the percentage fall in the one-month option premium is actually slightly greater at 20 per cent as against 19.7 per cent. The shorter and further out of money the option, the more pronounced is this effect.

Table 15.3 Effect of a fall in volatility on premium: at-the-money call option

Expiry	Volatility	Premium
1 month	15%	2.5 cents
1 month	12.5%	2.0 cents
12 months	15%	7.6 cents
12 months	12.5%	6.1 cents

Using the same situation but with a $1.65 sterling call option – that is, 5 cents out of the money, our tabulation might be as shown in Table 15.4. Again, the absolute loss is much larger for the twelve-month call than for the one-month option – that is, 1.4 cents as against 0.4 cent. And the percentage loss is 24 per cent compared with 44 per cent for the one-month option. The percentage loss due to a decline in volatility is known as 'vega elasticity'. The option writer who anticipates a fall in implied volatility will make more dollars by writing a long-dated, at-the-money, high vega option, but he will make more in percentage terms by writing out of-the-money, short-dated options.

Table 15.4 Effect of a fall in volatility on premium: out-of-the-money call option

Expiry	Volatility	Premium
1 month	15%	0.9 cent
1 month	12.5%	0.5 cent
12 months	15%	5.8 cents
12 months	12.5%	4.4 cents

15.5 Option pricing models

A mathematical model for pricing stock market options was referred to in detail in Chapter 14. Their model has been adapted by Garman and Kohlhagen[2] for pricing currency options. The Garman and Kohlhagen model for pricing currency options is an adaptation of the Black and Scholes model applied to a slightly different environment. Their model for the valuation of a currency call option at an exercise price of E is given by:

$$C = \frac{FN(\text{dist 1}) - EN(\text{dist 2})}{e^{pt}}$$

In this case the notation (where different from Black and Scholes) is as follows:

C = price of the currency option
F = the forward exchange rate
E = the exercise price
p = the risk-free interest rate differential (that is, domestic rate less foreign rate for comparable deposits) expressed on a continually compounded basis

$$\text{dist } 1 = \frac{\ln(F/E) + (r + {}^1\!/_2\sigma^2)t}{\sigma\sqrt{t}}$$

$$\text{dist } 2 = \text{dist } 1 - \sqrt{t}$$

σ^2 = the variance of the continuously compounded annual rate of change of the exchange rate

There are many other models for pricing currency options. One of these, the Leland[3] model, is interesting – it is a Black and Scholes variant which incorporates transaction costs. The formula developed by Leland allows direct comparison of the effects of changes in transaction costs or in the 'revision interval' – that is, the frequency with which a position is rehedged. One of the features of option management is that a hedged portfolio of options and currencies (or shares) must be rehedged every time the exchange rate (or share price) moves. In the Black and Scholes model, continuous rehedging is implicit. Clearly, in reality, transaction costs preclude such a policy. Traders generally hedge their position only at certain regular intervals when the original hedged position is seen to be imperfect. Leland's model allows for this with a revision interval term (Δt).

Nowadays most banks use computer models based on formulations similar to the above for pricing currency options. Many institutions are using their own in-house formulae for valuing currency options but these are similar to the Black and Scholes, Garman and Kohlhagen, or Leland models summarised above.

What all of the models have in common is the logic they apply to the problem of pricing a currency option. Effectively, it follows the routine set out in Figure 15.3. As we mentioned

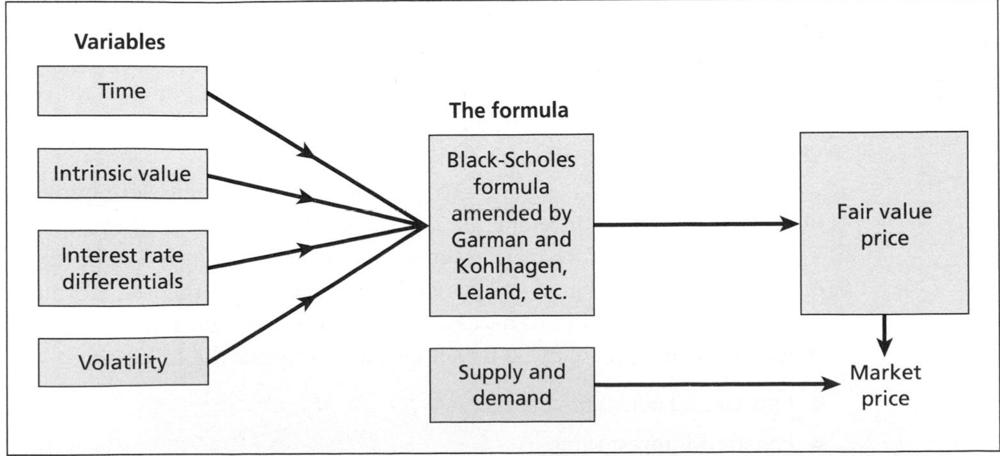

Figure 15.3 How a currency option is priced

in Chapter 14, what is most interesting is not the variables that are used in the formulations but those that were left out. No mention has been made of market direction or bias as an appropriate input. An implicit assumption of the models is that the market moves in a random fashion. In other words, while prices will change, the chances of a positive return are the same as the chances of a negative one. In fact, plots of currency price movements are usually found to be skewed, or log-normal. This arises partly because, while currency prices can rise without limit, they cannot fall below zero. Remember, too, it is possible that when there is government intervention in foreign exchange markets, a bias is introduced into currency movements – as noted in Chapter 6. And, it is also critically important to be aware that at the time of crisis-induced volatility, the models may give very deceptive results.

The Black and Scholes model explains well the option premium for a European call on equities. Garman and Kohlhagen's extension of the formula to cover currency options allows for the fact that currency pricing involves two interest rates, not one, and that a currency can trade at a premium or discount forward depending upon the interest rate differential.

Cox, Ross and Rubinstein[4] and Cox and Rubinstein[5] developed a variant of the currency-pricing model which accounts for the early exercise provisions of American-style options. Using the same approach as Black and Scholes, they incorporated a binomial method, to evaluate the call premium. This same binomial model is now used alongside the Garman and Kolhagen version of Black and Scholes to price currency options. Assuming that early exercise will take place only if the advantage of holding the currency is greater than the time value of the option, the binomial method involves making a series of trial estimates over the life of the option, each estimate being a probability analysis of early exercise for each successive day. Thus, for a one-year option the probability of a rise or fall in the currency is estimated for every day until expiry. The theoretical premium for the option, given various probabilities over time, is compared with the cost of holding the cash hedge position. Once the time value of the option is worth less than the forward points of the currency hedge, the position becomes too expensive to carry and the option should be exercised. In practice, the computation of 360 trials (one for each day of the year) would take too long, even for most computers. Most binomial-pricing models therefore reduce the number of iterations to a compromise level where the calculation process is reasonably fast and the approximation is not too great.

A less complex version was developed by Barone-Adesi and Whaley[6] using a simple quadratic approximation to value American-style currency options. Its essential mathematics are summarised in Tucker, Madura and Chiang.[7]

The early exercise provision in American options can make a significant difference to the premium value of some options, namely calls on higher interest rate currencies and puts on lower interest rate currencies. When early exercise is unlikely, however, the Black and Scholes and the binomial models give identical results.

There is a danger in taking the premium derived from the option-pricing model too literally. The market price and the fair-value price may well differ considerably, and while it is always possible for an arbitrageur to sell what is believed to be an overpriced option, or to buy an option that is underpriced compared to the theoretical value according to the pricing model, this will not necessarily guarantee profits. The main reason is that the key inputs to the model are by no means certain. Consider the following:

- known and constant volatility;
- constant interest rates;
- no transaction costs and/or taxation effects;

- continuous trading;
- no dividends;
- no early exercise;
- log-normal distribution of outturns.

Interest rate differentials may vary over the life of an option – and sometimes erratically so. The foreign exchange market does have transaction costs in the bid/ask spread, and when conditions become thin or volatile the spreads widen. And *ex-ante* volatility estimates may vary from one trade to another and will presumably be different from past volatility. The big unknown, is, of course, by how much. Also, the assumption of normal or even log-normal distribution of such movements is questionable as far as the foreign exchange markets are concerned. Research work on the behaviour of currency markets have identified biased price movements – there have been frequent occasions when prices do not behave in a neat distribution. Note our first paragraph in this chapter.

Before moving on to consider how well the Black and Scholes formula stands up in practice, we briefly take the concept of volatility a little further. Consider an option that is held entirely for insurance purposes. The value of the option depends upon the chance that the spot price will be above or below the exercise price of the option at the maturity date. In turn, this probability depends upon the uncertainty about the spot rate at the time the option matures. The standard deviation of the distribution of possible levels of the spot rate at the maturity date describes this uncertainty – and this is what volatility is all about. There is a simple relationship between volatility over a short period and over a long period. The standard deviation over t days is equal to the square root of t times the daily standard deviation. The standard deviation over three months is equal to approximately eight times the standard deviation over 1 day, since there are about 63 trading days in a quarter and the square root of 63 is approximately 8. Table 15.5 sets out standard deviations over different time periods. All of these are equivalent to a standard deviation of 10 per cent per annum. The market has adopted the convention of always quoting volatilities on an annalistic basis, just as interest rates and forward premiums are always quoted on an annual basis.

Volatility does not increase in a linear way with time. Over three months there is half as much volatility as over one year. Table 15.6 illustrates why this is so. Assume that a currency rate can move up or down by 1 per cent or stay the same over a single day. The standard deviation is 0.82 per cent. Over two days the standard deviation is 1.15 per cent, equal to $\sqrt{2} \times 0.82$ per cent. The two-day moves are not twice as scattered as the one-day moves, since sometimes when the currency moves up on the first day it moves back down on the second day and vice versa. This offsets part of the volatility contributed by the first day, resulting in the two-day standard deviation being less than twice the one-day standard deviation. Having said this, if both are annalist, they will give the same number.

Table 15.5 Volatility over different time periods

Time period	Standard deviation (%)
1 year	10.0
9 months	8.7
6 months	7.1
3 months	5.0
1 day	0.6

Table 15.6 Volatility over one and two days

Over one day		Over two days	
Move (%)	Probability	Move (%)	Probability
+1	1/3	+2	1/9
0	1/3	+1	2/9
−1	1/3	0	3/9
		−1	2/9
		−2	1/9
Standard deviation 0.82%		Standard deviation 1.15%	

Most currency options are hedged by some party. It may be that the bank writing the option takes cover; it may be that the market-maker in the option market carries out the delta hedging strategy. In theory, the company could, instead of buying an option, perform these trades itself and thereby replicate the option. Potential competition from company synthesisers of their own options forces prices towards the option model prices. This means that the spread of the market price over the model price is limited by the possibility of corporations and others synthesising their own options. The actual price paid by a corporation in the currency option market is likely therefore to be equal to the model price plus transactions costs of hedging by the option writer, plus a premium for risk of volatility changing plus a pure profit spread.

Companies synthesising their own currency options would save on the pure profit spread. Their cost would be based upon the model price plus transactions costs of replication by the corporation plus a premium for the risk of volatility changing.

15.6 Option pricing models for stocks and currencies: the empirical evidence

There are problems in carrying out empirical research to test the Black and Scholes model and other option-pricing models. First, any statistical hypothesis about how options are priced has to be a joint hypothesis to the effect that (1) the option-pricing formula is correct, and that (2) markets price financial instruments efficiently. If the hypothesis is rejected, it may be the case that (1) is untrue, that (2) is untrue, or that both (1) and (2) are untrue. A second problem is that future stock price volatility is an unobservable variable. One might estimate volatility from historical stock price data. Alternatively, implied volatilities can be used in some way – although this may result in circular reasoning. Another problem is to ensure that data on stock price and option price are obtained at the same time. Thus, if the option is thinly traded, it may be unacceptable to compare closing options prices with closing stock prices. For example, if the last option trade were at 11 a.m. while the closing stock price corresponded to a trade at 4.30 p.m., we would have something of a data problem.

Another problem concerns the normal curve assumption and the observations of fat tails. This was discussed in section 9.15 of this book. It is worth re-reading. Carefully.

Various research studies – see Buckley[8] – have sought to locate and test strategies to earn excess profits from option strategies. The majority of such published work supports the potential to earn higher than expected returns and many of these attribute this to

departures from log-normality. The Black and Scholes model assumes that the distribution of the asset price at some future time, conditional on its value today, is log-normal. Some tests of option pricing indicated that in-the-money and out-of-the-money options appear to be mispriced relative to at-the-money options. In other words, the volatility for which the Black and Scholes equation correctly prices at-the-money options causes it to misprice in-the-money and out-of-the-money options. These pricing errors can be explained by differences between the log-normal distribution assumed by Black and Scholes and the true distribution. And this will be the case with fat tail distributions.

Figure 15.4 shows four ways in which the true asset price distribution may be different from the log-normal distribution but still give the same mean and standard deviation for the asset price return. The features of these distributions are summarised in Table 15.7. For Figure 15.4(a), both tails of the true distribution are thinner than those of the log-normal distribution. For Figure 15.4(b), the right tail is thinner and the left tail is fatter. For Figure 15.4(c), the right tail is fatter and the left tail is thinner. In Figure 15.4(d) both tails are fatter. The true distributions in Figure 15.4 are derived from the log-normal distribution by removing probability mass from some areas and adding it to other areas in such a way that the overall mean and standard deviation of asset returns remain as before. Thus, in Figure 15.4(d) probability mass has been added to both tails of the distribution and to the central part of the distribution. This has been balanced by the removal of probability mass from those versions of the distribution that are between around one and two standard deviations from the mean.

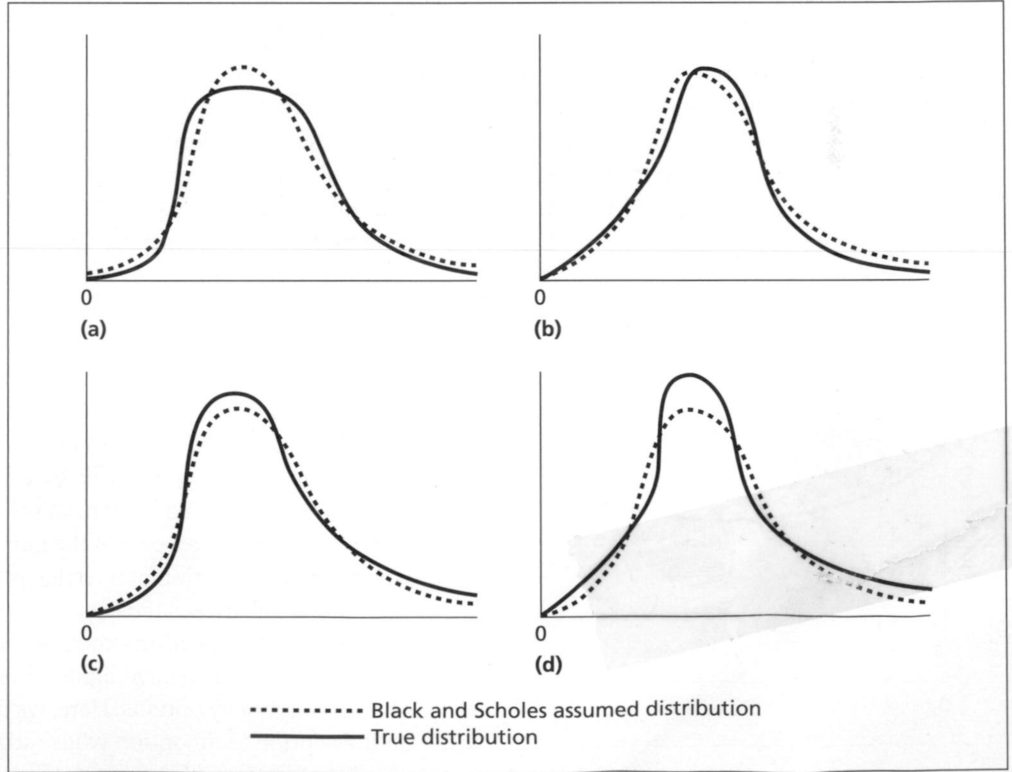

Figure 15.4 Possible asset price distribution

Table 15.7 Bias created by possible stock price distributions in Figure 15.4

Distribution in Figure 15.4	Features	Bias created
(a)	Both tails thinner	The Black and Scholes model overprices both out-of-the-money and in-the-money calls and puts.
(b)	Left tail fatter, right tail thinner	The Black and Scholes model overprices out-of-the-money calls and in-the-money puts. It underprices out-of-the-money puts and in-the-money calls.
(c)	Left tail thinner, right tail fatter	The Black and Scholes model overprices out-of-the-money puts and in-the-money calls. It underprices in-the-money puts and out-of-the-money calls.
(d)	Both tails fatter	The Black and Scholes model underprices both out-of-the-money and in-the-money calls and puts.

So, what would be the difference between correct option price and the Black and Scholes model price that would be observed in these four situations? This difference is sometimes termed bias. Consider a call option that is significantly out of the money. It will have a positive intrinsic value only if there is a large increase in the asset price. Therefore, its value critically depends only on the right tail of the terminal asset price distribution. The fatter this tail, the more valuable the option. Consequently, the Black and Scholes model will tend to underprice out-of-the-money calls when the asset price distribution is as illustrated in Figure 15.4(c) and (d), and it will overprice out-of-the-money calls in the cases shown in Figure 15.4(a) and (b). We now turn to a put option that is significantly out of the money. It will have a positive intrinsic value only if there is a large decrease in the asset price. Therefore, its value critically depends only on the left tail of the terminal asset price distribution. The fatter this tail, the more valuable the option. Thus, the Black and Scholes model will tend to underprice out-of-the-money puts when the asset distribution is as illustrated in Figure 15.4(b) and (d), and it will overprice out-of-the-money puts in the cases of Figure 15.4(a) and (c). The findings of Rubinstein[9] tend to conform to the asset price distribution shown in Figure 15.4(b).

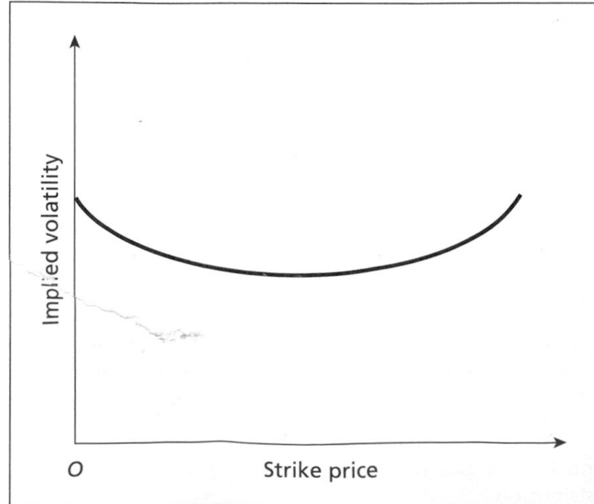

Figure 15.5 Volatility smile for foreign exchange options

It is worth noting that Tucker and Pond[10] and Tucker[11] found that a currency option-pricing model which incorporates discrete jumps in exchange rates outperforms the Black and Scholes model in pricing Philadelphia-traded currency options. The source of such jumps might be central bank intervention or realignments within a currency float group.

Volatility smile is a plot of the implied volatility of an option as a function of its strike price. For options on foreign exchange, a typical volatility smile is shown in Figure 15.5. Out-of-the-money and in-the-money options both tend to have higher implied volatilities than at-the-money options. Here, we define an at-the-money option as an option whose strike price equals the forward price of the asset. Figure 15.5 is therefore consistent with Figure 15.4(d).

15.7 Corporate use of currency options

If a company wishes to leave open the possibility of making a currency gain on a receivable or payable, while protecting itself against adverse movements in the exchange rate, it can do so via the currency option market. Currency options are of particular interest to the treasurer where a future currency cash flow is uncertain, as in the case of putting in a contract tender or issuing a foreign currency price list. In the case of a tender, if the contract is not awarded, the company merely lets the currency option lapse – or, if it pays it to do otherwise, it sells it on at a profit. If the company obtains the contract tendered for, it will exchange the currency option for a forward option running out to the payment dates under the contract.

But treasurers may also use currency options to hedge a contractually agreed deal in order to protect the downside exchange risk on a receivable or payable, while leaving open the upside potential. Currency options have become particularly attractive to corporate treasurers in times when there is substantial volatility in the foreign exchange markets. In 1984 the dollar was strengthening rapidly against most currencies, although many corporate treasurers felt that it was clearly overvalued in terms of purchasing power parity criteria. Given that trends in the market and purchasing power parity considerations pointed in opposite directions, it might have been an apposite time to use currency options. Of course, it would have been better not to hedge dollar receivables at all, but this view only emerges with the benefit of hindsight.

A price has to be paid to secure the benefit of an option. This is the front-end non-returnable premium which the option writer receives whether or not the company exercises its option. The decision to use currency options needs to be assessed carefully, taking into account the likelihood of the currency flow occurring, the volatility of the exchange rate until the funds are received and the cost of the premium. The answer to the criticism made by some treasurers to the effect that currency options are expensive comes back loud and clear. Why not write options yourself then?

Of course, one of the major problems with currency options traded on the Philadelphia, London or Amsterdam Stock Exchanges is that they have specific expiration dates which will usually differ from the date up to which cover is required. Because of this there has developed an over-the-counter (OTC) market in which tailor-made options are bought and sold privately between banks and their customers. The growth of exchange-traded and of OTC currency options are really complementary. The exchange-traded markets are used most frequently by banks hedging OTC positions. The OTC currency option business is largely made up of corporate activity. Increased volume in one market supports increased activity in the other. There are obvious reasons why a large volume of corporate currency option business has been channelled through the OTC market rather than directly through exchange markets. First and foremost is the fact that OTC options are tailor-made to meet a company's specific needs. A company, therefore, may ask a bank to quote a price on a currency option which exactly matches its hedge requirements with respect to the currency to be bought and sold, the amount, the price and the time period to be covered. The option specifications of exchange-traded products are standardised, so that a company's precise needs will not easily be met through this market place.

Corporate treasurers are also attracted by the fact that OTC transactions are operationally straightforward and are rather similar to forward foreign exchange dealing procedures.

It should be noted that there is no formal secondary market in OTC currency options, which makes them less flexible than exchange-traded options. But the company may sell its OTC option back to the bank writing it, or enter into an OTC option with exactly the reverse characteristics of the original one. OTC options do have far greater flexibility for companies in terms of expiry dates, amounts involved and the possibility of dealing in currencies not quoted on the traded exchanges. Banks may be prepared to tailor options in a range of currencies wider than that quoted on the currency options markets. In Table 15.8, a comparison between exchange-traded and OTC options is tabulated.

Table 15.8 Exchange-traded and OTC options compared

	Exchange traded	OTC
Contract terms, including amounts	Standardised	Fixed to suit circumstances; terms are not standard
Expiration	Standardised	Determined by requirements of customer
Transaction method	Stock exchange type medium	Bank-to-client or bank-to-bank
Secondary market	Continuous secondary market	No formal secondary market
Commissions	Negotiable	Negotiable, but usually built into the premium
Participants	Exchange members and clients	Banks, corporations and financial institutions

The currency option market is an innovative one. A variant of the basic option contract which has been introduced is the cylinder option, or zero-cost option as it is sometimes called. Its interest to corporate treasurers arises because, in times of high volatility, it enables the treasurer to lock into a narrow band in the exchange rate range. The workings of the cylinder option will become apparent with the help of a numerical example.

Assume that a UK company has a dollar receivable. The treasurer has a range of possible options in respect of the asset. The treasurer may, among other actions:

- leave the dollars uncovered;
- sell the dollars forward;
- buy a sterling call option;
- buy a sterling option cylinder.

Assume that the spot rate at the date when the treasurer is considering taking action amounts to \$1.86 and the forward rate for the maturity of the receivable is \$1.85. Assume also that the premium for an option to sell dollars at \$1.90 for the appropriate period is 4.50 cents. Having been informed of the premium by the bank, the treasurer expresses the opinion that it is expensive, to which the bank replies that it will write a zero-cost option. What this involves is as follows. To counter the premium payable on the \$1.90 option bought, the client writes an option to sell dollars to the bank at \$1.80 with a premium of 4.50 cents payable by the bank to the client. The two premia set off against each other, giving rise to the zero cost. If the client takes the zero-cost option, then the client will be in a position:

- To carry the profit or loss for exchange rate movements between $1.80 and $1.90. If the rate moves to $1.82 on maturity, the client takes the profit from the dollar strengthening from $1.86 to $1.82. Should the maturity rate be $1.88, the client takes the loss.
- To limit profit or loss should the exchange rate on maturity move outside the cylinder $1.90 to $1.80. So should the rate on maturity go to $1.92, the client bears a limited loss based on $1.90 less $1.86 and the bank bears the remainder of the loss from $1.92 to $1.90. In a reverse direction, if the rate on maturity is $1.76, the client makes a gain based on $1.86 less $1.80 and the bank takes the remaining profit based on the dollar strengthening from $1.80 to $1.76.

Effectively, the cylinder option in the example provides the treasurer with total cover against the dollar weakening beyond $1.90 and gives a gain to the company from the dollar strengthening to $1.80: but the company limits its gain should the dollar strengthen beyond $1.80.

Ignoring interest rate considerations, Table 15.9 shows comparative results from leaving the dollars uncovered versus taking forward cover versus buying a sterling option cylinder. Gains and losses shown in the table are in US cents against a base rate of $1.86. What the option cylinder hedge does is to allow the corporate treasurer to fix an exchange rate within a narrow band for a nil net front-end premium. This is achieved by the treasurer writing an option in the opposite direction to that in which cover is desired. The rate at which the option is written is such that its premium is equal to the premium on the option to be bought or sold to give cover for the receivable or payable.

Table 15.9 Comparative results of option cylinder (data as given in text)

Maturity exchange rate	Dollar uncovered gain (+) or loss (–)*	Forward sale: profit forgone (–) or loss saved (+)*	Buy sterling cylinder option: gain (+) or loss (–)*
1.92	–6	+7	–4
1.91	–5	+6	–4
1.90	–4	+5	–4
1.89	–3	+4	–3
1.88	–2	+3	–2
1.87	–1	+2	–1
1.86	0	+1	0
1.85	+1	0	+1
1.84	+2	–1	+2
1.83	+3	–2	+3
1.82	+4	–3	+4
1.81	+5	–4	+5
1.80	+6	–5	+6
1.79	+7	–6	+6
1.78	+8	–7	+6

* Gains and losses shown in US cents versus spots of $1.86.

Before leaving the topic of corporate use of currency options, it is worth mentioning that there are some treasurers who are of the opinion that currency options have one basic use: to protect profitability. Consider an example. Assume that a company imports wine from the United States, priced in dollars, into the United Kingdom. It has only one direct competitor importing US wine, although a host of importers deal in French, German, Italian and other wines. Against its immediate competitor it may suffer a disadvantage if it hedges via the forward market and its competitor does not and the dollar weakens. Obviously, the competitor might now gain market share by pricing down. It is just to avoid this competitive disadvantage, so the argument goes, that the currency option is designed. If the importer were covered by a currency option, its competitor would not be put at an advantage by exchange rate changes, since, whether the dollar hardened or weakened, the importer covered by the option can match whatever tactic its competitor employs without incurring loss – except of the currency option premium, of course. Given the above scenario, the covered wine competitor will, should the dollar harden, be in a position to gain at its uncovered competitor's expense. By carefully planning its tactics, the company might, through an aggressive competitive stance at such times, more than recoup the cost of the total currency premium paid out in the past.

Currency options may also, at least in theory, be employed to hedge economic exposure. Again consider an example. Imagine a UK exporter competing with a Japanese company for US market share. It has a transaction exposure against the dollar, and an economic exposure against the yen. It could hedge against the dollar exposure by selling dollars forward for sterling. But it could also hedge against its Japanese rival by buying yen put options. If the yen falls, the UK firm can use its option profits to match the Japanese firm's price cuts in the Unites States. If the yen rises, the options expire worthless, but the UK firm has the price advantage anyway.

In the above example, the hedging of the transaction exposure requires the existence of long-term forward contracts – these are available up to ten years for major currencies against the dollar. But the hedging of economic exposure in the above example requires an availability of long-term currency options. At the time of writing, OTC options are available for a few currencies against the US dollar up to a maturity of 10 years or more. Not all banks are prepared to quote them and because of this lack of competitiveness many corporate treasurers reckon them to be expensive. The long and short is, therefore, that exposures for only a limited period can currently be hedged with currency options. Clearly, in the example above, the UK firm has a long-run exposure against the yen which cannot be covered via options.

Of course, there are other ways of hedging economic exposures, such as seeking overseas sourcing or even relocating to the same countries as one's competitors. But care has to be taken that short-term exchange rate movements are not interpreted as long-run changes – as the US manufacturer of earth-moving equipment, Caterpillar, did. In the early 1980s Caterpillar moved some of its manufacture abroad to offset the impact of the strong dollar on its costs, compared with those of its Japanese competitor, Komatsu. Overseas production went from 19 per cent of total sales in 1982 to 25 per cent in 1986; overseas sourcing rose fourfold. Then the dollar started to fall. Caterpillar lost out. It might have been better to stay put and hedge its exposure via currency options.

Having now considered hedging and a range of derivatives, readers may like to look at Press Cutting 15.1. The next test bank contains questions based upon it.

PRESS CUTTING 15.1

Dealing with the dollar – retailers produce some fancy moves to cover their exposure

Steve Johnson says currency hedges are just one of the ways companies are coping with the weak dollar

Jeyes, the household products group, has shifted production from Europe to Mexico. Vesuvius UK, the ceramics company, is sourcing more raw materials from China. Retailers of goods ranging from clothing and bicycles to tickets to US theme parks have been forced to slash their prices.

These are just some of the repercussions of the slump in the value of the dollar that UK companies are grappling with. The swings in the currency markets have brought bad news for some and good news for others, but a need to be nimble is a unifying factor.

Jeyes, the Parozone-to-hair-care products group taken private in a management buy-out backed by Legal & General Ventures in 2002, has the bulk of its production based in Europe. As a result, the falling dollar has threatened to damage margins for the 10–15 per cent of sales generated in the US.

'We saw in the autumn of 2003 the start of the weakening of the dollar, so we extended the degree of foreign exchange cover we had and moved costs out of sterling and the euro and into US dollars', says Nick Flanagan, group treasurer at Jeyes.

'We were keen to use raw materials from in and around the US for our North American sales and we already had a manufacturing facility in Mexico. We are now increasing the size of this facility threefold. It's something we were doing anyway, but the weakness of the dollar has accelerated the process.'

Significantly, although the main aim of Jeyes' Monterrey plant is to service the US market, the plant may also become a source of products for Europe – a trend aided by the Mexican peso being one of the few currencies to underperform the dollar in 2004.

The Mexican move gave Jeyes a larger natural currency hedge, but the company also chose to extend the length of the hedges it had in place in the foreign exchange market to buy more time in which to restructure.

This protection means Jeyes is repatriating profits from its US operations at levels more advantageous than the current spot rate of $1.891.

Vesuvius UK, the speciality ceramics and refractory products arm of Cookson Group, has faced similar dilemmas. On the plus side, a growing proportion of raw materials now come from China, which has a rigid dollar peg.

Unfortunately, the currency benefits of this have been more than wiped out by the effect of rising global commodity prices on many of Vesuvius's inputs.

'We have seen big increases in commodity costs. We are seeing sterling equivalent costs going up despite the currency advantage', says Richard Sykes, finance director.

Contracts for materials such as alumina, zirconia and magnecite are typically being renewed at rates between 7 and 15 per cent higher in sterling terms. At the same time, the sterling value of the 10 per cent of turnover Vesuvius generates in the US has fallen by 20–25 per cent.

'We do have to accept lower margins', says Mr Sykes. 'We have to trade through the currency cycle. If we made decisions based on the currency cycle we wouldn't have any customers.'

Vesuvius operates a rolling hedge for its net currency exposure, typically covering 100 per cent for the coming three months, down to 70 per cent for exposure four quarters on. But, as Mr Sykes concedes, this merely delays the inevitable. If the dollar continues to weaken, hedges will be set at increasingly less advantageous rates.

Vesuvius, which generates half of its turnover from continental Europe, has at least started to benefit from recent sterling weakness against the euro, which has risen from £0.658 to £0.686 since August 2004.

But Mr Sykes warns that if commodity strength and dollar weakness continue, Vesuvius will have to consider withdrawing from one of its market segments, or at least outsourcing production from the UK, where it has five manufacturing facilities.

Companies importing goods from Asia for sale in the UK are net gainers from dollar weakness. Unfortunately for shareholders, many of the gains are being eroded by commodity price rises and high street price deflation.

Universal Cycles imports 600,000 bicycles a year from countries such as China, India, Vietnam and the Philippines, most of which are sold through retailers

Press cutting 15.1 (*continued*)

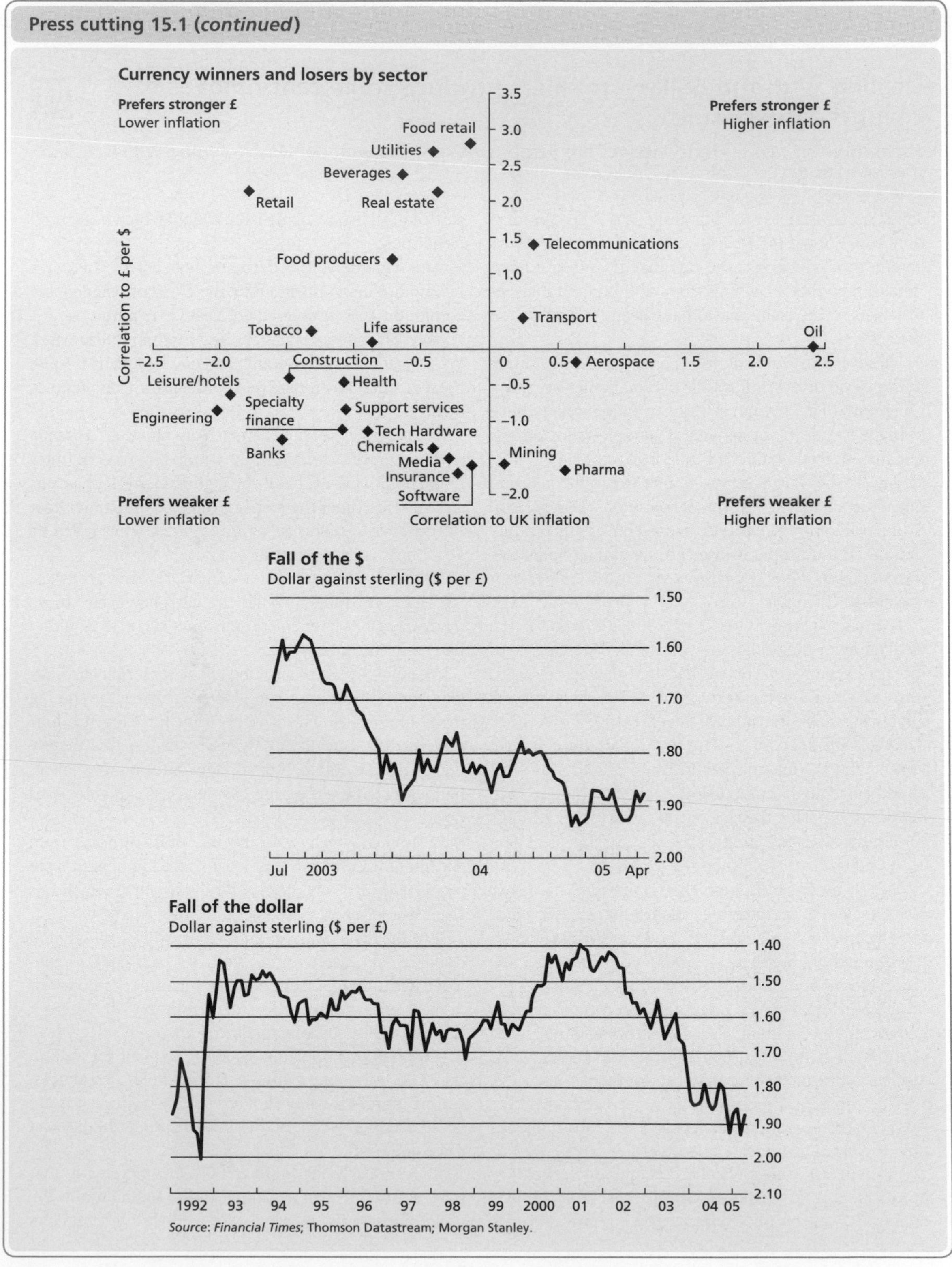

Source: *Financial Times*; Thomson Datastream; Morgan Stanley.

such as Argos, Toys R Us and Halfords. It has also diversified into garden furniture, battery-operated cars and pool tables.

Despite buying 95 per cent of its products in dollars, Universal has not had things all its own way.

'In the past 18 months raw material costs have increased quite dramatically. They have probably gone up 90 per cent in the past year alone', says Tony Brown, group finance manager. Shipping costs have risen by 20 per cent in the past year.

Universal has found it difficult to pass on cost increases, but Mr Brown says price rises were likely this year. Indeed, he sees widespread inflationary pressure if the pound falls below $1.80.

If that happens, Universal will be protected in the short-term, having hedged its dollar exposure forward until the end of the year.

Steven Kinsella, group financial controller of East, the women's fashion chain, also predicts a burst of inflation if the dollar shows signs of life.

As befits a retailer with a pronounced 'ethnic' slant, virtually all of East's range is imported from China, the Philippines and India. This has boosted margins in the past 18 months.

'A lot of clothing retailers work on $1.50 [to the pound], although this is moving up now and we are seeing price deflation on the high street', says Mr Kinsella.

He believes mass-market companies such as Next and Marks and Spencer have been forced to pass on all their cost savings, but that niche traders such as East have more pricing power.

'People operating in our niche market are not passing on the full impact of dollar weakness', he says. As such margins have risen, East has been able to invest in shop refits and its design, buying and merchandise teams.

East has moved to lock-in this happy position by hedging its currency exposure for the next 12 months, when historically six months has sufficed. Narrowing interest rate differentials between the UK and US have helped reduce the cost of this hedging, and Mr Kinsella says that most fashion retailers would have followed suit.

However, he believes that any sustained strengthening of the dollar against the pound would unleash inflation back on to the high street, with mass-market retailers being forced to pass on at least some of their rising costs.

Source: Financial Times, 12 April 2005.

Groups suffer a rude awakening

By Steve Johnson

With so many companies trading internationally in some way, few are immune to the effects of currency fluctuations. But recent violent movements will have come as a rude shock to many in the UK.

In the past 17 months the pound has rallied against the weak dollar, pushing as high as $1.945. With most Asian countries pegging their currencies against the dollar or intervening to limit appreciation against the greenback, sterling has also lost competitiveness against the world's manufacturing hub.

The pound traded in a range of $1.40–$1.70 between 1993 and November 2003. It had not come close to $2 since just before Black Wednesday in 1992.

Chris Towner, a consultant with corporate risk management service HIFX, which advises companies on managing foreign exchange risk, said many businesses assumed this $1.40–$1.70 pattern was permanent.

'They were in a hibernation period and it is only now that the wake-up call has come', he said. 'Dollar sellers [exporters to the US] have been waiting for the dollar to strengthen back to the $1.40–$1.70 level [against sterling] but the support level is now $1.85.'

Mr Towner added that these exporters were now suffering from a 'double whammy'. Not only had the exchange rate moved against them, but narrowing interest rate differentials between the UK and US meant dollar sellers were able to hedge two-years forward at a rate less than 3 cents better than spot, compared with 9 cents better than spot a year ago.

However, many UK companies importing from the 'dollar bloc' countries of Asia have seen import bills fall, further encouraging outsourcing to this region and fuelling the deflation in parts of the high street.

Source: Financial Time, 12 April 2005.

Press cutting 15.1 (*continued*)

How sterling's strength goes against the dollar revenues from ticket sales

A UK company selling US theme park tickets to British tourists might be expected to be a sure-fire winner from dollar weakness, with no commodity or shipping costs to muddy the waters, writes Steve Johnson.

But Oliver Brendon, managing director of American Attractions, which turns over £30m a year re-selling tickets to venues such as Disney World and Universal Studios, is hoping for a period of dollar strength.

Sterling has risen from $1.40 since American Attractions was launched in March 2002, but the 'cut-throat' nature of the business meant the company had been forced to pass all the cost savings to its customers, said Mr Brendon.

The company aims to minimise currency risk by buying one-month forward contracts and participation options.

The latter allows American Attractions to protect half its exposure for the coming year, with the option of either protecting the remainder or buying on the spot market, whichever is more advantageous.

With most of American Attractions' rivals simply relying on the spot market, and setting their prices accordingly, 'we would benefit from a period of dollar strength', said Mr Brendon.

'We can only make a profit on the exchange rate if we get a good forward rate', he added.

Source: Financial Times, 12 April 2005.

Summary

- Currency options provide the right, but not the obligation, to buy or sell a specific currency at a specific price at a time prior to a specified date or on a particular date.
- Users of currency options obtain insurance against adverse movements in the exchange rate while still retaining the opportunity to benefit from a favourable exchange rate movement. The maximum risk that is incurred by the buyer of an option is the premium cost of the said option.
- Currency options come in two forms. There are traded currency options and over-the-counter options. Be sure that you know the distinction between these two.
- Currency options may be classified as American or European options. Be sure that you know the difference. It is made clear in the text.
- Should a company wish to leave open the possibility of making a currency gain on a receivable or payable while protecting itself against adverse movements in the exchange rate, it may do so via the currency option market.
- Currency options are of particular interest where a future currency cash flow is uncertain as in the case of a tender on a contract or an overseas takeover bid.
- Currency options provide an easy way for a company to take positions and to speculate in foreign currency with limited downside risk.
- In competitive terms, currency options can provide valuable benefits. Take an example. Company A buys imports from overseas in foreign currency and sells in the home market for home currency. Its biggest competitor – indeed the market leader – has the same cash input and output profile. If the market leader decides not to hedge its foreign

currency payables while company A does hedge, a problem arises. Company A may gain in competitive terms if the foreign currency strengthens but it may lose out should it weaken. The currency option provides the wherewithal to back both horses. But it can be expensive. At the time of writing, sterling/dollar 12-month at-the-money American options were costing 5 per cent or so, while similar but European options were running at 4 per cent.

- Make sure you understand what in-the-money, at-the-money and out-of-the-money mean. If you have difficulty remembering, try this mnemonic. In the money options have intrinsic value. Do you see? 'In' the money = 'in'-trinsic value.
- Also make sure you understand what the Black and Scholes formula is saying. Remember the essence of Figure 15.3. If you are going to become an *aficionado* of option pricing you will need to be able to manipulate Black and Scholes. If not, merely understanding how it works will be enough. But do not be afraid of it. Remember the relatively user-friendly table for pricing options in Chapter 14.
- It is worth spending a little time ensuring that you know how to use an average rate option in order to hedge a foreign currency profit and loss account exposure.

End of chapter questions

15.1 When should a firm consider purchasing a call option for foreign currency hedging?

15.2 When should a firm consider purchasing a put option for foreign currency hedging?

15.3 Why should a firm consider hedging net payables or net receivables with currency options rather than forward contracts? What are the disadvantages of hedging with currency options as opposed to forward contracts?

16 Interest rate risk

Interest rate risk is concerned with the sensitivity of profit, cash flows or valuation of the firm to changes in interest rates. Viewed from the perspective of this definition, the firm should analyse how its profit, cash outturns and value change in response to changes in interest rate levels. Should its profits and cash flow fall when interest rates rise, then the risk-averse company, seeking to stabilise profit trends, will finance itself with fixed rate funds. A speculative housebuilder might be a company falling into this category. However, some companies' profits and cash flows move directly with interest rates – this is true of many financial institutions. Such firms might, if they were risk averse, fund themselves with floating rate finance. Having said all this, firms may back their view of the market by funding themselves in a particular way. Thus the housebuilder which anticipates a fall in interest rates might source from floating rate funds. **Interest rate exposure** arises from two sources. There is macroeconomic exposure – the kind that the housebuilder in the example faced. And there is the exposure that the lender faces in respect of interest receivable on its deposit and, similarly, that the borrower faces relating to interest to be paid on loans drawn down.

We take interest rate risk much further later in this chapter, but first of all it is necessary to consider the term structure of interest rates because this topic is at the centre of so much of our analysis.

16.1 The term structure of interest rates

The term structure of interest rates can be thought of as a graph of interest rates on securities of a particular risk class at a particular time, in which the interest rate is plotted on the vertical axis and time to maturity on the horizontal axis. Term structure theory is concerned with why the term structure has a particular shape at a particular time. Analysts sometimes refer to the term structure as being flat (same interest for all maturities), upward sloping (long-term interest rates higher than short-term interest rates) or downward sloping (short-term interest rates higher than long-term rates). Figure 16.1 illustrates these three situations.

The best known explanation of the term structure is the expectations theory. According to this hypothesis, expectations of future interest rates constitute the key determinant of the yield/maturity relationship. Each investor can either buy long-term securities and hold them or buy short-term securities and continually reinvest in shorts at each maturity over the holding period. In equilibrium, the expected return for each holding period will tend to

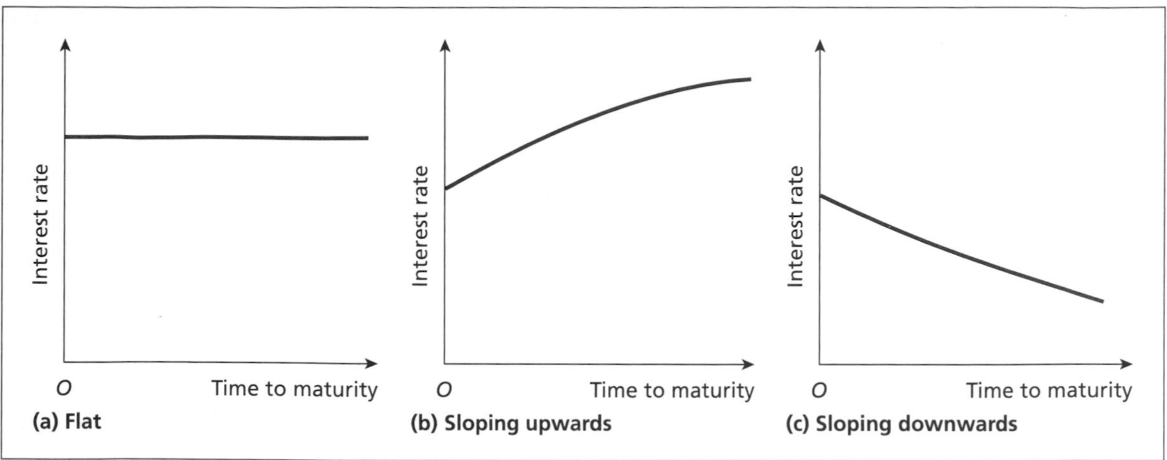

Figure 16.1 Types of term structure

be the same, whatever alternative or combination of alternatives was chosen. As a result, the return on a long-term bond will tend to equal an unbiased average of the current short-term rates and future short-term rates expected to prevail to maturity of the long-term bond. With this background, one can calculate the implicit or expected short-term rate for any future period based upon actual rates of interest prevailing in the market at a specific time. Expectations theory contends that the term structure of interest rates is entirely a function of investors' expectations about future interest rates.

Most evidence underpins the importance of interest rate expectations in the term structure of interest rates. However, Hicks and others have argued that long-term rates in fact tend to differ from the average of expected short-term rates because market participants prefer to lend short unless offered a premium sufficient to offset the risk of lending long. Hicks[1] argues that these liquidity premiums tend to be greater, the longer the maturity of the bond. His findings support the liquidity preference theory of the term structure of interest rates. Advocates of this theory believe that for the most part investors wish to lend short, and organisations aim to borrow long, so that liquidity premiums are positive – that is, the forward rate exceeds the expected future spot interest rate. If liquidity preference theory is right, the term structure should be upward sloping more often than not. A positive liquidity premium rewards investors for lending long. The reward manifests itself in high long-term rates of interest. Of course, if future spot rates were expected to fall, the term structure could still be downward sloping – but liquidity preference theory would predict a less dramatic downward slope than expectations theory.

A third theory, the preferred habitat hypothesis of Modigliani and Sutch,[2] argues that bond markets are segmented by maturity, and that the maturity preferences of market participants are so strong that investors tend to borrow and lend only in a particular range of maturities. Therefore, in each different credit market, interest rates tend to be determined by supply and demand rather than by interest rate expectations. This explanation is sometimes called the market segmentation theory, or the hedging pressure theory.

Finally, there is the inflation premium theory. Like the liquidity preference explanation, this theory argues that long-term interest rates reflect investors' expectations about future short-term interest rates plus a premium for risk. However, advocates of the theory contend that the principal source of risk is the rate of inflation. They argue that investors are interested in real returns and that the primary determinant in the term structure of interest rates is investors' expectations of inflation over different holding periods, which is the critical factor by which investors translate nominal interest rates into real expected returns.

Whichever theory of term structure seems to predominate in the domestic market should hold for the offshore market too. In the absence of capital controls, arbitrage would ensure the virtual equality of internal and external rates at each maturity, and whatever holds for the domestic market would also hold for offshore rates. In other words, there is normally no independent offshore dollar term structure of interest rates.

If capital controls are in place and they affect all maturities equally, the internal term structure might not be identical to the external one, but since offshore rates should tend to be at the same position relative to internal rates for each maturity, a nearly identical term structure should hold. As in the domestic market, if offshore currency investors think interest rates will drop, they will try to lock into long-term deposits; this will tend to lower the long-term yield to maturity.

The term structure of offshore currency interest rates will be consonant with the market's interest rate forecasts if, and only if, the yield on a long-term deposit equals the expected yield obtained from investing in short-term securities and reinvesting the proceeds successively in short-term deposits at the interest rate expected to prevail during each future period.

The above point can be observed easily by reference to a numerical example. Assume that a firm has money to invest for, say, six months. It might invest now for the whole six-month period. Or it might invest now for only three months and then reinvest for a further three later on. Clearly, if the interest is for six months now, the firm will receive a quotation for a fixed rate for the whole six-month period, with interest being credited at the end of the period. Also, if the firm invests for three months expecting to extend the investment by reinvesting at the end of that period for a further three months, it can expect to receive an offer of a fixed rate for three months with interest credited at the end of the period. But the firm could also obtain a forward/forward fixed interest rate for the period from the beginning of month 4 to the end of month 6. By pursuing this latter policy, the firm would have manufactured exactly the same investment as locking in for the whole six months – so the proceeds should, in present value terms, be the same. After all, the two investments are exactly equal in terms of risk, so they should yield the same returns.

If the firm invests for six months in accordance with the first scenario above, the proceeds of investing £1 now will be:

$$£1\left[1+r_6\left(\frac{6}{12}\right)\right] \tag{16.1}$$

where r_6 is the annual (as bankers quote it) interest rate for six months. Investing according to the second scenario, the terminal proceeds of investing £1 now would be:

$$£1\left[1+r_3\left(\frac{3}{12}\right)\right]\left[1+r_{3/6}\left(\frac{3}{12}\right)\right] \tag{16.2}$$

where r_3 is the annual interest rate for the first three months and $r_{3/6}$ is the annual interest rate from the beginning of month 4 to the end of month 6.

Generalising from equation (16.1), we could say that the terminal proceeds for the former scenario amounted to:

$$1+\left(r_{t_2}\times\frac{t_2}{12}\right) \tag{16.3}$$

where r is the interest rate and t_2 is the far term in months. Similarly, the terminal value of the latter scenario can be said to be equal to:

$$\left[1+\left(r_{t_1}\times\frac{t_2}{12}\right)\right]\left[\left(r_{t_{1\to2}}\times\frac{t_{1\to2}}{12}\right)+1\right] \tag{16.4}$$

where t_1 is the near term in months and $t_{1\to2}$ is the difference between the near and far terms in months.

Since the proceeds from the two investments should be the same, it follows logically that:

$$\frac{1+\left(r_{t_2}\times\frac{t_2}{12}\right)}{1+\left(r_{t_1}\times\frac{t_1}{12}\right)}=1+r_{t_{1\to2}} \tag{16.5}$$

The figure obtained from the above additions for $r_{t_{1\to2}}$ may be annualised to put it into terms used by bankers.

This forward rate is, of course, essentially the market's best estimate of a future interest rate based upon the term structure of interest rates, from which both forward quotes of interest rates are derived. An understanding of these very basic ideas is useful because it is the underpinning of various quotations to do with interest rates – for example, forward rate agreements and some other instruments which we will encounter in this chapter.

16.2 Interest rate exposure

Besides the exposure of the firm's operating income stream to changes in interest rate, there are at least two other types of interest rate exposure: these are called basis risk and gap exposure. Basis risk occurs when the basis upon which interest rates are determined for assets and liabilities is different. Consider a bank that has lent £5m to a corporate customer for three months based on LIBOR, but assume that the bank has funded itself with three-month **certificates of deposit (CDs)**. In three months, the bank itself anticipates rolling over both the assets and the liabilities. The bank is exposed to interest rate changes, inasmuch as the basis on which interest is determined on the bank's asset and liability is different. A 1 per cent change in LIBOR need not necessarily lead to an exactly equal change in CD rates.

By contrast, gap exposure arises from timing differences in the repricing of assets and liabilities that are sensitive to interest rates. Consider a bank that has invested heavily in six-month CDs issued by other banks. It has funded itself by issuing its own three-month CDs, thus creating a gap exposure. The basis on which interest is calculated on both assets and liabilities is similar – CD rates. But the timing of repricing is different. The bank will have to roll over its borrowings in three months' time. Should rates have increased, then the cost of financing will increase but the bank's income stream will not change for a further three months. Its profit on this transaction will be affected. Should the bank have had a greater proportion of liabilities being repriced before assets, it would presumably have been expecting rates to fall.

Managing interest rate exposure begins with its measurement. Gap management techniques focus upon just this problem. They are concerned with the exposure of net income to changes in interest rates during a period. If fixed rate liabilities exceed fixed rate assets, there is a positive gap. With a positive gap, a rise in short-term rates increases margins, while declining rates reduce margins. By contrast, if fixed rate liabilities are less than fixed rate assets, there is a negative gap. With such a gap, net interest margins decline if short-term interest rates rise and margins increase if rates fall. There are three widely used techniques of gap management: maturity gap modelling, duration analysis and simulation techniques. These are briefly considered in order.

The essential approach of maturity gap modelling is best illustrated by an example. Assume that for a particular gap period, interest-rate-sensitive assets are £6m while interest-rate-sensitive liabilities are £10m. At first sight, the analysis suggests a gap of £4m. While this is correct, it might be misleading. For example, assume that the firm is financing itself via 90-day CDs and that the assets in which it has invested are 90-day commercial paper. If it is the case that the historic volatilities of these two instruments vary – say, CDs are 110 per cent as volatile as the 90-day financial future while commercial paper is 85 per cent as volatile as the same financial future – then the interest rate exposure (volatility adjusted) can be estimated as £5.9m (see Table 16.1).

In this kind of analysis, the choice of financial futures as a standard is preferred for two reasons – first of all, their rates are market determined and, secondly, they can be used to adjust the gap in the desired direction by hedging without further correlation calculations being necessary – although, of course, volatilities can change.

Duration analysis is different and is again best explained by means of an example. Consider a bond. Its final maturity is often considered – erroneously – to be its key component. This concentrates simply on the final cash flow, rather than the whole configuration of cash flows throughout the bond's life. A 10 per cent bond with a 10-year life is not the same as a 5 per cent bond with a 10-year life, but both have the same final maturity. The concept of duration is designed to encapsulate all of the cash flows accruing under a bond, duly allowing for the incidence of their timing.

Assume two bonds. Each has a 15-year term to maturity and each sells to yield 10 per cent to maturity. The first bond is priced at par while the second sells at a substantial discount because its coupon is only 5 per cent. Much more of the first bond's total present value is received during the earlier years to maturity. This bond has a shorter maturity in a present value sense. Deep discount bonds are much more price sensitive to rate movements

Table 16.1 Maturity gap modelling

	Cash flow (£m)	Volatility (% v. financial futures)	Financial futures equivalent (£m)
Assets	6	85	5.1
Liabilities	10	110	11.0
Gap	4		5.9

than regular bonds. Also, on questions of default, the expected value of any loss on the second bond is greater because a larger proportion of the investors' outlay is riding on the more distant payments.

The concept of duration explicitly takes account of the timing of the return of value to a bondholder. Essentially, duration is the weighted average maturity stated in present value terms. The number of years into the future when a cash flow is received is weighted by the proportion which that cash flow contributes to the total present value of the bond.

If a bond has one coupon payment a year, then duration, D, may be defined, in algebraic terms, as:

$$D = \frac{\sum_{t=1}^{n} \frac{tC}{(1+r)^t}}{p}$$

where

n = the life of the bond;
C = the cash receipt at end of year t – this will be equal to the annual coupon, except for the last year, which is equal to the annual coupon and the repayment amount;
r = the yield to maturity as a percentage;
t = the number of years from now in respect of which each cash receipt, C, is receivable;
p = price of bond.

The top half of the expression is the present value of a single year's cash receipt weighted according to the year in which it is received. The denominator is the price of the bond or the sum of all of those cash flows that make the present value of the bond. Table 16.2 shows the calculation of the duration of a £1m bond with a 10 per cent coupon bond priced at par with five years to maturity.

The duration of a bond is less than the life of the bond. The duration can never exceed the term to maturity. A **zero-coupon bond** will have a duration equal to its maturity. The difference between duration and term to maturity increases as the term to maturity increases.

The notion of duration can be applied to a portfolio of assets too. By multiplying the duration of the individual asset in the portfolio by its weight in the value of the portfolio, an average duration can be calculated. This is valuable because it may be shown that a change in bond price with respect to a change in discount factor is approximately equal to its duration with the sign reversed. So, if a bond's duration is known, then it is possible to calculate how much the price will change as the yield of the bond changes. If the yield

Table 16.2 Duration of a 10 per cent five-year bond priced at par (face value of bond £1m)

Year	Cash flow (£000)	Discount at 10%	Present value of ($000)	Proportion of PV	Duration (years)*
1	100	0.909	90.9	0.0909	0.0909
2	100	0.826	82.6	0.0826	0.1652
3	100	0.751	75.1	0.0751	0.2253
4	100	0.683	68.3	0.0683	0.2732
5	1,100	0.621	683.1	0.6831	3.4155
			1,000.0	1.0000	4.1701
		Duration of bond = 4.17 years			

* Each year, proportion of PV is multiplied by number of years, i.e. column (5) is multiplied by column (1).

increases by, say, 1 per cent, for a bond with a duration of 4.73 years, the price should decrease by 4.73 per cent. For a portfolio of bonds with a duration of 6.38 years, every 1 per cent change in interest rates will lead to a change in the market value of the portfolio by approximately 6.38 per cent.

The final technique of gap management is simulation analysis. This merely consists of building a mathematical model of the financial flows of the corporation, incorporating the assets and liabilities from the current and projected balance sheets, given changes in interest rates. Clearly, for simulation models to be effective, the assumptions and data analysis need to be accurate and realistic.

Having identified and quantified interest rate exposure, the next step is to hedge the risk. This involves transferring risk from one party to a counterparty. The counterparty may have an opposite exposure to one's own or be willing to take on that position. Many interest rate instruments are available to do this. These include forward rate agreements, financial futures, interest rate swaps, options and options on interest rate swaps. Although some of these have already been briefly discussed in this book, they are now looked at in more detail.

16.3 Forward rate agreements

Forward rate agreements (FRAs) allow borrowers or investors to lock in today a LIBOR rate accruing from a forward start date for a given period – for example, for month 3 in the future to month 6. The FRA is currently an off-balance-sheet instrument. It is widely used to cover short-term interest rate exposures for periods up to two or three years. It is a contract between two parties to agree an interest rate on a notional loan or deposit of a specified amount and maturity at a specific future date and to make payments between counterparties computed by reference to changes in the interest rate. FRAs involve no exchange of the principal amount. They are concerned only with the interest element. To hedge an interest rate exposure, the notional amount of the FRA contract is made equal to the principal amount of the underlying asset or liability.

A borrower desirous of hedging an interest rate exposure in three months' time for a period of three months would purchase a three-month FRA starting in three months. This is known as purchasing a '3s *v.* 6s' FRA (or 'threes' against 'sixes'). An investor with floating rate assets wishing to lock in an investment rate for a similar period would sell an FRA contract. To see how FRAs work, assume that a borrower has a one-year floating rate loan that has to be rolled over every three months based on three months' LIBOR. For the first three months, LIBOR has already been fixed. The borrower is concerned about a short-term increase in interest rates and wishes to hedge this exposure for the following three months. This can be achieved by purchasing an FRA in respect of the next interest period and for a notional amount identical to the underlying loan transaction.

In three months' time, the borrower continues to borrow from the original source of finance. The FRA contract that the borrower has entered into will have the same start date as the next interest rate repricing date. On that day, the three-month LIBOR rate is compared with the rate agreed under the FRA contract. If the FRA rate is greater than LIBOR, then the borrower will pay the seller of the FRA contract the difference between the two rates. The borrower's cost of borrowing will be equal to the market LIBOR rate plus the difference paid to the FRA as counterparty. The all-in rate will be the same as the rate agreed under the FRA contract. If the FRA rate is less than LIBOR, then the FRA counterparty will pay the borrower the difference between the two rates. This time the cost of borrowing will be the three-month LIBOR rate less the difference received from the FRA counterparty. Similarly, the net cost to the borrower will be the same rate as agreed under the FRA contract.

In the FRA market it is common practice to discount the net interest amount and settle at the beginning of an interest period. The discount factor used is the prevailing LIBOR rate. By dealing an FRA contract, the borrower can fix the borrowing costs for, say, the next six months. The borrowing cost can be fixed for the rest of the year by purchasing a strip of FRAs – a borrower will purchase not only a '3s *v.* 6s' but also a '6s *v.* 9s' and a '9s *v.* 12s' contract.

As an example, assume that a corporate borrower deals a $10m 3s *v.* 6s FRA on 10 September 2004 for settlement on 10 December 2004 based on a maturity date of 10 March 2005. The contract rate is 9.65 per cent and the contract period is 90 days. If, on 10 December 2004, the three-month LIBOR fixing is at $10^1/_8$ per cent, the settlement amount payable on that date would be:

$$\frac{(0.10125-0.0965)\times 10{,}000{,}000\times 90/360}{1+(0.10125\times 90/360)}$$

$$= \$11{,}581.83 \text{ payable to the buyer of the FRA}$$

The above settlement formula is virtually standard in the business nowadays.

The price of each FRA contract is a function of the yield curve. It will be priced in the manner explained by reference to forward/forward interest rates earlier in this chapter.

16.4 Interest rate futures

Chapter 13 on financial futures explained how futures contracts could be used to hedge exposures. They are traded on exchanges and are standardised. Such standardised features include a set contract size, a specific settlement date and a specific interest period. These standard features make them less than utterly appealing to corporations as hedging tools because they do not allow for specific exposures. However, they are widely used by banks and financial institutions for hedging their portfolios. These institutions are not generally concerned with matching, with 100 per cent exactitude, their underlying exposures.

As we have mentioned in earlier chapters, financial futures contracts are for standardised amounts and delivery dates. The number of instruments traded is limited and they are traded off-balance sheet. All futures contracts are registered with the clearing house, which becomes the counterparty to any deal, and there are obligatory initial and variation margin requirements for all futures contracts.

16.5 Interest rate swaps

Interest rate swaps provide another means of eliminating interest rate exposure. Swaps were the topic of Chapter 12, where they were dealt with extensively. To spend more time on them here would be repetitious.

16.6 Interest rate options

Interest rate options include caps, floors and collars. Their mechanism, theory, advantages and disadvantages are just like those of currency options, which were discussed in Chapters 14 and 15. Such instruments as caps, floors and collars were covered in Chapter 12 on swaps.

Swaps, futures and FRAs lock in an interest rate. The company is protected against any adverse movements of interest rates, but it cannot take advantage of favourable movements of interest rates.

Interest rate options overcome this. They provide the right but not the obligation to fix a rate of interest, on a notional loan or deposit, for an agreed amount, for a fixed term, on a specific forward date. The buyer of the option has the right but not the obligation to deal at the agreed rate. The buyer is protected against adverse rate movements but is able to take advantage of a favourable movement in interest rates. The seller guarantees an interest rate if the option is exercised. The seller receives a fee – the premium – for providing this guarantee. The factors that determine the price of interest rate options are similar to those that determine currency option prices. Remember Black and Scholes, volatilities and all that? If not, refer again to Chapters 14 and 15.

The most common type of interest rate option available to borrowers as a hedge against rising interest rates is the interest rate cap. Interest rate floors protect investors against falling interest rates.

An interest rate cap is an arrangement where, in return for a premium, the seller of the cap undertakes, over an agreed period, to compensate the buyer of the cap whenever a reference interest rate (for example, three- or six-month LIBOR) exceeds a preagreed maximum interest rate (the cap rate). In addition to having this protection whenever the reference rate exceeds the cap rate, the buyer of the cap can benefit when the reference rate is below the cap rate. This is because, at such times, the borrower is not locked into a fixed rate and can take advantage of the lower market rates.

If an investor purchases a floor, he or she will be compensated by the seller whenever, say, three-month LIBOR falls below a pre-agreed minimum rate. The buyer will exercise the option only if rates fall below the agreed level and, therefore, is able to enjoy the benefits if interest rates remain at levels above the agreed rate.

Interest settlement procedures for a cap or floor transaction are straightforward. A borrower is compensated by the seller of the cap whenever the reference rate exceeds the cap rate. A floor investor is compensated whenever the reference rate falls below the floor rate.

Just as we mentioned in Chapter 15 that there are zero-cost options, so there are similar interest rate instruments – collars. Effectively, the simultaneous purchase and sale of a cap and a floor is known as a 'collar'. To illustrate how collars work, assume that a treasurer wishes to protect his or her interest income by buying a floor struck at 10 per cent. But he or she does not wish to pay the full premium and therefore sells a cap struck at, for example, 13 per cent. In this case, the cost of buying the floor exactly matches the premium received from selling the cap. So we have a zero-cost collar. By undertaking these transactions, the company has an investment that pays a minimum of 10 per cent if the floating rate is at or below 10 per cent and a maximum of 13 per cent when the floating rate is at or above 13 per cent on the interest determination date. If the floating rate is between 10 per cent and 13 per cent, then the return equals the reference rate.

Dealing an interest rate collar is always cheaper than buying the straight interest rate cap or floor, since the buyer is forgoing some of the upside benefit if rates move favourably. This is exactly the same as the zero-cost currency option.

Another interest rate exposure instrument is worth mentioning: this is the option on an interest rate swap, often called a swaption. It allows a company to protect itself against unfavourable interest rate movements but at the same time to benefit from favourable interest rate movements by initiating a swap transaction during a specific period at a predetermined rate. Interest rate swaps are similar to caps and floors although less flexible – the rate of borrowing or investing in the future is fixed once a swaption is exercised. With a cap or floor transaction, the buyer would continue to enjoy any benefits of favourable movements in interest rates during the period of the hedge. Swaptions are cheaper than interest rate caps or floors. The swaption premium is a function of market volatility together with factors such as the period of the option, the period of the underlying swap and the rate on the underlying swap. Like currency options, a swaption may be European style, where the buyer may exercise the option only on a specific day, or American style, where the buyer can exercise the swaption at any time during the option period.

Summary

- Interest rate risk is concerned with the sensitivity of profit, cash flows or valuation of the firm to changes in interest rates.
- Given this definition, the firm should analyse how its profits, cash outturns and value alter in response to movements in interest rate levels.
- If a firm's profits and cash flows are likely to fall when interest rates rise, the risk-averse firm will finance itself with fixed-rate funds. A speculative housebuilder, for example would fall into this category.
- For some companies, profits and cash flows move directly with interest rates. This is true of many financial institutions. Risk-averse firms that fall into this category might be more attracted to floating rate interest in terms of funding themselves.
- The term structure of interest rates can be thought of as a graph of interest rates on securities of a particular risk class at a particular time. Interest rate is plotted on the vertical axis and time to maturity on the horizontal.
- Note that the term structure of interest rates may be flat, upwards sloping or downwards sloping. There are various explanations of the term structure.
- Expectations theory suggests that anticipation of future interest rates by market players constitutes the key determinant of the term structure.
- According to the liquidity preference theory of the term structure of interest rates, market participants prefer to lend short rather than for longer periods. This merely reflects a view about risk. It means that liquidity premiums tend to be greater the longer the maturity of a bond, and this tends to suggest an upward-sloping term structure more often than not, all other things being equal.
- According to the preferred habitat theory of the term structure of interest rates, bond markets are segmented according to maturity. Within the various segments, a bargaining

process takes place between lenders and borrowers and the piecing together of these mini-term structures for each segment by maturity gives us the overall shape of the term structure.

- According to the inflation premium theory of the term structure of interest rates, it is argued that investors are interested in real returns. This means that in order to get to, for example a twelve-month interest rate, investors look to the real return and adjust in line with expected inflation for the next 12 months. A similar kind of process would operate in respect of interest rates over a two-year period. Investors would look for a real return and adjust this in accordance with expected inflation over a 24-month period. Thus the nominal interest rate for a particular period reflects the real return adjusted for expectations of inflation over that period.
- Note how equation 16.5 in the chapter works. It is underpinned by the notion that an investor can buy either long-term securities and hold them or buy short-term securities and continually reinvest in shorts at each maturity over the holding period. In equilibrium, the expected return for each holding period will tend to be the same whichever alternative or combination of alternatives is chosen. As a result of this, the return on a long-term bond will tend to equal the average of the current short-term rates and future short-term rates expected to prevail to maturity of the long-term bond. Equation 16.5 is important because it underpins the pricing of FRAs and forward/forward interest instruments.
- Note the definition of duration. It is the weighted average maturity of all payments on a security, coupons and principal, where the weights are the discounted present value of the payments. This means that the duration of a bond is shorter than the stated term to maturity on all securities except for zero-coupon bonds, where they are equal.
- Choices between fixed and floating rate funding should be based upon a careful analysis of the firm's interest rate exposure and a view of future rate movements given the level of risk aversion of the management.
- FRAs, interest rate futures and interest rate swaps may all be used to lock in interest rates for the firm.
- There are also interest rate options. These give the firm the right but not the obligation to fix a rate of interest on a notional loan or deposit, for an agreed amount, for a fixed term, on a specific forward date. Caps, collars and floors are all examples of interest rate options. As one would expect, they are priced according to the Black and Scholes model of option valuation.

End of chapter questions

16.1 (a) How does a company become exposed to interest rate risk?
(b) How does a bank become exposed to interest rate risk?

16.2 How might a company attempt to reduce interest rate risk?

16.3 How might a bank attempt to reduce interest rate risk?

17

Financial engineering

The term 'financial engineering' sounds complicated. Engineers are generally good at understanding the complexities of finance – they are numerate and logical, which financial management requires. But most finance people make poor engineers. Perhaps this is why financial engineering sounds esoteric. But, as Smithson[1] points out, financial engineering is 'usually nothing more difficult than using the box of financial LEGOs'. What he means is that the essence of financial engineering involves simple building blocks which can be bolted together to make a complex financial construction. And Smithson also points out that using an approach that derives from simple financial ideas to analyse complex financial instruments has a timelessness about it. The techniques of financial engineering will not get out of date even though many of the products built by the financial engineer may. Even though banks introduce innovative instruments, all that it is necessary to do to understand them is to break them down from their complicated financial construction into simple Lego components. Using this methodology, the analyst cannot get out of date and he or she does not have to learn new tricks – the analyst simply disaggregates the complicated new financial edifices into simple old ones. So what are the simple tools necessary to analyse the most complex financial instrument? The answer is easy – merely forwards and options and an idea of the risk profile which they create. Let us see whether we can make financial engineering easy then. We begin by looking at forwards.

17.1 Forward contracts

Eliminating a foreign exchange receivable exposure can be achieved, using on-balance sheet methods, by borrowing in the foreign currency concerned. Chapter 11 suggested various ways of doing this. Or a forward contract could be used – this involves off-balance sheet cover.

To analyse the effect of a forward contract, the resulting payoff from buying the forward may be superimposed upon the original risk profile. So, let us first of all look at the original risk profile without forward cover. If the actual exchange rate movement is adverse, the inherent risk will lead to a decline in profit, cash flow and hence the value of the firm. But with forward cover, this decline is exactly offset by the profit on the forward contract. Hence, from the risk profile illustrated in Figure 17.1 it can be seen that the forward contract provides the perfect hedge. In the figure, ΔV refers to the resulting change in the value of the firm and ΔP measures the difference between the actual price and the expected price.

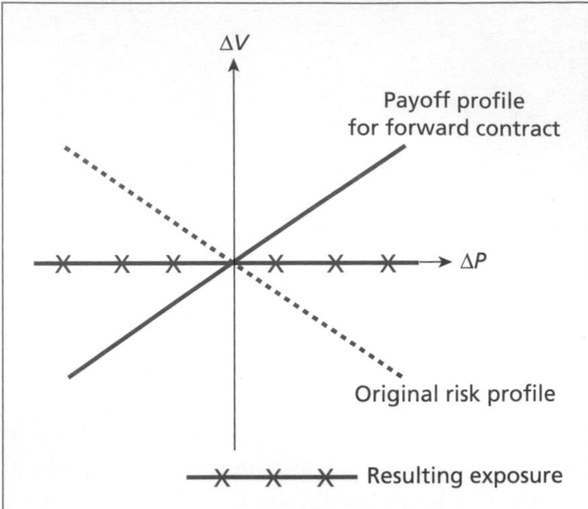

Figure 17.1 **Payoff profile for a forward contract**

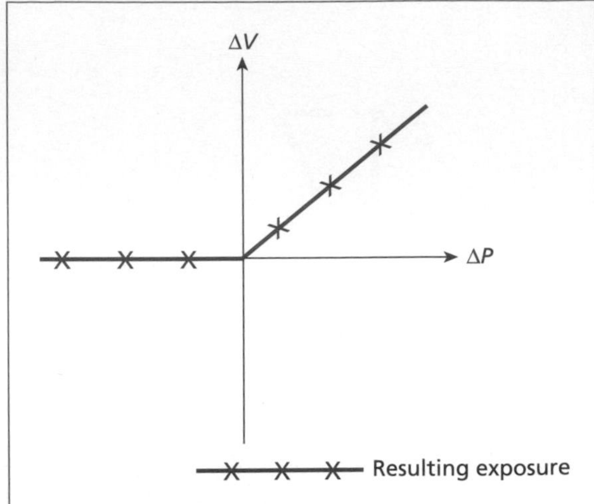

Figure 17.2 **Payoff profile for a call option**

As we know from earlier chapters, the forward contract is entered into and is subsequently closed out and settled at its maturity. A futures contract is really very similar. Yes, there is an initial margin requirement and top-up, or variation, margins may be called for during the course of the contract's life as it is marked to market daily. It is this feature that led Black[2] to liken a futures contract to 'a series of forward contracts. Each day, yesterday's contract is settled, and today's contract is written.' Certainly, a futures contract is really just like a sequence of forwards. The forward written on day 1 is settled on day 2 and is replaced, in essence, by a new forward reflecting day 2 expectations. The new contract is itself settled on day 3 and replaced, and so on until the day the contract ends at its ultimate maturity.

Just as a futures contract is very similar to a forward, so is a swap. Each is priced off interest rate differentials and, at least in theory, what can be achieved by a swap can be achieved by a forward. There may be occasions when one is more appropriate than the other, but essentially futures, forwards and swaps are very close relatives – not quite identical, but not far off. Admittedly, on the question of default risk, there are differences – the futures contract has the clearing house guaranteeing performance whereas the swap involves collateralisation of one loan against the other rather in the manner that the forward contract does. But the point is that the essential mechanics of futures, forwards and swaps are the same and the idea behind covering using forwards which was summarised in Figure 17.1 works similarly for futures and swaps. For forwards, swaps and futures contracts, the original risk profile is exactly offset by the payoff profile of the contract assumed. In short, the rationale of Figure 17.1 is equally applicable to futures and swaps as it is to forwards.

17.2 Option contracts

Option contracts are different. An option gives its owner the right, but not the obligation, to purchase or sell an asset. A generalised model of the payoff profile for an option is provided in Figure 17.2. Here, as in Figure 17.1, the financial price, *P*, might be an interest rate, a

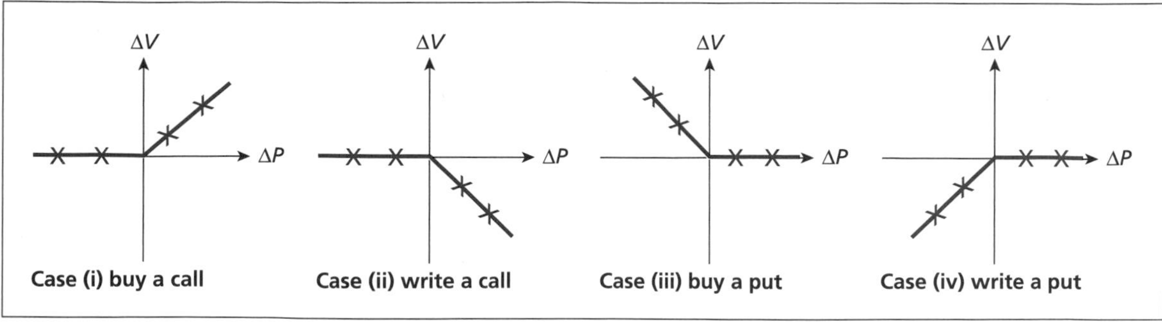

Figure 17.3 Payoff profiles for puts and calls

foreign exchange rate, a commodity price or the price of another financial asset (e.g. a share) – in short, whatever it is that the option relates to. The owner of the contract illustrated has the right to purchase the asset at a price agreed upon today. So, if *P* rises, the value of the option goes up. But the option contract holder is not obligated to purchase the asset if *P* goes down – so the value of the option remains unchanged, at zero, if *P* declines.

The option whose payoff profile is illustrated in Figure 17.2 and repeated in case (i) of Figure 17.3 is referred to as a call option; the option holder has bought the right to buy the asset at a specified price – the exercise, or strike, price. The payoff profile for the party selling the call option, known as the call writer, is shown in case (ii) of Figure 17.3. In contrast to the buyer of the call option, the writer of the call option has the obligation to perform. Thus, if the owner of the option decides to exercise his or her option, the seller of the option is required to sell the asset. Note that the buyer of a call has limited downside – the premium, which in any case is a sunk cost – but unlimited upside. The payoff profile for the unhedged option writer is exactly opposite. He or she has limited upside – the receipt of the premium – and unlimited downside risk.

There are also options to sell an asset at a specified price – this is the put option. The payoff to the buyer of a put is shown in case (iii) of Figure 17.3 and the payoff for the writer of the put is shown in case (iv). The points referred to in the previous paragraph about unlimited upside and downside continue to apply in the case of the put option.

All too often, one encounters confusion about the terminology used in option markets and in ways of achieving cover. Always remember that there is more than one way of skinning a cat (with apologies to cat lovers). Back to terminology first. The reader must remember that, for a dollar/sterling option, a call on dollars is equivalent to a put on sterling. And the same kind of idea applies to interest rates and bond prices. Remember too that when interest rates go up, bond prices go down. The problem about terminology here is best explained by way of an example. Suppose that a firm carries an interest rate exposure – a rise in interest rates adversely affects profit and value. As illustrated in case (i) of Figure 17.4, this downside risk might be eliminated by buying a call on the interest rate – commonly termed an interest rate 'cap'. In the figure, Δi represents a change in the interest rate and ΔV represents a change in the value of the firm. The same hedge effect could be achieved by buying a put on bonds. Remember that bond prices move in the opposite direction to interest rates. Case (ii) of Figure 17.4 illustrates the point. In these diagrams ΔP_{bond} represents a change in the bond price.

In the payoff profiles for options considered so far, we have not taken account of the premium paid by the buyer to the seller. In Figure 17.5 we remedy this. Case (i) in the figure

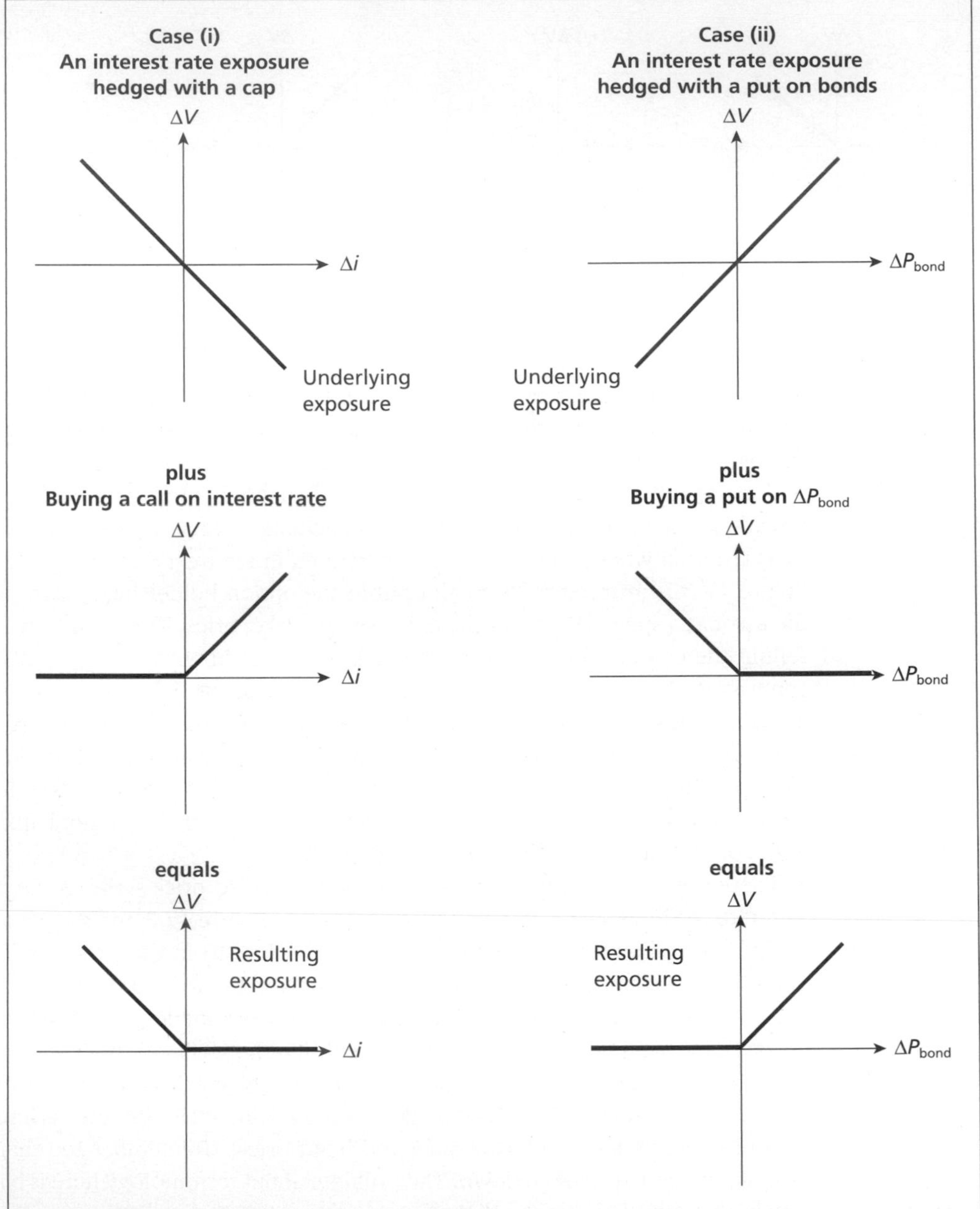

Figure 17.4 Using options to hedge exposures

shows the payoff profile for an at-the-money call option with the premium taken into account. In other words, the strike price is at the prevailing expected price as implied by the market. If the risk profile of this option is superimposed upon the underlying exposure, we obtain case (ii) in Figure 17.5. Note the shape of this new resulting exposure – this is obtained by merely combining the original exposure with the option inclusive of the premium. The premium for a call option falls as the strike price increases relative to the prevailing

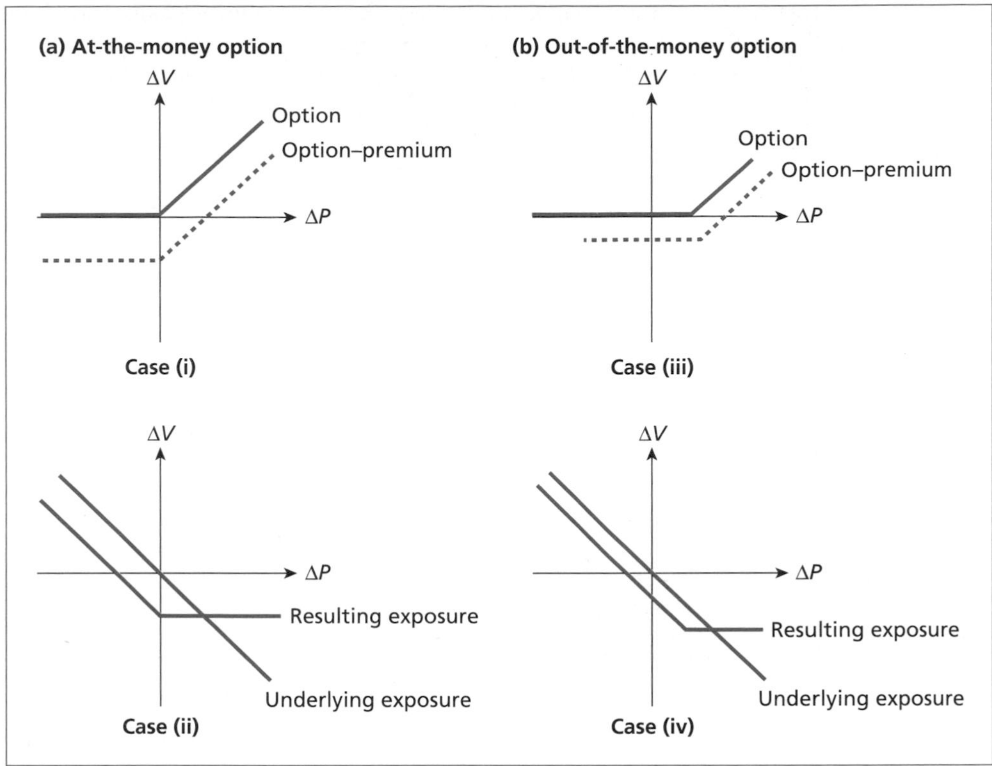

Figure 17.5 **Hedging with at-the-money call option and an out-of-the-money call option**

price of the asset. An option buyer seeking to lower the premium cost may do so by using an out-of-the-money option. As case (iv) of Figure 17.5 indicates, the buyer will incur larger potential losses. This simply reflects the fact that the buyer has paid a lower premium – has bought less insurance. The diagrammatic representation in case (iii) of Figure 17.5 shows the out-of-the-money option with the premium cost built in and case (iv) of the figure shows the underlying exposure and how the resulting exposure appears after allowing for the option's effects. The out-of-the-money option gives less downside protection, but the premium is significantly less. In other words, the option buyer can alter the payoff profile simply by changing the strike price; this will alter the premium cost too.

Clearly, options have a payoff profile which differs significantly from forwards, futures or swaps. However, an option's payoff profile may be replicated by a combination of forwards and risk-free securities. This point was tellingly made by Black and Scholes;[3] their argument may be summarised by reference to Figure 17.2, which describes the payoff profile for a call option. For increases with financial price *P*, the payoff profile for the option is that of a forward contract. For decreases in *P*, the value of the option is constant – this part of the payoff profile for the option is akin to a riskless security such as a treasury bill. Black and Scholes go on to demonstrate that a call option could be replicated by a continuously adjusting portfolio of two securities – forward contracts on the underlying asset and riskless securities. As the financial price *P* rises, the call option equivalent portfolio contains an increasing proportion of forward contracts; it contains a decreasing proportion when *P* falls. Arbitrage activity should ensure that the value of the portfolio is close to the market price of the exchange-traded option. Effectively, then, the value of a call option is determined by the value of its option equivalent portfolio of forwards and riskless securities.

From this, it should be evident that options do have more in common with the other instruments than was immediately apparent. As discussed earlier, futures are effectively nothing more than portfolios of forward contracts. And options are akin to portfolios of forward contracts and risk-free securities.

This is further borne out when we consider ways in which options may be combined. Take a portfolio constructed by buying a call and selling a put with a common strike price. As case (i) in Figure 17.6 shows, the resulting portfolio – long a call, short a put – has a payoff profile equivalent (assuming premiums are disregarded) to that of buying a forward contract on the asset. And case (ii) of Figure 17.6 shows that a portfolio created

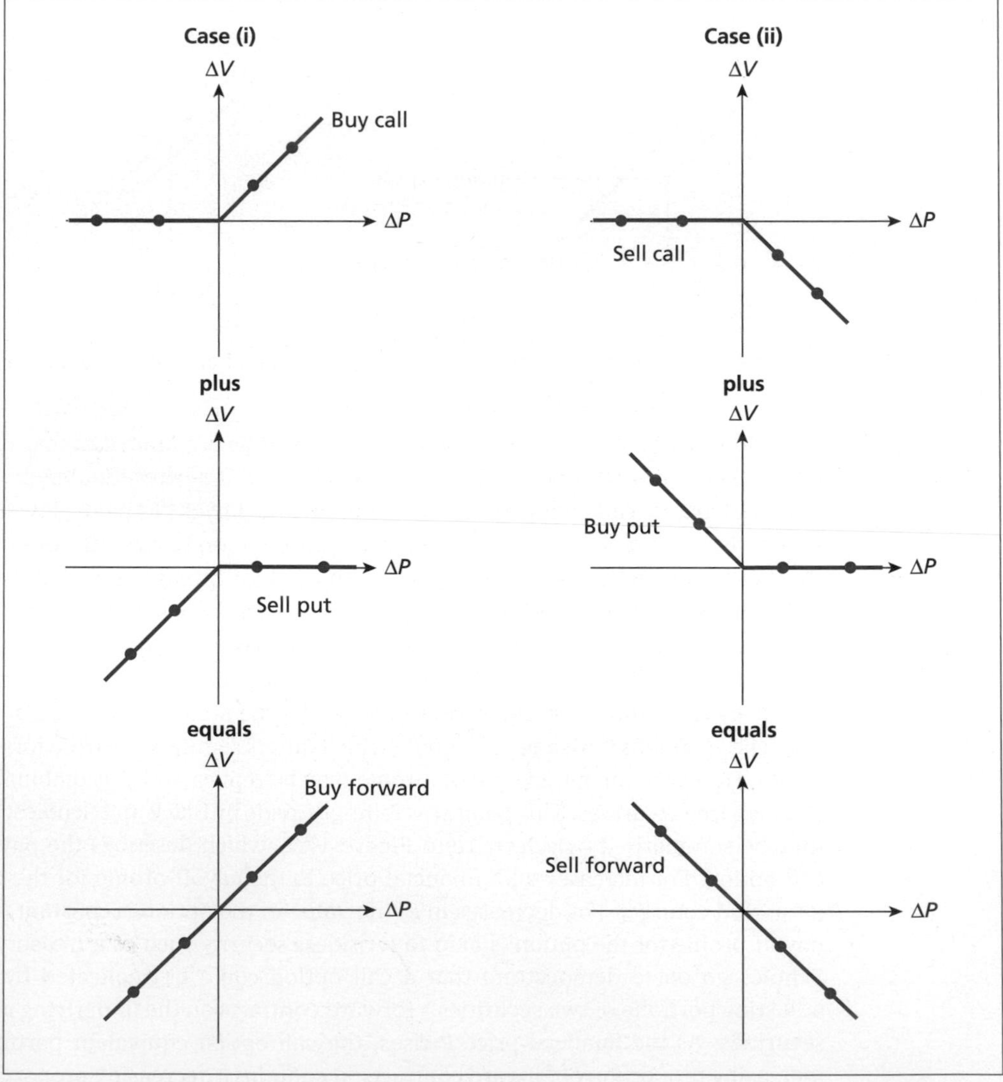

Figure 17.6 Dealing puts and calls can be like forwards

by selling a call and buying a put – that is, short a call, long a put – is equivalent to selling a forward contract.

The relationship summarised by Figure 17.6 is known more formally as the 'put–call parity' of the option parity theorem. According to this theorem, buying a European call and selling a European put is equivalent to being long forward. In other words:

$$\text{Buy call} + \text{Sell put} = \text{Long forward}$$

If the foreign currency appreciates relative to the strike price, it is profitable to exercise the call. By contrast, if the foreign currency depreciates relative to the exercise price, the buyer of the put exercises the option, forcing the seller of the put to buy in the foreign currency at the strike price. In effect, then, the simultaneous purchase of a call and sale of a put at the same exercise price is similar to the purchase of a forward contract at that exercise price. Note that this equivalence is only perfect for European options, which, it will be recalled, may only be exercised at maturity – not before. This equivalence does not hold for American options, which may be exercised before maturity and can consequently result in a position in the foreign currency prior to the maturity of the forward contract.

Going back to the option parity equation, it can be shown, by rearranging the terms, that:

$$\text{Buy call} + \text{Short forward} = \text{Buy put}$$

Remember that, algebraically, minus sell put would equal plus buy put. And minus long forward equals plus short forward.

As Smithson[4] states, 'we discovered two LEGO-like relations between options and the other three instruments: (1) Options can be replicated by snapping together a forward, futures, or swap contract together with a position in risk-free securities; (2) Calls and puts can be snapped together to become forwards.'

Caps and floors are, of course, nothing but fancy names for options. The collar, sometimes called the zero-cost option or cylinder, is simply manufactured by snapping together a put and a call at different strike prices such that the premium on the put and the premium on the call equal each other. Banks are perpetually introducing new financially engineered products to corporations – their understanding, and indeed their replication, is not difficult with the tools summarised in this chapter. To quote Smithson again, 'financial engineering is hard. Building innovative financial products with LEGOs is not.'

17.3 Some financial instruments

In the past, commercial banks have made a lot of money from slightly differentiated financial products which were made up from the simple snapping together of financial LEGOs. Different banks made it difficult for treasurers immediately to identify how one bank's product differed from another's by calling the same instrument different names. Salomon's 'range forward' is almost exactly the same as Citibank's 'cylinder option'.

Although their financial instruments are much less profitable now than heretofore, banks continue to produce their financially engineered products to meet the perceived needs of corporate customers. The corporate treasurer, in turn, tries to analyse the product in terms of its basic LEGOs in order to establish a fair price for the engineered product. We consider some of these products in turn.

Non-deliverable forward (NDF)

A non-deliverable forward is a foreign exchange forward outright where, instead of each party delivering the full amount of currency at settlement, there is a single net cash payment to reflect the change in value between the forward rate transacted and the spot rate two working days before settlement.

Imagine that one party wished to transact a forward outright but one of the currencies was not fully convertible or had no forward market. It is not possible for that currency to be delivered to, or by, a non-resident of that country. The need to deal an **outright forward** might arise because of the required precaution of a hedge for a commercial transaction or because of the apparent attractiveness of a speculation in that currency.

In the case of non-**convertibility**, normal outright forwards are either not permitted or highly government-regulated. If the purpose of the deal were speculation, the NDF would be sufficient. It provides a cash settlement yielding the same economic effect as if a normal forward outright had been dealt and then closed out two days before maturity by an offsetting spot deal. If the purpose of the deal were to hedge a commercial transaction, the same economic effect as a normal outright forward may be achieved by first transacting and settling the NDF, and buying or selling the non-convertible currency for spot value at the same time as the NDF is settled.

An NDF also has the effect of reducing counterparty risk, as the risk is limited to the settlement amount and does not involve the usual settlement risk on the whole nominal amount of the deal. Consequently, the rationale for NDFs is not limited just to non-convertible currencies.

Any contract for differences (CFD) resembles the NDF in that it comprises any transaction which is cash settled against a reference rate, rather than delivered in full. In other words, a net cash payment is made from one party to the other to reflect the difference between a price or rate agreed at the time of transaction and a reference price or rate determined later, or between two such reference prices or rates.

Banks are able to hedge net NDF positions that they have entered into either via their positions with their appropriate associated overseas bank, or by laying off their net exposure to another bank, or by undertaking money market hedges – see section 11.3.

Barrier options: knock-out option and knock-in option

A barrier option is a class of options (including knock-out and knock-in options) which are either cancelled or activated if the underlying price reaches a predetermined barrier or trigger level. A knock-out option is an option which is cancelled if the trigger level is reached. A knock-in option is an option which is activated if the trigger level is reached.

Barrier options are straightforward European options until, or from, the time the underlying reaches the trigger level. With a knock-out option, the option exists in the usual way (and either it is exercised at expiry or it expires worthless, depending upon the underlying price at that time) unless the underlying price reaches an agreed trigger level before then. If it does, the option is immediately cancelled.

With a knock-in option, the option cannot be exercised at expiry, regardless of the underlying rate at that time, unless an agreed trigger level has been reached at some time during the life of the option. If the trigger level has been reached, the option becomes a standard European option from that time onwards.

Due to these cancelling or activating features, barrier options are usually cheaper than ordinary options. This is because there are some situations under which a normal option would be exercised, but with a knock-in or knock-out option, exercise is not possible in these circumstances. There is less probability of the seller of the option paying out on the option; hence the lower value attaching to it. Consequently, barrier options can provide a hedge at a lower cost than a straightforward option, while still providing adequate protection. For example, the trigger level may be set by the buyer so that, if the trigger point is reached, the purchaser is then happy not to be protected, because the underlying provides a better bet.

Also, because of the lower premium, barrier options provide a more leveraged speculative instrument than a straightforward call or put. If the underlying moves as anticipated, the buyer achieves the same profit for lower initial cost.

Barrier options have an extensive jargon associated with them. They are also known as trigger options, exploding options and extinguishing options – four terms for the same instrument. The trigger level in a knock-out option is also known as an outstrike. The trigger level in a knock-in option is also known as an instrike.

An up-and-in option and a down-and-in option are knock-in options where the trigger is respectively higher than, or lower than, the underlying rate at the inception of the option. An up-and-out option and a down-and-out option are knock-out options where the trigger is respectively higher than, or lower than, the underlying rate at the birth of the option.

A reverse knock-out option (or kick-out option) and a reverse knock-in option (or kick-in option) are types of knock-out and knock-in option, where the trigger level is such that, at the point of its being triggered, the option would be in-the-money rather than out-of-the-money.

A double knock-out option and a double knock-in option refer to a knock-out option and a knock-in option with two trigger levels – one above and one below the underlying rate at the start – either of which will trigger the cancellation or activation of the option.

A path-dependent option is a general term for options such as barrier options, American options and average options, where the decision or ability to exercise them, and hence their value, depends not only on the underlying price at expiry, but also on the path that the price of the underlying has taken during the life of the option. Finally, the term exotic option refers to any complex option, including barrier options.

The financial engineering of barrier options basically derives from combining puts and calls at difference strike prices with forwards. Clearly, the precise nature of the engineering will vary depending on the nature of the barrier option involved.

The cylinder or zero-cost option

First of all, we consider the zero-cost option – sometimes called a cylinder option. On interest rates, the term 'collar' is used. Cylinders offer cover at reduced cost in return for the customer forgoing part of the profit potential if rates move favourably.

A cylinder enables the corporate treasurer to reduce the premium payable on the purchase of an option by simultaneously writing a second option to the bank for the same premium amount and tenor but at a different strike price. The treasurer selects the degree of risk to be taken, or the profit potential to be forgone, by choosing the strike prices of the two options that form the ceiling and the floor of the cylinder. By so doing, the treasurer can eliminate the premium altogether.

As an example, assume that a UK company is due to receive dollars from export sales in three months' time. The spot rate is $1.85, although the treasurer had budgeted for sales at $1.90. The premium to buy a normal currency option with a strike price of $1.90, matching the budget rate, is 1 per cent of the transaction amount. This is a low premium already, as the option is five cents 'out of the money' – that is, less favourable than the current spot. The treasurer still considers the hedge expensive and decides to negotiate a cylinder under which:

- the company buys an out-of-the-money option to sell (put) dollars at $1.90;
- the company simultaneously writes an out-of-the-money option to the bank, for the bank to buy (call) the same amount of dollars at a strike price such that the net premium the treasurer pays comes out at zero (or whatever amount the treasurer wants).

The range forward

Next, let us look briefly at the range forward. Like a zero-cost option, no up-front premium is payable. The contract specifies the top and bottom of a range of exchange rates. Within this range, the hedger can benefit from positive movements while having a limit to the downside. If, when the contract ends, the exchange rate falls within the range, the contract to buy or sell is effected at the spot exchange rate.

Getting into the range forward, the hedger chooses one of the two ends of the range plus the expiry date of the contract. It is left to the bank to choose the other end of the range, depending on the level of put and call premiums. Part of the calculation will include a small spread.

For example, assume that a US corporate needs to purchase sterling three months forward. The spot rate is $1.8200 to the pound and the three-month forward rate is $1.8085. The company is worried that rates may go against it, and it is looking for downside cover. The bank offering the range forward allows the company to pick the dollar rate above which it cannot afford to go. So one end of the range is fixed at $1.8700 to the pound. The bank decides it can offer $1.7520 at the other end. It could work the other way round, with the company setting the rate on the upside and the bank working out the downside. Either way, if in three months' time the exchange rate is between the two rates, the hedger deals spot. If the rates push outside the range agreed upon, the hedger deals at the top or bottom rate.

Obviously, the range forward, like the cylinder, is engineered via a put and call contract at differing strike premiums.

The participating forward contract

Next we consider the participating forward contract. Like the range forward, the participating forward requires no up-front payment. The contract represents a commitment to buy or sell foreign currency above an agreed floor exchange rate without setting any limit on potential movements in the buyer's favour. In the event of a positive movement, the buyer pays for the downside protection by taking less than 100 per cent of the favourable currency move.

The instrument is appropriate to hedgers who think their currency exposure has positive potential but who would like to buy downside protection. In volatile markets, the instrument comes into its own: participation in large movements, even if not 100 per cent, can render handsome returns. The participating forward is engineered via the currency option. The premium forgone by the bank is simply made good by its participation in resulting profits.

The break forward or fox (forward with optional exit)

The break forward, or fox, is a forward foreign exchange contract which can be unwound at a predetermined rate. It therefore combines many of the features of the conventional forward contract and the currency option. Like conventional forwards, break forwards allow the buyer, usually a corporate customer, to hedge against adverse exchange rate movements by locking in a fixed rate. Unlike conventional forwards, the customer can benefit from favourable exchange rate movements by breaking the deal at any time with only limited loss and then dealing at the more favourable spot or forward rate. As with currency options, the customer may take advantage of upside potential. But unlike currency options, the break forward does not require the payment of an up-front premium – this is rolled forward to settlement. A further advantage is that the tax treatment is more favourable than for currency options.

Under the break forward, the customer chooses the fixed rate, below which full downside protection is received, by agreeing to a loading – in effect the option premium of, say, 2 per cent – on the normal outright forward rate. The bank then calculates the rate at which the forward deal can be unwound – the break rate. Alternatively, the customer can nominate the break rate and the bank then calculates the fixed rate. Once entered into, the customer can unwind the break forward at any time if the current spot or forward rate looks better. In addition, if the funds being hedged are to be paid or received early, they can be bought/sold spot and the break forward then unwound at the break rate or the prevailing spot rate, whichever is more advantageous to the customer.

The break forward or fox is engineered through an American option with the premium compounded and taken by the bank in ultimate settlement.

The forward spread agreement (FSA)

Engineered via the forward rate agreement (FRA), but closer in function to the forward/forward currency swap, the FSA allows two counterparties to come to an agreement on the spread or interest rate differential between two currencies. Unlike the forward/forward currency swap, or back-to-back FRAs, the FSA involves no currency risk.

A banker funding, for example, a yen asset with a dollar liability, might want to insure against a widening of the interest rate differential in three-month deposits in the respective currencies. If the interest rate on the dollar liability rises, or the rate on the yen asset falls, opening the spread, the banker suffers. With an FSA, one contract covers exposure in two currencies where it would previously have required two FRAs, each FRA guaranteeing a forward rate in either the yen or dollar deposit. Another advantage is that bankers covering a yen exposure do not have to worry about **illiquidity** in the non-dollar FRA market. FSAs are dual currency instruments. While one side of the deal must be in US dollars, the other can, in principle, be for any other currency.

The deal-contingent forward

This instrument is well explained in Press Cutting 20.1. It looks rather like an option and banks sell them to clients who may need foreign currency were a deal to go through, for example in a cross-border takeover where there is a large element of uncertainty as to whether the bid will be successful in terms of achieving sufficient acceptances and meeting regulatory requirements. If deal-contingent forwards appear to be at no cost or at a relatively cheap price, perhaps this might have something to do with the scale of the banker's fee in acquisition situations. The option premium may get added in there.

Summary

- Financial engineering involves the coupling of two or more simple financial instruments to create a more complex one.
- Financial engineering involves simple building blocks which can be bolted together to create complex financial constructions.
- Even though banks may introduce innovative, complex financial instruments, they can easily be analysed by breaking them down into their more simple components. The analyst simply disaggregates the complicated new financial edifice into the simple old ones.
- The simple tools that are necessary to analyse the most complex financial instruments merely involve forwards and options. It is these that are bolted together to create the complex instrument.
- The text shows how this process can be used to produce some of the banker's most complicated new financial instruments to a simple combination. And, of course, their pricing should reflect the simple underlying components that make up the complex new product.

End of chapter questions

17.1 Describe the essentials of financial engineering.

17.2 Some companies have come unstuck dealing financially engineered instruments. Why do you suppose this is?

17.3 Banks pay big salaries to financial engineers. What traits do the financial engineers need to succeed?

Part E

FINANCIAL CRISIS 2007–8

The financial crisis of 2007–8 has been estimated to have wiped between USD2.5 trillion and USD3 trillion off the value of assets thanks to some rather reckless financial management by banks and governments aided and abetted by regulatory failure. US investment bank Lehman Brothers collapsed. AIG, Fannie Mae and Freddie Mac were rescued by the US government. Bear Stearns failed and was taken over by JP Morgan. The largest US mortgage lenders went out of business or were taken over under distress, including Indy Mac Bank, Countrywide Financial Corporation and New Century Financial. In the UK, notable collapses included Royal Bank of Scotland (RBS) and HBOS, rescued first by Lloyds Banking Group and subsequently bailed out by the UK government, which holds well over 50 per cent of both RBS and Lloyds. The finger is often pointed at the subprime mortgage business. But this only totalled some USD1.3 trillion and not all subprime mortgages defaulted – far from it. The size of the problem was magnified by the credit default swap (CDS) and the credit guarantee (almost the same as a CDS). We have seen what swaps are about (Chapter 12): we examine here a certain kind of swap – the CDS and we focus upon its role in the crisis.

To put the above figures into context the GDP of the USA in 2010 was around USD14.6 trillion; for the whole of the EU it was USD16 trillion and for Britain it was USD2.2 trillion.

18

Credit default swaps

This chapter is the first of two devoted to the topic of the financial crisis of 2007–8. Whilst we saw some value to these chapters appearing as the beginning of this book, we have decided not to pursue this route. The reasons for this are as follows. The crisis itself was underpinned by some astonishing casino banking (speculation) involving the credit default swap (CDS). To understand the CDS it is useful to have covered swaps. We did this in Chapter 12. Our consideration of the crisis itself follows the chapter on the CDS. So much for this brief explanation of our logic.

We now turn to the CDS. In relation to the financial crisis, if the problem created by subprime debt is rated 10, that created by credit default swaps and related **toxic assets** justifies, as we will show, a rating of 100 or more. In most newspaper articles and radio and television documentaries at the time of the financial collapse the central cause of the problem was portrayed as the **subprime mortgage** market. The CDS was barely mentioned. It seemed to be a bit player. How and why can this be so? Perhaps the commentators at the time found the CDS difficult to understand. And even if they did understand it, they couldn't explain it. Perhaps they thought that the public would find the CDS too complicated. Or, maybe there are other reasons – Buckley.[1] Naturally, your author gives the CDS its rightful position as a star player in the history of the financial crisis of 2007–8.

18.1 What are they?

So what is a CDS? It is a swap contract in which one party (A) makes a series of payments to a counterparty (B) and, in exchange, B would pay to A a capital sum if the credit instrument to which the CDS relates defaults (the capital instrument could be a bond or a loan of company C). The credit default that triggers the payment from B to A would typically be non-payment of interest or failure to make a capital repayment of a loan. In our example above, if company C were to default, the same result would be achieved and B would have to pay A. It should be mentioned that even if there is no default yet, the cost of credit default swap cover for new contracts goes up as a result of the party to which the credit default relates (party C in the example) looking more likely to default. Given this situation, in the secondary market (the market for existing credit default swaps) the value of B's position would fall and A's position becomes more valuable. There are features of CDS selling that make it akin to option writing – in particular that one can face wipeout from both. But

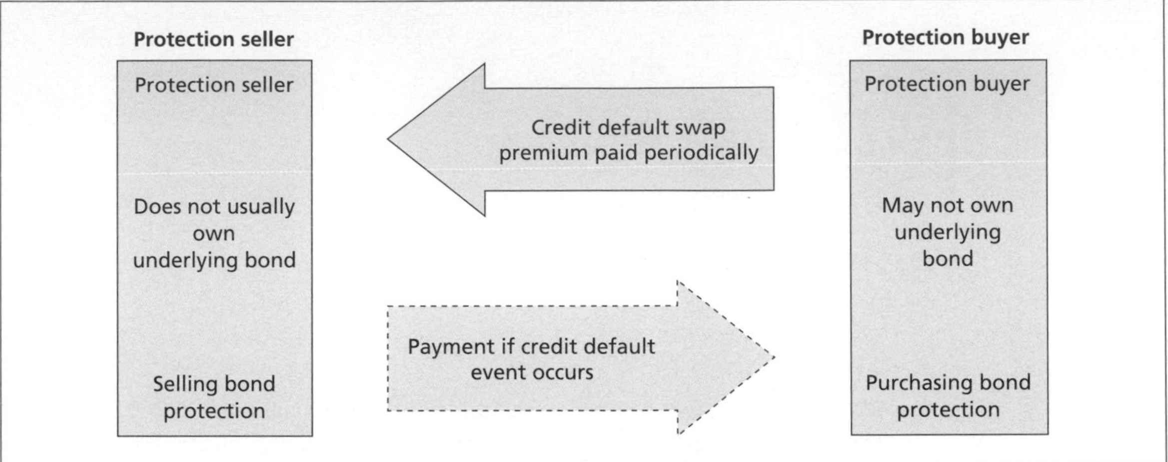

Figure 18.1 Credit default swap transaction

the CDS is not an option. With a CDS contract, there is a right and an obligation. With an option, there is a right but not an obligation. A better analogy is between a CDS and an insurance contract.

Just in case it is a little difficult to understand, we suspect that Figure 18.1 might help. It is worth looking at carefully. Of course, credit default swaps have a specified contract life – they don't last for ever.

If things still seem complicated, take an example. We quote from Larry McDonald[2] who provides an inside story of the Lehman Brothers collapse. Referring to the CDS business with Lehmans as the insurer (counterparty B in the example above) he states that, 'so far as the bank (Lehmans) was concerned, that was pretty good business. For absolutely nothing, they (Lehmans) would be paid a fee of USD9 million a year. That was great – unless, of course, the corporation went down, in which case the bank (Lehmans) would hold a USD1 billion liability. More often, the bank would sell the CDS to a hedge fund, which was more willing to take the risk. The bank would pick up a fast USD200,000 fee and be rid of the hassle.' A bit clearer? We hope so.

Note that there is now a secondary market in which CDS instruments can be traded. So, in our example above, both A and B could sell their CDS positions on in the secondary market. Assume that B bought the CDS for 100 and that the CDS relates to a bond of company C. If company C suffers a **credit rating** downgrade following poor trading or some other unexpected event, the CDS that B holds would fall in value to, say, 85 because B is more likely to have to pay out since a default by company C is now more likely.

CDS contracts are rather like insurance but there are differences, for example:

- Neither party to a CDS needs to own the **underlying security** (bond, loan or debt) to which the instrument relates. Neither the buyer nor the seller of the CDS has to suffer a loss from the default event (assuming that the CDS were not held by either party). This contrasts with insurance where the insured has to have an **insurable interest** under which he or she can demonstrate a potential loss should the default event occur.
- Neither party to the CDS needs to be regulated.

- The insured party in an insurance contract is bound by utmost good faith rules which require disclosure of all material facts and failure on this point can invalidate the contract. This is not so for a CDS where the maxim 'buyer beware' probably applies.
- The party responsible to pay under default is not required to set aside any specific amounts to pay the other party were the default to occur.
- Insurers manage risk by setting loss reserves based on the law of large numbers. Dealers in CDSs may manage risk by offsetting liabilities under a CDS by hedging using a reverse transaction with another counterparty.
- CDS contracts are generally subject to **mark to market** accounting, with income statement and balance sheet impacts. This is not the case in insurance accounting. Mark to market accounting involves revaluation of the instrument for financial statement purposes with gains, since the last reporting date, being taken into income or corresponding losses being charged against profit. Clearly, with respect to highly volatile instruments this can cause massive swings in reported profit and affect undistributed reserves. And result in big bonus escalation at banks. The mark to market accounting rules are currently under revision.
- The causal event for payout under an insurance policy is fairly clear. It is less so with a CDS. Technically, payment under a CDS contract is triggered by a credit event, the legal term for the process that would cause payment. A default and a credit event are legally distinct. A debt restructuring may constitute a credit event just as a default may. It falls to the International Swaps and Derivatives Association (ISDA), the representation body of the derivatives market that designs CDS contracts, to declare a credit event. The initial step in deciding whether a credit event has occurred is a request by an investor or interested party to the ISDA Determinations Committee requesting a judgment. In Europe, this committee comprises ten banks, including Barclays, Goldman Sachs and UBS, amongst others, whose representatives will together vote on whether a credit event has occurred. If they decide a credit event has not occurred, then the CDS will not pay out. This could mean that even if a country, say Greece, were not to declare default but restructure debt, ISDA might decide a credit event had occurred and a Greek CDS would pay out.

18.2 How do credit default swaps work?

Evidently, a CDS is a credit derivative contract between two counterparties. The buyer makes the periodic payments to the seller and in return receives a payoff if an underlying financial event (the default) occurs. As an example, assume that investor X buys CDS protection from bank Y where the underlying reference entity is company Z and the CDS has a five year life. Investor X will make annual payments to bank Y. If company Z defaults on its debt by missing an interest payment or does not repay capital as required, investor X receives a one-off payment from bank Y and the CDS is terminated.

If investor X owns debt in company Z, the CDS would be a hedge against that risk. If investor X bought the CDS contract without owning any company Z debt, this would be a speculative transaction betting against company Z. Also, even though investor X owned no debt in company Z, the above transaction could be a hedge against debt that it does hold in companies similar to Z. In this case company Z debt would be a proxy for the debt of the similar company or companies.

The spread on a CDS is the annual amount that the protection buyer (investor X above) must pay the protection seller (bank Y) over the life of the contract. It is stated as a percentage of the nominal amount of the CDS contract. If the CDS spread for company Z is 100 basis points (that is 1 per cent), then investor X buying USD20 million worth of protection from bank B must pay the bank USD200,000 per year. Such payments continue until the CDS contract expires, five years later in our example, or until company Z defaults.

Via the CDS, investors may speculate on changes in CDS spreads of company debt. For example, assume that hedge fund A does not rate company C highly to the extent that it feels that it will soon default on its debt. Hedge fund A buys USD20 million worth of CDS protection for three years from bank B with company C as the underlying reference entity, at a spread of, say, 400 basis points per annum. If company C does default after, say, two years, then hedge fund A would have paid USD1.6 million to bank B but would receive USD20 million, making a profit of USD14 million. Bank B will incur a USD18.4 million loss unless the bank has hedged the position by entering into a reverse deal to eliminate its exposure. Of course, if company C does not default, then the CDS contract will run for three years, and hedge fund A will have paid out USD2.4 million without any return, hence incurring a loss. There is also the possibility that before year 3, hedge fund A might sell on the CDS in the secondary market. If company C looks more likely to fail than when hedge fund A bought the CDS it will make a profit on the sale and the amount of profit will depend upon the new price of the CDS which, in turn, will depend upon the increased likelihood of company C's failure.

CDS contracts took off from virtually nothing in the 1990s to around USD632 billion in 2001 and to the astounding figure of over USD60 trillion before falling back to USD55 trillion in terms of value of contracts outstanding immediately following the crash – see Figure 18.2. To put this into context, world GDP totalled USD60 trillion in 2008. Admittedly, comparing these two figures involves a stock versus a flow. Nonetheless, the comparison is a telling one. Note that much of the total of USD60 trillion of CDS outstanding would involve hedging contracts. The point here is that if a bank has sold a contract to a customer, the bank itself may enter into an offsetting buy transaction to hedge, or cover, its exposure. Gillian Tett[3] describes, in colourful terms, a weekend-away session for JP Morgan bankers in which the brainstorming topic is the understanding and development of the credit default swap – well worth reading.

The CDS market attracted considerable concern from regulators in the 2008 Crash, particularly with the collapse of bankers Bear Stearns. In the run up to Bear Stearns' collapse, the bank's CDS spread increased dramatically. A surge of buyers were taking out protection against the bank's failure. This widening of its CDS spread had the effect of further increasing Bear Stearns vulnerability as it restricted Bear's own access to wholesale money markets eventually leading to its forced sale to JP Morgan in March 2008. It is an open question as to whether that surge in CDS protection buyers was a symptom or a cause of Bear's collapse. Investors saw that Bear Stearns was in trouble and sought to hedge exposure to the bank – or even, speculate on its failure. In September 2008, the same kind of scenario impacted Lehman Brothers. And, in that same month, American International Group (AIG) required a government bailout because it had been selling vast amounts of CDS protection (without hedging) against the possibility that various reference entities might decline in value. This exposed AIG to potential losses over USD100 billion. **Fannie Mae** and **Freddie Mac**,

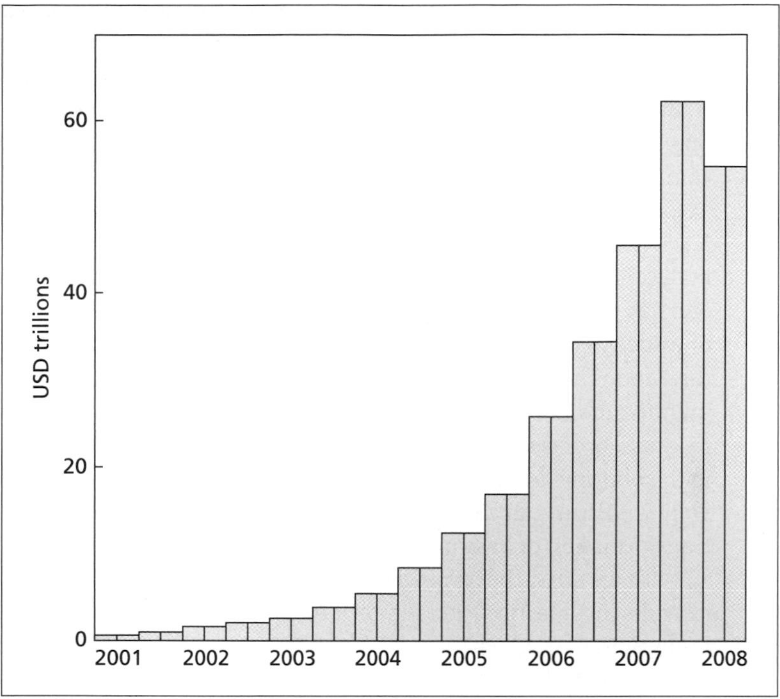

Figure 18.2 Outstanding value of credit default swaps (in USD trillions)

US **government sponsored enterprises** but with stock market quotations, were providing, at a fee, credit guarantees on mortgages and **mortgage-backed securities** (packages of mortgages which are sold on to investors). Basically, these were credit default swaps under another name. Fannie Mae and Freddie Mac were in this game bigger than AIG. In 2008 there was no clearing house for CDS transactions. All such deals were done over the counter (OTC). Since then, in November of 2008, a clearing facility for CDS trades has been introduced, covering a proportion – but by no means all – of the market. Also interesting is a newly introduced international standardisation of CDS contracts designed to prevent legal disputes in cases where it is not clear what a payout should be.

18.3 Drivers of the CDS market

The CDS market exploded from virtually nothing in the 1990s to USD55 trillion in 2007. So what was the prime mover of the CDS market's growth? In the early years of this century, US investment banks were packaging subprime debt into mortgage backed securities – and they seemed to be making big profits for their banks and big bonuses for themselves in doing so. But, the US market for subprime debt totalled only USD1.3 trillion in terms of outstanding debt as at 2007 – its peak. What the investment bankers were looking for was a new product that could out-do the subprime mortgage market. In short, there just was not enough subprime debt to go round. The bankers found the answer to their prayer in the CDS. Once a subprime mortgage has been packaged into a mortgage backed security (MBS) or a **collateralised debt obligation (CDO)**, it is used up and cannot be packaged again. There is a finite amount of subprime debt. Believe it or not, the bankers were running out of risky assets.

Enter the CDS. There is no limit to the amount of credit default swaps that can be written on company X. The company may have an equity market capitalisation of USD20 billion: company X may have USD5 billion (in market value terms) of debt all traded on stock exchanges, giving it an entity value of USD25 billion. But credit default swaps on company X are not limited to USD5 billion or to USD25 billion. They can be written for USD100 billion, or USD200 billion, or any amount you like. There is no limit. Unlike insurance where one has to have an insurable interest – that is to say, suffer a loss through the occurrence of a specified event (in this case, default on a debt) – with a CDS there is no limitation of this kind. The CDS does not require an insurable interest. So, one could, in theory, sell an infinite amount of CDS on company X debt. The bankers were hardly likely to run out of risky assets of this sort. And the bankers' efforts were rewarded as they packaged CDS assets with subprime loans into collateralised debt obligations (CDOs). And they knew that they would not run out of them. No chance. To many bankers, this was sheer alchemy – the transformation of base metal into gold.

With an MBS, the subprime loan would create inflows of interest: adding a CDS, would provide income from its annual protection payment rather like income from insurance premiums.

It was argued that, by adding a CDS to a pool of mortgages the effect would be that the quality of the asset pool would be enhanced and might justify a higher credit rating. So, by adding a CDS to a mortgage asset **pool**, a higher rating might be obtained. Now, we would have a mortgage pool but with the added presence of CDS inputs to create a collateralised debt obligation (CDO) pool.

During the crash, these acquired the epithet of 'toxic asset'. The toxicity is best illustrated by an example. With no default, or only a low probability of default, a CDS might have a positive value of, say, 100 based on the expected income stream from insurance-like premiums exceeding the expected outflow under default. But with defaults looming, the worth of the CDS could alter and acquire a negative value as the probability of having to pay out under the CDS exceeds the probability of receiving inflows (the insurance premiums). What was an asset, worth 100 in our example, may become a liability worth minus 100 or minus 500. The description toxic asset, also known as toxic debt, is truly justified. When defaults began to look more and more likely, these toxic assets were changing shape into infectious liabilities on bank balance sheets and, like a contagious plague, undermining their very health and existence. The disease was terminal for Lehman Brothers and would have been equally final for many other banks and financial institutions were it not for government rescues.

But we are advancing the story too fast. The creation of the CDO did not stop with the injection of CDSs. It involved more than subprime debt and credit default swaps. As we show in Figure 18.3, the addition of higher quality debt from prime mortgages was mixed in to give some credibility but so was low grade debt which ranged from credit card debt to emerging market debt to lowly rated corporate debt to private equity debt. Leveraged buyout debt often carries debt to equity ratios for the bought out firm of 80 per cent to 90 per cent versus typical corporate debt standards of 30 per cent to 40 per cent. Also, leveraged buyout debt might have an interest cover ratio – profit before interest and tax versus total interest – of 1.5 times versus a normal debt standard of 4 times or so. Lower quality

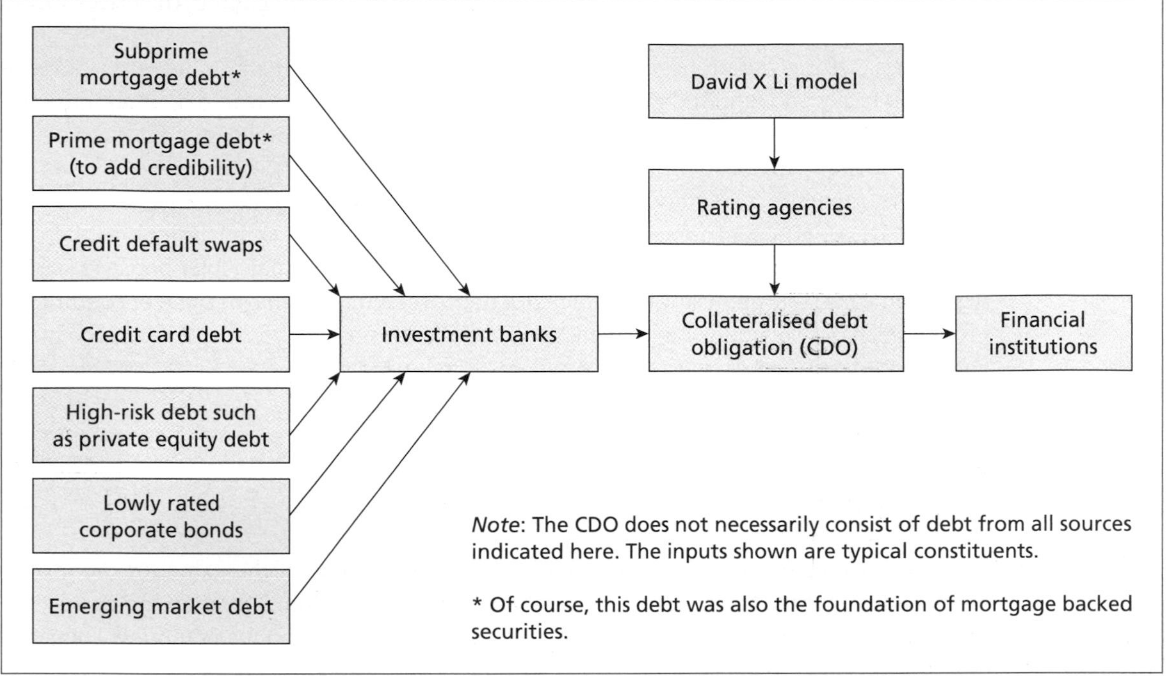

Figure 18.3 The collateralised debt obligation food chain

debt invariably carries higher interest rates than normal debt. This seemed great to the investment bankers who were cobbling together the CDOs. As we will see, having somehow managed to get a triple A rating on swathes of CDOs, the interest rate that would be paid to holders would be lower than that received from the debt and credit default swap assets. Magic? Sleight of hand? We shall see.

With the constituent crew on board the CDO, the trick was that the investment banks had to convince the rating agencies that the lack of **correlation** between the portfolio created by the various crew members (plus CDS insurance) would justify an enhanced credit rating compared to the individual credit ratings for the constituent members on their own.

Correlations are not as simple as they might at first sight appear. In illustrating this point, we draw on an example quoted in Salmon.[4] Assume a schoolgirl, A. The probability that her parents will get divorced this year is, say, 5 per cent. The risk of her getting head lice is 5 per cent. The chance of her seeing her teacher slip on a banana skin is 5 per cent. The likelihood of her winning the class spelling bee is also 5 per cent. If the market were trading securities based on these chances, they should all trade at the same price.

But, now, assume two schoolgirls, A and B, who sit next to each other and are great friends. If B's parents get divorced, what is the likelihood of A's parents getting divorced? Still about 5 per cent. The correlation is clearly low. If B gets head lice, the chance that A will also get head lice is high, maybe 50 per cent – the correlation is of the order of 0.5. If B sees her teacher slip on a banana skin, what is the chance that A will see it also? High, since they sit next to each other in class and are great friends, the chances are that they will both see the event. It could be 95 per cent, a correlation close to 1. If B wins the spelling bee, the chance of A winning it is zero, a correlation of minus 1. Now, if the market were trading securities based on the chances of these things happening to both A and B, the prices would be difficult to predict because the correlations vary a lot.

Clearly, getting the probabilities on the individual events for the schoolgirls A and B would be tricky enough. And getting the conditional probabilities would be more difficult. Looking at past data might help but these things get really fraught when it comes to conditional probability inputs and estimating errors.

With mortgages, correlations are tricky – as are conditional probabilities. What is the chance that a particular home in state X will decline in value? One can look at the past history to obtain some idea. And what is the chance that another particular house in state Y will fall in value? Again, historical data might help. Then there is the problem of conditional probability. And it's not just a problem about two homes but all of the houses in the mortgage backed security. An intractable problem? Maybe. Maybe not.

18.4 Correlations and credit ratings

We now introduce a new player to the CDS scene. The name of the game for the investment banks marketing the CDO is to enhance the credit rating, thereby increasing the price of the CDO, creating greater profit potential and greater bonus potential. The actor entering the stage is David X Li. Armed with an MBA and a PhD in statistics, his banking experience was at Canadian Bank of Commerce and Citibank where he was head of credit derivatives research. He was the sort of bright, young 'rocket scientist' that Wall Street loves to recruit. Li had moved from China where he was born (Xing Lin Li) in the 1960s. Writing in the *Financial Times* (24 April 2009), Sam Jones described Li as 'the world's most influential actuary'. Why? How did Li earn this epithet? Basically, by making the CDS a more marketable security. Basically, by helping to justify the triple A rating. Basically, by helping to create the vast market for toxic debt that would boomerang back to the innovating financiers.

Whilst working as a banker, Li[5] wrote and published a paper in the peer-reviewed *Journal of Fixed Income*. It was called 'On Default Correlation: A Copula Function Approach'. A **copula**, in statistics, is a way of formulating a multivariate distribution given various types of dependence. Referring to our earlier example of the schoolgirls, we have a number of variables – the divorce, the head lice, the banana skin and the spelling bee – and a number of dependences. There are various copula functions, the Archimedean copula, the Clayton copula, the Frank copula, the Gaussian copula, the Gumbel copula, and a number of others too. In short, the copula is used to couple the behaviours of two or more variables.

In Li's paper, he did not model default correlation but he used market data about the prices of CDS. These prices change as default risk rises and falls. Rather than waiting to assemble historical data on actual defaults, which are relatively rare in the real world, Li used historical prices from the CDS market. The critic might point out that the CDS market had a relatively short life up to the year 2000, when Li's paper was published, and had not experienced any big failures. So, his data were based on non-turbulent times and on assumptions of the market pricing CDS products efficiently. Li developed a model that used price rather than real-world default data, making the assumption that financial markets in general, and CDS markets in particular, price default risk correctly. Li's pricing model used the Gaussian copula, based upon the normal distribution or bell curve. Another target for the critic of the normal distribution.

According to the Li paper, huge amounts of risk diminished when risky assets were pooled in a CDO, with the implication that a large share of the pooled investment might be rated AAA. Word spread. Mathematicians and other quants in banks explained the model of derivatives structures. The bankers got the rating agency analysts interested. Wall Street derivatives arrangers started to pool risky assets using the new methodology of David X Li's formula. Banks created swathes of new CDOs backed by low-rated corporate bonds, emerging markets debt, subprime mortgage loans and CDSs. They split the CDOs into **tranches**, with the bottom tranches carrying most risk (because they would fail first if there were a default) and also being remunerated with the highest interest rate. High tranches would only fail as default crept up the pyramid and this relative less risk would be rewarded with lower interest than that for lower tranches. The rating agencies were willing to rate many CDO tranches AAA, even though the underlying assets carried much lower ratings. The bankers loved David X Li. And the bankers paid the rating agencies over and above their normal fee. Remarkably, as pointed out by Johnson and Kwak,[6] in 2005 only eight US companies had triple A ratings. They were AIG, Automatic Data Processing, Berkshire Hathaway, Exon/Mobil, General Electric, Johnson & Johnson, Pfizer and United Parcel Service.

According to Frank Partnoy,[7] 'The driving force behind the explosion of subprime mortgage lending in the US was neither lenders nor borrowers. It was the arrangers of CDOs. They were the ones supplying the cocaine. The lenders and borrowers were just mice pushing the button.' We would add that was even more true for the CDS market.

Wall Street banks now knew that they could use credit default swaps to create spiralling amounts of CDOs. They developed new repackaging transactions, using credit default swaps instead of subprime mortgages that, when pooled, could generate high ratings. These CDOs are technically known as synthesised collateralised debt obligations because of their artificial nature.

By 2006, there were more synthetic CDOs backed by credit default swaps than there were CDOs backed by real mortgage loans. And there were credit default swaps written on packages of subprime debt (CDS on MBS). Insurance companies like AIG had joined the banks as players in the CDS market.

All of these derivatives were unregulated. None of the financial institutions disclosed details about their CDS derivatives. Most just grouped credit default swaps with other derivatives in their published accounts. No one could assess the exposure to the CDS market. Banks bought large amounts of AAA tranches of synthetic CDOs but precise details – or even half precise details – were not apparent in published figures.

And here was the problem. Essentially, the banks dealing CDS products or CDOs based upon the CDS would receive an annual payment but have to pay out on default. However, even without default, they would suffer a reduction in value in the secondary market if the credit rating of the underlying company bond or mortgages upon which the CDS was written were to fall. If there were a default, one party to the CDS (counterparty B in our earlier example) would lose out having to pay the full nominal amount of the CDS. So, the seller gets an annual fee, rather than an up-front option premium, and has substantial downside risk – counterparty B could lose the whole amount of the CDS. So, rather than bear the potential downside if default were to occur the bank packages the CDS into the CDO.

So, for a CDS based on subprime loans, banks selling them. They received periodic payments from their CDS counterparties but carried exposure to pay out in the case of a default. But, of course, the package was rated AAA. It looks like insurance. But, as we pointed out earlier, it is not subject to insurance law. In which case, should the insurable interest requirement discussed in the section 18.1 of this chapter, be a requirement? We rather think so. Of course, for bankers creating the CDS market, calling the CDS a swap was a great marketing ploy. And the bank packaging the CDS liability into a CDO where it sits as a swap is satisfied. It sounds less risky. And, getting the AAA rating was a massive marketing ploy too.

Directors of financial institutions dealing CDOs based on subprime mortgages did not inform their shareholders of the massive risks they were carrying in respect of US house prices declining and defaults on subprime mortgage loans increasing and becoming highly correlated with other assets in the CDO. A decline in the price of subprime homes would put the homeowners in negative equity, with little incentive or ability to repay their debts. Many would default at the same time. It was an accident waiting to happen. Bank directors either hid, or did not understand, this risk. If either is the truth they are unfit to be directors of a public corporation – let alone a bank.

Whilst housing prices remained high, or flat, the banks and their employees would earn large profits from the subprime CDOs. And large bonuses too. But if housing prices collapsed, many banks would be wiped out. Awareness of this led several hedge funds and others to place big bets against the subprime mortgage markets and the banks. This involved them either in buying credit default swap protection on the bank so that in the case of default the hedge fund would gain in a big way or via the short-selling of stock in the at-risk banks.

18.5 The credit guarantee

As its name implies, the credit guarantee is an undertaking to reimburse losses on the default of a mortgage or other debt obligation. Whilst the biggest player in the pure CDS market was the US insurance giant AIG, the largest players in the credit guarantee market were the government sponsored entities (GSE), Fannie Mae, Freddie Mac and **Ginnie Mae**. Thanks to the passing of numerous laws in the USA, lending to weaker credit customers, especially via mortgages, expanded greatly in the decade spanning the new millennium. Cajoled by the newly created agencies set up under government legislation to widen home ownership, the three GSEs referred to were providing guarantees to underwrite mortgage backed loans, comprising loans to poor credits amongst others. This was accompanied by low prevailing interest rates, misselling of loans, fraudulent statements about income by borrowers, usually aided and abetted by mortgage salesmen, and inappropriate products being sold – such as mortgages which would be fixed at low rates for a short period before escalating to higher rates later. For the mortgage salesman the name of the game was closing the deal because this was the source of commission and most salesman were on very low basic rates of pay plus sales bonuses. Clearly, if the housing market in the USA were to head south and mortgage defaults and foreclosures occurred, the AIG and GSEs business model would look sad. And, of course, this is precisely what happened.

18.6 The unwinding

The unwinding started in the subprime housing market. Defaults increased in late 2006. Initially, the banks were not worried. Their models assumed that there would be minor defaults all over the US and these would not be correlated. The defaults kept coming. By early 2007, it was clear that the US subprime market had a problem. By the summer, subprime homeowners all over the US were defaulting on their mortgages. The cheap debt made available by subprime lenders had looked like an accident waiting to happen – and now it was happening. The subprime loans should never have been made – least of all at low interest rates. The Li model failed to predict the correlated defaults which most thinking persons would have said were likely to happen. Credit default swaps that had previously been worth considerable positive dollar amounts were now beginning to register negative value for reasons that we explained earlier. The banks began taking staggering losses on their holdings of CDOs. Institutions grew fearful about one another's solvency. They stopped lending to each other and liquidity dried up. The problem spread from asset class to asset class. In a globalised financial market with international linkages, the problem of disappearing liquidity spread like a disease across frontiers. Every bank was suspicious of every other bank. Interbank lending, an essential part of any capitalist economy, dried up. This was the credit crunch. The banks' pain spread to the real economy. Suddenly, everything was highly correlated.

Why had Li's formula not anticipated this? It assumed events tended to cluster around an average – as in the normal distribution. The whole model was bell curve based. But, the range of possible outcomes was more complicated. The mortgage market was far more prone to extreme correlation scenarios than most. At crisis times, security prices move away from their bell curve behaviour. Why did no one notice such an obvious fault in the Li formula?

There had long been warnings against reliance upon Gaussian bell curve behaviour in financial markets, Benoit Mandelbrot,[8] Nassim Nicholas Taleb,[9] and Pablo Triana[10] remind us that stock prices do not follow a Gaussian bell shaped distribution. Mandelbrot made this clear as long ago as the 1960s. Taleb makes the point that

> If the world of finance were Gaussian, an episode such as the crash [19 October 1987] (more than 20 standard deviations) would take place every several billion lifetimes of the universe . . . According to the circumstances of 1987, people accepted that rare events take place and are the main source of uncertainty. They were just unwilling to give up on the Gaussian as a central measurement tool.

Taleb goes on to remind us that

> 1987 was not the first time the idea of the Gaussain was shown to be lunacy. Mandelbrot proposed the scalable to the economics establishment around 1960, and showed them how the Gaussian curve did not fit prices then.

Maybe some would defend the use of the Gaussian normal distribution because it works well most of the time. If so, they must stress 'most of the time'. It is utterly not the immutable describer of market behaviour that is often taught. And theorems based upon it must be recognised as only right most of the time. For example, Black and Scholes option pricing theory derives the well-known formula which is based upon log-normal stock returns. Gaussian again. Press Cutting 18.1 makes the point tellingly.

PRESS CUTTING 18.1

Don't blame luck when your models misfire

By John Kay

When the financial crisis broke in August 2007, David Viniar, chief financial officer of Goldman Sachs, famously commented that 25 standard deviation events had occurred on several successive days. If you marked your position to market every day for a million years, there would still be a less than one in a million chance of experiencing a 25-standard deviation event. None had occurred. What had happened was that the models Goldman used to manage risk failed to describe the world in which it operated.

If the water in your glass turns to wine, you should consider more prosaic explanations before announcing a miracle. If your coin comes up heads 10 times in a row – a one in a thousand probability – it may be your lucky day. But the more likely reason is that the coin is biased, or the person who flips the penny or reports the result is cheating. The source of most extreme outcomes is not the fulfilment of possible but improbable predictions within models, but events that are outside the scope of these models.

Sixty years ago, a French economist described the Allais paradox, based on the discovery that most people treat very high probabilities quite differently from certainties. Not only do normal people think this way, but they are right to do so. There are no 99 per cent probabilities in the real world. Very high and very low probabilities are artifices of models, and the probability that any model perfectly describes the world is much less than one. Once you compound the probabilities delivered by the model with the unknown but large probability of model failure, the reassurance you crave disappears.

Techniques such as value at risk modelling – the principal methodology used by banks and pressed on them by their regulators – may be of help in monitoring the day-to-day volatility of returns. But they are useless for understanding extreme events, which is, unfortunately, the main purpose for which they are employed. This is what Mr Viniar and others learnt, or should have learnt, in 2007.

Yet the use of risk models of this type is one of many areas of finance in which nothing much has changed. The European Union is ploughing ahead with its Solvency II directive for insurers, which – incredibly – is explicitly modelled on the failed Basel II agreements for monitoring bank solvency. Solvency II requires that businesses develop models that show the probability of imminent collapse is below 0.5 per cent.

Insurance companies do fail, but not for the reasons described in such models. They fail because of events that were unanticipated or ignored, such as the long-hidden danger from asbestos exposure, or the House of Lords judgment on Equitable Life. They fail because underwriters misunderstood the risk characteristics of their policies, as at AIG, or because of fraud, as at Equity Fundings.

Multiple sigma outcomes do not happen in real life. When all the Merchant of Venice's ships are lost at sea during the interval, we know that we are watching a play, not an account of history. Shakespeare, no fool, knew that too. In Act V Antonio was able to write back his loss provisions in full even if it was too late to fulfil his banking covenant to Shylock.

But today the modellers are in charge, not the poets. Like practitioners of alchemy and quack medicine, these modellers thrive on our desire to believe impossible things. But the search for objective means of controlling risks that can reliably be monitored externally is as fruitless as the quest to turn base metal into gold. Like the alchemists and the quacks, the risk modellers have created an industry whose intense technical debates with each other lead gullible outsiders to believe that this is a profession with genuine expertise.

We will succeed in managing financial risk better only when we come to recognise the limitations of formal modelling. Control of risk is almost entirely a matter of management competence, well-crafted incentives, robust structures and systems, and simplicity and transparency of design.

Source: *Financial Times*, 2 March 2011.

Returning from our important digression, in April 2008, New Century, the second largest subprime lender in the United States, filed for bankruptcy. Shortly afterwards, Countrywide, the largest subprime lender, went into free fall. Hedge funds increased their short positions and the value of subprime mortgage loans dropped like a stone. And the same thing happened to CDOs and to bank stocks.

In June 2008, Moody's downgraded the ratings of USD5 billion of subprime mortgage-backed securities and put 184 CDO investments on review for downgrade. S&P placed USD7.3 billion on negative watch. Banks began announcing massive losses from investments backed by CDS and subprime mortgage derivatives.

Bear Stearns imploded and was bought by JP Morgan: Lehman Brothers filed for bankruptcy: Merrill Lynch sold out to Bank of America, which also bought Countrywide: the US government rescued AIG, the world's leading insurance company and the biggest pure CDS player, and it also took into conservatorship (nearly a takeover) Fannie Mae and Freddie Mac. In the UK, Northern Rock, the mortgage bank, had failed: as had Bradford and Bingley, a similar bank: the UK government rescued HBOS and Royal Bank of Scotland following idiotic investments in CDSs and, for RBS the most disastrous takeover of Dutch bank ABN Amro. In late 2008, alarm focused upon domino effects. Banks that were liable to pay out under CDS contracts could not meet their obligations. This led to chaos in CDS and CDO markets and resulted in prices of contracts dropping like a stone midst a lack of liquidity. If the above banks and institutions had all been allowed to fail without government intervention, they could, through their indebtedness to other banks, have pulled down the good banks too. The whole system could have been facing the abyss. And, the impact of this for business could have been utterly catastrophic because business after business could have failed as bank loans would be called in. This could have been worse than the Great Depression – much worse. With co-ordinated action by governments, the doomsday scenario was averted. Nonetheless, it remains the biggest financial crisis since the Great Depression.

Without derivatives, including CDS, CDO, MBS and credit guarantees, the total losses from subprime mortgage defaults would probably have been relatively small and containable. Without derivatives, the defaults would have hurt some, but not that much. The total of US subprime mortgage loans outstanding was around USD1.3 trillion. The decline in the value of these subprime loans on their own during 2008 was a couple of hundred billion USD topside. It represents less than 10 per cent of the estimated bailout losses by the International Monetary Fund as at April 2010. Where did the other 90 per cent come from? CDOs and credit default swaps is the answer. The amount outstanding in the CDS market in 2007 was USD60 trillion. Now, let us look at the following situation. It is an example but it may bear some resemblance to reality. Assume that, of the USD60 trillion outstanding, 70 per cent represents hedge contracts. This leaves 30 per cent unhedged CDS position – that is USD18 trillion worth. If half of these were not caught up in the CDS squall, that would leave 50 per cent that were. And this would involve USD9 trillion. If half of these were winners and half were losers, this would mean USD4.5 trillion of loss-making contracts. Assume that, on average, these contracts incurred losses of 65 per cent. That would mean losses of USD2.925 trillion. Not all of these would have required bailouts. Some would be borne directly by the banks concerned. Some may have been made good from the proceeds of bank recapitalisations – rights issues and injections from sovereign wealth funds (funds owned mainly by oil exporting states but also China, with surplus monies). However, because some banks would have had a concentration of positions resulting in losses and because these losses would have been so large that, without a government bailout, the bank would have failed, monies were forthcoming from government sources. If around USD0.5 trillion came from bank sources themselves, this would leave government bailouts of USD2.4 trillion. This is within a whisker of the IMF's April 2010 estimate of USD2.3 trillion. In truth, we cannot be sure of the amount at this stage. The figures are just what we say – estimates. And, there may be losses unrelated to CDSs and these could be worth over USD0.5 trillion. But whilst the problem first manifested itself in the subprime market squall, it multiplied into a toxic debt tsunami that might have become a second Great Depression.

We feel that it is worth mentioning a quote from John Cassidy.[11] He observes that, in May 2005 Alan Greenspan sang the praises of credit derivatives, saying their development 'has contributed to the stability of the banking system by allowing banks, especially the largest, systemically important banks, to measure and manage their credit risks more effectively'. Cassidy goes on to say,

> In the case of derivatives such as CDSs, Greenspan was merely stating the official view of the **Fed** and other international banking regulators. After he retired in January 2006, his successor, Ben Bernanke, made no effort to reverse the Fed's hands-off stance. The idea that CDSs facilitated the spreading and management of risk had attained the status of official dogma, and so had faith in VAR-based risk management. Unless something disastrous happened, none of the regulatory authorities would seriously question the Wall Street line.

But clearly derivatives, CDS, CDO and MBS, multiplied the losses from subprime mortgage loans and took the world staggeringly close to financial meltdown. As investors learned about these excesses, they lost confidence in the system. Without government intervention, the system would have crashed completely. Governments managed to prop up the tumbling dominos – just.

Finally in this chapter, we refer to Press Cutting 18.2 in which John Kay likens the game of selling CDSs and credit guarantees to tailgating – it's a brilliant analogy. And if the reader refers back to Figure 18.1, it should be apparent how CDS tailgating would work. The CDS seller picks up an annual income from the protection buyer and banks were taking this to profit in the income statement. But when tailgating turns to crash, the bank has to pay out to the protection buyer – a charge to the income statement. Whilst the tailgating was working, the dealers were being lauded, the bankers were being praised by their non-executive directors. Everyone was looking at the income statement and saying that this is great: that this is a money machine. Where you see money machines, ask questions, ask more questions and keep asking questions – because money machines are illusions. Was there a single non-executive bank director or regulator questioning this? And was anyone within the banks suggesting that provisions should be made against potential future payments under CDSs if the credit default event were to occur? Or would this adversely affect the bankers' bonuses? Also, is there some similarity between the carry trade and tailgating? If so, it is clear why carry traders have to move real fast to reverse their exposures when tailgating starts to look like a crash.

Your author cannot leave this chapter without mentioning the account (humorous in places) by Michael Lewis[12] and another by Gregory Zuckerman[13] on how big bucks were made on credit default swaps and other toxic instruments in the run-up to the financial crisis by betting against the continued housing boom and the likely subsequent impact on CDS and CDO prices. This involved arranging the purchase of protection by a speculator in anticipation of a housing price collapse – the speculator was said to be shorting the market. Some of the CDS involved paid out on accrued losses prior to total failure of the assets with a mark-to-market feature kicking in as batches failed – a pay as you go type of contract, termed PAUG (to rhyme with hog). The report of the US Senate permanent subcommittee on investigations[14] provides excellent coverage.

PRESS CUTTING 18.2

Tailgaters blight the markets as well as the motorways

by John Kay

Some people have described the process as picking up dimes in front of a steamroller. A more vulgar account refers to a creature that 'eats like a bird and shits like an elephant'. There is a more academic description: a strategy based on writing options that are substantially out of the money. But the analogy I prefer is tailgating, the practice of driving close to the bumper of the car in front at high speed.

However described, it is the same thing: a distribution of returns that produces frequent small profits punctuated by occasional very large losses. A high proportion of trading – and business – strategies in financial markets have this tailgating characteristic. I call it the Taleb distribution, after the author of *Fooled by Randomness* (an earlier, and better, book than the more widely read *Black Swan*), which gives numerous instances.

The distribution has been central to recent financial crises. Buying emerging market debt was a seemingly profitable activity with a remote possibility, eventually realised, of large losses. So was holding internet stocks of no fundamental value in the (usually correct, but ultimately false) belief that they could be sold on at a profit to a greater fool. The creation of bogus synthetic securities of investment grade, which offered a higher yield than genuinely good credits because their inherent risk was underestimated, led to the credit crunch. The issue was not just that these distributions displayed Taleb characteristics: these market activities were devised with Taleb characteristics in mind.

The power of the tailgating metaphor is that it captures other essential aspects of the process – above all, the self-satisfaction of the tailgaters, a self-satisfaction that is mirrored in financial markets. These guys have talent, or so they believe. They get to their destination faster than other people because of their driving skill and finely judged risk control. Such self-delusion is possible because cognitive dissonance separates the occasional accident from the frequent success. When an incident occurs, it is someone else's fault. The driver in front made an unexpected move, there was an obstruction on the road ahead that no one could have anticipated.

There is always an element of truth in these accounts of disaster. Most tailgating drivers will never be involved in an accident. A few will end their journey at the mortuary. This means the pool of people who have learnt by experience that tailgating is dumb is therefore small. Tailgaters think the view that their behaviour is dumb is based on a purely theoretical analysis, which is refuted by the tailgaters' practical experience. And so the culture of self-confident, self-congratulatory tailgaters perpetuates itself.

You might think that the sight of the worst highway pile-up in half a century would be followed by safer driving, but you would be wrong. The sight of an accident does lead drivers to be more careful for a short time, but it is often observed that this effect wears off very quickly. And so it is in financial markets.

The investment banks currently reporting their profits and bonuses are able to reassure us that tailgating still pays. In fact, tailgating has become even more rewarding, because governments are making special efforts to keep the roads clear, and the traffic police are all at conferences on safer driving.

Governments themselves have become infected by tailgating behaviour. Some officials think that government guarantees of private sector liabilities don't cost anything, because they probably won't be called on. Others tell you that governments will make a profit on their injections of emergency funds into financial institutions. These are precise analogues of the tailgater who congratulates himself on his skilful driving. The nature of guarantees and capital injections is that they often cost you nothing, but when they do cost you they cost you loads. The taxpayers who are paying for Icelandic banks and Fannie Mae have discovered that, but the wider lesson has not been grasped. Tailgating gets you to your destination faster – except when it doesn't.

Source: *Financial Times*, 20 January 2010.

Summary

- A credit default swap is a swap contract in which one party (A) makes a series of payments to a counterparty (B) and, in exchange, B would pay to A a capital sum if the credit instrument to which the CDS relates defaults (the capital instrument could be a bond or a loan of company C).
- The credit default that triggers the payment from B to A would typically be non-payment of interest or failure to make a capital repayment of a loan. In our example above, if company C were to go bankrupt the same result would be achieved and B would have to pay A.
- Even if there is no default yet, the cost of credit default swap cover for new contracts goes up as a result of the party to which the credit default relates (party C in the example) looking more likely to default. Thus the value of B's position would fall and A's position becomes more valuable.
- CDS contracts are rather like insurance but there are differences – see the next six bullet points.
- Neither party to a CDS needs to own the underlying security (bond, loan or debt) to which the instrument relates. Neither the buyer nor the seller of the CDS has to suffer a loss from the default event (assuming that the CDS were not held by either party). This contrasts with insurance where the insured has to have an insurable interest under which he or she can demonstrate a potential loss should the default event occur.
- Neither party to the CDS needs to be regulated.
- The insured party in an insurance contract is bound by utmost good faith rules which require disclosure of all material facts and failure on this point can invalidate the contract. This is not so for a CDS where the maxim buyer beware probably applies.
- The party responsible to pay under default is not required to set aside any specific amounts to pay the other party were the default to occur.
- Insurers manage risk by setting loss reserves based on the law of large numbers. Dealers in CDSs may manage risk by offsetting liabilities under a CDS by hedging using a reverse transaction with another counterparty.
- CDS contracts are generally subject to mark to market accounting, with income statement and balance sheet impacts. This is not the case in insurance accounting. Mark to market accounting involves revaluation of the instrument for financial statement purposes with gains, since the last reporting date, being taken into income or corresponding losses being charged against profit. Clearly, with respect to highly volatile instruments this can cause massive swings in reported profit and affect undistributed reserves. And result in big bonus escalation at banks. Accounting rules are currently under review.
- Closely allied to the CDS is the credit guarantee – essentially the same kind of instrument.

End of chapter questions

18.1 Compare and contrast credit default swaps and credit insurance.

18.2 How did packages of relatively poor quality debt and CDSs achieve the status of AAA ratings by credit rating agencies?

18.3 Discuss why it might be the case that the Gaussian distribution seems to fail when crises occur. What are the causes and effects?

19

The financial crisis of 2007–8: a synopsis

In recent years we have experienced one of the most momentous events in financial history – namely, the financial crisis of 2007–8. Although not directly part of the study of international finance, we would contend that any serious student of finance needs a deep understanding of what created and drove the crisis. Hence, in this section, we build upon the previous chapter to focus upon this issue. Inevitably, it is not possible to cover all of the spectrum of the crisis in one chapter and we would recommend other texts, for example Buckley[1] and 'The Financial Crisis Inquiry Report'[2] if it is desired to obtain a better understanding.

19.1 The good times

The roots of the crisis were planted in the decade before 2007. In this ten-year period, real interest rates – arrived at by taking the actual quoted interest rate and deducting the actual achieved rate of inflation – were exceptionally low and public expenditure was growing rapidly. A quick look at Table 19.1 will show that real interest rates were actually negative in the USA in three of the first seven years of the twenty-first century – and in one other year the rate was zero. Low real rates were not just a feature of the US economy.

Table 19.1 Real interest rates in the USA and UK

Year	USA (%)	UK (%)
2000	1$^1/_2$	3.1
2001	3	3.2
2002	1$^1/_2$	2.3
2003	minus $^1/_2$	0.7
2004	minus $^3/_4$	1.5
2005	minus 1	1.7
2006	0	1.5
2007	1	1.2
2008	1	0.5
2009	$^1/_2$	0.5

This was an almost global phenomenon. It appeared that governments around the world were talking to each other to co-ordinate low real rates. Many meetings of finance ministers had an unwritten agenda as bonding meetings to ensure that no single nation broke the coalition of low interest rates. And this fuelled boom times and a bubble in house prices in the USA, in the UK and elsewhere. Furthermore, banks, amongst others, were taking advantage of these low rates by increasing their debt levels as a proportion of total financing. Because debt was cheap, this was viewed as an efficient move. But because debt interest ranks above dividends and because debt repayment ranks above shareholders' capital on liquidation it is also a source of greater risk from the standpoint of shareholders. A post-war figure for banks' debt to equity ratios of 10 to 1 moved nearer to 25 to 1 with some institutions having ratios of more than 33 to 1. At this latter figure, a drop in the worth of a bank's assets by a mere 3 per cent would wipe out the balance sheet value attributable to the ordinary shareholders. This represents risk-taking of staggering proportions. Typical manufacturing and service businesses reckon that one part debt versus two parts equity is reasonable – and some banks were running at 33 parts debt to one part equity. Sure, every kind of business is different and every industry has different ratio standards. But the point is simple. Banks were taking on burgeoning debt. And too much debt equals too much financial risk.

On American main streets and on British high streets low interest rates fuelled a spend, spend, spend mentality. Much of the US spending spree was on goods made in China. This had an effect on Chinese government policy. Chinese exporters were in receipt of US dollars from their exports to the USA. China's central bank was a buyer of US dollars from Chinese exporters. The central bank of China recirculated these dollars by purchasing US government bonds. If the Chinese had sold the US dollars and bought their own currency, this would have weakened the dollar and strengthened the Chinese renminbi (also known as the Chinese yuan) and this would lessen, somewhat, China's competitiveness. Since China was simply investing its dollars in US government bonds, no such disadvantage for exporters accrued. At the same time, through being a purchaser of US Treasury bonds, China's willingness to acquire trillions of dollars worth of US dollar government securities meant that the USA was getting its funds to balance its deficits more cheaply than might otherwise have been the case. All jolly convenient for the USA because it kept its interest rates low. All jolly convenient for the Chinese in terms of their trade position. All jolly convenient for the US citizen who continued to enjoy low interest rates and cheap products from China.

American and European governments were undoubtedly influenced by the pleas of lobby groups to keep the boom going. The influence of lobbyists was also a major force in hastening deregulation of the banking systems. Around the world governments were basking in the glory of booming economies with happy consumers (therefore happy voters), bingeing on borrowed money, buying properties that they could not afford and enjoying a wave of consumerism that, seemingly, would never end. Presidents and finance ministers had a new mantra – 'we have conquered boom and bust'.

If the reader looks at Figure 19.1, the explosion in household debt at the start of the twenty-first century can be seen to be staggering. As can the take-off in UK and US average house prices in Figures 19.2 and 19.3 respectively. Look too at Figure 19.4 showing average annual house price inflation in real terms for the decade to 2006. Clearly, a bubble was being inflated in many countries. In truth though, what began as a bubble was rapidly becoming a balloon.

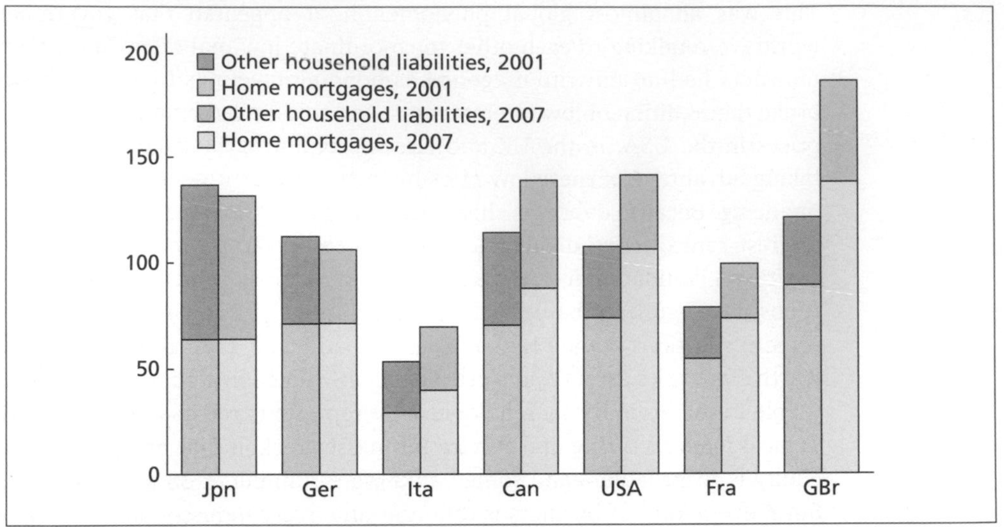

Figure 19.1 Household indebtedness (per cent of nominal disposable income)

Sources: Reuters DataStream; OECD.

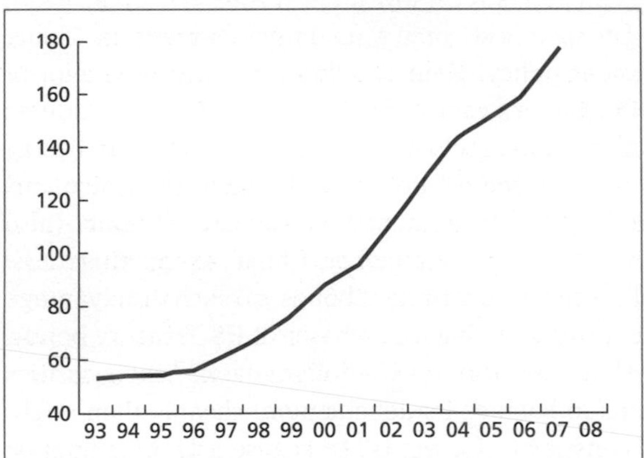

Figure 19.2 Index of UK house prices

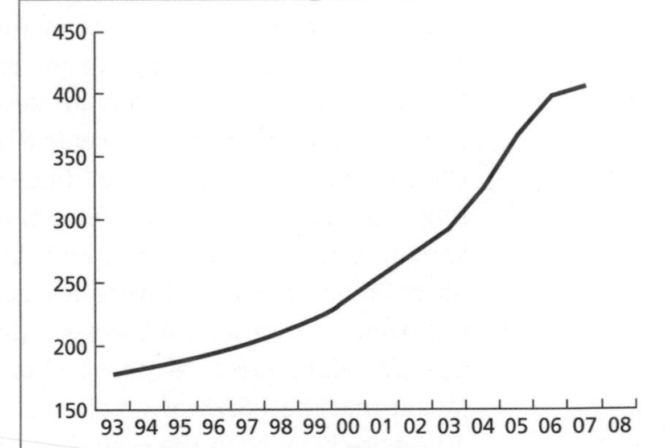

Figure 19.3 Index of US house prices

Source of Figures 19.2 and 19.3: Adapted from Graham Turner, *The Credit Crunch*, Pluto Press, 2008, Oxford Economic Forecasting and GFC Economics.

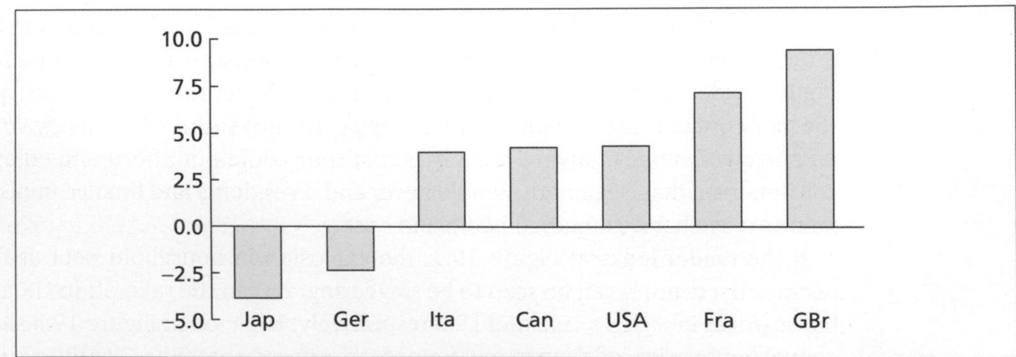

Figure 19.4 Real house price inflation – average annual increase over decade to end 2006

Source: OECD.

19.2 New models of lending

Since the middle nineties, the US government had been singing the virtues of wider home ownership and they had set up various agencies aiming to make this easier. This process was helped by the changing nature of bank lending. This involved a move away from the traditional model of **originate-to-hold** to the new model of **originate-to-distribute**. What does this mean? Under the traditional model, a mortgage bank would lend against the security of a home and the bank would hold the debt and receive interest and capital repayments. Under the originate-to-distribute model, things are different. The bank lends against the security of a home, but, instead of holding the debt, the bank sells on the debt to another bank or to a specialist financial institution where many similar loans, bought from various mortgage banks, are parcelled together and sold on to others as a package called an MBS (mortgage backed security). Alternatively, the financial institution which has bought the mortgages may mix them up with other debts – such as motor car loans, credit card debt, corporate loans and others – and the bundle is sold on as a CDO (collateralised debt obligation). This process is called **securitisation**. There are many other kinds of securitisation too. It should be clear that where the bank holds the mortgage debt under the traditional originate-to-hold model for, perhaps, 20 or 25 years it will be likely to be careful about its customers' abilities to repay and it will carry out a diligent appraisal in this area. However, under originate-to-distribute, one might expect that screening of borrowers to be at a lower level of care. And this was the case.

It wasn't just mortgage banks that were selling debt to be repackaged. As may be seen in Figure 18.3, commercial banks (those that take customers' deposits and make lendings to their customers) were doing the same in respect of loans to companies and credit card debt. The consequence of all of this was that the exacting standard and procedures that banks had worked to in terms of credit analysis were being jettisoned. The disciplines that had been built up over generations were being dumped. The argument was that since the bank was selling on the loan to someone else, why should the bank go to costly lengths involving diligent credit analysis.

Mortgage loans were being sold on to third parties for securitisation and the model of lending had moved to originate-to-distribute. Figure 18.3 tabulates the essence of the process. Given this background, mortgage lenders were more inclined to respond to government cajoling – and there was a lot of it, especially in the USA – to lend more to weak credit customers. After all, the banks were not holding these sub-prime loans on their own balance sheets but selling them on. The oil to grease the wheels of subprime lending was gushing from government goading and securitisation.

The lax nature of mortgage banks' appraisal procedures under the new model of originate-to-distribute meant that dodgy deals developed. For example, there were scams in which mortgage brokers and builders – and sometimes lawyers too – would collude to receive monies from lenders in excess of market value. This frequently involved buy-to-let properties and frequently involved off-plan homes where the properties had not yet been let or sold. Often, houses were described to lenders as having been sold off-plan without any such deal having been made – but with a fictitious purchaser invented as part of the scam. Another dirty trick involved borrowers indicating that they would occupy a property when, in reality, purchasing it as an investment to let or, more likely, to trade on – flipping. Figures 19.2 and 19.3 indicate why flipping might have been viewed as a good bet. Also, mortgage brokers were aiding borrowers to falsify their employment history and/or income level by creating fraudulent documents – the liar loan. This might involve hiding critical information. And some lenders were even accepting self-certified income figures. That is self-certified by the borrower. This facility was on offer from a vast percentage of the lenders in the market. What sort of diligence is this?

Mortgage lending criteria which had traditionally been on the basis of the lower of three times the borrower's income or 90–95 per cent of the value of the property mortgaged were being stretched. Some lenders were offering loans of 100 per cent plus on homes. Northern Rock – a UK mortgage bank – was offering, via its 'Together' brand, a deal of 125 per cent based on 95 per cent of the property value plus a 30 per cent top-up unsecured loan and a lending facility based on six times income.

19.3 The time bomb ticks

Add to all this, a new kid on the block – the credit default swap (CDS) which we described in the previous chapter. As we pointed out in that chapter, estimated losses accruing from the failure of the CDS and CDO market may have totalled approaching USD3 trillion or more, although it is too soon for us to be wholly certain of this amount. The fact is that it is big bucks. Compare it with the total income of America. The GDP of the USA was around USD14 trillion in 2009.

From virtually nothing in 2000, the value of outstanding credit default swaps had grown to over USD60 trillion in 2007 and was fuelling the income statements of many and various financial institutions (for example, AIG, Fannie Mae and Freddie Mac) and investment banks such as Lehman Brothers. The CDS and the associated credit guarantee had become favourite sons. To mix metaphors, the transformation of frog to prince was reversed back to frog when defaults began. Mortgage holders failed to meet their obligations. Borrowers on credit cards failed to make repayments. The income stream of the CDO was adversely affected. And there were credit default swaps written on CDOs. If you think that this looks like a pyramid of debt, you'd be right. All of this had negative implications for many CDS positions. As we have seen, with no default or only a low probability of default, a CDS might have a positive value, say 100 based on the expected income from the stream of insurance-like premiums exceeding the expected pay-out under default. But with defaults looming and then actually happening, the worth of the CDS could alter and even move to a negative value as the chances of paying out to the protection purchaser (the insured) increase. What was an asset worth 100 in the example may become a liability worth minus 100 or minus 500. And this is what happened. It was a time bomb that exploded and wiped out Lehman Brothers and, but for government intervention, would have done the same to AIG, Fannie Mae and Freddie Mac in the USA, and HBOS and RBS – among others – in the UK plus a good many other famous banks too. Some aspects of the Lehman debacle are briefly described in Press Cuttings 19.1, 19.2 and 19.3. Incidentally, the press cuttings refer to repos. There is a section in Chapter 30 on repos.

PRESS CUTTING 19.1

Valukas report finds few heroes

By Justin Baer in New York

Anton Valukas's 2,200-page report to the bankruptcy court on Lehman Brothers will not be the first account of the legendary securities firm's demise to captivate Wall Street.

For the many Lehman creditors with millions of dollars in claims at stake, his may be the only one that counts.

Mr Valukas was appointed in January 2009 by a court trustee to determine the causes of what was the largest bankruptcy filing in US history.

The examiner earlier this year submitted his report to the court, where it remained sealed until many of the key players agreed to release their rights to keep aspects of the document confidential.

In Mr Valukas's grim synopsis of Lehman's final days, there are few heroes and numerous alleged culprits.

'There are many reasons Lehman failed, and the responsibility is shared', Mr Valukas wrote in his report, which was made public by the court yesterday. 'Lehman was more the consequence than the cause of a deteriorating economic climate.'

Mr Valukas took aim at many of Lehman's leaders, including Dick Fuld, the firm's long-time chief executive, and former finance chiefs Chris O'Meara, Erin Callan and Ian Lowitt, and alleged he found colorable claims, or instances where there is enough credible evidence to support a claim, against each of the executives.

In his report, Mr Valukas claimed that Lehman's financial plight 'was exacerbated by Lehman executives, whose conduct ranged from serious but non-culpable errors of business judgment to actionable balance sheet manipulation; by the investment bank business model, which rewarded excessive risk taking and leverage; and by government agencies, who by their own admission might better have anticipated or mitigated the outcome.'

By the time Lehman imploded, $25bn in capital was supporting $700bn of assets and liabilities, a leverage ratio that was regarded as extremely high. In an effort to maintain favourable ratings from the rating agencies, Lehman engaged in what was referred to internally as Repo 105, a sort of window dressing which involved getting $50bn of assets off the firm's balance sheet at the end of both the 2008 first- and second-quarter balance sheets. The examiner quotes a Lehman executive saying, 'there was no substance to the transactions'.

The examiner alleged: 'Lehman did not disclose, however, that it had been using an accounting device (known within Lehman as "Repo 105") to manage its balance sheet – by temporarily removing approximately $50bn of assets from the balance sheet at the end of the first and second quarters of 2008.'

The examiner also alleged that a 'limited amount of assets' were 'improperly transferred' to Barclays, the UK bank that acquired Lehman's US brokerage business following the collapse.

Barclays declined to comment.

In a statement, Mr Fuld's attorney, Patricia Hynes, of Allen & Overy, said: 'The examiner believes the Lehman estate has a colorable claim against Dick Fuld because Lehman did not provide enhanced disclosures about certain financing arrangements called Repo 105 transactions.

'Mr Fuld did not know what those transactions were – he didn't structure or negotiate them, nor was he aware of their accounting treatment. Furthermore, the evidence available to the Examiner shows that the Repo 105 transactions were done in accordance with an internal accounting policy, supported by legal opinions and approved by Ernst & Young, Lehman's independent outside auditor. At no time did Lehman's senior financial officers, legal counsel or Ernst & Young raise any concerns about the use of Repo 105 with Mr Fuld who throughout his career faithfully and diligently worked in the interests of Lehman and its stakeholders.'

'In the three months during which he held the job, Mr Lowitt worked diligently and faithfully to discharge all of his duties as Lehman's CFO', according to a statement from Mr Lowitt's lawyer. 'Any suggestion that Mr Lowitt breached his fiduciary duties is baseless.'

Ms Callan and Mr O'Meara could not be reached for comment.

In addition, the examiner's report reiterates allegations that shortly after Lehman raised $6bn in a public offer in early June, Hank Paulson, then Treasury secretary, warned Mr Fuld that if Lehman reported further losses in the third quarter, without having a buyer or a definitive survival plan in place, Lehman's existence would be in jeopardy.

Source: *Financial Times*, 12 March 2010.

PRESS CUTTING 19.2

Accounting: fooled again

By Jennifer Hughes

On March 18 2008, Erin Callan, Lehman Brothers' chief financial officer, told a conference call that the bank was 'trying to give the group a great amount of transparency on the balance sheet' by providing more details. The analysts on the line even thanked her for it.

But what Ms Callan did not tell them is that Lehman had shifted $49bn (€36bn, £32bn) off its balance sheet in the quarter just ended, using a process it nicknamed Repo 105. That was expressly to help bring down the bank's reported leverage – or the ratio of assets to equity – the very reduction of which she was promoting to the analysts.

That and other similar deals came to light last week in a 2,200-page report by Anton Valukas, the bankruptcy court-appointed examiner. With little or no economic rationale, they are simply a form of the age-old accounting wheeze of window dressing the books to look better temporarily.

What has grabbed attention two years on is the matter-of-fact way the arrangements were discussed inside the bank by senior executives and were accepted by its counterparties – other financial groups with which Lehman did business before its collapse that September.

Yet even inside Lehman, not everyone saw the mechanism in so benign a way. Bart McDade, who became chief operating officer in June 2008, called Repo 105 'another drug we [are] on' in an e-mail and planned to slash its use, amid howls of protest from some departments. Martin Kelly, global financial controller, warned his bosses about the 'headline risk' to Lehman's reputation if the deals were to become public.

The process even cost the bank money. As one e-mail from another staffer put it: 'Everyone knows 105 is an off-balance sheet mechanism so counterparties are looking for ridiculous levels [of prices] to take them.'

But the pressure to do more of the deals grew in 2008, as did the outside world's obsession with the bank's precarious finances, particularly its leverage. Internal e-mails exhorted managers to work harder to get assets off the books. Although Dick Fuld, chief executive until its demise, has said through a lawyer that he could not recall discussions of Repo 105, Mr McDade told the examiner he had given his boss a June presentation on the topic.

Among the questions the Valukas report raises about the appropriateness of the accounting – and the auditing conducted by Ernst & Young – lies a bigger issue: how did this sort of financial engineering come to be considered a legitimate business tool and what, if anything, can be done about it?

Window-dressing the accounts is not new and can take many forms, ranging from the relatively benign to outright fraud. In manufacturing companies, for example, a manager might engage in 'channel stuffing' – shifting products just before quarter-end, even if they have not been expressly ordered – to help meet targets and boost reported revenues. This is not far removed from the retail store manager who, knowing he or she has achieved the monthly target, delays recording sales for a couple of days to help meet the next one.

Gimmicks to manipulate reported income are more common than those that, like Lehman's Repo 105s, focus on the balance sheet. But the US bank was hardly alone.

Indeed, one reminder came only yesterday with the arrest of Sean FitzPatrick who, also in 2008, resigned as chairman of Dublin-based Anglo Irish Bank following the revelation that he had for years concealed personal loans worth up to €87m ($119m, £77m). He did so by transferring them to another bank just before his bank's year-end, then returning them after the balance sheet date.

Two years before Mr FitzPatrick's departure, the US Securities and Exchange Commission forced a group of Puerto Rican banks to restate their accounts following its investigation into several misdemeanours, including managing earnings through a series of simultaneous purchase and sale transactions with other banks.

The practice is hardly recent; in 1973, the UK's London and County Securities collapsed after a government-initiated credit squeeze helped fulfil widespread market suspicions about its rocky finances. Eerily like the latest crisis, the failure of L&C threatened confidence in

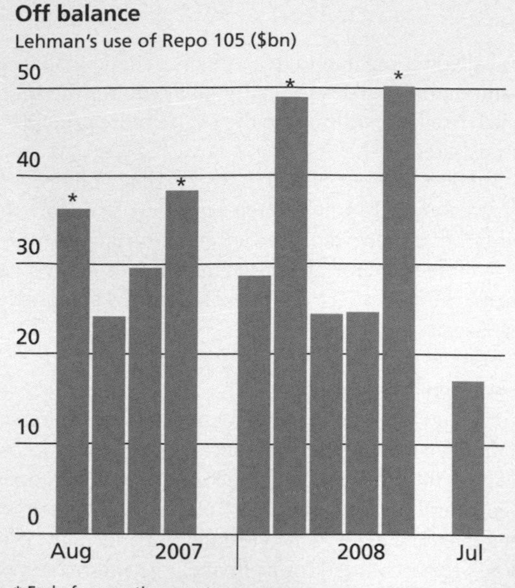

the country's banking system and forced the Bank of England to launch a rescue to keep its rivals afloat.

On unpicking L&C's accounts, the liquidators found, among many sharp practices, a window-dressing system involving a ring of banks that deposited funds with each other just before year-end to boost their reported liquidity.

Lehman's Repo 105s have attracted attention because attempts to hide assets by shifting them off the balance sheet are associated with dodgy accounting and best known for the interminable tangle of vehicles created by Enron, the failed US energy group, to hide its debts.

But the reason this issue keeps rearing its head in so many guises is that the question lies at the very heart of accounting, which was originally intended to give a company's owners a fair report of its business activities. Therefore, what goes on, and what stays off, the books is a permanent area of debate.

In spite of rulemakers' repeated, and increasingly lengthy, efforts to clarify matters, accountants and company managers know there remain many grey areas. This makes it a middle ground where managers can challenge their auditors – with some comfort – that, in spite of the shadiness implied by the term 'off balance sheet', they are legitimately debating an area without absolutely definite rules for all situations.

'It's always easier to break a rule than to draft a general rule in this area that says what the treatment ought to be', says Allan Cook, a former technical director of the UK Accounting Standards Board. He recalls receiving a series of letters from accountants and managers suggesting specific rules for off balance-sheet accounting and giving examples in which they would apply. 'The problem is you can't write a standard as a series of good solutions to individual situations; the rules have to be phrased in general terms', he adds.

Before the UK rulemaker was set up in 1990 (17 years after its US equivalent, the Financial Accounting Standards Board, began life) accountants from the era recall a series of running battles with clients and their lawyers over what should, and should not, be allowed.

Sir David Tweedie, now head of the International Accounting Standards Board, described the 1980s, when he was a partner at KPMG, as an era of 'creeping crumple' where clients tested boundaries. '[It was] the picking off of auditors by investment bankers, selling a scheme that perhaps was just within the law to a client, persuading two major auditing firms to accept it, whereupon it became accepted practice and [lawyers] would tell a third auditor that he could not qualify [the company's financial report]', he said in a 2008 speech.

Some of these transactions used the sort of financial vehicles heavily implicated in the recent crisis. Other schemes were seemingly more prosaic, such as allowing retailers to 'sell' their stores to their bank but with an agreement that they can buy any of the properties back at any point. Accountants were – and are – leery of calling that sort of deal a true sale since in reality, the seller has retained control. But one accounting expert says: 'I remember investment bankers telling us that we'd never stop it.'

All this means that it is unclear in many real situations exactly where the line falls between the legitimate exploitation of accounting rules, questionable window-dressing and sharp, or actually fraudulent, practice.

'One way of getting the lowest possible cost of funding is getting your presentation right', says one senior accountant of Lehman's Repo 105s. 'Put yourself in a position where analysts are constantly writing about your leverage and you believe you're technically entitled to reduce the cost of money by presenting your accounts this way. Its not then quite so unreasonable for you to say, "well, they've written the rules and I am within them".'

Press cutting 19.2 (*continued*)

But Lynn Turner, former chief accountant of the SEC, is more scathing about Lehman's use of Repo 105s. 'I don't think it's just financial engineering, I think it's cooking the books. It is just amazing to me that we're back here again', he says.

Privately, US auditors will talk of meetings with clients where they have been asked bluntly, 'tell me where it says I can't do this'.

'In financial reporting, no one wants to be left behind and have their competitors steal a march on them. It is a bit like an arms race, or a bloodsport', says Jack Ciesielski, editor of Analysts' Accounting Observer, a research service on the investment impact of accounting issues. 'The best analogy in real life might be a tax return and how some people feel they're being a chump if they don't go right up to the line, taking every deduction they can.'

The Valukas report has dragged accounting and auditing back into the spotlight. Ernst & Young says it retains confidence in its actions, adding that the last audited accounts of Lehman, to November 2007, were 'fairly presented' in accordance with US accounting principles.

Senior staff at rival firms among accountancy's 'big four' wonder privately what might have been uncovered if other failing institutions, from AIG and Bear Stearns to Royal Bank of Scotland, had been put under a similar year-long microscope that had access to three petabytes of information – equivalent to roughly 350bn sheets of paper.

Internally, the profession has for years been arguing over how to bring in broad-based principles in a world where auditors increasingly face the risk of litigation. In court, detailed rules can provide better protection. Now, the Group of 20 leading economies has called on regulators to settle on a single global set of standards by 2011. In reality, this requires the US to switch from its own rules to the IASB's more principles-based system.

But the cynics are already warning that while sweeping statements can help force managers to follow the spirit, rather than simply the letter, of the law, they also leave more room for individual interpretation. In other words, the sort of grey area exploited by Lehman will never really go away.

How Repo 105 worked

Banks use repurchase agreements, known as repos, all the time for short-term financing. One borrows cash and gives the other securities, such as government bonds, as collateral. Both agree to unwind the arrangement on a set date. The deals, which usually run only for days or weeks, are accounted for as financings, and remain on the books with banks recording an asset – the cash – and a matching liability in the promise to buy back the collateral.

Lehman's 105 was different – instead of handing over securities equivalent to the cash it received, the bank gave more than was necessary. The point was to exploit a loophole allowing such over-collateralised deals to be accounted for as true sales. Lehman then reported its obligation to repurchase the securities at a fraction of the full cost, and used the cash it had received to pay off its liabilities, thereby 'shrinking' its balance sheet.

Use of Repo 105 spiked sharply at the end of each accounting quarter – more so in 2008 as pressure grew on Lehman to reduce its leverage – and fell just as dramatically soon after the new accounting period began, as deals were unwound.

Rules and regulations

'With complicated transactions, you'll get complicated accounting.'

When the US Financial Accounting Standards Board first drew up the rules under which Lehman Brothers conducted its Repo 105 deals, the Securities and Exchange Commission told the body that the standard needed further work before publication.

Such an intervention from the regulator is extremely rare, and underlines the difficulties in developing rules regarding financial instruments.

'Perhaps, in retrospect, I should have gone back again and said no', says Lynn Turner, then the SEC's chief accountant, 'but they had addressed our issues'.

The rewritten SFAS 140 came into force in 2001, replacing a set of rules that were just six years old. It enhanced the old standard with new rules about exactly what qualifies as a sale – which was the very angle later used by Lehman in its Repo 105.

While accounting is relatively straightforward in the bricks-and-mortar world, it is far less so with financial instruments, where the 'slicing and dicing' of the past decade has made the job harder. As finance evolves, so the accounting has to keep up, leading to increasingly long and complex standards.

'Any time you deal with a complicated transaction, you're going to get complicated accounting', says Kevin Stoklosa of the FASB. 'If we were talking about selling a pair of shoes, then 10 people would probably come up with the same accounting treatment. With financial instruments in all their complexity, you get 10 different answers.'

Accountants are aware that allowing more assets on to the books would result in complaints too from investors.

'That would just gross up the balance sheet with all sorts of things that might not belong there – then people would accuse us of inflating the books', says one accounting expert. 'It's a real balancing act.'

In spite of the fuss over Lehman's actions, experts say that conducting trades merely for an accounting benefit, as the bank did, is rare.

'People will structure things for tax reasons because it saves them cash', says one senior accountant. 'It's actually very rare to see people go out of their way where the only benefit is accounting because it often costs them money – as it did Lehman – and is so badly looked upon.'

Source: *Financial Times*, 19 March 2010.

PRESS CUTTING 19.3

Overpaid CEO award

Take your pick. The crop of entries for the inaugural Lex Overpaid CEO of the year award was richer than any could have dared imagine. The term 'rewards for failure' scarcely did justice to a broken model of executive compensation that brought the global financial system to within an ace of collapse. From Europe, Sir Fred Goodwin, ousted as chief executive of Royal Bank of Scotland in October, was a popular choice among readers, after taking home a total of £8.2m in 2007 and 2006. Ditto the bosses of the Icelandic banks: they managed to sink not just their own companies, but an entire country.

But their packages look positively stingy when compared to the payouts offered to the disgraced titans of the US financial sector. Daniel Mudd, who pocketed $23m for his last two years' service at Fannie Mae, and Dick Syron, paid $33m by Freddie Mac over the same period, were both stand-out candidates. They were the two men who arguably did most to stoke the housing bubble that pushed the world's largest economy into recession. Both men made enough to set up their descendants for generations. Then they threw the government-sponsored enterprises into the arms of the taxpayer.

In the end, though, there could only be one winner: Dick Fuld. The Lehman Brothers boss made many tens of millions of dollars in the years preceding the bank's collapse in September, an event that triggered an earthquake in global markets. His stubborn refusal to sell the bank when he had the chance was the single worst trade of the year. Picking up $34m in 2007 and $40.5m in 2006, (nodded through by Sir Christopher Gent, a member of the board's four-person compensation committee), he set a high standard for the 2009 award. All suggestions for shortlistable candidates for next year should be e-mailed to lex@ft.com or posted online at www.ft.com/overpaidceos.

Source: *Financial Times* Lex Column, 22 December 2008.

On 3 March 2009, testifying to the US Senate budget committee, Federal Reserve Bank chairman, Ben Bernake responded to a quote from a senator relating to the AIG bailout saying that 'We have been doing what we can to break the company up, to get it into a saleable position . . . If there's a single episode in this entire 18 months that has made me more angry, I can't think of one (other than) AIG.' Acharya, Richardson, Nieuweburgh and White[3] state that 'Bernake is referring to the Financial Products Group at AIG that wrote . . . USD450 billion of CDS on AAA-rated products with little or no capital. His anger is understandable but perhaps should have been carried through to the GSEs as well. AIG's CDS positions were peanuts in comparison to the GSEs' writing USD3.5 trillion worth of credit guarantees on much riskier assets and similarly with little capital (albeit in accordance with regulatory requirements) and all in one direction'. These writers continue to say that 'If Fannie and Freddie were allowed to fail, USD3.5 trillion worth of guarantees held by the banking sector, pension and **mutual funds**, foreign governments and other entities would now be in a state of flux.' Had the US government not bailed out Fannie and Freddie, a domino effect involving the failure of counterparty after counterparty would have occurred. Such banking concerns would have joined Lehmans with the epitaph 'failed in the biggest crash since 1929'. Reported by *Inside Mortgage Finance* there was USD5.2 trillion outstanding in MBS guarantees by Fannie Mae, Freddie Mac and Ginnie Mae.

19.4 The time bomb explodes

The CDO and CDS markets involve some banks and financial institutions as sellers and other banks and financial institutions as buyers. With so many CDSs written on MBSs and CDOs containing mortgage debt, declines in the housing market would have a massively magnified negative impact on values for such securities and financial products. Remember that you could have securitised mortgages of USD10 billion but have credit default swaps totalling USD500 billion or even more written on them. Hence, the magnification. And this adverse effect would not be felt just in terms of values but it would impact market liquidity – which could quite easily dry up completely.

That is just what happened. The US Federal Funds rate was 1 per cent in 2005. By 2007, it had jumped to 5 per cent. When foreclosures on properties started to occur as the housing market began to head south, mortgage interest and capital repayments were not forthcoming and this was the income of the MBS and part of the income of the CDO and other similar instruments with housing debt mixed into them. Their market prices started to fall. First a trickle, then a cascade then a storm – the metaphors gush. And they are no exaggeration. No one wanted this alphabet soup of CDOs, CDSs and MBSs. Liquidity was at a standstill.

Over 2007, the drop in existing home sales was the steepest since 1989. In the first quarter of 2007, the S&P/Case-Shiller house price index for the USA recorded its first year-on-year fall in nationwide home prices since 1991. The subprime mortgage business was collapsing as interest rates peaked – see Figure 19.5 – and foreclosures accelerated.

In the economics textbooks, models nearly always assume that there is liquidity in markets – the price falls until buyers first nibble, then bite and this kickstarts (sorry, mixed metaphor) the upward trajectory. Reality in the latter half of 2007 was not like the textbook.

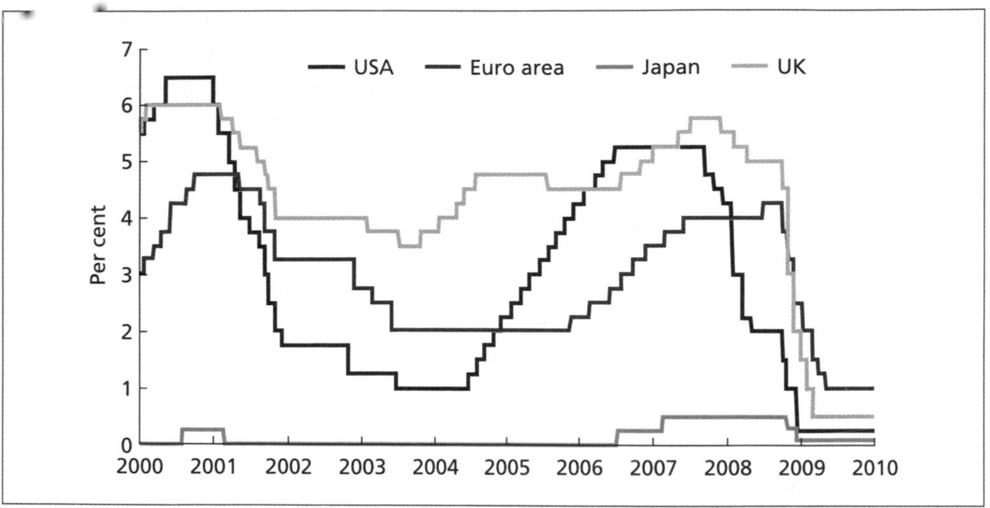

Figure 19.5 Official interest rates 2000–2010

With liquidity under pressure, it stalled when the players in the market started suspecting each other of having vast liabilities to pay out under credit default swaps. Banks had ceased dealing these instruments with one another. Worse, they stopped lending amongst themselves too. The interbank market was freezing over. This is normally an essential part of the banking business enabling financial firms to square off positions arising from their daily cash in versus their daily cash out. Fear and panic were features of Wall Street, the City of London and elsewhere in the late summer of 2008. And, of course, stockmarkets were hit too.

19.5 Why? Oh why did no-one see it coming?

Why didn't banks foresee this? After all, interest rates in the USA had been heading northwards for some time. The answer to this question may lie in the risk management systems used by banks. Expectations of financial market fluctuations were substantially based upon movements in line with the normal distribution, or bell curve. The fact is that, whilst this may be almost true most of the time, it is an oversimplification because markets seem to behave according to fat tail models and this means that extreme events, both positive and negative, occur more frequently than the bell curve model suggests. Bank risk management models are supposed to be augmented by 'what if?', simulation and scenario analysis. And, if one looks at Figure 19.5 harbingers of problems were there as interest rates climbed.

One of the remarkable things about markets is that their deviations from the bell curve are substantial. Had the Dow Jones index of industrial shares moved in accordance with the normal distribution, it would have moved by 4.5 per cent or more on only six days in the period from 1996 to 2003. In reality, it moved by at least this amount 366 times during the period.

Regulation of banks and financial institutions left something to be desired in the run-up to the financial crisis. This is an understatement. There are instances referred to in Buckley,[4] where the exploits of Bernard Madoff and his massive fraud were challenged by financial analysts but regulators failed to find anything untoward, where risk managers in banks discussed their worries with bullying CEOs whose ego trips involved certainty that existing policies were unquestionably right. And when such matters were discussed with regulators, they too failed to react. Additionally, there was the slow and possibly flawed reactions of accounting bodies who wished to maintain inflexibility in their mark-to-market rules and, with liquidity waning in CDO and CDS markets, values evaporated. Regulators were widely guilty of groupthink and their common thought was that the housing boom was set to continue as interest rates seemed likely to remain low. Bankers, governments and consumers were also sucked into this naïve groupthink frame of mind.

Meanwhile, the carrot of massive bank bonuses led dealers in financial institutions to chase CDOs and CDSs and related instruments even when markets started to look dodgy. Dealers were getting big buck bonuses for selling CDSs but were incurring massive risks for their banks. A lot of these ex-dealers have moved on nowadays and own mansions and estates in the country. Bonuses were calculated individually year by year with no deductions or repayments when the day of reckoning arrived. In fact, for most bonus-bloated bankers, the day of reckoning did not arrive.

The underpinning causes of the crisis lay in an environment of lax government and financial excesses with AIG, Fannie Mae and Freddie Mac and some investment banks prominent in their culpability. Financial institutions prefer to point the finger at subprime mortgages with little reference to the inverted pyramid of credit derivatives arranged on them. Press Cutting 19.4 raises this issue and a few more too.

PRESS CUTTING 19.4

Fantasy causes for credit crisis touted

By Pablo Triana

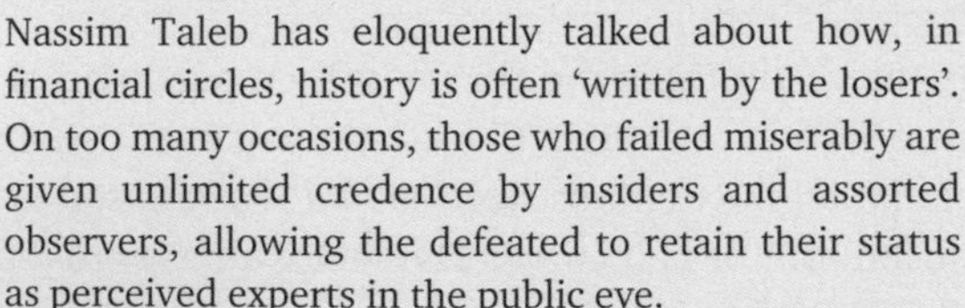

Nassim Taleb has eloquently talked about how, in financial circles, history is often 'written by the losers'. On too many occasions, those who failed miserably are given unlimited credence by insiders and assorted observers, allowing the defeated to retain their status as perceived experts in the public eye.

Thus, when the world gets to hear about the state of affairs in Financeland, the explanations often come from people with a demonstrably lacklustre record. We have seen this time and again when it comes to blown-up financiers, flawed financial theorists, off-the-mark analysts, yet-more-off-the-mark economic forecasters, or misleading credit raters. Even after demonstrating incompetence and enabling unbearable damage, many of those actors are neither castigated, nor banned from the premises. Losers, the argument would go, are allowed to stay.

As bad as the process that Mr Taleb describes may be, history 'written by the confused' could be worse. Here we would be talking about those instances when the financial script the populace is being fed is utter fantasy. This is potentially dangerous, as presenting a fake storyline would by default prevent the true causes from emerging and the core problems from being addressed and remedied.

It is crucial that current and future investors, policy-makers, and reporters are not confused by fantastical tales that would indirectly sanction a repeat of the bad practices of the past.

We are currently going through such a misinformation process. A few months ago a book on the academic intrigue behind the development of the efficient markets theory was released. Influenced by the publication of the text, many decided to concur in blaming said theory for the credit crisis. This idea has now become conventional wisdom in media quarters, from where the dictum is spread out to the masses.

I have explained in the past why it is odd to blame efficient markets theory for the malaise (basically, no one in the markets operates under its dictates; those who provoked the meltdown were not abiding by the construct, or even aware of its existence).

But the oddness goes beyond fingerpointing a creed that is clearly not followed out there. The author of the book does not blame the theory, which was rejected by the academic community decades ago. We now know that even the creator of the theory thinks it nuts to posit that his mathematical baby was the culprit, for the simple reason that it was never wholeheartedly adopted by professionals.

This is what Chicago professor Eugene Fama recently said when asked about the responsibility of his theory for the chaos: 'The premise is fantasy. Most investing is done by active managers who don't believe that markets are efficient . . . Despite my taunts of the last 45 years, about 80 per cent of mutual fund wealth is actively managed . . . The recent problems of commercial and investment banks trace mostly to their trading desks and their proprietary portfolios, and these are always built on the assumption that markets are inefficient. Indeed, if banks and investment banks took market efficiency more seriously, they might have avoided lots of their recent problems . . . I continue to believe the efficient markets theory is a solid view of the world for almost all practical purposes. But it's clear I'm in the minority. If the theory took over the investment world, I missed it.'

When the person with the most interest in portraying the tool as a widely embraced success is so open about its failure to become popular with financial punters, it is hard to conclude that those gorging on subprime CDOs were religiously following the academic doctrine.

The key question, of course, is why anyone would want to focus attention on a factor that was clearly irrelevant, based on a source that does not espouse the message they derive from it. What is behind the spreading of such a disturbingly confused narrative?

All the while, the true factors behind the troubles (things like the regulatory framework, the overt quantification of risk management, the reliance on credit ratings, and even born-again CDOs) are not being properly covered or denounced. And that is most likely why they continue to be in our midst, ready to strike and enable harm again.

Pablo Triana is the author of *Lecturing Birds on Flying: Can Mathematical Theories Destroy the Financial Markets*?

Source: *Financial Times* FTfm, 30 November 2009.

19.6 Escape

The economists' solution to banking crises is the mantra – throw money at the problem and mop it up afterwards.[5] Essentially, this is what governments did in order to breathe life into a banking system which was stalked by fear that counterparties might be wiped out – as some were. Some banks were nationalised, others received massive government injections of money in return for majority ownership in some cases, minority ownership in other instances. Some received guarantees from governments. A few were allowed to go bankrupt. Governments put money into the economy, sometimes via cheap loans to banks to encourage them to lend or at least not to sit on their hands and do nothing. Some of the impact of the money to the economy was via cuts in some taxes. All of this averted the possibility of another Great Depression. But the mopping up of this input is creating harder times for some, austerity for others.

Reinhart and Rogoff[6] warn, because financial crises require bailout funds for banks, that the impact of this is invariably a **sovereign debt** crisis. This is afflicting numerous countries, particularly some in the eurozone of the European Union for whom improvement is restricted due to their membership of the euro and despite having experienced divergent inflation rates.

19.7 The eurozone's problems

When the common currency was instigated, the conversion rates for the old national currency into the euro was set at such a level as to ensure competitiveness between themselves. This rate was an estimate of the equilibrium rate. Although, as we have seen in Chapter 3, there are minor differences between economists' views, an equilibrium exchange rate is normally taken as one which would create a current account balance of payments result of zero. This would mean that exports and imports of goods and services would be equal.

Consequently, to maintain equilibrium, within the eurozone, different countries should exhibit similar inflation rates – or more or less so. Inevitably, in reality, different inflation rates exist within a country. Inflation in the South-East of England may be different from that in the North-East. Inflation in New York may differ from that in the Mid-West. The actual cost of living and pay rates may be very different. But we would expect that the actual inflation rate differences would not be excessive.

Returning to the actual picture of inflation in the eurozone, the scale of the problem becomes clear. Labour costs in Germany rose 7 per cent between 2000 and 2008 versus 34 per cent in Ireland, 30 per cent in Spain, Portugal and Italy, 28 per cent in Greece and the Netherlands and 20 per cent in France. Over this period, Germany recorded an accumulated figure of exports minus imports of EUR1261 billion while Spain saw a deficit of EUR598 billion and Greece also achieved a minus figure amounting to EUR273 billion.

This picture is brought into relief if one tracks the real effective exchange of certain eurozone members from the beginning of the euro project up to the end of 2009. Remember, the real effective exchange rate is arrived at by looking at the actual exchange rate versus an index of foreign prices versus home prices. Also remember that if purchasing power parity is holding, the **real effective exchange rate** remains constant. Figure 19.6 shows the real effective exchange rate for certain countries in the eurozone. The conclusion that can be drawn from the graph is that Spain, Ireland, Portugal and Greece have all become relatively weak competitively at the euro exchange rate given their excessive inflation versus Germany which has controlled inflation and is competitively strong versus its eurozone partners.

The impact of these relative competitive positions for eurozone countries can be seen in Figure 19.7 which shows exports as a percentage of GDP from 1999 to 2009. Clearly Germany has been a winner and Greece, in particular, has been a loser.

A further tabulation shows the effect of all of this upon the balance of payments current account as a percentage of GDP and various countries' budget (government inflows versus outflows) deficits as a percentage of GDP. This appears in Table 19.2 which also shows consumer price increases for the last available year, unemployment rates and interest rates. The table shows data for the USA and the Britain as well as some eurozone countries. What is clear from the exhibit is the massive impact of inflation relativities within the eurozone. Of the countries in the table, the plight of Greece and Spain stand out with high negatives showing up on budget deficit data. The same is true for Britain and the USA. What also shows up are Germany and the Netherlands' current account positivity on balance of payments. Also, on the interest rates front, some big differences in eurozone ten-year interest rates. This is interesting. Since eurozone countries all have the same currency and all have interest rates set by the ECB, why should longer term interest rates diverge so much? After all, short term rates are exactly the same. Shouldn't German long-term rates be the same as Greek long-term interest rates? But, what if something odd happened. Like Greece quitting

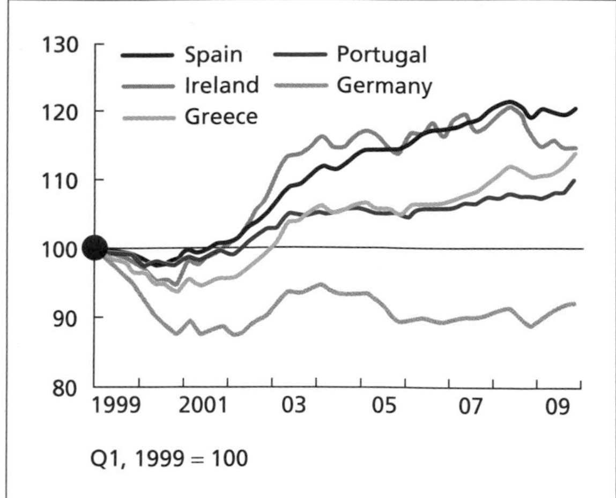

Figure 19.6 Real effective exchange rates 1999–2009, based on GDP deflators

Source: European Central Bank.

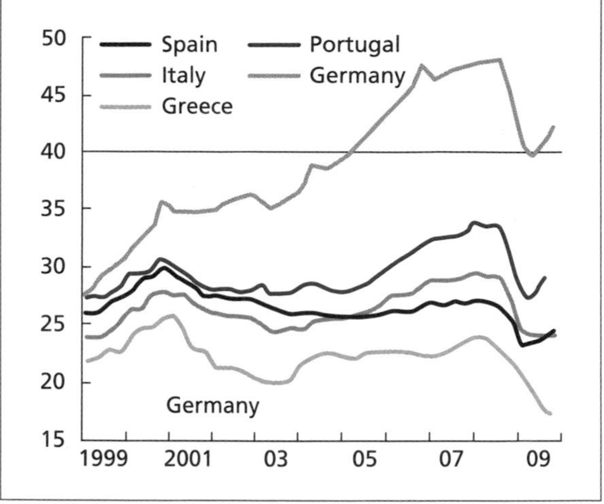

Figure 19.7 Export of goods and services (as a percentage of GDP)

Source: Thomson Reuters Datastream.

Table 19.2 Economic data for various countries (table prepared mid-May 2011)

Country	Consumer price increases % per annum	Unemployment rate %	Interest rates		Balance of payment current account versus GDP %	Budget deficit versus GDP %
			Three-month rate % per annum	Ten-year rate % per annum		
Austria	+3.1	4.3	1.42	3.66	+2.9	−3.4
Belgium	+3.4	7.7	1.42	4.26	+1.4	−3.8
France	+2.1	9.5	1.42	3.64	−2.0	−6.4
Germany	+2.4	7.1	1.42	3.28	+5.2	−1.7
Greece	+3.9	15.1	1.42	15.25	−4.5	−8.4
Italy	+2.6	8.3	1.42	4.78	−3.3	−4.0
Netherlands	+2.1	5.1	1.42	3.56	+5.7	−4.3
Spain	+3.8	20.7	1.42	5.23	−3.6	−6.7
Euro area	+2.8	9.9	1.42	3.09	−0.3	−4.4
USA	+2.7	9.0	0.21	3.22	−3.6	−9.9
Britain	+4.0	7.8	0.83	3.38	−2.0	−9.1

the eurozone. If this were to happen and Greece went back to its old national currency – the drachma – there would be every chance that the drachma would fall in value against the euro to make Greek exports competitive again. Is the interest rate market charging Greece a higher rate than other eurozone members because it expects that to happen? Is the premium the market charges Greece something to do with political risk? Does the market expect Greece to default on its debt? Or **reschedule** its debt? Maybe a bit of all of these. Incidentally, note that European countries outside the eurozone do have the luxury of currency depreciation – Britain, for example – as a way of helping them move towards the solution of their economic problems.

Table 19.3 Selected data for government debt to GDP (2010)

Country	Percentage
Greece	142.8
Italy	119.0
Belgium	96.8
Ireland	96.2
Portugal	93.0
Germany	83.2
France	81.7
UK	76.5
Austria	72.3
Netherlands	62.7
Spain	60.1
USA	58.9

Another worrying feature is the issue of public debt as a percentage of GDP. Remember that one of the Maastricht criteria for the eurozone is that government debt should be below 60 per cent of GDP. Table 19.3 shows figures from Eurostat for EU countries and the USA for further comparative purposes. There are some standout data, especially the Greek figure.

The phenomenal figures for Greece really have their roots way back in Greece's entry into the euro when it met the Maastricht criteria thanks to some remarkable financial engineering to reduce its apparent debt level – repos again.

At the time of writing (May 2011) Greece, Ireland and Portugal have all received bailout loan packages from the EU and the IMF. Some have received more than one bailout package. All three countries have experienced profligate inflation which has impacted their real effective exchange rates – see Figure 19.6.

Ireland's plight lay in inflation plus massive bailouts from the Irish government in the wake of a gigantic property boom which moved into reverse from 2007. On top of this, some of the leading banks in the country had an undiversified lending book to property companies and this plus some crony banking and equally crony regulation accompanied by a fair amount of fraud at some banks meant that the Irish government's rescue of banks precipitated an unsustainable financial position which subsequently required an EU and IMF bailout.

Possible routes out of the eurozone problem might include:

- Austerity programmes to continue in the high inflation countries. At best the risk is social tension. At worse, the risk is political upheaval and possible overthrow of existing regimes – in other words, revolution.
- Massive privatisations of state-owned monopolies to reduce government debt. Greece has substantial potential here.
- The high-inflation countries could quit the euro and return to their old national currencies. There would be short-term turmoil in the capital markets but this would settle down.
- There might be a half-way house which would be politically acceptable whereby weaker eurozone countries would adopt a new 'soft euro' which would involve a depreciation

against the existing euro – the 'hard euro'. We suspect that this would lead eventually to a return to national currencies for weaker eurozone members.

- New accessions to the euro could be put on hold – maybe permanently.

Your author rules out the other possibility which would be for Germany, in particular, to run high inflation for a few years to catch up that already experienced elsewhere in the eurozone. In theory it could work, but in practice it's highly unlikely. It's thinking the unthinkable.

Is it also unthinkable that these strains could create pressure to curtail the whole European Union project? Note that your author used the word curtail – not abandon. There are iconoclasts who have long expressed doubt about the expansion of the project. Their voices will be heard louder now. And if the project is curtailed, would it be such a bad thing? We include here various press cuttings which relate to eurozone bailout problems.

Some economists who look at the issue of an optimal currency area have expressed doubt about the eurozone. So what is an optimal currency area?

PRESS CUTTING 19.5

The eurozone's journey to defaults

By Martin Wolf

FT

A story is told of a man sentenced by his king to death. The latter tells him that he can keep his life if he teaches the monarch's horse to talk within a year. The condemned man agrees. Asked why he did so, he answers that anything might happen: the king might die; he might die; and the horse might learn to talk.

This has been the eurozone's approach to the fiscal crises that have engulfed Greece, Ireland and Portugal, and threaten other member states. Policymakers have decided to play for time in the hope that the countries in difficulty will restore their creditworthiness. So far, this effort has failed: the cost of borrowing has risen, not fallen (see chart). In the case of Greece, the first of the countries to receive help, the chances of renewed access to private lending on terms that the country can afford are negligible. But postponing the day of reckoning will not make the Greek predicament better: on the contrary, it will merely make the debt restructuring more painful when it comes.

Greek debt is on a path to exceed 160 per cent of gross domestic product. Unfortunately, it could easily be far higher, as a paper from Nouriel Roubini and associates at Roubini Global Economics notes. Greece may fail to meet its fiscal targets, because of the malign impact of fiscal tightening on the economy or because of resistance to agreed measures. The real depreciation needed to restore competitiveness would also raise the ratio of debt to GDP, while a failure to achieve such a depreciation may well curtail the needed return to growth. The euro may appreciate, further undermining competitiveness. Finally, banks may well fail to support the economy.

Given such a debt burden, what are the chances that a country with Greece's history would be able to finance its debt in the market on terms consistent with a decline in the debt burden? Extremely small.

Assume that interest rates on Greek long-term debt were 6 per cent, instead of today's 16 per cent. Assume, too, that nominal GDP grows at 4 per cent. These, note, are highly optimistic assumptions. Then, even to stabilise debt, the government must run a primary surplus (before interest payments) of 3.2 per cent of GDP. If Greek debt is to fall to the Maastricht treaty limit of 60 per cent of GDP by 2040, the country would need a primary surplus of 6 per cent of GDP. Every year, then, the Greek people would need to be cajoled and coerced into paying far more in taxes than they receive in government spending.

What might persuade investors that this is sufficiently likely to justify funding Greece? Nothing I can imagine. But remember that 6 per cent would be a spread of less than 3 percentage points over German bunds. The default risk does not need to be very high to make this extremely unappealing.

Press cutting 19.5 (*continued*)

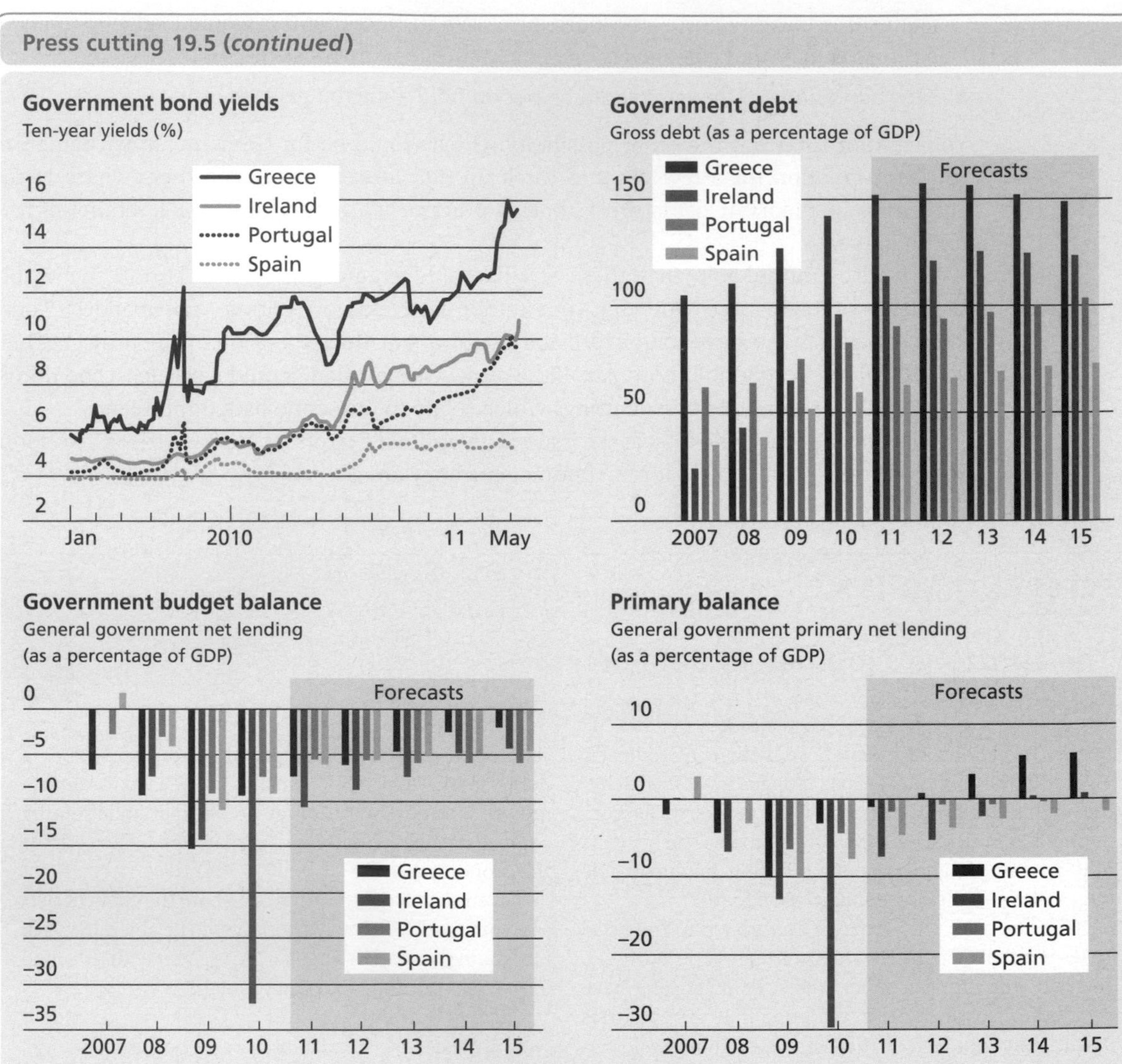

Sources: Thomson Reuters Datastream; IMF.

In short, Greece is in a Catch 22: creditors know it lacks the credibility to borrow at rates of interest it can afford. It will remain dependent on ever greater quantities of official financing. However that creates an even deeper trap.

Assume, for example, that half of Greek debt were to be held by senior creditors, such as the International Monetary Fund and the European stability mechanism, which is to replace the current European financial stabilisation mechanism in 2013. Suppose, too, that the reduction in debt needed to secure lending from private markets, on bearable terms, were to be 50 per cent of face value. Then private creditors would be wiped out. Under such a dire threat, no sane lender would consider offering money on bearable terms. A take-over of Greek debt by official funders makes return to private finance even more unlikely.

If one takes seriously the view that any debt restructuring must be ruled out, advanced by Lorenzo Bini Smaghi, an influential Italian member of the board of the European Central Bank, official sources must finance Greece indefinitely. Moreover, they must be willing to do so on terms sufficiently generous to make a long-term reduction in the debt burden feasible. That is possible. But it is a political nightmare: the moral hazard involved would be enormous. Greece would lose almost all sovereignty indefinitely and resentments would reach boiling point on both sides.

Non-European members would also prevent the IMF from offering such indefinite largesse. The burden would then fall on the Europeans. It seems unlikely that needed agreement would be sustained.

The alternative is a pre-emptive restructuring of the debt, perhaps next year. Since market prices tell us that this is what investors expect, it should not come as a shock to them. A restructuring ought to raise the country's creditworthiness and increase the incentives to sustain a programme of stabilisation and reform. Moreover, with a planned, pre-emptive restructuring the authorities could also prepare the needed support for banks, both inside Greece and outside it.

Many ways of restructuring debt exist, some more coercive than others. Fortunately, 95 per cent of Greek public debt is issued under domestic law, which should reduce the legal problems of enforcing the desired deep restructuring.

Needless to say, this would still be a big mess. Moreover, there is no certainty that a restructuring would return Greece to growth, since the country also suffers from a lack of competitiveness. Inside the eurozone, no simple way of resolving the latter weakness exists. The country may be doomed to prolonged deflation.

However unpopular restructuring might be, the alternative would be worse. The debt would then need to be financed indefinitely. This, then, would be a backdoor route into a fiscal support mechanism for members far more extreme than that for the states of the US. The saga is most unlikely to end with Greece. Other peripheral countries – Ireland and Portugal, for example – are also likely to find themselves locked out of private markets for a long time. In neither case is a return to fiscal health in any way guaranteed, given the extremely difficult starting points.

Overindebted countries with their own currencies inflate. But countries that borrow in foreign currencies default. By joining the eurozone, members have moved from the former state to the latter. If restructuring is ruled out, members must both finance and police one another. More precisely, the bigger and the stronger will finance and police the smaller and the weaker. Worse, they will have to go on doing so until all these horses can talk. Is that the future they want?

Source: *Financial Times*, 11 May 2011.

PRESS CUTTING 19.6

Eurozone reprofiling

Europe's financial leaders appear to have staged a hasty retreat from their attempt to persuade investors that there is a significant difference between restructuring (reducing the payments on bonds) and reprofiling (extending bond maturities without increasing the interest rate).

Anyone who understands the time value of money – which, it is to be hoped, includes every active European government bond trader – knows that both have the same effect (assuming the normal yield curve, in which longer maturities come with higher yields) of reducing the net present value of a bond.

Therefore, Tuesday's semantic development, that Jean-Claude Juncker, the president of the eurozone finance ministers, referred to reprofiling as 'soft restructuring', is moderately encouraging. It suggests that investors should take the process at least somewhat seriously.

The EU now accepts that some Greek sovereign debt restructuring is inevitable. This is realistic. For months, the market has been signalling a sharp cut in the debt's net present value. Indeed, the market valuation suggests a larger cut in NPV than can be obtained by almost any maturity extension.

The EU, the European Central Bank, the Greek government and Greek bond holders all wish the market is wrong. They want as 'soft' a restructuring as possible. A mere reprofiling would probably be mild enough to avoid some of the hazards of a 'hard restructuring', to which Mr Juncker says he is firmly opposed. Little wonder, since that would trigger immediate write-downs in banks' hold-to-maturity portfolios and claims on credit default swaps. Those might spawn financial chaos, especially if the restructuring tendency spread around the EU periphery.

Still, one way or another, Greece will end up paying back less – in terms of present value – than it originally promised. And there are advantages to calling such a financial adjustment by its proper name: a default.

Source: *Financial Times* Lex Column, 18 May 2011.

PRESS CUTTING 19.7

ECB hits out over Greek debt plan

By Ralph Atkins in Frankfurt, Quentin Peel in Berlin and Kerin Hope in Athens

This month Jean-Claude Trichet, ECB president, walked out of a meeting hosted by Jean-Claude Juncker, Luxembourg's prime minister. According to people familiar with events at the meeting, Mr Trichet was angry at talk of a so-called 'soft' restructuring that could involve an extension of Greek debt maturities.

After a meeting of eurozone finance ministers on Monday, Mr Juncker said a soft restructuring of Greek debt would be an option once Athens had taken further steps to bring its public finances under control.

Lorenzo Bini Smaghi, an ECB executive board member, responded on Wednesday, saying: 'Given how markets work, one should beware of using meaningless phrases, as Greece will then have to pay a price.'

The ECB fears a soft restructuring would be seen as a precursor to a 'hard' restructuring and spook markets across the eurozone. ECB officials instead want Greece to accelerate its privatisation programme. Mr Bini Smaghi said Athens needed to 'convince its citizens to pay taxes' and 'retire at 65 as everyone else does in the western world'.

Separately, Jürgen Stark, another ECB executive board member, criticised 'vested interests' in the UK and US who were hostile to Greece's reform efforts – an apparent attack on investors who have bet on a Greek default. In a further sign of European policy divisions, it emerged on Wednesday that the ECB and some eurozone countries are at odds with Germany's determination to involve private creditors in any future debt restructuring, for fear of scaring investors.

Berlin is pushing for a legal commitment to be written into the treaty establishing the European stability mechanism – the €500bn (£441bn) permanent rescue fund to be set up in 2013.

The ECB, which has bought about €45bn of Greek bonds over the past year, believes that eurozone governments should provide further loans if Greece requires additional help.

Source: *Financial Times*, 19 May 2011.

PRESS CUTTING 19.8

Greek debt talks cast doubt over sovereign CDS

By David Oakley and Tracy Alloway

In one sense, Greece may be about to get its revenge on the speculators blamed by politicians for exacerbating the country's debt crisis.

If eurozone leaders press ahead with plans to extend Greek bond maturities in a 'soft' or voluntary debt restructuring, then traders in credit default swaps could be one of the main casualties.

Sovereign CDS, which insure investors against the risk of a bond default, are facing a critical moment in their short history. The first sovereign CDS trades were made about 10 years ago and the question of whether or not this insurance will pay out could soon be put to the test.

A voluntary restructuring of Greek debt, or 'reprofiling', as European Union policymakers describe it, threatens to undermine the intrinsic value of buying the derivatives because such a restructuring is unlikely to amount to a so-called 'credit event'.

This means that the banks and investors who had bought CDS protection against any restructuring would receive nothing in recompense for any losses in interest due or principal invested in Greek bonds.

The failure to trigger a pay-out would raise questions over the usefulness of financial instruments that have been in hot demand over the past year as banks have scrambled to protect themselves from a default.

The cost of buying protection against a Greek default has swelled to 1,318 basis points – or $1.3m to insure $10m of debt annually over five years – from 641bp this time a year ago.

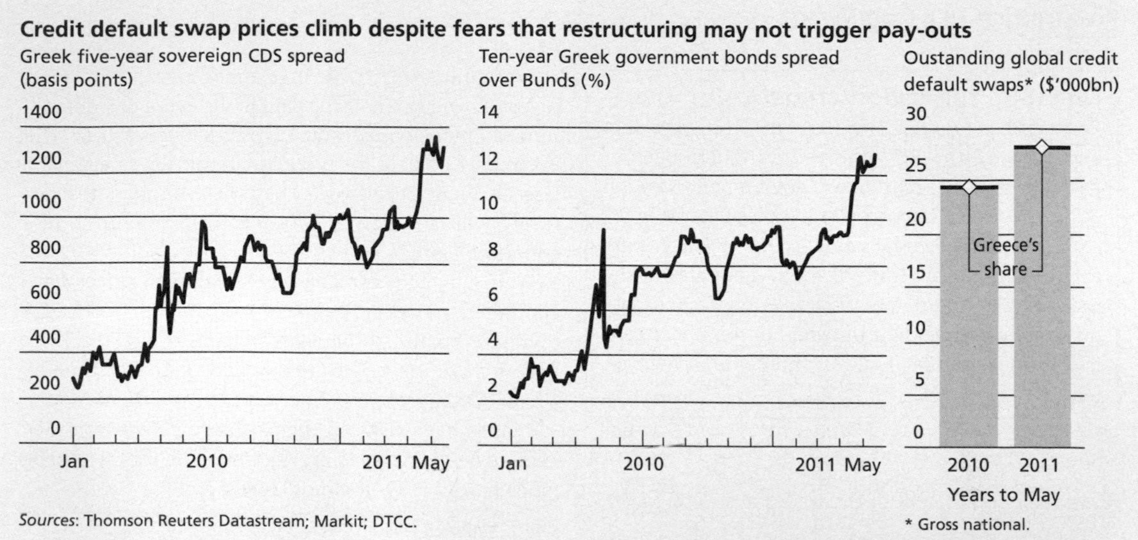

The discussion at this week's EU finance ministers' meeting, where 'reprofiling' appeared to gain traction, has worried some hedge fund managers.

'What is the point of me buying Greek CDS if I'm not going to get paid. This could kill the market, while it is still in its infancy', says the head of sovereign debt at one of Europe's biggest hedge funds.

Indeed, London law firms have been inundated with inquiries from hedge funds and banks wanting to know where they would stand in the event of a voluntary restructuring.

Gregory Venizelos and Rajeev Shah, BNP Paribas analysts, told investors last month: 'If a restructuring was to be voluntary, our CDS specialist expects that CDS would not trigger, thus invalidating such a wide spread.'

The irony over last year's fierce attacks on the CDS market by Greek prime minister George Papandreou is not lost on fund managers and bankers either.

In a series of speeches, Mr Papandreou said 'profiteering CDS derivatives' were threatening to 'blow up whole countries'. Now Greece may get its revenge, bankers say.

So, what exactly would constitute a credit event or trigger a pay-out?

For sovereigns, a credit event is defined by the International Swaps and Derivatives Association as a failure to pay a coupon interest payment or principal, a restructuring – changing the terms of an agreement – or the repudiation of or moratorium on debt.

Precedents are few and far between. Lawyers say one of the templates for a sovereign CDS pay-out occurred in Ecuador after it defaulted on one of its bonds in 2008. The ISDA was able to rule that the default was a credit event and initiate a recovery auction.

However, a Greek restructuring would be unlikely to lead to the same result.

Ultimately, the decision is in the hands of eight of the world's largest banks, four of the biggest US hedge funds and Pimco, which runs the world's largest bond fund. They are the voting members on the so-called determinations committee, which meets under the auspices of Isda and decides whether a restructuring is a credit event.

Should Greece extend debt maturities without cutting the final principal payment on a bond or imposing haircuts on investors in a voluntary bond exchange or restructuring, then the committee is likely to rule there has been no credit event

This is important because billions of euros in payouts from eurozone banks, therefore, would not be activated.

That would avoid a crisis in the European banking sector, but would leave those who bought CDS protection out of pocket. If contracts are deemed valueless, the market could wither.

Many bankers, though, believe the sovereign CDS market will survive, in spite of this risk.

They argue that the market has been reshaped by events in Greece. Most participants are now the banks exposed to possible losses on Greek debt and who want to hedge that risk, rather than the speculators fingered by politicians. The teams in the banks responsible for hedging risk to countries such as Greece are responsible

Press cutting 19.8 (*continued*)

No let-up for Lisbon on debt

Portugal has raised €1bn ($1.4bn) in its first debt auction since the EU approved its €78bn bail-out package, but the caretaker government saw no easing in its cost of borrowing, writes Peter Wise.

The IGCP, Portugal's public debt agency, paid an average interest rate of 4.657 per cent on the issue of two-month Treasury bills on Wednesday, marginally higher than the yield of 4.652 per cent it paid for a similar issue of three-month debt on May 4.

for at least 60 per cent of the trades in sovereign CDS, they say.

Voluntary restructurings, moreover, are rare. Investors will normally be paid in the event of a default. Indeed, most banks and investors expect they will eventually be paid for protecting themselves against a Greek default, because they believe a voluntary restructuring will be followed by a forced restructuring in a couple of years.

This may help explain why Greek CDS prices have continued to rise. Banks stress, too, that the Greek CDS market is small, so the repercussions of not receiving pay-outs are unlikely to resonate widely. Outstanding Greek CDS represent 0.3 per cent of the CDS market.

'Banks have risks on their balance sheets that they need to hedge or transfer. Without CDS, that would be much harder', says a senior lawyer.

Source: *Financial Times*, 19 May 2011.

PRESS CUTTING 19.9

IMF tells Greece to speed up reforms

FT

By Kerin Hope in Athens

The International Monetary Fund has warned that Greece's economic recovery programme risks being derailed unless the socialist government accelerates structural reforms.

Poul Thomsen, head of an IMF mission assessing the country's progress, said the country would not emerge from recession next year without 'stepped-up reforms'.

'The view that seems to be taking hold is that the government programme is not working', Mr Thomsen told a conference in the Greek capital on Wednesday.

'Without a determined reinvigoration of structural reforms in the coming months, I think the programme will start going off-track.'

The IMF official spoke the day after European Union leaders for the first time raised the possibility of rescheduling Greek debt repayments – but only if the country first implemented 'unpleasant' economic reforms and relaunched a stalled privatisation process.

Greece is likely to need further financial support of €60bn–€80bn ($85.6bn–$114bn) over the next two years on top of its current €110bn bail-out package.

'We are in a situation that if we do not accelerate structural reform, the deficit will get entrenched where it is now – about 10 per cent [of gross domestic product]', Mr Thomsen said.

George Papaconstantinou, finance minister, said the government was committed to meeting reform targets and was prepared to reverse its policy of preserving public sector jobs.

'We cannot move ahead without taking into consideration that, when public sector organisations shut down, shrink or are merged, there may also be dismissals', Mr Papaconstantinou said.

Source: *Financial Times*, 19 May 2011.

PRESS CUTTING 19.10

Europe to issue €5bn bail-out bond

By David Oakley

The European Union will launch a multibillion-euro bond as early as next week to raise money for the rescues of Portugal and Ireland in an important test of investor sentiment after rows over the Greek debt crisis.

Bankers say there is strong demand from European banks, pension funds and insurance companies for an expected €3bn–€5bn ten-year bond issue that is likely to price at yields of about 3.6–3.7 per cent, or 50–60 basis points over.

One investor said: 'I think there will be strong demand as this is a European bond that has the backing of the whole region, yet it offers a decent yield pick-up over Germany.'

Strategists hope a successful auction will ease tensions in the eurozone after heated arguments between European Central Bank technocrats and EU politicians over a potential restructuring of Greek debt.

ECB officials have warned that any move to delay repayments would be a dangerous distraction from Athens' economic and fiscal reform plans.

The triple A-rated bond will be the third sold by the EU as part of the rescue of Ireland and now Portugal. The first in January led to overwhelming demand for the paper from investors round the globe. The second bond issue in March was also a success.

The EU said on Thursday that it would look to sell bonds between May 23 and July 15, but it is likely to launch the first of these issues early as confidence has risen that it will attract a big order book.

Some investors said the EU may announce the banks that will be involved in selling the bonds as early as this Friday.

The bond is the first to be launched since Portugal's €78bn bail-out was agreed. A second EU bond, likely to be a five-year maturity, is expected to follow a week later.

These bonds will be issued under the auspices of the European Financial Stabilisation Mechanism, the body run by the EU commission responsible for €60bn of Europe's rescue funds.

The European Financial Stability Facility, which is headed by Klaus Regling and is overseen by eurozone governments, is then expected to follow with two bonds. The EFSF made its debut sale in January.

The EFSM and EFSF will both provide up to €26bn each to be disbursed over three years for Portugal. Further support will be made available through the International Monetary Fund for up to €26bn.

Subject to market conditions and the needs of those countries being bailed out, the EFSF plans a total of seven bond sales – including the one in January – in 2011, compared with three under the original calendar announced in December.

The EFSM plans a total of six debt sales – including the two in the first quarter – this year instead of four to five under the original schedule.

In 2012, the Luxembourg-based EFSF intends to raise as much as €13bn under the revised bail-out calendar since Portugal requested help, compared with €10bn in the original schedule.

The success of the European bond issues so far this year has contrasted with difficulties the peripheral countries have faced in raising money in the markets.

Source: *Financial Times*, 20 May 2011.

PRESS CUTTING 19.11

Watch out for tail risks hanging over Treasuries

By Gillian Tett

Three years ago, investors received a brutal lesson in why it can be risky for banks or other financial institutions to fund long-term holdings with short-term debt. But could it be time for investors to relearn that concept in relation to sovereign debt?

That is a question hovering over the $14,300bn US Treasuries market as the political fight about US fiscal policy intensifies.

In recent months, the atmosphere in the Treasuries market has been eerily calm, so much so that this week ten-year yields dropped to their lowest level this year.

That is striking, given that the Treasury technically hit the debt ceiling this week (the limit to how many bonds it can legally issue), and could even tip into a technical default in August if Congress fails to reach a deal to raise that debt ceiling by then.

But while it is reassuring to see that investors are continuing to gobble up US debt, even amid this political uncertainty, investors and politicians would do well to look also at what type of debt the US is selling today – and, more importantly, what it has sold in the past.

The issue revolves around the average maturity of the Treasuries market, or how frequently the government needs to sell new bonds to replace expiring ones.

This average maturity is now about 61 months, meaning around a ninth of the stock must be replaced each year.

By the standards of recent US history, this does not look too odd.

Since 1980, the average maturity has moved between 45 and 70 months. In 2008 it fell as low as 48 months, because the US government issued a large quantity of short-term debt to calm the financial markets.

However, when viewed with a wider lens, this US pattern looks unusual and unnerving.

In the UK, for example, the average maturity of sterling government debt is 13 years. While the UK is somewhat extreme in its duration, even in much of continental Europe the maturities are between seven and nine years.

The Treasury is keenly aware that this pattern makes the US something of an outlier, and unsurprisingly has been trying to extend the maturity profile.

It has already had some success, at least compared with 2008.

Indeed, these days T-bills – the shortest form of debt – account for less than 20 per cent of outstanding marketable debt, the lowest proportion since the 1960s.

But do not expect the Treasury to push out maturities too much further, too fast.

One problem is that US officials think it important to maintain the health of the T-bill market for overall financial stability, and thus are committed to continued hefty issuance there.

They also want to ensure that the ten-year bond market remains well supported, since this is central to the structure of US housing.

Doubts abound on whether there is even much investor appetite for ultra-long-term US debt. Although non-US investors have been buying a higher proportion of long-term debt, domestic institutions do not have the same appetite as, say, in the UK.

This creates at least two potential risks.

The most dramatic, and less likely, danger is that the short average maturity profile means the government could find it hard to keep rolling over its debt at a reasonable price – if at all – if there was ever a full-blown collapse of confidence.

The more subtle and likely problem is that the US government could also see the cost of financing the debt rise sharply if inflation surges, because it will need to roll over its debt at (rising) market rates.

The Congressional Budget Office, for example, recently projected what would happen to the US debt to gross domestic product ratio if inflation rose by 3 percentage points.

It concluded that this would fall from 72 per cent in 2012 to under 70 per cent in 2020, if bond rates remained stable (and all else remain unchanged). However, if rates rose by 2 percentage points, the debt burden rises to 76 per cent.

Inflation, in other words, will not ‘fix’ the US debt burden, or not unless the government finds a way of forcing market rates down with controls.

Right now, this does not matter. Those ten-year bond rates are still laughably low, meaning financing costs are cheap. But if sentiment ever swings violently, there could be a nasty wake-up call.

That is a sobering thought at a time when Washington is also living with a form of political ‘rollover’ risk, namely the danger that Congress keeps staving off any stable, long-term debt deal and resorting to short-term, temporary budget fixes, which like those bonds need to be continually renewed in a peculiarly hand-to-mouth way.

Source: *Financial Times*, 20 May 2011.

19.8 Optimum currency area

An optimum currency area (OCA) – also known as an optimal currency region (OCR) – is a geographical region in which it maximises economic efficiency to have the entire region share a single currency. OCA theory describes the optimal characteristics for the merger of currencies.

The development of the theory was stimulated by a paper written by Robert Mundell[7] discussing the ideas of a currency union in which states or nations replace their national monies with a single common currency.

To analyse whether joining a currency union serves its economic interests, a country needs to evaluate whether the benefits outweigh the costs. Adopting a common currency implies that the regions will henceforth have a fixed exchange rate with other members of the currency region.

Adopting a common currency implies that the two regions will henceforth have the same monetary policy. Each region loses its monetary autonomy. A monetary authority for the whole area decides upon a common interest rate for all members. It is argued that if a home country and its potential currency union partners are more economically similar or symmetric – meaning that they face symmetric shocks and few asymmetric shocks – then it is less costly for the home country to join the currency union. But benefits also need to be considered. The net benefits equal the benefits minus the costs. It is suggested that:

- As market integration rises, the efficiency benefits of a common currency increase.
- As symmetry rises, the stability costs of a common currency decrease.

So, OCA theory suggests that if market integration or symmetry increases, the net benefits of a common currency will rise. If the net benefits are negative, the home country should stay out of the union based on its economic interests. If the net benefits are positive, the home country should consider joining the union based on its economic interests.

But, of course, we know that to have a single currency, inflation rates in participant countries should be close to each other. Whilst a common monetary policy may be conducive to ensuring this, fiscal policy (government spending and taxation) often remains independent even within the currency union. This may create large divergences in inflation rates between different member countries. This was the case in the eurozone in the first decade of this century. Of course, in the eurozone, whilst member countries do have a common monetary policy, they do not have a shared fiscal policy.

Furthermore, an optimal currency area presupposes that all participants should be closely interlinked through trade, and similar in economic structures. A single currency area that consisted of two economies, one whose sole product was wheat, the other banks, would be unlikely to work. A slump in world wheat prices would hurt one badly while leaving the other relatively unaffected. Thus OCA countries are likely to be exposed to similar economic shocks and able to respond to them in a common way.

There are four oft-quoted criteria for a successful currency union area. These are:

- Labour mobility across the union. This includes the physical ability to travel across boundaries, lack of cultural barriers to free movement, which may include languages, and institutional arrangements (such as the ability to have pensions transferred throughout the region). In the eurozone labour mobility is low especially when compared with the USA.

- Capital mobility and price and wage flexibility across the region. This should enable market forces to distribute money and goods to where they are needed. Eurozone members trade heavily with each other. It is reckoned that the euro effect has increased trade by over 10 per cent within the eurozone.
- A system such as an automatic fiscal transfer mechanism to redistribute the money to sectors which have been adversely affected under the first two bullet points. This usually takes the form of tax transfers to less developed areas of a country or region. The eurozone was somewhat successful on this score up to the recent financial crisis. Since 2007–8, it has achieved less.
- Participant countries have fairly similar business cycles. Hence, booms and busts should not be much out of kilter.

While the eurozone scores well on some of the above criteria, it has lower labour mobility than the USA and has not performed well in smoothing out regional economic disturbances. And, inflation rates in member countries diverged significantly in the first decade of the new century.

If we contrast the eurozone's experience to date with that of the USA's single currency area, we see a different picture. In America's dollar area, the federal budget works well. If there is a downturn in California, Washington can provide direct help through larger assistance payments. At the same time automatic stabilisers operate. California during a downturn pays fewer taxes into the federal budget which aids the state in getting through its difficulty.

Is the eurozone an optimal currency area? Before the launch of the euro, many believed that the small group of countries at its heart – Belgium, France, Germany, Luxembourg and the Netherlands – fitted the notion. Few believed that it was true for other entrants – especially Ireland, Italy, Portugal, Spain and Greece, to say nothing of some of the more recent arrivals. The lack of geographical mobility of labour and wage flexibility hardly satisfy optimal currency area requirements. Nor does the EU's miniscule central budget of less than 2 per cent of GDP, which is far below the 25 per cent of GDP widely reckoned to be needed. (This is not a plea to increase the central budget!)

And, if we think about the need for market integration and symmetry of shocks, the financial crisis has demonstrated an absolute asymmetry with Ireland, Greece, Spain and Portugal far from being in line with Germany and the Netherlands.

19.9 Sovereign debt crises

It is not unusual that sovereign crises follow banking crises. The classic sovereign debt crisis involves a government finding itself unable to pay its debts (interest and scheduled capital repayments) as they fall due. The sovereign debt crisis reaches its peak with default.

Banking crises typically follow boom to bust routes involving:

- deregulation;
- periods of low interest rates leading to easy money;
- a rise in Keynes' animal spirits in the boom;
- an increased risk appetite in the personal, corporate and banking sectors;

- consumer business and banker overconfidence;
- the burgeoning of questionable financial practices ranging from off-balance sheet devices to granting loans to weaker and weaker borrowers to outright scams and Ponzi schemes;
- credit appraisal standards fall;
- malinvestment;
- increases in debt at personal, corporate and banking levels;
- significant increases in real housing prices;
- excessive use of short-term borrowing to finance longer term investment with rollover refinancing risk;
- so-called financial innovation;
- bubbles in parts of the economy – for example housing, equities or the like;
- low margins of safety meaning that relatively small drops in value create financial problems, especially where accompanied by high gearing;
- a shock that bursts the bubble leads to losses, recall of loans, sale of collateral and requests for government rescues by highly geared parties, including banks exposed to excessive risk;
- this leads to the inevitable bailout which causes governments to offer guarantees and pay out actual funds;
- contraction of Keynes' animal spirits in the bust;
- reduction of confidence of consumers, businesses and banks;
- debt repayment.

The reason that sovereign crises often arrive in the slipstream of financial crises is fairly well documented and its essence involves:

- the bailout increases government borrowing;
- as a consequence of the bailout, banks tighten lending, calling in some loans to weaker customers who should not, in all probability, have been advanced funds in the first place;
- lower levels of business activity follow;
- lower profit levels, and losses in many instances, accrue;
- as unemployment increases (jobs being cut at public and private levels) tax revenues fall and unemployment benefit payments increase;
- falling consumer spending and lower real estate transactions depress tax revenues further;
- an inevitable increase in government borrowing ensues;
- markets lower the standing of government debt with the corollary of increased interest cost;
- foreign exchange rate problems may ensue especially where currencies are overvalued due to a fixed exchange rate or presence in a currency union prevents devaluation.

With government debt increasing and government interest costs also rising plus an attendant fall in GNP it becomes increasingly likely that the sovereign will become less able to pay debts as they fall due.

There are key ratios for assessing government liquidity just as there for assessing corporate profitability and stability. Some of these are referred to later in Chapter 25. As Reinhart and Rogoff[8] observe, for middle income countries at the time of defaults or debt restructurings, data from 1970 and 2008 indicate that the average level of:

- external debt to GNP was 69.3 per cent with a range from 12.5 per cent to 214.3 per cent;
- external debt to exports was 229.9 per cent with a range from 73.1 per cent to 447.3 per cent.

The wide range of figures arises because maturity of debt clearly enters the equation. Mammoth debt, all due next year, presents a greater problem than a similar amount of borrowings with repayments evenly spread over the next fifteen years. At the time of writing (August 2011), numerous participants in the eurozone are exhibiting symptoms of financial frailty on the above criteria, reinforcing the probability of a finite life for the euro. Surely its epitaph awaits. EUR : RIP.

Summary

- The financial crisis of 2007/8 can be split into events up to 2007 which provided the wherewithal for the fall and the period after 2007 where events took a turn for the worse and reached disastrous economic proportions.

Up to 2007

- Expansion of credit availability with household debt reaching very high levels.
- Emergence of dangerous debt products – credit default swaps, CDOs, MBSs and others. Being on the wrong side of these products made banks more risky.
- Credit default swap bubble.
- Increasing ratios of debt in bank balance sheets making them more risky.
- Very low interest rates sometimes negative in real terms.
- Binge in high street consumption.
- Public sector spending rising fast.
- Rise in real incomes.
- Strong rise in subprime mortgage lending aided and abetted by government initiatives to win popularity and votes.
- Housing market boom reaching bubble proportions.
- Shock to the system – house prices go into reverse.

From 2007

- Subprime housing market crashes.
- Crash in CDS, CDO and MBS markets causing bank balance sheets to show financial distress and worse.

- Some banks fail. Others bailed out by governments.
- Governments throw money at their economies to prevent depression.
- Money supply loosened to ward off deflation, recession and depression.
- Unemployment increases but not on crippling scale.
- Sovereign debt downgraded. Harbingers of default loom.
- Bailouts for Greece, Ireland and Portugal with EU and IMF loans.
- In particular, the case of Greece's original entry into the eurozone was achieved by meeting the Maastricht criteria on financial ratios by means of a swap transaction in which Goldman Sachs (the investment bank) advanced cash to Greece (to help repay debt) in return for deferred income from airport fees and lottery proceeds, amongst other things – see *The New York Times*[9].
- Questions remain, as at 2011, about default possibilities in weaker eurozone countries. And there's a bigger question too. Is the eurozone past its sell-by date?

End of chapter questions

19.1 List and briefly discuss the major factors that underpinned the financial crisis of 2007–8.

19.2 Distinguish between the originate-to-hold and originate-to-distribute models of lending. Why did banks prefer to move to the latter model and what were some of the consequences?

19.3 What were the sources of problems for the weaker members of the eurozone?

6 Netting achieves all but one of the following:

(a) foreign exchange movements between subsidiaries are reduced;
(b) transactions costs are lowered;
(c) currency conversion costs are reduced;
(d) transaction exposure is reduced.

7 Which of the following statements is true about designing a good reporting system on foreign exchange exposure?

(a) Central control with virtually no input from the local level is essential.
(b) Reports should be generated by currency as well as by subsidiary.
(c) Reports should concentrate on translation exposure because this will affect earnings per share which is the key to corporate valuation.
(d) Routine reports should concentrate upon economic exposure, rather than translation or transaction exposure, because this represents the present value of future cash flows which is the key to corporate valuation.

8 On a Tuesday in January an operator contacts his financial futures broker. He wishes to speculate on the £/$ exchange rate. He sells seven March Sterling contracts at $1.7200. On the Thursday of that week he buys seven March Sterling contracts at 1.7100. Given that the tick size is 0.01 cent and the value of the tick is $2.50, what is the net of commission gain or loss achieved by the operator? Commission on the round trip is $120 per contract. In your answer ignore all aspects of interest (including interest on margin) and opportunity cost.

(a) $230 profit;
(b) $1,610 profit;
(c) $1,750 profit;
(d) we cannot say because we are not told the contract size;
(e) none of the above is correct.

9 Which of the following is true of foreign exchange markets?

(a) The futures market is mainly used by speculators while the forward market is mainly used for hedging.
(b) The futures market is mainly used by hedgers while the forward market is mainly used for speculating.
(c) The futures market and the forward market are mainly used for speculating.
(d) The futures market and the forward market are mainly used for hedging.

10 Which of the following is not a logical tactic for a US firm that will have to pay for a machine in euros in the future and desires to avoid exchange rate risk assuming the firm has no offsetting position in euros?

(a) buy a call option on euros;
(b) enter into a forward contract to buy euros;
(c) sell a futures contract on euros;
(d) buy euros now and put them on deposit to meet the payment when it falls due;
(e) none is illogical; (a), (b), (c) and (d) are all logical.

Part F

INTERNATIONAL CAPITAL BUDGETING

Analysing capital investment decisions involves comparing cash inflows with cash outflows from a project. Investment appraisal systems are frequently collectively termed capital budgeting, and this focuses upon expected incremental cash flows associated with a project. The specification of these flows for the overseas project creates the usual difficulties found in a domestic capital project, but international project analysis is much more complex. Although the basic pattern follows the same model as that suggested by corporate financial theory, the multinational firm must consider factors peculiar to international operations. These differences are very considerable and are focused upon in this section.

around the world. By 1960, the United States accounted for over 48 per cent of world FDI. Since then, we have witnessed the re-emergence of European, Japanese and Chinese multinationals.

But the great puzzle about FDI remains. Why do companies do it? As opposed to going to the trouble, risk and expense of setting up and managing manufacturing operations in a foreign country, why not export? If transport costs are prohibitive, why not license? Or sell technology and/or brands to an overseas firm which knows the territory well, and can manage and adapt to local conditions?

Any theory of FDI must address the following key questions:

- Why do firms move abroad as direct investors?
- How can direct-investing overseas firms compete successfully with local firms in the host country, given the disadvantage of operating in an unfamiliar foreign territory?
- Why do firms choose to enter a foreign country via FDI instead of exporting or licensing?

Before we move on to look at theories of the evolution of international business, we focus upon the sequential nature of the development of corporate international involvement.

20.2 The sequential process

The dynamic view of corporate internationalisation as involving a sequential process was identified by Johanson and Vahlne[1] and Luostarinen.[2] It normally moves through exporting to the setting up of a foreign sales subsidiary, to licensing agreements and similar contracts before actual investment in foreign production facilities takes place. This evolutionary approach may act as a risk-minimising process given the relative uncertainty associated with operating in a foreign environment. By internationalising in stages, the firm gradually moves from a relatively low risk, but easily reversible export-oriented policy, to a higher risk, but less reversible strategy involving production in other countries; at the same time, the profit payoff should multiply. The typical sequence of overseas expansion is depicted in Figure 20.1.

The firm with international ambitions typically makes its initial moves in this direction by exporting to a foreign market. Exporting has significant advantages over more fully fledged involvement. Capital requirements are minimal, risk is low, the decision is easily reversed and profits are immediate. Exporting provides a steep learning curve effect about the ways and business culture of the foreign country concerned. This is especially so in the areas of supply and demand conditions, competition, channels of distribution, payment

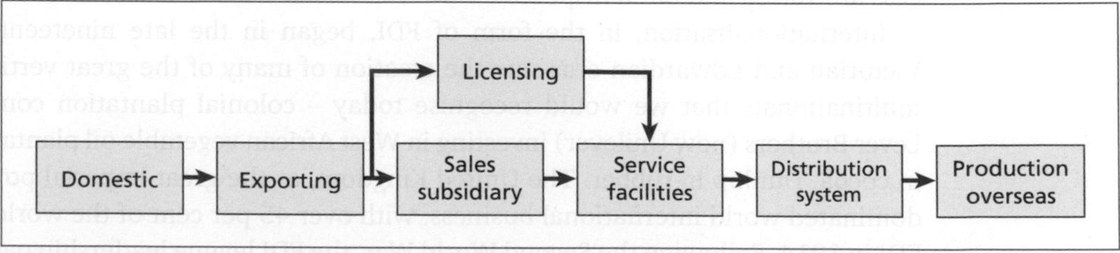

Figure 20.1 Typical foreign expansion sequence

conventions and the methods of foreign financial institutions. Building on export success, the firm may expand its marketing organisation abroad. It may switch from using export agents and similar intermediaries to dealing direct with foreign agents and distributors. As knowledge is built through increased communication with customers, the firm may establish its own sales subsidiary and service facilities. The culmination of this marketing expansion is often control of its own foreign distribution system.

As Figure 20.1 indicates, another route towards foreign expansion involves licensing as opposed to the overseas sales subsidiary. Licensing involves a local firm in the manufacture of another company's products in return for royalties and/or other forms of payment. For the home-based company, the main advantage of licensing is the minimal investment required. However, the corresponding cash flow may also be relatively low. There are sometimes problems in maintaining quality standards and it may be difficult to control exports by a foreign licensee. Indeed, a licensing agreement may create a competitor in some markets, with a resultant loss of future revenues to the licensing firm. Despite the risks, it appears very frequently that licensing, on its own, is the preferred method of penetrating foreign markets.

Some firms follow a policy of selling technology for equity in foreign joint ventures plus royalty payments. This kind of route towards internationalisation is really somewhere between licensing and developing overseas production facilities on one's own. It often results in a network of associate companies around the world. Other firms evolve to become fully fledged multinationals with production facilities overseas without passing through the licensing (or quasi-licensing), phase – hence, the mode of evolution summarised in Figure 20.1.

One of the disadvantages with both exporting and licensing is their inability to realise the full potential of a product in a foreign market. And licensing may create a significant competitor in some markets unless carefully controlled. Setting up a firm's own production facility overseas overcomes these drawbacks and enables the firm to keep up to date with local market developments and adapt its products and production and marketing methods to meet changing local tastes and conditions while also providing better after-sales service. At the same time, establishing local production facilities demonstrates a greater commitment to the local market and an increased assurance of supply stability. This is important for firms that produce intermediate goods for sale to other companies, rather than for the end-user. Tied in to the firm's decision to produce abroad is the question of whether to create its own subsidiaries and associates organically or to acquire going concerns. An advantage of the acquisitive route is the greater capacity to effect a speedy transfer overseas of parent skills, such as innovative production technology. And, the inorganically acquired local firm may provide ready-made marketing networks. This could be important if the parent is a late entrant to the market. Many firms use the acquisition route to gain knowledge about the local market or about a particular technology. The disincentive to use of this route is, of course, the cost of the acquisition.

The incremental model set out in Figure 20.1 owes a useful pedagogic approach to internationalisation and is undergoing continuous empirical investigation. It has a number of shortcomings. The dynamics of progress from one stage to another are not necessarily fully understood. The model is unidirectional and, as such, does not explain divestment or strategic reorientation. Also, the sequential nature of the process does not allow for the leapfrogging of stages, which has, in fact, been observed by Welch and Luostarinen.[3] The model has also been criticised for representing a process of great complexity in too simple a format. And the unidirectional orientation of the model assumes, or at least suggests, a cause and effect relationship that may be less than justified. The complexity of the process, plus the possibility of feedback loops representing reorientations, aggravates the neat ordering of the variables. Clearly, empirical testing in the area is difficult. In short, the model is by no means proven. Export seems, certainly, to be first step in the process of internationalisation. Like many of our models in the social sciences, the sequential route to full FDI illustrated in Figure 20.1 is not an immutable picture of a complex process. Nonetheless, it should not be given short shrift; it deserves healthy respect – and also a certain amount of suspicion. Augmented by the possibilities of leapfrogging, reversal, re-orientation (such as by moving to a strategic alliance, for example) and, indeed, withdrawal would enhance the model.

We would guess that there is a process of real option at work in which the multinational advances sequentially with the awareness that each step is an option which can be retracted if it proves unsuccessful or it can be capitalised upon with further advances if success occurs. In this sense, the cost of an advance forward is rather like an option premium which may be lost if success does not follow or provide a positive payoff if successful. Of course, this logic can be applied to many other investments. And, given this angle on the sequential approach, retraction has a clear place in the model, as it does in most investments. We briefly look at the ideas surrounding real options in Chapter 23.

Certainly empirical work underpins the deductive hypothesis that the initial move towards internationalisation is via the export route, and internationalisation as a process follows an incremental or sequential route. This may be seen as a learning process – an attempt to overcome the problems of information, language, culture, education, business practice and legislation, that constitute, for many organisations, a 'psychic distance' from strange foreign markets. Incremental development provides the cautious route that tends to overcome any lack of experience, knowledge or market information that would otherwise create strong barriers to international development.

We now turn to the next of our key theories of multinational strategy – it is the market imperfections approach.

20.3 Market imperfections

The most important idea in developing theories of FDI is that firms engaging in international production are at a disadvantage compared with local firms. This is generally assumed to be so because of their unfamiliarity with local market conditions. The operation of a subsidiary in a foreign market probably requires a greater commitment of time, attention and control compared with operating a subsidiary in the home market. Additional costs are incurred in terms, for example of communication, administration and transportation. For FDI to be successful, multinationals must, therefore, possess certain advantages not available to existing or potential local competitors.

The conditions required for multinationals to compete successfully with local firms in host country environments are discussed by Hymer.[4] He observes that foreign firms must possess advantages over local firms to make such investment viable and, usually, the market for the sale of the product or service is imperfect. FDI is motivated by market imperfections which permit the multinational to exploit its monopolistic advantages in foreign markets.

This view is elaborated further by Kindleberger,[5] who suggests that market imperfections offer multinationals compensating advantages of a magnitude that exceeds the disadvantages due to their lack of origins within a host environment, and it is the financial effects of this that underpin FDI. Again, FDI is a direct outcome of imperfect markets.

Market imperfections may arise in one or more of several areas – for example, product differentiation, marketing skills, proprietary technology, managerial skills, better access to capital, economies of scale and government-imposed market distortions, to name but a few. Such advantages give multinationals an edge over their competitors in foreign locations and thus serve to compensate for the additional costs of operating at a distance.

The suggestion, therefore, is that FDI may take place once the multinational has secured internally transferable advantages. These enable it to overcome its lack of knowledge of local conditions in host environments and to compete with local firms successfully. Market imperfections, created by the existence of an oligopolistic advantage for the multinational, may become a driving force for FDI.

Multinational firms are typically oligopolists. Virtually all multinationals enjoy considerable market power. The market in which they operate is usually one of international oligopoly with shades of monopolistic competition. Maybe this is because of the sizeable set-up costs involved in establishing an overseas plant. Only large firms may be willing to incur this entry cost. In a UK study, Dunning[6] identified oligopoly as a distinguishing feature of markets in which multinationals operate, confirming many other investigators' findings.

Establishing overseas subsidiaries is not compatible with perfect competition. In a perfectly competitive industry there are many small firms enjoying common access to knowledge and earning normal returns. Oligopoly power provides an insight as to why certain firms establish cross-border plants. Entry barriers are critical in maintaining high profits. As these are eroded in the domestic market, the firm may find it expedient and profitable to set up plants overseas. Of course, the firm need not be under pressure of eroding margins in the home market to stimulate scanning the world environment to seek to replicate its domestic market imperfections overseas. This may be a natural part of corporate strategy. It is merely an observation that expected adverse trends in home profits, owing to increased competition from rivals, may goad a firm into analysing its options elsewhere in the world carefully – something it is less likely to do under tranquil competitive conditions.

Logically, the question that follows concerns the whereabouts of any planned overseas plant. Considerations of locational efficiency concern market demand and comparative production and distribution costs; these obviously help to explain where production occurs. But they may not be the only factors at work. The multinational must have some firm-specific advantage – the source of market imperfection – giving it an edge over would-be indigenous producers. Michalet and Chevalier[7] cite over 30 reasons given by French multinationals for setting up overseas plants. Prominent were the importance of access to a particular market, the desire to spread risks, and adverse trends in the home market, although there seemed to be no single overriding factor at work. However, most of those cited related to some form of market imperfection.

Giddy[8] neatly summarised the situation saying that 'the maintenance of an oligopoly depends on the existence of barriers to competitive entry'. Hence, if domestic oligopolists are to become global ones, the sources of their domestic advantage must be transferable abroad. In addition, these advantages must be monopolistically held, for without such market imperfections foreign direct investment would be unlikely to occur. National firms would be better placed to meet the market need. The incentive for foreign investment is based, in part, on the advantages of internalising markets across national boundaries. So, what exactly do we mean by internalising?

Market imperfections arise from imperfect competition or imperfect information. If the supplier of a critical factor input to a firm's production process has some monopoly power, then the supplied firm may be faced with the possibility of having to pay a higher price for the input than it would under conditions of perfect competition. In such circumstances, it may pay the firm to internalise supply by buying up the supply source. This is sometimes termed 'integration backwards'. It simply makes the supplying firm part of the buying firm's production process. If the firm supplying the internalised goods or services happens to be located in another country, then the firm that undertakes the internalisation automatically moves along the path towards becoming a multinational business.

Multinationals obviously have intangible capital in the form of trade marks, patents, general marketing know-how and other organisational skills. These create market imperfections too. But it may be argued that local firms have an inherent cost advantage over foreign investors. After all, the multinational must bear the costs of operating in an unfamiliar environment. The multinational can, theoretically, only succeed abroad if its monopolistic advantages cannot be purchased or duplicated by local competitors. Of course, in the fullness of time, all barriers to entry erode. Then, the multinational firm must find new sources of competitive advantage. To survive as a multinational enterprise, the firm must create and preserve effective barriers to direct competition in product and factor markets worldwide.

Let us return to the pioneering work of Hymer,[9] in terms of explaining the application of market imperfections to FDI. He suggested that the decision of a multinational to invest in an overseas market can only be explained if the company has, and can utilise, certain advantages not possessed by its local competitors. These advantages may derive from skills in management, marketing, production, finance or technology. They may refer to preferential access to raw materials or other inputs. Whatever the source, the market for the sale of these advantages must be imperfect. Kindleberger[10] went further when he suggested that market imperfections are the reason for FDI.

Another requirement is that the specific advantages possessed by the multinational must be easily transferable within the firm, often over long distances. The facts that such firm-specific advantages exist, are transferable, and cannot easily be marketed, is not a sufficient explanation for the firm's decision to locate manufacturing facilities overseas. It might, alternatively, produce at home and export, or license production to an overseas partner. Other location-specific advantages – for example, input prices, transport and communication availability and costs, existence of trade barriers, sophistication of infrastructure – are said to be required in order to evolve necessary and sufficient conditions for the decision to locate production in foreign countries. Most theories of FDI flow from this premise.

Many of the insights into the role of market imperfections in impelling foreign direct investment derive from the work of Hymer. In pursuing foreign direct investment, it would seem that an organisation must possess a specific advantage to such an extent that this outweighs its fear, in terms of language, culture, physical distance and so on, of doing business in an environment where local practices are different from the home market. The argument goes that this advantage must be sufficient to offset the presumed potential of competition from locally situated organisations in order for foreign investment to occur. Such specific advantages may reside in barriers to entry. The most powerful source of specific advantage is product differentiation through, for example, a patented product or via production technology or marketing investment in branding, styling, distribution and/or service. But other sources are significant in creating competitive advantage – for example, economies of scale, access to capital and raw materials, integration backwards or forwards, skills such as managerial know-how, research and development and so on.

Market imperfections may be created in a number of ways:

- Internal or external economies of scale often exist, possibly because of privileged access to raw materials or to final markets, possibly from the exploitation of firm-specific knowledge assets, possibly from increases in physical production. The oligopolies which may result do not react as would firms in perfectly competitive markets. Knickerbocker[11] has shown that oligopolistic competitors tend to follow one another into individual foreign markets – behaviour that may not always be justified by pure profit potential.
- Effective differentiation – not only to products and processes but also to marketing and organisational skills – may create substantial imperfections.
- Government policies have an impact on fiscal and monetary matters, on trade barriers and so on. Multinationals are often able to borrow at lower rates than indigenous firms. Due to their stronger credit ratings, multinationals may often borrow funds in international markets at favourable rates when host government policies make domestic capital expensive or unavailable for indigenous firms. And multinationals are able to build efficient portfolios of FDI – thus reducing the risk involved in any one host's intervention. This may not be available to more regional competitors.

Market imperfections enable firms to use the power of their specific advantage to close markets and obtain superior rents on their activities. To quote Hymer, multinationals are propelled for monopolistic reasons 'to separate markets and prevent competition between units'. Clearly, if markets were open and efficient, organisations would not be able to sustain monopolistic advantages and, perhaps, the amount of FDI would be less.

Essentially, then, theories of international investment, based on the existence of market imperfections, suggest that foreign investment is undertaken by those firms that enjoy some monopolistic or oligopolistic advantage. This is because, under perfect market conditions, foreign firms would be non-competitive due to the cost of operating from a distance, both geographically and culturally. Presumably, the firm that invests abroad has some unique advantage, whether it be in terms of product differentiation, marketing or managerial skills, proprietary technology, favourable access to finance or other critical inputs. Oligopoly theory may also explain the phenomenon of defensive investment, which may occur in concentrated industries to prevent competitors from gaining or enlarging advantages that could then be exploited globally – see McClain.[12]

The more modern ideas expounded by Porter[13] on strategic management, which emphasise the role of building generic strategies on sustainable competitive advantages behind entry barriers, can be traced, partially, to Hymer's work, which in turn has been substantially influenced by Bain[14] and, further back, by Coase.[15]

It may be worth mentioning, in passing, that organisations operating in oligopoly but with a relatively undifferentiated product, for example, timber, tend to be involved in vertical-type foreign investments, while oligopolists with differentiated products are more generally involved in horizontal-type FDI.

There are other important insights of Hymer's work. He tells us that 'profits in one country may be negatively correlated with profits of another . . . an investor may be able to achieve greater stability in his profitability by diversifying his portfolio and investing part in each country'. Hymer recognised diversification as a motivating force in international investment, enabling risk to be spread in the portfolio of an individual or a corporation. The point is of particular importance where costs of carrying out the transactions internationally for individuals are greater than those for organisations. In strategic management terminology, companies balance their portfolios of strategic business units internationally so as to reduce the risk component of their returns by investing in economies at different stages of the business cycle, ultimately to prevent overexposure to recessions in individual economies. Given that Hymer's contribution was published in 1960, before the advent of the capital asset pricing model with its relatively similar focus, his insight is remarkable and significant.

At this point it is worth referring to another theory of the multinational which is based on diversification in order to smooth earnings. Products are diversified geographically and income is thereby earned in a variety of different currencies. As a result of constraints which may exist in capital markets through exchange controls, a company may undertake international diversification that cannot be replicated by shareholders. Whether the multinational achieves superior results through this policy is an empirical question but there is some weak evidence that it may – see Rugman.[16] Multinationals' policies of diversification by product and by region in their attempt to stabilise earnings look reasonable in this light.

Hymer might also have been influential in another direction. His comparison of multinational business strategy as 'contractual collusion' among oligopolists may, partially, have steered host governments to increase regulation and to perceive multinationals as creaming profits, a view which was prevalent in the 1960s and 1970s. The opinion was then rife that the multinational was a huge, terrifying, ruthless, stateless organisation capable of exploiting the poor, manipulating governments and flouting popular opinion. Vernon[17] observed that 'the multinational enterprise has come to be seen as the embodiment of almost anything disconcerting about modern industrial society'.

Nowadays it is only a slight exaggeration to say that the multinational is seen as the reverse – the embodiment of modernity, the prospect of wealth, full of technology, rich in capital, replete with skilled jobs. Governments around the world, and particularly in developing countries, are queuing up to attract multinationals.

Hymer's significant contribution to our understanding of multinational strategy failed, though, to address the geographic and spatial dimensions of internationalisation. It went some way to explaining why FDI occurs, but not where.

Moreover, Hymer's insights do not extend to the question of why FDI is the chosen route towards internationalisation. Why not licensing? To some extent the answer advanced turns around transaction costs (examined in more detail in the next section). What do we mean by this? Essentially, it is concerned with the costs of doing transactions in a particular way. Take a general example. We have seen that it is the possession of a specific advantage that enables international organisations to overcome the home advantage of local firms and thereby, partially, influences them to enter foreign markets. If the specific advantage is knowledge-based, for example if it is related to research and development, there is an obvious problem, namely retaining control of this intangible asset. Might an unscrupulous licensee steal it and exploit the advantage itself? How does the organisation provide sufficient information on such an asset without revealing its critical formula for success? The predicament is resolved if the organisation continues to exploit the underlying asset itself by retaining control over it. As Hennart[18] argues, in these circumstances FDI can be expected to be more frequent among technologically intensive companies, intent on sheltering trade secrets.

These considerations also impinge upon our views relating to internalisation. In circumstances where there is an exchange relationship, matters would be easy if all parties to a transaction were honest, reliable, fair, would abide by their word, and did business 'our way'. In reality, this is hardly immutably the case. Thus costs are incurred to minimise risks on these fronts whenever business is done with third parties. The intent is to reduce uncertainty. Will a monopoly supplier of raw materials hike the price? Can a supplier be depended upon to move heaven and earth to get the goods to us? These transaction costs can be minimised through internalisation – getting processes done within the group rather than by third parties, or external agents. These ideas about internalisation may help organisations select between different routes when it comes to expansion overseas – the choice between exporting, licensing and FDI. The decision between licensing and FDI may depend on such factors as the risk of knowledge dissipation, enforcement costs, the state of proprietary technology, probabilities of substitute products and so on. If there is a low risk of dissipation, licensing may be preferred over FDI, all other things being equal.

The choice between exports and FDI may be influenced by expectations of changes in tariff and non-tariff barriers. If tariff barriers are low, exports may be preferred over licensing and FDI. And it may make sense for the organisation to substitute internal markets (FDI) for licensing or for export, if exporting is ruled out on the grounds of transportation and/or tariff factors and if licensing is unattractive because of knowledge dissipation possibilities.

This approach has its critics. They tend to focus on whether internalisation is a general and predictive theory. Buckley[19] suggests that it is a 'concept in search of a theory'. He contends that it is tautological inasmuch as firms automatically internalise imperfect markets until the cost of so doing outweighs any benefits. Casson[20] states that 'internalization is, in fact, a general theory of why firms exist'. And Kay[21] observes that 'internalization does not satisfy the condition of refutability that is required for theory'. In defence of internalisation as an approach, rather than as a theory, Rugman[22] argues in its favour because of its potentially explanatory power as to when organisations internalise markets or otherwise. This, he claims, is a big contribution to our insights and understandings of FDI. So, let us look a little more closely at the ideas surrounding internalisation. But before we do, an overview of a closely related theory – that of transaction costs – is presented.

20.4 Transaction cost theory

Most theories of multinational enterprise attempt to identify and explain the conditions conducive to the multinational firm's existence. They seek to answer the question as to why the international organisation of economic activity within a multinational firm might be preferred to a network of arm's-length contractual arrangements with third parties.

Coase[23] argues from the starting point that the firm carries on various activities to achieve the end result of profitable production of goods and services. These activities, encompassing, for example, marketing and research and development, are related through flows of intermediate products – mostly, according to Buckley and Casson,[24] in the form of knowledge and expertise. Because of imperfections in intermediate product markets, there will be an incentive to bypass them and create internal markets. Activities that were previously linked by the market mechanism are brought under common ownership and control in a market (if market is the right word) internal to the firm. As Buckley and Casson observe, where markets are internalised in this way across international boundaries, multinational firms are created.

According to transaction cost theory, as conceived by Coase and further developed by McManus,[25] Williamson[26] and Teece,[27] the firm (termed the 'hierarchy' in their theories) and the market are alternative methods of organising exchange. The choice between intrafirm and arm's-length market exchange with third parties is based upon relative costs. Coase's view is that the main reason for a firm to exist as a hierarchy of interrelated transactions is that it is more costly for the market to handle a transaction. The firm may therefore bypass the regular market and use internal prices to overcome the excessive transaction costs of an outside market. Coase goes on to suggest that, given transaction costs, firms will tend to expand until the marginal cost of organising an extra transaction within the firm becomes equal to the marginal cost of carrying out the same transaction by means of an exchange in the open market.

In perfect markets – that is, by definition, with zero transaction costs – prices convey information about the consequences of actions and provide agents with the information necessary to reach optimal decisions. The large number of buyers and sellers makes prices exogenous and eliminates incentives for bargaining. Thus, market outcomes tend to be efficient when competition is strong. Competitive pressures drive parties to perform effectively at low cost and to deal with others fairly and honestly. Consequently, the firm will not internalise whenever the supplier market is competitive.

Of course, in the real world, markets are seldom perfectly competitive. Thus transaction costs are positive. When the number of potential buyers and/or sellers falls, prices are no longer exogenous and bargaining becomes possible. Consequently, given imperfect markets, internalisation is likely to have compelling efficiency properties.

To undertake a market transaction, it is necessary to research who to deal with and on what terms. It is also necessary to consider competing deals, to conduct negotiations leading up to the bargain, to draw up a contract and to undertake the inspection necessary to ensure that the terms of the contract are being observed. Market exchanges of information will therefore be costly relative to intrafirm exchange. In many circumstances, therefore, firms are efficient alternatives to markets. The most important efficiency property of the multinational arises from an organisational mode that is capable of transforming knowledge abroad in a relatively efficient fashion. As Teece observes, it is less costly to monitor activities and enforce proprietary rights over information within an internal organisational hierarchy than it is to enforce such rights in contractual market relationships with third parties. In short, the choice of arm's length and open market exchanges depends upon relative transaction costs.

20.5 Internalisation and firm-specific advantages

Internalisation theory and transaction cost theory are closely related. Internalization theory suggests that a firm internalises a transaction whenever the cost of using markets or contractual agreements is higher than that of organising it internally. Applied to multinationals, the suggestion is that international markets may be difficult to organise, monitor and control. Multinationals will tend to develop and use their own internal organisational hierarchy whenever intrafirm transactions are less costly than market transactions. The internal market within the firm therefore substitutes for the external market.

Perhaps we now have the wherewithal to answer the key question. Why go to all the lengths of FDI when exporting, licensing or selling technology and/or brands can be less risky and promise very fair returns? As mentioned earlier in this chapter, Pilkington pursued this route with float glass and General Foods followed it in exploiting the Birds Eye frozen food brand. Coase[28] gave us a hypothesis which he originally applied to the multiplant indigenous firm, but which may be applied equally to multinational activity. He suggested that the external market mechanism inflicts high transaction costs in areas such as defining and accepting contractual obligations, fixing the contract price, taxes to be paid on market transactions, and so on. He argued that these activities might be internalised by the firm wherever this is more effective in cost terms than using the external market mechanism. Obviously, internalisation is as much a feature of a multiplant domestic firm as of a multinational.

Buckley and Casson[29] developed this into an explanation of multinational activity, arguing the influence of market imperfections as a causative factor leading to internalisation. They emphasised the importance of imperfections in intermediate product markets, particularly those of patented technical knowledge and human capital. Such imperfections provide an incentive for the firm to internalise, for example, the knowledge market. The incentive to internalise depends upon the four key groups of factors:

- industry-specific factors, for example, economies of scale, external market structure, and so on;
- region-specific factors, for example, geographical distance and cultural differences;
- nation-specific factors, for example, political and fiscal conditions;
- firm-specific factors, for example, management expertise and technical know-how.

The multinational may realise valuable cost savings via the process of internalisation. According to Giddy,[30] such economies may arise through bypassing any of the following:

- concentrated markets for raw materials and arm's-length supply which may be both expensive and risky;
- imperfect markets for the firm's resources, for example as created by brand names;
- imperfect markets for outputs due to monopolistic control over distribution channels – a significant factor in many small countries;
- imperfect markets for product resources, perhaps because of government-imposed barriers to entry, such as tariffs.

Of course, internalising markets through FDI also imposes further costs, for example:

- additional communication costs which will vary with geographical and cultural distance;
- the cost of operating in an unfamiliar environment;
- the cost of overcoming political and social preferences for domestically owned firms;
- the administrative cost of managing an internal market.

The significance of the work of Buckley and Casson, and others who have developed the internalisation approach, is that it extends and deepens the market imperfections analysis by focusing upon intermediate product markets rather than on final product markets.

Effectively, their key hypothesis is that when the costs of internalisation are outweighed by the benefits, FDI aimed at harvesting this potential may follow. Magee,[31] writing on the theory of FDI, closely echoes the views of Buckley and Casson, and Hymer too. For example, he claims that 'Many of the reasons for choosing not to license arose from the imperfect nature of the market for the advantage. These imperfections prevented the appropriation of all the returns to the advantage.'

Perhaps internalisation provides answers to some aspects of the FDI puzzle. Rugman[32] points out that firms may prefer to co-ordinate their international transactions by hierarchy because of the specific problems of overseas trade. A lack of legal and managerial control, with associated uncertainty about the flow of goods and services, together with possible distortions and problems created by tariffs and customs delays, make international markets much less efficient and predictable than domestic ones. Teece[33] argues that research and development and branded assets are particularly difficult to trade internationally, being especially hard to value. He suggests, therefore, that knowledge-intensive industries are particularly likely to set up their own operations overseas and he actually finds that the extent of multinational operations by US corporations is positively correlated with the importance of advertising and research and development expenditures – although there may be a spurious correlation here deriving from size.

From the internalisation point of view, multinationals are merely searchers after efficiency, ready to substitute hierarchies for markets (and, possibly, vice versa too) as the balance of transaction costs changes. The internalisation argument does not assume a precise, risk-adjusted analysis of markets against hierarchies – in practice, such an analysis would be difficult and complex, if not impossible. The assumption is that the competitive forces of the market will normally render extinct, rather like evolution, those multinationals which do not get the balance right. This line of argument is suggested by Hennart.[34]

20.6 Location-specific advantages

Hood and Young[35] advance four factors that are relevant to the location-specific theory of FDI, which involves the multinational in seeking locations such that the differences between benefits and costs are maximised. Their four key factors are follows:

- *Labour costs*. Real wage costs vary, not only between developing and industrialised countries, but also within these groupings. Thus low-technology international industries may logically locate in low-wage economies. A similar movement is observed in other industries as technology becomes standardised.
- *Marketing factors*. FDI decisions may be affected by host-country characteristics such as market size, market growth, stage of development and the presence of local competition.
- *Trade barriers*. Such impositions are used by many host countries trying to encourage inward investment. Often multinationals set up local production facilities to protect an already developed export market when trade barriers are erected or mooted.
- *Government policy*. This may have a significant effect on the investment climate in a particular host country, either directly through fiscal investives, monetary policies or the regulatory regime, or indirectly through the prevailing social environment.

Hood and Young's analysis is mainly couched in terms of cost advantages. Work by Ronstadt[36] and Lall[37] into the location of international R&D facilities has indicated that non-price benefits may arise from foreign dispersal of research and development.

20.7 The product life cycle

One of the theories advanced to explain foreign direct investment is associated with product life cycle ideas. It is based on the concept that most products go through a number of clearly defined stages from birth to eventual old age. Much of the work in this area has been developed by Vernon[38] and modified by Wells.[39] The essence of Vernon's ideas is presented first, then the ideas are looked at in more detail. Vernon's early work[40] suggested that research and development of new products are undertaken in the most advanced countries whose population has sufficient income to demand the new product. Once developed, the product is introduced to the home market. As demand increases, it enters the growth stage in which the product is improved, standardised and economies of scale gained. As production increases, new export markets are opened. The success of exports may encourage firms in host countries to enter the market. This tends to result in the firm from the advanced country considering the setting up of local production facilities to maintain its advantage. The motive for foreign direct investment at this stage is defensive. The product eventually moves into the maturity stage when growth levels off. Competition from new products occurs, competition for market share heightens and margins are squeezed. Price competition may be so severe that the labour-intensive stages of production are actually undertaken, via foreign direct investment, in less-developed countries where labour is cheap. The multinational's decision to invest abroad depends on both the desire to protect and prolong an innovation lead and on relative labour and transportation costs, economies of scale, currency changes and legal/tax factors. Competitive multinationals do not wait for the product cycle to run its course; instead they have learnt to anticipate and accelerate it. Figure 20.2 summarises the typical product life cycle according to this view of the world of multinational business.

The product life cycle theory is based on four key assumptions, which set it apart from traditional trade theory. These are summarised below:

- Tastes differ in different countries.
- The production process is characterised by economies of scale.
- Information flows across national borders are restricted.
- Products undergo changes in their production techniques and marketing characteristics over time. The pattern of these changes is largely predictable.

The above represents merely a summary of some of the main aspects of the theory. It certainly deserves more detailed consideration and this now follows. According to product life cycle theory, the stimulus to innovation in the development of new products or processes is typically provided by a perceived opportunity or threat in the firm's major, generally the home, market. This market provides both the source of stimulus for the innovation and the preferred location for the product development. Various reasons account for this. The expense of research and development precludes duplication in numerous locations. Such

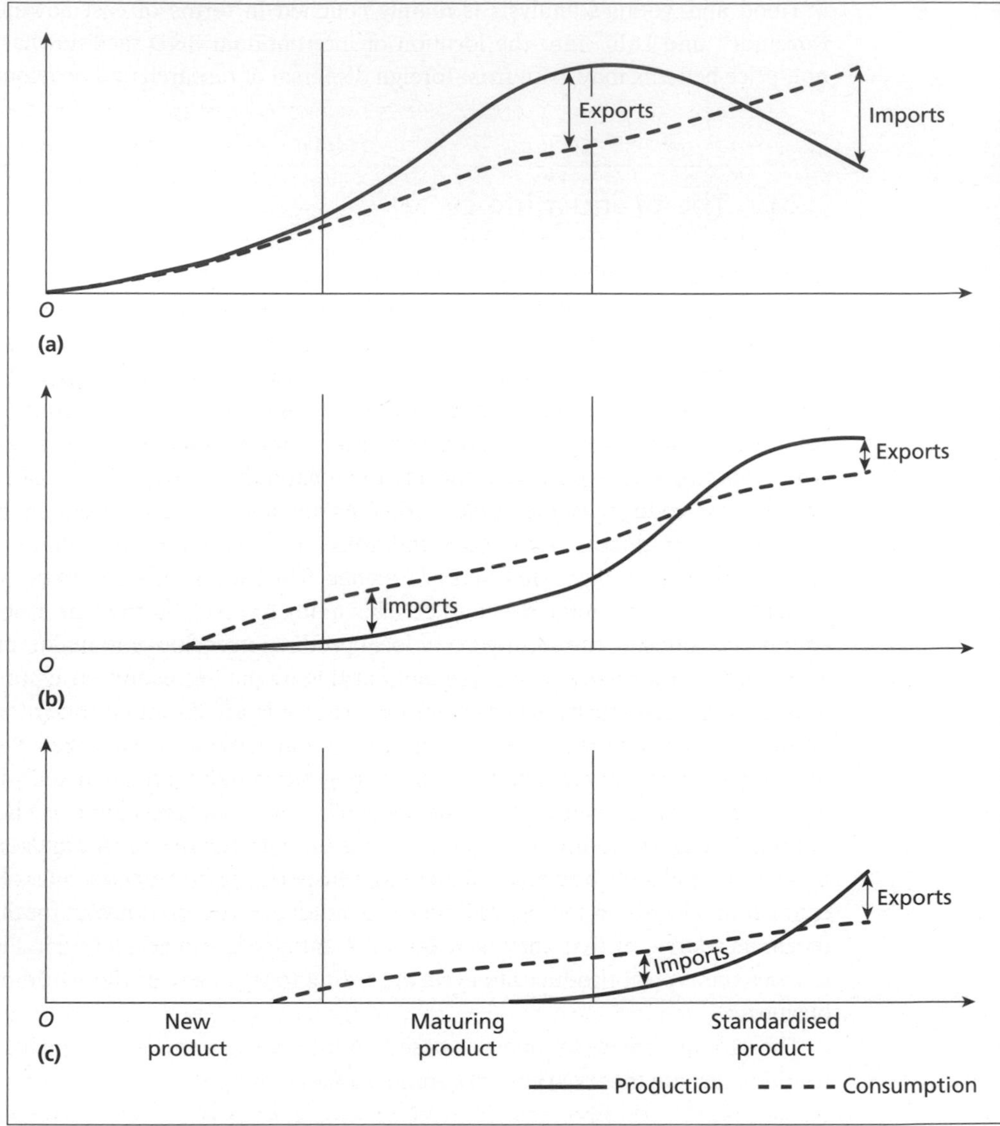

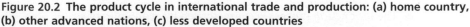

Figure 20.2 The product cycle in international trade and production: (a) home country, (b) other advanced nations, (c) less developed countries

activities are generally centralised near to the organisation's headquarters owing to their long-run strategic importance and to the necessity of keeping major breakthroughs in-house. There are other benefits to be gained by central location of R&D activities. These include maintenance of close links and communications among scientists and engineers and tight co-ordination between R&D activities and such functions as planning, production, marketing and finance. It is necessary to keep close to prospective customers and to monitor competitive developments. The nature of product development also influences the decision to begin production first in the home market. Vernon suggests that the transitions from development project to pilot plant to first commercial production are generally incremental in nature – they are bolted on. Specifications are frequently changed until the proper process and designs are established before the prototype for volume production is prepared. If this view is correct, close physical proximity between R&D and production is beneficial.

One corollary from conducting R&D within the home territory may be, as Vernon suggests, that innovations tend to reflect the characteristics of the home market. Perhaps this is why US firms have tended to develop and manufacture products that are both labour-saving and respond to relatively high-income needs. This line of argument would tend to suggest, as is possibly the case, that European firms would develop and manufacture products that are raw material-saving and labour-saving. And Japanese and European firms might take the lead in energy-saving innovations.

Product life cycle theory in international business recognises four phases. During the first of these, the innovating firm produces and markets solely in the home market. On commercial introduction, costs and prices tend to be high. If the product is sufficiently differentiated from other existing products, the innovating firm may benefit from monopolistic advantages with initial buyers relatively insensitive to price. If the product succeeds, there is a rapid expansion of the market, eventually providing increasing economies of scale, lower unit costs and possibly a further expansion of the market. Such success encourages the entry of competitors, especially as production becomes more standardised. Eventually the home market will tend to become saturated and profits will decline. Phase two is then looming.

In phase two, bigger markets and greater economies may be available through exporting. An underpinning assumption is that there is an imperfect market for knowledge and technology and that the original advantage held by the innovator in the home market may be applied abroad. Firms in the United States have typically sought markets in Canada and Europe first of all. These markets are frequently large enough to be attractive, and the demand patterns of many industrialised countries are relatively similar; this avoids the requirement to adapt the product substantially for the foreign market. Success in exporting prolongs the life of the product. In time, competition emerges from domestic firms in the targeted export market. At first it tends to be weak owing to the normal start-up problems and to the lack of economies of scale. But eventually this new competition tends to strengthen sufficiently to pose a real threat, given its lesser transport costs and nil import tariff. Phase three is at hand.

Phase three is typified by overseas producers gaining a substantial market share by honing their production techniques and by gaining economies of scale sufficient to cause a challenge to the original exporter, who incurs the added costs of transportation, tariffs and communication. Cultural distance may also become a factor for exporting firms less familiar with the market. Foreign governments often undertake protectionist actions to facilitate development and/or to enhance the competitiveness of local producers. In phase three, these factors become serious; they adversely affect exports. The exporting firm starts to consider shifting its strategy towards the location of production facilities abroad in the market that has heretofore been served by exports. This seemed to be the pattern applicable to the two decades following the Second World War, but its relevance now seems much less pronounced.

For very labour-intensive products for which mass manufacturing technologies are feasible, a fourth stage in the life cycle is apparent. This final phase involves the original innovating firm ceasing production in parts of the world with high labour costs. In this phase, the home market is serviced through imports from foreign subsidiaries located in low-wage countries abroad. These production locations will tend to be in rapidly developing countries, such as the currently emerging dragons of the Koreas, China, Vietnam, the Philippines, Indonesia, India and Thailand – where low labour costs are combined with sufficient infrastructure and potentially high productivity levels.

A modified version of the original product life cycle model was advanced by Vernon[41] in which he categorised multinationals within various stages of the development cycle. He distinguished three types of multinational oligopoly as follows:

- *Innovation-based oligopolies*. These firms create barriers to entry through continuous introduction of new products and aggressive differentiation of existing ones, both at home and abroad. Such firms tend to have a high ratio of R&D expenditure to sales and a low ratio of direct employees to sales. Firms in this category behave very much in accordance with product life cycle theory. However, the most aggressive of these firms are observed to exploit foreign markets without waiting for the product life cycle to run its course.
- *Mature oligopolies*. These firms tend to share markets in the traditional oligopolistic way long after their products have become standardised, through the maintenance of entry barriers via experience curve effects and economies of scale in marketing, production and/or transportation. These oligopolies may rely on high fixed costs as a barrier to entry, and adopt stabilising strategies including:

  (i) follow-the-leader behaviour in entering new countries or product lines;
  (ii) pricing conventions;
  (iii) mutual alliances, including joint subsidiaries and joint contracts.
- *Senescent oligopolies*. These tend to occur when existing barriers to entry erode. Multinationals either drop out of the particular market to concentrate on newer products or move production to low-cost locations.

The product life cycle theory is not fully accepted by economists. Some see it as a concept that has outgrown its usefulness. Amusingly, Giddy[42] feels that the theory has experienced growth, maturity and decline as a concept in explaining international investment patterns. He points to some of the shortcomings of the model, as follows:

- It is unable to predict correctly international patterns in many manufactured goods – for example, new products including digital watches and disposable razors, and mature products such as processed foods and toiletries.
- Raw materials trade cannot be predicted by the model.
- The model does not address the question of why multinationals do not license or export, but prefer to pursue an FDI strategy.
- The model does not examine the systematic advantages that foreign firms possess to enable them to overcome inherent disadvantages versus local firms.

Giddy acknowledges that the theory still has a degree of explanatory power in some cases, but, to him, it is not a fully blown theory of FDI.

The product life cycle now

By no means discredited, the product life cycle theory seems to have less relevance now compared with its heyday two or three decades ago. Certainly the theory represents an attempt at explaining trade in manufactured products that require some degree of technical sophistication in their invention, design and development. In some cases, the theory seems to fit the facts. Colour television was invented in the United States. In the early days of the product, the United States produced and exported these goods. Over time, the production of colour televisions shifted almost entirely to countries such as Japan, Taiwan, Korea and elsewhere in the Far East. And the product life cycle model has also been suggested as an explanation for the relative decline of the US semiconductor industry. But for other sophisticated products – for example, aircraft – the model seems to fit less well. The United States, which took the lead in their development, still retains comparative advantage despite the fact that aircraft are now a relatively mature product. The fundamental weakness of the product life cycle model is its inability to generalise its predictions in terms of industry or the timing of the changes in the location of comparative advantage.

Why have the predictive powers of the theory waned in recent years? There are possible explanations. First of all, there has been an undoubted increase in the geographical reach of many of the enterprises involved in the innovation process due to their having established subsidiaries abroad already. Secondly, the national markets of advanced industrialised countries now are far more homogeneous.

During the 30 or so years immediately following the Second World War, there was a rapid growth in foreign investment. For all of this period, the process of innovation, export and foreign investment probably ran full tilt, as predicted by the theory. One consequence is that one now rarely finds major innovative firms that do not already have extensive overseas operations. This has had at least two significant effects. First, the time interval between the introduction of a new product in the home market and its first production in a foreign location has substantially decreased. New facilities are easily bolted on to hasten the transfer of new technology abroad. Secondly, there is now a significant reverse flow of technology through innovations, by subsidiaries abroad, which are subsequently introduced into the original home market. This has, in part, been a consequence of the narrowing of differences between the markets of the industrialised countries.

Even if it is less applicable now than in the past, the product life cycle theory has not utterly passed its 'sell-by' date. It certainly continues to provide numerous insights. The model links the demand side to the theory of comparative advantage, and presents the argument that the pattern of many exports and imports is better explained by competitive factors at the firm level rather than at the national level. It suggests that international trade follows markets, and that international investment responds to potential and real threats to export markets. In short, product life cycle ideas attempt to describe how the export, import and location of manufacture of a product changes through time as firms respond to changing competitive conditions and as domestic and foreign markets for the product grow, mature and decline.

So, product life cycle theory has been important because it explained international investment. The theory recognised the mobility of capital across countries in contrast to traditional assumptions of factor immobility and it shifted the focus from the country to the product. This meant that it was important to match the product by its maturity stage with its production location in order to examine competitiveness.

But product life cycle theory has limitations. It is clearly most appropriate for technology-based products. These products are likely to experience changes in production process as they grow and mature. Others, for example resource-based products, such as minerals and other commodities, and services, which mainly employ human capital, are not so easily characterised by stages of maturity. Product life cycle theory is most relevant to products that involve mass production and cheap labour costs. However, product life cycle theory has bridged a wide gap between older trade theories and the newer, with more globally competitive markets in which capital, technology, information and firms themselves are more internationally mobile.

20.8 The eclectic theory

The ideas summarised above about firm-specific advantages, location-specific advantages and internalisation have been melded by Dunning[43] in his eclectic theory of international production. For him, these sources of profit are competitive advantages to the multinational and are defined in the following terms:

- *Firm-specific advantages*. The multinational possesses ownership advantages which may be held temporarily or permanently and are held exclusively. They promise superior returns over competitors in foreign markets. Firm-specific advantages include intangible assets such as expertise or patents.
- *Location-specific advantages*. These include factors specific to a particular place and have to be used in that place. They would embrace trade barriers that restrict imports, labour advantages, natural resources, proximity to final markets, conditions of transportation and communication, favourable government intervention and cultural factors.
- *Internalisation advantages*. These include factors for which a company gains by using its ownership internally instead of buying or selling on the market from or to third parties, respectively. These factors include possession of raw material sources and downstream consumption within the company, the ability to cross-subsidise products, the ability to avoid transaction and negotiation costs, avoiding uncertainty about buying and selling, the ability to control supplies of inputs and their conditions of sale, and so on.

Dunning formulated his main hypothesis in the following way. Given the possession of net ownership advantages over local firms, the most profitable development for the multinational is to internalise them by extending its own activities. It must then be beneficial for the multinational to combine these internalised advantages with some factor inputs in some foreign countries – otherwise foreign markets would be served entirely by exports and home markets by home production.

This model has received support from various empirical studies and it has survived criticisms that throw some doubt on its universality as a general theory of international operations. For example, Kojima[44] suggested that the eclectic model is built on the experience of US multinationals and has less relevance to non-US firms – for example, the Japanese. This suggestion is refuted, in part at least, by work by Dunning and Archer.[45] In a study of fifteen UK-based multinationals active between 1914 and 1983, they found that the eclectic model fairly adequately explained sources of competitive advantage enjoyed by these firms and explained the geographical orientation of their FDI.

Also, the eclectic theory seems more appropriate to greenfield operations than to acquisitions, which seem to be motivated more by reason of strategic development than by economic advantage – for example, the follow-the-leader oligopolistic reaction referred to earlier. Furthermore, a growing proportion of FDI is carried out to acquire technology – the eclectic theory has little to offer in this respect. However, in an appraisal of the empirical work carried out in testing the eclectic theory, Hood and Young[46] refer to difficulties of data deficiency, problems in devising empirical tests for internalisation factors and numerous statistical problems. They concluded that a satisfactory test of the eclectic theory had yet to be devised. But that was in 1979, and more recent work has cast some doubt on the immutability of the eclectic model. Perhaps that is almost inevitable in the social sciences where our models are rarely valid 100 per cent of the time.

Even if we are not wholly satisfied with the eclectic model, it cannot be denied that it has given us great insights into the logic and process of FDI. The first question on FDI is: why does the firm extend its activities to other countries? Dunning's theory suggests that there are location-specific advantages available in the host country. The question that follows is: how do foreign firms compete with domestic firms of the host country? The eclectic theory points to firm-specific advantages. Then there is a further question to be answered: why should the firm choose FDI instead of exporting or licensing? The response lies in internalisation. These three advantages may be sufficient to explain FDI, but are they necessary? The answer seems to be in the negative since location-specific advantages and internalisation advantages seem to be sufficient to explain multinational activity – thus rendering firm-specific advantages redundant. Some economists go so far as to claim that the concept of internalisation alone is sufficient to explain multinational activity, and that the theory of internalisation is the theory of FDI – see, for example, Casson.[47]

Porter[48] provides insights into the FDI conundrum. He argues that, in seeking competitive advantage, multinationals should seek either a low-cost strategy or one concentrating upon product differentiation. Internationally, these two generic strategies may be operated within four strategic contexts; Porter refers to these as follows:

- *Country-focused strategy*. Here the full range of the value adding activities is located in each country with little or no co-ordination between the various subsidiaries – for example, as in food manufacturing, retailing, and service industries such as insurance, advertising, banking, management consultancy.
- *High foreign investment with extensive co-ordination among subsidiaries*. This route is often followed with a view to protecting intangible, but strategically important, rights – for example, research and development, technology, etc. In the pharmaceutical industry, for instance, research and development activities may be spread across a number of countries. Such dispersion calls for global co-ordination of research and development to maximise its utility and minimise overlap and waste.
- *Export-based strategy with decentralised marketing*. This is surely the simplest form of international strategy and is widely used by companies new to the international arena.
- *Purest global strategy*. Here a high degree of co-ordination and concentration of activities is aimed at producing standardised products for a global market. For example, well into the 1980s, Toyota concentrated manufacturing in Japan, with activities such as advertising, servicing and spare parts decentralised. Many of these activities could be standardised, but they all had to be closer to the final buyer than was the case for manufacturing.

Porter's focus reflects current trends in international investment and strategy, for example:

- FDI is expanding with more players from more countries.
- Products sold around the world are becoming more homogeneous in nature and/or appearance, although local markets in some sectors are simultaneously becoming more highly segmented.
- There is a distinct trend for service industries to become more globalised.
- In a growing number of industries, concentration of activities is becoming less attractive as economies of scale may be reaching their limits.
- As telecommunications technology and costs drop quickly, the ability of firms to improve the efficiency of co-ordination grows.

20.9 International joint ventures

Over recent years there has also been a plethora of international joint ventures. Indeed it is fair to say that one of the most common FDI routes in the 1980s was joint ventures with a local partner. As an alternative to outright ownership and control over foreign assets, such ventures have interesting properties. Sharing ownership rights spreads the risks of ownership and provides incentives for trading partners to invest in specific assets or to dedicate them to specific uses in a way that they might be unwilling to do if transacting on a purely arm's-length basis. But such ventures also pose hazards for either or both of the partners and these should always be borne in mind when entering a joint venture or considering the qualities of a partner. The hazard is that one party to the venture may behave opportunistically once the investment has been made and attempt to appropriate value for itself at the expense of the joint venture partner. This temptation often looms large in international joint ventures, making them a potentially unstable form of long-term investment which may provide one of the partners with an incentive to assume complete control.

20.10 International acquisitions

Cross-border mergers and acquisitions are common. In such a merger or acquisition, a domestic parent acquires the use of a productive asset in a foreign country by way of one of three methods. These are:

- cross-border acquisition of assets;
- cross-border acquisition of stock;
- cross-border merger.

An acquisition of assets is the most straightforward. Capacity is acquired and only the asset is purchased. None of the liabilities supporting that asset are transferred to the buyer. Clearly, a major consideration is the purchase price. The cost of buying an existing manufacturing plant in a foreign country should be compared to the cost of building a similar plant through foreign direct investment.

In an acquisition of stock, the multinational buys an equity interest in a foreign company. This is easiest to accomplish where there are active public equity markets. The purchaser may make a friendly offer to management or, possibly, a hostile offer directly to stockholders through the financial markets.

In a merger, two firms pool their assets and liabilities to create a new company. Shareholders swap their holdings in the original firms for shares in the new company according to a negotiated exchange ratio.

Cross-border mergers can be difficult to achieve. Usually, a large proportion of shareholders in each company must approve the merger, but the merger may also have to be approved by governments in each country. Mergers frequently have antitrust implications, and government agencies in different countries may have different views on what is in the public interest. The meeting of public interest requirements is a frequent criterion in mergers and acquisitions. Press Cutting 20.1 presents some interesting financial issues relating to cross-hyphen border takeovers and provides a useful revision vehicle.

PRESS CUTTING 20.1

Choose the correct path for a viable deal

By James Politi

In May 2000, Air Products & Chemicals came out with a sobering announcement. Because of opposition from regulators at the US Federal Trade Commission, the Pennsylvania-based industrials group would drop an $11.2bn deal to buy British rival BOC that it had sealed with France's Air Liquide a year earlier.

In addition to being forced to abandon a crucial strategic move, there was another reason for Air Products and its investors to be gloomy. A strong fluctuation in the dollar/pound exchange rate in previous months meant Air Products would have to take a charge of nearly $300million, mostly from losses on the currency hedge that the company had put in place for the BOC deal in January 2000.

The Air Products case illustrates the challenges facing corporate chiefs and investment banks as they study ways to manage foreign exchange risk during M&A deals. A tricky balance has to be struck between properly managing currency exposure, and not hedging so much that it undermines the economics of a deal.

Paul Huck, chief financial officer of Air Products, grappled with these issues. Speaking to the FT today, he believes his company had little choice but to put a hedge in place once it expected the BOC takeover to be approved. Air Products was paying for a collection of assets outside the UK in sterling – Air Liquide was slated to take over the British BOC business – and as such was heavily exposed to any movements in the UK currency between announcement and closing.

'We still feel we did the right thing in hedging the transaction', says Mr Huck. 'When you do M&A you worry about having the economics of a deal change because of currency movements, and we're not in the business of making currency bets.'

The trouble with the hedge put in place by Air Products – a mix of options and forward contracts – is that its structure may have been too optimistic. While forwards are less expensive than options because they carry no fee, they leave the company heavily exposed to a currency shift in the wrong direction if the deal does not close. Options, on the other hand, can be expensive, carrying hefty up-front fees. However, if the currency moves in the wrong direction and the deal does not close, the company can simply let the options expire.

'If I had been willing to do this [use more options and less forwards] and pay higher premiums, it would have been very expensive, and might have hurt the deal [if the FTC had approved it]', says Mr Huck.

Hedging currency risk in M&A deals has become an increasingly popular product in the universe of risk management.

As global M&A volumes have grown, and the markets for derivatives – the primary hedging instruments – have become increasingly liquid, banks have been able to match supply and demand on foreign exchange risk with a series of customised hedging packages.

Below is a list of the pros and cons of different options for corporate and private equity executives when they are implementing their currency hedging strategies.

'Natural hedge'. 'A natural hedge would essentially be issuing the debt for the acquisition in the target's local currency, which would negate the need for foreign exchange hedge', says Courtney McLaughlin, head of the foreign exchange capital markets group in the investment banking division at Credit Suisse.

'If the deal is signed and the currency appreciates, the acquirer will pay more for the business in dollar terms, but because they are issuing debt in the local currency market they are getting more (in dollar terms) for the debt they are issuing, thereby creating the natural hedge.'

'Do nothing'. 'Clients may adopt this strategy, particularly early in the M&A process, as the uncertainty surrounding deal completion can be significant', say Leo Civitillo, North American head of foreign exchange and interest rate sales and structuring for corporates, and Steve Zannetos, executive director, North American foreign exchange sales and structuring for corporates at Morgan Stanley. 'When the deal progresses and the probability of completion increases, execution of a currency hedge is typically warranted. However, there may also be other considerations that drive a decision not to hedge, including a view on the market, the implied costs of hedging and accounting considerations. The risk of remaining unhedged is that the currency could significantly move against the company and adversely affect the economics of the acquisition.'

Press cutting 20.1 (*continued*)

'Foreign exchange option'. According to Mr McLaughlin at Credit Suisse, a foreign exchange option gives the buyer of the option the right – not the obligation – to purchase the currency at a specific price (known as the strike price). The client would buy a call option to protect itself against a rising currency and would pay a premium for the option – typically in the range of 50–200 basis points (depending on the maturity and price of the strike). Unlike a forward, the most money one can lose on an option is the premium that one pays for it, which makes it a particularly good strategy in the context of cross-border M&A. With an option, like insurance, you will always know how much you will spend on your hedge, which makes budgeting for the hedge relatively easy. An option is also a marketable asset, albeit a depreciating one, and could be sold in the free market in the event the hedge needs to be liquidated. The only real disadvantage of an option is its upfront cost.

'Foreign exchange forward'. 'FX forwards are simply an obligation to exchange one currency for another at a specified rate on a future date', say Mr Civitillo and Mr Zannetos at Morgan Stanley. 'We typically do not recommend that clients employ vanilla FX forwards to hedge the currency risk embedded in a cross-border transaction until we are absolutely certain that the deal will close. The reason is that the potential breakage or unwind cost of an FX forward can be significant, if the underlying transaction does not close as expected. However, assuming that all of the deal risks have passed, forward contracts can be a very efficient and cost effective way to lock-in the price of a foreign asset. Many clients initially execute option-based strategies and ultimately convert them into FX forwards to ensure that they have the funds needed to close the underlying strategic transaction.'

'Deal-contingent forward'. A deal-contingent forward is very similar to a vanilla forward with two key differences: the ability of the client to walk away from the contract if the deal is not consummated, and its price, explains Credit Suisse's Mr McLaughlin. A deal-contingent forward allows a client to exchange one currency for another at a specified rate on a future date. The client would define contingencies that, if met, would allow the client to walk away from the forward with no cost or obligation. The client is, in essence, transferring the unwind risk it is unwilling to shoulder to the bank that is selling the deal-contingent forward. Typical contingencies are: material adverse change clauses, shareholder approvals and regulatory approvals. A deal-contingent forward has an implicit cost that is paid for by striking the forward rate slightly off market (higher in the case of a buyer). A deal-contingent forward allows the client to enjoy the efficiency of a forward without the out-of-pocket cost of an option. They are a very popular product at the moment.

Source: *Financial Times*, 25 January 2007.

A further variant is the international joint venture where an investment-based agreement between two or more companies enables them to pool their resources in order to achieve some goal. A new company is usually created to accomplish this. Resource commitments, responsibilities and earnings are generally shared according to a specified formula. Joint ventures are useful when companies in the same industry or in similar industries wish to share the risk of a large venture, for example the development of a new product or market in a new territory.

In an international joint venture, the incentive to act opportunistically and violate the terms of the agreement can be great once a foreign partner has input the technology necessary for production. The partner can become a competitor, sometimes even reversing into the parent's home market. Because of this threat, multinationals using a joint venture have to find the right partner and structure the deal to their mutual advantage at the same time keeping proprietary technology at arm's length from the partner. Companies in technology-intensive industries, such as pharmaceuticals, electronics, and biotechnology, aim to maintain control of patents, trademarks, and production technologies. Where the risk of technology loss is high, another mode of market entry is usually preferred.

Another form of entry into a foreign market entry is through a strategic alliance. Such an alliance is a collaborative agreement that is designed to achieve some strategic goal. Strategic alliances are used to reduce the costs and risks of product development in industries with heavy R&D requirements, and to penetrate foreign markets in which domestic firms have little expertise or experience.

20.11 Globalisation

No overview of international business strategy would be complete without reference to globalisation. Levitt[49] comments upon

> the emergence of global markets for standardized consumer products on a previously unimagined scale of magnitude. Corporations geared to this new reality benefit from enormous economies of scale in production, distribution, marketing, and management. By translating these benefits into reduced world prices, they can decimate competitors that still live in the disabling grip of old assumptions about how the world works.

Stopford and Turner[50] have given us a model summarising forces which may influence global positioning. Their focus is upon three key issues and how these are influenced. Factors that impact global positioning are:

- Policy co-ordination, affected by:
  - worldwide information management;
  - global brand names;
  - common products;
  - phased product launches.
- Location, affected by:
  - key strategic markets;
  - regulation;
  - real exchange rates;
  - local learning.
- Operational integration, affected by:
  - multicountry scale economies;
  - international sales force;
  - common technology;
  - international logistics.

Analysis by Cvar[51] suggests that industries which become global have a series of characteristics. The model is as follows:

- Industries which become global:
  - high levels of demand for standardised products;
  - economies of scale.

- Triggers for globalisation:
  - common segments identified;
  - product defined globally;
  - supply sources consolidated.
- Successful global companies:
  - pre-emptive strategy;
  - performance measured globally;
  - R&D higher than average;
  - managed all elements globally;
  - overcome barriers to globalisation.

20.12 Game theory and international strategy

On the multinational business stage, the players are oligopolists. And game theory, associated with von Neumann and Morgenstern[52] and Oster[53], gives us insights into oligopolistic behaviour. Game theory focuses upon interactions between competitors and explains foreign investment in these terms rather than by comparing transaction costs. In game theory, the international moves and countermoves of oligopolists have less to do with maximising efficiency than with defence of market position.

In oligopolistic game theory, competitors are relatively few and are identifiable and well known by all players. Strategic moves by one party are highly visible and are likely to have a significant impact on the profits of other players. The competitors in an oligopolistic industry are generally stable over time. They engage in repeated interactions and negotiation and collusion with a fairly stable equilibrium becoming possible. Aggression tends to provoke punitive responses. Competition in oligopoly is not unlike the restraint observed by nuclear powers. The peace depends upon all parties knowing that disturbance of the equilibrium can set off a mutually disastrous course of events.

Game theory provides significant insights on FDI decisions. FDI may give one player the competitive advantage that would enable it to make a more menacing attack upon fellow oligopolists. In other words, it may create a change in the league table of competitive power – see Knickerbocker.[54] The first venture abroad in a particular market may enable the prime mover to gain market knowledge, economies of scale and other advantages over its rivals that have remained at home. In consequence, other players in the home oligopoly may tend to match each other's moves abroad to reduce this risk. By shadowing rivals' moves, they may not be left behind – no single player then gains a possibly destabilising competitive advantage versus the others. A matching of moves of this kind is precisely what Knickerbocker found in a study of FDI by US corporations between 1948 and 1967. He observed that FDI activity tended to concentrate in relatively clear and short time spans. Some 47 per cent of all FDI by 197 US corporations was clustered in particular three-year periods. He concluded that moves by one company into a particular country sector prompted a rush by its domestic rivals into that same country group. Bunching of FDI was marked in oligopolistic industries. Game theory may also illuminate international strategies of rivals from different countries. For Graham,[55] FDI in different countries can be seen as an exchange of threats between oligopolistic players in the same industry. A move by a foreign multinational into the home market may then be matched by home-based multinationals responding in kind.

The greater the extent of multinationality, the greater the ability of the multinational to exchange threats. A proliferation of country investment improves the ability to retaliate against competitors. The firm may fire warning shots in minor markets first of all and build up to a battle in major markets if the aggressor fails to back down. Additionally, a spread of markets makes it possible to cross-subsidise such battles. Networks of international joint ventures and alliances also improve information sources on competitor moves.

Underpinning game theory explanations of international competition is the premise that all players are acting according to the same rules. The expected outcome is a kind of collusive equilibrium, in which exchange of threats ensures an equilibrium, where established multinationals continue to enjoy oligopolistic profits. Multinationals become, to use the term coined by Porter,[56] 'good competitors'. They offer sufficient threat to prevent complacency but never enough to disrupt the equilibrium. According to Porter, powerful players should offer gentle competition as opposed to striving for complete dominance. Others might shelter under the umbrella of the market leader rather than offering all-out attack. If competitors perceive these as the rules, destructive battles may be avoided.

In global competition 'good competitors' may be thinner on the ground than in the domestic market place. Competitors from different countries may well have different philosophies of business and different objectives, particularly if backed by their government. This tends to be supporting the expansionist strategy of long-term investment in market share that has been so typical of Far East companies as part of their attack upon Western markets.

The game theory school might view international strategy, including FDI, as a chess game of pre-empting and countering competitors; others would perceive international moves as seeking to internalise activities to obtain competitive advantage, while others still would be sceptical, favouring behavioural and imperialistic goals. Perhaps the major lesson is to point out that not all players in multinational business have the same rule book.

20.13 The new trade theory

World trade developments in the 1980s led to criticism of existing theories. Although there was rapid growth in trade, much of it was not explained by prevailing theories. Two new contributions to trade theory emerged. Helpman and Krugman[57] developed a theory of how trade is altered when production of specific products possess economies of scale. A second development was associated with Porter[58] who examined the global competitiveness of industries rather than relying on country-specific factors.

Economies of scale and imperfect competition

Krugman's major contribution focused on costs of production and how costs and prices drive international trade. He highlighted two types of economics of scale: internal economies of scale and external economies of scale.

When there are economies of scale that accrue to the individual firm, we talk of internal economies of scale. The larger the firm the greater the scale of benefits and the lower the cost per unit. A firm possessing internal economies of scale could potentially monopolise an industry both domestically and internationally by lowering the market price. Such a firm would be using its internal economies of scale to create, first, imperfect competition and, potentially, a monopoly.

The link between the domination of domestic industry and influencing international trade comes from taking the assumption of imperfect markets back to the concept of comparative advantage. For the firm to expand sufficiently fully to enjoy its economies of scale, it must divert resources from other domestic business units in order to expand. Conflated to a country level, a nation's range of products in which it specialises narrows, providing an opportunity for other countries to specialise in these abandoned product ranges. Countries again search out and exploit comparative advantage. An implication of internal economies of scale is that it provides an explanation of intra-industry trade, an area in which traditional trade theory failed to provide an explanation. Intra-industry trade occurs when a country apparently imports and exports the same product, an idea inconsistent with traditional trade theory. According to Krugman, internal economies of scale lead a firm to specialise in a narrow product line. Firms in other countries may then produce products that are similar but were relinquished by the former firm. If consumers in either country wish to buy both products, they will be importing and exporting products that are, for purposes of national statistics, the same.

Turning briefly to external economies of scale, these are said to derive when the cost per unit of output depends on the size of an industry, not the size of the individual firm. Thus, an industry in one country may produce at lower costs than the same industry that is smaller in other countries. A country might dominate world markets in a particular product, not because it has one massive firm producing enormous quantities, but rather because it has many small firms that interact to create significant, competitive, critical mass – for example, crystal glassware in Germany. No one firm may be large, but all small firms in total create such a competitive industry that firms in other countries cannot break into the industry.

Unlike internal economies of scale, external economies of scale do not necessarily lead to imperfect markets, but they tend to result in an industry dominating its field in world markets. This provides an explanation as to why all industries do not necessarily move to the country with the lowest cost energy, resources or labour. What gives rise to this critical mass of small firms and their interrelationships is a complex question. Porter's work provides a partial explanation as to how these critical masses are sustained.

The competitive advantage of nations

The focus of early trade theory was on the country or nation and its inherent, natural endowment that might give rise to increasing competitiveness. As trade theory evolved, its focus moved to the industry and product level, leaving the question of national competitiveness behind. More recently, attention has moved to the question of how countries, governments and private industry can alter the conditions within a country and aid the competitiveness of its firms.

The prime mover in this area has been Porter.[59] He observes that national prosperity is created, not inherited. It does not merely grow out of a country's natural endowments, as classical economics suggests. To Porter, a nation's competitiveness depends on the capacity of its industry to innovate and upgrade. Thus, companies gain advantage against world competitors because of pressure and challenge. They benefit from having strong rivals domestically, aggressive local suppliers and demanding customers in the home market. Porter concludes that, ultimately, nations succeed in particular industries because their home environment is most forward-looking, dynamic and challenging.

Porter argues that innovation drives and sustains competitiveness. A firm must avail itself of all dimensions of competition which he categorises into the four components of the diamond of national advantage:

- *Factor conditions*. Most important, for Porter, is the ability of a nation continually to create, upgrade and deploy its factors of production, such as resources and skilled labour, rather than the initial endowment.
- *Demand conditions*. This embraces the spirit of competition that the firm faces in its domestic market. Highly competitive and demanding local markets are most likely to give rise to competitive edge. The character of the market, rather than its size, is paramount in promoting and maintaining the competitiveness of the firm. For Porter, character of the market translates into demanding customers.
- *Related and supporting industries*. This refers to the competitiveness of related industries and suppliers to the firm. The firm that is operating within a mass of related firms and industries gains and maintains advantages through close working relationships, proximity to suppliers and timeliness of product and information flows.
- *Firm strategy, structure and rivalry*. The conditions in the home market influence the ability to compete internationally. But no single operating strategy, form of ownership or management style can be said to be universally appropriate – flexibility becomes of essence.

These four components constitute what nations and firms must create and sustain locally as a forerunner to international success.

Some more recent theories are summarised in Buckley.[60] We also like the explanatory approach of Feenstra and Taylor.[61]

Summary

- Although many multinational firms appear to pursue a haphazard approach to overseas expansion, there is invariably an underlying rationale.
- Generally, this involves understanding and then capitalising on those factors that led to success in the past – and this usually involves a variety of market imperfections.
- These imperfections include barriers to entry, product differentiation, control of raw materials, patents, know-how, trademarks, marketing and organisational skills and so on.
- Theories of international business and foreign direct investment are summarised in this chapter.

End of chapter questions

20.1 King Company and President Inc. are automobile manufacturers that desire to benefit from economies of scale. King Company has decided to establish distributorship subsidiaries in various countries, while President Inc. has decided to establish manufacturing in various countries. Which firm is more likely to benefit from economies of scale?

20.2 Why do you suppose that foreign governments provide MNCs with incentives to undertake FDI in their countries?

20.3 Explain the theory of comparative advantage as a motive for foreign trade.

21 Exchange controls and corporate tax in international investment

Two of the major distorting features of international investment appraisal, which are absent in the domestic counterpart, are exchange controls and international corporation tax. In this chapter, a summary of the potential problems that they create is set out. So, as a prerequisite to arriving at a logical model for international capital budgeting, we present an overview that is highly specific to the task of analysing and appraising international investment opportunities.

21.1 Exchange controls

One of the major differences between domestic and international capital budgeting is the possible distorting effect of exchange controls. Not all host countries impose exchange controls but a significant number do – hence the overview of this topic in this chapter. Exchange controls refer to regulations that forbid or restrict the holding of assets denominated in foreign currency and foreign exchange transactions of residents insofar as they affect the earning, holding and spending of foreign currencies or the acquisition, retention or disposal of assets and liabilities situated abroad and/or denominated in foreign currency; exchange controls may also circumscribe the actions of non-residents in the host country. In connection with controls, currency is said to be convertible if the authorities of the country allow it to be exchanged without restriction or the need for permission into currencies of other countries. Complete freedom for all residents of a country and for all holders of a national currency to buy foreign currency or foreign-currency-denominated assets is termed full convertibility or free convertibility. It exists in a significant number of Western economies and for a number of developing countries.

When faced with problems such as recurring deficits on balance of payments, governments frequently resort to various controls. Exchange control is one such form. Confronted with inadequate reserves to finance deficits, or faced with increasing liquid liabilities to foreigners on a scale that threatens to create future difficulties if redemption of these liabilities is requested, exchange controls are often invoked in an effort to prevent problems becoming worse. Exchange rate movements affect such broad segments of the economy that governments, faced with financial difficulties, often resort to supporting exchange rates within some range or band. Exchange controls take many forms and they affect international transactions. In balance of payments terms, they are intended to have positive effects – or perhaps less negative effects than would otherwise be the case – upon current account and capital account outturns.

The imposition of exchange controls usually follows a consistent pattern. Payments to foreigners exceed receipts from foreign countries. Depreciation of the value of the country's currency is anticipated and in an effort to strengthen the home currency, exchange controls are invoked. The government legislates that those who obtain foreign exchange through exports and other transactions must sell their foreign exchange to the government or designated banks. The government must allocate this foreign exchange to importers and other purchasers of foreign goods and services. The host government usually keeps its exchange rate at a level at which it is overvalued, even though this means that demand for imports increases and exporting becomes less profitable and more difficult. In turn, this means that demand for foreign currency is greater than its supply. Hence, some of those who wish to buy foreign exchange cannot be permitted to do so.

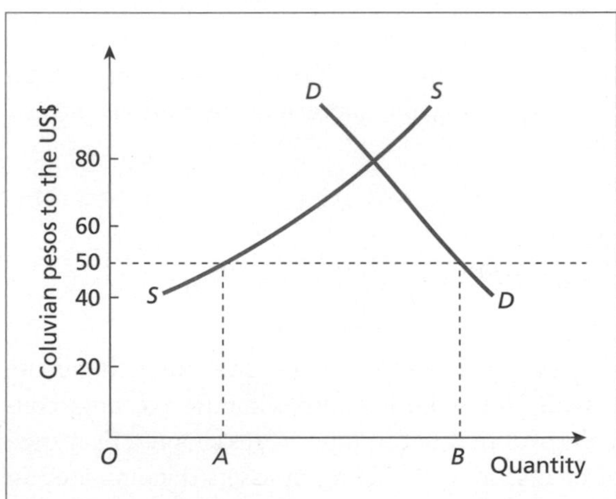

Figure 21.1 Foreign exchange market under exchange controls

The situation is illustrated in Figure 21.1 in which it is assumed that the Coluvian government attempts to keep the exchange rate of the Coluvian peso equivalent to 50 pesos to the dollar. Demand and supply in a free market would result in an equilibrium rate of 80 pesos to the dollar. At the exchange rate of 50 pesos, holders of foreign exchange would be reluctant to surrender it since they know that the equilibrium rate is 80 pesos. So the government must force the sale of the supply of foreign exchange, *OA*, to it or to designated banks, and it must allocate that supply to those who wish to buy it. At the official rate of 50 pesos to the dollar, rather than the equilibrium rate of 80, demand for dollars and indeed goods priced in foreign currency will be greater than at the equilibrium rate. The government, therefore, has created a problem which it must solve by dictate. It has to nominate who may purchase foreign exchange or it must simply restrict purposes for which foreign currency may be purchased. At 50 pesos to the dollar, the quantity *OB* would be purchased, but this is legally prevented since the country only has *OA*. Hardly surprisingly, significant black markets begin to develop in foreign currency with the black market price reflecting that rate which would hold in equilibrium rather than the official rate.

Exchange controls restrict imports to a level less than under free-market conditions. When a country maintaining exchange controls devalues its currency, imports increase – if permitted. In Figure 21.1, if Coluvia were to devalue its currency from 50 pesos per dollar to 80 pesos per dollar, the supply of foreign exchange would tend to increase and therefore the purchase of foreign exchange for imports would also tend to increase.

Typically, exchange controls apply to residents of a country. The nature of the transaction for which foreign exchange is required is invariably important as is the location to which foreign currency is to be transferred and the location of the party with whom the transaction is being carried out. All companies operating in a given country are usually treated, for exchange control purposes, as resident in that country. That the head office or controlling staff reside in another country does not affect residence for exchange control purposes. Where financial institutions import and export large amounts of foreign currency, special rules usually apply. Residence for exchange control purposes is determined by a different set of rules from that which determines residence for tax purposes.

The applicability of exchange control rules is governed by the type of transaction involved, but such rules normally embrace:

- imports, including obtaining the foreign currency required and licences, if any;
- exports and the disposition of foreign exchange proceeds;
- invisibles;
- investment abroad, including direct and portfolio investment;
- operation of multiple currency rates (this would include different exchange rates for different purposes);
- borrowing abroad by residents;
- permissions for non-residents to open bank accounts in the host country;
- permissions for residents to hold foreign currency accounts;
- limitations on the use of some foreign exchange management techniques;
- profit repatriation out of the host country.

It is the last bullet point that is particularly relevant for international capital budgeting. It is especially worthy of separate focus, and this now follows.

21.2 Profits repatriation

This is a critically important and complex topic. Profits made and cash flows earned in a foreign country are of no value to the international corporation if they cannot ultimately be repatriated to the home country for distribution to shareholders.

Many developed countries allow free repatriation of all profits and capital at any time. Normally under exchange control regulations, capital put into a country may be repatriated but the return of profits is strictly limited. Given that international companies have sought to circumvent the profits repatriation constraint by the use of billings for royalties, research and development, consultancy fees and the use of transfer pricing distortions and so on, it is hardly surprising that countries with exchange controls have responded by drawing up tough regulations and limiting repatriations in general. Many countries with exchange controls limit the amount to be returned to a given percentage of total capital invested and/or to a proportion of retained profit. This has the effect of forcing reinvestment of some of the profit in the host country. Frequently, profits that cannot be repatriated for a specified time – blocked profits – have to be invested in specified government bonds; upon maturity of the bond, they may be sent abroad. Since such government bonds attract low interest rates and since they are frequently used in high-inflation countries, their effect is hardly advantageous to the multinational corporation.

Sometimes countries with exchange controls segregate investments according to whether they are of an approved or of an ordinary status. Approved status projects have a privileged profits repatriation position or they may attract advantageous exchange rates on repatriation. From the international company's point of view such stipulations are critical in evaluating overseas investment projects.

Rules on profit distribution are so complex and varied and subject to such frequent change that investing international companies make it a policy to scrutinise carefully local regulations and they often negotiate a specific watertight agreement with the host nation in respect of capital and profit repatriation. But even this may not be sufficient. Such agreements have been renounced by existing governments. And new incoming governments may also disregard agreements made by their predecessors. Compensation guarantees from home governments are available for some countries – however there is, inevitably, a cost involved.

21.3 Circumventing profit repatriation restrictions

Various means are available to the international company for moving funds and profits from one country to another. These include:

- transfer pricing;
- fees and royalty agreements;
- leading and lagging;
- dividends;
- loans;
- equity versus debt considerations;
- currency invoicing;
- reinvoicing centres.

Exchange control authorities have become well aware that multinational companies use transfer pricing, royalties and leading and lagging to move funds and, consequently, have put impediments in the way of these techniques. Tight controls on invisibles, validation of import and export prices and constraints on leading and lagging are all examples of ways in which host governments have attacked this problem.

The making and repaying of intercompany loans which originally involved the input of foreign finance into the host country is often one of the few legitimate ways to transfer funds from a country with tight exchange controls. But, because foreign debt capital is subject to political risk and because funds may become blocked in foreign countries, multinationals have resorted to the use of parallel loans, **back-to-back loans** and currency swaps. Parallel loans are effectively a pair of loans made simultaneously in two countries. A parallel loan transaction involves two parties, who simultaneously make loans of the same value to one another's foreign subsidiaries. The parent, company A, will extend a loan in its home country and currency to a subsidiary of company B, whose foreign parent will lend the local currency equivalent in its country to the subsidiary of company A. **Drawdown** of the loan, repayment of principal and payments of interest are arranged to occur simultaneously. It should be noted that such transactions involve two separate loans but no cross-border movement of funds. Normally, there is some arrangement whereby, legally, the loans may be set off one against the other. But loans cannot be offset in the respective consolidated balance sheets. Such loans appear as both assets and liabilities. Payment of interest is made by both parties. This is based upon the cost of money in each country.

Back-to-back loans are often employed to finance associates located in countries with high interest rates or restricted capital markets – particularly when there is a danger of currency controls, or where different rates of **withholding tax** are applied to loans from a financial institution. As an example, assume that the parent company deposits funds with a bank in country A which in turn lends the money to a subsidiary in country B. In this sense, the back-to-back loan is an intercorporate loan channelled through a bank. The bank simply acts as an intermediary and from the bank's point of view the loan is risk-free because the parent's deposit provides collateral for the loan. Back-to-back loans of this sort create advantages where countries apply different withholding tax rates to interest paid to a foreign parent and interest paid to a financial institution. Furthermore, should currency controls be imposed, governments usually permit the local subsidiary to honour the repayment schedule of a loan from a major multinational bank. However, host government monetary authorities may have few reservations about placing impediments in the way of repayment of a straight intercompany loan. Back-to-back financing therefore provides better protection than an intercompany loan against exchange controls or expropriation.

Currency swaps achieve similar objectives to parallel loans but they are somewhat simpler. They involve two parties and one agreement. The two companies involved may sell currencies to each other at the spot rate and undertake to reverse the exchange after a specified term. Currency swaps have one or two advantages over parallel loans: they are reported off balance sheet, they have simpler documentation and they afford greater protection in the event of a default.

We now turn to considerations of debt versus equity in financing an overseas subsidiary. Generally speaking, financing an overseas subsidiary with debt from the parent company, as opposed to equity, provides greater flexibility. It is usually the case that a firm has greater latitude to repatriate funds in the form of interest and loan repayments than as dividends or reductions in equity. Furthermore, reductions in equity may be frowned upon by the host government. In addition, the use of loans as opposed to equity investment confers possibilities for reducing taxes. This arises on two fronts. Interest paid on a loan is usually tax deductible in the host nation, whereas dividend payments are not. Also, unlike dividends, loan repayments do not normally constitute taxable income to the parent company. To counter this, host countries' exchange controls may incorporate thin capitalisation rules whereby debt maximum levels are assumed and imposed in terms of interpreting exchange control regulations.

Capital controls may be circumvented by the judicious use of currency invoicing. The choice of currency in which an invoice is billed may enable a firm to remove blocked funds from a country that has exchange controls. Assume that a subsidiary is located within a country which restricts profit repatriation. If a devaluation of the host currency is forecast, this may provide the firm with an opportunity to move excess blocked funds elsewhere. This may be achieved by invoicing exports from that subsidiary to the rest of the corporation in the local currency of the devaluing country at a contracted price. As the local currency depreciates, profit margins are reduced in that subsidiary as opposed to what they would have been had billing been in a hard currency. But elsewhere within the corporation, they are improved. Effectively, cash from the devaluing country is shifted to another part of the group.

Multinationals also consider the use of reinvoicing centres. They are mainly used by multinationals as part of the exposure management function but they are sometimes used to disguise profitability, avoid government scrutiny and co-ordinate transfer pricing policy for tax purposes. The reinvoicing centre may be used to counter exchange controls by setting it in low-tax countries. These centres take title to all goods sold across frontiers, whether by one subsidiary to another or by sale to a third-party customer, although the goods themselves move directly from the factory to the purchaser. The centre pays the seller and the centre receives payment from the purchaser. While reinvoicing centres create obvious opportunities for using transfer pricing to the best advantage, they also give the international company considerable flexibility to utilise currency invoicing techniques. Needless to say, tax authorities and exchange control authorities are very suspicious of transactions which move through reinvoicing centres, especially when they are located in a **tax haven**.

It is also worth mentioning four other techniques that are used for circumventing exchange controls. These involve:

- purchase of capital goods with **blocked currency** where the equipment is for corporate-wide use;
- purchase of local services with blocked funds when such services are for use throughout the group;
- conducting and paying for research and development in the host country when the benefits accrue throughout the group;
- hosting corporate conventions, vacations and other expenses in the host country and paying for them with blocked currency.

The above techniques all involve purchasing goods or services locally which may aid the firm in other countries, thus achieving some measure of unblocking.

We now turn to a series of other techniques which can be categorised as **countertrade** but embrace barter, counterpurchase, industrial offset, buy-back and switch trading. All may be used by multinationals with the objective of unblocking funds which would otherwise be trapped in a host country by virtue of its exchange control regulations.

Countertrade

One method of profit remittance frequently used involves countertrade deals. Countertrade involves a reciprocal agreement for the exchange of goods or services. The parties involved may be firms or governments, and the reciprocal agreements can take a number of forms – for example, barter, counterpurchase, industrial offset, buy-back and switch trading. So what distinguishes the different types of countertrade?

Barter is the simplest form of countertrade. It involves the direct exchange of goods and services from one country for the goods or services of another. No money crosses frontiers, so there is no need for letters of credit or drafts, or trade financing or credit insurance. Frequently, one of the parties in a barter deal does not want the goods that are received, and so a third party that specialises in brokering arranges to sell them on for a fee. An oft-quoted example of a barter deal was the transfer in 1978 of the Polish international footballer, Kazimierz Deyna, for photocopiers and French lingerie.

Barter requires a mutual coincidence of wants. The ultimate parties in the transaction must each want what the other party has to offer, and want it at the same time. Such complete coincidence is unlikely, and to account for this, a different form of countertrade, called counterpurchase, has evolved and is now more common than barter. Under counterpurchase, the seller agrees with the buyer either:

- to make purchases from a company nominated by the buyer (the buyer then settles up with the company it has nominated); or
- to take products from the buyer in the future.

Counterpurchase may involve a combination of the above two possibilities. Counterpurchase may involve partial compensation with products and the balance in cash. Such types of countertrade deals are, strictly speaking, called compensation agreements.

Another form of countertrade involves industrial offset. A large part of countertrade involves reciprocal agreements to buy materials or components from the buying company or country. Thus, an aircraft manufacturer might agree to buy engines from a buyer of its aircraft. Or the deal might involve the aircraft manufacturer buying aircraft engines from a foreign producer with the engine manufacturer's country buying a large number of the aircraft.

Buy-back is a frequently encountered form of countertrade: it is common with capital equipment. In a buy-back agreement, the seller of the capital equipment agrees to buy the products made with the equipment it supplies. Thus a maker of mining equipment might agree to buy the output of the mine for a given period, maybe ten to fifteen years. Sometimes the equipment buyer pays partly in terms of its own product and partly in cash. Again, buy-back agreements of this latter kind are correctly called compensation agreements.

Switch trading is different. It occurs when the importer has received credit for selling goods or services to another country at a previous time, and where this credit cannot be converted into financial payment, but has to be used for purchases in the country where the credit is held. The owner of the credit switches title to its credit to the company or country from which it is making a purchase. Thus, a UK firm might have a credit in blocking country X for manufacturing equipment it has delivered. If a UK firm finds a product in France that it wishes to purchase, the UK firm might pay the French firm with its credit in country X. The French firm might agree to this if it wished to buy goods from country X. Most switch deals are arranged through brokers.

21.4 Other techniques of unblocking funds

A checklist and skeleton explanation of thirty methods used by international companies to enable profit remittance in the presence of exchange controls can be found in Buckley.[1] The whole point about the techniques referred to, including countertrade in all of its forms, is that they are relevant to international capital budgeting because they may provide the wherewithal to convert blocked cash generation in an overseas project into parent cash flows – but, of course, at a cost. Dependent upon the foreign country concerned, fees may range from 5 to 35 per cent – or even more.

Having completed a quick overview of exchange controls, we now move on to consider the essentials of international corporate taxation as it impacts upon cross-border investment appraisal.

21.5 International corporate taxation

One of the essential steps in domestic capital budgeting is the allowance for corporate taxation in order to arrive at incremental net of tax cash flows. Of course, domestic capital budgeting essentially involves only home country taxation. A similar step applies to international capital budgeting, but it is of greater complexity since it may involve tax outflows at both host and home country levels.

We continue this section with words of warning. This is, by no means, intended to be the sole reference on international taxation and tax planning. These topics are exceedingly complex and require detailed knowledge of the domestic tax code, foreign tax systems and bilateral tax treaties. This section can do little more than scratch the surface. Beware.

Clearly, every aspect of corporate tax in every country cannot possibly be covered here – even briefly. However, there are certain common themes that do recur in the domain of international taxation and it is upon these that we focus. For the purposes of this overview for international capital budgeting purposes, the focus is upon key aspects of international corporate tax – namely, withholding taxes, branch versus subsidiary and taxation of dividend remittances. But the topic is really a vast one and has far more facets than these. What follows in the next three sections in this chapter is an essential simplification. It is necessary to understand this before embarking upon the analysis of international capital projects.

Withholding taxes

Withholding taxes are collected from foreign individuals and/or corporations on income they have received from sources within a country. If a UK resident earns dividends in Canada, taxes will be withheld and paid to the Canadian revenue authorities. Credit is generally received at home for taxes withheld overseas. So the level of withholding primarily affects the amount of taxes received by the respective tax authorities. If the UK resident in the example above has 15 per cent withheld in Ruritania (a fictional country) and is in a 20 per cent marginal tax bracket in the United Kingdom (assuming the tax rate on dividends to be 20 per cent, which is not actually the case at the time of writing), the UK tax payable will be reduced to 5 per cent after credit for the 15 per cent is given. Higher withholding rates therefore generally mean that more tax is collected by the foreign authorities and a smaller amount by the home government. This is the essence of a particular topic that is extremely complicated in reality and is, of course, subject to regular change. In fact, one recent change that has occurred in many European countries is that no further tax in the home country is paid on remittance to the parent. This has made relocation, for tax purposes, very attractive to many companies and has explained the shift from Britain to other European centres.

Branch versus subsidiary

A key aspect of corporate tax planning concerns whether to operate abroad via a branch or through a subsidiary. Because of taxation, this is a key factor in many locations, but not all. A branch is a foreign operation that is incorporated at home – not in the host territory. A subsidiary is incorporated in the host country.

If a foreign activity is not expected to be profitable for a number of years, there may be an advantage to starting out with a branch so that negative earnings abroad may be used to offset profits at home. The tax laws of some countries allow branch income to be consolidated in this way. If a company expects positive foreign income, and this income is not to be repatriated, there may be tax advantages to a foreign subsidiary. Foreign branches may pay home taxes on income as it is earned. Foreign subsidiaries do not pay home taxes until the income is repatriated to the home country.

Dividends

The description in this section varies from country to country. We aim here to point out the problem that can arise. Whenever one is dealing with tax regulations, the advice that one examines local tax rules carefully applies. They are not always logical. Readers should note the last two sentences in the section header 'Withholding taxes' (above).

In the example which follows, we look at a holding company in Bigland with an overseas business in Ruritania. If a Bigland-resident company makes investments abroad, the company is liable to corporation tax on income received before deduction of foreign taxes. This rule applies to foreign subsidiaries and also to the chargeable fraction of any capital gains on the disposal of foreign assets.

Where a business is carried on through a foreign subsidiary, the Bigland company's liability arises on actual amounts received from the subsidiary by way of interest or dividend. Double tax relief is available in respect of the foreign tax suffered on both income and other gains.

Normally, only direct foreign taxes are taken into account for double tax relief, but if a Bigland company receives dividends from a foreign company in which it owns a reasonable holding, say 10 per cent or more of the voting power, underlying taxes on the profits out of which the dividends are paid are taken into account as well. In this case, the amount included in Bigland profits is the dividend plus both the direct and underlying foreign taxes. Double tax relief is given, but it should be noted that the relief on overseas income cannot exceed the Bigland corporation tax payable on overseas income. Table 21.1 is included to show how this treatment works in numerical terms for a UK group that owns 100 per cent of a business in Ruritania.

The assumptions at the head of Table 21.1 are important. They indicate the underlying position of the Ruritanian business relative to its Bigland parent and they set out Bigland and Ruritanian rates of corporate tax. In particular, it should be noted that when the Ruritanian business is a subsidiary of the Bigland parent, the distribution before overseas dividend tax is grossed up to obtain the amount subject to Bigland tax (see halfway down columns 1 and 2 in the table). This sum is taxed at the Bigland corporate tax rate but a **foreign tax credit** is available. This is given in respect of all the dividend withholding tax borne and for a proportion of foreign profits tax paid. In the example, the foreign profits tax credit, amounting to BLD214,000, is obtained by taking the amount of foreign profits tax paid (the equivalent of BLD600,000) and multiplying it by the amount paid out as dividend (the equivalent of BLD500,000) divided by the profit available for distribution (the equivalent of BLD1,400,000).

Note also that if there are excess taxes paid, as in column 2 of Table 21.1, Bigland will impose additional taxes but will, in fact, allow the use of these excess taxes paid as an offset

Table 21.1 Tax position of Bigland company with overseas income

Holding company in Bigland owns 100 per cent of the Ruritanian business.

Columns 1 and 3 assume that the Bigland corporation tax rate is 50 per cent.

Columns 2 and 4 assume that Bigland corporation tax is 35 per cent.

Columns 1 and 2 assume that the Ruritanian business is a subsidiary.

Columns 3 and 4 assume that the Ruritanian business is a branch of the Bigland.

Ruritanian profits are, in Bigland currency terms, BLD (Bigland dollars) 2m pre-tax. In Ruritania, businesses are subject to a 30 per cent tax. Where the local business is a subsidiary, the Ruritanian company pays a dividend equal to BLD500,000 and this is subject to a local withholding tax on dividends of 10 per cent. In the case of the branch, there is no distribution.

Ruritania as a subsidiary (BLD000)			Ruritania as a branch (BLD000)	
50%	35%	Bigland corporation tax rate	50%	35%
2,000	2,000	Pre-tax profits	2,000	2,000
600	600	Foreign profits tax	600	600
1,400	1,400	Profit available for distribution	1,400	1,400
500	500	Paid out as dividend	–	–
900	900	Profit retained	1,400	1,400
450	450	Bigland net receipt of dividend	–	–
50	50	Withholding tax thereon	–	–
500	500	Distribution gross of dividend tax	–	–
714	714	Grossed up for Bigland tax purposes (multiply by 100/70)	–	–
714	714	Subject to tax	2,000	2,000
357	250	Bigland tax rate applied	1,000	700
		Foreign tax credit		
(214)	(214)	Profits tax	(600)	(600)
(50)	(50)	Withholding tax	–	–
93	nil	Additional Bigland tax payable	400	100
–	14	Excess taxes paid	–	–

against Bigland taxes due on other income arising from that country. In other words, credit for foreign taxes is given on a source by source basis.

An overseas holding company (or dividend cleaning company) may be interposed between a foreign operating company and group head office with the function of bringing together foreign dividends paid out of profits that have suffered tax at high and low effective rates. The resulting dividends from the overseas holding company will be regarded as a single source and as having suffered foreign tax at the weighted average of the effective rates attaching to the dividends that it has received from subsidiaries. The proportion of dividend income into the mixer company may be planned to produce the best underlying rate on dividend flows to the parent – see Figure 21.2.

Assume that Bigland allows companies to mix high and low tax dividends within an intermediate offshore holding company. This can enable a Bigland company with subsidiaries operating in high tax rate locations and low tax countries to mix dividends so that no further tax is paid on distribution to the parent – see Figure 21.2.

Foreign tax credits are not available in all jurisdictions and some countries operate an exemption rather than a credit system, in which case dividend planning needs will be different.

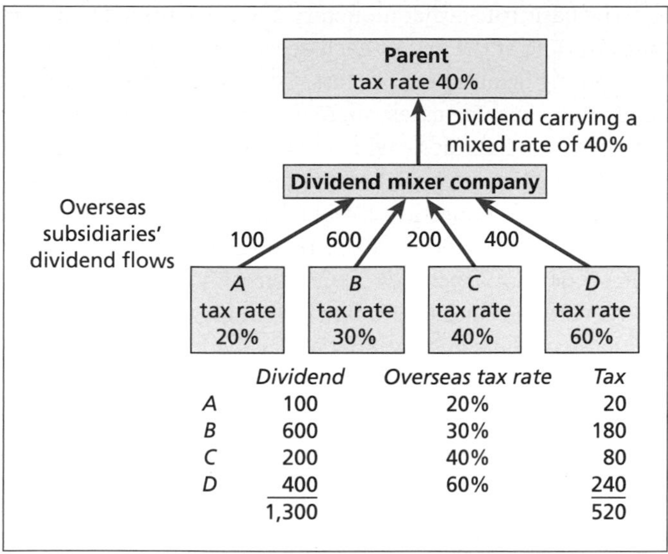

	Dividend	*Overseas tax rate*	*Tax*
A	100	20%	20
B	600	30%	180
C	200	40%	80
D	400	60%	240
	1,300		520

Figure 21.2 **Operation of a dividend mixer company**

Another important feature of dividend planning is the operation of intermediate holding companies to accumulate investment income. For example, a holding company might be formed and dividends received from lower-tier subsidiaries are retained there, rather than sending them by dividend to the parent company. Such treasury planning is, however, subject to anti-avoidance tax legislation in many countries. Intermediate holding companies are also used to take advantage of tax treaties in order to reduce withholding taxes. It may be possible, by correct choice of the intermediate company, to reduce a withholding tax rate to zero.

Furthermore, many companies arrange for high profit deals to be channelled through low-tax vicinities. And they may attempt to arrange transfer pricing amongst overseas subsidiaries to minimise the overall tax take.

Evidently, the process is so complex that corporate treasury executives and tax experts need to get together to consider the possibilities before them created by non-symmetrical tax treatment of dividends – and of other features as well. The whole point of this section is, of course, to present the sinews of international taxation given its relevance in international capital budgeting.

21.6 Taxation of UK multinationals

We now turn briefly to the tax regime facing many multinationals (including UK-based multinationals) with respect to the tax position on foreign exchange positions. In essence, the legislation sets down two acceptable accounting methods for foreign exchange taxation purposes – accruals or mark to market. Under the tax rules, foreign exchange differences arising on most monetary assets and liabilities will be taxed or relieved as income. Assets within the scope of the regime include cash, foreign currency and debts. Liabilities include debts and tax-deductible trading provisions; foreign currency contracts are also included.

The basic rule is that monetary items denominated in foreign currency will be translated into sterling at the end of each accounting period and the difference taken into account in computing taxable profit or loss. Complications arise where accounting rules allow a different result. In some cases, there may be an accounting versus tax mismatch. In other cases there are special rules – which require elections to be made within tight time limits – under which an alternative tax treatment is applied to reflect more closely the accounting treatment. Complications are likely to arise, for example, in relation to anticipatory hedging, particularly in relation to gains realised on rolling forward contracts, and also to hedging of transactions or exposures of one company by another company.

As with the rules for foreign exchange, the rule for the taxation of financial instruments is that payments and receipts under the instruments covered by the legislation, including most interest rate and currency swaps, floors, caps, collars, futures and FRAs, will be taxed as income or allowed as deductions from profits. Where the lifetime of the instrument spans more than one accounting period, income or expense is to be recognised each year according to either mark-to-market criteria or on an accruals basis.

21.7 Multicurrency management centres

Multinational corporations frequently set up currency management centres to focus and control currency management. Foreign exchange deals and covering by subsidiaries are usually routed through such centres. The mere existence of such centres often creates suspicion in the minds of local tax authorities. There may be problems in persuading tax authorities to accept such centres as legitimate business ventures rather than as tax avoidance vehicles. Nonetheless, where a multicurrency management centre has been created, it can provide possibilities for tax minimisation.

The centre is likely to be the focus of foreign exchange transactions and will probably carry the currency exposure risk of the total corporation. Clearly, the tax implications of the location of such a centre need to be carefully studied. A tax haven may reduce the tax charge on foreign exchange gains but will not provide relief for any losses or the cost of administrating the centre itself. The centre should be set in a location that has tax treaties with other countries and in which there are advantages for the corporation as a whole. Tax on interest or dividends withheld should be available to reduce local taxes, and foreign tax credits should be similarly available. An extremely careful assessment of the worldwide tax burden of the corporation must precede choice of centre.

Should the multinational corporation wish to charge foreign exchange losses and administration costs of the centre to its various subsidiaries, it will probably have to prove the need for the centre other than as a tax avoidance device. The charging of a fee for the use of the centre's services to subsidiaries at a rate, for example of $^1/_2$ per cent of the value of each deal helps in this context. Such charges should be in line with fees charged by independent consultancy services. However, tax authorities view with great suspicion fees paid to offshore multicurrency management centres located in areas where the corporation tax rate is very low.

Multicurrency management centres may be the focus of intercompany pricing. A company has scope in choosing the currencies in which it will undertake its intercompany transactions. This choice may be neutral before tax but far from neutral after tax. Take an international company that manufactures in a low-tax area with a strong currency and sells to an affiliate in a high-tax area with a weak currency. It is preferable to invoice in the strong currency and have the exchange loss realised in the high-tax area. This is preferable to invoicing in the weak currency and recognising the exchange loss in the low-tax territory.

21.8 Co-ordination centres

The Netherlands, Luxembourg, Belgium, Dublin and Switzerland have become popular domiciles among European companies for the location of financial subsidiaries designed to reduce tax payments. A checklist for where to locate a financial subsidiary would include the following criteria:

- political and economic stability;
- favourable tax laws;
- hard currency;
- no exchange controls;
- low stamp duty rates;
- low capital taxes;
- good banking and other financial infrastructure;
- no withholding taxes on interest payments and dividends;
- no (or low) taxes on interest income;
- good tax treaty network;
- no securities turnover tax;
- no (or low) taxes on foreign participation.

Belgium has become very popular among companies in the United States and Europe for siting co-ordination centres. Co-ordination centre legislation, enacted in Belgium, provides tax incentives for international groups which centralise their co-ordination activities in Belgium. The legislation permits the multinational, in agreement with the Belgian government, to construct a tailor-made centre to meet its needs. Such centres may carry out a wide variety of financial and managerial services on a virtually tax-free basis. The following activities are permitted for co-ordination centres:

- to establish in-house banks which can engage in intergroup lending, netting, reinvoicing, factoring, leasing and centralising foreign exchange management;
- to raise external loans and issue **Euronotes** and Eurobonds;
- to centralise marketing, research and development and other group support activities.

Legislation can provide the following cash advantages to co-ordination centres:

- 10-year tax exemption;
- no capital registration tax;
- no tax on real estate used by the company;
- tax withholding credits, exemption from withholding taxes and from foreign exchange regulation, and tax and social security exemptions for expatriate employees.

Two sorts of business activity are permitted under co-ordination centre rules. The first includes advertising, information collection and dissemination, insurance and reinsurance, research, government relations, accounting and data processing and centralised purchasing. The second group covers intercompany financial transactions whose objective is to centralise treasury management.

To qualify, the co-ordination centre must be part of an international group with a specified level of aggregate capital and annual turnover. Financial institutions are excluded from obtaining the tax benefits of co-ordination centres in Belgium. The co-ordination centre rules include that at least ten full-time employees by the end of the second year of operations with no restriction on their nationality – although it is probably prudent to have some Belgian nationals. If legislation designed to attack these facilities were introduced, they would not disappear but merely relocate to a territory outside any newly enacted rules.

The effect of taking advantage of co-ordination centre legislation is that the multinational can readily centralise treasury and other cross-border activities in a low-tax environment while creating tax-deductible intercompany costs for subsidiaries in high-tax countries.

21.9 Foreign exchange rate strategy

The range of local tax rules on foreign exchange gains and losses makes the achievement of an optimal foreign exchange tax strategy difficult. Complexity is compounded by frequent changes in tax legislation.

The objective of tax strategy is to maximise distributable net-of-tax profit. As such, tax planning is part of the overall corporate strategy. But tax strategy may have important behavioural implications. If the multinational decides to devolve maximum autonomy to its foreign subsidiaries, it is not likely to permit a tax tactic of repaying loans to obtain tax credits to compromise its style of decentralised management. Low profits in certain foreign subsidiaries, created and manipulated for tax reasons, may lower morale of key staff in a foreign subsidiary.

Nonetheless, tax treatment of exchange gains and losses provides a rich and broad seam for the skills of the corporate treasurer. In this area, particular attention must be paid to the lack of symmetry in tax laws.

Devising a tax strategy involves tabulating tax rules, exchange controls and tax rates in each territory in which the multinational corporation operates. This represents the framework within which tax strategy operates. Another important step towards the specification of a fruitful tax strategy is the tabulation of expected cash flows and assets and liabilities held in each currency. This may already have been done as a stage in normal foreign exchange exposure management. Examination of tax effects of future transactions – in particular, loans in foreign currencies, forward cover and translation gains or losses, plus a schedule of the benefits and costs of channelling such transactions through an offshore tax haven – should also be considered. Treatment of individual transactions will depend upon the local tax laws and exchange control regulations existing. Hodder and Senbet[2] note the key role that tax arbitrage plays in developing an international capital structure and they set out a number of mechanisms for tax arbitrage transactions.

Examples abound of policies designed to maximise distributable post-tax cash flows. Financial assets may be moved between subsidiaries so that gains occur in countries where the tax on gains is nil or very low. Intercompany debt repayment may be accelerated (or retarded) to achieve optimal tax treatment. Subsidiaries may borrow from one another in weak foreign currencies if the exchange gain on the loan devaluation is not taxed in one centre but the loss is tax allowable elsewhere. And they might borrow in strong currencies if the loss on loan revaluation is allowable in one centre while the profit is not taxable in the other. The tax effect in either case may be a key factor in the decision as to where and in which currency to borrow. If the unrealised loss on a foreign loan is not allowed against tax until the loan is repaid, it may be tax efficient to repay it and refinance. Allowable exchange losses should be located in those countries where tax rates are highest. Subsidiaries in weak currency countries may be funded by foreign loans if the exchange loss can be set against local profits. Ensuring that debt is concentrated in countries where operations are profitable and where the tax rate is high is tax efficient. Financing a venture with short-term roll-over funds which are exchange loss allowable against tax, rather than with a long-term loan which is allowable only on termination of the loan, may be tax efficient. Making all currency contracts assignable may also be a useful tactic. Schemes of this sort have to conform to local exchange control regulations, but within such constraints there is plenty of scope to maximise post-tax profits.

We now have the wherewithal to examine the topic of international capital budgeting in more depth; we do so starting in the next chapter.

Summary

- The tax treatment of foreign exchange gains and losses varies from one country to another. Great care must be taken to ensure that local tax regulations are properly and comprehensively understood if optimal tax treatment is to be obtained for a multinational group.
- Within the confines of a general text, it is only possible to describe a series of general principles.
- Under the UK tax rules, foreign exchange differences arising on most monetary assets and liabilities denominated in foreign currency will be taxed or relieved as income, usually in line with accounting treatments. The same idea applies to revenues and expenses on financial instruments. By and large, this puts the UK tax treatment on a similar footing to that in the United States.
- Exchange control regulations forbid or restrict the holding of assets denominated in foreign currency and foreign exchange transactions of residents of the country which has instituted the control. Exchange controls also circumscribe the actions of non-residents in the host country.
- Currency is said to be convertible if the authorities of the home country allow it to be exchanged, without restriction or the need for permission, into currencies of other countries.

- Exchange controls take many forms which range from requirements that residents surrender all holdings of foreign currency to restrictions on the acquisition of foreign-currency-denominated assets and liabilities, from the stipulation that foreign companies meet certain requirements for setting up businesses in the host country to restrictions on remittances out of the host country.
- In response to exchange controls, multinational companies have developed techniques to mitigate some of their adverse impacts. These include the use of transfer pricing, royalty payments, leading and lagging, matching, reinvoicing centres, parallel loans and many others.
- Living with exchange controls clearly presupposes a detailed knowledge of the actual regulations. Resort to a local consultant is often the wisest course because of complexities and unwritten interpretations of regulations and because of the scope for arranging individual agreements with host governments – and, not to put too fine a point on it, the availability of corruption when implementing regulations.

End of chapter questions

21.1 Why do you suppose countries impose foreign exchange controls?

21.2 Do you think that, long-term, foreign exchange controls will encourage or discourage inward foreign investment?

22

The international capital budgeting framework

Like domestic capital investment decisions, international capital budgeting focuses upon expected incremental cash flows associated with a project. The specification of these flows for the international project creates the usual difficulties found in a domestic capital project, but international project analysis is more complex. Although the basic pattern follows the same model as that suggested by corporate financial theory, the multinational firm must consider factors peculiar to international operations.

A project may be estimated to produce very considerable cash flows in a foreign territory but, because of exchange control restrictions, the bulk of these foreign cash flows may not be distributable to the parent company. In these circumstances, looking at the project purely in terms of cash flows accruing in the foreign territory may indicate that it is worth investing. But is this good enough? Surely the present value to the parent company is a function of future cash flows accruing to it which are distributable to the parent company's investors. If the bulk of foreign territory cash flows were blocked by exchange controls, it would only be incremental cash flows which are remittable back to the parent company that add value for its investors. International capital projects may be looked at from at least two standpoints: incremental project cash flows and incremental parent cash flows. To the international company it is only incremental parent cash flows that can add shareholder value.

Complexities often arise in multinational companies because overseas investment projects have substantial knock-on effects on other operations elsewhere within the group. For example, an international engineering company, contemplating the establishment of a plant in Spain, may find that the proposed investment will affect the operations of other units within the multinational group. This may arise, in part, through the new project's effect on sales of other parts of the group within Europe – for example, sales deriving from the UK and Danish plants. But it may also arise through vertical integration by, for example, affecting the output of a mining operation in South America that it owns. It could be the case that the new plant is expected to absorb output from the mine. Where such knock-on effects exist, the firm needs to evaluate the project by aggregating all incremental cash flows accruing. Thus, while cash flows in Spain are clearly relevant, so are reduced cash flows accruing to the UK and Danish operations, and so are increased flows accruing to the South American mine. To get to grips with the difficulties of multinational capital budgeting, it is necessary to take cognisance of such effects.

This chapter gives a simplified overview of international capital budgeting. This is accompanied by a summary of the findings of various surveys of international project appraisal techniques used by US-based multinationals. That these tend to fall short of normative theory will become apparent. The development of a full spectrum of preferred practices in international capital budgeting follows in the chapters immediately following.

22.1 The international complications

There is a handful of complexities in international capital budgeting. These embrace situations where:

- project cash flows and parent cash flows differ;
- part of the parent input is via equipment;
- exchange rates are not expected to be constant throughout the project's life;
- different rates of tax apply in the country of the project and in the parent's country;
- royalties and management fees are involved;
- full remittance of cash flows arising from a project are restricted in terms of payment to the parent.

In international capital budgeting, a significant difference usually exists between the cash flow of a project and the amount that is remittable to the parent. The main reason for this may be the existence of exchange controls in the host nation. Management in an overseas subsidiary can be excused for focusing only upon project cash flows accruing locally. Overseas managers often ignore the consequences of an investment upon the rest of the corporation – in particular the impact of the project at the level of distributable cash flows of the parent company. At the level of the project itself, the appropriate incremental cash inflows are those additional cash outturns resulting from new operations after adjustment for local corporate taxes. From the parent's view, the critical incremental cash flow figures are the additional remittable funds to the parent treasury in London or New York or Amsterdam or wherever. From the central treasury's point of view, the important cash flows relating to a new investment are incremental cash flows that are distributable to the multinational's headquarters. This means that management fees (net of the costs of providing supervision), royalties, interest, dividend remittances, loan inputs and repayments and equity inputs are all key cash flows.

According to corporate financial theory, the value of a project is determined by the net present value of future cash flows available for the investor. Generally, the parent multinational values only those cash flows that are available for repatriation. Valuation would logically be done net of any transfer costs, since it is only these remaining funds that can be used to pay interest at home and corporate dividends. The estimation of parent cash flows involves us in focusing upon incremental remittable cash flows. Whether they are actually remitted or not is immaterial – we need to home in on flows that may be remitted.

International project evaluation might embrace two key stages of analysis. First, project cash flows might be computed from the overseas subsidiary's standpoint, as if it were a separate free-standing entity, that is as if it were being evaluated by a resident of the host country. Focus in the second stage of analysis moves to the parent. Here analysis requires forecasts of the amounts and timing of distributable cash flows. It also requires information about taxes payable. The cash flow projections to the parent may be checked in terms of

Table 22.1 Parent cash flows for an international investment in a country with exchange controls

Equity put into overseas project
Dividends remittable back from overseas project
Equity capital remitted back to parent
Loans put into overseas project
Loan interest
Loan repayments
Management fees received from overseas project net of supervision costs
Royalties
Equipment or inventory contributed to overseas project (here the opportunity cost is the relevant figure)
Contribution accruing to the parent or to a subsidiary within the group on incremental sales to the project. This effect may be positive or negative
Appropriate tax effects on remittance
Remittable value of real operating options
Terminal value of remittable dividends
Terminal value of remittable royalties, management fees, contribution from intragroup sales, etc.
Terminal value of blocked funds multiplied by factor to allow for probability of unblocking by the terminal value date

logic by considering what the parent distributable cash flows would be without the investment and then considering the parent distributable post-investment cash flows and subtracting the former from the latter. It is distributable parent cash flows that matter from the standpoint of the multinational.

For an overseas investment in a country where there are no restrictions on remittance, incremental cash flows accruing to the multinational corporation might be forecast in local currency and then converted into the multinational corporation's home currency in accordance with expected exchange rates prevailing when such cash flows accrue. Where a project is in a country from which cash flow repatriation is restricted, the relevant focus should be upon remittable incremental parent cash flows. Analysis might embrace the cash flows set out in Table 22.1. The simplification described in the table is expanded upon in later chapters of this text.

Theoretically, the arguments in favour of considering only distributable parent cash flows in international capital budgeting decisions are substantial. However, we should be prepared to be pragmatic – as we will show in Chapter 26.

A major complication in international capital budgeting arises in situations where the headquarters company puts up part of its equity or loan capital in an overseas subsidiary by way of equipment or inventory. Clearly, the project should be debited with this input for the purpose of calculating project returns. But parent returns are of paramount importance, so how should we treat this factor at the level of parent incremental cash flows?

The home territory company has surrendered value – in the form of equipment or inventory – in the expectation of obtaining greater value later on in terms of remittable, incremental parent cash flows. The problem that the financial analyst has is to put a value on the equipment or inventory surrendered. There is an ideally suited technique for valuing the property put in by the home territory company – and this involves the use of the concept of deprival value. This was defined by Bonbright[1] as the 'adverse value of the entire loss, direct or indirect, that the owner might expect to suffer if he were to be deprived of the property'. Effectively, in subscribing equipment or inventory, the home territory company is voluntarily being deprived of assets in favour of the foreign business. Bonbright advances three meaningful bases for valuation of an asset:

- The current purchase price of an asset in a comparable state of wear and tear. This is replacement cost (RC).
- The net realisable value (NRV) of the asset. This is the current net disposable value.
- The present value of the expected future earnings stream flowing from the asset (PV).

An individual asset may be valued on each of these three alternative bases. But there are six ways in which values may be ranked in order of magnitude:

1 NRV > PV > RC

2 NRV > RC > PV

3 PV > RC > NRV

4 PV > NRV > RC

5 RC > PV > NRV

6 RC > NRV > PV

It should be noted that replacement cost in all of these circumstances would be the cost of replacing the asset in a condition and location similar to that deprived – this means in a comparable state of wear and tear, of comparable output and cash-generating capacity and in the same place as before deprival.

In cases 1 and 2, the firm would be best advised to dispose of the asset concerned. However the maximum loss suffered on disposal of the asset in these two cases is not NRV but RC. By purchasing another asset of the same type, the firm would restore the opportunity to obtain NRV. Thus, the correct basis for valuation would be replacement cost.

In cases 3 and 4, the firm would be advised to use the asset in the business, thus realising its present value, which is the greatest payoff. However, if the firm were deprived of the asset concerned, it could simply replace it and thereby achieve the PV, which is the most advantageous outturn. In cases 3 and 4, the replacement cost is evidently the relevant deprival value involved.

In case 5, if the firm were deprived of the asset, the amount forgone would be the PV. Evidently what the firm has forgone is the asset with which to earn future cash flow. Since the PV of future cash flows exceeds the NRV, the amount lost by the firm would be the PV. Note that in this case if the firm were deprived of the asset there would be no point in replacing it – hence the amount of RC is irrelevant here.

Likewise in case 6, if the firm were deprived of the asset, there would be no logical reason to replace it because RC exceeds both PV and NRV. This time, if deprived of the asset, the firm has surrendered the NRV rather than the PV. It would have paid the firm to obtain the NRV by selling it off rather than to concentrate upon PV by working the asset.

This approach was, in fact, the recommended method of asset valuation in Sandilands Committee report on *Inflation Accounting* (1975) in the United Kingdom. Although inflation accounting is not the focus of this chapter, the Bonbright approach seems the relevant and

Table 22.2 Basis of an asset valuation

Case	Circumstances	Correct basis
1	NRV > PV > RC	RC
2	NRV > RC > PV	RC
3	PV > RC > NRV	RC
4	PV > NRV > RC	RC
5	RC > PV > NRV	PV
6	RC > NRV > PV	NRV

logical way to assess the value forgone by the home territory company in surrendering assets to an overseas venture. The correct basis of valuation is summarised in Table 22.2.

Cases 1, 2 and 4, where NRV exceeds RC, are likely to be relevant where inventory is input to a project. These cases are much less likely to apply to fixed assets. The most common basis for equipment valuation is likely to derive from case 3, where the purpose for which the equipment is used in the home territory is likely to be ongoing. But cases 5 and 6 might also be encountered. Case 5 implies that the purpose to which the asset is put has a limited life since presumably when it was worn out it would pay to cease operations. Case 6 clearly implies that, rationally, the asset should be sold off immediately anyway.

Obviously, when an asset subscribed to an overseas venture is completely unnecessary to the home operations, then the relevant valuation basis would be NRV. Having identified the appropriate valuation method in respect of the asset subscribed to an overseas project, this becomes the initial minus item in the parent cash flow projections against which subsequent estimated inflows are set. It is worth noting that, whether in a domestic or international situation, were one company to subscribe equipment and inventory to another company in return for a share of its equity, deprival value would provide the correct basis for valuing the input as part of the process of investment appraisal.

We now turn to the third area of complication – exchange rates. If exchange rates are in equilibrium at the time the project commences and if future exchange rates move in line with inflation differentials and if, further, project cash inflows and outflows move in line with general inflation in the overseas territory, then, assuming that there are no exchange control restrictions and assuming that host territory and home country taxes are at similar rates, project cash flow analysis will give exactly the same indication about investment viability as parent cash flow analysis. Rarely, if ever, will all these conditions hold. Because of this, it is recommended that estimated future project cash flows (net of local tax) are shown in money terms (that is, gross of expected host country inflation) and that the project net present value is calculated by following the application of a money terms host country discount rate.

Parent cash flows should be estimated by applying the expected future exchange rate to host country net cash flows if there are no exchange controls, or to remittable net cash flows if exchange controls are in place or are expected to be introduced. Due allowance must be made for host and home country taxation impacts and a parent net present value would be estimated following the application of a risk-adjusted parent discount rate, which might be based upon a weighted average cost of capital where the NPV method is used or upon the ungeared cost of equity in adjusted present values (APV) calculations – see the next section in this chapter.

Estimation of future exchange rates might follow projections of inflation rates. In reality, movement of rates in this way tends to hold in the long term; in the short term, movements in exchange rates often follow discontinuous paths with governments supporting currencies for long periods before giving in and letting the economics of inflation rate differentials have their full effect. Thus, exchange rate movements are often discontinuous and financial analysts may wish to reflect this in their forecasts – although the time at which the full effect of inflation differentials is likely to reassert itself is incredibly difficult to predict. Perhaps this problem is best handled via sensitivity analysis, with various sets of figures being prepared for different timings of purchasing power parity re-establishing equilibrium. More detail on these points appears in the next chapter.

The fourth area of complication concerns taxation. Clearly, project cash flows should be estimated net of local taxation and parent cash flows should be calculated net of host and parent taxation. On this point, reference should be made to Chapter 21 on relevant aspects of international corporate taxation. Also, if royalties and management fees are charged by a home-based company to an overseas operating subsidiary, then these should be shown as a debit to the project cash flow and as a credit in the parent cash flow analysis. Strictly speaking, of course, income to be forgone and/or incremental costs to be incurred in deploying management in pursuit of the project should be set against parent cash inflows.

To reiterate, situations where full remittance of net cash flow from project to parent is restricted are the major source of difficulty in international capital budgeting.

22.2 NPV or APV?

Under the net present value method, all cash flows are discounted to present value at the required rate of return (sometimes called the criterion rate or cut-off rate or hurdle rate). The net present value of an investment proposal is given by:

$$\text{NPV} = \sum_{t=0}^{n} \frac{A_t}{(1+k)^t} \tag{22.1}$$

where k is the required rate of return and A_t is the cash flow in year t.

The NPV approach is not the only one available. Another line of attack is through the adjusted present value. Its pedigree is undoubted. Sired by Modigliani and Miller,[2] this thoroughbred has been trained by Myers.[3]

Remember Modigliani and Miller's proposition that the total market value of the firm and its cost of capital are independent of its capital structure. Thus, the total market value of a firm is given by capitalising the expected stream of operating earnings at a discount rate appropriate to its risk class. It follows that this cut-off rate for investment purposes is completely independent of the way in which investment is financed. Remember too that their original propositions were developed with assumptions of a world without taxes, among other things. Relaxing this assumption, as they did in their 1963 article, they conceded that because the payment of interest is deductible for corporate tax purposes, leverage lowers the cost of capital – but only to this extent. Their valuation model assumes that after-tax operating flows are capitalised at the appropriate capitalisation rate for a firm with no debt in the risk class specified plus a further increment to value resulting from the present value of lower tax payments consequent upon the use of debt and hence the deduction of interest.

Myers' APV approach to discounting cash flows from an investment opportunity, which gives rise to debt capacity, disaggregates sources of value accruing to the project into:

- the capitalised value of the unleveraged project's operating cash flows; plus
- the capitalised value of the tax shield associated with the debt capacity of the project itself.

These cash flows are logically discounted at different rates, a function of their different risks. Naturally, the former are viewed as being more risky. The adjusted present value of a project is given by:

$$\text{APV} = \sum_{t=0}^{n} \frac{\text{OCF}_t}{(1+k^*)^t} + \sum_{t=0}^{n} \frac{k_\text{d} D T_\text{c}}{(1+k_\text{d})^t} - \text{initial investment} \tag{22.2}$$

where OCF_t is the after-tax operating cash flow in period t. The required rate of return in the absence of leverage – that means all-equity financing – is k^*. The cost of debt financing is given by k_d. The value of debt financing sustainable by the project is D and T_c is the corporate tax rate. The discount rate applied to unlevered cash flows, k^*, does not, of course, include any allowance for the impact of debt financing. The notion is simply to disaggregate the financing effect of a project from its operating cash flow effect. The discount rate applied to the tax shield is that applicable to the source of this effect – namely the cost of debt funds. The affinity between Modigliani and Miller's tax adjustments approach and Myers' APV should be self-evident. It should be mentioned that the relationship in equation (22.2) is better expressed as the sum of the present value of operational cash flows and the value of the tax shield less initial investment assuming a constant debt ratio through time. By using a constant amount of debt, D, in the above formulation, the implication is that the outstanding debt in future periods is determined by initially expected market values inclusive of the value created by the project under consideration itself.

It is also worth mentioning that there is scope for debate about the discount rate to be applied to tax savings due to the deductibility of interest from profit for corporation tax purposes. In developing the argument here, one of the key assumptions is that the firm has sufficient profit to cover interest payments and thus render the effective cost of debt to the firm as equal to the net of tax cost.

But should the discount rate applied to the tax savings in equation (22.2) in order to quantify the present value of the tax shield be k_d before tax or k_d $(1 - T)$, that is, after tax? The appropriate tax rate is represented by T. While we prefer the post-tax rate, the answer comes out the same whether the pre-tax approach is adopted and correctly applied.

22.3 Foreign investment and the cost of capital

A reasonable question is whether foreign investment justifies a higher rate of return than does comparable domestic investment. Intuitively, managers often feel that a higher real return is justified for overseas investment given that the company is moving outside a geographical market which its executives know and in which it is presumably already successful. However, one might argue that international diversification lowers a firm's beta. This topic is discussed in Chapter 24 where it is pointed out that there is conflicting and rather weak statistical evidence as to whether multinationality affects beta. A fairly simple routine is also presented for computing the cost of equity capital (in home country terms and therefore in a manner suitable for application to remittable cash flows) for emerging market investments – see the end of section 24.8.

22.4 The basic model

There is sometimes confusion about the order of calculation necessary to arrive at a home country net present value for a project where a multinational corporation is contemplating investment in a country that puts no restrictions on remittance of cash and profit flows. At least four methods may be followed to arrive at the present value. The methods themselves and the stages of evaluation involved in each are summarised in Table 22.3. They all give the same result as long as purchasing power parity holds throughout the period of analysis and as long as taxes are ignored.

Corporate tax is an important issue in international capital budgeting. **Free cash flows** in the overseas territory are obviously critical in analysing potential profitability. These must be stated net of local taxation. Assuming that no exchange controls exist, all incremental foreign cash flows should (**notionally**) be treated as if they were remitted to the parent. In turn, this means that overseas free cash flows net of local taxes have to be subjected (again notionally) to overseas withholding tax, then converted to home currency where they will (probably) bear further tax. Before proceeding to the detailed model for international capital budgeting model, it is obviously necessary to be aware of the problems posed by international corporate taxation; this was the subject matter of Chapter 21.

Of course, the firm might hold foreign free cash flow either in the host country or in a tax haven prior to passing it on, perhaps, to another investment elsewhere in the world, rather than back to the parent. In such circumstances, does it make more sense to focus upon incremental cash flows without subjecting them to home territory taxes? This is one

Table 22.3 Framework for the evaluation of an international investment decision

Stage	Method 1	Method 2	Method 3	Method 4
1	Estimate future cash flows in local currency and in money terms	Estimate future cash flows in local currency and in money terms	Estimate future cash flows in local currency and in money terms	Estimate future cash flows in local currency and in money terms
2	Convert to home currency using forecast exchange rates	Calculate present value using local currency money terms discount rate	Reduce to real terms flows in local currency by discounting for local inflation	Reduce to real terms flows in local currency by discounting for local inflation
3	Calculate present value using home currency money terms discount rates	Convert to home currency present value using spot rate	Convert to home currency using spot exchange rate	Calculate real terms present value in local cash using real terms discount rate
4			Calculate present value using real terms discount rate	Convert to home currency present value using spot rate

of many problems that needs to be addressed. In fact, it receives further attention in later chapters.

Returning to Table 22.3 it is suggested that the superior approach to capital budgeting in countries with no regulations preventing the repatriation of funds would be to use method number 1, duly adjusted for taxation, and might involve the following steps:

- Forecasting local currency, money terms, free cash flows after local taxes. Given the existence of inflation, this better simulates reality than does calculation in real terms.
- Converting these to home currency, money terms, free cash flows net of all taxes – host and home. Conversion would involve forecasts of exchange rates, whether using an allowance for inflation differentials for all years of the project, or a correction for disequilibrium followed by a trajectory reflecting inflation differentials.
- Discounting of home currency, money terms, free cash flows net of all taxes to net present value using a home currency, money terms, risk-adjusted, net of tax discount rate.
- If the project's assumptions are reasonable and if it promises a positive NPV under these most stringent tax assumptions, the project is likely to be attractive.

Even where exchange controls are an impediment to full distribution of project cash flows, the same order of routine as that suggested in the bullet points above is the preferred method since it takes account of host inflation which may have a big effect on a project. But, clearly the analysis has to be restricted to remittable flows only. This creates some problems in terms of cash flow analysis – but consideration of these is best deferred until the next chapter. The discount rate applied would logically be a risk-adjusted weighted average cost of capital in NPV calculations or the ungeared cost of equity in APV calculations.

22.5 Empirical studies of international investment appraisal

A number of surveys of US multinationals' practices of international capital budgeting have been published and they seem to indicate that actual procedures are far from what theory would suggest. A summary is available in Buckley.[4] In the following chapters we formulate a normative model for international capital budgeting.

Summary

- Analysing capital investment decisions involves comparing cash inflows with cash outflows from a project.
- Investment appraisal focuses upon expected incremental cash flows associated with a project.
- Overseas projects possess the usual difficulties found with respect to domestic capital projects but international project analysis is much more complex.
- The same basic model as that suggested by corporate financial theory is used in international capital budgeting, but the multinational firm must consider factors peculiar to international operations.

- A project may be estimated to produce considerable cash flows in a foreign territory but, because of exchange control restrictions, the bulk of these foreign cash flows may not be distributable to the parent company.
- In the circumstances above, looking at a project purely in terms of cash flows accruing in the foreign territory may indicate that it is worth investing – but is this good enough?
- The present value to the parent company of a multinational is a function of future cash flows accruing to it which are distributable to the parent company's investors.
- Remember that for an overseas project some cash flows may be blocked by exchange controls.
- Only incremental cash flows are remittable back to the parent company which add value for its shareholders. Where there are no exchange controls, such problems are minimised – but note that they still exist. It is always possible that a host government may impose exchange controls sometime in the future.
- An overseas capital project may be looked at from at least two standpoints. The first of these is incremental project cash flows. This angle is concerned with foreign currency cash flows. The second angle is incremental parent cash flows. This means cash flows that may find their way back to the parent. To the multinational company, it is only incremental parent cash flows that matter.
- There are six key categories of complexity in international capital budgeting. In reality, of course, at least one of these is equally applicable to domestic capital budgeting. The six categories embrace situations where:

  (i) full remittance of cash flows arising from a project is restricted in terms of payment to the parent;
  (ii) part of the parent input is via equipment;
  (iii) exchange rates are not expected to be constant throughout the project's life;
  (iv) different rates of tax apply in the country of the project and in the parent's country;
  (v) royalties and management fees are involved;
  (vi) there are knock-on effects impinging upon group operations elsewhere in the world.

  Difficulties raised by these six points are considered in more detail in Chapter 23. Be fully conversant with the problem.
- Many poor international investment decisions have been made because of the failure of the management of the multinational company fully to comprehend that it is distributable parent cash flows that matter rather than mere project cash flows.

End of chapter questions

22.1 Why should capital budgeting for projects in an overseas subsidiary be assessed from the parent's perspective rather than just the subsidiary's cash flow perspective?

22.2 What additional factors deserve consideration in multinational capital budgeting that may not normally be relevant for a purely domestic project?

23 The international capital budgeting model

Analysing capital investment decisions involves comparing cash inflows with cash outflows from a project. Investment appraisal focuses upon expected incremental cash flows associated with a project. As we pointed out in Chapter 22, overseas projects possess the usual difficulties found with respect to domestic capital projects plus a few more which makes international project analysis more complex. The same basic model as that suggested by corporate financial theory is used in international capital budgeting, but the multinational firm must consider factors peculiar to international operations.

A project may be estimated to produce considerable cash flows in a foreign territory but, because of exchange control restrictions, the bulk of these foreign cash flows may not be distributable to the parent company. In these circumstances, looking at a project purely in terms of cash flows accruing in the foreign territory may indicate that it is worth investing – but this level of analysis may not be good enough.

The present value to the parent company of an international investment is a function of future cash flows accruing to it which are distributable to the parent company. But, for an overseas project, there may be some cash flows that are blocked in the host territory by exchange controls. It is only incremental cash flows which are remittable back to the parent company that add value for its shareholders. Where there are no exchange controls, such problems are minimised – but many of the complexities referred to in Chapter 22 still exist. And it is always possible that a host government may impose exchange controls sometime in the future.

An overseas capital project may be looked at from at least two standpoints. The first of these is incremental project cash flows. This angle is concerned with foreign currency cash flows. It would be the relevant angle from which a local partner would look at an overseas project. The second perspective is incremental parent cash flows. This means that focus is upon cash flows that may find their way back to the parent. To the multinational company, it is only incremental parent cash flows that matter. So this would be the right focus for a multinational in appraising overseas projects.

In Chapter 22, a handful of sources of complexity in international capital budgeting were pointed out – in fact, there were six. In reality, of course, at least one of these is equally applicable to domestic capital budgeting. The categories embrace situations where:

- full remittance of cash flows arising from a project are restricted in terms of payment to the parent;

- part of the parent input is via equipment;
- exchange rates are not expected to be constant throughout the project's life;
- different rates of tax apply in the country of the project and in the parent's country;
- royalties and management fees are involved;
- there are knock-on effects impinging upon group operations elsewhere in the world.

Various texts point out the source of difference between project cash flows and parent cash flows. This may, in the main, be due to:

- exchange rate movements not reflecting purchasing power parity;
- different rates of host and home corporate taxation;
- full remittances of overseas cash flows being restricted.

Note that enabling blocked cash flows to become remittable – for example, through countertrade – may reverse the original categorisation of a project as inferior, on the basis of apparent parent cash flows, to acceptability while still using the same set of decision criteria.

23.1 International project appraisal

Domestic and international investment appraisal may be similar in some respects but there are very significant differences. The essential message is that, while domestic project appraisal is concerned with establishing the present value of future cash flows at home, international capital budgeting focuses upon the present value of remittable future cash flows.

The six problem areas highlighted earlier impinge upon international investment such that any overseas opportunity possesses Janus-like qualities. Its two-facedness becomes manifest in that, viewed from the project standpoint, its appearance is unlike the image presented when seen from the parent's angle. The argument has been advanced that it is remittable cash generation that matters in terms of adding value for the corporation. When there are no exchange controls creating an impediment, project cash flows should all be remittable – although changing exchange rates and parent taxation will present difficulties to be borne in mind. When there are exchange controls, a further complexity is in place. In these circumstances, remittable parent cash flows may be achieved by:

- dividends;
- royalties and management fees;
- loan repayments;
- countertrade;
- other means of unblocking.

Such remittable flows must, of course, take account of changing exchange rates and parent tax rates, as would be the case if cash generated by a project were not fettered by exchange control regulations. Note that loan repayments are specified as a means of hastening remittance when exchange controls are in place – the whys and wherefores are discussed later in this chapter. It follows that, where there are remittance constraints, the role of financing international investment may be critical in terms of parent NPV. In these circumstances, financing can affect the present value of investments – and significantly.

In short, international project appraisal needs to take account, in home currency parent cash flow terms, of capital outlays (allowing for equipment transfer effects), maximum remittable cash flows (including royalty and management fee flows and loan repayments), and tax and exchange rate effects, and these flows have to be discounted at the appropriate risk-adjusted opportunity cost of capital. One of these problem areas is taxation – it is to this topic that we now turn.

23.2 Taxation

It will be noted that the approach advocated here involves investment appraisal from the parent standpoint, with profit flows arising in the host territory first of all falling into the local tax net. Then, on distribution (or assumed distribution) they may be subjected to a withholding tax and, finally, in the home territory they may fall into the tax net again, depending upon home taxation legislation.

Assume that a company with a proposed project in an overseas territory expects to earn the foreign currency equivalent of $1m in both pre-tax profit and cash generation terms. With an overseas tax rate of 15 per cent, a withholding tax of 10 per cent and a home corporation tax rate of 33 per cent, the figures that go into the project appraisal would be as shown in Table 23.1.

Of course, it may be the case that the multinational decides to reinvest all of the profit post-foreign tax in the host country – this would involve a reinvestment of the equivalent of $850,000. In other words, no withholding tax or home tax would be paid. Equally, it may be the case that the multinational decides to pay out profits to an intermediate holding company. And the cash so distributed would be onward re-routed for reinvestment elsewhere in the worldwide operations of the multinational. Under this scenario, the amount available for reinvestment would equal $765,000 (that is, the amount before home country tax but after foreign and withholding taxes – see Table 23.1). Evidently, by taking credit for only $670,000, we are applying a scenario that is the harshest possible in tax terms. If the investment exhibits a positive NPV in parent cash flow terms under this

Table 23.1 Project appraisal: parent cash flows net of taxes

	$	$
Profit and cash generated before tax		1,000,000
Foreign tax equivalent of		150,000
Withholding tax equivalent of $850,000 @ 10%		85,000
Home country tax		
$1m @ 33%	330,000	
Less foreign tax credit	235,000	
		95,000
Giving net of tax profit flow of		670,000

scenario, then clearly, assuming monies generated by the investment are either reinvested in the host country or routed elsewhere in the multinational's global operations, the effect will be to enhance the anticipated outturn.

If the project fails to promise a positive NPV in parent terms under this harshest scenario but does look acceptable if these assumptions are relaxed on the basis of re-routing funds around the world without their being returned to the home country, then top management has further information upon which to make a decision. Whether it gives such a project the green light or not is a matter of judgement. At least the project appraisal is producing data that would be valuable in reaching that goal for which management is paid – a wise decision based upon informed judgement.

In any case, using the harshest tax scenario could be said to take cognisance of the corporation tax rules in various countries applying to controlled foreign companies (CFCs). Legislation on CFCs has been introduced to counter the following two perceived abuses that inland revenue authorities believed had resulted in tax avoidance:

- the accumulation of income by subsidiaries in low-tax areas;
- the artificial diversion of business profits away from the home country when otherwise those profits would have been subject to home country tax.

CFC legislation seeks to impose home country tax on home country companies in respect of the unremitted profits of certain types of companies located in low-tax countries. The legislation is complex and varies from country to country.

The essential point is that the application of host and home taxation in terms of arriving at cash generation in home country currency is the harshest tax treatment. But does it best take account of the real world of the multinational? To answer the question, consider an example. Imagine a multinational based in the United States but with no home operations – all of its businesses are overseas. Suppose that dividends to group shareholders and amounts to cover head office costs are paid out of dividends remitted from the European subsidiaries. Assume further that the group has interests in the Far East, Australasia and Africa. These are profitable but pay no dividend to the headquarters in the United States. Surely, given such a scenario, it would be illogical to apply home and host tax to new investments in Europe only, but debit Far Eastern, Australasian and African projects with host country taxation only – in other words, to allow them to avoid home tax for evaluation purposes.

If the illogicality is not immediately apparent, we could take as an example an otherwise similar group except that this second multinational pays for group dividend and head office costs out of profit remittances from the Far East, Australasia and Africa – in other words, the European subsidiaries would remit no dividends in this instance. Clearly, it would not be sensible for the first multinational to give investments in the Far East, Australasia and Africa a free ride as far as US tax is concerned and for the latter to exempt European project proposals from US tax.

The author of this book has come across evidence of more than one multinational charging all of its overseas projects (for investment appraisal purposes) with a hypothetical average home tax rate based on evening out the above anomaly. Perhaps the best approach is to look at overseas projects with the harshest tax treatment in a base case and run sensitivity analysis scenarios assuming zero home tax and with an average home tax rate (see the previous sentence). This should give group directors the wherewithal to exercise informed judgement.

Before leaving this section, it should be mentioned that some home country tax legislation does not impose any further tax on remittance of dividend. Clearly, in international capital budgeting, companies with tax headquarters in these countries will gain in value terms – and this value gain is entirely as a result of a tax imperfection.

We now turn to the analysis of international capital budgeting decisions where there are no exchange controls in force.

23.3 Project evaluation with no exchange controls

Whether a project is subject to exchange controls or not, the initial appraisal invariably begins with an analysis in host country currency. Such an appraisal involves the basic cash flow techniques of domestic capital budgeting incorporating the computation of a net present value or internal rate of return. The methodology might incorporate NPV or APV figuring, using the logic of the respective frameworks as summarised in Chapter 22 with discount rates reflecting required returns in local currency terms. Clearly, this would indicate how a local partner might view a particular project. But it would not be this perspective from which the multinational should evaluate a foreign capital investment decision. To the international corporation, the relevant focus is upon remittable cash flows. In terms of adding value, it does not matter whether the flows are actually remitted; the fact that there is no impediment to remittance should, logically, create value for the corporation. Thus, it is assumed that all available incremental free cash flow (normally profit before interest and tax, add back depreciation, less fixed capital inputs, less working capital inputs, less tax payable) is paid out and remitted to the multinational headquarters. The parent will, for project evaluation purposes, convert to home currency at the anticipated exchange rate and also allow for notional home territory corporate tax.

In the analysis which follows, we approach the problem of international project evaluation without exchange controls on the assumption that the parent company owns all of the equity in the foreign subsidiary. This assumption is relaxed later on. Although Shapiro[1] points out that 'incremental cash flows to the parent can be found by subtracting worldwide parent company cash flows (without the investment) from post-investment parent company cash flows', the more usual approach is to concentrate from the very beginning upon incremental cash flows to the parent, focusing substantially upon the project rather than the entire company. This latter method usually involves less computation, but where there are knock-on effects, great care has to be exercised. By this is meant those kinds of situation where, for example, investment in a new plant in Spain affects output and cash generation in, say, the French and Belgian subsidiaries. This kind of situation is encompassed by the third bullet point in the next paragraph. Of course, whether the route to incremental cash flows is via worldwide remittable cash flows or through remittable cash generation at the level of the project itself, the final decision should be the same.

Where a multinational company contemplates an overseas investment on the basis of 100 per cent ownership, as is frequently the case, and when there are no exchange controls, the present value calculation, from the parent's viewpoint, should include:

- The multinational's incremental free cash flow year by year (net of host and home tax).
- Royalties, management fees and the like, if any (net of home tax).

- Any **cannibalisation effects** must be allowed for in the evaluation. For example, if the multinational were exporting direct to the host country prior to implementation of the project and subsequently it is to be locally sourced, the loss of contribution, net of tax, must be built into the calculation.
- If any subsidised interest is involved, the present value of the subsidy must be incorporated. For example, use of purchased US equipment by a European-based multinational, undertaking investment in the Far East, may attract a lower than market interest rate for dollars based on **Exim Bank** finance. The subsidy, net of tax, should be discounted year by year at the market rate for dollar finance, net of tax, to arrive at a present value. Of course, where such subsidised finance is available in a foreign currency, the question of covering the exposure must be considered and appropriate action taken.
- Where part of the parent's contribution to the overseas project is via equipment input, this must be allowed for. If the equipment input is without actual cost passing, but would otherwise be used within the parent's ongoing business, Table 22.2 in Chapter 22 sets out an appropriate basis of valuation. If the circumstances are as above, except that cash is paid, the consideration, net of any tax effects, must be incorporated.
- The multinational's opportunity to exploit any growth opportunities over and above the base case valuation of incremental cash flows. These kind of opportunities are frequently called real operating options. How any such options might be valued is also considered later in this chapter.
- If incremental free cash flows are forecast over a finite time period only, the question of a terminal value has to be addressed. Various approaches to calculating this are considered later in this chapter.

Table 23.2 provides a summary of generally encountered incremental cash flows as sources of value in international capital budgeting without exchange controls. Table 23.3 shows this information in a slightly different format. The items in Table 23.3 are considered in turn.

Table 23.2 Summary of relevant cash flows: international investment with no exchange controls

Value	Approach used	
	NPV	APV
Value of investment inputs	✓	✓
Value of incremental free cash flow of overseas investment	✓	✓
Value of management fees and royalties	✓	✓
Value of any cannibalisation effects to the group	✓	✓
Value of any subsidised interest involved	✓	✓
Value of any growth opportunities in excess of value of incremental free cash flows	✓	✓
Allowance for terminal values	✓	✓
Value of tax shield due to debt; the amount will vary from classical to imputation tax system		✓

Table 23.3 Valuation of overseas project from parent's perspective: no exchange controls

Value of overseas project	=	−	Value of investment inputs
		+	Value of incremental free cash flows of investment
		+	Value of management fees and royalties back to parent
		−	Value of any cannibalisation effects to the group
		+	Value of any subsidised interest
		+	Value of growth opportunities in excess of value of incremental free cash flows
		+	Allowance for terminal values
		+	Value of tax shield due to debt capacity created by project in cases where the APV method is used

The value of investment inputs embraces fixed capital and working capital required to undertake the project. This might be thought of as a gross amount, in local currency terms as at year of the project. In our initial scenario there are no minority interests, but we should nonetheless focus upon the present value of this amount, converted to home currency at the time-zero exchange rate less any allowances for the opportunity cost of any parent equipment input along the lines suggested in Table 23.2.

The next item in Table 23.3 is the value of incremental free cash flows. The specification of this item is relatively straightforward, with flows converted to home currency net of taxes using expected exchange rates for each year of cash generation. Of course, if free cash flow is forecast for a finite period only, it will be necessary to incorporate a terminal value – see Table 23.3. Where the valuation of free cash flow is based on forecasting to infinity, this would not be necessary.

Table 23.3 next specifies the value of management fees and royalties. These should be specified net of host country withholding taxes and home currency corporate taxes. It is suggested that, to avoid double counting, incremental free cash flows of investment should be calculated net of management fees and royalties.

Again, assessing forecasts for a finite period, it would logically follow that a terminal value of royalties and management fees should be incorporated in the valuation exercise. Where the forecast is done on a simplified assumption of being to infinity, this would not be necessary. The same kind of idea also applies in respect of cannibalisation effects, the next of our valuation parts in Table 23.3.

In international capital budgeting, it is often the case that a new investment may have knock-on effects. For example, a new plant in a host country may mean lost exports to the host country from elsewhere in the group, or it may mean a new scheduling of production and sales with the new facility taking output from elsewhere in the group. The contribution on such lost turnover (net of taxes) should be allowed for in the capital budgeting proposal if accurate simulation of reality is to be achieved. Of course, for an integrated group of companies, there may be positive upstream and/or downstream effects, the contribution from which should be included in the analysis.

Referring back to Table 23.3, we next look at subsidised interest. As mentioned earlier, this frequently arises as a result of equipment purchase involving the equivalent of the Exim Bank in the country of supply. So, the subsidy may be in a currency other than that of host or parent, in which case forward cover or swapping has to be considered. For example, a

Dutch parent company considering investment in Malaysia but purchasing Japanese equipment may find that it can access yen at below the market rate. The amount of the interest subsidy would be given by the annual interest payment in yen versus the market rate annual interest payment in yen – less costs of forward cover assuming the company wishes to avoid foreign exchange risk on such interest payments. Usually such subsidised finance is only available for relatively short periods. The discount rate used to value this item is the market rate for the currency in which the subsidy is denominated. This contrasts with earlier value calculations where the discount rate is the appropriate rate representing either a risk-adjusted weighted average cost of capital for the project concerned or the ungeared cost of equity, dependent upon whether the calculation is based upon NPV or APV methods respectively.

A different approach is adopted in this case because we would normally discount at a rate reflecting the riskiness of the cash flow stream concerned. To apply the weighted average rate to our interest rate stream is not an acceptable practice. The riskiness of the interest-related stream of cash flows should be taken into account by discounting at the market interest rate – and this is clearly very different from the weighted average cost of capital. If this is accepted, the next question concerns whether the discount rate should be pre-tax or post-tax. In capital budgeting exercises we are always concerned with post-tax incremental cash generation so it follows that the logical discount rate should be an after-tax rate. Since we are concerned with home country value creation, the relevant tax rate to apply to both the interest subsidy and to the discount rate would logically be the home country corporate tax rate. Note that this tax rate should be applied to both numerator and denominator to ensure consistency.

If we revert to Table 23.3, it will be noted that our next source of value creation is growth opportunities. Since this topic is moderately complicated, we return to it under a separate heading (see the next section).

According to the order of considering topics in Table 23.3, terminal values come next. When we forecast incremental cash generation for a project out to year *n* and this is a finite period, we may or may not expect the project to cease at that time. If we do expect it to cease, we should get back the value of invested working capital and something for fixed capital too. This must be allowed for as a terminal value.

If we do not expect the project to cease but are merely truncating it at some finite number of years for analysis purposes, then we should allow for a terminal value to take account of operations beyond the conveniently assumed truncation date. In such cases the terminal value should embrace the value of:

- free cash flows from the investment converted to home currency and net of host, withholding and home taxes;
- royalty and management fees, net of all taxes;
- cannibalisation effects beyond the truncation date, net of all taxes.

While the former is usually allowed for in calculations, the latter two are frequently forgotten in international investment appraisal.

The suggested methodology for estimating the value of an international investment to the multinational corporation in a situation where there are no exchange controls has so far been approached on the assumption that the project does not have minority interests. Where there are minorities in the overseas investment, the valuation process needs to be changed marginally, since the minorities will participate in some cash flow streams, but not all. Note that, normally, of the cash flow categories listed in Table 23.2, the minority partners will participate pro rata in:

- value of incremental free cash flows of the overseas investment;
- value of subsidised interest;
- value of growth opportunities accruing in the host country.

The minority might not share pro rata in the investment inputs. Remember that the parent may sell, or transfer for value, equipment to the overseas venture; clearly such effects have to be allowed for in investment appraisal from the home-based parent company's standpoint. Management fees, royalties and cannibalisation effects also have to be allowed for but these are invariably exclusively for the parent – the minority does not participate in such effects at all. Similarly, when it comes to calculating a terminal value and this is based on future free cash flows of the project, future royalties and future cannibalisation effects, clearly the minority interests would only be participants in the first of these values – and adjustment needs to be made appropriately.

23.4 Growth opportunities – a.k.a. real operating options

Real options analysis is one way of looking at, and attempting to value, growth opportunities. Indeed, real options are often referred to as reflecting the present value of growth opportunities (PVGO). Valuing projects with growth opportunities may readily be undertaken by:

- Making cash flow projections for a base case scenario, perhaps with a fairly modest growth assumption, for example in line with the growth of the economy. The point is that this base case scenario might be written around most likely outturns.
- On top of the base case cash flow projections, the analyst might superimpose further projections based on more optimistic outturns with the firm pursuing a more growth-orientated strategy, if this is compatible within the market place.
- The net present value of the base gives a good idea of most likely outturns.
- The net present value of the superimposed expansionary situation (assuming that it is supported by reasonable assumptions) gives an idea of PVGO.
- With sensitivity analysis logically applied to the base case outturns and to the PVGO scenario, a realistic view of the project's expectations may be obtained.

This kind of methodology is a perfectly good way to look at valuing growth opportunities. Indeed, discounted cash flow analysis is the gold standard of valuation and, as such, is necessarily the cornerstone of any valuation process.

Real options analysis may provide a raincheck on the magnitude attached to the value of growth opportunities. But we would stress that the valuation by discounted cash flow comes top of the league of valuation techniques. Real options analysis is something of a reinforcement. So, how does it work?

The central argument for a real options approach is that the standard discounting process adopts a static analysis. While this is true, using sensitivity analysis stops the analysis being too static. The standard discounting process is static in the sense that operating decisions are viewed as being fixed in advance and, as such, give rise to the base case set of incremental cash flows. This feature is at the heart of why the pure discounted cash flow techniques, used by so many companies, may be less than perfect in simulating the business world.

In reality, good managers are frequently good because they pursue policies that maintain flexibility on as many fronts as possible and maintain options that promise upside potential. For investment decision-making, this means keeping open the opportunity to make decisions contingent upon information that may become available in the future. For example, dependent upon actual levels of demand, or competition, or cost, the rate of output of a new product may be accelerated, existing facilities may be extended or, should outturns be less attractive than expected, they may be closed temporarily or even abandoned altogether.

Research and development is an obvious case in point. Testing a new market via a pilot operation is clearly another. Oil exploration obviously falls into this category, levels of exploration and investment being highly contingent upon oil prices prevailing. Mining and quarrying are similar kinds of investment – extraction, temporary closure or even abandonment being obvious courses of action that will depend on actual prices of and/or demand for the product concerned. International investment is another example. Invariably it begins with a small commitment which may be scaled upwards should the environment prove profitable, or it may be curtailed should the host country appear to offer less attractive cash flows than anticipated. Of course, many purely domestic investments are rather like this, having scale-up possibilities.

All of these examples have one key feature in common: the firm has flexibility in terms of its course of action depending upon outcomes and factors that are unknown at the time of the project's inception. Qualitatively, the idea is fairly straightforward, and we can take it further by incorporating numerical data.

23.5 Valuing real operating options

Let us look at a very simple numerical example and consider how the decision tree approach can be used to value real operating options. Following on from this example, we will show how further complexity can be built into the model as necessary.

Imagine a European firm, United Chemicals and Colloids plc (UCC), confronted with a foreign investment which is likely to absorb €9.5m and promises a best estimate of remittable future net cash flows, in real terms, amounting to:

Years 1 and 2	€1.1m p.a.
Years 3 to 12 inclusive	€1.45m p.a.

The firm forecasts remittable cash flow for 12 years only and uses a 10 per cent discount rate to evaluate the project. As shown in Table 23.4, the investment promises a best estimate net present value of €0.23m (negative).

However, note the probability distribution of potential remittable cash flows. This is summarised in Table 23.5 and it shows that there is a 5 per cent chance (based on subjective probability estimates) of the project yielding annual remittable cash generation equal to €4m per annum from year 3 through to year 12. But if this level of outturn were achieved,

Table 23.4 UCC case: best estimate net present value (euro million)

	Years		
	0	1–2	3–12
Investment	–9.50		
Remittable net cash flow		+1.10 p.a.	+1.45 p.a.
Discount at 10%	–9.50	+1.91	+7.36
Net present value = euro 0.23m (negative)			

Table 23.5 UCC case: expected remittable cash flows (and their probabilities) (euro million)

	Years				
	0	1–2		3–12	
		Probability	Amount	Probability	Amount
Investment	–9.50				
Remittable cash flow		0.4	+2	0.05	+4*
		0.4	+1	0.50	+2
		0.1	0	0.30	+1
		0.1	–1	0.10	0
				0.05	–1

* At this level of outturn, UCC would invest a further €30m in year 4 with best estimate remittable cash generation for years 5 to 12 inclusive of €16m per annum.

the firm would, most likely, scale up and invest the equivalent of a further €30m in year 4 and would, according to best estimates, achieve very creditable returns reflecting the potential buoyancy which would translate into remittable cash flows of foreign currency giving €16m per annum from year 5 to year 12 inclusive.

What should be apparent is that, with the scale-up decision incorporated into the analysis, the NPV of the project will now be different. As shown by Table 23.6 (overleaf), the new NPV of the project comes out at €0.94m positive. In other words, the value of the call option embedded in the project may be said to approximate €1.17m.

Clearly, the project referred to is simplistic. This is deliberately so to illustrate the basic routine required. Obviously the €16m forecast beyond year 4 with the scale-up option is a single number estimate and fails to incorporate probabilities.

To pursue the problem of evaluating real options further, we now consider a single project that requires a capital outlay of £10m. In return, the company receives an asset with present value of net inflows of £9m. Assume that both of these figures, and all others in this example, are in real terms. Assume also that the asset is risky and its value is likely to change. Returns on the asset have a standard deviation of about 40 per cent per year and the company can wait for up to three years before deciding to invest or not. The appropriate discount rate is 5 per cent. Viewed conventionally, this project's NPV is £9m minus £10m. That is £1m negative. But having the opportunity to wait three years and see what happens is a valuable option. In effect, the company owns a three-year American call with an exercise price of £10m on underlying assets worth £9m. With an

Table 23.6 UCC case: calculation of net present value with scale-up option (euro million)

	Years								
	0	1 and 2		3 and 4		4		5–12	
		Probability	Amount	Probability	Amount	Probability	Amount	Probability	Amount
Investment	−9.50					0.05	−30		
Remittable cash flow		0.4	+2	0.05	+4			0.05	+16
		0.4	+1	0.50	+2			0.50	+2
		0.1	0	0.30	+1			0.30	+1
		0.1	−1	0.10	0			0.10	0
				0.05	−1			0.05	−1
Expected PV at 10% discount rate	−9.50		+1.91		+2.08		−1.02		+7.47
Expected NPV = euro 0.94m (positive)									

American call option on a stock which pays no dividend, it is not optimal prematurely to exercise it. In this case, an American option is valued as a European call option. Now, if we use the Black and Scholes approach and the notation of Chapter 16, NPV_q for this option is £9m ÷ [£10m/$(1.05)^3$]. This equals 1.04. The option has a cumulative variance of 0.40 times $\sqrt{3}$, or 0.69. The Black and Scholes matrix table, which was introduced in Chapter 16, shows that an option with these characteristics is worth 28.4 per cent of the value of the underlying asset, or 0.284 (£9m). This equals £2.556m positive. Compare £2.556m positive with £1m negative.

The simple project just examined had an NPV, traditionally measured, of minus £1m. But valued inclusive of option value, its worth is around £2.5m positive. Is this contradictory? What should the company do? In fact, the traditional NPV and the option value do not contradict one another. The company should not invest in the project now. If it does, it will forfeit the option and waste £1m. But neither should it discard the project. It should wait, watch and actively cultivate the project over the next three years. Although the project's traditional NPV is less than 0, the project is very promising because NPV_q is greater than 1. Although $E > S$, these two variables are relatively close to one another and $S > PV(E)$. By the end of three years, there is a good chance that the NPV will exceed zero and the option will be exercised. In the meantime, the option on the project really is worth over £2.5m, not minus £1m, provided the company does not, suboptimally, exercise it now.

This example could be likened to a biotechnology project which a firm is thinking of selling off because it is not part of its core research and development focus. The project may not promise a positive net present value if developed now, but if the firm were to dispose of it, what price should it ask? Naturally, the asking price would be based upon jam tomorrow. One way to put a value on this might be via real options analysis. Incidentally, another approach would be to use discounted cash flow valuation of various possible outturns plus subjective probabilities attached to these scenarios.

In the example of UCC, valuation of the growth option was approached via subjective probabilities. The solution to the valuation problem in this case could have been achieved by specifying volatilities, a time factor relating to the exercise period and, finally, an exercise price.

A question that the reader is likely to ask, in connection with the valuation of real options, concerns estimating the volatility of a project. There is not one single guaranteed approach here but there are at least three possible routes to putting a figure on volatility:

- *One might take a guess*. What is a high standard deviation? Returns on leading US stocks have a standard deviation of about 21 per cent per year. For the United Kingdom, the figure is nearer 26 per cent per year. For small US companies, the figure is 36 per cent per year. Individual projects will have higher volatilities than a diversified portfolio like a company. Volatility of 20–30 per cent per year is not remarkably high for a single project.
- *One might gather some data*. Volatility can be estimated for some businesses using historical data on investment returns in certain industries. Alternatively, implied volatilities can be computed from quoted option prices for a very large number of traded equities.
- *One might do a simulation*. Spreadsheet-based projections of a project's future cash flows, together with a probability distribution for project returns, might be helpful.

The question of the magnitude of t in real options valuation is also critical. The big issue here is how long the firm is likely to maintain a profitable, value-enhancing competitive advantage. This is a matter of judgement but there are major concerns that might be raised in attempting to quantify this competitive advantage period (CAP). They relate to barriers to entry, patent positions and ferocity of competition, among others – for a considered view on this topic, see Buckley, Tse, Rijken and Eijgenhuijsen.[2]

Sometimes multinationals pursue an almost scatter-gun pre-empting strategy which creates numerous minor real operating options. For example, the firm might make a number of small investments in a few Eastern European countries with the expectation that at least one will be highly successful and, maybe, provide the location for a scale-up in that country and for export to other nearby buoyant economies too. The point is that the physical presence in a multiplicity of countries may deter competition and provide a portfolio of question marks (to use Boston box jargon), of which at least one is expected to be very successful. In the above kind of instance, the evaluation might be undertaken to reflect the strategy of pre-emption with cash outflows for the various different countries in year zero aggregated and with inflows expected for a small number of years from all of these locations also aggregated, followed by the expected scale-up allowed for in the quantitative analysis using real operating option valuation methods as above. Of course, this type of scatter-gun strategy would be likely to be the exception rather than the rule. On such occasions, evaluation using this approach truly reflects the firm's strategic choice of intended pre-emptive action.

The message should be apparent. A strategy that adds corporate value is to maintain flexibility through structuring investments in a manner paralleling options. Investments of this kind, which includes most international commitments, should be analysed beyond the traditional DCF model. This means evaluating them to embrace the option characteristic. Structuring investment decisions in such a way as to confer an option element enhances shareholder value over and above the base case present value scenario. Failure to evaluate investments of this kind to allow for this option aspect may, at best, result in an understatement of the potential shareholder value created and may, at worst, mean that firms fail to undertake growth strategies and ultimately pack their product portfolios with yesterday's winners but today's dogs.

23.6 Project evaluation with exchange controls

Rather like project analysis where no exchange controls are operative, investment appraisal with controls normally begins by focusing upon the host country currency cash flows. This would be the perspective from which a local partner would appraise the investment – but it would not be the angle that the multinational would find most relevant. Again, as in the case where no exchange controls were assumed to exist, the focus of the international group would be upon remittable cash generation. And, of course, the existence of exchange controls create a significant barrier to such remittability.

When exchange controls exist, it is very frequently the case that investment is undertaken in conjunction with a local partner – sometimes this is a legal requirement in the host country, sometimes it is of the multinational manager's own volition. Given this tendency, the analysis here assumes the involvement of a local partner.

Where a multinational firm contemplates an overseas investment and where there are exchange controls impacting upon potential remittances to the parent, then the present value calculation, from the parent company's standpoint, would include the following:

- The multinational's investment input. There are complications here since such subscription may be via equity or parent debt. Subscribing by the debt route may allow cash generated by the project to be returned to the home country by debt repayment and interest whereas, were subscription to be via equity, such flows might be blocked by controls.
- Remittances of cash generated back to the parent, primarily, through dividend payment. Of course, not all cash generated would be remittable because of exchange control constraints. Thus, forecasts of annual profit and loss accounts and balance sheets – not just cash generation details – will be critical to the evaluation since, when exchange controls exist, remittance is invariably based upon a proportion of profit or some formula related to profit in conjunction with capital employed (or capital originally subscribed from outside the host country plus retained earnings).
- Remittances back to the parent by way of parent debt service – capital plus interest – and management fees and royalties, although these are invariably subject to very careful scrutiny and to ceilings set by exchange control authorities and regulations.
- Allowance for investment from local debt raised as part of the initial financing. Against this, one should logically include debt repayment and interest thereon. The virtue of an analysis which embraces investment financed by third-party debt and its service is that it ensures that all capital required is accounted for in the project appraisal. Some analysts, by contrast, leave these items out of the analysis altogether. If the project generates sufficient blocked cash flows to repay debt and accrued interest, this latter approach is entirely acceptable (it will, incidentally, achieve the same bottom-line result as the approach recommended). If this is not the case, then the more conservative approach is to reduce the dividends assumed to be distributed to take account of the repayment schedule. The data for this more conservative approach are less readily available if local debt raising and its service are left out of the cash flow equation – see Buckley[3] for further detail on this point.
- As in the earlier example, where no relevant exchange controls were in existence, cannibalisation effects must be built into the equation.

- When we are confronted with exchange controls on an overseas project and where finance with a subsidised interest rate is raised by the overseas venture, we do not need to take account of any subsidised interest as a separate item in the cash flow analysis – as was the case where no exchange controls were present. Remember that when there were no exchange controls, we would undertake our cash flow appraisal by applying a discount rate to cash generation before interest. So the worth of the interest subsidy must be calculated separately. By contrast, where exchange controls are present, the bottom line of the forecast profit and loss account will already have taken into account interest charges – including the effect of the subsidy itself. However, when host country exchange controls are present but the multinational raises soft debt, specifically and unequivocally tied to the project, in a company outside the host country, then the case for including the value of the subsidy as a parent cash flow is clear. Indeed, the multinational may structure the financing deal to ensure that it receives the full benefit of the subsidised interest itself.
- Allowances, as in the case where there are no exchange controls, for parent contribution of equipment as part of its input. The cash flow analysis, of course, may well have different values for the equipment compared with the local balance sheet figure for initial input.
- Invariably, in international capital budgeting with exchange controls, blocked cash flows remain after allowing for dividend distribution (whether expected or notional) and debt service. There are a number of approaches to valuing these. But, first of all, let it be said that if such cash were permanently blocked with no means available to get cash back to the parent then the value of such blocked funds must be zero. In reality, this is rarely the case. First, countertrade and such techniques present ways of unblocking. And, second, there is usually some expectation of existing controls being relaxed or removed altogether. A probability factor may be applied to model such expectations. Care has to be taken to avoid double counting: we refer to this later on in this section.
- An allowance for any terminal values.

Table 23.7 provides a summary of the generally encountered sources of value in international investment appraisal with exchange controls. Table 23.8 shows the same information along slightly different lines. We now examine the items in the tables in more detail and in turn.

The value of the parent's share of investment inputs may cover fixed and working capital required to undertake the project, with equipment inputs valued in accordance with the asset value concept referred to in Table 23.2. The parent's share of capital inputs would logically be valued in home currency terms and the split between equity and debt input would be a question of the particular contractual agreements between parent and overseas operating business.

The next item in Table 23.8 concerns locally raised debt. There are two approaches available with respect to this item. First of all, we might leave this out of the analysis entirely and we might compensate for this by disregarding local debt service. This is entirely acceptable as long as it is remembered that there may be cash effects in terms of reduction in assumed dividend where insufficient cash is generated to service debt and dividend in an individual year. Thus, for evaluation purposes, payment of dividend may be constrained by shortages of cash in particular years. The alternative approach is to include investment financed by local debt and, to compensate, to allow for debt service in the cash flow analysis. This latter

Table 23.7 Summary of relevant incremental cash flows: international investment with exchange controls

	Approach used	
	NPV	APV
Share of equity inputs allowing for subscription via equipment, etc.	✓	✓
Share of input as parent debt	✓	✓
Share of input as local debt*	✓	✓
Value of remittable dividend stream	✓	✓
Value of management fees and royalties	✓	✓
Value of cannibalisation effects to the group	✓	✓
Value of any subsidised interest involved only if it is raised and serviced outside the host country and, presumably, in a territory without exchange controls	✓	✓
Repayments of parent debt and interest thereon	✓	✓
Repayment of local debt and interest thereon*	✓	✓
Value of any real operating options	✓	✓
Share of blocked cash flows allowing for: • countertrade remittability; or • multiplying by factor for discontinuance of exchange controls	✓	✓
Allowance for terminal value	✓	✓
Value of tax shield due to debt: the amount will vary from classical to imputation tax system		✓

* Some analysts exclude both of these items – see text for an overview and commentary on this problem.

Table 23.8 Valuation of overseas project from parent's perspective but with exchange controls

Value of project	=	–	Value of share of equity input allowing for subscription via equipment, etc.
		–	Value of input as parent debt
		–	Value of input as local debt*
		+	Value of remittable dividend stream
		+	Value of management fees and royalty stream
		–	Value of any cannibalisation effects to the group
		+	Value of any subsidised interest only if it is raised and serviced outside the host country and, presumably, in a territory without exchange controls
		+	Value of parent debt repayment and interest thereon
		+	Value of local debt repayment and interest thereon*
		+	Share of value of any real operating options
		+	Value of blocked cash flows assuming either unblocking via countertrade and similar means or multiplying by a factor representing the probability of discontinuance of exchange controls
		+	Allowance for terminal values
		+	Value of tax shield due to debt capacity created by project in cases where the APV method is used

* Some analysts exclude both of these two items – see text for further details on this problem.

approach ensures the full control of cash flow, and this may be valuable when it comes to undertaking sensitivity analysis with lower than expected outturns.

The next item is the value of the parent's share of remittable dividend stream. Of course, in order to determine the estimated level of remittable dividend to the parent, forecast profit and loss accounts and balance sheets for the overseas venture will have to be prepared. Any dividend remittance will only be payable out of the balance on profit and loss account after taking off such items as royalties and interest payments.

The value of management fees and royalties is, in fact, the next item listed in Table 23.8. This value should be stated net of host country withholding taxes and net of home currency taxes too.

As we mentioned earlier in this chapter, cannibalisation effects in international capital budgeting have to be taken into account in terms of the present value of the lost margin, net of taxes, in home currency terms arising from knock-on effects.

Next we turn to subsidised interest. Note that Tables 23.7 and 23.8 state that its value would only, logically, be included if it were raised and serviced outside the host country's exchange controls – indeed, presumably, in a country without exchange controls thus enabling the multinational to acquire the full value of the subsidy. The whole point here is that if the debt is raised in the host country, by the operating company there, its financial effects will already be felt in profit and loss account terms before determining dividends remittable. By contrast, if raised outside the host country, the subsidy will not have been built into the equation. Essentially, the earlier remarks under the sixth bullet point at the start of this section should make the point clear. If such subsidised funding is outside the host territory, its value should be determined in exactly the same manner as suggested in the section on subsidised debt in cases where there are no exchange controls.

When we refer back to Table 23.8, we see that the next items are parent and local loan repayments and interest. Clearly, the inclusion of local debt service will be a function of whether or not it has been allowed for in the initial cost of the investment. (This was discussed earlier in this section.) There is no such problem with parent debt – this should unequivocally be included in our cash flow analysis. The objective of the multinational putting in some of its subscription as parent debt is to enable payments to the parent to occur in the presence of host country exchange controls. Of course, host governments respond by restricting debt levels, for exchange control purposes, through thin capitalisation rules, which allow the host to refer to notional leverage levels for parent debt service purposes. Aside from such problems, the cash flow implications for the parent in the home country are clear. Capital and interest would normally be denominated in home currency terms. This would ensure that debt service was in parent currency terms and would result in relatively straightforward cash flow implications from the parent's standpoint.

We next turn to the value of blocked cash flows. Clearly, if blocked for ever, with no possibility of unblocking, the value of such cash to the parent can only, logically, be zero. Usually, in the real world, there are possibilities of unblocking based on:

- such devices as countertrade;
- the probability of the host country relaxing exchange controls.

Both of the above bullet points mean that we might put a value on blocked cash which is 'unblockable'. For capital budgeting purposes, this might involve estimating the amount of blocked cash to be built each year, taking the multinational's share, allowing for countertrade costs and then estimating the net of tax value in parent currency terms.

Another approach, in terms of valuing blocked cash flows, is to assume that they build up within the company in the host country, earning appropriate interest up to some terminal value date and then to apply a probability factor to take account of potential unblocking as of that date.

Of course, it should be mentioned that these ideas apply also to the value of real operating options. A portion of the value of the multinational's share might be blocked and must be valued in a manner approximately consistent with the approach suggested immediately above.

In Table 23.8, terminal value comes next. When we focus upon cash flows over a finite period, we might or might not expect cash flows to cease then. If we do expect them to cease, we should get back a share of invested capital in terms of working capital released, any residual values of fixed capital and any blocked cash. Clearly, the multinational's share of this represents a terminal value in the project – although care may have to be exercised to ensure that no double-counting of blocked cash occurs and it is also necessary to allow for the impact of controls to be in place at the end of the project's life.

If it is not expected that the project will cease but it is merely being truncated after a finite period for ease of analysis, then a terminal value should be allowed for on the basis of expected operations and their cash flow implications beyond the assumed truncation date. In such a case, the terminal value should embrace the value of:

- dividend flows in home currency terms net of all taxes;
- blocked cash generation beyond the truncation date capitalised as suggested above; this might include, of course, blocked real operating options;
- royalties and management fees net of all taxes;
- cannibalisation effects beyond the truncation period net of all taxes.

Of course, it is assumed that all loans (especially to the parent) have been repaid by the truncation date; if not, then appropriate amounts with their specific timing should be duly taken into account.

Finally, in terms of items listed in Table 23.8, there is the question of whether the NPV or APV criterion is being used to estimate value. Where the APV route is adopted, the appropriate tax shield calculations must be made – the coverage given to this topic in Chapter 22 applies equally in the case of international investment appraisal with exchange controlling.

23.7 Debt–equity swaps

Debt–equity swaps became popular with corporations as a means of reducing the cost of investment in less developed countries (LDCs). Debt–equity swaps are financial transactions in which LDCs exchange part of their debt with foreign commercial banks for equity rights which are sold to an interested party. The purchasers of these equity rights may be either the same lenders – the foreign banks – or firms that pay the lenders for these rights. Debt–equity swaps can be a profitable source of advantage for firms that exploit their key benefit – access to local currency at exchange rates more favourable than the official rate.

Debt–equity swaps have their roots in the international debt crisis of the 1980s and the resultant difficulties suffered by debtor nations, banks and the international financial community. Commercial banks have been swapping their problem loans into equity investments because the debtors have insufficient hard currency to make interest payments, let alone to pay back principal. They make the swaps either directly, as an exchange for other loans with which the bank invests abroad, or indirectly, by selling the loan in the secondary market.

The commercial bank which has lent to the LDC has an asset. Since there is some possibility of rescheduling and even default, the asset may be worth less than $100 for a face value debt of $100. The bank will evaluate this worth and also what might be paid for it in the secondary market. If the bank decides to sell, it may negotiate (in discount terms) a level that will satisfy its financial requirements. When the bank's discounted loan is matched by an offer from a corporate investor, the loan may be sold. In some cases, the investor may be a domestic corporation in the LDC which has access to hard currency, perhaps as a result of previous capital flight. The debtor country then redeems the debt in local currency. The first of the above transactions is a debt sale in hard currency. Lending banks sell debt obligations in hard currency in the US secondary loan market, at a price lower than their nominal (or face) value.

Next in the debt–equity swap process, a currency exchange takes place. The acquired hard currency debt is presented by the purchaser to the country's central bank, which redeems it for local currency. The redemption rate is roughly equal to the debt's original dollar face value but converted at the official exchange rate minus a transaction fee. The debt–equity swap is concluded when the corporate investor purchases, in local currency, equity rights to existing ventures or invests in the start-up of new ones.

Clearly, from the standpoint of the corporate investor, entry into a developing country via the debt–equity swap market is achieved at a cost lower than would otherwise be the case. In capital budgeting terms, then, the initial capital cost is lowered. From the point of view of the Third World country, debt is redeemed and increased investment is encouraged. Obviously, this topic is one that is particularly relevant in the case of international capital budgeting with exchange controls since most of the LDCs with the potential for undertaking attractive debt–equity swaps are nations with significant exchange controls.

Brady bonds

With their roots in the international debt crisis of the 1980s, there were also **Brady bonds**, named after Nicholas Brady, then the US Treasury Secretary. These were dollar-denominated bonds issued mostly by Latin American countries. In exchange for commercial bank loans, defaulting countries issued new bonds for the principal sum and unpaid interest. These were tradable and sometimes had guarantees, of varying strength, attached. The innovation of the Brady bond was to allow the commercial bank to exchange its claim on developing countries into a tradable instrument, allowing the banks to get the debt off the balance sheet. Countries involved in the early rounds of Brady bond issuance were Argentina, Brazil, Bulgaria, Costa Rica, Dominican Republic, Ecuador, Mexico, Morocco, Nigeria, Philippines, Poland, Uruguay and Venezuela.

The Brady bond process ended during the 1990s. However, many of the innovations involved became commonplace in later sovereign restructurings. This was the case for Russia's debt reprofiling, for example. Various countries have since repaid after restructuring. Of course, a few defaulted on their Brady bonds, for example Ecuador in 1999.

23.8 Sensitivity analysis

So far, both under the heading of international capital budgeting with and without exchange controls, a route has been suggested towards the estimation of value. Naturally, the usual capital budgeting considerations as regards beginning the analysis with a best estimate picture of cash flows and then adjusting outturns to allow for the effects of a number of 'what if?' scenarios would apply. In addition to the usual changes to market share, lower demand, late commissioning of plant and so on, one might allow for variations from the harshest tax treatment, using different exchange rates, estimating terminal values using different methodologies, and assessing the sensitivity of outturns to varying levels of political risk (see Chapter 25) and to varying assumptions about real operating options.

Summary

- When analysing international capital budgeting propositions it is necessary to distinguish two very different kinds of situation. The first of these is where there are no exchange controls in the host country. The second is where there is partial blockage of overseas cash generation. Distinguishing which category a particular project falls into is necessary because the recommended methodology of analysis varies from one to the other.
- We look, first of all, at the situation where there are no exchange controls in the host country. In this kind of situation, we may do our analysis in terms of project cash flows or in terms of parent cash flows. Really, though, it is the result of the parent analysis that matters. Project cash flow forecasts, duly discounted, usually give the same indication as to attractiveness of an investment opportunity as parent cash flow analysis – but this is not necessarily the case. To reiterate, it is parent cash flows that matter from the standpoint of the investors in the multinational company.
- Project cash flows, of course, involve the comparison of cash outflows and cash inflows in local currency terms. Such an analysis will lead to the calculation of an internal rate of return or a present value for the project under consideration. Calculation may involve the APV or NPV techniques. Be sure that you are clear as to how the APV and NPV methods differ.
- Since we are dealing, first of all, with a situation where there is no restriction on remittances of bottom-line cash generation from a territory without exchange controls, cash generation in the host country is just as good as cash generated in the United Kingdom or in the United States or in Germany. In situations where there are no exchange controls, there is no point in restricting the analysis in parent cash flow terms merely to the dividend remitted.
- Calculations in terms of parent cash flows should begin by undertaking an analysis of overseas cash flows in local currency terms, at local rates of inflation and then converting them to home currency flows by using expected future exchange rates, allowing for home taxes and then discounting at a risk-adjusted rate which allows for anticipated inflation in the home country. Exchange rate movements should be consistent with these different inflation levels except for corrections of previously prevailing disequilibria.

- The valuation of growth opportunities is a recommended step in valuing overseas investments, whether with or without exchange controls.
- It is usual, in undertaking analysis of an overseas project in terms of home parent cash flows, to subject potential cash generation available for remittance to withholding taxes and home taxes. Since not all overseas cash generation will be remitted to the parent company, this is really the harshest tax treatment possible. If the project stands up on this severest set of tax assumptions, it must also stand up assuming a less strict tax burden. And it may, of course, be possible to engineer a less tough tax impact through the use of tax havens and other devices.
- In terms of converting host currency cash generation into home currency terms, we have suggested that exchange rates prevailing in future years should be estimated. Note that this may be done simply by using the forward rate or through a purchasing power parity analysis. We believe that it is useful to undertake the analysis in home currency terms using both methodologies.
- We now have the wherewithal to undertake a full analysis of the potential of the project in home currency terms. We have details of capital outflows and capital inflows translated back into home currency terms. In addition, where there is subsidised finance, we need to calculate the present value of this subsidy in home currency terms and, if we are using the APV approach, we will need to estimate the value of the tax shield of the debt capacity of the project in home currency terms. All of this can readily be done and the summation will give us full present value details of the project in home currency terms.
- We now turn to the situation where there is some blockage of cash flows in the host country. This usually arises because of exchange controls. The bullet points from here onwards relate to the situation where there is some constraint upon remittance of cash generated in the host country.
- Only remittable cash flows out of an overseas territory create added shareholder value. Cash permanently blocked in an overseas territory adds no value.
- The multinational may remit monies to the parent company in a number of ways. This may include dividend payments, but, in addition, it may involve royalty payments and interest payments on parent loans. This represents a departure from the rules which students have learned in respect of domestic capital budgeting, but debt repayment is a genuine technique by which multinationals hasten the transfer of monies out of a blocking host territory and this needs to be reflected in international capital budgeting analysis. It reinforces the idea that financing does affect parent cash flows in capital appraisal when exchange controls create constraints on remittances. This is a very important point.
- If it is possible to hasten repayment through parent loans, a pertinent question follows. Why not finance all overseas projects by parent loans? In fact, host countries rarely allow it – their exchange controls frequently require a substantial equity input from the parent company. Often, exchange controls stipulate that if an overseas company has an excessively high debt level, then thin capitalisation rules may be invoked under which part of the debt is reclassified for exchange control purposes as equity. Secondly, excessive use of parent debt closes one route by which political risk is minimised, namely the use of local funding. This technique is dealt with in Chapter 25.
- One route towards avoiding remittance constraints involves royalties and loan interest and capital repayments on parent loans. In international capital budgeting terms, these

24.2 The new international evidence

New evidence suggests that the figures in Table 24.1 should be revised. This emerges from in-depth work by Dimson, Marsh and Staunton,[4] who set out to eliminate some of the biases contained in previously published data. Their original study covered one hundred years to 2000 and has been updated annually. Their work was justified because returns had been derived from index figures, there was a bias towards successful firms – weakly performing companies, perhaps affected by financial distress and falling market capitalisation, tend to be demoted from indexes of top stocks. Correcting for this kind of bias and others relating, for example to small index sizes and incorrect rights issue adjustments, among others, enabled Dimson, Marsh and Staunton to focus upon international equity, bond and bill returns over the period from 1900 to 2000. As they say:

> Good indexes follow an investment strategy that could be followed in real life. Apart from dealing costs, an investor should in principle have been able to replicate index performance. Indexes, especially when they are constructed retrospectively, must therefore be free from any look-ahead bias. They must be constructed solely from information that would have been available at the time of investment. Serious bias can arise if index constituents are tilted towards companies that subsequently survived or became large, or towards sectors that later became important.

Having corrected for various biases, Dimson, Marsh and Staunton produced key tables of returns. These are brought together in our composite Table 24.2. This shows returns accruing to capital gains and dividends, or interest, on a per annum basis from equities, government bonds or government bills (three-month bills) for selected Western economies over a very long period. The figures here show lower returns than the Ibbotson and Sinquefield data because of the elimination of various biases. It is our opinion that the new data carries greater authority than that quantified earlier.

On the topic of the equity risk premium (that is, $R_M - R_F$), data on past worldwide returns allow us to put a figure upon this key piece of information, for various countries. Statistics are reproduced in Table 24.3.

The data shown in Table 24.3 may be helpful when applying the capital asset pricing model (see the equation at the start of this chapter) approach in estimating a firm's cost of equity capital in various parts of the world. However, there are pitfalls in expecting their returns to perpetuate in the future. One of the arguments favouring the arithmetic mean

Table 24.2 Real (inflation-adjusted) equity, bond and bill returns around the world from 1900

Country	Equities (% pa)			Bonds (% pa)			Bills (% pa)		
	Geometric mean %	Arithmetic mean %	Standard deviation %	Geometric mean %	Arithmetic mean %	Standard deviation %	Geometric mean %	Arithmetic mean %	Standard deviation %
Ireland	4.8	7.0	22.2	1.5	2.4	13.3	1.3	1.4	6.0
Japan	4.5	9.3	30.3	−1.6	1.3	20.9	−2.0	−0.3	14.5
The Netherlands	5.8	7.7	21.0	1.1	1.5	9.4	0.7	0.8	5.2
Switzerland†	5.0	6.9	20.4	2.8	3.1	8.0	1.1	1.2	6.2
United Kingdom	5.8	7.6	20.0	1.3	2.3	14.5	1.0	1.2	6.6
United States	6.7	8.7	20.2	1.6	2.1	10.0	0.9	1.0	4.7

† Premia for Switzerland are from 1911.

Source: Dimson, E., Marsh, P. and Staunton, M., *Triumph of the Optimists*, Princeton University Press, Princeton, NJ, 2002.

Table 24.3 Worldwide equity risk premia relative to long-term bonds and treasury bills from 1900

	Annual equity risk premium relative to long-term government bonds			Annual equity risk premium relative to three-month treasury bills		
Country	Geometric mean %	Arithmetic mean %	Standard deviation %	Geometric mean %	Arithmetic mean %	Standard deviation %
Ireland	3.2	4.6	17.4	3.5	5.4	20.6
The Netherlands	4.7	6.7	21.4	5.1	7.1	22.2
Switzerland†	2.7	4.2	17.9	4.3	6.1	19.4
United Kingdom	4.4	5.6	16.7	4.8	6.5	19.9
United States	5.0	7.0	20.0	5.8	7.7	19.6
World	4.6	5.6	14.5	4.9	6.2	16.4

† Premia for Switzerland are from 1911.

Source: Dimson, E., Marsh, P. and Staunton, M., *Triumph of the Optimists*, Princeton University Press, Princeton, NJ, 2002.

flows from looking at a simple example. Assume that a share moves from 100 in year 0 to 120 in year 1 and back to 100 at the end of year 2. It pays no dividends. Clearly, the return on the investment is zero. And, the geometric mean return comes out at zero whilst the arithmetic mean calculation is of an annual return of 1.6667 per cent – see below for calculations.

$$\text{Geometric mean} \quad \sqrt{(1.2)(0.8333)} - 1 = 0\%$$

$$\text{Arithmetic mean} \quad \frac{20\% + (-16.6667\%)}{2} = 1.6667\%$$

Note that the percentage return on investment for year 1 is plus 20 per cent and for year 2 is minus 16.6667 per cent (since the price falls from 120 to 100). We are sure that the geometric mean return looks more realistic.

Another argument which favours the geometric mean derives from looking at the outturn, year by year, as annual independent draws for a stable distribution of returns. Thus, suppose that a two-period investment has equally likely outcomes of a 40 per cent return and a minus 20 per cent return. Average returns might be computed thus:

$$\text{Arithmetic mean} \quad \frac{40\% + (-20\%)}{2} = 10\%$$

$$\text{Geometric mean} \quad \sqrt{(1.4)(0.8)} - 1 = 5.8\%$$

On this basis, which is the more realistic measure?

The expected result at the end of the two-year period can be computed thus. Assume \$1,000 is invested and that the returns conform to the expected frequency distribution below:

$$\begin{aligned}
\$1{,}000 \times (1.4) \times (1.4) \times (0.25) &= \quad \$490 \\
\$1{,}000 \times (1.4) \times (0.8) \times (0.25) &= \quad \$280 \\
\$1{,}000 \times (0.8) \times (1.4) \times (0.25) &= \quad \$280 \\
\$1{,}000 \times (0.8) \times (0.8) \times (0.25) &= \quad \underline{\$160} \\
\text{Expected value} \quad &= \underline{\underline{\$1{,}210}}
\end{aligned}$$

Clearly, we are looking at an expected outturn at the end of year 2 of $1,210. This expected return is the arithmetic average return given by:

$$\$1,000 \times (1.10)^2 = \$1,210$$

The incorrect argument is that the expected outturn at the end of the investment period is given by:

$$\$1,000 \times (1.4) \times (0.8) = \$1,120$$

To be sure, the latter figure of $1,120 may accrue but, as shown above, it only has a 50 per cent probability of occurrence. What is ignored is the *ex-ante* possibility of outturns amounting to $1,960 (given by $1,000 × 1.4 × 1.4) and $640 (given by $1,000 × 0.8 × 0.8). Each of these has a 25 per cent probability of occurrence. Allowing for these probabilities, we obtain an expected value at the end of two years amounting to $1,210. Note that, according to this argument, the false return conforms to the geometric return. In the context here, its falsity relates to the fact that it does not take into account the binomial-type distribution of potential outturns.

Viewed from a standpoint before the event, by undertaking a risky investment, we are exposed to a broad spread of potential results. We require a higher return on this risky investment, compared with an investment with a certain return, to compensate for the spread of possible outturns. The arithmetic mean takes into account the full distribution of potential results. The question that follows is what is the appropriate time interval to use? Is it one year? Or are investors single period expected utility of terminal wealth maximisers, given a two-year period? Or a three-year period? Lengthening the time interval increases the precision of the estimate of the mean return. But lengthening the time interval also strains the plausibility of the assumption that returns are drawn from a stable distribution.

To reiterate, the simple argument favouring the geometric mean is as follows. If a share falls by 50 per cent in the first year and then doubles – that is, it increases by 100 per cent – in the second, the investor breaks even. The total return is zero. The geometric return conveys this precisely:

$$\sqrt{(1-0.5)(1+1)} - 1 = 0$$

However, the arithmetic mean return comes out at 25 per cent per annum, given by:

$$\frac{-0.5+1}{2} = 0.25$$

But investors can really only be expected to realise geometric returns over the long time frame. Indeed, the compound rate of return to a buy and hold strategy would tend to be measured by the geometric, rather than the arithmetic, mean. The geometric mean return is always less then the arithmetic mean return, except when all yearly returns are exactly equal. There is an approximate relationship between the two means such that the geometric mean is roughly equal to the arithmetic mean minus one half of the variance, σ^2, of yearly returns. Thus:

$$\bar{R}_g \approx \bar{R}_a - {}^1\!/\!_2\sigma^2$$

Another idea occasionally quoted as suggesting the use of a geometric mean flows from the view that both it and the internal rate of return (IRR) are essentially based on compound interest arithmetic. The argument that one should compare like with like would militate in favour of comparing a geometrically derived IRR with a geometrically derived mean in capital budgeting (similar to the point about a buy and hold strategy mentioned earlier).

There is other evidence favouring the use of a geometric mean. In essence, it derives from ideas of mean reversion of share returns to a trend. If share returns were expected to revert to a trend, then this would suggest the use of a geometric mean since the geometric mean is, by definition, an estimate of a smoothed long-run trend. Referring back to the example of the investment offering an equal chance of a 40 per cent return and a minus 20 per cent return period by period, mean reversion would tend to chop off the more extreme outturns in the distribution of potential payoffs. Of course, it is these less likely outturns that give the pattern of potential payoffs its binomial distribution. It is the likelihood of achieving this kind of distribution that is at the heart of the argument preferring the arithmetic mean over the geometric counterpart. With mean reversion, and hence a more narrow range of outturns than the full binomial distribution, this line of argument breaks down. The fact is that there is now a substantial body of evidence identifying mean reverting behaviours in stock returns. This empirical observation is one of the strongest arguments supporting the use of the geometric mean in estimating the cost of equity capital for the firm. Given this background, we will be returning to the topic of mean reversion later on.

24.3 Mean reversion

There is now a significant body of research which has sought to identify mean reversion in stock returns. While some studies have found evidence of mean reversion in stock returns, it is relatively weak. Furthermore, the findings of many of these studies have been criticised on statistical or methodological grounds in follow-up papers. We refer in detail to this evidence in Buckley.[5]

Many financial economists (but not all) believe that there is good evidence of mean reversion in stock returns. This means, for example that a poor year for stock market returns is slightly more likely to be followed by a good year, rather than by another poor year. Similarly, good returns are more likely to lead to weak subsequent returns rather than another good year. Thus, bad years would cancel out good years and vice versa. Over long periods of time, the risk of equities is reduced and if there is more mean reversion with stocks than with bonds, stocks eventually become less risky than bonds. Of course, it is possible to argue that the mean reverting behaviour of stocks versus the mean averting behaviour of bonds has a lot to do with unexpectedly large inflation levels after the Second World War and this is merely a fleeting phenomenon – at least, the mean averting behaviour of bonds might be.

The problem with data on mean reversion is that they go back only a few decades and we do not have very many independent and non-overlapping 20-year periods from which to draw inferences. Formal statistical tests have been unable to establish convincingly that there is absolutely certain mean reversion in stock returns, even though the raw numbers suggest it. If there were no mean reversion in stock returns, there would be no reason to believe that stocks would become less risky than bonds over long horizons – unless bonds themselves were to exhibit mean aversion.

But there are psychological hypotheses underpinning mean reversion. According to behavioural finance (see, for example, Thaler[6]), if investors become overly optimistic about economic prospects and push stock markets to levels that are unreasonably high, then sobering news may lead investors to correct this error, forcing markets back down. Bubble correction phases of this type generate mean reversion in returns.

Mean reversion is frequently viewed with scepticism because it seems to imply a conflict with the idea that markets are efficient and prices tend to be right. It is a misconception that if prices reflect fundamental value they should move randomly. Mean reversion can be consistent with a world where prices are rational. All that is needed is that the risk perception for stocks, in general, changes over time. Following a big market setback, investors may find stocks more risky. Higher risk should be compensated by a higher expected return. So, after a stock market setback, we might see higher average returns and we would call this mean reversion. The whole idea of market efficiency has been subject to more and more scepticism as evidence for market crashes and crises has accumulated. As a theory it has one foot in the grave.

Indeed, another view of the risk/return paradox is that by looking at stock returns on existing stock markets, we miss the risk of collapse of a particular stock market. Advocates of this idea are quick to point out that of all of the stock exchanges that existed in 1900, half have since then experienced significant interruptions or have been completely abolished. Looking only at data for the United States and a handful of Western-type markets misses this kind of risk because these markets have never experienced collapse. However, the risk of future collapse is always there. Perhaps high return on stocks relative to bonds simply reflects the possibility of a complete market collapse. This is, really, a rather frail argument because this kind of risk might not just limit itself to the stock market. A shock that could bring down stock markets would surely also affect bond markets. Indeed, this is usually the way things have happened.

24.4 The equity risk premium

So where does all this leave us in terms of estimating the value of the equity risk premium, that is (R_M minus R_F)? We use data from the United States. We have to confront the significant problem of the use of a geometric or an arithmetic mean. According to the new evidence, a figure of 5.8 per cent to 7.7 per cent, depending upon which of the respective means is used, looks like the appropriate amount, given that R_F is measured by reference to treasury bills. The figure is 5 per cent to 7 per cent if R_F is measured against long-term government bonds. But are these returns sustainable in the future? Humbly, we have to admit that we cannot be sure. Perhaps a way around this problem is simply to take the real return achieved from stocks in the past and use this as an estimate for a firm with a CAPM **beta** of 1. Given a geometric mean basis, this would imply a real return from equities of 6.7 per cent for the United States. If bonds were expected not to be outmanoeuvred by inflation and to yield a real return of between 2 and 4 per cent, this would suggest an equity premium of around 3 to 5 per cent.

It is also worth mentioning that mean reversion in stock returns is not the same as mean reversion in corporate investment project returns. However, Fuller, Huberts and Levinson[7] find that earnings per share growth numbers for corporations seem to revert to the mean after seven years or so.

Furthermore, we cannot be completely certain as to whether arithmetic or geometric means should be used in valuation exercises. Perhaps the evidence of mean reversion is sufficient to make a strong case for the geometric mean – but the jury is still deliberating. So, vendor and purchaser, regulator and regulated can continue their discussions. Certainly, using more than a single discount rate in valuation is realistic. Of course, such a methodology would result in a range of value. Once again, this is surely realistic.

24.5 The international risk premium

The issue of whether we should add in a country risk premium in non-domestic investment appraisal is, with practitioners at least, a vexing one. The answer depends upon an assessment of whether country risk is systematic or unsystematic. If the risk is unsystematic, it should, according to CAPM theory, not be included in the cost of equity.

For a company operating primarily in an advanced European country or the United States, it may be argued that investment in less-developed countries would provide greater diversification benefits than investment in developed countries because the economies of less developed countries are less closely linked to those of industrialised nations. However, the systematic risk of projects in less developed countries is unlikely to be too far below the average for all projects, since such countries are still ultimately tied in to the world economy. According to this view, the systematic risk of projects in less developed countries might be only marginally below that of comparable projects in industrialised countries. A Zambian copper mine may represent a capital project in a less developed country but its systematic risk will be near to that in industrialised countries because the world demand and the world price of copper are functions of the state of economies in industrialised countries.

If stock markets take cognisance and are influenced by domestic and international operations of firms, then it follows, according to CAPM, that it is reasonable for foreign operations to be set required rates of return based upon systematic risk. Many investigations have attempted to test the hypothesis that investors take account of the foreign involvement of multinational firms. Severn[8] found that the greater the foreign involvement of a firm, the lower the **covariance** of its earnings per share with the earnings of the Standard and Poor's index. But multinationals are larger than most domestic corporations and the reduction in earnings variability found by Severn might have been due to size and greater product diversification rather than to foreign earnings. Consistent with this view, Haegele[9] showed that, while multinationals' systematic risk is lower than for domestic corporations, these differences disappear once the results are adjusted for firm size. In this area, Agmon and Lessard[10] examined the stock market behaviour of US multinational corporations. If investors recognise and reward international diversification, they argued, price movements of multinational shares should be more closely related to a world market factor and less to a domestic US market factor, and this should be more pronounced the greater the degree of international operations. While their regression analysis, based on portfolios of US multinationals with an increasing proportion of their sales outside the United States, weakly supports this hypothesis, their results are very low on statistical significance. Similarly, Aggarwal[11] failed to locate any statistical relationship between multinationality and the cost of equity capital.

Perhaps, then, investors do not recognise the portfolio effects of a multinational corporation's foreign activities. Perhaps international diversification by companies has an insignificant effect upon systematic risk. But, according to Hughes, Logue and Sweeney,[12] who developed indices using portfolios of solely domestic and multinational firms, their results suggest that the performance of the multinational is clearly superior to that of its purely domestic counterpart.

Of course, there are also the well-known pieces of work on portfolio diversification undertaken by Solnik[13] and Jacquillat and Solnik.[14] Comparing the results achieved in terms of reduction of variance by an international portfolio versus a portfolio of internationally diversified companies, they concluded that, while multinational firms do provide diversification for investors, international portfolio diversification is a far superior source of elimination of variance. Furthermore, investors are able, in the absence of restrictions on portfolio investment, to action this superior diversification on their own. The lower co-movement between the returns on securities in a portfolio, the better the diversification – again see Buckley.[15] There is now a wealth of literature to the effect that international portfolio diversification can increase returns without increasing the standard deviation of returns.

In fact, there is conflicting evidence as to whether we should use different required rates of return for comparable international and domestic projects, given ultimate measurement in home currency terms. The empirical evidence gives us little more than a partial answer.

If country risk were unsystematic it would not, in the context of a CAPM approach, be included in the cost of equity. Exploratory work by Roll[16] suggests, in an arbitrage pricing theory (APT) framework, that the systematic country factor is significant in the case of many emerging, as opposed to industrialised country, equity markets.

Rather than attempting an adjustment to beta, some firms, including some City of London and Wall Street bankers, add on a risk premium derived from adjusting for the basis points spread of the country's bonds against UK government bonds or US Treasuries of similar maturity and other terms. We give an example of this approach in section 24.8 on emerging markets. A more explicit way of dealing with country risk is to make adjustment in the numerator of the present value calculation, that is in the cash flow forecast for the project itself. Clearly, using both of these approaches in a particular case would be double counting.

24.6 Gains from international diversification

By adopting an international approach to stock market investment, it is possible to maintain returns while lowering risk. This is documented in Dimson, Marsh and Staunton[17] and many other studies. Dimson, Marsh and Staunton exemplify this with their data from equity portfolios that the standard deviation of 29.1 per cent for the single-country investment falls to 17.3 per cent for an equally weighted 16-country portfolio – a dramatic fall in risk. If one were to use market capitalisation weightings, the above process reduces the standard deviation of returns from 20.2 per cent to 17.0 per cent.

Maybe risk reduction nowadays is falling as world equity markets are more integrated than was the case over the whole of the period from 1900 to 2000, the period covered by Dimson, Marsh and Staunton.

24.7 The international capital asset pricing model

We now turn to another approach in terms of looking at excess returns achieved from equity investment around the globe. Let it be stated clearly, at the outset, that the findings here are by no means conclusive – indicative is certainly the best that can be said. They concern evidence of an international capital asset pricing model (ICAPM). Essentially, what we are looking at concerns the nature of international capital markets. Two extreme views are possible:

- International capital markets are integrated and risky assets are priced according to their undiversifiable world risk, that is, a world (or international) CAPM applies. The relevant risk measure would be a beta measured against the world market portfolio.
- International capital markets are segmented and risky assets are priced relative to domestic assets only – that is, domestic systematic risk is the basis of asset pricing. The relevant risk measure in pricing assets is the beta measured against the domestic market portfolio.

No single national capital market has been found to be fully segmented or fully integrated with world markets at all times. The capital markets of most industrial countries are much more integrated today than they were a decade ago. A second tier seems to be moving towards integration with industrial countries' capital markets.

Capital market segmentation is a financial market imperfection driven either by government constraints or investor perceptions and regulations – or both. The most important imperfections are information barriers (including accounting and regulatory disclosure quality), transactions costs, foreign exchange regulations, the nature of the market for corporate control, small country bias (due, often, to illiquidity factors), political risk, regulatory barriers (including remittance restrictions and a number of other controls) and, finally, equity market controls, regulations and lack of transparency.

The extent to which capital markets are segmented is likely to have a significant impact on the cost of capital. In a fully segmented market, it is likely to be higher than in other capital markets. On the issues of integrated versus segmented capital markets, there have been numerous empirical studies – see Buckley.[18] Sadly, findings suggest that neither hypothesis could be rejected in favour of the other. But some empirical support has been found for an International Capital Asset Pricing Model (ICAPM).

Evidence tends weakly to suggest increasing integration of world capital markets, although it is certainly not an issue that has been resolved. Having said this, the next part of this section, which is based upon ideas of equity market integration, is essentially consistent with an ICAPM.

Despite evidence for and against, if it is accepted that major stock markets around the globe have some tendency to move in sympathy with one another, we might think of a world excess return relationship in which the monthly excess returns for a particular market, for example the UK equity market, might be related to the monthly excess return on the world index. In algebraic terms, we might be thinking of a relationship of the following kind:

$$(R_C - R_F) = \alpha_C + \beta_C(R_W - R_F) \qquad (24.1)$$

In the above equation, R_C represents the monthly return in, for example, US dollar terms for the equity market in country C, R_F represents the monthly riskless rate of return, again to ensure consistency, expressed in US dollar terms, proxied by the return on US treasury bills, α_C is the monthly risk premium for country C, β_C is the beta for country C and R_W represents the monthly return, expressed in US dollar terms, from equity investment in the world index.

24.8 Emerging markets

There then remains the perplexing problem of the appropriate discount rate for corporate investment in emerging markets. On this topic, there is a polarisation of views which is exemplified by the recommendations of Lessard[19] and Godfrey and Espinosa.[20] So what are their contrasting standpoints?

All other things being equal, it is generally agreed that projects in emerging markets are more risky than similar projects in domestic and developed markets. To take account of these higher risks and, also, greater unfamiliarity, many companies build an extra premium into the discount rate to be applied to projects in emerging markets. But, usually, the basis for these adjustments is arbitrary. Consequently, companies often over-discount projected cash flows and, in so doing, unduly penalise projects.

The view that the extra premium required is modest is the stance taken by Lessard. He suggests other assets, its information advantage and its ability to manage these risks. Although more volatile in themselves, investments in emerging economies generally contribute relatively little to the volatility of a company's cash flows and its shareholders' portfolios compared with domestic projects, which would probably have less diversification effect. Furthermore, political risks, such as the threat of expropriation, shifts in policy and exchange inconvertibility, can be roughly allowed for by incorporating a premium reflecting the risk of non-payment on government bonds. This is represented by the credit spread on government bonds above the cost of similar term US government bonds and it is Lessard's view that this should be added as a risk premium to the normal required return in evaluating the return on remittable home currency cash flows. Finally, Lessard suggests that unfamiliarity with an emerging market host country should not be factored into the discount rate. The effects of unfamiliarity should decrease over time, as opposed to increasing at a compound rate as would be implied by adjusting the discount rate.

Having developed the idea of country betas in the previous section, one of the first ideas that might occur to the reader is the use of country betas for emerging market projects. Immediately, a problem arises. In their estimates of costs of equity capital by country, Godfrey and Espinosa found that all developed countries had betas in excess of 0.5. But, by contrast, for emerging markets, calculation of country betas (for the period from 1989 for some countries, 1991 and 1993 for others, up to 1996) revealed that 15 out of 26 major emerging markets in the world had betas below 0.5 and four of these countries had betas that were negative, thus implying, via the CAPM equation, discount rates below the risk-free rate. The reason for the low betas for emerging markets is the low correlations between returns from equity investment in these countries and returns from the world equity portfolio. In fact, the correlation between developed market returns, on average (unweighted), and world market returns was 0.6; for emerging market versus the world market, the correlation was 0.2. This low correlation essentially suggests that emerging markets are not integrated with developed capital markets and, as such, it implies that an ICAPM is not totally applicable.

Like Godfrey and Espinosa, Lessard reports similar findings on low – and some negative – correlations. This led him to suggest an approach other than one that is based on country betas. In terms of specifying a premium, Lessard agrees that bond risk premia reflect the market's assessment of potential losses due to rescheduling or default. These events do not exactly match the events that would jeopardise the generation or the remittance of cash flows from an overseas investment. For example, in the case of Argentina, despite repeated negotiations and non-payment of interest on sovereign debt in the 1980s – to the point where the secondary market price of Argentine government debt fell to 15 per cent of its **face value** – dividends from businesses were fully convertible.

On the other hand, adverse factors may impact the direct foreign investor without the event of rescheduling or default on government debt. Despite these reservations, bond risk premia provide objective measures of potential payments difficulties that may be closely correlated with problems that a direct investor would encounter. Therefore, government bond spreads on US Treasuries do provide fair measures of the impact of downside country risks.

Godfrey and Espinosa argue for an even greater premium. Their first step is to suggest a premium on the US risk-free rate for country credit quality, as above. However, to this they add a further premium – the premium for business volatility. They argue as follows. The measure of an asset's systematic risk, or beta, is calculated as:

$$\text{Beta} = \frac{\text{cov}(r_{\text{i}}, r_{\text{m}})}{\sigma_{\text{m}}^2} = \rho_{\text{i,m}}(\sigma_{\text{i}}/\sigma_{\text{m}})$$

where σ_i and σ_m are, respectively, the volatilities of the asset and the market. Cov(r_i, r_m) is the covariance between the asset and the market portfolio of all risky assets and, finally, $\rho_{i,m}$ is the correlation between the asset and the market portfolio. So, beta is the product of the correlation between the investment and the market and the ratio of the asset's volatility to the volatility of the market. The latter ratio is an indication of the relative risk of the asset versus the market. If this ratio is greater than 1, the asset is more volatile than the market. If it is less than 1, it is less volatile than the market. The correlation coefficient, ρ, measures the degree of co-movement between the asset and the market. Beta thus adjusts the individual stand-alone risk (that is the ratio-of-volatilities term) to reflect only the non-diversifiable (that is the correlation term) aspects of the risk.

Accepting that empirically determined country betas for emerging markets are less than reliable, their argument continues thus. In calculating the premium for business volatility they use an adjusted beta that is equal to the ratio of an individual country's equity volatility to that of the US market. In essence, in the equation for beta above, this assumes that the correlation coefficient is equal to one. In short, their adjusted beta is equal to:

$$\sigma_{\text{i}}/\sigma_{\text{US}}$$

For the purpose of generating their business risk premium, they simply multiply this adjusted beta by the US equity market risk premium. This approach to calculating emerging market discount rates focuses on total risk – not just systematic risk as in CAPM.

Godfrey and Espinosa concede that by allowing for a country's credit quality and the volatility of the local equity market, there is an element of double counting. Yes, but how

End of chapter questions

24.1 Explain how characteristics of MNCs can affect the cost of capital.

24.2 From an investor's standpoint, have small companies, in general over the past, been more profitable than their larger brethren?

25

Country risk analysis and political risk

Multinational firms constantly assess the business environments of the countries in which they are operating as well as those that they are considering for investment. Likewise, investors are interested in assessing which countries offer the best prospects for sound investment. This is what **country risk** analysis is about – the assessment of potential risks and rewards associated with making investments and doing business in a country. Essentially, we are interested in whether reasonable economic policies are likely to be pursued because this creates a business environment in which firms may flourish. But political factors may lead countries to pursue economic policies that are adverse to business and to their own economic wellbeing. Because of this, the focus of country risk analysis cannot be purely economic in its approach. It must also study political factors that give rise to economic policies.

The international economic environment is dependent upon the policies that individual nations pursue. Given the linkage between a country's economic policies and the degree of exchange risk, inflation risk and interest rate risk that multinational companies and investors face, it is vital to study these areas and attempt to forecast them. One cannot assess a country's risk profile without an insight into its economic and political policies and how these policies affect the country's prospects for economic growth. Forecasts at exchange rates, inflation rates and interest rates are enhanced by understanding the economic factors affecting national policies.

25.1 Country risk analysis

Country risk analysis took off in the 1960s and 1970s in response to the banking sector's attempts to define and measure its exposure to cross-border lending. At one time, before widespread international lending, country risk was often called transfer risk – that is, the risk that a government might impose restrictions on debt service payments abroad. When governments themselves became major bank borrowers, the concept of **sovereign risk** emerged. Sovereign risk is wider than transfer risk. It embraces the idea that even if the government is willing to honour its external obligations, it might not be able to do so if the economy cannot generate sufficient foreign exchange. Country risk began to include transfer risk and sovereign risk.

Political risk came to be used by industrial firms to describe adverse foreign events of a macroeconomic, social, political or strategic nature that might affect their business.

The globalisation of financial markets and the growth of portfolio investment brought further demand for country risk analysis since a significant part was viewed, in capital asset pricing model terms, as unsystemic risk that could be diversified away. Nowadays, the term country risk is synonymous with cross-border risk or international business risk, terms which have recently gained currency. These terms are widely used and are used interchangeably.

25.2 Sources of country risk

The sources of country risk are numerous. They embrace all aspects of a country's economic, financial, social and political organisation as well as its geographic location and strategic importance. A comprehensive checklist of risk sources specified by Nagy[1] includes the following:

- war;
- occupation by a foreign power;
- civil war, revolution, riots, disorders;
- takeover by an extremist government;
- politically motivated debt default, renegotiation or rescheduling;
- unilateral change in debt service terms;
- state takeover of an enterprise;
- indigenisation (forced relinquishment of control by foreign owners of enterprises);
- natural calamities;
- depression or severe recession;
- mismanagement of the economy;
- credit squeeze;
- long-term slowdown in real GNP growth;
- strikes;
- rapid rise in production costs;
- fall in export earnings;
- sudden increase in food and/or energy imports;
- over-extension in external borrowing;
- devaluation or depreciation of the currency.

All of the above headings, according to Nagy, include a set of sub-headings, sometimes extending to over two dozen such subsidiary events. Country risk analysis usually begins by specifying a country's position in accordance with Nagy's list and placing the country on a five (or seven) point scale depending on its likelihood to suffer the risk sources detailed above.

25.3 Measuring country risk

In terms of measuring country risk, it is possible to use a form of ratio analysis to allow us to augment the qualitative approach described above. In corporate finance, financial gearing or leverage plays a major role in determining financial risk. Financial gearing is measured by the extent to which the assets of the firm are financed with debt. It shows up in the income statement, as an interest expense, causing variability in net income over and above the variability in operating income caused by operating risk.

With macroeconomic risk, the same type of effect is present. But, in the absence of a macroeconomic balance sheet, we are forced to look at other proxies. In standard economic risk assessment, analysts combine variables to generate ratios considered to be significant indicators of the ongoing and prospective economic situation. One set of ratios aims at assessing the prospects for long-term growth in GDP or GNP. It includes:

- gross domestic fixed investment/GDP (or GNP);
- gross domestic savings/GDP (or GNP);
- marginal capital/output (the number of dollars of increase in investment necessary to increase output by one dollar);
- net capital imports/gross domestic fixed investment;
- gross domestic savings/gross domestic fixed investment.

The ratio of gross domestic fixed investment to GDP measures the economy's propensity to invest. Usually, a higher rate of investment leads to increased output and higher rates of growth of GDP. The extent to which this applies depends on the marginal capital to output ratio. This ratio claims to measure the marginal productivity of capital. It is usually calculated by dividing gross fixed domestic investment in one period by the increase to GDP in one or two periods later. A lower ratio signifies a higher productivity of capital and the higher the productivity of capital, the better the outlook for growth in GDP. The net capital imports over gross domestic fixed investment ratio indicates the extent to which GDP growth is dependent on goods from abroad. The higher the ratio, the more dependent the economy is upon overseas imports. Through the gross domestic savings to gross domestic fixed investment ratio, one obtains an insight into how dependent the economy is on foreign resources. The lower the domestic savings to domestic investment ratio, the more dependent is the economy. Usually, dependence on foreign resources is interpreted as a negative factor in economic risk assessment. Whether or not this is true is a moot point. For example, the resource gap may be large due to profitable investment opportunities and the willingness of foreigners to lend. This is hardly a negative. However, in the absence of profitable investment opportunities, the resource gap may be large due to a high propensity to consume. This is a negative because it signals that current consumption is being financed with foreign borrowing and that the rate of return on domestic investment is lower than the cost of the foreign resources.

Other ratios are used to indicate price stability – these are:

- government budget deficit/GDP (or GNP);
- percentage increase in the money supply.

As high inflation is generally considered to be undesirable, the outlook for price stability and economic performance should be more favourable when both the government budget deficit and the growth in the money supply are, relatively speaking, low.

The main ratios for assessing potential changes in the balance of payments are:

- percentage change in exports/percentage change in world GDP, or the GDP charge for the main customer countries (this represents the income elasticity of demand for exports);
- percentage change in imports/percentage change in GDP (this is, of course, equal to the income elasticity of demand for imports);
- imports/GDP;
- commodity exports/total exports;
- official reserves/imports.

A high income elasticity of demand for exports (first bullet point) and a low income elasticity of demand for imports (second bullet point) is usually considered to be favourable for the balance of payments. A high ratio of imports to GDP is usually considered unfavourably. Because of the possible volatility of commodity prices, a high ratio of commodity exports to total exports is usually viewed unfavourably, while a high ratio of reserves to imports is viewed as a plus.

A country's financial risk refers to its ability to generate enough foreign exchange to meet payments of interest and principal (together this is termed debt service) on its foreign debt. The debt crisis of many developing countries in the 1980s provides a well-known example of financial risk. Because of over-borrowing and the unproductive use of borrowed resources, the countries in crisis were unable to honour their debts to the banks that had lent to them, causing big losses for the banks and economic sacrifices from defaulting countries.

Financial risk analysis for a country involves an assessment of the country's foreign obligations compared to its current and prospective economic situation. The variables used in assessing cross-border financial risk include those already cited plus ratios concerned with the country's foreign debt and interest, for example:

- total external debt (EDT), which may be broken down into:
  - long-term public and publicly guaranteed debt outstanding and disbursed (DOD);
  - long-term private non-guaranteed outstanding debt;
  - short-term debt;
  - use of IMF credit;
- total debt service (TDS) which can be broken down into:
  - interest payments (INT);
  - principal payments.

Information on a country's external debt can be combined with the economic and balance of payments data to generate a number of significant ratios on the ongoing and prospective financial situation. The most common of these include:

- total external debt/exports (EDT/X);
- total external debt/GNP (EDT/GNP);
- official reserves/total external debt (RES/EDT);

- official reserves/imports (RES/M);
- long-term public and publicly guaranteed debt outstanding and disbursed/exports (DOD/X);
- long-term public and publicly guaranteed debt outstanding and disbursed/GNP (DOD/GNP);
- total debt service/exports (TDS/X);
- total debt service/GNP (TDS/GNP);
- interest payments/exports (INT/X);
- interest payments/GNP (INT/GNP);
- official reserves/long-term public and publicly guaranteed debt outstanding and disbursed (RES/DOD).

As mentioned earlier, financial leverage plays a major role in determining financial risk in the corporate finance arena. This is also the case with assessment of a country's financial risk. Here financial leverage shows up as an interest expense, affecting the variability of GDP less interest paid and exports net of debt service. Given this background, analysts often look at such ratios as EDT/X, EDT/GNP, DOD/X and DOD/GNP as measures of the company's financial leverage. The lower these ratios are, the better the country's financial position. As with a company's financial ratios, these country ratios should be used with caution – their measurement may be less than 100 per cent accurate, especially for developing countries.

Other ratios used in corporate finance, like times interest earned and cash flow coverage are used to determine the extent to which current obligations are covered by current income. The interest cover ratio relates earnings before interest and taxes to interest charges and the cash flow cover ratio relates earnings before interest and taxes to total annual debt service including payments for interest and principal. So, INT/X and INT/GNP are akin to a times interest earned ratio. TDS/X and TDS/GNP are like cash flow coverage ratios. Again, lower ratios indicate a stronger financial position, all other things being equal.

Note that these ratios use exports and GNP, which are gross of costs and do not reflect the net flows such as earnings or net exports (X – M) that the country generates to honour its external financial obligations.

Finally, the ratio RES/M resembles a liquidity ratio in corporate finance. Liquidity ratios measure the firm's ability to meet maturing short-term liabilities. The RES/M ratio measures a country's ability to maintain import levels out of gold and foreign exchange reserves.

Clearly, just as ratio analysis is available to help assess the financial strength of a company, so it has a place in country analysis in quantifying the strength of national economies. In the hands of skilled analysts, both are potent forces in determining financial and economic strength. But neither form of ratio analysis is a simple black box that throws up an answer. Their interpretation is an art – but a potentially valuable and telling one.

25.4 Political risk

In most countries, governments intervene in their national economies. This increases the political risk that multinational firms face. Political risk takes various forms, from changes in tax regulations to exchange controls, from stipulations about local production to expropriation, from commercial discrimination against foreign-controlled businesses to restrictions on access to local borrowings. Political risk can be defined as the exposure to a change in value of an investment or cash position resultant upon government actions. When viewed from the multinational corporation's standpoint, the effect of changes in government policies may be positive as well as negative.

Although political risk poses severe threats and may create profitable opportunities for multinational companies, firms have been found to view and to react to political risk without formal planning or systematic analysis. This is naive; a formal assessment of political risk and its implications for the multinational firm is important for decision-making and it is towards the specification of such a framework that this chapter is aimed.

Formal assessment of political risk usually involves three key steps:

1 The recognition of the existence of political risk and its likely consequence: this stage is concerned with measuring political risk.
2 The development of policies to cope with political risk: this stage is concerned with managing political risk.
3 Should expropriation occur, the development of tactics to maximise compensation: this stage is concerned with developing post-expropriation policies.

25.5 The measurement of political risk

There are two ways to approach the measurement of political risk. First of all there is the country-specific route (this is also called the macro approach) and there is also the firm-specific route (this is frequently called the micro approach).

Various political risk-forecasting services are available. These services normally develop models leading to country risk indices which purport to quantify the level of political risk for each nation analysed. These indices generally reflect the stability of the local political environment. Such measures generally take cognisance of changes of government, levels of violence in the country, internal and external conflicts, and so on. Indices of this sort are intended to assess whether the government in power at a particular point in time will be there in the future and hence the extent to which the existing political status quo can be expected to continue.

The rating method developed by Haner[2] is worth mentioning because its approach is systematic and its rationale is not dissimilar to many others. Haner rates, on a scale from 0 to 7, a number of factors that cause internal political stress. These include:

- fractionalisation of the political spectrum and the power of resulting factions;
- fractionalisation by language, ethnic or religious groups and the power of resulting factions;
- restrictive measures required to retain power;
- xenophobia, nationalism, inclination to compromise;
- social conditions, including extremes in population density and the distribution of wealth;
- organisation and strength of a radical left government.

To these scores are added ratings arising from external factors. These include:

- dependence on or importance to a hostile major power;
- negative influence of regional political forces, possibilities of border wars and disruptions arising from such sources of conflict.

Finally, additional ratings relating to estimated symptoms of problems are computed and aggregated. These include:

- societal conflict;
- political instability.

Scores are aggregated and updated regularly as the world political environment changes. Countries are then rated as to:

- minimal risk – 0 to 19 rating points;
- acceptable risk – 20 to 34 rating points;
- high risk – 35 to 44 rating points;
- prohibitive risk – 45 rating points and over.

A not-dissimilar method of country risk evaluation is prepared regularly by the monthly financial magazine, *Euromoney*. Its rating draws on the weighting implied in Table 25.1. *Euromoney* polls a cross-section of experts. These specialists are asked to give their opinions on each country with regard to one or more of the factors in the scheme. Three broad categories are considered: analytical indicators (40 per cent), credit indicators (20 per cent) and market indicators (40 per cent). Each of these is further subdivided into more detailed components as shown in Table 25.1.

The analytical indicators include economic factors, a political risk evaluation and an economic risk view. The economic indicators included reflect the ability to service debt and are obtained from currently available data involving the ratio of external debt to GNP, the

Table 25.1 Country risk evaluation system used by *Euromoney*

	Weighting (%)
Analytical indicators	
Economic indicators	15
Debt service to export ratio	
Balance of payments to GNP	
External debt to GNP	
Political risk	15
Economic risk	10
Credit indicators	
Debt service record	15
Ease of rescheduling	5
Market indicators	
Access to bond markets	15
Selldown of short-term paper	10
Access to forfaiting market	15
	100

ratio of the balance of payments to GNP, and the ratio of debt service payments to exports – see section 25.3 above. The economic risk evaluation is provided by a panel of expert economists who are asked to take a forward look. Likewise, a political risk evaluation is obtained by polling specialists in assessing political risk.

Credit indicators are based on how easily a country is viewed as being able to reschedule debt payments, and how well the country has performed in meeting payments in the past. As can be seen from Table 25.1, the payments record carries more weight than the rescheduling ability.

Market indicators are based on the risk premia that financial markets are placing on a country's bonds, its short-term securities and the non-recourse loans made to its exporters. Large premia are a sign of high market-perceived risk. Of course, the market does consider factors already included elsewhere in Euromoney's rating scheme in pricing country debt, so there is an element of double counting.

Another financial monthly, *Institutional Investor*, also publishes country risk ratings based on a panel of banks' scores for creditworthiness. A number of similar systems are available for subscription; however, their approaches vary only slightly and most rely on a combination of objective data and subjective estimates. Frequently, their input data are different – for example, inflation rates, balance of payment deficits and surpluses, and other macroeconomic factors are used. The objective is always to assess whether there is a high risk of adverse changes resulting from government intervention. The development of political risk models is becoming more sophisticated and the ability of political risk models to forecast the timing of changes in the environment is important. However, research in this area is at too rudimentary a stage to be anything like conclusive. As a rule, the models used by rating agencies have not been consistently successful. It is worth mentioning that most models have not evolved out of discriminant analysis techniques, which would, perhaps, be the most scientific approach to the rating of country-specific political risk.

One exception to this comes from recent research by Morgan[3] who did use discriminant analysis to assess the influence of variables on the likelihood that a country would need to reschedule loan repayments. Morgan found the following characteristics of rescheduling countries:

- a relatively high ratio of total debt to exports;
- a relatively high proportion of floating rate loans to total loans;
- a relatively low rate of growth in GDP.

Work in the area of the use of data drawn from statistical analysis as an aid to forecasting political risk is in its infancy, but it seems set to experience considerable growth.

It needs to be stressed that some firms may gain by the same event that harms other firms. A firm relying on imports will be adversely affected by trade restrictions, but an import-competing firm may well be the beneficiary of such regulations.

Political risk has a different impact on different firms. Generalised political risk indices must be used cautiously and subjected to careful analysis to assess the full impact upon a particular company. Governments rarely expropriate foreign investments indiscriminately. The greater the benefits of a foreign operation to the host country and the more expensive the replacement of such facilities by a purely local operation, the lower the degree of political risk to the firm. Governments select expropriation targets according to criteria other than purely political ones.

Firms frequently incorporate the consequences of political risk into investment decisions via the following:

- shortening the minimum payback period;
- raising the required discount rate for the investment;
- adjusting cash flows for the cost of risk reduction – for example, by charging a premium for overseas political risk insurance;
- adjusting cash flows to reflect the impact of a particular risk;
- using certainty equivalents in place of expected cash flows.

Of the above methods, the last is the least fraught with theoretical objections, but it is probably the least used.

25.6 Managing political risk

A firm may take action to control its exposure to political risk. Having analysed the political environment of a country and assessed its implications for corporate operations, it has to decide whether or not to invest there. If it decides to go ahead, it should structure the investment so as to minimise political risk. It needs to be reiterated that the impact of political risk is a function of the firm's activities. The firm's overseas investments determine its susceptibility to political risk. Political risk may be controlled at the pre-investment stage or in the course of operations – or both. There are four approaches aimed at minimising risk in the pre-investment period. These can be classified as avoidance, insurance, negotiating the environment and structuring the environment.

The simplest approach to the management of political risk is to avoid it. Many firms do this by simply deciding against going ahead with investments in politically uncertain countries. If the international firm does decide to go ahead, the key question is the extent of political risk which a company is prepared to tolerate and whether the investment promises an appropriate return to compensate for it. Avoiding countries likely to be politically unstable ignores the possible high returns available from investment there. Business is all about taking risks and ensuring that sufficient returns are earned to compensate for them.

The second approach to pre-investment planning for political risk is insurance. Having insured assets in politically risky areas against expropriation and lesser risks of a political kind, the international firm can concentrate upon managing the business rather than worrying about political risk. Specific government departments of most developed countries sell political risk insurance to cover the foreign assets of domestic companies. In the United Kingdom, ECGD offers a confiscation cover scheme for new overseas investments only. Lloyd's of London also offers the company opportunities to insure against political risk, including expropriation. Its cover applies to new and existing investments on a comprehensive, non-selective policy. Lloyd's is, in fact, the only private insurer against expropriation. Fees vary according to country and the type of risk insured, with cover usually limited to 90 per cent of equity participation.

In addition to insurance, many firms try to reach an agreement with the host government before making an investment. This 'concession agreement' defines rights and responsibilities on the parts of both parties. Effectively, it specifies the rules under which the firm can operate locally. Such agreements have frequently been resorted to by multinationals operating in less-developed countries. They are often negotiated with weak governments. However, they have frequently been repudiated following a change in government and, therefore, cannot guarantee the international company avoidance of political risk. Concession agreements have carried less weight in the Third World as time has gone on; nonetheless they are usually observed in developed countries.

Having decided to invest in a country, a firm may minimise its exposure to political risk by structuring its operating and financial policies to make its posture acceptable and to ensure that the multinational remains in charge of events. A strategy of keeping the foreign company dependent upon group companies for markets and/or supplies is one such tactic. With virtually integrated production in different countries, there is little point in a government in a host country expropriating assets, since it would continue to be dependent upon the multinational corporation for supplies. This policy is one of the approaches used by international motor companies.

For companies that depend heavily upon research and development facilities and proprietary technology, concentrating these facilities in the home country enables a firm to lower the probability of expropriation. Similarly, establishing a single global trademark that cannot legally be duplicated can be effective. Sourcing from various plants reduces the host nation's ability to hurt the worldwide firm by seizing a single plant. And encouraging external local shareholders is another risk-reducing policy. This may involve raising capital from the host government, international financial institutions and customers, rather than employing funds supplied or guaranteed by the parent company. But it may not necessarily be the cheapest way of raising capital.

Obtaining unconditional host government guarantees is another way of minimising financial aspects of political risk. Such guarantees enable creditors to initiate legal action in foreign courts against any commercial transactions between the host country and third parties should a subsequent government repudiate the original obligations. Such guarantees provide the international company with sanctions against a foreign nation without relying upon the support of its home government.

Operating policies may also be resorted to as a ploy to avoid political risk. In such a category we would put planned divestment, short-term profit maximisation, creating benefits for the host nation, developing local shareholders and adaptation. Each of these is now briefly considered.

Planned divestment speaks for itself and is a policy commonly used to minimise political risk. Under short-term profit maximisation, we include policies of withdrawing the maximum amount of cash from the local operation. Cutting reinvestment to the bare minimum, deferring maintenance expenditures, cutting marketing expenditures and eliminating training programmes are all tactics aimed at short-term cash generation. These policies are not unusual in the light of clear expropriation threats as they ensure that the company will have a short life locally. However, this behaviour is likely to hasten expropriation. International firms also try to manage political risk by changing the benefit/cost split between the multinational and the host country. If a local government's objectives are concerned with economic benefits and costs, then the international firm may attempt to reduce the perceived advantages of nationalisation or expropriation. Policies include ensuring that benefits accrue locally. Such approaches embrace training local workers and managers, developing export markets for the host nation and manufacturing a wide range of products locally as substitutes for imports. Another common strategy is the encouragement of local stakeholders, including customers, suppliers, employees, bankers and so on, all based in the host nation. This policy includes concentrating operations upon joint venture partnerships with local firms. Another tactic for political risk management involves adaptation to potential expropriation and the development of policies to earn profits following expropriation. Many oil companies whose properties have been nationalised or expropriated receive management contracts to continue exploration, refining and marketing. Such multinationals recognise that they do not have to own or control an asset to earn profits and create cash flow.

Financial tactics designed to minimise political risk embrace a whole spectrum. Threats exist because of the possibility of confiscation of assets and the possibility that a foreign currency will become less convertible. If funds are not convertible, it is best to borrow locally as much as possible rather than risk funds becoming permanently blocked overseas. Methods by which multinationals reduce political risk through financing tactics include the use of a very high proportion of local gearing, minimising intragroup sources of finance and avoiding parent or group guarantees. It also pays the multinational to try to ensure that profit arises in the United Kingdom, through such devices as royalty payments, transfer pricing and so on, rather than leaving surplus funds in a country where political risk may be perceived to be high. No medals should be won for building up blocked funds overseas.

25.7 Post-expropriation policies

Expropriation does not come out of the blue. Generally, there are cues and signals that precede expropriation. Recognition of these gives the international firm opportunities to open discussions with the host government. In anticipated expropriation situations, the international firm frequently moves from rational negotiation, to applying power, to legal remedies and then to management surrender. When expropriation occurs, the aim of negotiation changes. Trying to persuade the host government of its folly comes first. The multinational corporation often quotes the future economic benefits that it will provide, but presumably the host government has already assessed these and its own actions have already taken them into account. If confiscation was merely a bargaining ploy on the part of the host nation to gain concessions, then this approach is likely to be successful. The multinational that perceives host government sabre-rattling to be of this kind may resort to a policy of retreat aimed at profitably keeping in the battle.

The firm may bargain with the government in an attempt to persuade it to reconsider. Mutual concessions may be suggested with the intention of the firm continuing its operations. Such concessions may include the following:

- hiring national managers;
- raising transfer prices charged from the locally based firm to other parts of the group;
- accepting local partners;
- changing expatriate management;
- investing more capital;
- contributing to political campaigns;
- releasing the host government from concessionary agreements;

- supporting government programmes;
- suspending payment of dividends;
- surrendering majority control;
- removing all home-country personnel;
- reorganising to give greater benefit to the local company.

Of the above concessions, the first four are the most attractive to the international firm. As a rule, the second four are the next most attractive and the final four are the least attractive.

If the above concessions do not work, then the firm begins to apply negative sanctions. These may take the form of supporting an opposition political party or invoking home government support for the firm's position. But these political tactics rarely work. By contrast, the international firm may agree at this stage to relinquish control in return for compensation, thereby saving the host government and the firm itself a considerable investment in negotiating time.

While rational negotiation and applying power continue, the firm may also begin to seek legal redress. It is a rule of law that legal remedy must first be sought in the courts of the host country. After this route has been exhausted, the international firm may proceed to put its case in the home country and in international courts. Where host courts are impartial, seeking local redress is likely to be moderately effective. But where the judiciary is subservient to the government, the international firm can expect little payoff here and it may be most expeditious to seek judgments against the host country's property in the home or third countries.

Efforts to sue national governments are frustrated by the doctrine of sovereign immunity and the act of state doctrine. The former says that a sovereign state may not be tried in the courts of another state without its consent. And the latter doctrine implies that a nation is sovereign within its own borders and that its domestic actions may not be questioned in the courts of another nation, even if those actions violate international law. However, the doctrine of sovereign immunity is normally waived when it comes to a foreign country's commercial activities.

Another route is to lobby in the home country in an attempt to restrict the import of raw materials and other products from the host country. Arbitration of investment disputes is another alternative; this is now moderately effective since the establishment of the International Centre for Settlements of Investment Disputes, set up in 1966 by the World Bank. Created to encourage foreign direct investment by providing a forum for settling international investment disputes, the centre provides binding arbitration, although in practice its influence is small.

Should the firm have experienced a lack of success during the phases of negotiation, applying power and seeking legal redress, eventual surrender follows and attempts at salvaging some of the investment ensue. This usually involves settling for whatever insurance and other payments may be obtained.

25.8 Political risk analysis in international capital budgeting

Companies undertaking overseas projects explicitly take on an element of political risk which is related to host government actions. Shapiro[4] details a series of models designed to quantify, in an interesting way, whether that risk is acceptable or not. One route is via a break-even probability analysis for a particular government action. The sinews of his approach are summarised in this chapter. Essentially, the aim is to develop a generalised formula for assessment of political risk in investment appraisal. This approach enables analysts to assess the impact of various political risk factors, one by one.

The basic argument is developed by looking at the effects on project outturns of a number of political risk events. Here we consider, in turn, expropriation, blocked funds and increased taxes. And following on from this we develop our generalised model.

So, first of all, we consider expropriation. The base case net present value of a project in a foreign territory can be written as:

$$-I+\sum_{i=1}^{n}\frac{X_i}{(1+k)^i}$$

where I represents the present value of the capital investment inputs, X_i refers to the remittable net cash flow generated by the project in year i, and k represents the appropriate discount rate. Now, should expropriation occur in year h, the net present value of the project will fall, to:

$$-I+\sum_{i=1}^{h-1}\frac{X_i}{(1+k)^i}+\frac{G_h}{(1+k)^h}$$

The notation above remains as before except that the amount represented by G would embrace not only direct compensation paid by the host government, political risk insurance and so on, but also the effect of tax deductibility (if any) and capital repayment of obligations which might be avoided resultant upon the expropriation. We have allowed for G being paid in year h in the equation above. In the real world it may not be the case that payment is so prompt – but the sentiment remains, and the effect of timing of payment of the sum, G, must be incorporated into the equation.

We now take things a little further. Suppose that the probability of expropriation in year h is p_h and zero in all other years, then the project's net present value becomes:

$$-I+\sum_{i=1}^{h-1}\frac{X_i}{(1+k)^i}+p_h\frac{G_h}{(1+k)^h}+(1-p_h)\sum_{i=h}^{n}\frac{X_i}{(1+k)^i}$$

If the project exactly breaks even under expropriation, its net present value will be zero. So, if we set the above equation equal to zero, we can find the break-even value of p_h. Doing this and rearranging terms, it can be seen that:

$$p_h\left[\sum_{i=h}^{n}\frac{X_i}{(1+k)^i}-\frac{G_h}{(1+k)^h}\right]=-I+\sum_{i=1}^{n}\frac{X_i}{(1+k)^i}$$

And rearranging the above terms further, the break-even value of p_h can be found thus:

$$p_h=\frac{\displaystyle\sum_{i=1}^{n}\frac{X_i}{(1+k)^i}-I}{\displaystyle\sum_{i=h}^{n}\frac{X_i}{(1+k)^i}-\frac{G_h}{(1+k)^h}}$$

In a particular expropriation case, if we find that the break-even value of p is, for example, 0.25, we need not spend time worrying about whether the likely value is 0.10 or

0.15 – suffice it to say that, being less than 0.25, the project is acceptable. By a similar line of argument, if the probability of expropriation is somewhere between 0.40 and 0.50, clearly the project is not acceptable.

As an example of the use of the above formula, consider an investment with a capital cost of £1m, a project life of five years, an annual net remittable cash flow of £500,000 and a discount rate of 20 per cent per annum. The project's net present value can be calculated as £495,305. Expropriation data involve a possible nationalisation of the project at the end of year 2 with compensation from the host government estimated at £200,000. Using the break-even formula above it can be shown that this value comes out at:

$$\frac{495{,}305}{731{,}416-138{,}889}=0.84$$

If, incidentally, compensation were zero, the break-even probability would be:

$$\frac{495{,}305}{731{,}416}=0.68$$

The same series of arguments leads to a similar kind of proposition with respect to blocked funds. Our deductions begin with the base case net present value of the project at:

$$-I+\sum_{i=1}^{n}\frac{X_i}{(1+k)^i}$$

If we assume that funds become blocked in year j and beyond, the project's net present value can be stated as:

$$-I+\sum_{i=1}^{j-1}\frac{X_i}{(1+k)^i}+\sum_{j}^{n}\frac{X_i(1+r)^{n-i}}{(1+k)^n}$$

The above formulation assumes a reinvestment rate of r per cent per annum in the blocking territory, with all blocked proceeds ultimately remitted in year n; otherwise all notation is as earlier.

If the probability of blocking in year j is q_j and zero in all other years, then the net present value of the project becomes:

$$-I+\sum_{i=1}^{j-1}\frac{X_i}{(1+k)^i}+q_j\sum_{i=j}^{n}\frac{X_i(1+r)^{n-i}}{(1+k)^n}+(1-q_j)\sum_{i=j}^{n}\frac{X_i}{(1+k)^i}$$

The break-even value of q is obtained when the value of the above equation is zero. In this circumstance it can be shown that:

$$q_j\left[\sum_{i=j}^{n}\frac{X_i}{(1+k)^i}+\sum_{i=j}^{n}\frac{X_i(1+r)^{n-i}}{(1+k)^n}\right]=\sum_{i=1}^{n}\frac{X_i}{(1+k)^i}-I$$

And the above formulation can be rearranged to give the break-even probability as:

$$q_j=\frac{\sum_{i=1}^{n}\frac{X_i}{(1+k)^i}-I}{\sum_{i=j}^{n}\frac{X_i}{(1+k)^i}+\sum_{i=j}^{n}\frac{X_i(1+r)^{n-i}}{(1+k)^n}}$$

Again, take a simple example. Assume that a project involves a capital investment of £1m, has a project life of five years and creates annual remittable cash generation, net of taxes, of £375,000 per annum. With a 20 per cent per annum discount rate, the project's net present value comes out at £121,625. On the question of blocking, it is considered that this is likely immediately after year 1 and the host government is expected to insist on a reinvestment rate of 5 per cent per annum. The break-even blocking probability comes out, using the above formula, as:

$$\frac{121{,}625}{808{,}975-649{,}555}=0.76$$

Turning now to the political risk of increased taxes, an almost exactly similar line of argument can enable us to identify a break-even probability which may be useful in assessing political risk in international project appraisal. The base case net present value, as before, is given by:

$$-I+\sum_{i=1}^{n}\frac{X_i}{(1+k)^i}$$

With a tax increase coming in year m, and where π represents taxable profit and Δt is the change in the tax rate, the project's net present value falls to:

$$-I+\sum_{i=1}^{m-1}\frac{X_i}{(1+k)^i}+\sum_{i=m}^{n}\frac{X_i-\pi_i\Delta t}{(1+k)^i}$$

If the probability of a tax increase in year m is p_m and zero in all other years, then the net present value of the project becomes:

$$-I+\sum_{i=1}^{m-1}\frac{X_i}{(1+k)^i}+p_m\sum_{i=m}^{n}\frac{X_i-\pi_i\Delta t}{(1+k)^i}+(1-p_m)\sum_{i=m}^{n}\frac{X_i}{(1+k)^i}$$

Using the normal methodology developed in the immediately preceding section, the break-even value of p_m is where the net present value of the project becomes zero:

$$0=-I+\sum_{i=1}^{n}\frac{X_i}{(1+k)^i}+p_m\sum_{i=m}^{n}\frac{X_i-\pi_i\Delta t}{(1+k)^i}+(1-p_m)\sum_{i=m}^{n}\frac{X_i}{(1+k)^i}$$

And this simplifies to give:

$$0=-I+\sum_{i=1}^{n}\frac{X_i}{(1+k)^i}-p_m\sum_{i=m}^{n}\frac{\pi_i\Delta t}{(1+k)^i}$$

Rearranging, we can establish that the break-even value of p_m is given by:

$$p_m=\frac{\sum_{i=1}^{n}\frac{X_i}{(1+k)^i}-I}{\sum_{i=m}^{n}\frac{\pi_i\Delta t}{(1+k)^i}}$$

Again, let us take a numerical example. Assume, as before, that the base case data are as follows. The investment has a cost of £1m and a project life of five years, it generates £375,000 per annum of remittable cash flow, net of tax, and the relevant discount rate is 20 per cent per annum. As before, the base case net present value comes out at £121,625. If there is a possibility of an increase in the tax rate from, say, 25 per cent to 50 per cent, immediately after year 2, then the break-even probability comes out as:

$$p_m = \frac{121{,}625}{\sum_{i=3}^{5} \frac{500{,}000 \times 25\%}{(1.20)^i}} = \frac{121{,}625}{182{,}695} = 0.67$$

So far, we have developed three models to analyse political risk in international capital investment appraisal; in turn these have been concerned with expropriation, blocked funds and tax increases. But we can generalise. The base case net present value, in all instances, is:

$$-I + \sum_{i=1}^{n} \frac{X_i}{(1+k)^i}$$

With political risk built in, the base case is reduced by the probability of the political risk occurrence multiplied by the present value of the forgone cash flows resultant upon the occurrence. So the net present value becomes:

$$-I + \sum_{i=1}^{n} \frac{X_i}{(1+k)^i} - p\ (\text{PV of forgone cash flow})$$

where p is the break-even probability of occurrence of the political risk event. Rearranging the above equation, we can establish that the generalised formula is:

$$p = \frac{-I + \sum_{i=1}^{n} \frac{X_i}{(1+k)^i}}{\text{PV of forgone cash flows}}$$

Or, to present it another way, the break-even probability always equals:

$$\frac{\text{NPV of investment (base case)}}{\text{PV of forgone cash flows following implementation of political risk factor}}$$

We believe that this formula provides a most useful way of analysing political risk in capital investment appraisal. The method advocated here is not dissimilar to that advanced elsewhere in which political risk is allowed for by multiplying the cash flow in any year of operations by the probability of survival and dividing this by the sum of the discount rate and the probability of confiscation. By summing such terms for each year of operations, and allowing for the initial capital input, a net present value can be arrived at for the project – see, for example, Levi.[5]

Summary

- Political risk can be defined as the exposure to a change in the value of an investment of cash position resultant upon government actions.
- Governments intervene in their national economies and, in so doing, increase the level of political risk that the multinational firm faces. Political risk ranges from exposure to changes in tax legislation, through the impacts of exchange controls to restrictions affecting operations and financing in a host currency.

- Multinationals are concerned with the measurement and management of political risk. There are various approaches to the measurement of political risk – most of them are subjective in nature.
- In terms of managing political risk, one way is clearly to avoid it by deciding against going ahead with investments in political uncertain countries.
- Another approach is through insurance. Assets may be insured in politically risky areas against expropriation and other risks of a political kind. Fees vary according to the country concerned and the type of risk insured and cover is usually limited to 90 per cent of equity participation.
- The multinational may reach an agreement with the host government prior to investment – although subsequent governments may renege on such concessions.
- Keeping the foreign subsidiary dependent upon group companies for supplies and markets – the integrated operations approach – is a useful means of management of political risk.
- Financing a local subsidiary with a high level of local debt is another tactic. If expropriated, the host government takes over the assets and liabilities of the local business. Liabilities of the subsidiary include the high level of local debt.
- Political risk in international capital budgeting is best taken into account at the *ex-ante* stage by the break-even probability approach. This involves estimating the probability of occurrence of a particular political risk factor such that the present value of the project moves from being positive to being zero. The generalised formula for the break-even probability always equals:

$$\frac{\text{NPV of investment (base case)}}{\text{PV of forgone cash flows following implementation of political risk factor}}$$

- Follow through some of the numeric calculations in the main text, rather than the algebraic. If you do this, it is relatively straightforward.

End of chapter questions

25.1 Explain an MNC's strategy of diversifying projects internationally to maintain a low level of overall country risk.

25.2 Once a project is accepted, country risk analysis for the foreign country involved is no longer necessary, assuming that no other proposed projects are being evaluated for that country. Do you agree with this statement? Why or why not?

25.3 Do you think that a full country risk analysis can replace a capital budgeting analysis of a project in a foreign country? Why?

26

International capital budgeting: the practicalities

Having homed in on the underlying theory of international capital budgeting in Chapters 22 and 23, we now apply this knowledge in the real world of business.

In this chapter we provide a fairly straightforward case study of international capital budgeting. It should be easily assimilated by students who have progressed this far in the text. The case is designed to illustrate, in a practical way, how the proposed method should be used to evaluate financially projects which involve overseas spending. The case is concerned with the situation where the host country constrains multinational freedom by restricting the flow of cash back to the parent or elsewhere in the world by the imposition of exchange controls. In this set of circumstances, the potential flow of moneys back to the parent may be hastened by, for example financial engineering. It follows that the role of financial ingenuity in international investment may be critical in terms of parent net present value; its importance is outstandingly marked where there are remittance constraints. In other words, in these circumstances, financial creativity can affect the present value of investments – and significantly. The calculations in the worked example in this chapter should bring out this point.

26.1 Net present value and adjusted present value

The calculation of the present value of a project may be approached by way of the net present value method or via the adjusted present value technique. Both have the backing of a sound theoretical underpinning. The net present value has its roots in the traditional theory of finance, which was well expounded by Solomon.[1] The adjusted present value draws on the Modigliani and Miller[2] approach to the cost of capital and has been developed by Myers.[3] The rationale and detail relating to both techniques are well covered in any of the thorough texts on financial management.

In practical terms, the prescriptions of the two methods were summarised in Chapter 23. Correctly applied, they should give similar answers. For a good discussion see Ross, Westerfield and Jaffe.[4]

We now turn to a worked example on international capital appraisal. It involves problems with partial blockage of overseas cash generation.

26.2 Overseas project appraisal: Alpha NV

Alpha NV (Alpha) is a multinational company headquartered in a eurozone country. It is engaged in the manufacture and distribution of electrical motors that find a broad spectrum of end uses in commercial and industrial applications in various parts of the world. So far, it has not made any sales in Olifa, a republic which is experiencing lift-off as a result of newly found mineral reserves which are planned to come on-stream in some two or three years' time. This is one of the main drivers of Olifa's attractiveness to Alpha. Olifa has a right-wing government which has been in power for 20 years (but with so-called democratic elections) but its citizens have a feeling of well-being in a country where success and upward mobility are highly rated. Olifa is encouraging industrialisation but also seeks to push multinationals entering the country to privatise their investments after five years. The government has specified a price earnings multiple around four times historic profits after tax for this purpose. Because of a 25 per cent industrialisation impost (which is not tax deductible) on all new inward investment, as opposed to a 50 per cent duty on other imports to Olifa, Alpha's project analysis team has concluded that direct investment appears to be the preferred mode of entry to Olifa. For this purpose, a wholly-owned Olifa subsidiary (Olifa Alpha Limited) is to be formed. This subsidiary is referred to as OAL.

The base case

Key financial data relating to the Olifan project is as follows:

- The local currency is the Olifan dollar (OLD). Olifa is currently experiencing inflation of around 15 per cent per annum and this is likely to continue into the foreseeable future. The exchange rate now (year 0) is 5 Olifan dollars to the euro. Inflation in the euro area, for the purposes of this example, is put at 3 per cent per annum over the next five years or so.
- The capital cost of the project is OLD200m plus an import duty of OLD50m. Under Olifan regulations, this capital must be subscribed from the overseas investor as equity capital in the Olifan subsidiary.
- Olifa has implemented fairly tough foreign exchange control regulations but they seem relatively transparent and honest (although some readers might say that an honest foreign exchange control was an oxymoron – a figure of speech which involves contradictory terms used in conjunction, like Hannibal Lecter being a beautiful killer). These involve a remittance of profits based on 10 per cent of profit after tax. When arriving at this profit level, initial entry costs (exclusive of the industrialisation impost) are to be depreciated on an historic cost basis, straight line over five years – that is, 20 per cent per annum. However, the profit on realisation at the end of year 5 – that is, the proceeds less the initial input (exclusive of industrialisation impost) – is to be taxed at 50 per cent. Furthermore, these realisation proceeds are not remittable to the parent until year 8. During this period, from year 5 to year 8, such proceeds must be deposited in a bank approved by the Olifan government at a zero interest rate. On remittance, these proceeds will attract an exchange rate (this is guaranteed by the Olifan government) of OLD12.0744 equals EUR1. This exchange rate is based upon inflation differences of 15 per cent per annum for Olifa and 3 per cent

per annum for the eurozone. This guaranteed rate will prevail whatever the market level for the EUR/OLD. Despite exchange controls, the OLD is a freely floating currency. In fact, in recent years, the OLD has followed, very closely, a purchasing power parity path.

- Under exchange controls, non-Olifan owned companies are precluded from earning interest on deposits in banks in Olifa.
- On selling out at the end of year 5, the retained profit within OAL may also be remitted to the multinational without any further imposition of Olifan tax but, otherwise, on the same conditions as those summarised in the last but one bullet point – that is deferment until year 8.
- These are the allowable remittances under Olifan foreign exchange regulations:
  - the tax rate on corporate profits in Olifa is 20 per cent, and this is guaranteed up to year 5 for multinationals investing in Olifa;
  - no withholding tax will be encountered on remittances of dividends and terminal value from Olifa to the eurozone;
  - remittances of profit will be assumed to have borne a tax rate of 20 per cent as a foreign tax credit for purposes of taxation in the home eurozone country of Alpha NV. This regulation applies for remittances of profit and the terminal value part of the year 8 remittance for retained profit;
  - the home country corporate tax rate is to be taken as 41 per cent. This means that the net amount of profit remittances in home country terms are to be grossed up at 20 per cent to allow for Olifan tax paid. This grossed up amount attracts a 41 per cent home tax rate but from this is deducted a 20 per cent foreign tax credit. So, if the taxed remittance were EUR5 million, the following home tax treatment would apply:

Remittance	EUR5m
Grossed up (multiply by 100 over 80)	6.25m
Total tax (41%)	2.56m
Less Olifan tax credit (6.25 – 5)	1.25m
Home tax payable	1.31m

  Note that there is a more straightforward way of calculating the home tax and this is simply to take the foreign tax rate (20 per cent) away from the home tax rate (41 per cent) giving home tax payable of 21 per cent of the grossed up remittance.

- To attract its investment, the Olifan government has guaranteed Alpha a monopoly of its market out to year 5. This is a normal procedure in Olifa.
- This has enabled Alpha's analysts to come up comfortably with estimates of best estimate outturns which are summarised in Table 26.1.
- Alpha uses a real rate of return expectation of 8 per cent to screen investments. Based upon the risk premium attaching to Olifa and to Oifan government securities, an additional 3 per cent is required to compensate for Olifan risk (the calculation of this is not shown). Remember, too, that Olifan inflation is estimated at 15 per cent per annum while eurozone inflation is estimated at 3 per cent per annum – and this is the inflation rate to be used for the home country concerned within the eurozone.

Although it is not of absolute interest (because the preferred angle of analysis in international capital budgeting is the parent viewpoint with parent cash flows as the appropriate input), we can calculate the net present value of the investment from a project viewpoint.

Table 26.1 Alpha Olifa best estimates of project cash inflows based on an Olifan inflation rate of 15 per cent per annum

Year	Units sold Thousands	Sales price (OLD)	Sales revenue (OLDm)	Variable costs at 50% of sales revenue (OLDm)	Fixed costs (OLDm)	Depreciation (OLDm)	Operating profit (OLDm)	Olifan tax at 20% (OLDm)	Profit after tax (OLDm)	Additional working capital* (OLDm)	Free cash flows† (OLDm)
1	160	2000	320	160	40	40	80	16	64	(48)	56
2	200	2300	460	230	46	40	144	29	115	(21)	134
3	250	2645	661	330	53	40	238	38	190	(30)	200
4	300	3042	913	456	61	40	356	71	285	(38)	287
5	360	3498	1259	629	70	40	520	104	416	(52)	404
6	Terminal value based upon P/E ratio of 4 times										1664

* Working capital is based on 15 per cent of sales.

† Free cash flow equals profit after tax, add back depreciation, less additional working capital. No new capital expenditure is assumed. Initial investment is reckoned to have a twelve-year life, even though the depreciation write off gives a five-year life – consistent with Olifan tax rules.

This is done in Table 26.2. Note that we use the more correct 28 per cent discount rate based on multiplying up risk premiums rather than the approximate rate of 26 per cent based upon their addition. This approach becomes a most relevant precaution when dealing with very high inflation economies.

As can be seen from Table 26.2, the investment in Olifa shows a fairly substantial net present value from a project standpoint – equal to OLD680m, that is EUR136m (OLD680m ÷ 5). But it is the parent standpoint return we are focusing upon, and this means further analysis. The project net present value may not be good enough for a eurozone investor because of remittance restrictions.

Table 26.2 Alpha Olifa calculation of net present value from a project standpoint

Step 1 The approximate discount rate:

Real terms requirement + Inflation + Risk premium for Olifa

8% + 15% + 3% = 26%

Step 2 The more precise discount rate:

(1 + Real terms requirement) (1 + Inflation) (1 + Risk premium for Olifa) – 1

(1.08) (1.15) (1.03) – 1 = 0.279

say 28%

Step 3 Calculation of the project standpoint net present value:

Free cash flow for year	0	1	2	3	4	5
Flow – see Table 26.1 (OLDm)	(250)	56	134	200	287	404
– terminal value* (OLDm)						1664
Discounted to present value at 28% (OLDm)	(250)	44	82	95	107	602
Net present value (OLDm)	680					

* No tax has been applied to the terminal value. In the Olifan information bullet points, the terminal value was assumed to attract tax on remittance. The cash flow analysis in Table 26.2 is from a project standpoint – that is, without remittance.

The next steps that we need to take to estimate the net present value of the Olifan project from a parent standpoint are as follows:

- We must estimate remittable profits to the eurozone country. To do this, we must look at the profit after tax as per Table 26.1 and build in a 10 per cent dividend which is sent back to the home country.
- To convert these remittances to euros, we must estimate future exchange rates. To do this, we assume a purchasing power parity trajectory. Of course, exchange rates rarely follow a PPP trend year in year out. But, past evidence points in this direction for the OLD versus the EUR. And, in any case, analysis with different scenarios is possible and these may prove useful for managerial judgement.
- We must also forecast the terminal value in terms of the estimated P/E multiple of 4 times; the capital profit arising here will be subject to Olifan tax at 50%. Additionally, retained profits within OAL may be remitted too. Both of these final remittances must be deferred to year 8. The former will be subject to a home capital gains tax of 41 per cent and the latter will be treated like any other profit remittance.
- Home remittances are discounted at the appropriate euro discount rate.

Covering all of these calculations, we have presented Tables 26.3 to 26.7. Their content is explained below:

- Table 26.3 – a PPP forecast for the OLD versus the EUR.
- Table 26.4 – dividend remittances from Olifa to the home country showing tax payable on their arrival in the home territory.

Table 26.3 Purchasing power parity forecast of the OLD against the EUR

- Note that the PPP equation (see Figure 3.1) is used. Subscript E represents the euro and subscript $_O$ represents the Olifan dollar, we use the equation:

$$\frac{p_E - p_O}{1 + p_O} = \frac{s_t - s_O}{1 + s_O}$$

Otherwise, the notation used in Figure 3.1 applies. In dealing with data in the equation, given our notation, we should use a direct eurozone quotation for currencies – again, see Figure 3.1.

- Calculations below follow PPP.

Year	Opening exchange rate	Euro inflation	Olifan inflation	Closing exchange rate
0	€0.2			
1		3%	15%	€0.17913 (OLD5.5825)
2		3%	15%	€0.16044 (OLD6.2329)
3		3%	15%	€0.14370 (OLD6.9589)
4		3%	15%	€0.12870 (OLD7.7700)
5		3%	15%	€0.11527 (OLD8.6753)
6		3%	15%	€0.10324 (OLD9.6862)
7		3%	15%	€0.09247 (OLD10.8143)
8		3%	15%	€0.08282 (OLD12.0744)

Table 26.4 Dividend remittances from Olifa to the home country

Year	Profit after taxes as per Table 26.1 in OLDm	Dividend at 10% of PAT OLDm	Exchange rates as per Table 26.3 OLD to one €	Dividend in €m	Dividend grossed up €m	Additional home tax at 21% €m	Net of tax dividends to home country €m
1	64	6.4	5.5825	1.15	1.44	(0.30)	0.85
2	115	11.5	6.2329	1.85	2.31	(0.48)	1.37
3	190	19.0	6.9589	2.73	3.41	(0.72)	2.01
4	285	28.5	7.7700	3.67	4.59	(0.96)	2.71
5	416	41.6	8.6753	4.80	6.00	(1.26)	3.54

Table 26.5 Net remittance of terminal value (based on P/E of 4) and retained profit

- Terminal value based on P/E 4

PAT year 5	OLD416m
Value (PAT × 4)	OLD1664m
Cost of investment (excl import duty)	OLD200m
Taxable amount	OLD1464m
Olifan tax at 50%	OLD732m
Net amount remitted	OLD932m (Value 1664 minus tax 732)

- Retained profit is given by total PAT (see Table 26.1) of OLD1070m less dividends paid of OLD107m to give OLD963m
- Remittances deferred until year 8

	Remittance based on 4 P/E OLDm	Remittance of retained profit OLDm	Year 8 exchange rate (contractual)	Euro amount remitted €m	Remitted profit grossed up €m	Home country capital gains tax* €m	Home tax @21% €m	Net cash flow €m
Cash flows (1)	932		12.0744	77.19		(11.15)		66.04
(2)		963	12.0744	79.76	99.70		(20.94)	58.82

* Based on 41 per cent of amount remitted less cost of EUR50m, assuming no indexation for capital gains tax purposes.

- Table 26.5 – terminal value and retained profit remittances in year 8 from Olifa to the home country with Olifan and home taxes shown.
- Table 26.6 – tabulation summarising the appropriate home country discount rate to be applied to flows from Olifa.
- Table 26.7 – an overarching table bringing together data from Tables 26.3–26.6 into a summary of home country cash flows which are then discounted to net present value.

Evidently, as Table 26.7 shows, the net present value in home currency parent cash flow terms is in negative territory to the extent of EUR2.76m.

Financially engineering the project

Is it possible to use financial engineering to improve parent cash flows? Perhaps there are three areas where this is feasible. The first concerns the possibility of overcoming the foreign exchange restriction relating to foreign companies earning zero interest from banks in Olifa.

Table 26.6 Appropriate discount rate to be applied to cash flows back to parent

- The approximate discount rate:

Real return requirement + Home inflation + Risk premium for Olifan project

8% + 3% + 3% = 14%

- More precise calculation:

(1 + Real terms requirement) (1 + Inflation) (1 + Risk premium) – 1

(1.08) (1.03) (1.03) – 1 = 14.58%

(say) 15%

Table 26.7 Parent net cash flows from Olifan project leading to parent net present value

Year	Outflow (EURm)	Dividends to home country (EURm) (See Table 26.4)	Final remittance deferred to year 8 (EURm) (See Table 26.5)	Parent net cash flow (EURm)	Present value of cash flows discounted at 15% (EURm)
0	(50)			(50)	(50)
1		0.85		0.85	0.74
2		1.37		1.37	1.04
3		2.01		2.01	1.32
4		2.71		2.71	1.55
5		3.54		3.54	1.76
8			124.86	124.86	40.83
Net present value					(2.76)

Could Alpha Olifa deposit surplus funds with, say, a European bank in Olifa at zero interest with the condition that the European bank would credit interest to Alpha in its home country? Obviously, this would be subject to negotiation as to rates – but perhaps it might involve receiving an amount in euros based on:

(Real rate) + (Inflation)

This might amount to around 6 per cent – probably, in reality, something less than this because the bank is accommodating Alpha. Under Olifan exchange controls, OAL probably loses an OLD interest rate of around 22 per cent given by:

(1 + Real interest rate) (1 + Inflation) (1 + Risk premium) – 1

(1.03) (1.15) (1.03) – 1

The second possibility of financial engineering is to hasten the year 8 terminal value to year 5. Could this be achieved by some financially engineered device, such as countertrade? For more on this issue, see section 21.3.

There is also a third route, again involving financial engineering via a commercial bank. The essential feature here is to hasten the final payments from year 8 to year 5. How might this be achieved?

It is apparent that by year 5, if all goes according to plan, Alpha NV can expect to receive €156.95m (77.19 + 79.76, see Table 26.5 in year 8 and it can expect to pay home taxes of €32.09m (again see Table 26.5, €11.15 + €20.94) on this remittance in year 8. Alpha

Table 26.8 Parent net cash flows from Olifan project plus securitisation of terminal payment

Year	Parent net cash flow as per Table 26.7 (EURm)	Securitisation effect (EURm)	Parent net cash flows after securitisation (EURm)	Present value of cash flows discounted at 15% (EURm)
0	(50)		(50)	(50)
1	0.85		0.85	0.74
2	1.37		1.37	1.04
3	2.01		2.01	1.32
4	2.71		2.71	1.55
5	3.54	124.62	128.16	63.69
8	124.86	(156.95)	(32.09)	(10.49)
Net present value				7.85

might approach its commercial bank with a view to securitising the receipt of €156.95m from year 8 to year 5. If the bank were to decide to charge Alpha a 2 per cent credit spread, the cost of such a financial transaction could be around 8 per cent per annum (given by real return; 3%, plus euroland inflation, 3%, plus credit spread 2%). So the bank would advance to Alpha NV at the end of year 5 the sum of:

$$\frac{\text{EUR156.95m}}{(1.08)^3} = \text{EUR124.62m}$$

and Alpha NV would repay the bank EUR156.95m, out of the proceeds of the remittance from Olifa, in year 8. The effect of this would be an alteration of the parent net cash flow schedule shown in Table 26.7 to the more favourable pattern shown in Table 26.8. This latter table shows a new net present value of parent cash flows amounting to EUR7.85m. Note that we are now in positive territory. In fact, this net present value understates the true figure because the discount on the 'securitisation' amount to EUR32.33m (156.95 – 124.62) would, in all probability, be tax deductible as interest payable.

So, our project which originally showed a positive net present value from a project cash flow standpoint but a negative net present value in terms of parent cash flows (base case) has been transformed. By financial engineering, we have turned the Olifan project into positive territory in terms of parent cash flows. In real life, these kinds of situation are frequently encountered.

Note that what we have presented here is, of course, a base case for the Olifan project. In the real world, it would be useful to run various pieces of sensitivity analysis or scenarios for the project. Testing underpinning project assumptions is a critical piece of analysis here. In truth, it is rarely the case that we home in on one immutable value for a project. What we arrive at is, rather, a range of values that might be useful in aiding management judgement about whether to go ahead with a project or not.

Note also that the case example has focused on a situation where remittances are constrained. Where one is dealing with a host country without any exchange controls, the total amount of free cash flow generated normally becomes remittable. Thus, with no exchange controls, complexities are far fewer than in the Alpha NV case. Overall, what we are concerned with here is the methodology.

26.3 The Olifan project with no home tax on remittance

In this section, we look at the Olifan project assuming that company Alpha was headquartered in a country which imposed no home tax on remittances of dividends but with a capital gains tax on final remittance from abroad. In fact, this tax treatment has been increasingly adopted by certain territories desirous of attracting (and keeping) companies into their areas for tax purposes.

Under the above scenario, clearly the project will produce a higher return to Alpha than in the case detailed in section 26.2. This arises because of the corporate tax imperfection. And, as mentioned, it is the case that more countries are operating according to this formula. This has made such countries more attractive as location centres for tax purposes and many multinational companies have moved their centre of operations for tax purposes for just this reason.

We now demonstrate the present value effects of such a tax scenario for company Alpha. We assume that all other data are the same as in the earlier scenario. The home tax on dividends remitted is the big difference then.

First of all, the dividend remittances from Olifa to the home country as shown in Table 26.4 are altered. The revised figures appear in Table 26.9 below.

Table 26.9 Dividend remittances from Olifa to the home country assuming no home tax on remittance

Year	Profit after taxes as per Table 26.1 in OLDm	Dividend at 10% of PAT OLDm	Exchange rates as per Table 26.3 OLD to one €	Dividend in €m	Additional home tax at 21% €m	Net of tax dividends to home country €m
1	64	6.4	5.5825	1.15	nil	1.15
2	115	11.5	6.2329	1.85	nil	1.85
3	190	19.0	6.9589	2.73	nil	2.73
4	285	28.5	7.7700	3.67	nil	3.67
5	416	41.6	8.6753	4.80	nil	4.80

Also, there has to be a revision, due to lower tax on remittances of profit deferred to year 8. However we assume that capital gains tax on the sale of the business would still apply. Revisions to Table 26.5 produce figures set out in Table 26.10.

Clearly, under this lower tax scenario, the project produces a positive parent net cash flow of over EUR6 million – see Table 26.11. Of course, were we to build on top of this the impact of financial engineering, we would be able to add further NPV.

Table 26.10 Net remittance of terminal value (based on P/E of 4) and retained profit

- Terminal value based on P/E 4

PAT year 5	OLD416m
Value (PAT × 4)	OLD1664m
Cost of investment (excl import duty)	OLD200m
Taxable amount	OLD1464m
Olifan tax at 50%	OLD732m
Net amount remitted	OLD932m (Value 1664 minus Olifan tax 732)

- Retained profit is given by total PAT (see Table 26.1) of OLD1070m less dividends paid of OLD107m to give OLD963m
- Remittances deferred until year 8

	Remittance based on 4 P/E OLDm	Remittance of retained profit OLDm	Year 8 exchange rate (contractual)	Euro amount remitted €m	Home country capital gains tax* €m	Home tax @21% €m	Net cash flow €m
Cash flows (1)	932		12.0744	77.19	(11.15)		66.04
(2)		963	12.0744	79.76		nil	79.76

* Based on 41 per cent of amount remitted less cost of EUR50m, assuming no indexation for capital gains tax purposes.

Table 26.11 Parent net cash flows from Olifan project assuming no further home dividend tax on remittance

Year	Outflow EURm	Dividends to home country EURm (See Table 26.9)	Final remittance deferred to year 8 EURm (See Table 26.10)	Parent net cash flow EURm	Present value of cash flows discounted at 15% EURm
0	(50)			(50)	(50)
1		1.15		1.15	1.00
2		1.85		1.85	1.40
3		2.73		2.73	1.80
4		3.67		3.67	2.10
5		4.80		4.80	2.39
8			145.80	145.80	47.68
Net present value					6.37

Evidently, the tendency of financial executives to seek advantageous tax locations to enhance NPV would seem self-evident.

Press Cuttings 26.1, 26.2 and 26.3 provide an interesting study containing contentious issues about the benefits of using overseas funds to pay for an acquisition.

PRESS CUTTING 26.1

Synthes confirms discussions with J&J

By Haig Simonian in Zurich

Shares in Synthes, the Swiss surgical products and medical services group, rose on Monday as it confirmed that it was in talks with Johnson & Johnson of the USA.

'In response to market speculation, Synthes confirms that it is engaged in discussions with Johnson & Johnson about a potential business combination transaction,' it said. 'No assurance can be given as to whether, when or on what.'

The group, which runs its business largely out of the USA, was responding to speculation late last week that it was in negotiations on a sale that could value Synthes at up to $20bn.

A Synthes official declined to comment.

The company's shares gained as much as 12 per cent, but eased back to trade up 6.6 per cent at SFr147.90 in afternoon Zurich trading.

Synthes shares trade only on the Swiss stock market, although the company is legally based in the US.

Its operations are split between Pennsylvania and Switzerland, with about a quarter of its employees and roughly half its production coming from the latter.

The group has its origins in the late 1950s, when a pioneering group of Swiss orthopaedic surgeons developed new techniques for fractures and resetting broken bones, using high-tech screws and plates.

Production was originally outsourced to two Swiss precision engineering companies. In the 1970s, a third group, Synthes USA, became involved.

Over the past decade, the groups involved consolidated, with Hansjörg Wyss, the Swiss entrepreneur behind Synthes USA, becoming dominant.

Synthes, as the group is now called, has expanded on the back of growing acceptance of the surgeons' pioneering techniques – institutionalised via the AO Foundation (Association for the Study of Osteo-synthesis), based in Davos.

J&J earlier this year made an unsuccessful bid for Smith & Nephew, the UK hip and knee replacement company that was said to be valued at nearly $11bn.

'J&J's modus operandi has been to do acquisitions', Les Funtleyder, a fund manager and healthcare analyst at Miller Tabak, said.

'But I would wonder if they would want to clean up their consumer unit before this kind of acquisition.'

Source: Financial Times, 19 April 2011.

Deal could be just what doctor ordered

FT

By Alan Rappeport in New York

A successful bid for Synthes, the Swiss medical device maker, could be timely medicine for Johnson & Johnson after a year plagued by product recalls and bribery allegations.

Healthcare analysts are optimistic that if the talks between the companies lead to a deal, J&J will become the leading participant in the fast-growing medical trauma market.

It will solidify its dominance in orthopaedics and gain increasing power when dealing with hospitals.

'The last couple of years have been challenging for J&J', said Rick Wise, an analyst at Leerink Swann, noting the company's series of recalls and the impact of the tough economy.

'What better time to make a major strategic move?'

Last year J&J took after-tax charges of $922m due to lawsuits related to its DePuy ASR replacement hip, which was recalled, and other product liabilities and litigation.

Recalls were a drag on the company in its latest quarter, pulling sales back by 30 per cent.

Earlier this month, J&J agreed to pay $70m to US regulators after admitting 'improper payments' to healthcare employees in Greece, Poland and Romania connected to the sale of medical devices, and kickbacks to the former Iraqi regime of Saddam Hussein.

Synthes specialises in plates, screws, saws and drills surgeons use when repairing skulls and spines.

Wells Fargo analysts estimate that if J&J acquires Synthes, its share of the orthopaedic market would grow to 28 per cent, and medical devices would account for 46 per cent of its overall sales, up from 40 per cent.

Synthes controls about 50 per cent of the market for trauma devices.

As with J&J, Synthes has had its share of problems.

Last October, Synthes and Norian, its subsidiary, agreed to pay $24m in penalties after US authorities charged them with wrongfully conducting trials of a bone cement device on human subjects, and misleading the Food and Drug Administration.

But Synthes has proved to be highly profitable, and last year group sales rose 8.6 per cent to $3.69bn while net profits increased nearly 25 per cent to $908m.

The $6bn market for trauma-related products has been growing at an average rate of 10 per cent over the

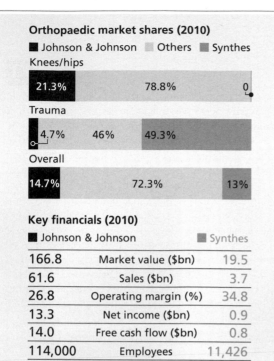

Orthopaedic market shares (2010)

■ Johnson & Johnson ■ Others ■ Synthes

Knees/hips

21.3% 78.8% 0

Trauma

4.7% 46% 49.3%

Overall

14.7% 72.3% 13%

Key financials (2010)

Johnson & Johnson		Synthes
166.8	Market value ($bn)	19.5
61.6	Sales ($bn)	3.7
26.8	Operating margin (%)	34.8
13.3	Net income ($bn)	0.9
14.0	Free cash flow ($bn)	0.8
114,000	Employees	11,426

Sources: Wells Fargo; Bloomberg.

past five years, and companies that sell pharmaceuticals have been looking to devices as a way to blunt losses from forthcoming patent expirations.

At a healthcare conference last month, Michael Mahoney, J&J's chairman of medical devices and diagnostics, underscored the importance of the device business.

He said healthcare reform legislation could provide a boost, as more insured patients require treatment.

He noted, however, that device prices remained under pressure and that the looming medical device tax would pose challenges.

'A major acquisition and use of cash would bring operational and expense synergies', Ben Yeoh, analyst at Atlantic Equities, said.

Larry Biegelsen, a healthcare analyst at Wells Fargo, suggested that such a merger could trigger further consolidation in the medical device industry as smaller rivals became acquisition targets.

He projected that a $20bn deal would add up to 5 per cent to J&J's earnings from 2012 to 2014.

Acquiring Synthes would please J&J investors by putting its $28bn in cash to good use.

'J&J has a lot of cash that was earned and is held outside the USA', Mr Wise said.

'It certainly could be enhancing to the company's sales, margins and returns to take low-earning cash and redeploy it to a high-margin business.'

Source: *Financial Times*, 19 April 2011.

Publicity-shy guiding light

By Haig Simonian

FT

If Synthes is bought by Johnson & Johnson, it will dispel years of speculation about the plans of Hansjörg Wyss, the group's publicity-shy guiding light.

Mr Wyss, 75, gave up operational management only three years ago, and remains the major shareholder, with 40 per cent owned directly and 8 per cent through family trusts.

Unlike the orthopaedic surgeons behind Synthes's products, Mr Wyss studied engineering. He discovered the medical business via friendship with a surgeon who helped develop the products behind Synthes's predecessor companies.

He progressively built his stake, later expanding the group through big mergers.

But succession was always unclear. Mr Wyss, long divorced, has a 38-year-old daughter not in the business. His time is divided between a home near Boston, a California vineyard and a Swiss mountain retreat.

In recent years, he has been gradually reducing his stake. His philanthropy includes a $25m gift to Harvard Business School, support for the Beyeler Foundation and various environmental causes.

Source: *Financial Times*, 19 April 2011.

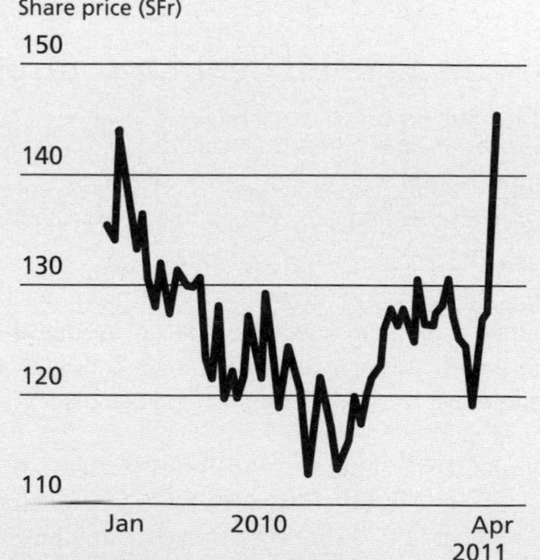

Source: Thomson Reuters Datastream.

PRESS CUTTING 26.2

J&J/Synthes

Fracture a bone anywhere in the world and the odds are good that Synthes will supply the materials to mend it. Snapping up the device maker for a cool $20bn may be just what the doctor ordered for Johnson & Johnson which, while not quite broken, has been prone to some nasty spills lately. It lost nearly $1bn in sales last year due to various product recalls and has been on the prowl since failing to consummate a big deal for British device manufacturer Smith & Nephew.

Buying Synthes is about much more than bolstering J&J's wounded portfolio though. A leader in other parts of the orthopaedic market, J&J remains a bit player in trauma, Synthes's forte. An ageing population translates to far more broken bones in coming decades, just as it means more artificial hips and knees (where J&J already has scale). Synthes controls about half of this business, valued at more than $5bn, around a fifth of the overall orthopaedics market. And its spinal products business would help J&J edge closer to market leader Medtronic.

Analysts at UBS reckon the rumoured price would be mildly accretive for J&J's earnings per share if financed mostly with cash. Moreover, as a US-based but Swiss-listed company, Synthes would allow J&J to deploy the large chunk of its $28bn gross cash position now held abroad and otherwise prone to US taxes if repatriated. Antitrust concerns are an issue but not a big one. J&J is so puny in trauma that its key competitors would face tougher hurdles, making counter bids less likely.

J&J remains mum on the deal, perhaps for good reason. Synthes has put itself into play by confirming talks, which may boost a mooted price that seems modest based on an unlevered earnings multiple. Synthes seems eager for players to take the stage, wishing them a hearty 'break a leg'!

Source: *Financial Times* Lex Column, 19 April 2011.

PRESS CUTTING 26.3

J&J seals $21.3bn deal for control of Synthes

By Haig Simonian in Zurich

Johnson & Johnson has agreed a $21.3bn takeover of Switzerland's Synthes to create the world's leading orthopaedic devices group.

J&J, which has a diversified healthcare business including drugs and devices, said on Wednesday it would pay SFr159 a share for Synthes, a 8.5 per cent premium over the Swiss company's closing share price on Tuesday.

Synthes shareholders will receive SFr55.65 in cash and the equivalent of SFr103.35 in J&J stock – approximately 1.7–2 shares – for each share they hold. The net cost to J&J will be about $19.3bn, given that Synthes has about $2bn in cash.

Shares in Synthes, which is based in the USA but quoted in Switzerland, have risen sharply in recent weeks on takeover talk. Synthes confirmed earlier this month it was discussing a deal, but gave no assurances about the outcome.

The deal marks the biggest takeover for J&J, which has expanded rapidly through acquisitions in recent years. Combining the two businesses will create a big orthopaedics player, combining J&J's existing activities with Synthes's dominant position in trauma surgery.

The sale also marks an exit for Hansjörg Wyss, the Swiss entrepreneur who created Synthes and expanded it through acquisitions.

Sales at Synthes reached $3.7bn last year on growing demand for its high-technology precision screws and plates, used for emergency surgery around the world.

Demand in the orthopaedics market, worth an estimated $37bn a year, is expected to grow strongly because of rising life expectancy.

Mr Wyss, aged 75, owns about 40 per cent of Synthes, with a further 8 per cent held through family trusts. He remains firmly identified with the company, having only given up management control three years ago.

The sale talk this month came as a surprise, as it had been widely expected in Switzerland that Mr Wyss would seek to maintain Synthes's independence, possibly through a long-term trust – a model similar to that at some other Swiss companies such as travel group Kuoni.

People close to the situation said Mr Wyss had examined all the options, including talks over the years with all the world's leading pharmaceuticals and medical equipment groups.

A clean break had emerged as the best solution, as this would also offer the best terms to the group's other shareholders.

The latest talks with J&J began last September, with the US group having emerged as the most suitable buyer, being big enough to afford the takeover and not so active in trauma products as to face serious competition constraints. J&J also had the reputation of leaving subsidiaries on a relatively long leash.

Credit Suisse advised Synthes. J&J was advised by Goldman Sachs.

Source: *Financial Times*, 28 April 2011.

Summary

- International capital budgeting and its domestic counterpart are different.
- It is hoped that, with the help of the case study in this chapter, it has become apparent that, under the general heading of international project appraisal, there are many complications.
- The financial analyst has to be more aware and more alert when confronted with international project appraisal than with its domestic cousin.
- You have been warned in this chapter of some of the pitfalls in cross-frontier investment analysis. There are undoubtedly more. Take care.

End of chapter questions

26.1 What is the limitation of using point estimates of exchange rates within the capital budgeting analysis?

26.2 Explain how simulation can be used in multinational capital budgeting.

Test bank 4

Exercises

1 The Inter-Continental Company is considering investing in a new chalet hotel at Verbier in Switzerland. The initial investment required is for \$2m, or CHF4m at the current exchange rate of \$1 = CHF2. Profits for the first ten years will be reinvested, at which time Inter-Continental expects to sell out. Inter-Continental estimates that its interest in the hotel will realise CHF6.5m in six years' time.

(a) Indicate what factors you would regard as relevant in evaluating this investment.
(b) How will changes in the value of the Swiss franc affect the investment?
(c) Indicate possible ways of forecasting the \$: CHF exchange rate 10 years ahead.

2 Compare and contrast international investment and financing decisions with their domestic counterparts.

3 One of the UK divisions of Global Enterprises plc wishes to set up a new manufacturing plant in Indonesia, because this would give it an important foothold in one of the fast growing parts of the world market, and would to a large extent deny this market to its main world competitors. The investment would amount to some £60m, of which the process plant would represent £40m.

The total effort of studying this proposal will be considerable and you, as treasurer, are asked to write a memorandum outlining the issues that you regard as critical to the decision to invest, other than purely commercial ones about product costs, markets and prices, and competition.

4 You are the treasurer of Development Properties Ltd and are considering the funding of a project due for completion over the next six months. At the end of the six months payment will be received from the client for the total costs and the profit element, although a progress payment of £2m will be received in one month's time.

The funding of the project is maintained separately from the remainder of the funding of Development Properties and a special loan facility has been arranged at a cost of LIBOR + 1/2 per cent p.a. £4m of costs require to be funded immediately and a further £5m in three months' time.

Interest rates quoted are:

LIBOR	%
1 month	14–13 7/8
2 months	13 7/8–13 3/4
3 months	13 7/8–13 5/8
6 months	13 1/2–13 1/4

FRA quotes have also been obtained:

1 v 3 13.70–13.50

3 v 6 12.70–12.50

(a) Identify the cheapest method of borrowing overall for the project for the next six months.
(b) What factors would you consider if you believed interest rates would fall by 1/4 per cent within the next month?
(c) What other mechanisms would you consider to manage the interest rate if you believed that interest rates might increase sharply over the next few weeks?

5 In connection with Press Cuttings 26.1, 26.2 and 26.3 how much do you estimate that J&J has saved, if anything, in terms of its financing of the Synthes acquisition? Explain your reasoning.

Multiple choice questions

1 A US multinational is setting up a subsidiary in France with local operations only and French competition only. Funds from the subsidiary will be regularly sent to the parent. *Ceteris paribus*, the ideal situation from the parent's standpoint is:

(a) a stable euro after the subsidiary is established;
(b) a weak euro after the subsidiary is established;
(c) a decision by the French government to leave the euro because this would be congruent with free market economics so beloved of American capitalists;
(d) a strengthening euro after the subsidiary is established.

2 A Japanese-based multinational has a German subsidiary that annually remits DM20 million to Japan. If the mark ________ against the yen, the yen amount of remitted funds _______.

(a) appreciates; decreases;
(b) depreciates; is unaffected;
(c) appreciates; is unaffected;
(d) depreciates; decreases.

3 The degree of political risk faced by a European company operating in an Asian country:

(a) may be specified objectively by using a political risk index;
(b) depends on the benefits provided by the firm;
(c) depends on how the firm has structured and financed its Asian operations;
(d) is given by the net present value of the Asian investment divided by the present value of cash flows relating to the political risk factor.

4 A Belgian multinational anticipates cash flows of EUR10m, EUR12m and EUR16m, respectively, for the first three years of a project in Ruritania. The initial investment is EUR79m. The firm expects a perpetuity of EUR20m in years 4 and beyond. If the required return on the investment is 17 per cent, how large does the probability of expropriation in year 5 have to be before the investment breaks even in NPV terms? Assume that the total cash flow in year 5 in the event of expropriation is equal to EUR36m.

(a) 22 per cent;
(b) 31 per cent;
(c) 40 per cent;
(d) 47 per cent;
(e) 79 per cent.

5 When trying to establish whether to go ahead or not with an international capital project, which of the following factors is not relevant?

(a) future inflation;
(b) exchange control blockages;
(c) remittance provisions;
(d) sales cannibalisation;
(e) home and host country taxation;
(f) expenditures already made in the host country.

6 A multinational company based in Switzerland is considering establishing a two-year venture in Malaysia with an initial investment equal to CHF30m. The firm's weighted average cost of capital is 10 per cent and the required rate of return on this project is 12 per cent. The project is expected to generate cash flows of M$12m at the end of year 1 and M$30m at the end of year 2, excluding salvage value. Assume no taxes, and a stable exchange rate of M$1.35 per Swiss franc over the next two years. And further assume that all cash flows are remitted to the parent. What is the approximate break-even salvage value? Note that M$ represents the Malaysian ringitt.

(a) M$1.39m;
(b) M$1.88m;
(c) M$5.45m;
(d) M$7.36m.

7 The cost of capital for a project in Australia but evaluated in home currency on the basis of converted remittable cash flows, should theoretically:

(a) equal the parent's weighted average cost of capital;
(b) equal the minimum rate of return necessary to induce investors to buy or hold the multinational firm's shares;
(c) equal the average rate used by Australian investors to capitalise corporate cash flows;
(d) be a function of the riskiness of the project itself.

8 From the viewpoint of a foreign subsidiary, the required nominal rate of return on a project (i.e. the discount rate used to find the NPV):

(a) is usually lower than the rate of inflation in that country;
(b) should be equal to the required money terms rate of return used in the parent country for a project of the type being analysed;
(c) should be equal to $(1 + p)(1 + r)$ where p is the expected inflation rate in the foreign country and r is the required nominal return used in the parent country for a project of the type being analysed;
(d) should be the local required nominal rate of return for a project of the type being analysed;
(e) should always be higher than that in the home country to allow for the additional risk;
(f) two of the above are correct.

9 An international firm preparing to site production facilities in the Far East has been offered direct investment incentives worth US$25m from Thailand and US$15m from Malaysia but Singapore has offered no investment incentives. According to this scenario:

(a) it will definitely cost $10m less to build the plant in Thailand than in Malaysia;
(b) it will definitely cost $15m less to build the plant in Malaysia than in Singapore;
(c) the incentives may be available to offset higher costs of production in Thailand and Malaysia;
(d) all of the above.

10 The government of a host country with no exchange controls offers a multinational a ten-year \$50m loan at 12 per cent to set up a local production facility. The principal is due for repayment in a bullet at the end of six years. The market interest rate on such a loan is 18 per cent. With a marginal tax rate of $33\frac{1}{3}$ per cent, how much is this loan worth to the multinational? Assume that tax is paid in the year that profit on which it is assessed is earned. Assume that the multinational is in a tax-paying situation.

(a) \$3.50m;
(b) \$4.11m;
(c) \$8.22m;
(d) \$10.49m;
(e) None of the above.

Part G

INTERNATIONAL FINANCING

Companies – whether they operate within national boundaries alone, or beyond – may borrow in their own domestic capital markets or they may move further afield and tap international markets to finance their operations. International borrowing enables companies to lower their average cost of finance and it may be an important part of the funding equation for companies whose base is within countries with shallow capital markets, as well as for major multinational companies. This section is concerned with international financing, and finance for international trade.

27

Financing the multinational and its overseas subsidiaries

In addition to the general issues of financing which apply to any business, there are special factors which impinge upon the funding of a multinational company and its overseas subsidiaries. With respect to the financing of any business, management needs to consider exactly what is being financed, the extent to which the problem can be solved by more efficient operation of the assets owned (for example, better working capital management can reduce the needs for funds), the extent of debt, the blend of short-term and long-term funds, the maturity structure and evaluation of the true relative costs of different sources of capital. But on the multinational financial stage there are more considerations that have to be borne in mind. In this chapter we present an analysis of these features peculiar to the financing of overseas operations. An approach to the problems of domestic financing can be found in any of the good standard texts on financial management.

In terms of global financing considerations, this chapter first of all sets out a framework designed to minimise taxes, manage currency and political risk and exploit financial market distortions. It then moves on to look at special features of financing overseas subsidiaries. Here we shall cover factors that impinge on overseas subsidiary financing, such as the presence of political risk, exchange control risk, currency risk, losses earned by subsidiaries, intercompany credit, taxation effects, dividend policy, other methods of profit transfer, parent company guarantees and the problem of partly owned subsidiaries. It is our contention that rational recommendations on the financing of an overseas subsidiary can flow only from a careful study of all the special features above and an evaluation of how they are likely to impact upon a company confronted with an overseas opportunity which it wishes to finance. But first of all we attempt to develop a series of guidelines for global financing. In this section, a debt is acknowledged to an excellent article by Lessard and Shapiro.[1]

27.1 The international financing choice

At least three factors play a major part in multinational financing choices – the opportunities to minimise global taxes paid, the possibilities to manage currency risk and political risk, and the windows of opportunity that may be available to exploit financial market distortions to raise money at rates below the normal market rate.

Financial theory has long discussed whether there is an optimal capital structure for the corporation which maximises the value of the firm. In a world where taxes play a major part in the financial equation, it now seems pretty clear that the search for this holy grail is justified.

As discussed earlier, we believe that hedging of currency and other risks does have a value. We would agree that the capital asset pricing model suggests that reducing corporate risks that are diversifiable at the portfolio level should not benefit shareholders. But we would also agree that diversifiable risks, if left unmanaged, may have significant effects on the expected spread of outturns in respect of the firm's profits and cash flow. Excessive earnings variability may affect a number of issues which would be detrimental to shareholder interests. For example:

- Excess earnings volatility may lower a firm's credit rating, resulting in higher interest costs. It may also adversely affect access to bank credit and thereby prevent the firm from taking advantage of interest tax shields.
- Earnings volatility, with the increased risk of financial distress may adversely influence the willingness of suppliers, customers and employees to enter into relationships with the firm.
- Excess earnings volatility may hinder management in taking a long-run view which would be in the best interests of investors.

The contention is, therefore, that the objective function of the firm might be postulated in the following form:

$$\text{Maximise } V_F = \sum V_i - P(\sigma)$$

where V_F is the value of the firm, V_i is the present value of each of the firm's divisions, strategic business units or projects, and $P(\sigma)$ is a penalty factor that reflects the impact on expected after-tax cash flows of the total risk of the firm. According to this formulation, the value of the firm is adversely affected by expected variability of cash flow. This form of objective function has been proposed by Adler and Dumas[2] and is reinforced by Lessard and Shapiro.[3]

The inclusion of a penalty cost in the above formulation reflects the possibility that the firm may wish to hedge those unsystematic risks which might contribute significantly to the expected variability of its cash and profit flows. Admittedly, such hedging transactions will have a zero present value in their own right. We nonetheless feel that they can be justified because of their effect in reducing the penalty factor specified in the above objective function. We now turn to the three major issues briefly referred to earlier: taxes, hedging and financial market imperfections.

27.2 Minimisation of global taxes

Non-symmetrical tax treatment of various components of financial cost means that equality of before-tax costs may lead to inequality at the after-tax level. The fear of countries imposing withholding taxes on dividends and interest paid to foreign investors by entities operating in the host country has led to a multiplicity of foreign finance subsidiaries designed to avoid this additional tax inconvenience. Financing choices designed to minimise corporate taxes are frequently concerned with:

- selecting the tax-minimising currency, jurisdiction and vehicle for issue;
- selecting the tax-minimising mode of internal transfer of currency and/or profit.

Interest payments on debt are tax deductible; dividends are not. It follows that, all other things being equal, there is an incentive to increase the firm's gearing. Also, because inter-group dividend payments may lead to tax consequences different from those of interest and principal payments, parent company financing of its affiliates in the form of debt rather than equity may have frequent tax advantages.

Furthermore, where there is asymmetrical tax treatment of foreign exchange gains and losses, or where interest expenses are subject to one tax treatment and dividend payments are subject to another, the expected after-tax cost of financing will differ across countries even if their expected before-tax costs are the same. Clearly, the firm will wish to structure its international borrowings in such a way as to minimise global tax deductions. This may favour very high debt levels in certain territories – but there are problems. Limits to the extent to which debt may be substituted for equity may be set by the regulations in a number of countries concerning thin capitalisation rules. These set a limit on the gearing ratio. Beyond this specified debt level, capital is simply treated by the tax authorities as equity. The implication of this is that interest on debt above the acceptable maximum is not tax deductible and payments may be subject to dividend withholding tax. The United States is the most notable example of a country concerned about thin capitalisation. Although no formal statement has been made by the US tax authorities, a commonly used rule of thumb is that a debt to equity ratio in a range between 2.5 to 1 and 4 to 1 is the maximum acceptable.

Tax arbitrage is clearly a source of reduction in the total tax burden. It basically involves moving revenues and/or expenses from one tax jurisdiction to another with the specific objective of lowering the global tax bill. Of course, in terms of assessing underlying management performance, the distorting effect of such movements should be eliminated.

27.3 Managing risk

Financing to manage foreign exchange risk essentially involves offsetting unanticipated changes in the currency value of operating cash flows with identical changes in the same currency in terms of the cost of servicing liabilities. Perfect hedging is difficult because of the uncertainty in estimating the expected effects of currency changes on operating flows. Thus, a firm with a sizeable export market might hold a portion of its liabilities in the currency of determination of the export revenues – this might be the currency of competitors or it might be the currency of the buying country. Any reduction in operating cash inflows due to an exchange rate change would be offset by a reduction in the debt service cash outflows.

In using financing hedges to offset exchange risks, the firm seeks to finance in such a way that it balances the currency risks inherent in the operation. In using financing to reduce political risk, the idea is that, as political risk increases, the mode of financing reduces potential adverse effects overall. For example, firms may reduce the risk of currency inconvertibility by appropriate inter-affiliate financing. Parent funds may be invested as debt rather than as equity. Back-to-back and parallel loans may be arranged. As much local financing as possible may be sought.

Another approach to managing political risk draws upon project finance techniques. Instead of supplying subsidiaries with direct or guaranteed capital, the sponsoring company raises project finance for a foreign investment from (perhaps) the host and other governments, international development agencies, overseas banks – or even from customers. Repayment is tied to the project's success. For the sponsoring firm or consortium, the project finance creates an international network of banks, government agencies and customers with a vested interest in the fulfilment of the host government's contract with the consortium. An expropriation threat is likely to upset relations with customers, banks and governments worldwide. Kennecott, the minerals company, in financing a major copper mine expansion in Chile, exemplifies the value of a firm stand by the corporation and its associated banks in the project finance network – see Moran.[4] In spite of the subsequent rise to power of the Allende regime, which promised to expropriate all foreign holdings in Chile with zero compensation, Allende was forced to honour commitments to Kennecott. A much fuller picture of project financing is provided in Buckley.[5]

27.4 Financial market distortions

One of the most important aspects of global financing strategy is to gain access to a broad range of fixed sources to lessen dependence on any one single source. At the same time, the multinational is concerned with minimising the cost of funds so raised. The hypothesis is that the cost of international borrowing is below the cost of pure domestic funding. The corporate treasurer accessing international capital markets hopes to ensure that this hypothesis works for his or her firm by exploiting financial market imperfections, distortions and inefficiencies. Subsidised finance is often the source of such potential saving.

Government credit and capital controls may lead to deviations from equilibrium in capital markets. Governments frequently intervene in domestic financial markets to achieve goals other than economic ones. A government might limit corporate borrowing in an effort to hold down interest rates, thus providing its finance ministry with a lower-cost source of funds to meet a budget deficit. Where governments do restrict access to local credit markets, local interest rates are usually at a level below equilibrium on a risk-adjusted basis. If there is a viable offshore market for the currency, the controls will result in a difference between domestic and offshore rates, giving rise to arbitrage opportunities. Firms might borrow in domestic markets and, to the extent that it is feasible, on-lend in offshore markets. In fact, the firm should borrow as much as possible, *ceteris paribus*, in the subsidised market.

Other financial market distortions may be available because many governments offer incentives to multinationals to influence their production and export-sourcing decisions. Direct investment incentives include interest rate subsidies, very long loan maturities, loan guarantees, official repatriation guarantees, direct grants related to project size, favourable prices for land and favourable terms for the building of plants, to say nothing of favourable tax incentives. All of these – and a great many further variants – create possibilities for drawing down finance at a cost below the fair market rate.

Also, governments of developed nations have export finance agencies whose purpose is to boost local exports by providing long repayment periods, low interest rates and low-cost political and economic risk insurance. These export credit agencies may frequently be used to advantage by multinationals, depending on whether the firm is seeking to export or import goods or services. Firms engaged in projects with sizeable import requirements may also be able to finance their purchases on attractive financial terms via the appropriate export-financing agency. The basic tactic remains. Shopping around among the various export credit agencies for the best possible financing arrangement can pay dividends. As an example, in connection with the financing of the Russian gas pipeline to Western Europe, Russia played off various European and Japanese suppliers and their export-financing agencies against each other and managed to get quite extraordinarily favourable credit and pricing terms.

27.5 The multinational's capital structure

Should the multinational obtain finance in such a way that its debt structure conforms to parent company norms? Or should it operate throughout the world conforming to the debt/equity capitalisation norms for each country in which it operates? Or should it vary its subsidiaries' capital structures to take advantage of opportunities to minimise taxes, offset risks and exploit distortions in capital markets? Students of international financial management often ask these questions. The answer surely flows from the view that, when deciding on a wholly owned subsidiary's funding, any accounting version of a separate capital structure for the subsidiary is illusory unless the parent is willing to allow its affiliate to default on its debt. As long as the multinational group has a legal or moral obligation to prevent the affiliate from defaulting, the individual unit truly has no independent capital structure. Its true debt/equity ratio is equal to that of the consolidated group.

Evidence on parent willingness to guarantee their affiliates' debts is provided by two surveys – one by Stobaugh[6] and the other by Business International.[7] In the survey by Stobaugh, not one of a sample of twenty medium and large multinationals said that they would allow their subsidiaries to default on debt – even though it did not have a parent company guarantee attached. And of the small multinationals reporting, only one out of seventeen indicated that it would allow a subsidiary to default on its obligations. The Business International survey of eight US-based multinationals had similar findings. The majority of firms interviewed said that they would make good the non-guaranteed debt of a subsidiary that defaulted on its borrowings. These surveys appear to indicate that most multinationals view subsidiary financial structures as having little relevance. Perhaps the third option above, namely to vary subsidiary financial structure to take advantage of local financing opportunities, appears to be the best course of action.

In spite of the argument that a subsidiary's capital structure is relevant only in so far as it affects the parent's consolidated worldwide debt ratio, some firms still follow a policy of not providing parent financing and guarantees beyond the initial investment. Why should this be so? Their rationale for this policy may be understood in the context of agency theory. Forcing the foreign affiliate to stand on its own feet means that the parent firm is, by implication, admitting that its power of surveillance over foreign subsidiaries and associates is limited. In effect, the parent is turning over some of its monitoring responsibilities to local financial institutions. At the same time, affiliate managers are presumably working to improve local operations, thereby generating the internal flows that will negate the need for parent financing. The existence of agency costs also affects corporate policy regarding parent guarantees. When a parent provides an affiliate with a loan guarantee, it explicitly loses the bank as a partner in the risk, with an attendant reduction in the need to monitor and control the loan – since the bank will probably be repaid irrespective of whether it monitors the affiliate loan or not. On the other side of the equation, of course, the bank will doubtless insist on inserting tougher covenants when there is no loan guarantee from the parent.

27.6 Political risk

Chapter 25 of this book was devoted to the topic of country risk and political risk. In the context of financing an overseas subsidiary, we need to consider confiscation risk, commercial political risk and financial political risk.

Subsidiaries operating in most stable, industrialised countries might consider themselves free from confiscation risk. However, even countries such as the United Kingdom and Canada have shown, for example in their postures on oil exploration, that US multinational companies run a risk in this area. Obviously, exposure in advanced industrialised countries is less than in, say, Nicaragua or Iran, but it nonetheless exists. The parent company may partially counter such risk by the way in which it finances its overseas subsidiaries. It may also resort to confiscation insurance. Many government-aided agencies, such as the ECGD in Britain, offer confiscation cover for new overseas investments, and Lloyd's offers cover for existing and new investments in a comprehensive, non-selective form. Financial tactics designed to minimise this risk embrace the use of high levels of gearing (preferably local gearing), maximum use of local sources of funds, including local debt and equity where a partly owned subsidiary is deemed acceptable, minimising the use of intergroup sources of finance and avoiding parent company guarantees. The essential idea is that, should the subsidiary be confiscated, the host government takes over the liabilities as well as the assets of the multinational's local operations.

The second class of political risk considered here is commercial political risk, which is best explained by an example. Consider that an overseas country is taken over by a left-wing government which imposes regulations of high minimum wages and freezes price levels, resulting in falling profit margins. This kind of exposure may affect all businesses in the country or it may be designed specifically to attack foreign-owned operations. Exposure to discrimination against foreign-owned businesses may take various guises, such as not awarding government contracts to them, giving advantages and subsidies to local-owned competitors, restricting import licences for key raw materials, refusing to grant work permits to non-indigenous staff and so on. By taking in local shareholders, it may be possible to create an influential body of opinion which would result in avoidance of some of the worst aspects of commercial political risk.

Financial political risk takes such forms as restricting access to local capital markets, restricting the repatriation of capital and dividends, imposing heavy interest-free import deposits and so on. Financing tactics designed to beat such impediments are not always easy to access. If the problem is merely the non-availability of cheap local capital markets, then the company must weigh up the relative merits of funds from outside the country versus the more expensive version of local funds. Restrictions on dividend remittance favour financing using parent debt or other debt borrowed from outside the host country. Interest and capital repayments will, in all probability, be remittable. If dividend remittances are severely restricted, analysis of parent cash flows as recommended in Chapter 23 may show a lack of economic viability for the whole operation.

27.7 Exchange control risk

Frequently, exchange controls affect the multinational company because an overseas subsidiary has accumulated surplus cash in the country in which it operates and this may not be remitted out of the overseas territory. This surplus cash may arise from profits earned or as sums owed for imports into the overseas country. As an example of how this latter constraint works, France used to have a regulation that stipulated that intergroup trade debts of a French subsidiary to an associated company, if not paid within one year of import, became blocked as an unremittable sum of capital invested in the subsidiary.

Goods shipped to some countries, notably Nigeria and India, which were denominated in the local currency became blocked since the host country's currencies were virtually totally inconvertible. The rule of thumb for the international company, irrespective of whether it is shipping to a subsidiary or to a third party, is not to ship goods without guaranteed clearance from exchange control and licensing authorities.

Where blocked funds are likely to accrue, the logical financing tactic for the international group is to finance overseas subsidiaries with as high a proportion of local borrowings as is possible; blocked funds resulting from earning non-remittable profits may subsequently be used to repay these borrowings.

27.8 Currency risk

Currency risk needs to be managed for the group as a whole and it is preferable if it is managed for the subsidiary too – even if this be by way of hedging with the group treasury. For the risk-averse company, the preferred policy is to match assets and liabilities in the same currencies both at group and at subsidiary level. In the overseas subsidiary, this would probably be assisted by drawing down as much local debt as is feasible. If local debt cannot be obtained by the overseas subsidiary because of its foreign ownership, the group treasurer may seek to borrow offshore the currency of the overseas subsidiary. If this cannot be drawn by the local company because of exchange controls, it may be logical for the parent to do the borrowing.

If the only source of finance for the risk-averse overseas subsidiary is hard currency debt – for example, US dollars or Swiss francs – then, if available, forward cover should be arranged for principal and interest payments. In evaluating competing sources of hard currency finance, if such has to be resorted to, it is assumed that the treasurer will not fall into the interest rate trap. Take the example of 'cheap' Swiss franc finance versus 'more expensive' US dollar funds. If the respective interest costs are 3 per cent per annum and 6 per cent per annum, the market is expecting the dollar to weaken over the borrowing period to eliminate this difference – this is what the international Fisher effect would be predicting. But remember that all this is on a pre-tax basis. To allow for tax effects, we have to take cognisance of the tax system under which the borrower is liable to pay tax on its income. According to most tax systems in the world, the total amount of interest (including any foreign exchange losses due to currency depreciation in the territory of operations relative to the currency of borrowing) is tax deductible. But in some countries, currency losses on principal repayment are not. The conclusion is that in such circumstances, all other things being equal, it is cheaper and safer to pay the higher interest rate rather than to incur relatively large unrelieved losses on repayment of principal.

27.9 Losses earned by subsidiaries

Although there may be no currency exposure position for the group as a whole, it could be the case that local exchange controls mean that an overseas subsidiary carries an exposed position which could make the subsidiary insolvent should adverse currency movements materialise. This may result in trading becoming illegal.

The parent company may overcome this problem (and, for that matter, the general problem occasioned by local losses leading to insolvency) by injecting further capital or by advancing new loans and subordinating them to the other creditors. Alternatively, the parent may subordinate any existing intercompany debt to the other creditors, or it may guarantee all debts of the subsidiary, provided that these courses of action are acceptable under local legal rules. However, such policies leave any resultant losses unrelieved for tax purposes.

When trading losses have a high probability, it is perhaps better that the overseas business should be set up as a branch of the home operation – in which case losses would be tax allowable against the home territory tax liability. Alternatively, an agreement may be made between a home territory exporting subsidiary, which is liable to tax, and the overseas operation to which it sells products, whereby it agrees to guarantee each year to meet the shortfall should overseas expenses exceed revenues. To be effective, this kind of revenue subvention must be defensible in the sense that the expense legitimately belongs in the home country. There is a defensible case where a substantial volume of goods is shipped from the home subsidiary to the overseas counterpart. It would not, of course, be a defensible argument were there no intercompany trade.

27.10 Intercompany credit

The reader of this chapter so far is probably convinced that a very low parent input plus substantial local borrowing represents the ideal solution to the problem of financing the overseas subsidiary. Such a mix of funding creates problems should the subsidiary be subject to unforeseen setbacks. While emergency lines of local credit may solve the short-term problem occasioned by a temporary reverse of profit or cash flow, it may be the case that these dry up in adverse circumstances. It then falls upon the group to provide funding.

While the input of parent company equity or borrowing sourced from other than the local territory would solve the problem, the suddenness of the onset of the financing problem may favour another solution, which may be recommended in the short term because it is more prompt and easy to set up. This short-term solution simply lies in a variation of the terms of intercompany credit. This means, in the context of the situation described, that the overseas subsidiary would pay intergroup creditors more slowly than originally prescribed and that intergroup receivables due to the overseas subsidiary would be paid more rapidly. The process is rather like leading and lagging but it is this time triggered by an unforeseen deterioration of local outturns, rather than an imminent movement of exchange rates. Resort to such a tactic must, of course, fall within the latitude on payment terms permitted by exchange control regulations.

27.11 Taxation effects

International taxation is a complex topic. Clearly, different countries have different tax systems with different rates of tax on profits. The scope for arranging an international group's affairs in order to minimise taxation is therefore extensive and this is true for tax corollaries of financing.

It is worth bearing in mind the almost immutable rule that there is no tax relief against consistent losses in any one country. The best approach is therefore to arrange a group's affairs such that losses are avoided in any one country. To the extent that such losses are caused by artificial practices, such as high transfer pricing, it is far better from a purely tax standpoint to discontinue such dysfunctional tactics.

27.12 Dividend policy

As part of their exchange control regulations, many developing countries erect barriers that discriminate against dividends being paid to overseas shareholders. While such practices tend to reduce the flow of funds out of the developing country, they also have the effect of discouraging direct investment inwards, which might otherwise hasten the diffusion of technology, help the growth of the developing economy and provide much-needed employment. Governments of developing countries argue that they prefer to keep a greater proportion of their industrial cake in the hands of local investors; multinationals argue that the cake becomes smaller than would otherwise be the case.

The critical question for the international company, though, is not an altruistic one: it concerns cash flows out of and remittable back to the parent. If a project fails to stand up when judged on these criteria the international company should not consider investing.

27.13 Other methods of profit transfer

Because of their actions in the past, multinationals obtained a reputation for avoiding taxes and transferring cash around the world in spite of exchange controls by such devices as manipulating transfer prices, management fees, service charges, royalty payments and non-commercial interest payments. Over the past twenty years or so, tax authorities have become adept at frustrating such manipulation. It is frequently difficult to make even fair cross-frontier charges between group members without investigation. In short, the pendulum has swung so far in the direction of the taxing authorities that multinationals are basically very concerned about avoiding paying more than their fair burden of tax in many developing countries. Nowadays arm's-length transfer pricing has become the preferred policy of most enlightened multinationals and the use of artificial means of profit transfer as a medium for shifting cash around a group has tended to fall into disrepute, although it is still encountered.

27.14 Parent company guarantees

The use of high levels of debt – especially local debt – to circumvent political risk has been recommended. Where parent company guarantees are given to an overseas subsidiary's creditors, the benefits gained by using high local debt levels tend to evaporate. Many multinationals make it a policy never to give parent company guarantees, although on occasions it is impossible to avoid giving them – for example, if a contract tender is to be seriously considered. However, some treasurers would argue that the multinational company that walks away from its insolvent subsidiary is likely to have problems with lenders in all countries and that relatively little is gained by rigidly avoiding guarantees.

Letters of comfort are, of course, a different matter. These are letters given by the multinational parent to a lender, usually a bank, which acknowledge that the borrower is a subsidiary, that the parent is aware of the indebtedness and that the holding company intends to continue to own the subsidiary. Letters of comfort of this kind have no legal stature, but they do have a moral dimension. They are not guarantees and do not count as such for accounting purposes and for calculating covenant figures. However, letters of comfort that refer to the substitution of a guarantee in prescribed circumstances may be a different kettle of fish again. The key question concerns whether or not such letters constitute guarantees. Legal advice should be sought before signing a letter of this kind. Letters of comfort are sometimes called '**letters of awareness**' or 'letters of support'.

The topic is debatable at length. However, it is our belief that as a device to reduce the impact of political risk, particularly confiscation risk, the avoidance of parent company guarantees certainly has substantial advantages for the international company.

27.15 Partly owned subsidiaries

Deciding about whether an overseas subsidiary should be wholly owned or only partly owned is probably the most critical and far-reaching decision on the financing of overseas operations. The major argument advanced against the presence of outside shareholders is that it makes single-minded management to meet the goals of the majority investor difficult without conflicts of interest with the minorities. The presence of the minority shareholder imposes a need to manage the subsidiary by the most careful application of the arm's-length principle. Any other approach results in constant friction with the outside shareholders, who may become paranoid about the subsidiary's profits and cash flows being syphoned off for the benefit of the majority shareholder. This problem is frequently highlighted when one of the shareholders provides some local facilities for the subsidiary for which it requires financial recompense. At its worst, failure to apply the arm's-length principle results in substantially reduced motivation of local management, especially when such local managers are also minority shareholders. The presence of outside shareholders means that the two sets of investors may have very different objectives on dividend policy. The dividend may be the only tangible reward for the minority, and they may also suffer much less tax on it than the majority shareholder. Furthermore, and most importantly, the minority shareholders may be reluctant to bear their fair share of the burdens of keeping the subsidiary financed or guaranteeing its obligations. At its most acute, this problem may effectively rule out new equity or guaranteed finance. It would, after all, be unfair to the majority shareholders to require them to bear a disproportionate share of such burdens. Such factors have to be carefully weighted against the opposite side of the argument.

The case for having local minority shareholders is that in many countries it is required by law, and in many countries it is an absolute political necessity. It is often argued that, in some countries, influential local shareholders open vital doors to customers, contacts and government authorities and that they can protect the overseas subsidiary against political and commercial discrimination. Moreover, there are frequently very good commercial reasons for local participation in an overseas venture.

Where there are outside shareholders, important consequences ensue. Corporate objectives of the overseas subsidiary may differ from the wholly owned case. We have referred to some obvious examples already. But there are others. For example, in the context of currency risk, local minority shareholders are not interested in group exposure; they are concerned only with that of the overseas subsidiary. Where the local minority shareholders are also the management group, views on perquisites and other managerial trappings are frequently bones of contention.

As a general rule, overseas subsidiaries with minorities are generally very lowly geared and it is often difficult to agree with the minority on profit retentions, extra capital or other finance from shareholders and guarantees from shareholders. Guarantees are altogether impracticable where the minority share is held by the public. Indeed, where the partly owned overseas subsidiary is a company quoted on a local stock exchange, the above problems are reinforced. Public investors cannot give guarantees for such a company, and it is costly and time consuming to raise new capital from such shareholders. And where the law requires that local shareholders must hold a minimum percentage of the capital, the parent company does not even have the option of merely subscribing new capital itself. All these difficulties favour a generous initial capitalisation and, probably, a policy of high retention of profits.

There is no single, ultimate answer to the problem of whether an overseas subsidiary company should use outside equity finance or not. In this section we have merely tried to point out the advantages and disadvantages of each policy. Real-world decisions on this topic require careful analysis and commercial judgement, but it must not be forgotten that an investment by a parent company in an overseas subsidiary must stand up in terms of parent cash flow analysis along the lines advocated in the chapter on capital budgeting.

27.16 The advantages of borrowing internationally

Many companies carry on their main operations in countries whose domestic capital markets are comparatively small and possibly subject to drying up. Should the parent company be located in such a country and should that company have fairly substantial needs for cash to invest in order to compete in world markets, then its growth and competitive ability may be constrained by the existence of shallow domestic financial markets – unless it taps international financing sources. This was one of the major problems confronting Novo Industri A/S (see Stonehill and Dullum[8]), the Denmark-based pharmaceutical group, in 1978 when it launched its first dollar convertible Eurobond issue. The economics of the pharmaceutical industry, with its high added value, high research and development levels, high capital intensity and need for constant innovation, make access to deep capital markets a necessary precondition to successful competition on a world scale. Novo was aware that the scale of its corporate strategy turned on the availability of substantial cash resources on an ongoing basis. It saw its domestic capital market as small and subject to periods of illiquidity, which meant that, if it wanted to pursue its strategic plan, it was necessary to look outside domestic capital markets.

These kinds of consideration are much less critical for companies based in the United Kingdom or the United States but they can be very relevant in many other countries. Indeed, the lack of depth and the illiquidity of some countries' capital markets may be one of the historic reasons for most large multinational businesses being based in countries with sophisticated financing sources. This author believes that the lack of ready access to substantial domestic capital markets has constrained the growth of businesses in many smaller European countries and elsewhere in the world.

Besides the benefit of access to deeper financial markets, tapping capital markets outside one's own home country should enable the international company to take advantage of market imperfections that prevent the Fisher effect from holding in the short term. It will be recalled that, according to the four-way equivalence model developed in Chapter 3, real interest rates (that is, nominal rates adjusted for anticipated inflation) should tend towards equality. But, given that our model is rarely, if ever, totally in equilibrium, the company which has access to world financial markets, rather than just to its domestic one, should be able to lower its cost of borrowing. Schematically, we would suggest a relationship like that shown in Figure 27.1. It is worth mentioning, however, that when a company taps international financial sources for the first time, it generally finds itself paying slightly more than an established borrower in terms of coupon rates plus underwriting fees.

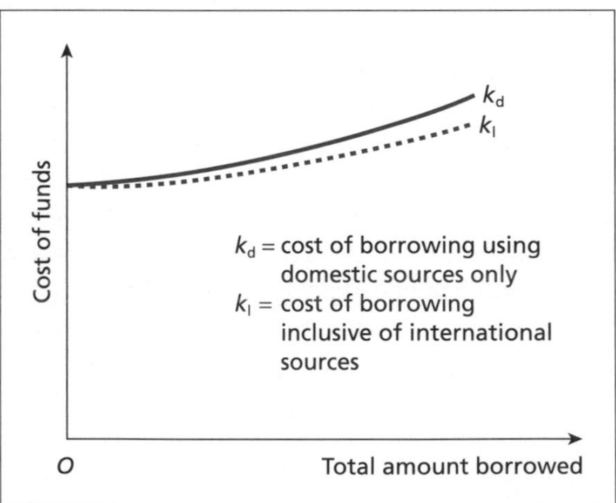

Figure 27.1 The international cost of borrowing

27.17 The risks of borrowing internationally

International financing can be broadly categorised into three classes embracing the following situations:

1 financing in the currency in which cash inflows are expected;

2 financing in a currency other than that in which cash inflows are expected, but with cover in the forward or swap market or otherwise hedged;

3 financing in a currency other than that in which cash inflows are expected, but without forward or swap or other cover.

Financing by way of the first two methods avoids foreign exchange risk. But with funds raised via the third method, foreign exchange risk is taken on.

If the international Fisher effect were always to hold as an immutable law and if foreign exchange markets were always in equilibrium, then the benefit accruing to the company through lower nominal interest rates on financing in a hard currency would be exactly offset by the amount by which the harder currency appreciated relative to the other currencies. In other words, if international Fisher holds, then the true cost of funds at the pre-tax level would be equal to the nominal interest rate in the home currency, and this rate would apply irrespective of whence the international company were to draw its funds. As we know from the discussion in Chapter 6, the international Fisher effect does not hold in the short term in the real world, and there is some doubt about whether it holds in the long term. If it is the case that we cannot feel confident about international Fisher asserting itself in the long run, and if it is also the case that exchange rate markets and the interest rate are not always in equilibrium, then the international treasurer may seek either to avoid financing risk by one or more of the techniques discussed earlier or to profit in this area by his or her own insights. Thus the treasurer may seek to raise money denominated in overvalued currencies for relatively long maturities, and by the same token will avoid raising funds in undervalued currencies.

Just as disequilibrium in international Fisher can give rise to financing opportunities for the astute corporation treasurer who is prepared to take on foreign exchange risk, so market imperfections that flow from different tax regimes also create opportunities. Tax legislation on foreign exchange gains and losses varies from one country to another. It is worth mentioning that two or more international financing propositions that appear to have the same pre-tax cost of funds after taking account of interest costs and expected strengthenings and weakenings of currencies may, on a post-tax basis, yield different costs. This phenomenon might result from the fact that corporate tax rates in different centres vary, but it might also flow from the fact that countries have different rules as to whether a capital loss or gain on repayment of an international borrowing is respectively tax deductible or comes into charge for tax.

Most of the discussion to date in this text has focused upon exchange risk problems associated with international financial exposure in the short term – that is, up to one year. In reality, the majority of financing decisions have a time dimension beyond 12 months. But the further we extend this time horizon, the greater become two key problems which impinge upon the international financing decision. First, forward exchange markets become thinner: for many currencies there may not be a forward market beyond 12 months. Secondly, in many developing countries around the world, longer-term local currency financing becomes much more difficult to find.

The non-availability of forward markets for a few currencies for periods beyond twelve months does not mean that the treasurer cannot obtain forward cover for long-term borrowings in foreign currencies. The astute treasurer can use the spot/forward method which was discussed in Chapter 11. Imagine a UK-based international company which has just made a 50m Batavian drac borrowing, requiring repayment of the total sum borrowed in three years' time. If there were no forward market beyond 12 months, the treasurer could manufacture three-year cover by a spot/forward swap. The technique would involve the process shown in Table 27.1.

Table 27.1 Spot/forward swap cover for three-year Batavian drac borrowing

End of year		
0	Buy BDc 50 million versus £	12 months forward
1	Sell BDc 50 million versus £	Spot
	Buy BDc 50 million versus £	12 months forward
2	Sell BDc 50 million versus £	Spot
	Buy BDc 50 million versus £	12 months forward
3	Use proceeds of forward purchase at end of year 2 to repay borrowing	

Remember that the difference between the spot rate and the twelve-month forward rate is underpinned by interest rate differentials. This means that, using the technique summarised in Table 27.1, the treasurer has manufactured three-year cover for the borrowing at an exchange rate equal to the twelve-month forward rate at the end of year 0 plus/minus the twelve-month interest differential at the end of year 1 plus/minus the twelve-month interest differential at the end of year 2. It should be borne in mind that when the treasurer begins this deal at the end of year 0 he or she is exposed in terms of not knowing what the interest rate differential for 12 months will be both at the end of year 1 and at the end of year 2. So this technique minimises risk, but does not totally eliminate it.

Of course, nowadays the widespread availability of swap markets may provide the ideal alternative route to obtaining cover for the exposure referred to above. Swap markets have far greater liquidity in maturities out to ten years than is available in the long-term forward markets. This usually makes swaps cheaper than long-term forward cover.

What if the treasurer decides not to cover the long-term foreign borrowing? How should the relative merits of competing borrowing propositions be assessed? In short, how should the treasurer assess the cost of international borrowing?

27.18 Foreign currency financing decisions

In a simple domestic financing situation the true cost of finance may be derived by solving a straightforward discounted cash flow calculation. The amount borrowed, the cash inflow to the company, is set against the interest and principal repayments in each year, the outflows for the company, duly discounted. After a discounting process, the rate that equates the present value of total inflows with the present value of total outflows is the true cost of the borrowing. The general equation may be written as:

$$\text{Amount borrowed} = \frac{[\text{interest paid}_1 + \text{capital repayment}_1]}{(1+r)} + \frac{[\text{interest paid}_2 + \text{capital repayment}_2]}{(1+r)^2} + \cdots + \frac{[\text{interest paid}_n + \text{capital repayment}_n]}{(1+r)^n}$$

where r is the true cost of the loan. The equation would derive from an incremental cash flow analysis in which additional inflows and outflows resulting solely from the financing decision would be specified. The true cost of the borrowing may be calculated on a pre-tax basis or using a post-tax approach. Clearly, if the post-tax cost is required, incremental cash flows must be expressed net of tax.

Where foreign exchange risk is undertaken in an international borrowing, the computation of the cost of the loan is somewhat more complex. But calculations involve the same basic principles. Incremental cash flows arising under a borrowing are specified and the discounted cost is computed. But in this instance we need to recognise that incremental cash flows in home currency terms embrace the initial borrowing, interest to be paid and capital to be repaid, with all of these cash flows duly adjusted to allow for expected or actual (if the analysis is an *ex-post* one) exchange gains and losses. The general equation, in home currency terms, may be expressed as:

$$\text{Amount borrowed} = \frac{\begin{array}{c}[\text{interest paid}_1 + \text{capital repayment}_1\\ (\text{inclusive of realised exchange gain or loss}_1)]\end{array}}{(1+r)} + \frac{\begin{array}{c}[\text{interest paid}_2 + \text{capital repayment}_2\\ (\text{inclusive of realised exchange gain or loss}_2)]\end{array}}{(1+r)^2} + \cdots + \frac{\begin{array}{c}[\text{interest paid}_n + \text{capital repayment}_n\\ (\text{inclusive of realised exchange gain or loss}_n)]\end{array}}{(1+r)^n}$$

The solution to the above equation for r gives us the true effective cost of a borrowing. Evidently, if the cost of a foreign borrowing is being made in advance of drawing down a loan, then estimates must be made of future exchange rate movements. For this purpose, the tools in the armoury of the international treasurer were discussed in earlier chapters. Where the currency of borrowing is overvalued or undervalued at the time the loan is drawn down, the treasurer needs to make estimates of the timing and extent of movements towards equilibrium – and this is a major problem.

The true effective cost of a borrowing from international sources may be computed on a pre-tax or on a post-tax basis. The post-tax computation is more complex because we need to consider not only the net-of-tax interest cost but also the foreign exchange gain or loss and whether this is recognised for tax purposes. Analysts also need to be careful in their calculations about whether a borrowing is an amortising loan or one with a bullet repayment. A bullet repayment involves a single lump sum repayment at maturity. A given currency movement virtually always results in a different true effective cost of funds if the loan is an amortising one as opposed to one involving a bullet repayment. Also the timing of an appreciation or depreciation of a currency can be extremely material in the calculation of the true cost of borrowing. The sooner the appreciation of a borrowed currency takes place, the greater the increase in the true cost of borrowing. The sooner the devaluation of a borrowed currency occurs, the bigger the decrease to the net effective cost of funds.

As an example, consider a UK company financing itself in dollars. The company draws down a five-year \$1m borrowing in year 0 and the loan carries a 10 per cent per annum coupon. Assume that the dollar appreciates from \$1.30 to the pound at the time of

Table 27.2 True effective annual cost of borrowing (%)

Year of $ appreciation	Repayment terms		
	Equal amortisation	50% by equal amortisation 50% by balloon repayment	Bullet repayment
1	14.5	13.7	12.8
2	13.3	13.0	12.6
3	12.3	12.2	12.3
4	11.3	11.7	12.1
5	10.6	11.3	12.0

drawdown to $1.17. The true cost of the loan on a pre-tax basis is shown in Table 27.2. The table shows this true cost on the basis that the dollar revaluation takes place in one go either in year 1 or in year 2 or in year 3 and so on. The true effective pre-tax cost in the table is based on a number of assumptions: these are as follows. First, the loan is repayable in equal installments; second, the loan is assumed to be repaid by annual amortisation of $100,000m plus a **balloon** in year 5 of $500,000m; third, the loan is repaid by a bullet repayment at the end of year 5.

The figures in the table emphasise the need to look beyond the coupon rate of interest. In our example, the devaluation of sterling against the dollar is not a large one by the relative standards of past experience in a floating currency regime. But the impact of that depreciation in the case of the equally amortising loan is staggering. The impact of a revaluation of the dollar of only around 10 per cent coming early, rather than late, in the borrowing is to raise the coupon cost from around 10 per cent per annum to an effective cost of approaching 15 per cent per annum. The management of a company would have good reason to be critical of the treasurer who talked in terms of this dollar loan as only costing around 10 per cent per annum before tax.

Movements of the Swiss franc and the Deutschmark against sterling through the early 1970s and the strengthening of the dollar in the early 1980s show how naive many corporate treasuries have been in talking their companies into borrowing in cheap interest currencies. Hopefully such financial executives and their companies have learned by bitter, and expensive, experience.

It is also necessary to take account of expected currency movements when calculating the cost of debt as part of a company's exercise of calculating its weighted average cost of capital. This simple procedure is frequently overlooked by financial and planning executives. And in many cases the effect can be very substantial indeed.

There is an increasing tendency for providers of finance in international capital markets to offer floating rate lending with interest tied to LIBOR or some other convenient interest rate base. This creates complexities for the treasurer of an international company. There is a strong temptation to argue that, if international Fisher holds in the long term, the treasurer need not worry whence any borrowing is arranged. Devaluations and revaluations should, according to this theory, cancel out against floating interest rate differentials. This simplistic approach is valid only if the relevant exchange rates move in accordance with the prediction of purchasing power parity and the Fisher effect during the whole course of the loan from drawdown to final repayment. Furthermore, interest and foreign exchange markets must be in equilibrium at the start of a borrowing period for this indifference to financial sourcing to be justified. This is a pretty tall order. Indeed, outside textbook models it will never be found.

This has practical implications for the international treasurer even in a world of floating interest rate finance. Imagine that a UK company is considering borrowing via a dollar floating rate loan at a time when the dollar is undervalued by reference to past movements of real effective exchange rates. Even though the loan carries a floating rate, should the dollar/sterling exchange rate move once and for all to correct the previous disequilibrium in PPP but thereafter the rates continue to move in line with international Fisher, then, if this is foreseen, the dollar borrowing will appear relatively expensive. So, even with floating rate notes, the treasurer needs to be very careful. The floating interest rate does not circumvent the problem of potential exchange rate movements.

This whole area of foreign currency financing without forward cover is one that is full of pitfalls. Short cuts are ill-advised. There is no substitute for careful analysis of the interaction between past movements of exchange rates, interest rates and inflation rates. And future estimates are necessary if logical predictions of future exchange rates are to be made over the period of a borrowing. This process is an essential prerequisite to the task of estimating, *ex ante*, the cost of an international borrowing. Hopefully, the framework of analysis laid down in this text should be helpful to potential international borrowers.

Summary

- The problems associated with financing an overseas subsidiary differ substantially from those of financing an independent company. The first question to ask is whether the subsidiary is wholly owned or not.
- Where it is only partly owned, it should be capitalised generously and would probably be lowly geared. The reason for this is that it is often difficult to agree with the minority on such things as profit retentions, extra capital needed or guarantees from shareholders. Indeed, guarantees are altogether impracticable where the minority is held by the public. All these difficulties suggest a generous initial capitalisation with only a low debt to equity ratio.
- Where the subsidiary is wholly owned, political risk may be reduced by virtue of financing with a high debt level. This was referred to in an earlier chapter.
- Financing, like many aspects of the multinational's activities, should provide an opportunity to minimise global taxes and exploit financial market distortions in order to raise funds at minimum cost. Furthermore, global financing is a means to gain access to a broad range of capital markets and to lessen dependence on any single source. This flexibility can be a great benefit in terms of monitoring and exploiting windows of opportunity to raise relatively cheap money due to capital market imperfections and also in terms of providing reassurances should some markets temporarily dry up.
- As long as the multinational group has a legal or moral obligation to prevent an overseas affiliate from defaulting, the individual unit really has no independent capital structure. The true debt to equity ratio is equal to that at the consolidated level.
- International borrowing may enable companies to lower their average cost of finance – see Figure 27.1.
- International borrowing is important for companies whose headquarters are within countries with shallow capital markets as well as for major multinationals.

- The true cost of various sources of financing should be calculated by all companies. This involves using the traditional discounted cash flow framework with the amount borrowed showed as an inflow in year 0 and outflows in respect of payment of interest, net of tax, and repayment of principal according to the repayment schedule.
- Calculating such a true cost is relatively easy in respect of domestic borrowings and those that are fully covered. Using the usual framework referred to above, an IRR in respect of the borrowing can be calculated. Where funding occurs in a currency other than that in which cash inflows are expected, but without forward or swap or other cover, its cost should be estimated with anticipated movements in exchange rate used. However, when presenting data on the costs of relative funding, particular attention needs to be drawn to such uncovered cases.

End of chapter questions

27.1 Why is it necessary to compute the present value when assessing the cost of financing for two alternatives?

27.2 Why might a US-based MNC issue bonds denominated in euros?

28

Financing international trade and minimising credit risk

Two problem areas dominate the financing of international trade: these concern foreign exchange risk and credit risk. The former topic is wide ranging and is considered in detail in various sections of this book. This chapter focuses upon credit risk. This may be defined as the risk that one may not be paid for goods or services supplied. Its complexities in an international arena arise because of the difficulties of taking repossession of goods following non-payment when they are outside the country of the supplier.

Before goods are shipped, the importer and exporter agree the terms of a transaction, including price, insurance, freight, dates of shipment and so on. The banking system provides several methods of making or receiving payment in international trade. Payment method usually lies among a number of choices including cash with order, open account, bills of exchange, documentary letters of credit and government assistance schemes. These choices are not mutually exclusive. For example, bills of exchange and letters of credit are often used as part of a package with government assistance as well. In this chapter we consider each of the above methods of financing international trade. It must be borne in mind that this whole topic is a broad one and the coverage here can only be superficial. In summary, the main trade finance possibilities are shown in Table 28.1. The trade finance solutions listed in the table are arranged in order of risk – from the highest risk to the exporter (which is the lowest risk to the importer) to the lowest risk to the exporter (which is the highest risk to the importer). An appendix explaining trade finance terms can be found at the end of this chapter. Readers dealing with the topics of financing international trade and minimising credit risk in the real world would be well advised to obtain advice from a banker or other specialist.

Table 28.1 Trade finance possibilities from highest risk to exporter (lowest risk to importer) to lowest risk to exporter (highest risk to importer)

Term	Description
Extended terms	Importer pays for goods over period of time during which they are used by importer, often three to 10 years. A set of promissory notes is normally issued upon shipment, payable at six-month or one-year intervals.
Open account, clean draft	Exporter makes shipment and awaits payment direct from importer. Any documents needed by importer sent directly by exporter when sale is invoiced though a draft may also be presented separately through banking channels.

28.3 Documentation in foreign trade

There are three important key documents involved in foreign trade. The first is bill of exchange or draft, which is an order to pay; the second is the bill of lading, which is a document involved in the physical movement of the merchandise by a common carrier; the third is the **letter of credit**, which is a third-party guarantee of an importer's creditworthiness.

Documentation in foreign trade is designed to ensure that the exporter will receive payment and the importer will receive the merchandise. Also, documents in foreign trade are used to eliminate non-completion risk, to reduce foreign exchange risk and to finance trade transactions.

The risk of non-completion is greater in foreign trade than in domestic transactions. Thus, exporters wish to keep title to the goods until they are paid for and importers are reluctant to pay until they receive the goods. Most domestic sales are on open account credit. Under open account, the buyer does not sign a formal debt instrument because credit sales are made on the basis of a seller's credit evaluation of the buyer. Buyers and sellers are also, usually, further apart, physically and culturally, in foreign trade than in domestic trade. Consequently, sellers are less able to ascertain the credit standing of their overseas customers. Buyers may also find it difficult to determine the reputation and integrity of their foreign suppliers. Much of the non-completion risk is reduced through the use of the bill of exchange, the bill of lading and the letter of credit.

Of course, foreign exchange transaction risk arises when export sales are denominated in a foreign currency and are paid at a later date. Forward contracts, swaps, currency options and currency denominating practices, referred to elsewhere in this text, may be used to reduce foreign exchange risk in foreign trade.

Because all foreign trade involves a time lag, funds become tied up in the shipment of goods for some period of time. Trade transactions become free of non-completion and foreign exchange risk due to well-drawn trade documents and forward contracts. Thus, banks are prepared to finance goods in transit and even prior to shipment. Financial institutions at either end of the trade offer a variety of financing alternatives that reduce or eliminate risk for both exporter and importer.

Drafts

A bill of exchange (or draft) is an order written by an exporter that requires an importer to pay a specified amount of money at a specified future date. Through the use of drafts, the exporter may use its bank as a collection agent on accounts that the exporter finances. The bank forwards the exporter's drafts to the importer, either directly or indirectly (through a branch or a correspondent bank), and then remits the proceeds back to the exporter.

A draft involves three parties – these are the drawer or maker, the drawee and the payee. The drawer is the person or the business issuing a draft. This person is usually the exporter who sells and ships the merchandise. The drawee is the person or the business against whom the draft is drawn. This person or business is usually the importer who must pay the draft at maturity. The payee is the person or the business to whom the drawee must eventually pay the funds. If the draft is not a negotiable instrument, it designates the person or bank to whom payment is to be made. Such a person, known as the payee, may be the drawer or a third party such as the drawer's bank. However, most drafts are **negotiable instruments**. Drafts are negotiable if they meet a number of conditions. The draft must:

- be in writing and signed by the drawer (the exporter);
- contain an unconditional promise or order to pay an exact amount of money;
- be payable on sight or at a specified time;
- be made out to order or to bearer.

If the draft is made to order, the funds involved would be paid to a person specified. If it is made to bearer, the funds should be paid to the person who presents the draft for payment.

When a draft is presented to a drawee, either the drawee or his bank accepts it. This **acceptance** acknowledges in writing the drawee's obligation to pay the sum indicated on the face of the draft. When drafts are accepted by banks, they are termed bankers' acceptances. Some bankers' acceptances are highly marketable. This means that the exporter can sell them in the bill marker or discount them at his bank. Whenever they are sold or discounted, the seller writes his endorsement on the back of the draft. In the event that an importer fails to pay at maturity, the holder of the draft will have recourse for the full amount of the draft from the immediately previous endorser and then the endorser before that – and so on.

Drafts are used in foreign trade for a number of reasons. First of all, they provide written evidence of obligations in a comprehensive and fairly standard form. Second, they allow both the exporter and the importer to reduce the cost of financing and to divide costs equitably. Third, they are negotiable and unconditional. This means that drafts themselves are not subject to disputes that may occur between the parties involved.

Drafts may be either sight drafts or time drafts. A **sight draft** is payable upon demand. Here, the drawee must pay the draft immediately or dishonour it. A time draft is payable a specified number of days after presentation to the drawee. When a time draft is presented to the drawee, he may have his bank accept it in writing or by stamping a notice of acceptance on its face. When a draft, or bill of exchange, is drawn on and accepted by a bank, it becomes a bankers' acceptance.

Drafts may be documentary drafts or clean drafts. Documentary drafts require shipping documents such as bills of lading, insurance certificates and commercial invoices. Most drafts are documentary since all of these shipping documents are necessary to obtain the goods shipped. The documents attached to a documentary draft are passed on to an importer either upon payment, for sight drafts, or upon acceptance, for time drafts. If documents are to be delivered to an importer upon payment of the draft, the draft is referred to as a D/P (documents against payment) draft. If the documents are passed on to an importer upon acceptance, the draft is called a D/A (documents against acceptance) draft.

When a time draft is accepted by an importer, it is termed a trade acceptance or a clean draft. When clean drafts are used in international trade, the exporter usually sends all shipping documents directly to the importer and only the draft to the collecting bank. The clean draft involves a fair amount of risk. Thus, clean drafts are generally used in cases in which there is considerable faith between exporter and importer or in cases in which firms send goods to their foreign subsidiaries.

Bills of lading

We now turn to bills of lading. A bill of lading is a shipping document issued to an exporter firm or its bank by the carrier which transports the goods. It acts as receipt, a contract and a document of title. As a receipt, the bill of lading indicates that the goods specified have been received by the carrier. As a contract, it is evidence that the carrier is required to deliver the goods to the importer in exchange for certain charges. As a document of title, it is evidence of ownership of the goods. So, the bill of lading is used to ensure payment before the goods are delivered. The importer cannot obtain title to the goods until he obtains the bill of lading from the carrier.

Bills of lading may be straight bills of lading or order bills of lading. A straight bill of lading requires that the carrier deliver the goods to a specified party, usually the importer. This technique is used where the goods have been paid for in advance. An order bill of lading requires the carrier to deliver the goods to the order of a specified party, usually the exporter. In this case, the exporting firm retains title to the goods until it receives payment. Once payment is forthcoming, the exporting firm endorses the order bill of lading in blank or to its bank. The endorsed document can be used as security for financing.

Bills of lading may be on-board bills of lading or received-for-shipment bills of lading. On-board bills of lading indicate that the goods have been placed on board the vessel. A received-for-shipment bill of lading merely acknowledges that the carrier has received the goods for shipment but does not guarantee that the goods have been loaded on the vessel. A received-for-shipment bill of lading may readily be converted into an on-board bill of lading by the appropriate stamp which shows the name of the vessel, the date and the signature of an official of the vessel.

In addition, bills of lading may be classified as clean bills of lading or foul bills of lading. A clean bill of lading indicates that the carrier has received the goods in apparently good condition. By contrast, a foul bill of lading bears an indication from the carrier that the goods appeared to have suffered some damage before the carrier received them for shipment. Foul bills of lading are, generally, not acceptable under a letter of credit. With a letter of credit it is important that the exporter obtain a clean bill of lading.

Letters of credit

We now turn to letters of credit. A letter of credit is a document issued by a bank at the request of an importer. In the letter of credit, the bank agrees to honour a draft drawn on the importer if the draft accompanies specified documents such as the bill of lading. Typically, the importer requests his or her local bank to write a letter of credit. In exchange for the bank's agreement to honour the demand for payment that results from the transaction, the importer promises to pay the bank the amount of the transaction plus a specified fee.

Letters of credit facilitate foreign trade and are advantageous to both exporter and importer. They give a number of benefits to the exporter. First, they mean that the exporter sells his goods abroad against the promise of a bank rather than a commercial firm. Because banks are usually better credit risks than most business firms, exporters are almost assured of payment if specific conditions are met. Second, exporters may obtain funds as soon as they have the necessary documents such as the letter of credit and the bill of lading. When shipment is made, the exporter prepares a draft in accordance with the letter of credit and presents it to his local bank. If the bank finds that all papers are in order, it advances the face value of the draft less fees and interest.

The letter of credit also gives a number of benefits to importers. It assures them that the exporter will only be paid if he or she provides certain documents, all of which are carefully examined by the bank. If the exporter is unable or unwilling to make proper shipment, recovery of the deposit is more easily achieved from the bank than from the overseas exporter. Also, the letter of credit enables the importer to remove commercial risk to the exporter in exchange for certain considerations. Moreover, it is less expensive to finance goods under a letter of credit than by borrowing.

Letters of credit may be irrevocable or revocable. Most letters of credit between unrelated parties are irrevocable. An irrevocable letter of credit cannot be cancelled or modified by the importer's bank without the consent of all parties. A revocable letter of credit can be revoked or modified by the importer's bank at any time prior to payment. Banks do not favour revocable letters of credit. Indeed, some banks refuse to issue them because of their potential for subsequent litigation.

Letters of credit may be confirmed or unconfirmed. A confirmed letter of credit is a letter of credit confirmed by a bank other than the issuing bank. Why might this be necessary? An exporter may want a foreign bank's letter of credit confirmed by a domestic bank when the exporter has some doubt about the foreign bank's ability to pay. In this case, these banks are obligated to honour drafts drawn in accordance with the letter of credit. Unconfirmed letters of credit are guarantees only of the opening bank. The strongest letter of credit is clearly a confirmed, irrevocable letter of credit. Such a letter of credit cannot be cancelled by the opening bank and, moreover, it requires both the opening and confirming banks to guarantee payment on drafts issued in connection with an export transaction.

Also, letters of credit may be either **revolving** or non-revolving. A revolving letter of credit is a letter of credit whose duration revolves, for example, weekly or monthly. Thus, a £50,000 revolving credit might authorise an exporter to draw drafts up to £50,000 each week until the expiry of the credit. A revolving letter of credit might be used when an importer has to make frequent and known purchases and payments. Most letters of credit are non-revolving. Thus, typically, letters of credit are issued and valid for a single transaction.

Other documentation

There is other documentation required too. In addition to the draft, the bill of lading and the letter of credit, some additional documents frequently required in international trade are commercial invoices, insurance documents and consular invoices. These, and some other documents, are required to obtain the goods shipped. Furthermore, they may be essential to clear the merchandise through customs at ports of entry and departure.

A commercial invoice is issued by the exporter. It contains a precise description of the merchandise, indicating unit prices, quality, total value, financial terms of sale and various shipping features. The commercial invoice may include other information such as the names and addresses of both exporter and importer, the number of packages, transportation and insurance charges, the name of the vessel, the ports of departure and destination, export or import permit numbers and so on.

Shipments in international trade are all insured. Most insurance contracts nowadays automatically cover all shipments made by the exporter. The risks of transportation range from damage to total loss of merchandise. Most ocean carriers do not have any responsibility for losses during the actual transportation except those directly attributed to their negligence. Therefore, some form of marine insurance is arranged to protect both the exporter and the importer. This additional insurance coverage ranges from limited cover for losses through collision, fire and sinking to the broad coverage of all risks.

Exports to some countries require a consular invoice issued by the consulate of the importing country. Specifically, a consular invoice is necessary to obtain customs clearance. It also provides officials with information necessary to assess import duties. The consular invoice does not carry title to the goods and is negotiable.

Various other documents may be required by the importer or may be necessary in clearing the goods through ports of entry or exit. These include certificates of origin, weight lists, packing lists and inspection certificates. A certificate of origin certifies the country in which the goods were manufactured or grown. A weight list specifies the weight of each item. A packing list identifies the contents of each individual package. An inspection certificate is a document issued by an independent inspection company to verify the contents and quality of the shipment.

28.4 Bills of exchange

In our analysis at the beginning of this chapter, one of the methods of making payment in international trade was identified as the bill of exchange (or draft). A bill of exchange is defined in UK law as an unconditional order in writing addressed by one person to another, signed by the person giving it, requiring the person to whom it is addressed to pay, on demand or at a fixed or determinable future time, a certain sum in money to, or to the order of, a specified person, or to bearer.

An exporter can send a bill of exchange for the value of goods through the banking system for payment by an overseas buyer on presentation. Typically, an exporter prepares a bill of exchange which is drawn on an overseas importer, or on a third party designated in the export contract, for the sum agreed as settlement. The bill of exchange, or draft, resembles a cheque; indeed a cheque is defined by the Bills of Exchange Act 1882 as a bill of exchange drawn on a banker, payable on demand. An example of a bill of exchange is given in Figure 28.1.

The bill of exchange is called a sight draft if it is made out payable at sight – that is, on demand. If it is payable at a fixed or determinable future time, it is called a term draft, since the buyer is receiving a period of credit, known as the tenor of the bill. The buyer signifies an agreement to pay on the due date by writing an acceptance across the face of the bill.

By using a bill of exchange with other shipping documents through the banking system, an exporter can ensure greater control of the goods because, until the bill is paid or accepted by the overseas buyer, the goods cannot be released. Also, the buyer does not have to pay or agree to pay until delivery of the goods from the exporter.

A UK exporter might pass a bill of exchange to a bank in the United Kingdom. The UK bank forwards the bill to its overseas branch or to a correspondent bank in an overseas buyer's country. This bank, known as the collecting bank, presents the bill to whoever it is drawn upon for immediate payment if it is a sight draft, or for acceptance if it is a term draft. This procedure is known as a 'clean bill collection' because no shipping documents are required. Clean bill collections have recently become more popular. Such collections provide more security than open account terms if there is some doubt about a buyer's financial status.

However, it is more likely that bills are used in a documentary bill collection method of payment. In this case, an exporter sends the bill to the buyer by way of the banking system

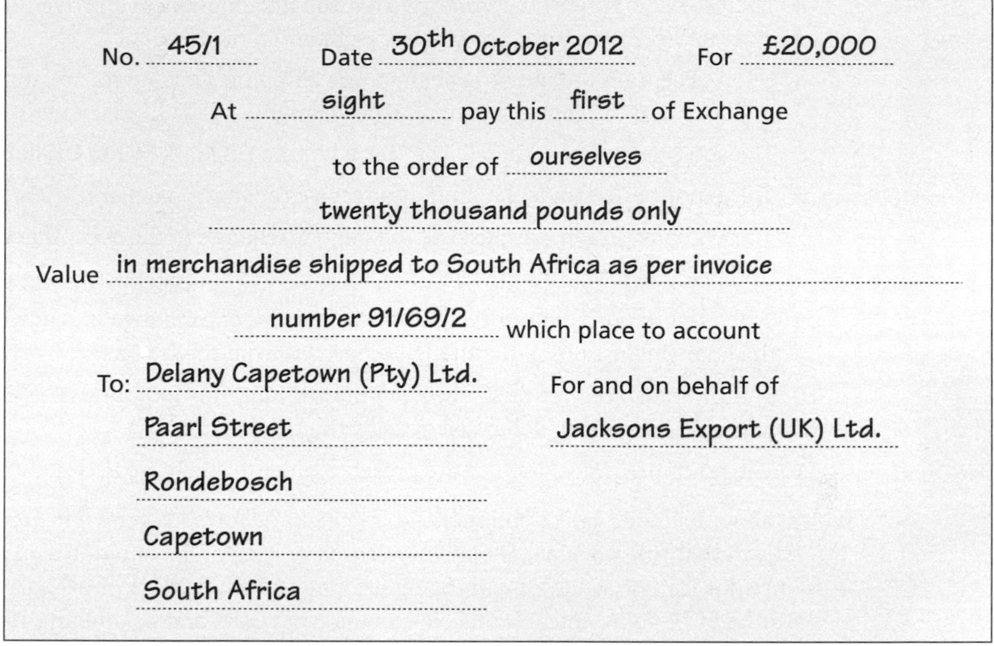

No. 45/1 Date 30th October 2012 For £20,000

At sight pay this first of Exchange

to the order of ourselves

twenty thousand pounds only

Value in merchandise shipped to South Africa as per invoice

number 91/69/2 which place to account

To: Delany Capetown (Pty) Ltd.
Paarl Street
Rondebosch
Capetown
South Africa

For and on behalf of
Jacksons Export (UK) Ltd.

Figure 28.1 Example of a bill of exchange (date change)

with the shipping documents, including the document of title to the goods, usually an original bill of lading. The bank releases the documents only on payment or acceptance of the bill by the overseas buyer. This was detailed in the previous section of this chapter.

An exporter may even use the banking system for a cash against documents (CAD) collection. In this case only the shipping documents are sent and the exporter instructs the bank to release them only after payment by the overseas buyer. This method is used in some European countries whose buyers prefer CAD to a sight draft if the exporter insists on a documentary collection for settlement of the export contract.

In all the methods of payment using a bill of exchange, or draft, a **promissory note** can be used as an alternative. This is issued by a buyer which promises to pay an exporter a certain amount of money within a specified time. For a UK exporter, it is also possible to send the documents and bill of exchange directly to an overseas buyer's bank, thus bypassing the UK bank. This system of direct collection is widely supported by US banks.

In order to make clear what procedures an exporter wants from a particular collection and what action should be taken if an overseas buyer does not meet the payment terms of the contract, most UK banks ask exporters to fill out a bank lodgement form. This is a check-list which ensures that all the instructions are remembered in order to make a successful collection.

As an illustration of how bills of exchange work, consider the following example of a US exporter and a UK importer using a 60-day sight draft.

1 The US exporter makes a shipment to a UK importer with the billing made out to the name of the exporter.
2 The exporter delivers the draft and shipping documents to the US bank, which sends the draft and shipping documents to the UK bank.

3 The UK bank notifies the importer that the documents have arrived and presents the draft to the importer for acceptance, payment in 60 days.

4 Upon accepting the bill of exchange, the shipping documents are surrendered to the importer and the shipment can now be claimed.

5 The accepted bill of exchange is returned to the US bank by the UK bank.

6 The exporter discounts the draft and receives advance payment.

7 The US bank, in turn, disposes of the bill of exchange in the acceptance market.

8 Upon receiving such funds, the US bank is now in a liquid position again.

9 When the sixty-day maturity approaches, the bill of exchange is sent to the UK bank by the financial institution that had purchased it from the US bank.

10 The UK bank receives payment from the UK importer in pounds sterling and the conversion of sterling to dollars is made by the UK bank.

11 The funds are transmitted to the present holder of the trade acceptance.

The above example can be summarised in schematic form, as shown in Figure 28.2.

Given that title documents may be released only upon payment, the exporter's position is superior to that achieved with open account exporting. Bills of exchange also have the advantages of being cheaper than documentary credits and of opening further arenas for financing. Bills of exchange may be discounted by negotiation. This means that a bank buys its customer's outward collection (that is, the foreign currency proceeds of an export) at the time that the collection is remitted abroad. This provides the exporter with short-term funds. Banks may also give an advance against an outward collection of bills of exchange.

Exporters of substantial creditworthiness may also use a merchant bank acceptance facility. Under this financing mechanism, documentary drafts drawn by the exporter on the overseas buyer become security and are handled as documentary collections by the merchant bank. These documents are pledged to the merchant bank. The exporter draws a draft on the bank and, after acceptance by the bank, the draft, now known as an accommodation bill, is discounted, usually with a discount house, and the proceeds are paid to the exporter.

Using bills of exchange offers less security to the exporter than obtaining cash with order or using letters of credit. Bills of exchange provide the importer with a period of credit and

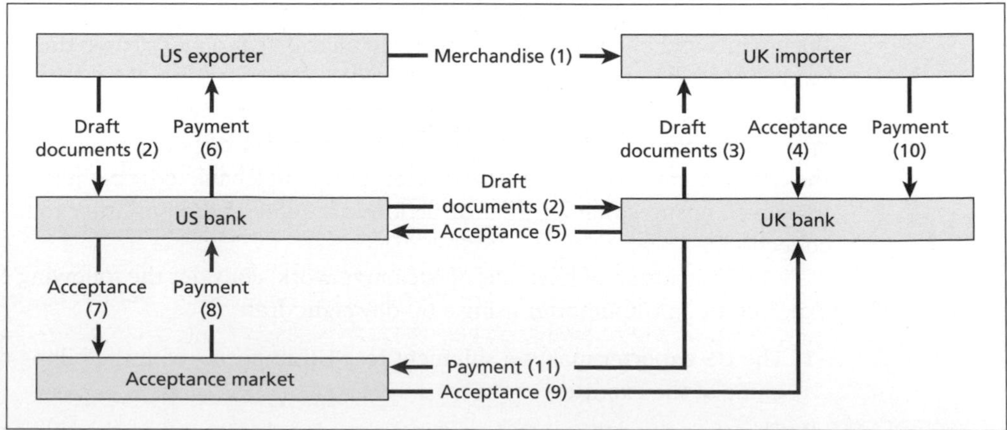

Figure 28.2 Example of international trade financing under a 60-day sight draft

the chance to ensure that the goods are what was ordered before payment is authorised. Transacting international trade via bills of exchange reduces the risk of non-payment. Although more expensive than cash with order and open account, bills of exchange are cheaper than trading via letters of credit.

28.5 Documentary letters of credit trading

As discussed earlier in this chapter, a documentary letter of credit is a credit under which drawings are honoured, provided the beneficiary delivers the documents evidencing shipment of the goods ordered. With a documentary letter of credit, exporters are able to receive payment for goods in their own country, once shipment has taken place. At the same time, the buyer is secure in the knowledge that payment will not have been made unless the terms and conditions of the credit have been met. With the security of the documentary credit, the exporter is able to produce goods knowing that it will receive payment promptly. At the same time the importer is as sure as it can be that the goods will be received when they are required.

The first contractual step in an export transaction is the sale contract. If it is agreed as part of the contract that a documentary credit is to be used for payment of the goods, then the buyer will make arrangements with its bank for the issue of the credit. The onus of drawing up the letter of credit lies with the importer, which gives its bank detailed instructions about the nature of the goods, their quality and price, the total value of the credit, the documents required, the dates between which documents may be presented for payment and any special provisions which may have been agreed between purchaser and seller. These terms and conditions will be contained in the advice of issue of the documentary credit sent to the seller, which is technically referred to as the beneficiary. The documentary credit is separate from the sales contract. As such the beneficiary checks that the terms comply with those agreed in the sale contract. If they differ, the beneficiary contacts the seller – technically known as the taker – and requests that the seller instructs its bank to issue an amendment to the credit.

Banks advise the beneficiary in one of three ways that a credit has been opened in its favour. They may advise the beneficiary direct, indicating a bank in the beneficiary's country where payment may be obtained against the documents. Secondly, they may address the advice of opening to the beneficiary and send it to their branch or correspondent for onward transmission. Thirdly, they may address it to their branch or correspondent in the beneficiary's country and request that the beneficiary should be notified.

Letters of credit are of various types. The most frequently encountered are revocable, irrevocable and confirmed irrevocable credits. The differences between revocable and irrevocable credits are important and have been referred to earlier in this chapter.

To reiterate, a revocable credit may be amended or cancelled at any time without prior notice to the beneficiary. However, the issuing bank is bound to reimburse a branch or other bank to which such a credit has been transmitted and made available for payment, acceptance or negotiation, for any payment, acceptance or negotiation complying with the terms and conditions of the credit, and for any amendments received up to the time of the payment, acceptance or negotiation made by such branch or other bank prior to receipt by it of notice of amendment or cancellation.

An irrevocable credit constitutes a definite undertaking of the issuing bank, provided that the terms and conditions of the credit are complied with:

- to pay, or that payment will be made, if the credit provides for payment, whether against a draft or not;
- to accept drafts if the credit provides for acceptance by the payment at maturity, if the credit so provides, for the acceptance of drafts drawn on the applicant for the credit or any other drawee specified in the credit;
- to purchase/negotiate, without recourse to drawers and/or bona fide holders, drafts drawn by the beneficiary at sight or at a tenor, on the applicant for the credit or on any other drawee specified in the credit, or to provide for purchase/negotiation by another bank, if the credit provides for purchase/negotiation.

A revocable credit is not a legally binding undertaking between the bank or banks concerned and the beneficiary, since it may be modified or cancelled at any time without the beneficiary being notified, though payment made before receipt of a modification or cancellation remains valid. Thus it is never a confirmed credit. An irrevocable credit may not be modified or cancelled without the consent of all the parties concerned.

The beneficiary of a credit may not know the standing of the opening bank. If the opening bank becomes bankrupt after the beneficiary's bank has negotiated the credit, but before it has been reimbursed, then the beneficiary's bank has recourse to the beneficiary. As a precaution, the beneficiary can ask its bank to confirm the credit for a fee, provided the bank is satisfied about the standing of the opening bank. Once confirmed, the confirming bank has no recourse to the beneficiary after negotiation of the credit. This constitutes a confirmed irrevocable documentary letter of credit.

After the beneficiary has received the documentary credit in the form required, and the goods are available for shipment, arrangements are made via an agent to draw up the documents. The agent receives a copy of the credit to ensure that the documents are prepared according to it. After the goods have been shipped, the beneficiary delivers all the documents to its bank, with the credit. The bank compares the documents with the credit. If it is satisfied that they are in order, the bank pays the beneficiary.

When an exporter has negotiated in the contract with a buyer for a confirmed irrevocable letter of credit, then security of payment, as far as is humanly possible, is achieved.

Whether or not the credit is confirmed, it is essential that the exporter checks the credit terms immediately to make sure that they are compatible with the sales contract made with the buyer. When dealing with documentary credits, the bank is concerned only with the documents to be presented and not with the goods or services involved. Documentary credits may provide for payment at sight or for acceptance of a term bill of exchange by either the issuing bank in a buyer's country or the correspondent bank in the United Kingdom. A schematic representation of the typical series of steps involved in trading under a documentary credit is set out in Figure 28.3.

Under a letter of credit transaction, the onus of financing falls squarely upon the buyer. The main benefit derived by the importer is the protection of a definite date by which the seller is required to ship goods. The buyer therefore expects prompt delivery. Also the buyer may expect to receive lower prices when a letter of credit is submitted, since difficulties are so fully safeguarded that the exporter finds it unnecessary to cover them in the price. Advance orders, or orders running throughout a period of time, are well protected by the

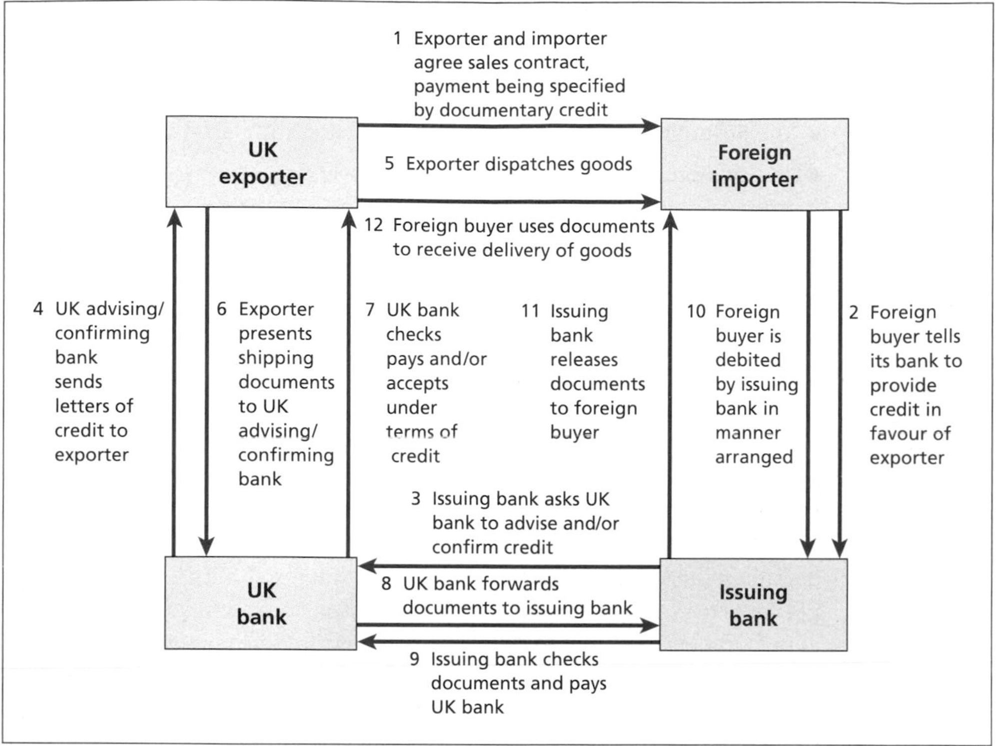

Figure 28.3 Documentary credit trading

expiration date of the letter of credit, as well as by the limit of the sum of money for which it is drawn. Attractive discounts are frequently offered to importers for providing letter of credit payment.

Letters of credit are of great benefit when the parties involved are relatively unknown to each other, or where one of the parties is in a country where political risk of non-payment is high. Over recent years, an increasing portion of world trade has been conducted between multinationals and their subsidiaries and associates, or between well-established trading partners. In these cases the risk of default is greatly reduced and trading on open account has reasserted itself.

Letters of credit do have drawbacks and there are popular alternatives. For example, a small importer wishing to open a letter of credit may be called upon by its bank to provide partial – or even full – cash cover. The cash flow impact of this may be so acute as to force the importer to find other ways of arranging payment. This may be via a confirming house or an international credit union which arranges extended payment terms. Exporters are usually happy to deal with the confirming house, which makes payment on behalf of the importer, without the security of a letter of credit. Exporters can also improve cash flows by selling their debt books to a factoring house. Factoring houses give the seller credit insurance by taking over its invoices as the goods are supplied, and they provide cash – either immediately or at some agreed future date – for up to three-quarters of the invoice value less various incidental charges.

Before entering the arena of trading via documentary credit, the reader should note that well over 50 per cent of the sets of documents lodged under letters of credit are rejected by banks upon first presentation because they are either incomplete or incorrect. Delays or refusals to pay inevitably ensue. The main reasons for this are as follows:

- the letter of credit has expired;
- the documents are presented after the period stipulated in the letter of credit;
- the shipment is late.

28.6 Government assistance schemes

Most countries operate a system of credit insurance through agencies such as the **Export Credit Guarantee Department (ECGD)** in the United Kingdom (this department has now been partially privatised). The overall services of these agencies vary from one country to another and for precise details it is necessary to refer to their booklets of services rendered. In the remainder of this chapter we concentrate upon ECGD's services in the export credit field.

ECGD insures exporters against the risk of not being paid, whether this results from the default of the purchaser or from other causes. It also offers unconditional guarantees of 100 per cent repayment to banks, thus creating security for banks to provide finance to exporters at favourable interest rates. ECGD insures new investment overseas against the risks of war, expropriation and the imposition of restrictions on remittance. It also provides protection against part of the increases in UK costs for large contracts with long manufacturing periods. For major contracts it supports the issue of performance bonds, and for members of a UK consortium it provides protection against losses arising through the insolvency of a member of the consortium.

ECGD classifies export trade into two categories. First, there is trade of a repetitive type, involving standard, or near standard, goods. Credit risk cover on these is provided on a comprehensive basis. The exporter must offer for cover all or most of its export business for at least a year in both good and bad markets. Secondly, there are projects and large capital goods deals of a non-repetitive nature, usually of high value and involving lengthy credit periods. This business is not suited to comprehensive treatment and specific policies are negotiated for each contract. Cover for this specific insurance is given in one of two ways. With a supplier credit, the manufacturer sells on deferred payment terms, borrowing from a UK bank to finance the period from shipment until payment is received. ECGD insures the exporter and often gives a guarantee direct to the bank. With a buyer credit, the exporter receives prompt payment from its buyer, which draws on a loan from a UK bank to provide this payment. The loan is repaid in instalments and ECGD guarantees the bank repayment by the overseas customer.

In the area of supplier credit, ECGD's comprehensive short-term guarantee provides an insurance on sales with credit periods of up to six months. The risks covered embrace the following:

- insolvency of the buyer;
- the buyer's failure to pay within six months of the due date for goods which it has accepted;
- the buyer's failure to take up goods that have been despatched (where not caused or excused by the policy holder's actions, and where ECGD decides that the institution or constitution of legal proceedings against the buyer would serve no useful purpose);

- a general moratorium on external debt decreed by the government of the buyer's country or of a third country through which payment must be made;
- any other action by the government of the buyer's country which prevents performance of the contract in whole or in part;
- political events, economic difficulties, and legislative or administrative measures arising outside the United Kingdom which prevent or delay the transfer of payments or deposits made in respect of the contract;
- legal discharge of a debt (not being legal discharge under the proper law of the contract) in a foreign currency, which results in a shortfall at the date of transfer;
- war and certain other events preventing performance of the contract, provided that the event is not one normally insured with commercial insurers;
- cancellation or non-renewal of a UK export licence or the prohibition or restriction on export of goods from the United Kingdom by law.

ECGD covers 90 per cent of the loss where it arises through the first two categories of risk. With the third, the exporter bears the first 20 per cent of the original price, and ECGD bears 90 per cent of the remainder. For the other risks, ECGD covers 95 per cent of the loss, except where the loss arises before the goods are despatched overseas. Here the loss is limited to 90 per cent.

Under comprehensive policies, the exporter offers for insurance a broad spread of business to be transacted over a future period. But transactions involving large projects or contracts are negotiated individually between the exporter and ECGD. This gives rise to a specific guarantee where cover runs from either the date of contract or the date of shipment. Risks covered are similar to those covered under the comprehensive policies, except that the top percentage of cover remains at 90 per cent.

ECGD also offers guarantees for supplier credit financing. Here the credit period must be less than two years from the date of export of goods or completion of services, and the buyer gives a promissory note or accepts a bill of exchange. ECGD may give an unconditional guarantee to the exporter's bank that it will pay 100 per cent of any sum three months overdue. ECGD agrees a limit for the finance it will guarantee based on experience and the exporter's financial standing. Operationally, the exporter presents the notes or bills to its bank after shipment of the goods with the appropriate documentary evidence and a standard form of warranty that its ECGD cover for the transaction is in order.

British banks have agreed to finance 100 per cent of the value of such transactions and to charge interest at a very small spread over base rate. The exporter signs a **recourse** undertaking to give ECGD the right to recover from the exporter should the bank claim sums due in advance of, or in excess of, claims payable under the standard policy. All classes of UK exports qualify for this facility.

With exports ranging from cash against documents to six-month credit, ECGD guarantees a straight loan from the bank to the exporter in respect of the export transaction and it guarantees 100 per cent of the bank loan.

A further area through which ECGD picks up credit risk is effectively via buyer credit financing. In many large contracts where specific supplier credit insurance is available, exporters may prefer to negotiate on cash terms and to arrange a loan to the buyer with repayment terms similar to the credit it might expect from the supplier. ECGD buyer credit guarantees are available to banks making such loans in respect of contracts of £1m or more.

A buyer credit guarantee normally involves the overseas purchaser in paying, direct from its own resources to the supplier, 15–20 per cent of the contract price, including a sufficient downpayment on signature of the contract. The remainder is paid to the supplier direct from a loan made to the buyer or a bank in the buyer's country by a UK bank and guaranteed by ECGD, as to 100 per cent of capital and interest, against non-payment for any reason. The contract may include some foreign goods and services, but the amount of the loan will then be less than the British goods and services to be supplied.

28.7 Sources of export finance

Buying credit risk can be expensive. So it pays not to duplicate cover – for example, by taking out ECGD cover together with an irrevocable letter of credit. On occasions this duplication may be unavoidable, such as where ECGD makes a confirmed irrevocable letter of credit a condition of its cover on a particular buyer. This happens when the buyer is especially risky and would not otherwise qualify for cover.

In Table 28.2 the various sources of short-term export finance are summarised. One of the headings in the table is important and its implications deserve further comment. This is the term 'recourse'. **Non-recourse** finance means that the lender has no right of action against the exporter due to the overseas buyer failing to meet its obligations. However, it is worth mentioning that ECGD retains a right of recourse against the exporter on two grounds. The first relates to the extra percentage cover given to the bank. The bank advancing funds is indemnified 100 per cent by ECGD should the buyer fail to pay, but the exporter's cover is for only 90 or 95 per cent. Thus ECGD may claim back the difference of 5 or 10 per cent from the exporter. Also the right of recourse may be retained in respect of the whole 100 per

Table 28.2 Sources of export credit

Source	Nature	Is buyer aware?	Is 100% advanced?	Is the exporter relieved of:		
				Sales ledger work?	Credit risk?	Recourse?
Overdraft	Borrowing	No	Yes	No	No	No
Acceptance credit	Borrowing	No	Yes	No	No	No
Advance against bills	Borrowing	No	Less	No	No	No
Negotiating bills	Sale of bills	No	Less	No	No	No
Factoring	Sale of book debt	Yes	Less	Yes	Yes	Yes
Invoice discounting	Sale of invoices	No	Less	No	No	No
Export merchant	Sale of goods	Yes	Yes	Yes	Yes	Yes
Confirming house						
Traditional	Sale of goods	Yes	Yes	Yes	Yes	Yes
Modern	Sale of book debt	Yes	Yes	Yes	Yes	Yes
Government-backed agency offering comprehensive bank guarantee						
Bills	Sale of bills	No	Yes	No	90/95%	Yes
Open account	Borrowing	No	Yes	No	90/95%	No
Forfaiting	Sale of bills	Yes	Yes	Yes	Yes	Yes

cent paid out by ECGD to the bank should ECGD consider that default has arisen due to a factor not covered in the comprehensive guarantee. In effect, this is where there is a dispute about the exporter's performance of its contract. The exporter does, of course, continue to enjoy 90/95 per cent immunity to pure default risk, irrespective of whether the default is commercial, arising from the buyer's financial weakness, or political.

The accounting impact of non-recourse finance is interesting. If the finance is with recourse, it appears on the exporter's balance sheet as a liability financing the receivable on the assets side. But if the finance is without recourse, it is treated as an outright sale of the receivable to the bank. There is then no liability on the balance sheet. For the six categories of export finance in which the response of 'no' appears in the last column of Table 28.2 – that is, where the finance is with recourse to the exporter – receivables and liabilities would be greater on the balance sheet than would be the case with non-recourse finance.

Referring to data in Table 28.2, various caveats should be noted. Regarding the column 'Is 100% advanced?', where less than 100 per cent is given under an export-financing source it will usually be above 80 per cent of invoice value. Factoring without invoice discounting essentially amounts to credit insurance and is expensive. Nowadays factors increasingly hold their own ECGD cover. Many have overseas associates and they often restrict their factoring to customers approved by such associates. Export merchants and confirming houses operating in the traditional mode buy goods as a legal principal, although the modern confirmer does not acquire title to the goods. Confirmers usually accept risks that exporters cannot deal with through their normal channels. Confirming is effectively a way of obtaining ECGD cover without incurring the substantial administrative cost of operating that cover. It should be noted that forfaiting normally differs from factoring in that it applies mainly to medium-term credit and requires that a guarantee, called an aval, of a local bank be obtained; this makes the credit costly. In some cases, buyers are asked to obtain this aval without being informed of the forfaiting operation. Forfaiting and factoring are both relatively expensive media of export finance.

The forms of finance set out in Table 28.2 are all fairly complex and readers desirous of obtaining a detailed insight of their real-world operation are referred to the fairly substantial literature on their practical use. In-depth descriptions are outside the scope of a book of this nature. However, since both forfaiting and countertrade are growing methods of international trade, brief sections are now devoted to each in turn.

The accounting impact of non-recourse finance is interesting. If the finance is with recourse, it appears on the exporter's balance sheet as a liability financing the receivable on the assets side. But if the finance is without recourse, it is treated as an outright sale of the receivable to the bank. There is then no liability on the balance sheet. For the six categories of export finance in which the response of 'no' appears in the last column of Table 28.2 – that is, where the finance is with recourse to the exporter – receivables and liabilities would be greater on the balance sheet than would be the case with non-recourse finance.

Referring to data in Table 28.2, various caveats should be noted. Regarding the column 'Is 100% advanced?', where less than 100 per cent is given under an export-financing source it will usually be above 80 per cent of invoice value. Factoring without invoice discounting essentially amounts to credit insurance and is expensive. Nowadays factors increasingly hold their own ECGD cover. Many have overseas associates and they often restrict their factoring to customers approved by such associates. Export merchants and confirming houses operating in the traditional mode buy goods as a legal principal, although the modern confirmer does not acquire title to the goods. Confirmers usually accept risks that exporters cannot deal

28.9 Countertrade

Countertrade involves a reciprocal agreement for the exchange of goods or services. The parties involved may be firms or governments, and the reciprocal agreements can take a number of forms – for example, barter, counterpurchase, industrial offset, buy-back and switch trading. Very brief details were discussed in Chapter 21.

Summary

- The usual methods of payment in international trade involve either cash with order, open account, bills of exchange, documentary letters of credit or government assistance schemes. Ensure that you understand the generalities of each. Note that government agencies, such as ECGD in the United Kingdom, will generally take up to 90 per cent of the credit risk on exports subject to the exporter paying a fee.
- Government agencies also provide supplier credits and buyer credits which are sources of finance to ease smooth export trading. Note how these work.
- Try to obtain, from your reading of this chapter, a reasonable idea of the hierarchy of letters of credit.

End of chapter questions

28.1 What is forfaiting? Specify the type of traded goods for which forfaiting is applied.

28.2 What is countertrade?

28.3 What motivates governments to establish so many guarantee and insurance schemes to aid international trade?

29

Practical problems in hedging

Consider the following example. A German airline purchased US aircraft, with the price denominated in USD, at a time when the value of the dollar was increasing. The price was set in dollars and the airline was afraid that the dollar would strengthen further, increasing the equivalent euro cost of the planes. The airline management entered into forward contracts for the dollars required to pay for the planes. In the event, the dollar weakened against the euro. The forward contracts cost the airline USD300 million more for the planes than if it had simply waited and purchased the dollars on the spot market. Of course, the actual outturn is not known at the time the hedging decisions is made. The example above, indicates one of the advantages of using options. The airline could have bought a call option to buy USD dollars for euros. Depending upon rates, the airline might even make a profit by such a strategy.

Of course, many firms use forwards to hedge receivables and payables (assuming that they have decided to hedge in the first place). They might argue that it is not their core business to try to profit from exchange rate differences. Suppose that your firm, a UK importer, has bought foreign currency forward against the pound in respect of your imported goods and/or services, and your competitors have not.

- If the GBP weakens, you will be at an advantage versus those competitors who did not hedge.
- If the GBP strengthens, your budgeted price will remain intact and your budget will contain the margin that you have priced in via the forward rate. But those of your competitors who did not deal forward have a margin gain from the strength of the pound versus the foreign currency. They may take the opportunity to price aggressively and gain market share at your expense.

The decision to hedge may be a function of knowledge of competitors' policies as well as a view on likely exchange rate movements. Often, through trade associations, firms discuss their hedging policies. Being too communicative on this score may not be the best policy for a relatively strong firm.

Currency risk shifting occurs where one party to a commercial contrct attempts to negotiate invoicing denominated in its domestic currency. Risk sharing is different. It typically involves a formula-driven arrangement where both parties end up bearing some of the risk. It represents a co-operative solution to the problem rather than risk-shifting.

29.1 Contingent, or pre-transaction, exposures (a.k.a. tender to contract exposures)

A contingent event is something that may or may not happen. A company may be exposed to a transaction event in the future, but the event is not 100 per cent certain. Whether an event will be transacted is not yet known.

An example is where a company is bidding for an overseas contract with the price fixed in foreign currency. If it wins the contract, the company will be exposed to exchange rate risk. The exchange rate may have moved between tender and award of the contract. If it does win the contract, the company may wish to hedge all of the resulting foreign exchange receivables. Therefore it might consider taking out forward cover. The problem is clear. If a forward FX contract is taken out at the time of the bid, the forward itself is a foreign exchange rate risk. If the contract is won, then the forward works as a hedge. But if the contract is not awarded, the forward itself acquires the nature of an FX risk. So, does the tenderer hedge at the time of bidding or when (and if) the contract is won?

Consider the following example. Brit plc, a British company, has requested tenders for a GBP300 million contract to commence in three months' time. Payment will be made at the commencement of the contract. Yank inc, a US corporation, is tendering for the contract.

The three-month forward rate for GBP/USD is 1.40.

Let us assume that in three months' time the dollar will either have:

- strengthened, the exchange rate will be GBP/USD1.25; or
- weakened, the exchange rate will be GBP/USD1.60.

If Yank were to hedge 100 per cent of its potential transaction exposure using forward contracts at the same time as the tender is sent to Brit, the situation may be summarised as below:

	Contract is won	**Contract is not won**
Dollar strengthens	Use forward contract as hedge	Actual exchange gain taken to the income statement
Dollar weakens	Use forward contract as hedge	Actual exchange loss taken to the income statement

If the contract is not won and if the dollar strengthens, the FX profit (excluding the time value of money) would be:

	USD
Dollars received from forward if exposure hedged (GBP300mn × 1.40)	420mn
Dollars paid to acquire GBP300mn (to deliver against forward (GBP300mn × 1.25)	375mn
Profit	55mn

If the dollar weakens and the contract is not won, the FX loss would be:

	USD
Dollars received from forward if exposure hedged (GBP300mn × 1.40)	420mn
Dollars paid to acquire GBP300mn to deliver against forward (GBP300mn × 1.60)	480mn
Loss	60mn

Clearly, the problem for Yank is whether to hedge the FX risk. It could hedge when the bid is made. But the numbers show that this is risky.

Even if Yank waits until the contract is awarded, there is risk because by the award date the FX rate could have moved. In this instance, if Yank wins the contract and should the pound strengthen, Yank will have more profit than expected. And if the pound weakens Yank's profit will be less than originally anticipated. Note that the gains and losses in this case are the reverse of the forward example given earlier.

With the forward, Yank acquired a sterling liability – the three-month forward. So if sterling weakens (i.e. dollar strengthens), and the contract is not awarded Yank will be able to buy GBP at a lower rate and thus make a profit.

If Yank waits to enter into a spot deal if the contract is won, Yank does not hold a sterling liability over the three months period. Given this comparative situation versus contingent forward cover, there will be a gain if sterling strengthens.

Of course, given that a **tender**-to-contract situation creates a contingent exposure, it may be argued that a currency option is the ideal situation for the tenderer; after all, a currency option is an instrument with contingency built into it. But, currency options do not come cheap.

It is possible that the firm calling for tenders could take out the currency option and sell the option with the tender award to the successful tenderer. Well yes, but there are problems. In the example of Brit and Yank above, this would work if Brit took out an option – GBP versus USD – and if all of the potential bidders were incurring costs in USD or were US based. But would it work if half of the bidders were from the eurozone and half from the USA with each sourcing costs in their local currency? Clearly, there is a problem.

It could be overcome if Yank were to bid in USD and eurozone competitors were to bid in EUR – this way currency risk is shifted. But, most likely, Brit would reject all such bids. Another possibility is that Yank puts in its bid with the caveat that the bid is only of effect if the exchange rate at the time of contract award is, say, at USD1.30 or better (meaning that if the FX rate were 1.25 at the time of award, Yank's bid would lapse). The chosen cut off would articulate with estimated dollar costs and dollar proceeds at the cut-off exchange rate.

The treasurer of Yank could consider acquiring a single three-month option to sell GBP300mn for USD. Whether or not Yank wins the contract, the option will expire, either in or out of the money, and Yank may recoup the option premium plus a profit or merely sell the contract on for time value if the option is out of the money. If the tender to contract period were three months with payment six months after this, then, if awarded the contract Yank would sell the option when awarded the contract and replace this with forward cover.

Note that in Press Cutting 20.1, we introduced the deal-contingent forward, a kind of option contract specifically aimed at needs for foreign currency in takeover situations.

29.2 The price list problem

It is worth briefly considering the price list problem. It arises in cases of competition with foreign producers. A company may advertise its product for a set period of time on a guaranteed price basis, no matter what happens to its exchange rate. There are good reasons for this. It is costly to have to change the advertised pricing schedules every time the economic environment changes. And, in markets where there is competition from suppliers from different countries, the price list problem is compounded. One solution to this problem is to argue that as exchange rates change you change your price list – or you adjust discount and incentive policies. It is often argued that adjusting discounts and incentives is an easier route than regular changes to price lists. However, nowadays with price lists posted on websites, the problem recedes.

29.3 The foreign competitor problem

This is an exposure to product price changes resulting from relative weakening in a competitor's exchange rate. A British company may be exposed to competitive pressures in Europe arising from a depreciation of the US dollar because there are US based competitors in the European market and FX rate movements may give them a cost advantage or disadvantage. This problem and the price list problem are sub-sets of the economic exposure problem. We now turn to the problem of attempting to quantify economic exposure.

29.4 Quantifying economic exposure

In this section, we attempt to indicate how to identify and measure the impact of rate changes upon the value of the firm. Also, we attempt to look at how this risk could be managed via commercial and treasury strategies. To achieve this, we need to undertake an analysis of the firm's cash flows:

- relating to operating activities;
- relating to investment activities (including capital spending);
- relating to financing activities (including borrowing currency effects).

To establish the effect of a currency change, such as a currency devaluation or revaluation, upon the market value of the parent firm requires two steps. These are:

1 an estimate of the impact on each of the above three types of cashflow as measured in the host currency;

2 a calculation to convert this to the home currency.

To illustrate, we work through a particular scenario with numerical detail. Assume that a British firm has an overseas subsidiary. The exposure to be analysed will be that of the offshore operation. As can be seen from the scheme in Table 29.1, we begin with pre-devaluation flows and, allowing for sensitivities of these items (the delta), we calculate post-devaluation flows.

When completed, Table 29.1 would show flows before and after local currency devaluation. This calculation is not simple. Following a currency devaluation (or revaluation), one cannot expect local operating cashflows to remain unaffected by the change in exchange rates. An understanding of the economic factors impacting on the trading performance

Table 29.1 Operating exposures in local currency

	Pre-devaluation flows	Deltas	Post-devaluation flows
Sales	*	→	†
Cost of sales	*	→	†
Overheads (admin., marketing, etc.)	*	→	†
Net profit	*	→	†
Tax	*	→	†
Add back depreciation	*	→	†
Net working capital requirements	*	→	†
Operating net cashflow	*	→	†

of the subsidiary is necessary in order to estimate the likely effects on revenues and costs. Will revenues and costs increase or decrease because of the exchange rate movement? We are looking to calculate local currency sensitivities, or deltas, before we even think about converting back to the parent company's currency.

The inputs to the Table 29.1 involve a number of tricky calculations. For example, these include:

- **The value of sales.** The two key issues here are price and quantity. The primary links between the two are provided by:
  - *price elasticity*: this refers to the product demand following price changes; and
  - *supply elasticity*: this refers to the extent to which quantity is likely to be adjusted following a price change.

  Elasticities depend upon such things as whether or not the product is differentiated from those of competitors. Wine, for instance, exhibits a varying degree of product differentiation, depending upon perceived quality. Vintage champagnes and very fine wines have low price elasticity. Less favoured wines have much higher elasticity.

  Following a local currency devaluation, the local subsidiary may find it difficult to raise its prices. This will probably be true where the product is price elastic. Usually, in such circumstances, when taken back to home currency, sales revenue will decline.
- **Cost (cost of sales and overheads).** The key question here concerns sourcing of inputs. If these are mainly local there should be little change in local currency terms. In home currency terms, following a devaluation of the host currency, inputs may appear cheaper. In this case, input costs as they appear in the table should decline. Local wage costs, though, may rise in response to a devaluation.
- **Net profit.** It follows from the above that the net profit change depends upon factors such as:
  - which sector of the local economy the subsidiary operates in (if it is the export sector, profit could improve);
  - the general matching or mismatching of currencies of sales with those of input costs;
  - the elasticity of demand for the product; the lower the better;
  - the elasticity of supply emanating from potential competitors; the lower the better;
  - the extent to which input costs, such as labour, adjust upwards in local currency terms following a devaluation;

29.5 Hedging gearing or net worth

In Chapter 8, it was argued that virtue probably resides in hedging cash flow exposures – even though we have seen, in the immediately preceding section that hedging economic exposure may be difficult. In Chapter 8, it was pointed out that hedging pure accounting exposures may have some virtue when the firm is close to bank covenant constraints and exchange rate changes could easily create problems wholly based upon the impact of pure accounting exposures. But there may be a problem.

To hedge the balance sheet gearing ratio may have effects on the firm's net worth (issued capital plus undistributed profit plus other accounting capital reserves). And vice versa – to hedge net worth may have impacts on gearing. We will illustrate this with a numerical example. But, before we do so, we will make the point that it is possible to hedge gearing and it is possible to hedge net worth – but not both at the same time. We now turn to an example – see Table 29.4. Here we assume that a UK company has a balance sheet consisting of UK assets, value GBP180 million, and US assets of USD90 million which translates to GBP45 million at the initial exchange rate of GBP1 = USD2. The company also has an initial net worth of GBP150 million and debt of the equivalent of GBP75 million – some in GBP, some in USD. This is reflected in column 1 of Table 29.4.

To hedge the net worth, the firm would raise debt split in such a way that the USD debt was equal to the USD assets – hence the debt would be split as to USD90 million (equal to GBP45 million at the starting exchange rate of GBP1 = USD2) and GBP30 million. If the FX rate were to move to, for example, GBP1 = USD1.5, it can be seen from column 2 of Table 29.4 that the net worth is maintained at GBP150 million. This will be true whatever FX movement is encountered. But note that in the position exemplified, the debt to net worth ratio has worsened from 50 per cent to 60 per cent.

To hedge the gearing ratio (debt to net worth), the firm would have to raise debt split in proportion to the initial split of assets – namely 20 per cent in USD and 80 per cent in GBP. With this background, Table 29.5 shows that when the FX rate moves to GBP1 = USD1.5, the gearing ratio is maintained at 50 per cent. But note that net worth has moved to GBP160 million.

Table 29.4 Example of hedge to maintain net worth

	Initial FX rate GBP1 = USD2 £million	**FX moves to GBP1 = USD1.5 £million**
Assets (USD90m)	45	60
Assets (GBP180m)	180	180
Total assets	**225**	**240**
Debt (USD90m)	45	60
Debt (GBP30m)	30	30
Total debt	75	90
Net worth	150	150
	225	**240**
Net worth maintained	150	150
Gearing changes	50%	60%

Table 29.5 Example of hedge to maintain gearing

	Initial FX rate GBP1 = USD2 £million	FX moves to GBP1 = USD1.5 £million
Assets (USD90m)	45	60
Assets (GBP180m)	180	180
Total assets	**225**	**240**
Debt (USD30m)	15	20
Debt (GBP60m)	60	60
Total debt	75	80
Net worth	150	160
	225	**240**
Gearing maintained	50%	50%
Net worth changes	150	160

Clearly, any move to hedge gearing in order to protect borrowing covenants is likely to lead to variations in net worth. And vice versa. Obviously, care is called for on this issue.

29.6 Translation exposure management

Translation exposure policies may reflect different risk profiles in treasury management. For example:

- A low risk (passive) translation risk policy would involve natural off-sets between assets and liabilities such that if the local currency does weaken, losses in asset values are accompanied by partially off-setting gains on the liability side. Given this standpoint, it is logical to have local operations financed by local currency borrowings. However, even here there may be problems because, for example, the present value of a foreign business may not equal its book value. Hence, hedging book value (say, RUD100 million) by local borrowings may be pointless if the present value of operations is near zero. Like most things in finance great case is necessary in designing a financial strategy.
- A higher risk (more aggressive or active) translation exposure risk management may involve attempting to balance assets and liabilities as between those currencies perceived to be stronger or more stable versus weaker currencies perceived to be at risk of depreciation or devaluation. This involves taking a view on the future of these currencies as against the local currency.

This higher risk policy may involve funds adjustment to alter the currency composition of assets, liabilities or cashflows to diminish asset exposure to weaker currencies and reduce liability exposures to stronger or hard currencies. Common examples include:

- investing in hard currency securities;
- replacing hard currency debt with soft currency debt;
- economising on working capital;
- pricing exports in hard currency and imports in the softer local currency;

- adjusting transfer prices as between the parent and subsidiary operations in order to reduce the FX risk;
- speeding up the payments of dividends, interest, royalties, or fees, or even adjustment of their amounts to take advantage of potential charges in FX mode;
- adjusting the leads and lags for payments to and from the subsidiaries in order to anticipate devaluations.

Again, care is needed with such financial tactics to ensure that the net of tax effects are as desired and accord with legislation. We would emphasise that there is always the danger that an unthinking treasurer might hedge non-cash exposures with a cash flow hedge (for example a forward).

The treasurer needs to ensure that the senior executives fully understand the nature of hedging before a hedge is put in place. Suppose the treasurer of a chemicals company hedges the cost of oil using the futures market. If oil prices fall, the actual price paid for oil is lower than the expected cost. But the futures contract will have been closed out at a loss. If the purpose of the hedge had not been explained before it was put in place, namely that there was a desire to fix the cost of oil for the next reporting period, Board members may be disappointed that a hedge has not actually lowered costs.

Currency matters impact competitive strategy. For example importers are exposed to currency rate changes. Commonly they will try to cope with increased costs as long as they can by trimming their profit margins. This will especially be the case when there is competition from local suppliers of the same product. Over time they will attempt to make small selling price adjustments (pass throughs) in response to exchange rate changes.

It works the other way too. For example, a sharp rise in the value of the yen relative to the US dollar could force Japanese car makers to raise the prices of the cars they sell in the USA in USD. In this situation, the US auto companies may maintain the former price of their models and, in so doing raise market share.

In a similar manner, currency changes may provide both the need and the opportunity to change product mix. A currency appreciation may be the ideal time to introduce new product lines while the exchange rate cushion exists against competitors. Also, an appreciation local currency will lead to locally based exporters coming under pressure in their overseas markets. They may decide to move up-market in an effort to re-brand their product into a more differentiated category.

Product sourcing for components is also a possible response to the threat or anticipation of long-term currency realignments. It can offer the advantages of both a weaker currency and cheaper labour costs. With multiple possible sources, as is the case for the international company, such producers can source components from any one of a number of different locations and/or suppliers. Automotive and related components sourcing has been a common response to the rising euro in recent years. Furthermore, the search around the world for cheaper sourcing has meant recent moves to India and China – the goal of lower labour costs being evident.

Also, a multinational corporation may locate product plants in several different countries. This is sometimes referred to as diversifying exchange rate risk. In fact, it has the character of a real option. By constructing its own overseas plants or sourcing from foreign suppliers, the multinational has bought for itself the option of obtaining imports from whichever currency bloc or labour source is temporarily most advantageous. But, as stated before, a more substantial motive for production relocation is usually to seek lower long term labour and other costs – subject, of course, to the maintenance of quality.

Paradoxically, currency fluctuations may have been a source of economic benefit. They may induce a firm to take action towards greater efficiency. This may arise by closing down or relocating plant, moving offshore, renegotiating labour agreements, reducing costs, improving product quality, or trimming excessive numbers of product lines. The world auto industry has come under such pressure during the past decades.

29.7 Currency risk policies

A one-size-fits-all policy of currency risk management is not possible. However, a systematic process of dealing with currency risk may be established for both high level policy decisions and downstream implementation.

On broad policy issues, the Board will be concerned to establish a checklist on some of the following questions:

- Should the firm ever take aggressive positions on foreign exchange? Should it ever speculate?
- Should the firm worry about FX fluctuations at all? Is any form of intervention against FX exposure likely to enhance or detract from the value of the firm? What is the risk appetite of shareholders, and are management more risk averse compared to shareholders who are able to diversify risk by investing in a number of different companies? How are other stakeholders, such as lenders, likely to react? Is there a danger of violating debt covenants?
- What is the correct risk response for transaction, pre-transaction, economic and translation exposures?
- Should currency risks be managed by commercial strategies or using financial markets based solutions?
- What of non-operating cashflows, such as investment, dividend payments, or intercompany transfers – should these be hedged? Do other special situations need special attention? And, if so, what are they?
- If exposure is to be hedged, what should be the time horizon? Is the policy immutable? Or may it be altered, subject to agreement, to take advantage of perceived short-term disequilibria? For example, hedging foreign currency receivables may be on a one-year selling basis. But, if the foreign currency is reckoned to be too strong would it be feasible to extend the hedge horizon? (Or is this speculation?)
- Should the firm attempt to make judgement calls about possible changes in exchange rates? Or should management seek a passive approach to currency risk? Is management mainly concerned with smoothing the impact of FX fluctuations or taking advantage of FX fluctuations? Do management have the expertise and resources to make informed decisions and to act on them?
- What hedging instruments are available? Which should be used? Do those responsible have the expertise to use them correctly? What is the view on currency options?
- And other questions too.

A typical corporate treasury, even for fairly large companies, will rarely amount to more than half a dozen people. Some use consultants for specialist functions, or to provide an occasional review of policy. In such circumstances, simple and robust rules or guidelines are demanded. One could expect these to vary with the nature of the business, as well as the size of the company. Therefore corporate foreign exchange policies can vary a good deal. However, many companies attempt to characterise their philosophies as a set of fairly basic rules.

Summary

- Companies face FX problems in connection with contingent exposures. Theoretical and practical solutions are looked at. However, it has to be said that judgement underpins the final choice of action.
- Quantification of economic exposure is complex. Estimates of various elasticities in response to exchange rate movements are called for as inputs into figuring on changes to cash flow. Then present value estimation in respect of movements in FX rates follows.
- Hedging gearing or net worth are practical considerations for the treasurer in financing the business. It is feasible to do either but not to do both. Note how the problem is approached.

End of chapter questions

29.1 Some experts consider the hedging of economic exposure to be the most complicated theoretical and practical problem in cross-border finance. Why?

29.2 What factors might lead the treasurer to hedge anyway? What factors might lead the treasurer to hedge net worth?

Part H

MISCELLANEOUS

30

Miscellaneous issues in international finance

In this chapter we focus on a number of topics which are much too important not to be covered in a book of this sort and are relevant to the study of international finance, but that do not warrant a separate chapter. In particular, parts of this chapter are devoted respectively to the questions of performance measurement, treasury centralisation versus decentralisation, the treasury of a profit centre or cost centre and transfer pricing.

30.1 Overseas subsidiary performance measurement

The development of a system for evaluating the performance of an overseas affiliate logically involves four distinct phases:

1 specification of the purpose of the system;
2 determining information requirements;
3 designing an information collection system;
4 assessing the system in cost/benefit terms.

The first step, then, is to specify the system's purpose. Immediately a key question arises: is head office management concerned with managerial performance or flows back to headquarters? In any case, how do we ensure that subsidiary management is insulated, in terms of evaluation, from factors beyond its control, such as exchange rate charges, local inflation rates and so on? We return to these questions later in this chapter.

First of all, we take a couple of steps back and ask what the main objectives of a system of performance evaluation are. They embrace the following:

- to provide a basis to aid global resource allocation;
- to provide an early warning system to highlight things going wrong;
- to ensure that adequate profit and/or cash are generated and to measure them;
- to provide a set of standards to motivate individual managers;
- to provide a basis for evaluating the performance of individual managers.

That seems fairly straightforward. So what are the problems?

30.2 Problems in overseas performance evaluation

Exchange rate movements create difficulties in terms of evaluating the performance of an overseas affiliate. The first difficulty is whether one should measure using home or host currency. If evaluation is in home currency terms, then, in drafting a budget, assumptions have to be made about exchange rates. But actual performance will be realised, in all probability, at some other exchange rate. An unbudgeted change in exchange rates automatically makes for a variance between budget and actual. If the firm in the overseas territory is involved in competing with imports or in exporting, this variance will impact upon local currency outturns. Furthermore, if performance is looked at in home currency terms, then there will not only be a variance due to the above economic exposure but there will also be one associated with translation.

Focusing just upon the impact of translation problems, Lessard and Lorange[1] point out that there are three exchange rates that can be used in setting a budget and these three can also be used to monitor (or track, as they refer to it) performance. The three exchange rates are the initial rate, the projected rate and the end rate, and their permutation in a 3×3 matrix produces nine possible combinations of budgeted and actual exchange rates. Lessard and Lorange summarise the situation as shown in Figure 30.1. Given that only three of these monitor on the same basis as budgeting, the logical contenders would appear to be:

- budget at initial rate, monitor at initial rate;
- budget at projected rate, monitor at projected rate;
- budget at ending rate, monitor at ending rate.

Lessard and Lorange prefer the second method. They show that two of the major criteria for good management control systems are satisfied. They claim that 'goal congruence exists because a corporate-wide point of view will prevail in making decisions in which exchange rate changes might have an impact'. Furthermore, they claim that operating managers are treated fairly, since they receive neither blame nor credit for variations in performance caused by exchange rate changes that are unanticipated.

Exchange rate used in budget	Exchange rate used to track performance versus budget: *Initial*	*Projected*	*Ending*
Initial	Budget – initial Track – initial	Budget – initial Track – projected	Budget – initial Track – ending
Projected	Budget – projected Track – initial	Budget – projected Track – projected	Budget – projected Track – ending
Ending	Budget – ending Track – initial	Budget – ending Track – projected	Budget – ending Track – ending

Figure 30.1 Exchange rates and control

Source: Lessard, D.R. and Lorange, P., 'Currency changes and management control: resolving the centralization/decentralization dilemma', *Accounting Review*, July, 628–37, 1977.

Stewart[2] proposes measuring performance by use of a normalised exchange rate, based on what the exchange rate would be if the market adjusted fully to purchasing power parity (PPP) over the short run. The argument advanced is that actual exchange rates fluctuate around an intrinsic value; sometimes the market rate is overvalued, sometimes it is undervalued. In the long run, exchange rates and local profitability return to PPP conditions. It follows that, should performance be measured by intrinsic value or normalised exchange rates, firms may avoid the ups and downs created by excessive exchange rate movements. Stewart asserts that, if asset values and operating profit are measured in the home currency using a PPP-normalised exchange rate, then rates of return on investment will tend to measure performance effectively. This approach assumes that exchange rates are in equilibrium in some base period. The disadvantage of Stewart's approach is that it fails to take account of economic exposure effects and homes in solely upon translation aspects of the problem. It does not, in other words, take account of competitive aspects of changing exchange rates. And it seems to focus upon a hypothetical state of the world rather than looking at the way it really is.

Lessard and Sharp,[3] taking up the challenge of this objection, propose a measure of performance that addresses the need both to translate foreign currency profits into home currency and to take cognisance of the impact of exchange rates on underlying profitability. They suggest the use of a technique that might be termed 'contingent budgeting'. Their recommended procedure involves three steps which they describe as follows:

1 Prepare a budget based on a 'most-likely' scenario. This is the traditional budget preparation process. It seems to be natural to prepare the budget in terms of local currency units.
2 Prepare an audit of the likely effect of a range of surprise deviations from existing exchange rate parities, in terms of impact on prices, costs and hence operating cash flows. The objective of this procedure is to develop, in advance, an expectation of the relationship between exchange rates, operating management's best efforts, and operating cash flows.
3 At the end of the year, when the exchange rates are known, use the results of the audit to compute a set of standards or benchmarks of performance, given the exchange rates that actually materialized. Actual results should then be compared with the contingent standards as the point of departure in discussing management performance.

Lessard and Sharp's approach is theoretically acceptable but whether it is cost effective and practical is another question. Admittedly, the whole budget process is bathed in subjectivity – Lessard and Sharp's recommended method seems to have more than its fair share.

In proposing an eminently practical approach, Carsberg[4] suggests that an affiliate's actual performance should be compared with budget using local currency. He argues that, rather in the manner used to assess performance of managers in home country subsidiaries, 'the performance of an overseas manager may best be judged in terms of the results measured in overseas currency, and set against standards of performance in the country concerned'. Carsberg admits that:

> [F]or the purpose of capital allocation, however, the home country financial management must attempt to estimate the effects of currency changes on the long-run profitability of proposed international investments; and control procedures will need to focus on a comparison of actual and estimated returns in the home currency.

Carsberg's pragmatic solution is summed up in his observation that:

> [T]he best way to assess whether an overseas investment has been satisfactory is to measure the net cash flows generated by the investment, translate them into terms of the home currency, and discount them at the appropriate cost of capital to obtain a net present value.

But any system of overseas performance evaluation needs to exclude the effects of certain multinational practices which may be deemed valuable at the level of the group but which are imposed upon subsidiaries – such practices include transfer pricing, funds flow adjustments (for example, leading and lagging) and group hedging requirements.

Transfer pricing can have a significant impact on an overseas subsidiary's performance. A manager who is deemed accountable for the influence of transfer prices on reported profits is likely to react in ways that are counterproductive to the group as a whole. Transfer pricing is virtually always a centralised decision emanating from the multinational headquarters. Its purpose may be tax minimisation or to inflate costs where prices are based on cost plus or something similar. In performing an appraisal of an overseas subsidiary, the distorting effect of less than arm's-length pricing should be eliminated. Certainly, managerial evaluations should be decoupled from the transfer prices being used. This decoupling may be done by charging purchasers market prices, if available, or by using the marginal cost of production and shipping plus a reasonable profit on sales. Managers of subsidiaries that produce solely for sale to other subsidiaries ought to be evaluated on the basis of their production costs, rather than their profits. After all, they are essentially cost centres with no control over the revenues, which are set at headquarters level to achieve maximum net-of-tax profits.

Decoupling in the way suggested above may present problems at times. Transfer prices of multinational drug companies are monitored closely throughout the world. To disclose, even with the group, the effect and level of transfer prices and true costs may not be expedient from the standpoint of the drug company concerned.

The next area that needs to be disaggregated for performance evaluation purposes is the effect of funds flow adjustment – in particular, the effects of leading and lagging and suchlike. Leading and lagging may be directed from the central treasury at headquarters with a view to maximising group profits. The results obtained at operating overseas subsidiary level would be unlikely to reflect that operating performance of managers in the host country – certainly, it is not them who usually instigate the action. Leading and lagging is likely to distort working-capital levels and ratios of affiliates. A subsidiary ordered to extend longer credit terms to another group company will require more working capital to finance its business and will show an increase in its debtors to sales ratio. Also, its interest expenses will increase. Since leading and lagging is a group policy, its effects should not be included when evaluating subsidiary management. These effects should be reversed by eliminating the cost of carrying intra-corporate debtors and adding these costs to those subsidiaries invoiced with intra-corporate creditors. Also, each affiliate's investment base should reflect only those corporate assets required for its operating business.

There is also the question of hedging. Foreign operational management may wish to hedge transaction exposure. If this is the case, performance evaluation should allow for covering even though all covering is only carried out at group level. It is usual to require that divisions do not use outside bankers to cover foreign exchange exposure but that all hedging be dealt with according to one of three approaches:

- Subsidiaries hedge all foreign exchange transaction exposures with the group treasury.
- Subsidiaries hedge only those foreign exchange transaction exposures that they consider wise with the group treasury.
- Subsidiaries hedge no foreign exchange transaction exposure at all but leave this function to the group treasury, to which all exposures are routinely reported.

Whichever system is used, all transaction exposure should be reported to the group treasury. And where the central treasury is used for covering, it is required to quote to divisions rates for forward cover which the divisions could get in the foreign exchange market.

For reporting purposes, we believe that the middle course is the preferred one. It ensures that subsidiaries are responsible for their selective hedging actions. Using this system, divisional management accounts will reflect operational outturns plus the results of covering which has been duly instigated by the subsidiaries concerned. It should be recalled that, even though this system is used, all hedging is done with the centre and the group treasury obtains information on all transaction exposures, whether hedged or not. So it can take action in response to the total group exposure.

Neither the first system nor the last gives operating management any discretion on hedging and the withdrawal of this discretion may be a demotivating factor. Given that we wish our control system to be functional as well as being a motivator, it is preferable for divisions to report all transaction exposures, but to hedge whatever they wish of this exposure with the head office treasury. This system is also preferable where there are minority interests in a subsidiary. Clearly, selective hedging at the level of the partly owned subsidiary may be beneficial to minority shareholders. If a system is to be designed that does not act against the interest of minority shareholders, which the 'hedge everything' or 'hedge nothing' system may do, then care must be taken to ensure that subsidiary results are not distorted by requirements which may be optimal at the group level but not at the subsidiary level.

The whole area of empirical work on overseas performance evaluation is somewhat under-researched. Choi and Czechowicz[5] found that budget compared with actual is the single most important performance criterion for 64 US multinational firms and for 24 non-US multinational firms; return on investment comes second. Interestingly, in their survey they found that US multinationals rate cash flow to the parent as more important than cash flow to the affiliate, whereas non-US multinationals reverse the ranking order. Persen and Lesig[6] also found that actual performance versus budget topped the list of evaluation criteria.

On the question of centralisation versus decentralisation of treasury control, Meister[7] indicates that, of a sample of multinationals, 85 per cent indicated that decisions involving repatriation of funds were made at the corporate level. Furthermore, where companies were minority partners in joint ventures, they appeared to have little control over the repatriation decision. On the issue of intersubsidiary financing, in most companies either the chief financial executive of the parent company or the treasurer, with the aid of tax advice, appeared to decide on intracorporate flows of money. And on the question of negotiation of funds, 85 per cent of firms indicated that all medium-term and long-term financing was approved at corporate headquarters, although many firms allowed their subsidiaries more leeway with regard to raising short-term finance.

An interesting study by Stobaugh[8] indicated different attitudes towards centralisation among small (average annual foreign sales of \$50m), medium (average annual foreign sales of \$200m) and large (average annual foreign sales of \$1bn) multinationals. The small-firm group generally allowed subsidiaries a lot of leeway in financial management, perhaps owing to lack of sophistication in international financial management at headquarters or to cost/benefit factors. Medium-sized firms tended to have very sophisticated control and reporting systems designed to optimise world results and cash flows. But the largest-firm group tended to reverse the centralisation trend to some extent by providing subsidiaries with formal guidelines but allowing them considerable leeway within these boundaries.

This latitude seemed to be due to a recognised inability to optimise in such a complex area as global financial flows.

30.3 Centralisation of exposure management

The argument against centralised control is simple. Central bureaucracies can be expensive, slow to respond to problems and inflexible – particularly from the viewpoint of the manager in the front line. But there are some decisions that cannot sensibly be delegated. Many financial decisions fall into this category. The case for centralising foreign exchange management rests on the following arguments:

- It ensures that the company as a whole follows a consistent policy.
- It facilitates the matching of exposures. Without a centralised approach, there is a big danger that one subsidiary might be buying a currency at the same moment as another is selling it.
- It helps to get the best rates in the market. Banks charge far wider spreads on their buying and selling rates when dealing for small amounts via branches. The finest rates may be obtained by dealing large amounts directly with the bank's own dealing room. Dealing through the local branch of the bank always results in a poorer rate of exchange and some loss of control of the transaction.
- It ensures the concentration of limited expertise. If centralised, exposure management will be handled by a team for whom it is a primary function rather than a secondary aspect of a divisional finance or accounting role. Concentration of skills in this way should ensure a better understanding of the problem and an enhanced execution.
- Centralisation will pool both skills and systems investment. It usually justifies proper dealing facilities, direct lines and computer systems for data management and communication.
- It helps integration with cash management.

By contrast, there are a number of arguments advanced to support decentralisation of exposure management. These include the following:

- There are substantial up-front costs in recruitment, office space and equipment in establishing a central foreign exchange expertise.
- Foreign exchange risk management is interesting and stimulating. Line managers may resist attempts to take this authority away.

A further, somewhat spurious, argument against centralisation is that it may demotivate divisional management by transferring authority and control from individual units and profit centres. Centralisation need not involve this. The approach recommended in this book is that individual units should regard the central treasury as their banker and run an account with head office. Divisions may or may not hedge exposure with the treasury; this should maintain their autonomy. They will, of course, report all exposures to the centre. A more valid argument against the centralisation of foreign exchange exposure activities is that divisional staff may become blind to the risks involved and the expertise necessary to handle foreign exchange problems as they inevitably arise in the course of their work. Clearly, good training of line managers who may come up against foreign exchange problems is essential.

Factors influencing the centralisation/decentralisation discussion are many. For example, the corporate philosophy on autonomy is pertinent, as is ownership. With a larger number of partly owned subsidiaries or associates with substantial minority holdings, it may be appropriate to adopt a decentralised approach. After all, minority shareholders will want optimisation at the level of their own investment – and this is not the group level.

The proportion of value or turnover exposed is obviously a relevant factor in deciding whether to centralise or not. Where performance will not be materially affected by changes in exchange rates, foreign exchange risk is unlikely to be an issue. But clearly, where group profit and balance sheet are substantially exposed to currency volatility, the reverse is true.

Large multinational groups, with a number of subsidiaries trading in different countries and with each other, will create complex exposures. There will be correspondingly greater opportunity for inconsistency in exposure management, unless centralised.

In a purely decentralised system, the unit looks after its own exposures only, having no regard for exposures occurring elsewhere in the group. It will decide on the timing of cover and implement that decision using external methods if necessary. Reports to the parent may not even identify the currency flows.

At the opposite end of the spectrum is the completely centralised system. Here the treasury receives and co-ordinates data and forecasts of currency flows from all group members to determine the total net position, and undertakes appropriate hedging action determined by group exposure positions and strategy. The subsidiary will not be consulted on group hedging strategy.

There are many intermediate variations possible too. The treasury may exist merely as an advisory function, directing when and how the subsidiary should hedge its exposures; this may be appropriate where a company has many relatively independent overseas subsidiaries. A centralised treasury may provide a dealing service to carry out the cover decisions of the subsidiaries. It may deal only with exceptional or very large currency exposures. Many companies operate a system under which the subsidiaries are obliged to report all exposures to the centre, and must undertake any cover they wish to put in place with the centre, but can choose if or when to hedge; the centre covers the group position according to overall exposure and policy, while the subsidiary remains in control of its own performance. If justified by cost/benefit considerations, this latter kind of approach is most effective.

Empirically, Evans, Folks and Jilling[9] have observed an increasing tendency towards centralisation in the US-based multinationals. Oxelheim[10] has found a similar trend with Swedish-based international groups, stimulated by improved global tax planning, knowledge concentration and other financial economies of scale.

To round off this summary of the centralisation/decentralisation debate, it must be stressed that, whatever system is adopted, it needs to be justified on cost/benefit grounds and it needs to be regularly checked to ensure that the system chosen continues to deliver the goods in cash terms. The need for *ad hoc* post-audits should be clear.

30.4 The treasury as a profit centre

The centralisation of foreign exchange exposure management creates the opportunity to run it as a profit centre. In this context, profit may accrue first from improved exchange rates on deals, secondly by taking selective hedging decisions and thirdly by generating profits from speculation in currencies.

The extent to which the treasury is allowed to play currency markets – to punt – is a matter for board decision, taking into account shareholders' best interests. Given the caveat about equity investors' interests, any position taking can be justified only by some superior knowledge possessed by a treasury executive or adviser. This would probably imply only minimal speculation. Whatever approach is used in terms of profit or cost centre, treasury performance needs to be measured. If the track record fails to indicate superior outturns given the level of risk incurred, then any position taking at all should be ruled out. Failure to match appropriate return levels for the amount of risk incurred presumably raises questions about whether the treasurer is up to the job.

The author is aware that some companies have set up their treasury with a remit to make money by taking positions in foreign exchange markets (with performance measured and controlled), rather as banks do.

30.5 Transfer pricing

The repatriation of profit by a multinational firm from its overseas operations can be a politically sensitive problem. In order to get monies out of an overseas subsidiary that restricts flows outwards, it may use transfer pricing. It may set high transfer prices on goods and services supplied to a foreign subsidiary by the head office or by divisions in environments that are less restrictive. Or the multinational may lower the transfer prices of products which the foreign division sells to the head office or to other divisions.

Transfer pricing is also used to reduce overall corporate taxes. The multinational may shuffle income to keep profits low in high-tax countries and relatively high in low-tax countries. The gains from profit shuffling via transfer prices are limited by the authorities in some countries; they may reallocate income if it is deemed that transfer prices have distorted profits.

Transfer prices may also be used to reduce import **tariffs** and to avoid quotas. When tariffs on imports are based on values of transactions, the value of goods moving between divisions may be artificially reduced by keeping down the transfer prices. This could put the multinational at an advantage over domestic firms. Also, where quotas are based on values of trade, the multinational can keep down prices to maintain the volume. Again, the multinational may turn this to advantage over purely domestic competitors. However, import authorities frequently adopt their own 'value for duty' on goods entering to help prevent revenues from being lost through transfer pricing manipulation.

For resource allocation in the multinational, it is important that divisional profitability be measured accurately. The record of profitability of different divisions is often relevant in allocating resources to capital projects and in sharing corporate resources. To discover the true profitability, the group should be sure that interdivisional transfer prices are the prices that would have been paid had the transactions been with independent companies – arm's-length prices. But there may be problems inasmuch as multinational group management may not want true profits to be known outside of a tight central coalition of executives.

30.6 Accounting for financial market derivatives

The growth of derivatives has created a need for accounting standards to recognise and report on derivatives usage. The merits of alternative accounting standards for financial market transactions, including derivative instruments, are being actively debated in academic, political, and business circles around the world, on an ongoing basis.

By and large, international accounting is agreed that:

- Derivatives are assets and liabilities that should be reported in financial statements, and not hidden away from accounting data.
- **Fair (market) value** is the most relevant way to report value.
- Derivative assets and liabilities should be reported on the balance sheet. Derivative income and expenses should be reported in the income statement.
- Special accounting rules should apply to qualifying hedge transactions.

Derivatives are included on the balance sheet at fair (market) value and derivative gains or losses are immediately recognised in earnings. If certain conditions are met, derivative instruments can be designated as a hedge to offset the risk of another asset, liability, or anticipated transaction. Hedge effectiveness is the test applied to a hedging instrument to ascertain whether it will be eligible for hedge accounting. Hedge accounting allows a hedging instrument to be exempt from the mark-to-market requirement of FAS 133 and IAS 39. If certain requirements are met the hedging instrument is carried on the balance at its fair market value but the gains and losses are instead posted to reserves and not to the income statement.

There are two types of hedge – cash flow hedge and fair value hedge. A cash flow hedge matches cash flows from an investment with predictable cash flows from a hedging instrument. A fair value hedge matches the changes in fair value in the underlying instrument with the changes in fair value of the hedging instrument.

To qualify for hedge accounting a hedging effectiveness of between 80 per cent and 125 per cent is normally required. This hedge effectiveness is calculated by performing an analysis on the underlying position and the hedge.

These accounting rules require substantially more effort on the part of financial managers and accountants to comply with the rules, especially on qualifying hedge transactions. To qualify for hedge accounting treatment under FAS and IAS rules, a hedge must also be clearly defined, measurable and effective. This requires that financial managers document their reasons for entering into or modifying a hedge. This documentation process may be complex and time-consuming. The rules allow hedge accounting where there is a clearly identifiable exposure that is offset with a clearly identifiable hedge transaction. This is not too difficult for a hedge of a transaction exposure to currency risk. An example is a foreign currency receivable due in 30 days that is hedged with a 30-day forward contract. Another example would be a rolling hedge in which a long-term transaction exposure is hedged with a succession of short-term forward contracts. It is extremely difficult to qualify as a hedge when there is not a clearly defined underlying exposure. This is the case for some operating exposures.

Non-hedge derivative gains or losses are recognised immediately in earnings, along with the offsetting losses or gains on the underlying exposure. For hedges of anticipated foreign currency transactions, the accounting rules recognise gains or losses in a balance sheet reserve account and then flow them into earnings when the underlying exposure is recognised and moved from the balance sheet. This allows both sides of the hedged position to be recognised at the same time.

At the time of writing, significant problems exist, especially in the area of accounting for financial institutions and banks. In 2005 the international accounting board, IASB, introduced the incurred loss system whereby poor lending is not charged to the income statement until the loans fail rather than being provided for as the loans become progressively bad. This has caused banks to overstate profit, pay bonuses and fail to set aside a sufficient cushion of capital against bad loans. The conclusion that dangerous risks may build up without being allowed for in accounting terms cannot be denied. And this played some part in the financial crisis of 2007–8.

There remain other accounting difficulties, many of which are exemplified by John Flower in Nobes and Parker.[11]

30.7 Repos

The **repo** market took off in the 1970s. Securities dealers often sold Treasury bonds with their relatively low returns to banks and conservative investors. They then invested the cash proceeds of these sales in securities that paid high interest rates. The security dealers agreed to repurchase the Treasuries – often within as short a period as a day – at a slightly higher price than what they sold them for. This repo transaction – essentially a loan – made it inexpensive and convenient for Wall Street firms to borrow. These deals were essentially collateralised loans: the securities dealers borrowed almost the full value of the collateral, minus a small cost – or haircut. Like commercial paper, repos were renewed, or **rolled over**, frequently. For that reason, both repos and commercial paper are borrowings that could be termed **hot money** because lenders could quickly move in and out of these investments in search of higher returns. The market could also be viewed as a risky source of funding because of potential defaults which might suddenly occur.

In 1982, two major borrowers, the securities firms Drysdale and Lombard-Wall, did default on their repo obligations, creating significant losses for lenders. In the fallout, the Federal Reserve acted as lender of last resort to support the market. The Fed relaxed the terms on which it lent Treasuries to securities firms, leading to a ten-fold increase in its securities lending. Following this episode most repo participants switched to a triparty arrangement in which a large commercial bank acted as intermediary between the borrower and the lender, thus protecting the collateral and the funds by putting them in escrow. This would have severe consequences in the financial crisis of 2007 and 2008 when banks became suspicious of the credit-worthiness of all other banks – but in the 1980s these procedures stabilised the repo market.

30.8 Syndicated loans

There are usually three categories of bank in a loan syndicate. There are lead banks, managing banks and participating banks. In large credits, there is a separate group called co-managers. This group comprises participating banks providing more than a specified amount of funds. Most loans are led by one or two major banks which negotiate to obtain a mandate from the borrower to raise funds. After the preliminary stages of negotiation with a borrower, the lead bank begins to assemble the management group, which commits itself to provide the entire amount of the loan, if necessary. Portions of the loan are then marketed to participating banks.

In the early stages of negotiation with a borrower, the lead bank assembles a management group to assure the borrower that the entire amount of the loan will be taken up. The management group may be in place before the mandate is received or may be assembled immediately afterwards. During this phase, the lead bank may renegotiate the terms and conditions of the loan if it cannot assemble a managing group on the initial terms. But, rather than renegotiate, many lead banks are willing to take more of the credit into their own portfolio than they had originally planned. The lead bank is normally expected to provide a share at least as large as any other bank. Once the lead bank has established the group of managing banks, it then commits the group to raise funds for the borrower on specified terms and conditions.

When the management group is established and the lead bank has received a mandate from the borrower, a placement memorandum is prepared by the lead bank and the loan is marketed to other banks which may be interested in taking up shares. Such lenders are termed the participating banks. The placement memorandum describes the transaction and gives information regarding the financial health of the borrower. The statistical information given in the memorandum is usually provided by the borrower.

The lead bank emphasises that the placement memorandum is not a substitute for an independent credit review by participating banks, and such participating banks generally sign a statement that they have performed an independent analysis of the credit. However, smaller banks tend to rely heavily on the judgement of the lead and managing banks.

The lead bank bears the chief responsibility for marketing the loan, although other members of the managing group assist in this respect. There are three main methods used to find participants for syndicated credits. The borrower may specify that a certain bank should be given the opportunity to participate because the borrower wishes to establish a relationship with that bank. Often banks contact the borrower expressing an interest in participating in a given credit. But the bulk of participants are banks invited by the lead bank to join the syndication. Each major bank maintains files on the syndicated lending activities of other banks. The files contain lists of banks that have joined various syndications. This information enables the loan syndication officers at the lead bank to estimate which banks might be interested in which borrowers. Once a first list of potential participants has been assembled, the lead bank, operating through informal contacts in London and elsewhere, will try to determine which of the banks are interested in expanding their portfolio to particular borrowers and on what terms, and which banks are unwilling to increase their credit exposure to particular countries. From this analysis the list is finalised.

When a bank is invited to participate in a syndication, the amount and the terms and conditions it is being asked to accept are set out in a telex sent by the lead bank. This short-cuts the negotiation process and expedites the credit.

The lead bank usually offers to sell off more of the credit than it really wishes, since some of the banks that receive invitations will opt not to participate. An experienced lead bank can usually gauge the appropriate number of participation invitations to be extended. If the credit is attractive, fewer banks will be contacted. If the credit (based on terms and conditions) appears hard to place, a greater number of invitations will be sent out. If the loan is oversubscribed, the borrower is usually given the opportunity to borrow more money than initially negotiated on the same terms. If the borrower does not choose to take advantage of this, the amounts assigned to each bank are scaled down pro rata.

In a successful loan syndication, once the marketing to participants is completed, the lead and managing banks usually keep 50–75 per cent of their initial underwritten share. The lead bank is generally expected to take into its portfolio about 10 per cent of the total credit. This rule of thumb does not apply to very large credits, where a 10 per cent commitment to a single borrower may, when taken with credits to the borrower already in the bank's portfolio, give the bank an excess exposure in relation to its capital. It is not acceptable market practice for a bank to lead and arrange a credit and not take any portion of the credit into its own portfolio. It takes from two weeks to three months to arrange a syndication, with six weeks as the norm – the more familiar the borrower, the quicker the terms can be set and the placement memorandum prepared.

The most common type of syndicated loan is a **term loan**, where funds can be drawn down by the borrower within a specified time of the loan being signed – this is called the 'drawdown period'. Repayments are subsequently made in accordance with an amortisation schedule. Sometimes amortisation of loans commences almost immediately following drawdown. For other loans, amortisation may not commence until five or six years after drawing down the loan. Sometimes term loans have no amortisation over the life of the loan and all repayment is due on maturity – this kind of loan is termed a 'bullet loan'. Loans that require repayment according to an amortisation schedule and include a larger final payment on maturity are termed 'balloon repayment loans'. The period prior to the commencement of repayment is termed the 'grace period'. The extent of the grace period is usually a major negotiating point between borrower and lead bank. Borrowers are usually willing to pay a wider spread in order to obtain a longer grace period.

Syndicated loans of the revolving credit type are occasionally encountered. In these, the borrower is given a line of credit which it may draw down and repay with greater flexibility than under a term loan. Borrowers pay a fee on the undrawn amount of the credit line.

Additional to interest costs on a loan, there are also **front-end fees**, commitment fees and occasionally an annual agent's fee. Front-end management fees are one-off charges negotiated in advance and imposed when the loan agreement is signed. These fees are usually in the range of 0.5 to 1 per cent of the value of the loan. The fees may be higher if a particular borrower insists upon obtaining funds at a lower spread than is warranted by market conditions and creditworthiness.

The relationship between spreads and fees is hard to quantify, as data on all fees are usually unobtainable. But there is some evidence to suggest that banks will accept lower spreads if compensated by higher fees, since they are interested in the total return on the loan. Some borrowers prefer to pay a higher fee, which is not published, while going on record as paying a low spread. Over time, demand and supply conditions determine both spreads and fees. During periods of easy market conditions, borrowers can command low fees and low spreads. During periods when banks are reluctant to extend credit, high spreads and high fees are the norm.

Front-end fees consist of participation fees and management fees. Each of these typically amounts to between 0.25 and 0.5 per cent of the entire amount of the loan. Participation fees are divided among all banks in relation to their share of the loan. The management fees are divided between the underwriting banks and the lead bank. The lead bank usually takes a *praecipium* – an overall fee – on the entire loan. The rest of the management fee is divided among the managing banks in proportion to the amount each agrees to underwrite prior to syndication.

In addition to front-end fees, borrowers may pay commitment fees. These fees are charged to the borrower as a percentage of the undrawn portion of the credit in return for the bank tying up part of its credit capacity on behalf of the borrower, even though the loan has not yet been drawn down and does not earn any interest for the bank. Commitment fees of 0.375 to 0.5 per cent per annum are typically imposed on both term loans and revolving credits.

The agent's fee, if applicable, is usually a yearly charge but may occasionally be paid at the outset. The agent's fee is relatively small; it may amount to as little as $10,000 annually. It is meant to cover minor administrative and incidental expenses related to the syndication. But the fee may be larger and negotiable.

To protect their margins, banks usually require all payments of principal and interest to be made after taxes imposed have been paid. If those taxes are not creditable against the banks' home country taxes, the borrower must adjust payments so that the banks receive the same net repayment. The decision as to whether the borrower or lender absorbs any additional taxes imposed by the country in which the loan is booked is negotiated between the parties. Additionally, a reserve requirement clause is generally inserted, stipulating that an adjustment will be made if the cost of funds increases because reserve requirements are imposed or increased.

There is usually no prepayment penalty. The charges on syndicated loans may be summarised as follows:

$$\begin{aligned}
\text{Annual payments} = {} & (\text{LIBOR} \times \text{spread}) \\
& \times \text{amount of loan drawn down and outstanding} \\
& + \text{commitment fee} \times \text{amount of loan undrawn} \\
& + \text{annual agent's fee (if any)} \\
& + \text{tax adjustment (if any)} \\
& + \text{reserve requirement adjustment (if any)}
\end{aligned}$$

$$\begin{aligned}
\text{Front-end charges} = {} & \text{lead bank } \textit{praecipium} \times \text{total amount of loan} \\
& + \text{participation fee} \times \text{face amount of loan} \\
& + \text{management fee} \times \text{face amount of loan} \\
& + \text{initial agent's fee (if any)}
\end{aligned}$$

30.9 Offshore currency interest rates and their linkage with domestic rates

Each offshore currency market, whether it be offshore dollars, offshore sterling or whatever, is linked through arbitrage to its domestic counterpart. Hence, offshore currency rates are strongly influenced by domestic rates. Because there is no regulating authority to set interest rates in the offshore markets and no one set of banks enforces administered rates, offshore currency interest rates are determined by the forces of competition.

Furthermore, domestic and external markets compete for funds. The essential starting point to the analysis of the relationship between domestic and external interest rates is a clear understanding of what the offshore currency market is. Using the United States and the US dollar for illustration, the offshore dollar market (external) and the domestic market (internal) are merely competing segments of the total market for dollar-denominated credit, intermediated by financial institutions operating either internally (domestic banks) or externally (**Eurobanks**). The offshore dollar market competes with the domestic US credit market for deposits and for the making of loans. Within this competitive arena, the offshore currency segment possesses certain unique characteristics:

- Eurobanks are not required to maintain reserves against their deposit liabilities.
- Eurobanks are less subject to regulation.
- Eurobanks are not subject to interest rate ceilings, whether imposed by government or by cartel.
- Eurobanks can take better advantage of low-tax locations.
- High degrees of competitiveness, and virtually unrestricted entry, force Eurobanks to keep margins small and overhead costs low.
- Eurobanks are less subject than domestic markets to pressure to allocate credit for socially valued but unprofitable purposes.
- Eurobanks are subject to greater risk than domestic banks (see later in this section).

Given that the offshore dollar market and the domestic dollar money markets deal in the same currency and that there is very considerable freedom for capital to move between these markets in response to interest rate differentials, it is no coincidence that interest rate structures are closely linked. In the absence of specific obstacles and barriers (such as exchange controls), arbitrage between the domestic and external segments of the dollar-denominated money markets ensures close correspondence both in terms of rate levels and in terms of timing and magnitude of rate changes. This close cleavage of rates has regularly been demonstrated in empirical work; but where exchange controls or the like are in place, the tendency for the close movement of rates in domestic and external markets is found to be much weaker. Indeed, an indication of the efficacy of capital controls can be seen in the degree of divergence of interest rates in the two markets. Wide divergences are associated with tight capital controls, and vice versa.

In our earlier discussions on the four-way equivalence model, we found that the major influences upon offshore currency interest rates, currency expectations and forward exchange rates might be summarised as follows:

- Offshore currency interest rate differential = forward premium or discount (this is known as interest rate parity).
- Forward premium or discount = expected change in exchange rate (expectations theory).
- Expected change in exchange rate = offshore currency interest rate differential (international Fisher effect).
- Offshore currency interest rate differential = difference in expected inflation rates (Fisher effect).

It should be recalled – and this is most important – that when using the four-way equivalence model, interest rate differentials must be based upon offshore currency interest rates. It should also be recalled that, empirically, interest rate parity is the only one of the above equivalences which is found to hold in the short term.

That offshore currency rates do not exactly equal domestic interest rates is explained in the main by regulatory factors such as reserve requirements affecting one market but not the other. The extent to which reserve requirements impinge upon rates can be demonstrated by a simplified numerical example. (In fact, the USA does not have reserve asset requirements, neither are interest rates as high as in our example). Assume that a US bank receives \$10m in domestic deposits and that the reserve requirement (which has to be deposited with the central bank and does not earn any interest) is 5 per cent. The effective funds received, then, amount to only \$9.5m – that is, 95 per cent of the deposit. Assume further that the bank pays 15 per cent per annum on the full \$10m. The effective cost of the funds in the domestic deposit is therefore given by:

$$\text{Effective cost of domestic deposit} = \frac{\text{Interest rate paid}}{1 - \text{Reserve requirement}}$$

$$= \frac{15\%}{1 - 0.05}$$

$$= 15.79\%$$

The additional cost of the reserve requirement is therefore 79 basis points. This is the extra amount that the bank can afford to pay on offshore dollar deposits (which avoid reserve requirements) to achieve the same true cost of funds.

Another major reason for different interest rate levels in domestic and external markets arises because of perceived differences in risk. These risk differences can best be explained with the help of an example. A US depositor in the offshore dollar market holds a claim in one location – for example, London – but may ultimately receive payment in the United States. The depositor might be deprived of its funds at maturity by an action of either the UK or the US government. In the case of a domestic deposit, it is only the actions of one government that can affect the deposit.

Of course, it is also possible to argue that offshore markets may actually reduce risk. In countries where new capital controls upon disposition of residents' funds are feared, external deposits might well be considered less risky by residents than leaving funds on domestic deposits. As well as indirect interference through government regulations, depositors may be concerned with direct government intervention. The government of the country in which the Eurobank operates may seize the assets of the bank and block repayment of liabilities or otherwise restrict its activities through political action. The scenario might be as follows. In a fit of nationalism or in an attempt to alleviate foreign exchange difficulties, the government of a country where offshore currency deposits and loans are made intervenes in the operations of branches of foreign banks within its territory. This is the kind of risk termed 'sovereign risk'. And, by definition, it is always present in the offshore currency business. Eurobanking involves attracting funds from non-residents and making loans to other non-residents. If very few of the Eurobank's assets are directly subject to the host country's jurisdiction, then offshore operations are at risk only if that government is able to press its claims in the jurisdictions of the borrowers against the competing claims of the parent bank. Another fear is that, while the central banks of various countries are often perceived as being ready to bail out any major bank whose domestic operations get into trouble, they might not do so for offshore branches. After all, who is the lender of last resort when difficulties originate from loans on the books of foreign affiliates?

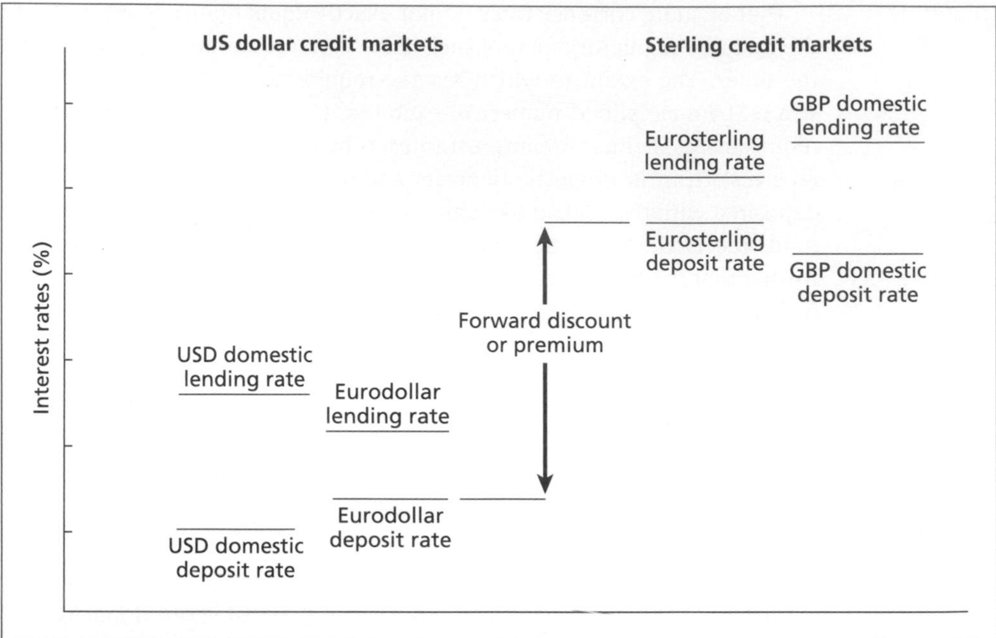

Figure 30.2 Interest relationships in domestic and offshore currency credit markets

In short, the risks associated with external dollar deposits and loans are usually greater than those associated with their domestic counterparts. These greater risks stem from the possibility of government intervention of not just one, but two or more countries, and from the possibility that central banks might not function as lenders of last resort for Eurobanks.

Just as there is a relationship between domestic and external interest rates, so offshore dollar interest rates of different maturities follow similar term structures to domestic rates. Interest rates of the same maturity move in tandem in the two markets. Generally, long-term rates are less volatile than short-term rates. This is because short-term rates are very sensitive to the near-term outlook for credit conditions, whereas long-term rates are affected to a greater degree by long-term inflationary expectations.

The relationship between domestic and offshore currency credit markets is summarised in Figure 30.2.

30.10 The international bond market

Money may be raised internationally by bond issues and by bank loans. This is done in domestic as well as international markets. The difference is that in international markets the money may come in a currency which is different from that normally used by the borrower. The characteristic feature of the international bond market is that bonds are always sold outside the country of the borrower. There are three main types of bond, of which two are international bonds. A domestic bond is a bond issued in a country by a resident of that country. A **foreign bond** is a bond issued in a particular country by a foreign borrower. Eurobonds are bonds **underwritten** and sold in more than one country.

A foreign bond may be defined as an international bond sold by a foreign borrower but denominated in the currency of the country in which it is placed. It is underwritten and sold by a national underwriting syndicate in the lending country. Thus, a US company might float a bond issue in the London capital market, underwritten by a British syndicate and denominated in sterling. The foreign bond issue would be sold to investors in the UK capital market, where it would be quoted and traded. It would be called a **Bulldog bond**. Foreign bonds issued within the United States are called **Yankee bonds**, while foreign bonds issued in Japan are called **Samurai bonds**. Canadian entities are the major floaters of foreign bonds in the United States.

A Eurobond may be defined as an international bond underwritten by an international syndicate and sold in countries other than the country of the currency in which the issue is denominated. An example of a Eurobond transaction would be an issue by a German company of dollar-denominated bonds through a consortium of UK merchant banks, a large German bank and the overseas affiliate of an American investment bank.

Eurobonds are generally issued by corporations and governments needing secure, long-term funds and are sold through a geographically diverse group of banks to investors around the world.

Eurobonds are similar to domestic bonds in that they may be issued with fixed or floating interest rates. But they possess a number of distinctive features:

- The issuing technique takes the form of a placing rather than formal issuing; this avoids national regulations on new issues.
- Eurobonds are placed simultaneously in many countries through syndicates of underwriting banks which sell them to their investment clientele throughout the world.
- Unlike foreign bonds, Eurobonds are sold in countries other than that of the currency of denomination; thus dollar-denominated Eurobonds are sold outside the United States.
- The interest on Eurobonds is not subject to withholding tax.

Bonds are usually issued through a special financing subsidiary, often in a tax haven, thus ensuring the absence of withholding tax. The subsidiary issuing the bonds, usually in the form of bearer bonds, has a parent company guarantee. Threats of governments to impose withholding taxes on Eurobond interest would be likely, were they to crystallise, to result merely in relocation to ensure the non-impact of such taxes.

There are a number of different types of Eurobond. A **straight bond** is one having a specified interest coupon and a specified maturity date. Straight bonds may be issued with a floating rate of interest. Such bonds may have their interest rate fixed at six-month intervals at a stated margin over the LIBOR for deposits in the currency of the bond. So, in the case of a Eurodollar bond, the interest rate may be based upon LIBOR for Eurodollar deposits. In the case of bonds based on euros, the interest rate will be related to EURIBOR. Floating rate notes have come to represent an increasing proportion of new issues on the Eurobond market. Interest on these bonds is paid at the end of each six-month period. Such bonds usually carry guaranteed minimum interest. If a bond has an interest rate of LIBOR plus 1 per cent with a minimum of 6 per cent and if LIBOR were to fall below 5 per cent, the interest would remain at 6 per cent.

A **convertible Eurobond** is a bond having a specified interest coupon and maturity date, but it includes an option for the holder to convert its bonds into an equity share of the company at a conversion price set at the time of issue.

The issue of Eurobonds is normally undertaken by a consortium of international banks. The procedures for placing are similar to those for syndicated loans detailed earlier in this chapter. The borrower may be a large corporation or a government. The borrower normally asks a major international bank to arrange the issue. A managing syndicate, including at least four or five leading banks, plus a bank from the borrowing country, is then organised. Eurobonds are placed, rather than formally issued, with the banks' clientele of international investors. In the past, Eurobond underwriting and fee costs have come out at between 2 and $2^1/_2$ per cent, divided between the following parts:

Management fee	0.375–0.5 per cent
Underwriting fee	0.375–0.5 per cent
Selling concession	1.250–1.5 per cent
Total gross spread	2.000–2.5 per cent

A record of the transaction called a 'tombstone' is subsequently published in the financial press. Those banks whose names appear at the top of the tombstone have agreed to subscribe to the issue. At a second level, a much larger underwriting syndicate is mentioned. The banks in the managing syndicate will have made arrangements with a worldwide group of underwriters, mainly banks and security dealers. After arranging the participation of a number of underwriters, the managing syndicate will have made a firm offer to the borrower, which obtains the funds from the loan immediately. At a third level, the underwriting group usually arranges for the sale of the issue through an even larger selling group of banks, brokers and dealers.

Eurobond issues have been made in a wide variety of currencies and composite currencies. These include US dollars, sterling, euros (and the predecessor currencies of the euro), Swiss francs, SDRs and so on.

In addition, there is the US domestic debt market. Over six times as large as its UK counterpart, it is one of the largest in the world. It is also the most technically complicated in which to borrow. This means that only the largest foreign companies are able to justify the investment in set-up costs necessary to tap the market.

The US Securities and Exchange Commission (SEC) is responsible for setting standards and reviewing the content of all issue prospectuses. It also sets the standard for certain routine reports that companies must comply with if they are listed on one of the US stock markets or have public bonds in issue. As a result of this involvement, the documentation associated directly and indirectly with a money-raising operation in the United States is much greater than in any comparable market. Although the amount of compulsory disclosure is high, it is not really significantly higher than that usually met voluntarily by most major UK companies.

Another novelty for the first-time borrower in the US domestic debt market is the requirement that it must be rated by the two rating agencies. It is from this rating procedure that the term 'triple A' for the very highest quality of credit comes. Moody's writes Aaa, while Standard and Poor's writes AAA. After triple A comes double A and then three gradations of single A: A+, A and A–. Then comes triple B, which is the lowest rating acceptable in the bond market for a domestic credit. A foreign borrower would have to be rated single A to borrow, but if it were an initial borrowing it would probably have to be A+. The rating largely determines the coupon rate. It should be noted that it is the bond issue that is rated rather than the company; a company's whole spectrum of bond issues will usually carry the same rating but need not necessarily do so because of the varying quality of security. Each bond floated is rated prior to issue and the agencies monitor the rating, and may change it, through its life. This normally involves an annual review with occasional changes in rating.

The representatives of each rating agency require a comprehensive statement of affairs from the intending borrower. The data required will be greatly reduced if the borrower has already had bonds rated in the market. The statement is usually as strong on business strategy as on finance. It is reinforced by a number of senior executives submitting to a detailed interrogation. A new borrower would certainly be expected to field its chief executive and finance director. During this process, borrowers need the support of their investment bankers. Rating agency staff are bright and sharp in debate. They specialise by industry. Given that they are being exposed to a great deal of confidential information, they have a very good insight into the strategies, structures and shares in market segments. The rating agencies give their rating decision to the borrower in confidence so that the company may withdraw the issue should the ratings be unacceptably low. The borrower may make representations at this stage, but the depth of analysis carried out makes it improbable that an agency will alter its rating. Agencies do not necessarily agree and split ratings are by no means unusual, but they persist only if they are one place apart. Should the gap be wider, a compromise will be reached with one or both agencies adjusting their rating. Where agreed, ratings are announced publicly and stand until they are adjusted on review. Comparisons of what is meant by various bond-rating agencies' categorisations is summarised in Table 30.1.

Table 30.1 What bond ratings mean*

	Moody's	Standard & Poor's	Fitch IBCA
Highest credit quality; issuer has strong ability to meet obligations	Aaa	AAA	AAA
Very high credit quality; low risk of default	Aa1 Aa2 Aa3	AA+ AA AA–	AA
High credit quality, but more vulnerable to changes in economy or business	A1 A2 A3	A+ A A–	A
Adequate credit quality for now, but more likely to be impaired if conditions worsen	Baa1 Baa2 Baa3	BBB+ BBB BBB–	BBB
Below investment grade, but good chance that issuer can meet commitments	Ba1 Ba2 Ba3	BB+ BB BB–	BB
Significant credit risk, but issuer is presently able to meet obligations	B1 B2 B3	B+ B B–	B
High default risk	Caa1 Caa2 Caa3	CCC+ CCC CCC–	CCC CC C
Issuer failed to meet scheduled interest or principal payments	C	D	DDD DD D

* Firms' precise definitions of ratings vary.

The scale of the US domestic bond market makes it attractive to large borrowers, but a significant sales effort is usually necessary, especially for first-time borrowers. Meetings to address investors are arranged, with a roadshow visiting financial centres; the quality of such presentations is a significant factor in the success of an issue.

It always has to be remembered that the United States is a highly litigious society. It is not expensive to lose a lawsuit in the United States because costs are not awarded in favour of the successful litigant. This means that it is always possible to find an attorney prepared to fight any fairly reasonable case on an opportunistic basis. If the attorney wins, he or she takes a percentage of the damages, but no basic fee is claimed, whether the case is won or lost. The managers of companies entering the US financial markets should not forget this. It means that they are exposed to the risk of action for damages from any investor which can demonstrate that it was misled by a prospectus. Consequently, documentation is intensively studied by the issue managers, their solicitors and the senior executives of the borrowing company to ensure its accuracy.

Before leaving this brief review of the US domestic market, reference must be made to the US commercial paper market. The term 'commercial paper' simply means an unsecured promissory note, essentially an IOU, usually issued by corporations for maturities from 1 to 270 days. This market is open to foreigners and has been tapped at extremely fine rates by UK and continental European companies. Other CP markets exist elsewhere in the world. There is, for example, a UK commercial paper market which is similar (but not exactly so) to USCP.

30.11 The advantages of the Eurobond market to borrowers

The Eurobond markets possess a number of advantages for borrowers. These include the following:

- The size and depth of the market are such that it has the capacity to absorb large and frequent issues.
- The Eurobond market has a freedom and flexibility not found in domestic markets. The issuing techniques make it possible to bypass restrictions, such as requirements of official authorisation, queuing arrangements, formal disclosure, exchange listing obligations and so forth, which govern the issue of securities by domestic as well as foreign borrowers in the individual national markets. All the financial institutions involved in Eurobond issues are subject to at least one national jurisdiction. National authorities can, and sometimes do, make their influence felt, especially when their own currency is used to denominate the issue.
- The cost of issue of Eurobonds, at on average less than 2.5 per cent of the face value of the issue, is relatively low.
- Interest costs on dollar Eurobonds are competitive with those in New York. Often US multinationals have been able to raise funds at a slightly lower cost in the Eurobond market than in the US domestic market.
- Maturities in the Eurobond market are suited to long-term funding requirements. Maturities may reach thirty years, but fifteen-year Eurobonds are more common. In the

medium-term range, five- to ten-year Eurobonds run into competition with medium-term Eurodollar loans. But the longer maturities provide the assurance of funds availability at a known rate.

- A key feature of the Eurobond market is the development of a sound institutional framework for underwriting, distribution and placing of securities.

30.12 The advantages of the Eurobond market to investors

There are a number of special characteristics of the Eurobond market which make it particularly attractive to investors. These include the following:

- Eurobonds are issued in such a form that interest can be paid free of income or withholding taxes of the borrowing countries. Also, the bonds are issued in bearer form and are held outside the country of the investor, enabling the investor to evade domestic income tax. But some countries' exchange control regulations limit an investor's ability to purchase Eurobonds.
- Issuers of Eurobonds have, on the whole, an excellent reputation for creditworthiness. Most of the borrowers – governments, international organizations or large multinational companies – have first-class reputations. The market is very much a name market.
- A special advantage to borrowers as well as lenders is provided by convertible Eurobonds. Holders of convertible debentures are given an option to exchange their bonds at a fixed price and within a specified period for the stock of the parent company of the financing subsidiary. A bond with a warrant gives the bondholder an option to buy a certain number of shares of common stock at a stated price. The more the price of the underlying stock rises, the more valuable the warrant becomes. Since warrants are usually detachable, the bondholder may retain the bond but sell the warrants.
- The Eurobond market is active both as a primary and as a secondary market. The secondary market expanded in the late 1960s and early 1970s. Eurobonds are traded over the counter both locally and internationally by financial institutions that are ready to buy or sell Eurobonds for their own accounts or on behalf of their clients. Just as telecommunications linkages have integrated foreign exchange markets, so they have integrated the secondary market in Eurobonds. Since 1968 international trading in Eurobonds has been greatly facilitated by a clearing house in Brussels and called Euroclear. Participants in Euroclear can complete transactions by means of book entries rather than physical movements of the securities. This has removed the main barrier to secondary market trading, which had been the inability to deliver bonds on time. There are now various other clearing arrangements in the market.

30.13 Cash management

Cash management is concerned with planning, monitoring and managing liquid resources. In general terms, the objectives of cash management are as follows:

- to ensure that the organisation has the wherewithal to pay its obligations as they fall due;
- to ensure the availability of funds at the right time, in the right place, in the right currency and at an acceptable cost;
- to reduce borrowing requirements and interest cost;
- to minimise idle balances;
- to optimise after-tax earnings on surplus funds;
- to reduce bank charges;
- to increase remittable funds to the parent company from divisions, branches and subsidiaries;
- to reduce tax liabilities.

Cash management has been greatly influenced in recent years by a number of innovations. These include the development of domestic and international cash transmission systems between banks and the rapid growth in electronic banking, allowing corporate treasurers to plan and monitor their cash position around the world. Value-dated transfer instructions via a personal computer or terminal are widespread, as are such techniques as cash pooling, intercompany netting, reinvoicing and factoring. For a further summary see Buckley.[12]

30.14 Project finance

Project finance is not exactly a newcomer to the international finance scene. Indeed, in 1856 financing for the building of the Suez Canal was raised by a variant of this technique. But it was not until some sixty years ago that early project finance techniques were used in the United States to fund the development of oilfields. Small Texan and Oklahoman wildcat explorers lacked sufficient capital to develop their oilfields and could not raise sufficient straight debt on their own credit standings. The bankers developed a form of production payment finance – instead of looking to the company's balance sheet for security, the banks relied on the specific reserves themselves with the direct proceeds of oil sales earmarked for the loan's repayment.

A number of variations on this theme developed, but it was not until the expansion in North Sea oilfields that project finance grew beyond production payment financing and assumed some of the variety that it has today. Subsequently, international banks have used project finance concepts first for major mineral developments, then for infrastructural development, and then in the manufacturing sector. Toll roads, tunnelling projects, theme parks, production facilities in the utilities industries, shipping and aircraft finance have also received funding via project finance techniques, although the popularity of particular industries waxes and wanes from time to time.

Project finance is illusive in terms of precise definition because there is no single technique that is immutably used – each facility is tailored specifically to suit the individual project and the needs of the parties sponsoring it. In essence, the expression project finance describes a large-scale, highly leveraged financing facility established for a specific undertaking, the creditworthiness and economic justification of which are based upon that undertaking's expected cash flows and asset collateral. It is the project's own economics rather that its sponsor's (usually the equity owners) financial strength that determines its viability. In this way, the sponsor isolates this activity from its other businesses. Through careful structuring, the sponsor may shift specific risks to project customers, developers and other participants, thus limiting the financial recourse to itself.

This process of sharing risk is not without costs. Project finance borrowing is normally more expensive than conventional company debt and the very large number of contracts that must be specified between the relevant parties entails additional time and expense. But the ultimate result may be more acceptable to the sponsors. Compared with direct funding, it is usually off-balance sheet and this may better reflect the actual legal nature of non-recourse finance.

Lenders may be attracted to project finance. In addition to higher fees, they can be sure that cash generation will be retained within the project rather than diverted to cross-subsidise other activities. The lenders further benefit in terms of their first claim to these funds. They are protected by a range of covenants from the sponsor and other parties. Spreading project risks over several participants lessens their dependence on the sponsor's own credit standing too. The typically large capital requirement necessitates syndication to a group of institutions, so that the credit exposure is shared across many lenders. A properly structured project finance facility does not necessarily entail more risk exposure than a normal corporate advance.

It can be seen that in project lending the focus is entirely upon the project being financed. The lender looks, mainly (often wholly), to the project as a source of repayment. Its cash flows and assets are dedicated to service the project loan. Clearly, the project cannot start to repay a loan until it is operational and continuing to operate soundly, so analysis by lenders is critical. If any major part of the project fails, lenders probably lose money. Projects lack a variety of products and their assets are highly specialised, equipment may be of relatively little value outside the project itself and may, sometimes be geographically remote. A project's assets may provide little in terms of the second exit route that bankers usually like in respect of a loan facility. Because of this, project finance is regarded by bankers as high risk/high reward money – although the risk may be reduced by careful structuring. The other side of the coin is that project cash flows are dedicated to debt repayment.

The owner's risk is often confined to whatever equity or guarantees are needed to make the project viable. Having said this, where the owner plays another role – perhaps contractor or operator – then the owner bears the normal risks associated with these roles. In recompense for the limited risk, the owner will often take nothing out of the project until debt has been repaid – only the strongest of projects can accommodate early withdrawal. Once the project becomes debt-free, then everything that remains is the owner's.

The specific features below distinguish project finance from conventional corporate borrowing. They may not all be present in a particular project financing instance.

- The project is usually established as a distinct, separate entity.
- It relies considerably on debt financing. Borrowings generally provide 70–75 per cent of the total capital with the balance being equity contributions or subordinated loans from the sponsors. Some projects have been structured successfully with over 90 per cent debt.
- The project loans are linked directly to the venture's assets and potential cash flow.
- The sponsors' guarantees to lenders do not, as a rule, cover all the risks and usually apply only until completion (coming on-stream).

- Firm commitments by various third parties, such as suppliers, purchasers of the project's output, government authorities and the project sponsors are obtained and these create significant components of support for the project credit.
- The debt of the project entity is often completely separate (at least for balance sheet purposes) from the sponsor companies' direct obligations.
- The lender's security usually consists only of the project's assets, aside from project cash generation.
- The finance is usually for a longer period than normal bank lending.

Project finance is most frequently used in capital-intensive projects which are expected to generate strong and reasonably certain cash flows and which may consequently support high levels of debt. Many oil companies, which are small relative to the sums involved in the development of major fields, have used project finance to enable them to pursue major new developments using a production payment loan on an existing field already in production to pay for the further development of a new field – rather as a property developer can mortgage existing properties to provide finance for new developments. These kinds of production payment loan tend to be on a limited recourse basis – that is, if the field fails to produce sufficient revenue, the lender has no recourse to the oil company itself except in limited circumstances, such as failure of the oil company to operate the field competently. In this way, the company sheds some of its risk while retaining the long-term benefits of its new discovery.

Further features including the following:

- In project finance, lenders usually take some degree of credit risk on the project itself.
- In deciding whether to finance a project, lenders must consider its technical feasibility and its economic projections. This means that the commercial, legal, political and technical risks of a project must all be evaluated.
- Having analysed the risks associated with a project, lenders try to establish a method of financing that covers those risks in the most effective way. It is necessary that the financial structure in project finance should be creative enough to allow the project to succeed.
- From the lender's point of view, effective security must be structured. Lenders are usually deeply concerned about the cost of over-runs and they frequently seek completion guarantees and performance bonds.
- Project financiers are very concerned about the availability of all raw materials and customers, and try to ensure ability to service and repay debt.
- Lenders frequently require assurances regarding the revenues which the project will generate. Evidence of sales contracts may be asked for with respect to the short to medium term or even the longer term. Provisions relating to price adjustments may be critical.

For a far more extensive summary, see Buckley.[13]

Summary

- On the topic of subsidiaries' performance measurement, on practical grounds, comparison of actual outturns with budgeted performance in foreign currency terms may be the most sensible, cost-effective approach. This is especially so if it is coupled with an emphasis upon cash generation in home currency terms which may then be discounted to provide a focus upon performance in present value terms. Performance evaluation based upon accounting outturns needs to be adjusted to allow for the effects of transfer pricing, funds flow adjustments (such as leading and lagging) and hedging policy.
- Exposure management may be centralised or decentralised. The case for centralisation involves the following arguments: it ensures that the company follows a consistent policy; it facilitates the matching of exposures; it helps ensure that the best rates in the market are obtainable; it ensures the concentration of limited expertise, skills and systems investment; it helps integrate with cash management. The case against centralisation involves the following points: there are substantial up-front costs in recruitment, office space and equipment in establishing a centralised foreign exchange expertise; foreign exchange risk management may be an interesting and stimulating aspect of the subsidiary company's life; taking this away from the subsidiary may, at the margin, be a demotivating factor. Centralisation need not involve this. The approach recommended in this book is that individual units should regard the central treasury as their banker and run an account with head office as if it were their banker. Divisions may hedge some exposures with the treasury – this means that autonomy will be maintained. They will, of course, report all exposures to the centre. Another argument against the centralisation of foreign exchange exposures is that divisional staff may become blind to the risks and expertise needed to handle foreign exchange problems.
- With a large number of partly owned subsidiaries, it may be appropriate to adopt a decentralised approach. Minority shareholders will want optimisation at the level of their own investment – not at group level.
- The proportion of value or turnover exposed is obviously a relevant factor in deciding whether to centralise or not. Where performance will not be materially affected by changes in exchange rates, foreign exchange risk is unlikely to be an issue. In a purely decentralised system, the unit looks after its own exposures only, having no regard for exposures occurring elsewhere in the group. At the opposite end of the continuum is the completely centralised system in which the treasurer receives and co-ordinates data from all group members determining a net position and undertaking appropriate hedging action. The subsidiary will not be consulted on group hedging strategy. Many intermediate variations are possible too. It must be stressed that whatever system is adopted, it needs to be justified on cost–benefit grounds and must be regularly checked to ensure that the system chosen continues to deliver the goods in cash terms. The need for *ad hoc* post-audits is clear.
- Whether the treasury should be a profit centre or a cost centre is a question frequently discussed. If foreign exchange exposure management is centralised, it creates the opportunity to run as a profit centre. In this context profit may accrue from improved exchange rates on deals, by selective hedging actions and, thirdly, by speculating in currencies. Of course, any position-taking can only be justified by some superior knowledge possessed

by a treasury executive or adviser. The result of this is that only minimal speculation – if any – could be justified. It is worth noting that non-bank organisations which involve themselves in interest rate mismatching and running the treasury as a profit centre are scored negatively by credit-rating agencies. One of the dangers of running the treasury as a profit centre is that it may go for profit by ripping off divisions.

- Transfer pricing may be used to get monies out of an overseas subsidiary that restricts flows upwards. The multinational may set high transfer prices on goods and services supplied to a foreign subsidiary by the head office or by divisions in environments that are less restrictive. The multinational may lower the transfer prices of products which the foreign division sells to the head office or to other divisions. Transfer pricing may be used to reduce overall corporate taxes. The multinational may shuffle income to keep profits low in high-tax countries and relatively high in low-tax countries. Transfer prices may also be used to reduce import tariffs and to avoid quotas. For purposes of resource allocation in the multinational, it is important that divisional profitability be accurately measured. To discover true profitability, the group should be sure that interdivisional transfer prices are the prices that would have been paid had the transactions been with independent companies – that is at arm's length. But there may be problems inasmuch as multinational group management may not want true profits to be known outside a tight central coalition of executives.
- The largest international debt market is in offshore currency. The offshore currency market is that market in which Eurobanks accept deposits and make loans denominated in currencies other than that of the country in which the bank is located.

End of chapter questions

30.1 Explain how transfer pricing can be used to reduce a MNC's overall tax liability.

30.2 Briefly describe the role of tax planning by the MNC. What are its key functions?

30.3 Describe the possible conflict of interests between centralised and devolved management.

30.4 What is syndicated lending? Why do banks sometimes prefer this form of lending?

30.5 What is the difference between Eurobonds and foreign bonds?

30.6 What are the objectives of the cash management function?

30.7 What is cash management essentially concerned with?

30.8 Project finance is difficult to define. What are its essential features?

30.9 When deciding whether or not to back a project finance proposition, what essential features do potential lenders home in on?

Test bank 5

Exercises

1 Global Enterprises plc (see balance sheet below) believes broadly in currency neutrality. The board prefers not to risk a loss to the sterling amount of shareholders' funds from exchange rate movements rather than to have the chance of making gains from such movements. The group had long had a surplus of some US $60m assets over US liabilities. It had been decided in principle to take corrective action. However, this was in 1980 when the spot rate was $2.30 = £1. You advised that the timing was not felicitous. In 1984 when the rate reached $1.20 = £1 you felt that the time had come to take immediate action, but you also judged that a desirable restructuring of the balance sheet for the longer term needed more time. For example, you had little short-term sterling debt that could be immediately repaid and you did not wish to increase the gearing in the meantime.

What immediate steps could you take to neutralise the $60 million exposure, and what options should you then investigate for a longer-term solution?

	£m		£m
Fixed assets	460	Capital reserves	590
Stocks and debtors	850	Minorities	50
Trade creditors	(380)	Loan capital	300
Tax & dividends	(50)	Cash and deposits	(270)
Other current liabilities, provisions & accruals	(210)		
	670		670

2 You are the treasurer of a major chemical producer, one of whose divisions has postponed a major plant on a greenfield site in the UK because of restrictions on resources in a period of high capital expenditure. An investment bank acting on behalf of the plant supplier proposes that you set up a special-purpose company to revive the project, financing it on a limited recourse basis. The £100m cost would be provided:

	£ million
Equity	
Your company	18 (of which £6m is to be preference shares)
Plant supplier	8
Plant contractor	4
	30
Debt	
Bank loans	70
	100

The concept would be that the banks would rely on the cash flow from the project to service the debt. Your company would be expected to manage the construction process as it would with any plant and purchase the end product but there would be no recourse to your company's general credit. At the point when the banks have been repaid, you would have the option to buy out the other shareholders at cost plus a rate of return equal to current interest rates. Your finance director asks you:

(a) What undertakings your company is likely to have to give in order to make the project bankable.
(b) How you would propose that the risks arising from the undertakings be managed.
(c) Whether to apply to the revived project your normal hurdle rate for greenfield projects. This is a 23 per cent after-tax discount rate and is based on a target corporate gearing of 65 per cent equity : 35 per cent debt.

Draft a response.

3 You are the international treasurer of a major multinational processing and selling food products. The fruit products division is planning a greenfield plant to produce canned orange juice from locally grown fruit in a high-inflation (currently 60 per cent p.a.) South American country. The equipment is available from the United States or from Europe. The production will be 25 per cent for the local market with the balance exported to meet existing demand in European countries. You will have to advise on the financing structure of the company being formed to own the plant (local regulations require a separate legal entity) and the impact on the group's situation.

What factors will you consider in formulating your advice?

Multiple choice questions

1 A multinational has one subsidiary in a 45 per cent tax rate country, and another in a 30 per cent tax rate country. To increase its overall after-tax earnings, the headquarters should arrange to:

(a) lower the price of supplies from the low-tax-rate subsidiary to the high-tax-rate subsidiary;
(b) move expenses from the high-tax rate subsidiary to the low-tax-rate subsidiary;
(c) have the low-tax-rate subsidiary lower its prices charged for materials transferred to the high-tax rate subsidiary;
(d) none of the above.

2 A firm produces goods for which substitutes are universally available. Depreciation of the firm's home currency should:

(a) reduce local sales because foreign competition in the home market is reduced;
(b) reduce the firm's exports denominated in the firm's home currency;
(c) reduce returns earned on the firm's foreign bank deposits;
(d) reduce payments required to pay for imports denominated in foreign currency;
(e) none of the above.

3 Which of the following creates an effective hedge of net payables in US dollars for a UK firm?

(a) purchase of a sterling put option;
(b) sale of pounds forward for dollars;
(c) sale of sterling futures;
(d) all of the above;
(e) none of the above.

4 A US-based multinational is due to receive Sfr8m in 90 days. The current spot rate of the Swiss franc is $0.62 and the 90-day forward rate is $0.635. Managers at the multinational have come up with the following estimate for the spot rate of the US dollar against the Sfr in 90 days:

	Probability
$0.61	10 per cent
$0.63	20 per cent
$0.64	40 per cent
$0.65	30 per cent

The probability that the forward hedge will result in more US dollars being received compared to the outturn assuming no hedging is:

(a) 10 per cent;
(b) 20 per cent;
(c) 30 per cent;
(d) 50 per cent;
(e) 70 per cent.

5 A multinational based in the United States is due to receive CHF10m in 180 days. The current Swiss franc/dollar spot rate is $0.50; the 180-day forward rate is $0.51. A Swiss franc call option with a strike price of $0.52 and a 180-day expiration date attracts a premium of 2 cents. A Swiss franc put option with a 180-day expiration date and an exercise price of $0.51 has a premium of 2 cents. The management of the firm reckons that the spot rate in 180 days might be:

	Probability
$0.48	10 per cent
$0.49	60 per cent
$0.55	30 per cent

Including the cost of the premium in your calculation, what is the probability that the forward hedge will result in more dollars received than the options hedge?

(a) 10 per cent;
(b) 30 per cent;
(c) 40 per cent;
(d) 70 per cent;
(e) none of the above.

6 *Ceteris paribus*, a firm will benefit from geographical diversifying if:

(a) the correlation between country economies is high;
(b) the correlation between country economies is low;
(c) the correlation between country economies is positive;
(d) two of the above are correct.

7 Financial theory suggests that achieving which of the following, all other things being equal, is likely to increase shareholder wealth?

(a) seeking to profit from capital market distortions;
(b) reducing the riskiness of operating cash flows;
(c) maintaining the debt to capital employed ratio;
(d) all of the above;
(e) none of the above.

8 A bank raises finance with a preponderance of fixed interest short-term borrowings and lends with a preponderance of longer-term lendings at fixed interest rates. It justifies its policy on the grounds that the term structure of interest rates is upwards sloping. If interest rates increase by 150 basis points ($1^1/_2$ per cent) all along the term structure, what effect does this have on the bank?

(a) It will make more money than that previously planned.
(b) It will make less money than that previously planned.
(c) It will be indifferent because the effect will be felt equally on its short-term borrowings and its longer-term lendings.
(d) It should increasingly resort to financial disintermediation by off-balance-sheet operations.
(e) None of the above is correct.

9 Transfer pricing:

(a) includes the pricing of goods, services and technology exchanged among associated companies in different countries;
(b) is used by multinationals to achieve a number of objectives;
(c) is subject to limitations imposed by tax authorities;
(d) may influence managerial incentives and performance;
(e) all of the above are correct.

10 A sterling call option exists with a strike price of \$1.60 and a 90-day expiration date and it attracts a premium of 3 cents per unit. A sterling put option with an exercise price of \$1.60 and a 90-day expiration date has a premium of 2 cents per unit. A US multinational plans to deal options to cover its receivable of £7m in 90 days. The options concerned are European options. The sterling/dollar spot rate is expected to be \$1.57 in 90 days. On this basis, what would be the dollar proceeds after allowing for the option premium?

(a) \$11.69m;
(b) \$10.99m;
(c) \$11.06m;
(d) \$11.43m;
(e) \$11.34m.

Suggested answers to end of chapter questions

Chapter 2

2.1 Under the fixed exchange rate system, governments attempted to maintain exchange rates within 1 per cent of a predetermined value. This would be achieved by government intervention. Devaluations and revaluations were necessary every so often. Under a freely floating system, government intervention is non-existent. The market arrives at a rate. Under a managed-float system, governments allow exchange rates to move according to market forces, but they intervene when they believe it is necessary.

2.2 Central banks may use their currency reserves to buy a specific currency in the foreign exchange market to place upward pressure on that currency. Central banks can also attempt to force currency depreciation by selling that currency in the foreign exchange market in exchange for other currencies, thus flooding the market.

2.3 Briefly, a freely floating system may help to correct balance of trade imbalances as the currency should adjust according to market forces. A strong current account balance should create a strengthening currency which, in turn, should dampen demand for the country's exports and, at the same time, increase imports into the country. The result of this should be a movement towards current account balance. A disadvantage of freely floating exchange rates is that firms have to manage their international exposures.

Chapter 3

3.1 Demand for pounds should increase, supply of pounds for sale should decrease, and the pound's value should increase.

3.2 The higher the real interest rate of a country relative to another country, the stronger will be its home currency, other things equal.

3.3 The Latin American countries concerned have very high inflation, which places downward pressure on their currencies. Effective anti-inflationary policies are needed to prevent further depreciation. They could begin by cutting inflation and controlling it via the money supply.

Chapter 4

4.1 Yes! One could purchase Swiss francs at Bank Y for $0.40 and sell them to Bank X for $.401. With $1 million available, CHF2.5 million would be purchased at Bank Y. These Swiss francs would then be sold to Bank X for $1,002,500, thereby generating a profit of $2,500.

4.2 The large demand for CHF at Bank Y will force this bank's ask price for CHF to increase. The large sales of CHF to Bank X will force its bid price down. Once the ask price of Bank Y is no longer less than the bid price of Bank X, locational arbitrage will no longer be profitable.

4.3 Yes. The appropriate cross exchange rate should be 1 Batavian drac = 3 Ulerican crowns. The actual value of the BTD in terms of ULC is more than it should be. One could obtain BTD with USD, sell the BTD for ULC and then exchange ULC for US$. With $1,000,000, this strategy would generate $1,006,667 – creating a profit of $6,667.

($1,000,000/$0.90 = BTD1,111,111 × 3.02 = ULC3,355,556 × $0.30 = $1,006,667)

Chapter 5

5.1 All other things being equal, a high inflation rate tends to increase imports and decrease exports, thereby increasing the currency account deficit.

5.2 A weakening home currency increases the price of imports purchased by the home country and reduces the prices paid by foreign businesses for the home country's exports. This should cause a decrease in the home country's demand for imports and an increase in the foreign demand for the home country's exports, and improve the current account balance.

5.3 A current account deficit is reflected in a net sale of the home currency in exchange for other currencies. This places downward pressure on the home currency's value. If the home currency weakens, it will reduce the home demand for foreign goods (since goods will now be more expensive), and will increase the home export volume (since exports will appear cheaper to foreign countries). In some cases, the home currency will remain strong even though a current account deficit exists, since other factors (such as international capital flows), other than the current account, can affect the forces on the currency by the currency account.

Chapter 6

6.1 PPP suggests that the purchasing power of a consumer will be similar when purchasing goods in a foreign country or in the home country. If inflation in a foreign country differs from inflation in the home country, the exchange rate will adjust to maintain equal purchasing power. So, higher inflation depresses the exchange rate of the high inflation country, all other things being equal.

Currencies of high inflation countries will be weak according to PPP, causing the purchasing power of goods in the home country versus these countries to be similar.

6.2 One method would be to track the currencies of two countries over time and compare their inflation levels over these periods. Then, you could determine whether the exchange rate changes were similar to what would have been expected under PPP theory.

A second method would be to choose a variety of countries and compare the inflation differential of each foreign country relative to the home country for a given period. Then, you might determine if the exchange rate changes of each foreign currency were what would have been expected based on the inflation differentials under PPP theory.

6.3 (a) The value of the dollar should rise as more rapidly rising GNP in the United States should lead to a relative increase in demand for dollars.

(b) The value of the dollar should fall in line with PPP.

(c) According to PPP, the exchange rate should remain the same.

(d) The value of the dollar should rise as the higher real rates attract capital from Japan that must first be converted into dollars.

(e) The value of the dollar should fall as foreigners find it less attractive to own US assets and the demand for dollars falls.

(f) Higher US wages and declining relative productivity weaken the American economy and make it less attractive for investment purposes. Assuming that a weak economy leads to a weak currency, the dollar will fall. From a somewhat different perspective, when a nation's productivity growth lags behind that of its major trading partners, the other countries will become more competitive. The depreciating currency is the market's way of restoring balance. The lagging country regains its balance, but only by accepting a lower real price for its goods. In effect, the cheaper currency is the market's way of cutting wages in the lagging country. From another perspective, US inflation rises relative to Japanese inflation and, through PPP, the dollar should fall.

Chapter 7

7.1 Transaction exposure is due to international transactions by a firm and affects cash flows. Economic exposure impacts the present value of future cash flows. The two are alike because they are cash flow exposures. They are different because economic exposure affects all future cash flows but transaction exposure involves a limited future time window for cash flows. Transaction exposure is easy to hedge. Economic exposure is very difficult to hedge perfectly.

7.2 If the firm competes with foreign firms that also sell in the same market, then the consumers may switch to foreign products if the local currency strengthens – or vice versa.

7.3 Most companies use strategic methods such as diversified production, marketing and financing. The biggest problem with the diversification strategy is the loss of economies of scale. The biggest advantage is that it can yield lower costs – subject to quality maintenance.

Chapter 8

8.1 (a) It affects consolidated financial statements, which are often used by shareholders to assess the performance of the MNC.
(b) Pure translation exposure does not affect cash flow. It simply reflects the impact of exchange rate fluctuations on consolidated financial statements rather than cash flow.

8.2 The typical first reaction to this question is to say that Walt Disney's world exposure must increase, as EuroDisney would generate revenues in French francs (latterly euros), which may be converted to dollars in the future. If the French franc (euro) were to weaken against the dollar, the revenues would be converted to fewer dollars – and vice versa – thereby increasing economic exposure.

But, Walt Disney Inc was already affected by movements in the French franc and other major currencies before EuroDisney was built. When major currencies weaken against the dollar, foreign tourism to the United States is likely to decrease and Walt Disney's revenue in the United States would fall. By having a European amusement park, Disney may offset the declining US business during strong dollar cycles, as more European tourists may go to the EuroDisney in France. So, Disney may become less exposed to exchange rate movements because of the existence of EuroDisney.

Chapter 9

9.1 Consideration of all cash flows in a particular currency is not necessary when some inflows and outflows offset each other. Only net cash flows between currencies are truly relevant when looking at transaction exposure.

9.2 The net exposure in each currency in US dollars is derived below:

Foreign currency	Net inflows in foreign currency	Current exchange rate	Value of exposure
Ruritania doppels (RUD)	+RUD 2 million	$0.15	$0.3 million
British pounds (GBP)	+GBP 1 million	$1.50	$1.5 million
Batavian dracs (BTD)	−BTD 1 million	$0.30	$−0.3 million

Since the RUD and BTD move in tandem against the dollar, their dollar value of net exposures cancels out. Their exposures should be offset if their exchange rates against the US dollar continue to be highly correlated. The firm's main concern about exposure should be the GBP net inflows.

9.3 No! Thus, past correlations will not serve as perfect forecasts of future correlations. However, historic data may still be useful if the correlations are reasonably expected to be pretty stable.

Chapter 10

10.1 Netting uses a centralised compilation of inter-subsidiary potential cross-border cash flow. It is designed to reduce currency conversion costs and processing costs associated with payments between subsidiaries. By specifying a single net payment to be made instead of all individual payments owed between subsidiaries, transaction costs may be reduced.

10.2 A subsidiary in need of funds would receive cash inflows from another subsidiary sooner than is required. This early payment provides the necessary funds. If the subsidiary in need of funds is making payment, it may be allowed by the MNC parent or recipient subsidiary to delay on its payment. The technique is particularly pertinent when devaluations are expected. In these circumstances you would wish to increase monetary liabilities in the devaluing currency and decrease monetary assets in the devaluing currency.

Chapter 11

11.1 The firm could borrow an amount of Swiss francs such that CHF100,000 to be received in 90 days could be used to pay off the loan. This amounts to (100,000/1.02), around CHF98,039, which could be borrowed now and converted to about $49,020 and invested in a US$ deposit for 90 days. The borrowing of CHF has offset the transaction exposure due to the future receipt of CHF.

11.2 If US Co Inc deposits BLW186,916 (computed as BLW200,000/1.07) into a bank account denominated in BLW earning 7 per cent over six months, the deposit would be worth BLW200,000 at the end of the six-month period. This amount would then be used to make the net BLW payments. To make the initial deposit of BLW186,916, USA Co Inc would need about $18,692 (computed as 186,916 × $0.10). If necessary, it could borrow these funds. The money market hedge eliminates transaction exposure.

11.3 It should be equal in terms of favourability. If IRP exists, the forward premium on the forward rate would reflect the interest rate differential. The hedging of future payables with a forward purchase provides the same results as borrowing at the home interest rate and investing at the foreign interest rate to hedge the payables.

Chapter 12

12.1 An interest rate swap usually involves an exchange of fixed (floating) rate interest payments for floating (fixed) rate interest payments in the same currency. A currency swap typically involves an exchange of principal plus interest payments in one currency for equivalent payments in another currency.

The credit risk on a currency swap is greater than that on interest rate swap. First, the credit risk on the interest rate swap is confined only to interest payments, while the credit risk on the currency swap involves both principal and interest payments. Second, because the exchange rate changes that occur during the lifetime of a currency swap may be large, the credit risk of the currency swap can be correspondingly larger.

12.2 In some instances, a domestic company may borrow money at a lower rate of interest in the domestic capital market than a foreign firm. Note that, we stress 'in some instances'. For example, a US company may borrow money at a better rate (versus foreign companies) in the United States, but it might have less favourable access to capital markets in Europe. At the same time, a European company may have good borrowing opportunities domestically (borrowing in euros versus market rates in euros) but less good opportunities in US$ (versus US$ market rates) in the United States. These rate differentials raise the possibility that each firm can exploit its comparative advantage in the domestic market and share the gains by reducing net borrowing costs. In fact, if the firm can access funds at below market rate in any currency, it may, via a swap, convert the borrowing to a currency in which it wants to raise funds. For example, a US firm building a new plant using Japanese equipment may, through the Japanese Exim bank, have access to JPY at below market rates. It might take the JPY although it has no other exposure to JPY and, through a swap, convert the borrowing to US$, the currency in which most of its operating cash flows arise. And this may yield a rate below the market rate for US$.

12.3 You prefer to pay a fixed long-term rate and receive a floating short-term rate. The initial short-term rate that you receive will merely be the spot rate that prevails today. However, if your expectation is correct, the short-term rate will rise more than the market expects and you will then receive that higher rate. Because your payments are fixed, you will gain from your insight.

Chapter 13

13.1 The US corporation could agree to a futures contract to sell GBP at a specified date in the future and at a specified price. This locks in the exchange rate at which the GBP could be sold.

13.2 The basis is the difference between the cash price (often the source of risk being hedged by a futures position) and the futures price. The performance of a futures hedge depends on whether or not the basis changes over the time of the hedge, or whether such changes are predicted and accounted for when the hedge is established. Unless anticipated *ex ante*, a change in the basis over the time of a hedge implies that the value of the cash position will change by a different amount than the value of the futures position, resulting in an unanticipated gain or loss. Basis risk is the risk associated with changes in the basis which will have a direct bearing on how well a hedge performs.

Changes in the basis are more likely when the characteristics of the cash position being hedged are more different from the characteristics of the future being used as a hedge. Ideally, one would choose the futures contract based on the same position being hedged in the cash market. This results in a minimal change in the basis over time and provides the most effective hedge. However, when futures contracts are not traded on exactly the same thing being hedged in the cash market, a greater degree of basis risk is inherent. Under these circumstances, the hedge is referred to as a cross-hedge since the hedge is being applied across markets. The more similar the futures instrument is to the cash instrument being hedged, the more likely their price movements will be equal over time and the less basis risk will be involved. A futures instrument which is very dissimilar to the cash instrument will involve greater basis risk than instruments (cash and futures) which have similar characteristics.

A mismatch in maturities between the futures instrument and the cash instrument being hedged can contribute to basis risk. Assume that 180-day Treasury Bills are being hedged with (90-day) Treasury Bill futures contracts. Even though Treasury Bills are involved in both the cash and futures positions, they are in different commodities. The value of the futures contract will be influenced by changes in expected 90-day interest rates whereas the value of the cash instrument will be influenced by 180-day interest rates. It is unlikely that changes in these rates will be exactly the same. At the same time the value of a 90-day Treasury Bill will respond differently to a unit change in interest rates than will a 180-day Treasury Bill. Even when rate changes are equal, price changes may not be equal and basis changes will occur.

13.3 (a) The December futures price would have decreased, because it reflects expectations of the future spot rate as of the settlement date. If the existing spot rate were $1.51, the spot rate expected on the December futures settlement date is also likely to be near to $1.51.

(b) You would have sold futures at the existing futures price of $1.59. That is equal to 'sell GBP at $1.59'. Then, as the spot rate of the pound declined, the futures price would decline and you could close out the futures position by purchasing a futures contract at a lower price. Alternatively, you could wait until the settlement date, purchase the pounds in the spot market, and fulfil the futures obligation by delivering pounds.

Chapter 14

14.1 An options premium is the sum of intrinsic value and time value. Both intrinsic value and time value are influenced by volatility of the underlying. With a currency contract, intrinsic value is the difference between the exchange rate of the underlying currency and the strike price of the currency option. Time value is the amount of money that options buyers are willing to pay for an option in the anticipation that the price of the option may increase over time.

14.2 Options have positive values even if they are out-of-the-money because investors will usually pay something today for out-of-the-money options on the chance of profit before maturity. They are also likely to pay some additional premium today for in-the-money options on the chance of an increase in intrinsic value before maturity.

14.3 An option is in-the-money if it can be exercised for a gross profit immediately. Gross profit here means that the profit excludes the initial price paid for the option. This means that a call is in-the-money when the value of the underlying security exceeds the exercise price. A put is in-the-money when the value of the underlying security is less than the exercise price.

Chapter 15

15.1 A call option can hedge a firm's future payables denominated in a foreign currency. It effectively locks in the maximum price to be paid for a currency.

15.2 A put option can hedge a firm's future receivables denominated in a foreign currency. It effectively locks in the minimum price at which a currency may be sold.

15.3 Currency options not only provide a hedge, but they provide flexibility since they do not require an actual commitment to buy or sell a currency (whereas the forward contract does).

A disadvantage of currency options is that a price (the up-front premium) is paid for the option itself. The only payment by a firm using a forward contract is the exchange of a currency as specified in the contract.

Chapter 16

16.1 (a) By having a mismatch in terms of inflows of cash falling as a consequence of an interest rate rise but the firm is financed by floating rate interest. Clearly, this kind of mismatch could also involve stable inflows financed by floating rate finance.

(b) By granting more floating rate loans for a particular maturity than it has deposits at floating rate for that maturity.

16.2 Using the interest rate swap market, or if it is exposed as in 1(a), it might finance at a fixed rate.

16.3 By ensuring that, within maturities, fixed rate deposits and fixed rate loans are equal and ensuring that, within maturities, the same is achieved for floating rates. Adjustments to imbalances may be achieved via swaps and futures.

Chapter 17

17.1 It really consists of bolting together financial instruments, LEGO-like. So options, and forwards or puts and calls of different maturities are bolted together to form a new financial instrument that can be priced according to its underlying LEGO pieces and in accordance with their logical prices.

17.2 Because their financial staff have failed to analyse instruments via their underlying components – their LEGO pieces and their LEGO prices.

17.3 The players need the ability to recognise the needs for financial instruments in corporate treasury (at least, this is true for the salesmen) and then they need the logic and mathematical ability to bolt together the underlying financial LEGOs to create a instrument that is profitable to the bank and meets the customer's needs.

Chapter 18

18.1 CDS contracts are rather like credit insurance but there are differences. These are shown in section 18.1. The major ones are:

- Neither party to a CDS needs to own the underlying security (bond, loan or debt) to which the instrument relates. Neither the buyer nor the seller of the CDS has to suffer a loss from the default event (assuming that the CDS were not held by either party). This contrasts with credit insurance where the insured has to have an insurable interest under which he or she can demonstrate a potential loss should the payment not be made.
- The insured party in a credit insurance contract is bound by utmost good faith rules which require disclosure of all material facts and failure on this point can invalidate the contract. This is not so for a CDS where the maxim buyer beware probably applies.

18.2 By arranging the writing of credit default swaps or credit guarantees on the debt package it was argued that this ensured that the holder of the debt package was insulated against loss. Furthermore, the dubious reasoning in David X Li's paper on correlations increased the argument in favour of enhanced rating.

18.3 It seems that fat tail distributions better describe the behaviour of financial markets. The evidence is clear and noted in the text. Is this related to the fact that in crises many factors are correlated? Probably. But is the greater reason that the whole idea of the applicability of the normal distribution to the behaviour of financial markets an unreasonable one not borne out by real world evidence? Again, probably.

Chapter 19

19.1 Factors impacting the financial crisis are many. They include:

- The manufacture by major governments around the world of an environment of low interest rates, easy credit and lax regulation: this created a spend, spend, spend mentality with the public who consumed at ever increasing levels on the high street and chased property prices higher and higher with purchases of property which they could barely afford. At the same time light regulation of financial institutions led them to take greater and greater risks with bank executives paying themselves bigger and bigger bonuses.
- On the issue of risk, banks were increasing their levels of gearing – taking on more financial risk – at the same time as their business model became riskier (they raised the level of business risk).
- The recirculation of China's surplus to the USA enabled the USA to keep its interest rates low. At the same time, China's tendency to keep its exchange rate too low meant that its exports worldwide was an enabling factor in the main street boom.
- Financial firms boosted the mortgage market by taking on an increasing level of subprime mortgages. This was influenced by government cajoling on providing finance for housing to poor credits.
- Securitisation of loans packaged into mortgage backed securities and collateralised debt obligations insured with credit guarantees from Fannie and Freddie and credit default swaps enabled banks to grant easy money and pass the liability on to others.
- Because banks were moving loans on via securitisation, they reduced their credit appraisal standards or even disposed of them altogether.
- Rating agencies dropped their standards, perhaps in search of easier and higher fees, and enabled weak debt to be rated triple A. At the same time tranching of debt was a big plus.
- The bank bonus culture meant that institutions sought higher returns (which helped the bonus) even though higher risk accompanied the returns (and this was not debited against the bonus). Fannie, Freddie and AIG were major culprits.
- Subprime lenders were exhibiting fraudulent policies as salesmen encouraged lying in their clients' applications.
- Financial regulation seemed almost to be comatosed. Asleep on the job is, perhaps, flattering.

There are, of course, other issues, but this needs to be a summary answer.

19.2 The originate-to-hold model of lending involved the lender keeping the loan it had made in its books as an asset. Originate-to-distribute meant that lendings were securitised and sold on to others. One of the reasons for this was that it took loans off the bank's balance sheet. A major consequence was the bank credit standards of appraisal fell since they were not going to hold the loans on their books.

19.3 The members of the eurozone entered the euro at around estimated purchasing parity – except, perhaps, Greece where economic data were massaged somewhat. In the boom prior to the crisis, their inflation was higher than the stronger members. At the same time, banks were creating problems as they advanced loans for housing and for housebuilders (Ireland and Spain) with the results that when their economies moved into reverse their governments found themselves bailing out banks. This led to government finances looking very sick as they borrowed from abroad to fund the bank rescues. So, essentially it was a package based on these two factors. Of course, inflation could be higher in some countries within the eurozone than others because fiscal policy (unlike monetary policy) resides with the constituent governments as opposed to the EU itself which, through the European Central Bank, is responsible for monetary policy.

Chapter 20

20.1 King Company is likely to benefit because it is maintaining all of its manufacturing in one area. All other things being equal, if President Inc. spreads its production facilities, it will incur higher fixed costs per unit of output. But, presumably, President Inc is seeking lower costs in countries into which it is directing its FDI. This could result in lower costs per unit (subject to maintenance of quality). But this is not an economy of scale.

20.2 Foreign governments sometimes expect that FDI will provide needed employment or technology for a country, or exports from the country, or reduced imports. For these reasons, they may provide incentives to encourage FDI.

20.3 The theory of comparative advantage implies that countries specialise in the production of goods which they can produce most efficiently and that they rely on other countries for other goods. Many countries can produce certain goods more efficiently than other countries because countries are endowed differently in their economic resources. You specialise where you can best apply your limited resources. And buy in the rest.

Chapter 21

21.1 Before and after a devaluation, they may wish to control companies' and individuals' abilities to move their money around as they wish. In other words, they wish to fetter free markets in financial assets to meet balance of payments objectives and other goals.

21.2 Probably, overall, discourage because they invariably involve restrictions on remittances. However, multinationals may still invest because they hope for changes in the regime later on, by which time they will have developed a strongly cash-generating business.

Chapter 22

22.1 When a parent allocates funds for a project, it should view the project's feasibility from its own perspective. It is possible that a project might be feasible from a subsidiary's perspective, but be infeasible when viewed from a parent's cash flow perspective (due to remittance restrictions, foreign withholding taxes or exchange rate changes affecting funds remitted to the parent).

22.2 Some of the more obvious factors are:

(a) exchange rates;
(b) whether remittance restrictions exist;
(c) the probability of a host government takeover;
(d) foreign demand for product;
(e) foreign attitude toward the firm; and
(f) tax effects.

Chapter 23

23.1 Debt–equity swaps allow the lender (or whoever has a claim on the debt) to exchange the claim for an equity investment in the borrower's assets. MNCs may consider purchasing claims on LDC debt in the secondary market to swap these claims for an equity investment in the LDC's assets. In this way, debt–equity swaps can increase activity in the secondary loan market. In fact, this has been a feature of the attempts at solving the debt crisis affecting developing countries.

23.2 Additional factors that merit consideration in a foreign project analysis include: the host government attitude toward foreign companies, exchange rates, currency controls, foreign demand for product, possible expropriation – and others too.

Chapter 24

24.1 The following characteristics of MNCs can influence the cost of capital:

- *Size*. MNCs may be stable firms which are better known and therefore receive preferential treatment by creditors.

- *Access to international capital markets*. MNCs have access to more sources of funds than domestic firms. To the extent that financial markets are segmented, MNCs may be able to obtain financing from accessing various sources at a lower cost.
- *International diversification*. If an MNC can achieve favourable tax breaks on foreign operations, it might enhance after-tax cash flows.
- *Country risk*. MNCs with subsidiaries in politically unstable countries may experience volatile cash flows over time and be more susceptible to financial problems. This may increase the cost of capital.
- *Host country interest rates*. MNCs may be offered subsidised loans to locate in some territories. This reduces their overall cost of capital.

24.2 Yes. But beware – their standard deviation of returns has been greater too. So, they have earned higher returns but they have exhibited higher risk.

Chapter 25

25.1 If the MNC can set up foreign projects in countries whose country risk levels are not highly correlated over time, then it reduces the exposure to the possibility of high country risk in all of these areas simultaneously.

25.2 Disagree! Even if the MNC is already in country X, it should always be asking should we continue here? Country risk needs to be monitored continually. If country risk is so high that there is great danger to employees, it may be argued that no expected return is high enough to warrant the project.

25.3 No. Country risk analysis is not intended to estimate all project cash flows and determine the present value of these cash flows. It is intended to identify forms of country risk and their potential impact. This is important for capital budgeting but it is not a substitute for an international project appraisal aimed at homing in on a parent net present value.

Chapter 26

26.1 Point estimates of exchange rates lead to a point estimate of a project's NPV. It is more desirable to have a feel for a variety of outcomes (NPVs) that might occur.

This might mean sensitivity or scenario analysis.

26.2 Develop a range of possible values that each input variable (such as price, quantity sold, exchange rates) may take on. Then apply a simulation model to these ranges. The result is a distribution of NPVs that may occur.

Chapter 27

27.1 Two alternatives could show similar cash outflows when summing all periods. Yet, the alternative with more of its outflows occurring later would be preferable because of the time value of money. It would probably have a better present value picture.

27.2 It may offset some exchange rate risk if it has cash inflows in euros. These euros could be used to make coupon payments.

Chapter 28

28.1 A forfaiting transaction involves an importer that issues a promissory note to pay for the imported goods over a period of three to seven years. Notes are offered to the exporter who sells them at a discount to a forfaiting bank. Forfaiting is mostly used for capital goods.

28.2 Countertrade involves the sale of goods to one country in exchange for goods from that country.

28.3 Governments may be able to boost exports by establishing policies that either protect the exporters from various types of risk, or encourage lenders to provide financing to exporters.

Chapter 29

29.1 Certainly the theory behind hedging economic exposure is not so complicated. It basically involves ensuring that the present value of the firm is immunised against exchange rate movements. Of course, substantial problems arise in the practical implementation of such a concept. And even more where the firm gets to grips with practical awareness. Numerous problems relating to changing elasticities ensue to say nothing of uncertain competitor reactions.

29.2 Basically, the answer to both questions lies with constraints that the firm may be near in terms of its loan or similar covenants. Whichever is the nearer and has the greater impact is likely to direct the treasurer's attention.

Chapter 30

30.1 The MNC could set a pricing policy (within provisions set out by the governments concerned) to impose high prices or interest costs on goods or funds transferred to those subsidiaries that are in high-tax countries and are profitable at a pre-tax level.

30.2 Tax planning involves (1) knowing the tax laws of each country (2) using the tax laws to analyse the feasibility of alternative policies and (3) minimising the MNC's overall tax liability.

30.3 If centralised management makes decisions to benefit the MNC overall, this may hamper one subsidiary at the expense of another (transfer pricing is an example). The subsidiary adversely affected by the policy may disapprove the MNC's tactics, thereby creating a conflict of interests.

30.4 Syndicated lending reflects a group of banks (called a syndicate) providing a large loan to a customer. This is sometimes desirable as a single loan may be highly damaging to a single bank if the borrower defaulted on the loan. With a syndicate, the potential loss to any bank is limited.

30.5 Eurobonds are bonds that are underwritten by a multinational syndicate of banks and sold simultaneously in many countries other than the country of the currency in which they are denominated. Foreign bonds are bonds which are sold in a particular country by a foreign borrower, and underwritten by a syndicate of members from that country; foreign bonds are denominated in the currency of that country.

30.6 Cash management is concerned with planning, monitoring and managing liquid resources.

30.7 Cash management is designed to ensure the availability of funds at the right time, in the right place, in the right currency and at an acceptable cost. It is concerned with ensuring that the organisation has the wherewithal to meet its obligations as they fall due. Cash management is concerned with borrowing facilities, interest costs, bank charges, idle cash balances and investment of surplus funds. It also has as its objectives the optimisation of remittable funds to the parent and the reduction of tax bills. Cash management is also concerned with banking relationships, electronic banking, cash collection and disbursement and short-term investment.

30.8 The term project finance covers a variety of financing structures. Generally and legally, project finance refers to funds provided to finance a project that will, in varying degrees, be serviced out of the revenues derived from that project. The level of recourse and the type of support given may vary from one project to another. In project finance, lenders usually take some degree of credit risk on the project itself.

30.9 In deciding whether to finance a project, lenders must consider its technical feasibility and its economic projections. This means that the commercial, legal, political and technical risks of a project must all be evaluated. Having analysed the risks associated with a project, lenders try to establish a method of financing that covers those risks in the most effective way. It is necessary that the financial structure in project finance should be creative enough to allow the project to succeed. From the lender's point of view, effective security must be structured. Lenders are usually deeply concerned about the cost of over-runs and they frequently seek completion guarantees and performance bonds. Project financiers are very concerned about the availability of all raw materials and customers, and try to ensure ability to service and repay debt. Lenders frequently require assurances regarding the revenues which the project will generate. Evidence of sales contracts may be asked for with respect to the short- to medium-term or even the longer term. Provisions relating to price adjustments may be critical.

Suggested answers to selected exercises

Test bank 1

1 (a)

New York	USD0.55	= CHF1
Zurich should be the same		
Zurich	USD0.55	= CHF1
Zurich (Direct)	CHF1.8181	= USD1

(b)

New York	USD0.55	= CHF1
i.e.	CHF1.8181	= USD1
Zurich should be	CHF1.8181	= USD1
Zurich is	CHF1.8500	= USD1
Arbitrage is:		
Buy CHF	Sell USD in Zurich, and	
Sell CHF	Buy USD in New York	

2 (a) New York USD0.55 = CHF1

USD1.60 = GBP1

We want CHF for GBP1

$$\text{GBP1} = \text{USD1.60}$$
$$= \text{CHF1.60} \times \frac{1}{0.55}$$
$$= \text{CHF2.9091}$$

(b)

New York	CHF2.9091 = GBP1
Zurich quote	CHF2.80 = GBP1
Arbitrage involves:	
Buy CHF	Sell GBP in New York
Sell CHF	Buy GBP in Zurich

3 (a) US$ investment

Proceeds in three months' time

$1,000,000 × 1.02 = $1,020,000

£ investment

Buy £ spot $1m ⇒ 1.8 = £555,556

Invest 90 days

£555,556 × 1.025 = £569,445

Sell proceeds forward at day 0 for 90 days

£569,445 × 1.78 = $1,013,612

£ investment in $ yields a riskless profit of $6,388 after interest costs.

(Using formula)

Forward discount

$$\frac{f_0 - s_0}{s_0} = \frac{1.78 - 1.80}{1.80} = -1.111\%$$

Interest differential

$$\frac{i_\$ - i_£}{1 + i_£} = \frac{0.02 - 0.025}{1.025} = -0.488\%$$

Interest rate parity not holding. Scope for covered interest arbitrage.
Keep forward discount constant. Interest differential needs 'more minus'.

$$i_£ \uparrow \qquad i_\$ \downarrow$$

(b) US$ investment proceeds – see question 3(a): $1,020,000.
Investment proceeds – see question 3(a): £569,445.
Equilibrium forward rate:

$$\frac{1{,}020{,}000}{569{,}445} = 1.7912$$

(Using formula)
Interest differential (3 months):

$$\frac{0.02 - 0.025}{1.025} = -0.004878$$

Forward discount (3 months):

$$\frac{f - 1.80}{1.80}$$

In equilibrium, interest differential equals forward discount:

$$\frac{f - 1.80}{1.80} = -0.004878$$

Solving: $f = 1.7912$

(c) Forward discount:

$$\frac{1.78 - 1.80}{1.80} = -1.111\%$$

Interest differential:

$$\frac{0.02 - 0.035}{1.035} = -1.449\%$$

Interest rate parity not holding. Scope for covered interest arbitrage.
Keep forward discount constant. Interest differential needs 'less minus'.
$i_£$ too high; $i_\$$ is too low. Borrow $; invest £.

(d) Three-month forward discount

$$\frac{1.78 - 1.80}{1.80} = -1.111\%$$

Interest differential – 3 months

$$\frac{0.02 - x}{1 + x}$$

In equilibrium:

$$\frac{0.02 - x}{1 + x} = 0.0111$$

Solving, $x = 0.0314$.
Three-month £ interest rate is 3.14%, that is, 12.56% p.a.

6 (a) We want to sell CHF, buy AUD and to buy CHF, sell AUD.
To get the rate for selling CHF, buying AUD, we go via

	Sell CHF	Buy USD	CHF1.5495
	Sell USD	Buy AUD	AUD1.7935
So	Sell CHF1.5495 = USD1		
	Sell USD1	= AUD1.7935	

CHF1 = AUD1.157470

Picking up opposite quotes will give us the offer quote of 1.158863. The answer is

CHF1 = AUD1.157470 – 1.158863

or AUD1 = CHF0.8629 – 0.8640

(b) We want the rate to sell GBP buy AUD and to buy GBP sell AUD. We go via

Sell GBP buy USD 1.6325
Sell USD buy AUD 1.7935
Sell GBP1 = USD1.6325
Sell USD1.6325 = AUD2.927889

Using the opposite quotes will give us the offer quote of AUD2.931316. The answer is:

GBP1 = AUD2.9279 – 2.9313
AUD1 = GBP0.3411 – 0.3415

Foreign exchange rates

FX rates matrix:

GBP against	US$	AU$	JPY
Spot	1.6325–1.6335	2.30–2.30 3/4	263.15–263.25
1 month	1.6250–1.6262	2.29 3/8–2.30 1/4	263.00–263.35
2 month	1.6190–1.6203	2.28 7/8–2.29 3/4	262.98–263.33
3 month	1.6122–1.6135	2.28 3/8–2.29 1/4	262.96–263.31

FX rates:

1 1.6335
2 262.96
3 1.6262
4 263.15
5 2.30
6 263.33
7 1.6190
8 2.28 7/8
9 2.29 1/4
10 263.35
11 1.6135
12 263.31
13 1.6135
14 263.00
15 2.30 1/4
16 2.28 3/8

17 $\frac{1.6250-1.6325}{1.6325} \times \frac{12}{1} \times 100\% = 5.51\%$ p.a.

US$ at premium: $i_{£} > i_{US\$}$

18 $\frac{1.6135-1.6335}{1.6335} \times \frac{12}{3} \times 100\% = 4.90\%$ p.a.

US$ at premium: $i_{£} > i_{US\$}$

19 Same as 18.

20 $\frac{263.135-263.20}{263.20} \times \frac{12}{3} \times 100\% = 0.10\%$ p.a.

Yen at premium: $i_{£} > i_{Yen}$

21 $\frac{262.96-263.15}{263.15} \times \frac{12}{3} \times 100\% = 0.29\%$ p.a.

Yen at premium: $i_{£} > i_{Yen}$

22 $\frac{2.2975-2.3075}{2.3075} \times \frac{12}{2} \times 100\% = 2.60\%$ p.a.

AU$ at premium: $i_{£} > i_{AUD}$

Test bank 2

2 (a) Transaction exposure in respect of export receipts from sales invoiced in foreign currency. Economic exposure in all markets against Japanese yen and the euro. This arises because the UK company concerned has its cost base in sterling (presumably) whereas competitors have theirs in yen and euros. (Note that this is a presumption since it is possible that all competitors could have their main cost inputs in dollars, for example.) If the presumption about cost bases being in the respective home currencies of the key competitors, then, should sterling's real effective exchange rate strengthen against the yen and the euro, the UK competition would lose out. Were sterling's real exchange rate to weaken, then the UK competition should gain.

(b) The economic exposure should be measured in terms of how the present value of the business alters as real exchange rates alter. This is not as easy as it sounds and would involve a lot of work (perhaps involving regression analysis, perhaps involving deductive reasoning) on cash generation, profit outturns and so on and how they change in response to exchange rate movements. This work would draw from analysis of various elasticities – but the essential point is that it is concerned with present value changes.

(c) Economic exposure may be reduced by establishing the same cost base as competitors. So relocation of manufacturing facilities to acquire cost inputs in yen and euros, of a relatively similar magnitude to competitors, should achieve a reduction in economic exposure.

3 Full quotations are:

	US$	NKr
Spot	1.2775–1.2785	11.2500–11.2600
1m	1.2719–1.2732	11.2475–11.26375
2m	1.2672–1.2686	11.2550–11.2725
3m	1.2625–1.2640	11.25875–11.2775

Answers:

(a) 11.2775
(b) If interpreted as option from day 30 to day 90 = 11.2475
If interpreted as day 60 to day 90 = 11.2550
(c) 1.2625
(d) 1.2686
(e) 11.26375
(f) 11.2475

4 (a) 13.8735
(b) 1.3900
(c) 1.3870
(d) 1.3915
(e) 13.8735
(f) 13.8575

5 The solution to this question involves us in preparing a multinational netting matrix similar to that set out below (figures in ax000):

	Receiving subsidiary				Total payments	Net	Eliminated
	Alpha	**Beta**	**Gamma**	**Delta**			
Alphaland	–	125		200	325	–	325
Betaland	250	–	100	300	650	275	375
Gammaland	–	150	–	250	400	175	225
Deltaland	200	100	125	–	425	–	425
Total receipts	450	375	225	750			
Net	125	–	–	325			
Eliminated	325	375	225	425			

The net result is that the Betaland and the Gammaland subsidiaries pay the equivalent of ax275,000 and ax175,000 respectively and this is received by the Alphaland and Deltaland subsidiaries as to the equivalent of ax125,000 and ax325,000. Transaction costs are saved on the eliminated transfers totalling the equivalent of ax1.35m.

Test bank 3

1 Justification for foreign currency borrowings might include:

	Ex ante	*Ex post*
• Matching against exposures	• versus projected foreign currency cash flows	• versus actual foreign currency cash flows
• Matching against translation exposures	• versus projected foreign currency net assets	• versus actual foreign currency net assets
• Matching against competitive exposure	• to neutralise, partially, expected foreign competition	• to neutralise, partially, actual foreign competition
• Accessing below market funds in foreign currency and covering to move liability to desired currency	• financial attractiveness of proposition	• financial attractiveness of proposition
• PPP disequilibria	• fundamental overvaluation of currency borrowed	• actual financial outturns

3 (a) Possible sources of cover

	Amount/maturity	**Comment**
Option:	$12m, 11 months	Excess cost, but opportunity for profit
	$10m, 11 months	May leave $2m exposed
	$12m, 8 months + swap	Excess cost, plus interest rate risk for months 8–11.
Forward:	$10m, 8 months + swap	May leave $2m exposed plus interest rate risk for months 8–11
	$12m, 11 months	Could be creating a $2m exposure
	$10m, 11 months	Could be leaving a $2m exposure
Combination:	$10m, 11 month forward plus $2m, 11 months option	The exposure is covered but the cost of the option may be unnecessary
	$10m, 11 months forward plus $2m, 8 months option + swap if necessary.	Exposure is covered and option premium reduced. Risk to interest rates on swap remain.

(b) Factors that could influence choice:

- *Cost*. Option premium cost increases as maturity is further away.
- *Forecasts*. If there is a firm view on rates (interest or currency) then the $12m option for eight months plus swap may be justified. The combination shown above might be appropriate if there is no firm view.
- *Year-end*. The hedge will, most likely, be in place over a year end. What are the implications of valuation of hedges in accounting and tax treatment terms?
- *Tax*. Will receipt and hedge be tax symmetrical?

4 (a) 4S has revenues in sterling and costs in US$ as well as euros, Moroccan dinars and other currencies. Relatively little of the cost may be assumed to be in sterling. This cost/revenue mismatch, coupled with the narrow net margin, at a mere 5%, means that small currency fluctuations may dramatically improve profitability or eliminate it altogether. Remember, there's also fuel costs in USD. So, at first sight, there is every reason to hedge most exposures.

(b) Should the largest competitor decide not to cover any of its exposures, this may lead to very high profitability relative to 4S or very low or negative outturns leading to either a stronger or weaker competitor. Depending on the concentration of the market this may be a very significant factor. For example, if there are only two participants, 4S and the competitor, then this would have a very significant impact on the competitive positions.

The competitor could, if rates moved favourably, offer discounts on holidays or reissue its brochure to gain market share. If the competitor gained significant market share this could impact on 4S's ability to fill the chartered and/or contracted aircraft seats and hotel accommodation. Clearly this would have an even greater impact on profitability.

While favourable exchange rate movements may lead to discounts, unfavourable movements may be more difficult to offset by surcharges, reversing the competitive situation.

There are therefore major risks to current year profitability, and to the relative strength of 4S and its major competitor for the future.

Even if the largest competitor did not hedge USD risk on fuel, surely 4S should.

(c) The question of management of the risk resolves into two issues, volume and price. Forecasts are required showing the level of demand that is reasonably certain as well as an expected level. It may be possible then to cover some of the volume risk by taking options on holiday accommodation and aircraft seats rather than straightforward contracts.

Regarding the price risk, forward contracts may be appropriate for the minimum expected sales, bearing in mind the payment profile; that is, when cash is expected to be received and when currency payments have to be made. The use of options is probably not appropriate for the majority of costs because of the premium involved relative to the narrow profit margin.

Other than these methods, it may be possible to include a surcharge option in the terms and conditions of sale. This, however, is likely to meet with customer resistance and impact further on the volume risk.

It may be possible in the future to sell holidays in the United States to provide a US$ revenue stream, or to sell in continental Europe and provide a euro revenue stream. It may also be possible to pay for hotel accommodation in either sterling or euro, although this may create further problems of hotels providing an unsatisfactory service if the exchange rate is unfavourable to them and no cover has been taken. Alternatively, the hotels may price less competitively if they are being asked to carry the risk. There are also such things as trade associations through which data on exposure and its management may be talked through and, possibly, standardised.

5 Managing the purchased call position

Action upon a rise in the underlying security

Options are potentially much more volatile than the underlying asset. It is therefore as important to take action over profits as over losses, because even substantial option profits can quickly be spirited away. Moreover, the extrinsic value will decay, reducing profits as expiry approaches, even if the asset does not decline.

The investor who is in the lucky position of owning profitable call positions has a choice of action. The choice must be made in the light of the investor's expectations of movements in the price of the underlying asset or of changes in implied volatility. The choice is:

1 The position can be closed out by selling the calls at a profit. This is appropriate if the investor considers that the underlying security price has reached its peak.

2 Sell the options and invest part of the proceeds in a series with a higher exercise price and perhaps a longer maturity. It may be possible to find a suitable exercise price/maturity combination that allows the original investment and some profit to be recouped and still open the new position.

Clearly such an aggressive attitude is appropriate only where the investor has strong expectations of a substantial upward movement in the underlying security.

3 The third action is to hold to maturity. This is risky because the underlying security may fall in price. In addition, any extrinsic value currently in the option premium will erode by expiry.

4 The fourth type of action is to convert a straight call position into a bull spread by selling an out-of-the-money call of the same expiry as the call purchased. This action is only appropriate if the underlying security is expected to rise modestly above the next exercise price. In particular, the security price should not be expected to be above the exercise price plus premium – and not below the exercise price at expiry.

Action upon a fall in the asset price

If the asset price falls and the investor changes his expectations of the price of the security, the most appropriate action is to close the position by selling the options. It must be remembered that when the option was purchased extrinsic value was paid in the premium, and extrinsic value will be eroding. To retain a position where expectations have changed means any remaining extrinsic value may be wasted. If the expectations have not changed, the option holder may:

1 Roll down the option position. However, this will entail paying extra premium as the now out-of-the-money option is sold and an at-the-money or in-the-money option purchased. It is important to consider whether this is not throwing good money after bad.
2 Roll forward the position – i.e. sell the current option and buy one with a later expiry. Again, this will entail paying more premium and should be carefully evaluated.

Action upon a change in the implied volatility

If the underlying volatility has risen, one must remember that, generally, that volatility will be mean reverting. Thus the option holder may wish to consider selling the current holding and buying an alternative option that has a lower implied volatility. However, such judgement must also take into consideration the expected movement in price and timing of that movement, and compare with the exercise price and expiry of the options with lower implied volatility.

If the implied volatility has fallen, but the option holder has unchanged expectations of the price rising, then the option position should be held. However, if the call has been purchased in the expectation of the implied volatility rising, and it has in fact fallen, then one's expectations of future implied volatility should be re-evaluated.

Managing the purchased put position

If the put position is showing a profit, the holder has a choice of any of the following actions:

1 Sell the put and realise the profit.
2 Continue to hold the put. However, as with calls, this is risky. In addition, if expiry is imminent, the position should not be held until expiry unless the holder wishes to sell assets that are held. This is because the transaction costs of exercising (i.e. on selling the asset) are much greater than closing the option position.
3 Roll down the position. Sell the in-the-money option and buy one that is at-the-money or out-of-the-money. This will provide exposure to any further fall in the price of the underlying asset, while crystallising some of the profit already gained.
4 Sell out-of-the-money puts against puts held. This converts a straight purchase into a vertical bear spread.
5 Buy a call at-the-money to protect some of the profit on the put position. The cost of the call is an insurance premium against the underlying asset rising in price. This cost will reduce the gains from further falls and will protect only if the rise is greater than the extrinsic value of the call premium.

Where the holder of a put is showing a loss, the choices are:

1 To sell the put and take the loss.
2 Roll up the option position. However, this will entail paying extra premium as the now out-of-the-money option is sold and an at-the-money or in-the-money option purchased. It is important to consider whether this is not throwing good money after bad.
3 Roll forward the position – i.e. sell the current option and buy one with a later expiry. Again, this will entail paying more premium and should be carefully evaluated.

The consideration regarding changes in implied volatility, already discussed with regard to calls, are equally applicable to long put positions.

6 (a) The bank would enter into a five-year swap to receive fixed and pay floating. A swap of Rassendylls 50 million would transform the cash flow on the debt from a fixed 10% to a floating STIBOR +2% (since the swap is 8% fixed for STIBOR). If the bank focuses on market values, it would be a better idea to contract for a swap amount of Rassendylls 53.99 million, the current market value of the debt.

(b) A = Rassendylls 100 million
L = Rassendylls 56.15 million
V = Rassendylls 46.06 million (if a Rassendylls 53.99 million swap were done)

7 No. On the loan, the bank stands to lose all interest payments $(8 + m)\%$ plus the principal of 100%. On the swap, the bank stands to lose only an interest rate differential (fixed minus floating) and no principal. Furthermore, if the floating rate rose above the fixed rate, the bank would have to pay the difference anyway, so the default of the other party does not worsen the situation. The credit quality markup on the swap μ should be much smaller than on the loan m.

8 The fourth factor is the risk-free interest rate. Future prices increase with increases in the risk-free interest rate. Investors can create portfolios having identical levels of risk by either investing directly in a diversified equity portfolio or purchasing an equivalent position in stock index futures and placing the remainder in risk-free assets. The stock portfolio earns the price appreciation of the stocks plus their dividends yield; the futures portfolio earns the price appreciation of the futures plus the risk-free interest rate. Since futures are marked to market, the futures price will equal the spot price of the stocks at the futures contract's expiration date. Market forces (arbitrage activity) result in stock index futures being priced such that their price is equal to the future value of the current spot price, using the 'cost of carry' as the discount rate. The cost of carry is the risk-free interest rate minus the dividends yield on the stock portfolio.

If the risk-free interest rate subsequently increases, it becomes more profitable to purchase the futures/treasury bill combination than to invest directly in the stocks themselves, because of the higher return on the Treasury bills now available. As a result, the price of the futures contract will be bid up until it is again equal to the future value of the current spot price of the equivalent stock price. Thus, there is a direct and positive relationship between the risk-free interest rate and futures prices.

Note that volatility is not part of the answer. Volatility would be part of the answer were it to relate to options and not to futures.

9 (a) The USD 10 million raised from the bond issue can be converted to CHF 15 million at the spot exchange rate. We therefore need to base the floating side of the swap on CHF 15 million.

Year	Bond cash flows	Swap cash flows	
1	– \$ 650,000	+ \$ 650,000	– (LIBOR – i) on CHF 15 mln
2	– \$ 650,000	+ \$ 650,000	– (LIBOR – i) on CHF 15 mln
3	– \$ 650,000	+ \$ 650,000	– (LIBOR – i) on CHF 15 mln
4	– \$ 650,000	+ \$ 650,000	– (LIBOR – i) on CHF 15 mln
5	– \$ 10,650,000	+ \$ 10,650,000 – CHF 15 mln	– (LIBOR – i) on CHF 15 mln

The NPV of the USD flows in the swap (using 6.8%) is 9,876,333. This is equivalent to CHF 14,814,499 at the spot exchange rate. If i = 0, the CHF flows in the swap would have an NPV of CHF 15,000,000. In order for the two side of the swap to match therefore, the NPV of $(i \times 15 \text{ million} \times 1/2 \times 365/360)$ each six months for 5 years must be (15,000,000 – 14,814,499) = 185,501.

Convert 4.5% per annum to an equivalent rate of 2.225% for a six-monthly period ($\sqrt{1.045} = 1.02225$). Then, using the TVM function of an HP calculator:

N = 10, 1% YR = 2.225, PV – 185,501, FV = 0 gives PMT = 20,895

You therefore need $15{,}000{,}000 \times i \times 1/2 \times 365/360 = 20{,}895$. This gives i = 0.27%. You can therefore achieve (LIBOR – 27 basis points) in CHF.

(b) Eclat might enter into the swap because:

- it has already raised USD funds at below market prices, perhaps tied to an Eximbank loan, but the currency of inflows is CHF and it wishes to hedge the CHF asset;

- it may be speculating that the CHF is likely to weaken – if this occurs, Eclat could swap back into a USD liability;
- it may need to balance group currency assets and liabilities;
- perhaps the USD liability was incurred some time ago to hedge USD assets and these assets have now been sold off;
- and probably more reasons too.

(c) What could go wrong?

- Counterparty default (choose A1 counterparty).
- Breach of covenant on USD bond (avoided by good treasury management!).

(d) If CHF asset sold in two years, this could be dealt with by:

- Reversing swap (being bought out or acquiring reverse cash flows or just swapping into logical currency liability on the basis of the firm's balance sheet as of the time of the disposal) after two years.
- Entering into a swaption now.

Probably, the first bullet point is to be preferred if the disposal is truly uncertain or conditional. If it is certain, then latter policy may be preferable – or a forward swap would, in these circumstances, be preferable.

Test bank 4

1 (a) Relevant factors are:

- assumptions underpinning the forecast;
- Swiss inflation;
- Swiss required rate of return;
- future exchange rate changes \$/CHF;
- US inflation;
- US required rate of return.

In essence the firm is concerned in the comparison of:

$$\$2\text{m now versus } \$\frac{6.5e}{(1+r)^6}\text{ million}$$

where e is the exchange rate six years out and r is the required dollar return on the investment or in purely domestic terms:

Sfr4m now versus Sfr6.5m 10 years out

(b) It is fluctuations in the real value of the Sfr that matter; fluctuations in the nominal value of the Sfr that are wholly offset by higher inflation in the US should not affect the investment. If the real value of the Sfr rises, the real dollar price of hotel service being sold by Inter-Continental should also rise. If demand for their services is elastic, which it may be given the heavy dependence of the Swiss hotel industry on foreign tourists, real dollar revenues will decline. Inelastic demand will lead to an increase in real dollar revenues. The hotel's real dollar cost of Swiss labour and services will rise. The overall impact is that if PPP holds, nominal currency changes should not affect Inter-Continental's Verbier investment. If PPP does not hold, an increase in the real exchange rate is likely to cause a decrease in the real value of the Verbier investment.

(c)
- Projection on the international Fisher effect, using nominal interest differentials between US and Swiss bonds with maturities of 10 years.
- Forecast relative US and Swiss prices and then use PPP to forecast the rate change.
- Use the forward rate if a ten-year swap can be found.

Over the long run PPP tends to hold leaving a relatively constant real exchange rate. But whether or not the exchange rates are in equilibrium at the date of Inter-Continental's initial investment is a material factor in estimating future exchange rate movements.

4 The cash flow profile of the project under consideration is set out, month by month, below:

Month (end of month)	0	1	2	3	4	5	6
Cash flow (£m)	−4	+2	–	−5	–	–	$(+7+\pi)$

(where π is the project profit)

(a) Students usually begin this question by trying to establish whether it is better to rely on LIBOR borrowing or to lock in an FRA rate, all other things being equal. From the interest rates quoted for LIBOR, the implied rates for 1 v 3 and 3 v 6 can be calculated as below:

Borrow	**Lend**
1 v 3 implied rate:	
$=\dfrac{1+(0.13875\times 3/12)}{1+(0.14\times 1/12)}$	$=\dfrac{1+(0.13625\times 3/12)}{1+(0.13875\times 1/12)}$
$=\dfrac{1.346875}{1.0116667}$	$=\dfrac{1.0340625}{1.0115625}$
$=1.0227553$	$=1.0222428$
1 v 3 rate $= 2.27553\% \times 6$ p.a.	1 v 3 rate $= 2.22428 \times 6$ p.a.
$= 13.65318\%$ p.a.	$= 13.34568\%$ p.a.
3 v 6 implied rate:	
$=\dfrac{1+(0.135\times 1/2)}{1+(0.13875\times 1/4)}$	$=\dfrac{1+(0.1325\times 1/2)}{1+(0.13625\times 1/4)}$
$=\dfrac{1.0675000}{1.0346875}$	$=\dfrac{1.06625}{1.0340625}$
$=1.0317125$	$=1.0311272$
3 v 6 rate $= 3.17125\% \times 4$ p.a.	3 v 6 rate $= 3.11272\% \times 4$ p.a.
$= 12.685\%$ p.a.	$= 12.45088\%$ p.a.

From the above calculation, the implied rates are:

1 v 3	13.65–13.35
3 v 6	12.68–12.45

It can be seen that these rates are lower than the FRA rates for comparable periods. *Ceteris paribus*, borrowing is preferred to FRA usage.

Given the cash flow profile in the question, the cheaper route is probably:

0–6	Borrow	£2m
0–1	Borrow	£2m
3 v 6	Buy FRA	£5m

Interest costs on this basis are calculated below. Remember that borrowing will be at a $^1/_2$% p.a. premium on LIBOR.

	£
0–6 $(13^1/_2 + {}^1/_2)$% p.a. on £2m	140,000
0–1 $(14 + {}^1/_2)$% p.a. on £2m	24,167
Interest thereon month 1–6 to put interest costs in terms of terminal value	1,359
3 v 6 FRA $(12.70 + {}^1/_2)$% p.a. on £5m	165,000
	330,526

There are other borrowing routes. Interest costs of some are shown below. The figures are calculated in terminal value terms. The first involves:

0–1	Borrow	£4m
0–3	Buy FRA	£2m
3–6	Buy FRA	£7m

Interest costs on this choice amount to:

	£
0–1 (14 + 1/2)% p.a. on £4m	48,333
Interest thereon 1 → 6 to put interest costs in terminal value	2,719
1 v 3 FRA (13.70 + 1/2)% p.a. on £2m	47,333
Interest thereon 3 → 6 to put interest costs in terms of terminal value	1,597
3 v 6 FRA (12.70 + 1/2)% p.a. on £7m	231,000
	330,982

Another borrowing route might be:

0–6	Borrow	£4m
1–3	Sell FRA	£2m
3 v 6	Buy FRA	£3m

Interest costs on this choice amount to:

	£
0–6 (13 1/2 + 1/2)% p.a. on £4m	280,000
1 v 3 Sell FRA (13.5)% p.a. on £2m	(45,000)
Interest thereon 3 → 6 to put interest costs in terms of terminal value	(1,491)
3 v 6 Buy FRA (12.70 + 1/2)% p.a. on £3m	99,000
	332,509

All of the above calculations reinforce the choice of action proposed originally.

(b) If interest rates were expected to fall within the first month we might adopt the original policy by borrowing £4m for one month and not doing any FRAs. This is clearly risky and the critical factor would be the strength of our opinion about the interest rate fall. Interest rate options could be built into the equation based on the original borrowing policy.

(c) If interest rates were expected to rise over the next few weeks we could finance the original borrowing suggested but add in caps or other interest rate option devices.

Test bank 5

1 Possible solutions would include:

(a) Do not worry about it if it were a pure translation exposure. However, note that gross gearing on a debt-to-equity ratio basis is 51 per cent although, on a net basis, it is only 5 per cent. Perhaps there is a covenant on gross debt-to-equity ratio level of around 50 per cent (which is not unusual) – in which case we may have to be more than concerned with the exposure.

(b) Drawdown $ debt to replace £ debt. Justified on grounds of matching against $ economic exposure. Need to generate sufficient $ inflows to service debt.

(c) Drawdown $ debt, convert to £. Pay dividend for US company to holding company?

(d) Drawdown $ debt. Lend $60m to holding company denominated in £. Repay £ debt.

2 (a) and (b) It is essential to identify and understand all the types of risks involved for the company and for the bank. The question should be raised of whether the company is so tied into this project as effective owner that it would not in practice be able to take advantage of the limited recourse package and walk away. Is the whole thing an expensive charade? If not, the following undertakings and risk management factors are relevant:

- *Completion risk*. The bank will want guarantees that:
  (i) the plant can be built for the price stated (demand fixed prices from supplier and contractor);
  (ii) the debt will be serviced if the plant is late on stream or does not perform to specifications (take liquidated damages equal to debt services from supplier/contractor; query; insure their credit; take bonds);
  (iii) they get paid if the plant is damaged (insurance).

  If there is residual risk left with the majority shareholder, recourse should be limited to a stated cash amount.
- *Sales risk*. The chemical company will have to commit to buying the product but it should avoid committing to purchase at a preset price. Risk of being tied into uncommercial sources when competitors get the benefit of failing costs, therefore commitment to be at market price.
- *Operational risk*. If the process is proven, banks may be prepared to take the risk of unexpected operating costs, but they will expect a commitment to provide management expertise.
- *Interest risk*:
  (i) During the construction period. It is probably sensible to arrange to fix (through FRAs, swaps) or cap interest rates to ensure that overall cost stays within finance available.
  (ii) During operational period. Fixing interest rates may make banks feel more secure about allowing a sales price tied to market rates.

(c) Hurdle rates for the non-recourse project. Obviously the fact that risk is reduced in the project should mean that the firm uses a lower hurdle rate than usual. It is clearly inappropriate for the normal hurdle rate to be applied to the overall pre-interest cash flows. It would probably be appropriate to look at the firm's cash out for equity versus cash back as dividends and terminal value (if any). Furthermore, the project finance alternative should be justified in terms of its NPV versus the NPV with the firm doing the project on its own with no limited resource finance.

3 There is no single answer to this question. The good answer needs to be structured to deal with:

- sources of funding;
- factors relevant to gearing;
- currency-related issues and exposure generally;
- wider issues.

Sources of funding:

- Local currency equity.
- Equity form debt/equity swaps.
- Local currency debt.
- International debt market.
- Local expatriate credit agencies.
- Parent funds.

Gearing-related issues:

- Arguments for debt:
  (i) High local taxes? Is this the case?
  (ii) Local withholding tax.
  (iii) Minimise translation losses.
  (iv) Minimise political risk if local debt.
- Arguments for equity:
  (i) Risk of low and fluctuating profit on project.
  (ii) Group policy re guarantees of subsidiary debt.
  (iii) Thin capitalisation rules.

Currency-related issues:

- Combined effects of inflation, interest rates, currency movements.
- Real costs of local debt – may be cheap.
- Mechanism for adjustments in exchange rate – automatic or big lag?
- Can hard currency income be obtained for debt servicing?
- Exposure effects – transaction, translation and economic on P & L, B/S, cash flow.
- Key question is how to protect economic value of project.
- Consider exposure issues re sales pattern, raw material costs, labour costs, plant depreciation, interest costs and overheads.

Wider issues. Discussion usually involves mention of the following:

- Debt service implications of 25/75 local/export sales split.
- Servicing hard currency purchase of equipment.
- High local tax rates suggest debt.
- Withholding taxes suggest debt.
- Export credits?
- Local versus international debt.
- Currency exposure.
- Interaction of inflation/devaluation/local interest rates.
- Currency controls.
- Thin capitalisation rules.

Solutions to multiple choice questions

Summary of answers

	Test bank				
Question	1	2	3	4	5
1	b	e*	b	d	d
2	c	c	a	d	e
3	d	e	e*	c	d
4	c	c	d	d*	c
5	a	e*	a	f	d
6	c	c	d	d*	b
7	a	b	b	d	a
8	d	a	e	d	b
9	c	b	a	c	e
10	c	a	c	c*	c

* Indicates complicated answers – see below.

Test bank 2

1 \$500,000 × 1.70 = CHF850,000
Invest at 10% gives CHF935,000
Convert to \$ 12 months forward 935,000 ÷ 1.76 = \$531,250
% return = 31,250 ÷ 500,000 × 100 = 6.25%

5 $\frac{(1+0.05)^5}{(1+0.08)^5} - 1 = -13\%$

$\$0.20\,[1+(-0.130)] = \$0.174$

Or, using $\frac{i_\$ - i_{kr}}{1+i_{kr}} = \frac{s_t - s_0}{s_0}$

We can come up with a year 1 rate of DKK/US\$ 0.194175
Repeating this constantly to year 5 gives DKK/US\$ 0.174 (approx.)

Test bank 3

3 Profit per unit = \$0.61 – \$0.58 – \$0.02
= \$0.01

Test bank 4

4 Cash flows (no expropriation)

	Year					
	0	1	2	3	4	5
Cash flow	−79	+10	+12	+16	+20	+20 → inf
PV at 17%	−79	+8.6	+8.8	+10.0	+10.7	+(117.6 × 0.5336) = 62.8

NPV (no expropriation) = −40.9 + 62.8 (1 − p)
p = probability of expropriation

Cash flows (with expropriation)

	Year					
	0	1	2	3	4	5
Cash flow	−79	+10	+12	+16	+20	+36
PV at 17%	−79	+8.6	+8.8	+10.0	+10.7	+16.4
NPV (with expropriation) = −40.9 + 16.4p						

Putting these two scenarios together, the expected NPV will be

$$-40.9 + 62.8\,(1 - p) + 16.4p$$

For break-even, we put this expression equal to zero and solve for p

$$-40.9 + 62.8 - 62.8p + 16.4p = 0$$
$$p = 47.2 \text{ per cent}$$

6 Cash flows

	Year		
	0	1	2
Cash inflows – M$ million		12	30 + x
FX rates		1.35	1.35
12% discount		0.8929	0.7973
Net present value in CHF million	−30	+7.94	17.72 + 0.5906x

Break even

$$-30 + 7.94 + 17.72 + 0.5906x = 0$$
$$4.34 = 0.5906x$$
$$x = 7.35$$

10 Gain $ = $3m per annum
Net of tax = $2m per annum
PV = $2m (annuity factor 6 year 12%)
= $2m × 4.1114
= $8.2m

Appendix 1
Present value of $1

Years hence	1%	2%	4%	6%	8%	10%	12%	14%	15%	16%	18%
1	0.990	0.980	0.962	0.943	0.926	0.909	0.893	0.877	0.870	0.862	0.847
2	0.980	0.961	0.925	0.890	0.857	0.826	0.797	0.769	0.756	0.743	0.718
3	0.971	0.942	0.889	0.840	0.794	0.751	0.712	0.675	0.658	0.641	0.609
4	0.961	0.924	0.855	0.792	0.735	0.683	0.636	0.592	0.572	0.552	0.516
5	0.951	0.906	0.822	0.747	0.681	0.621	0.567	0.519	0.497	0.476	0.437
6	0.942	0.888	0.790	0.705	0.630	0.564	0.507	0.456	0.432	0.410	0.370
7	0.933	0.871	0.760	0.665	0.583	0.513	0.452	0.400	0.376	0.354	0.314
8	0.923	0.853	0.731	0.627	0.540	0.467	0.404	0.351	0.327	0.305	0.266
9	0.914	0.837	0.703	0.592	0.500	0.424	0.361	0.308	0.284	0.263	0.225
10	0.905	0.820	0.676	0.558	0.463	0.386	0.322	0.270	0.247	0.227	0.191
11	0.896	0.804	0.650	0.527	0.429	0.350	0.287	0.237	0.215	0.195	0.162
12	0.887	0.788	0.625	0.497	0.397	0.319	0.257	0.208	0.187	0.168	0.137
13	0.879	0.773	0.601	0.469	0.368	0.290	0.229	0.182	0.163	0.145	0.116
14	0.870	0.758	0.577	0.442	0.340	0.263	0.205	0.160	0.141	0.125	0.099
15	0.861	0.743	0.555	0.417	0.315	0.239	0.183	0.140	0.123	0.108	0.084
16	0.853	0.728	0.534	0.394	0.292	0.218	0.163	0.123	0.107	0.093	0.071
17	0.844	0.714	0.513	0.371	0.270	0.198	0.146	0.108	0.093	0.080	0.060
18	0.836	0.700	0.494	0.350	0.250	0.180	0.130	0.095	0.081	0.069	0.051
19	0.828	0.686	0.475	0.331	0.232	0.164	0.116	0.083	0.070	0.060	0.043
20	0.820	0.673	0.456	0.312	0.215	0.149	0.104	0.073	0.061	0.051	0.037
21	0.811	0.660	0.439	0.294	0.199	0.135	0.093	0.064	0.053	0.044	0.031
22	0.803	0.647	0.422	0.278	0.184	0.123	0.083	0.056	0.046	0.038	0.026
23	0.795	0.634	0.406	0.262	0.170	0.112	0.074	0.049	0.040	0.033	0.022
24	0.788	0.622	0.390	0.247	0.158	0.102	0.066	0.043	0.035	0.028	0.019
25	0.780	0.610	0.375	0.233	0.146	0.092	0.059	0.038	0.030	0.024	0.016
26	0.772	0.598	0.361	0.220	0.135	0.084	0.053	0.033	0.026	0.021	0.014
27	0.764	0.586	0.347	0.207	0.125	0.076	0.047	0.029	0.023	0.018	0.011
28	0.757	0.574	0.333	0.196	0.116	0.069	0.042	0.026	0.020	0.016	0.010
29	0.749	0.563	0.321	0.185	0.107	0.063	0.037	0.022	0.017	0.014	0.008
30	0.742	0.552	0.308	0.174	0.099	0.057	0.033	0.020	0.015	0.012	0.007
40	0.672	0.453	0.208	0.097	0.046	0.022	0.011	0.005	0.004	0.003	0.001
50	0.608	0.372	0.141	0.054	0.021	0.009	0.003	0.001	0.001	0.001	

Years hence	20%	22%	24%	25%	26%	28%	30%	35%	40%	45%	50%
1	0.833	0.820	0.806	0.800	0.794	0.781	0.769	0.741	0.714	0.690	0.667
2	0.694	0.672	0.650	0.640	0.630	0.610	0.592	0.549	0.510	0.476	0.444
3	0.579	0.551	0.524	0.512	0.500	0.477	0.455	0.406	0.364	0.328	0.296
4	0.482	0.451	0.423	0.410	0.397	0.373	0.350	0.301	0.260	0.226	0.198
5	0.402	0.370	0.341	0.328	0.315	0.291	0.269	0.223	0.186	0.156	0.132
6	0.335	0.303	0.275	0.262	0.250	0.227	0.207	0.165	0.133	0.108	0.088
7	0.279	0.249	0.222	0.210	0.198	0.178	0.159	0.122	0.095	0.074	0.059
8	0.233	0.204	0.179	0.168	0.157	0.139	0.123	0.091	0.068	0.051	0.039
9	0.194	0.167	0.144	0.134	0.125	0.108	0.094	0.067	0.048	0.035	0.026
10	0.162	0.137	0.116	0.107	0.099	0.085	0.073	0.050	0.035	0.024	0.017
11	0.135	0.112	0.094	0.086	0.079	0.066	0.056	0.037	0.025	0.017	0.012
12	0.112	0.092	0.076	0.069	0.062	0.052	0.043	0.027	0.018	0.012	0.008
13	0.093	0.075	0.061	0.055	0.050	0.040	0.033	0.020	0.013	0.008	0.005
14	0.078	0.062	0.049	0.044	0.039	0.032	0.025	0.015	0.009	0.006	0.003
15	0.065	0.051	0.040	0.035	0.031	0.025	0.020	0.011	0.006	0.004	0.002
16	0.054	0.042	0.032	0.028	0.025	0.019	0.015	0.008	0.005	0.003	0.002
17	0.045	0.034	0.026	0.023	0.020	0.015	0.012	0.006	0.003	0.002	0.001
18	0.038	0.028	0.021	0.018	0.016	0.012	0.009	0.005	0.002	0.001	0.001
19	0.031	0.023	0.017	0.014	0.012	0.009	0.007	0.003	0.002	0.001	
20	0.026	0.019	0.014	0.012	0.010	0.009	0.005	0.002	0.001	0.001	
21	0.022	0.015	0.011	0.009	0.008	0.006	0.004	0.002	0.001		
22	0.018	0.013	0.009	0.007	0.006	0.004	0.003	0.001	0.001		
23	0.015	0.010	0.007	0.006	0.005	0.003	0.002	0.001			
24	0.013	0.008	0.006	0.005	0.004	0.003	0.002	0.001			
25	0.010	0.007	0.005	0.004	0.003	0.002	0.001	0.001			
26	0.009	0.006	0.004	0.003	0.002	0.002	0.001				
27	0.007	0.005	0.003	0.002	0.002	0.001	0.001				
28	0.006	0.004	0.002	0.002	0.002	0.001	0.001				
29	0.005	0.003	0.002	0.002	0.001	0.001	0.001				
30	0.004	0.003	0.002	0.001	0.001	0.001					
40	0.001										
50											

Appendix 2

Present value of $1 received annually for *n* years

Years (n)	1%	2%	4%	6%	8%	10%	12%	14%	15%	16%	18%
1	0.990	0.980	0.962	0.943	0.926	0.909	0.893	0.877	0.870	0.862	0.847
2	1.970	1.942	1.886	1.833	1.783	1.736	1.690	1.647	1.626	1.605	1.566
3	2.941	2.884	2.775	2.673	2.577	2.487	2.402	2.322	2.283	2.246	2.174
4	3.902	3.808	3.630	3.465	3.312	3.170	3.037	2.914	2.855	2.798	2.690
5	4.853	4.713	4.452	4.212	3.993	3.791	3.605	3.433	3.352	3.274	3.127
6	5.795	5.601	5.242	4.917	4.623	4.355	4.111	3.889	3.784	3.685	3.498
7	6.728	6.472	6.002	5.582	5.206	4.868	4.564	4.288	4.160	4.039	3.812
8	7.652	7.325	6.733	6.210	5.747	5.335	4.968	4.639	4.487	4.344	4.078
9	8.566	8.162	7.435	6.082	6.247	5.759	5.328	4.946	4.772	4.607	4.303
10	9.471	8.983	8.111	7.360	6.710	6.145	5.650	5.216	5.019	4.833	4.494
11	10.368	9.787	8.760	7.887	7.139	6.495	5.937	5.453	5.234	5.029	4.656
12	11.255	10.575	9.385	8.384	7.536	6.814	6.194	5.660	5.421	5.197	4.793
13	12.134	11.343	9.986	8.853	7.904	7.103	6.424	5.842	5.583	5.342	4.910
14	13.004	12.106	10.563	9.295	8.244	7.367	6.628	6.002	5.724	5.468	5.008
15	13.865	12.849	11.118	9.712	8.559	7.606	6.811	6.142	5.847	5.575	5.092
16	14.718	13.578	11.652	10.106	8.851	7.824	6.974	6.265	5.954	5.669	5.162
17	15.562	14.292	12.166	10.477	9.122	8.022	7.120	6.373	6.047	5.749	5.222
18	16.398	14.992	12.659	10.828	9.372	8.201	7.250	6.467	6.128	5.818	5.273
19	17.226	15.678	13.134	11.158	9.604	8.365	7.366	6.550	6.198	5.877	5.316
20	18.046	16.351	13.590	11.470	9.818	8.514	7.469	6.623	6.259	5.929	5.353
21	18.857	17.011	14.029	11.764	10.017	8.649	7.562	6.687	6.312	5.973	5.384
22	19.660	17.658	14.451	12.042	10.201	8.772	7.645	6.743	6.359	6.011	5.410
23	20.456	18.292	14.857	12.303	10.371	8.883	7.718	6.792	6.399	6.044	5.432
24	21.243	18.914	15.247	12.550	10.529	8.985	7.784	6.835	6.434	6.073	5.451
25	22.023	19.523	15.622	12.783	10.675	9.077	7.843	6.873	6.464	6.097	5.467
26	22.795	20.121	15.983	13.003	10.810	9.161	7.896	6.906	6.791	6.118	5.480
27	23.560	20.707	16.330	13.211	10.935	9.237	7.943	6.935	6.514	6.136	5.492
28	24.316	21.281	16.663	13.406	11.051	9.037	7.984	6.961	6.534	6.152	5.502
29	25.066	21.844	16.984	13.591	11.158	9.370	8.022	6.983	6.551	6.166	5.510
30	25.808	22.396	17.292	13.765	11.258	9.427	8.055	7.003	6.566	6.177	5.517
40	32.835	27.355	19.793	15.046	11.925	9.779	8.244	7.105	6.642	6.234	5.548
50	39.196	31.424	21.482	15.762	12.234	9.915	8.304	7.133	6.661	6.246	5.554

Years (n)	20%	22%	24%	25%	26%	28%	30%	35%	40%	45%	50%
1	0.833	0.820	0.806	0.800	0.794	0.781	0.769	0.741	0.714	0.690	0.667
2	1.528	1.492	1.457	1.440	1.424	1.392	1.361	1.289	1.224	1.165	1.111
3	2.106	2.042	1.981	1.952	1.923	1.868	1.816	1.696	1.598	1.493	1.407
4	2.589	2.494	2.404	2.362	2.320	2.241	2.166	1.997	1.849	1.720	1.605
5	2.991	2.864	2.745	2.689	2.635	2.535	2.436	2.220	2.035	1.876	1.737
6	3.326	3.167	3.020	2.951	2.885	2.759	2.643	2.385	2.168	1.983	1.824
7	3.605	3.416	3.242	3.161	3.083	2.937	2.802	2.508	2.263	2.057	1.883
8	3.837	3.619	3.421	3.329	3.241	3.076	2.925	2.598	2.331	2.108	1.922
9	4.031	3.786	3.566	3.463	3.366	3.184	3.019	2.665	2.379	2.144	1.948
10	4.192	3.923	3.682	3.571	3.465	3.269	3.092	2.715	2.414	2.168	1.965
11	4.327	4.035	3.776	3.656	3.544	3.335	3.147	2.752	2.438	2.185	1.977
12	4.439	4.127	3.851	3.725	3.606	3.387	3.190	2.779	2.456	2.196	1.985
13	4.533	4.203	3.912	3.780	3.656	3.427	3.223	2.799	2.468	2.204	1.990
14	4.611	4.265	3.962	3.824	3.695	3.459	3.249	2.814	2.477	2.210	1.993
15	4.675	4.315	4.001	3.859	3.726	3.483	3.268	2.825	2.484	2.214	1.995
16	4.730	4.357	4.033	3.887	3.751	3.503	3.283	2.834	2.489	2.216	1.997
17	4.775	4.391	4.059	3.910	3.771	3.518	3.295	2.840	2.492	2.218	1.998
18	4.812	4.419	4.080	3.928	3.786	3.529	3.304	2.844	2.494	2.219	1.999
19	4.844	4.442	4.097	3.942	3.799	3.539	3.311	2.848	2.496	2.220	1.999
20	4.870	4.460	4.110	3.954	3.808	3.546	3.316	2.850	2.497	2.221	1.999
21	4.891	4.476	4.121	3.963	3.816	3.551	3.320	2.852	2.498	2.221	2.000
22	4.909	4.488	4.130	3.970	3.822	3.556	3.323	2.853	2.498	2.222	2.000
23	4.925	4.499	4.137	3.976	3.827	3.559	3.325	2.854	2.499	2.222	2.000
24	4.937	4.507	4.143	3.981	3.831	3.562	3.327	2.855	2.499	2.222	2.000
25	4.948	4.514	4.147	3.985	3.834	3.564	3.329	2.856	2.499	2.222	2.000
26	4.956	4.520	4.151	3.988	3.837	3.566	3.330	2.856	2.500	2.222	2.000
27	4.964	4.524	4.154	3.990	3.839	3.567	3.331	2.856	2.500	2.222	2.000
28	4.970	4.528	4.157	3.992	3.840	3.568	3.331	2.857	2.500	2.222	2.000
29	4.975	4.531	4.159	3.994	3.841	3.569	3.332	2.857	2.500	2.222	2.000
30	4.979	4.534	4.160	3.995	3.842	3.569	3.332	2.857	2.500	2.222	2.000
40	4.997	4.544	4.166	3.999	3.846	3.571	3.333	2.857	2.500	2.222	2.000
50	4.999	4.545	4.167	4.000	3.846	3.571	3.333	2.857	2.500	2.222	2.000

Appendix 3
Table of areas under the normal curve

Graph of an Appendix 3 table value

z	0.00	0.01	0.02	0.03	0.04	0.05	0.06	0.07	0.08	0.09
0.0	0.0000	0.0040	0.0080	0.0120	0.0160	0.0199	0.0239	0.0279	0.0319	0.0359
0.1	0.0398	0.0438	0.0478	0.0517	0.0557	0.0596	0.0636	0.0675	0.0714	0.0753
0.2	0.0793	0.0832	0.0871	0.0910	0.0948	0.0987	0.1026	0.1064	0.1103	0.1141
0.3	0.1179	0.1217	0.1255	0.1293	0.1331	0.1368	0.1406	0.1443	0.1480	0.1517
0.4	0.1554	0.1591	0.1628	0.1664	0.1700	0.1736	0.1772	0.1808	0.1844	0.1879
0.5	0.1915	0.1950	0.1985	0.2019	0.2054	0.2088	0.2123	0.2157	0.2190	0.2224
0.6	0.2257	0.2291	0.2324	0.2357	0.2389	0.2422	0.2454	0.2486	0.2517	0.2549
0.7	0.2580	0.2611	0.2642	0.2673	0.2704	0.2734	0.2764	0.2794	0.2823	0.2852
0.8	0.2881	0.2910	0.2939	0.2967	0.2995	0.3023	0.3051	0.3078	0.3106	0.3133
0.9	0.3159	0.3186	0.3212	0.3238	0.3264	0.3289	0.3315	0.3340	0.3365	0.3389
1.0	0.3413	0.3438	0.3461	0.3485	0.3508	0.3531	0.3554	0.3577	0.3599	0.3621
1.1	0.3643	0.3665	0.3686	0.3708	0.3729	0.3749	0.3770	0.3790	0.3810	0.3830
1.2	0.3849	0.3869	0.3888	0.3907	0.3925	0.3944	0.3962	0.3980	0.3997	0.4015
1.3	0.4032	0.4049	0.4066	0.4082	0.4099	0.4115	0.4131	0.4147	0.4162	0.4177
1.4	0.4192	0.4207	0.4222	0.4236	0.4251	0.4265	0.4279	0.4292	0.4306	0.4319
1.5	0.4332	0.4345	0.4357	0.4370	0.4382	0.4394	0.4406	0.4418	0.4429	0.4441
1.6	0.4452	0.4463	0.4474	0.4484	0.4495	0.4505	0.4515	0.4525	0.4535	0.4545
1.7	0.4554	0.4564	0.4573	0.4582	0.4591	0.4599	0.4608	0.4616	0.4625	0.4633
1.8	0.4641	0.4649	0.4656	0.4664	0.4671	0.4678	0.4686	0.4693	0.4699	0.4706
1.9	0.4713	0.4719	0.4726	0.4732	0.4738	0.4744	0.4750	0.4756	0.4761	0.4767
2.0	0.4772	0.4778	0.4783	0.4788	0.4793	0.4798	0.4803	0.4808	0.4812	0.4817
2.1	0.4821	0.4826	0.4830	0.4834	0.4838	0.4842	0.4846	0.4850	0.4854	0.4857
2.2	0.4861	0.4864	0.4868	0.4871	0.4875	0.4878	0.4881	0.4884	0.4887	0.4890
2.3	0.4893	0.4896	0.4898	0.4901	0.4904	0.4906	0.4909	0.4911	0.4913	0.4916
2.4	0.4918	0.4920	0.4922	0.4925	0.4927	0.4929	0.4931	0.4932	0.4934	0.4936
2.5	0.4938	0.4940	0.4941	0.4943	0.4945	0.4946	0.4948	0.4949	0.4951	0.4952
2.6	0.4953	0.4955	0.4956	0.4957	0.4959	0.4960	0.4961	0.4962	0.4963	0.4964
2.7	0.4965	0.4966	0.4967	0.4968	0.4969	0.4970	0.4971	0.4972	0.4973	0.4974
2.8	0.4974	0.4975	0.4976	0.4977	0.4977	0.4978	0.4979	0.4979	0.4980	0.4981
2.9	0.4981	0.4982	0.4982	0.4983	0.4984	0.4984	0.4985	0.4985	0.4986	0.4986
3.0	0.4987	0.4987	0.4987	0.4988	0.4988	0.4989	0.4989	0.4989	0.4990	0.4990

Appendix 4
Black and Scholes value of call option expressed as a percentage of the share price

Square root of cumulative variance, that is $\sigma\sqrt{t}$

	Share price divided by present value of exercise price, that is $S/PV(E)$														
	0.30	**0.35**	**0.40**	**0.45**	**0.50**	**0.55**	**0.60**	**0.65**	**0.70**	**0.75**	**0.80**	**0.82**	**0.84**	**0.86**	**0.88**
0.05	0.0	0.0	0.0	0.0	0.0	0.0	0.0	0.0	0.0	0.0	0.0	0.0	0.0	0.0	0.0
0.10	0.0	0.0	0.0	0.0	0.0	0.0	0.0	0.0	0.0	0.0	0.0	0.1	0.2	0.3	0.5
0.15	0.0	0.0	0.0	0.0	0.0	0.0	0.0	0.0	0.1	0.2	0.5	0.7	1.0	1.3	1.7
0.20	0.0	0.0	0.0	0.0	0.0	0.0	0.0	0.1	0.4	0.8	1.5	1.9	2.3	2.8	3.4
0.25	0.0	0.0	0.0	0.0	0.0	0.1	0.2	0.5	1.0	0.8	2.8	3.3	3.9	4.5	5.2
0.30	0.0	0.0	0.0	0.1	0.1	0.3	0.7	1.2	2.0	3.1	4.4	5.0	5.7	6.3	7.0
0.35	0.0	0.0	0.1	0.2	0.4	0.8	1.4	2.3	3.3	4.6	6.2	6.8	7.5	8.2	9.0
0.40	0.0	0.1	0.2	0.5	0.9	1.6	2.4	3.5	4.8	6.3	8.0	8.7	9.4	10.2	11.0
0.45	0.1	0.2	0.5	1.0	1.7	2.6	3.7	5.0	6.5	8.1	9.9	10.6	11.4	12.2	12.9
0.50	0.2	0.5	1.0	1.7	2.6	3.7	5.1	6.6	8.2	10.0	11.8	12.6	13.4	14.2	14.9
0.55	0.5	1.0	1.7	2.6	3.8	5.1	6.6	8.3	10.0	11.9	13.8	14.6	15.4	16.1	16.9
0.60	0.9	1.6	2.5	3.7	5.1	6.6	8.3	10.1	11.9	13.8	15.8	16.6	17.4	18.1	18.9
0.65	1.4	2.4	3.6	4.9	6.5	8.2	10.0	11.9	13.8	15.8	17.8	18.6	19.3	20.1	20.9
0.70	2.1	3.3	4.7	6.3	8.1	9.9	11.9	13.8	15.8	17.8	19.8	20.6	21.3	22.1	22.9
0.75	3.0	4.4	6.1	7.9	9.8	11.7	13.7	15.8	17.8	19.8	21.8	22.5	23.3	24.1	24.8
0.80	4.0	5.7	7.5	9.5	11.5	13.6	15.7	17.7	19.8	21.8	23.7	24.5	25.3	26.0	26.8
0.85	5.1	7.1	9.1	11.2	13.3	15.5	17.6	19.7	21.8	23.8	25.7	26.5	27.2	28.0	28.7
0.90	6.4	8.5	10.7	13.0	15.2	17.4	19.6	21.7	23.8	25.8	27.2	28.4	29.2	29.9	30.6
0.95	7.8	10.1	12.5	14.8	17.1	19.4	21.6	23.7	25.7	27.7	29.6	30.4	31.1	31.8	32.5
1.00	9.3	11.8	14.3	16.7	19.1	21.4	23.6	25.7	27.7	29.7	31.6	32.3	33.0	33.7	34.4
1.05	10.9	13.6	16.1	18.6	21.0	23.3	25.6	27.7	29.7	31.6	33.5	34.2	34.9	35.6	36.2
1.10	12.6	15.4	18.0	20.6	23.0	25.3	27.5	29.6	31.6	33.5	35.4	36.1	36.7	37.4	38.1
1.15	14.4	17.2	20.0	22.5	25.0	27.3	29.5	31.6	33.6	35.4	37.2	37.9	38.6	39.2	39.9
1.20	16.2	19.1	21.9	24.5	27.0	29.3	31.5	33.6	35.5	37.3	39.1	39.7	40.4	41.0	41.7
1.25	18.1	21.1	23.9	26.5	29.0	31.3	33.5	35.5	37.4	39.2	40.9	41.5	42.2	42.8	43.4
1.30	20.0	23.0	25.9	28.5	31.0	33.3	35.4	37.4	39.3	41.0	42.7	43.3	43.9	44.5	45.1
1.35	21.9	25.0	27.9	30.5	33.0	35.2	37.3	39.3	41.1	42.8	44.4	45.1	45.7	46.3	46.8
1.40	23.9	27.0	29.9	32.5	34.9	37.1	39.2	41.1	42.9	44.6	46.2	46.8	47.4	47.9	48.5
1.45	25.8	29.0	31.9	34.5	36.9	39.1	41.1	43.0	44.7	46.4	47.9	48.5	49.0	49.6	50.1
1.50	27.8	31.0	33.8	36.4	38.8	40.9	42.9	44.8	46.5	48.1	49.6	50.1	50.7	51.2	51.8
1.55	29.8	33.0	35.8	38.4	40.7	42.8	44.8	46.6	48.2	49.8	51.2	51.8	52.3	52.8	53.3
1.60	31.8	35.0	37.8	40.3	42.6	44.6	46.5	48.3	49.9	51.4	52.8	53.4	53.9	54.4	54.9
1.65	33.8	36.9	39.7	42.2	44.4	46.4	48.3	50.0	51.6	53.1	54.4	54.9	55.4	55.9	56.4
1.70	35.8	38.9	41.6	44.0	46.2	48.2	50.0	51.7	53.2	54.7	56.0	56.5	57.0	57.5	57.9
1.75	37.7	40.8	43.5	45.9	48.0	50.0	51.7	53.4	54.8	56.2	57.5	58.0	58.5	58.9	59.4
2.00	47.3	50.1	52.5	54.6	56.5	58.2	59.7	61.1	62.4	63.6	64.6	65.0	65.4	65.8	66.2
2.25	56.1	58.6	60.7	62.5	64.1	65.6	66.8	68.0	69.1	70.0	70.9	71.5	71.6	71.9	72.2
2.50	64.0	66.1	67.9	69.4	70.8	72.0	73.1	74.0	74.9	75.7	76.4	76.7	77.0	77.2	77.5
2.75	70.9	72.7	74.2	75.4	76.6	77.5	78.4	79.2	79.9	80.5	81.1	81.4	81.6	81.8	82.0
3.00	76.9	78.3	79.5	80.5	81.4	82.2	82.9	83.5	84.1	84.6	85.1	85.3	85.4	85.6	85.8
3.50	86.0	86.9	87.6	88.3	88.8	89.3	89.7	90.1	90.5	90.8	91.1	91.2	91.3	91.4	91.5
4.00	92.0	92.5	92.9	93.3	93.6	93.9	94.2	94.4	94.6	94.8	94.9	95.0	95.0	05.1	95.2
4.50	95.7	96.0	96.2	96.4	96.6	96.7	96.9	97.0	97.1	97.2	97.3	97.3	97.3	97.4	97.4
5.00	97.8	97.9	98.1	98.2	98.3	98.3	98.4	98.5	98.5	98.6	98.6	98.6	98.6	98.7	98.7
6.00	99.5	99.5	99.6	99.6	99.6	99.6	99.7	99.7	99.7	99.7	99.7	99.7	99.7	99.7	99.7

Square root of cumulative variance, that is $\sigma\sqrt{t}$

	Share price divided by present value of exercise price, that is $S/PV(E)$														
	0.90	**0.92**	**0.94**	**0.96**	**0.98**	**1.00**	**1.02**	**1.04**	**1.06**	**1.08**	**1.10**	**1.12**	**1.14**	**1.16**	**1.18**
0.05	0.0	0.1	0.3	0.6	1.2	2.0	3.1	4.5	6.0	7.5	9.1	10.7	12.3	13.8	15.3
0.10	0.8	1.2	1.7	2.3	3.1	4.0	5.0	6.1	7.3	8.6	10.0	11.3	12.7	14.1	15.4
0.15	2.2	2.8	3.5	4.2	5.1	6.0	7.0	8.0	9.1	10.2	11.4	12.6	13.8	15.0	16.2
0.20	4.0	0.7	5.4	6.2	7.1	8.0	8.9	9.9	10.9	11.9	13.0	14.1	15.2	16.3	17.4
0.25	5.9	6.6	7.4	8.2	9.1	9.9	10.9	11.8	12.8	13.7	14.7	15.7	16.7	17.7	18.7
0.30	7.8	8.6	9.4	10.2	11.1	11.9	12.8	13.7	14.6	15.6	16.5	17.4	18.4	19.3	20.3
0.35	9.8	10.6	11.4	12.2	13.0	13.9	14.8	15.6	16.5	17.4	18.3	19.2	20.1	21.0	21.9
0.40	11.7	12.5	13.4	14.2	15.0	15.9	16.7	17.5	18.4	19.2	20.1	20.9	21.8	22.6	23.5
0.45	13.7	14.5	15.3	16.2	17.0	17.8	18.6	19.4	20.3	21.1	21.9	22.7	23.5	24.3	25.1
0.50	15.7	16.5	17.3	18.1	18.9	19.7	20.5	21.3	22.1	22.9	23.7	24.5	25.3	26.1	26.8
0.55	17.7	18.5	19.3	20.1	20.9	21.7	22.4	23.2	24.0	24.8	25.5	26.3	27.0	27.8	28.5
0.60	19.7	20.5	21.3	22.0	22.8	23.6	24.3	25.1	25.8	26.6	27.3	28.1	28.8	29.5	30.2
0.65	21.7	22.5	23.2	24.0	24.7	25.5	26.2	27.0	27.7	28.4	29.1	27.8	30.5	31.2	31.9
0.70	23.6	24.4	25.2	25.9	26.6	27.4	28.1	28.8	29.5	30.2	30.9	31.6	32.6	32.9	33.6
0.75	25.6	26.3	27.1	27.8	28.5	29.2	29.9	30.6	31.3	32.0	32.7	33.3	34.0	34.6	35.3
0.80	27.5	28.3	29.0	29.7	30.4	31.1	31.8	32.4	33.1	33.8	34.4	35.1	35.7	36.3	36.9
0.85	29.4	30.2	30.9	31.6	32.2	32.9	33.6	34.2	34.9	35.5	36.2	36.8	37.4	38.0	38.6
0.90	31.3	32.0	32.7	33.4	34.1	34.7	35.4	36.0	36.6	37.3	37.9	38.5	39.1	39.6	40.2
0.95	33.2	33.9	34.6	35.2	35.9	36.5	37.2	37.8	38.4	39.0	39.6	40.1	40.7	41.3	41.8
1.00	35.1	35.7	36.4	37.0	37.7	38.3	38.9	39.5	40.1	40.7	41.2	41.8	42.4	42.9	43.4
1.05	36.9	37.6	38.2	38.8	39.4	40.0	40.6	41.2	41.8	42.4	42.9	43.5	44.0	44.5	45.0
1.10	38.7	39.3	40.0	40.6	41.2	41.8	42.3	42.9	43.5	44.0	44.5	45.1	45.6	46.1	46.6
1.15	40.5	41.1	41.7	42.3	42.9	43.5	44.0	44.6	45.1	45.6	46.2	46.7	47.2	47.7	48.2
1.20	42.3	42.9	43.5	44.0	44.6	45.1	45.7	46.2	46.7	47.3	47.8	48.3	48.7	49.2	49.7
1.25	44.0	44.6	45.2	45.7	46.3	46.8	47.3	47.8	48.4	48.8	49.3	49.8	50.3	50.7	51.2
1.30	45.7	46.3	46.8	47.4	47.9	48.4	48.9	49.4	49.9	50.4	50.9	51.3	51.8	52.2	52.7
1.35	47.4	47.9	48.5	49.0	49.5	50.0	50.5	51.0	51.5	52.0	52.4	52.9	53.3	53.7	54.1
1.40	49.0	49.6	50.1	50.6	51.1	51.6	52.1	52.6	53.0	53.5	53.9	54.3	54.8	55.2	55.6
1.45	50.7	51.2	51.7	52.2	52.7	53.2	53.6	54.1	54.5	55.0	55.4	55.8	56.2	56.6	57.0
1.50	52.3	52.8	53.5	53.7	54.2	54.7	55.1	55.6	56.0	56.4	56.8	57.2	57.6	58.0	58.4
1.55	53.8	54.3	54.8	55.3	55.7	56.2	56.6	57.0	57.4	57.8	58.2	58.6	59.0	59.4	59.7
1.60	55.4	55.9	56.3	56.8	57.2	57.6	58.0	58.5	58.9	59.2	59.6	60.0	60.4	60.7	61.1
1.65	56.9	57.3	57.8	58.2	58.6	59.1	59.5	59.9	60.2	60.6	61.0	61.4	61.7	62.1	62.4
1.70	58.4	58.8	59.2	59.7	60.1	60.5	60.9	61.2	61.6	62.0	62.3	62.7	63.0	63.4	63.7
1.75	59.8	60.7	60.7	61.1	61.5	61.8	62.2	62.6	62.9	63.3	63.6	64.0	64.3	64.6	64.9
2.00	66.6	66.9	67.3	67.6	67.9	68.3	68.6	68.9	69.2	69.5	69.8	70.0	70.3	70.6	70.8
2.25	72.5	72.8	73.1	73.4	73.7	73.9	74.2	74.4	74.7	74.9	75.2	75.4	75.6	75.8	76.0
2.50	77.7	78.0	78.2	78.4	78.7	78.9	79.1	79.3	79.5	79.7	79.9	80.0	80.2	80.4	80.6
2.75	82.2	82.4	82.6	82.7	82.9	83.1	83.3	83.4	83.6	83.7	83.9	84.0	84.2	84.3	84.4
3.00	85.9	86.1	86.2	86.4	86.5	86.6	86.8	86.9	87.0	87.1	87.3	87.4	87.5	87.6	87.7
3.50	91.6	91.6	91.7	91.8	91.9	92.0	92.1	92.1	92.2	92.3	92.4	92.4	92.5	92.6	92.6
4.00	95.2	95.3	95.3	95.4	95.4	95.4	95.5	95.5	95.6	95.6	95.7	95.7	95.7	95.8	95.8
4.50	97.4	97.5	97.5	97.5	97.5	97.6	97.6	97.6	97.6	97.6	97.7	97.7	97.7	97.7	97.8
5.00	98.7	98.7	09.7	98.7	98.7	98.8	98.8	98.8	98.8	98.8	98.8	98.8	98.8	98.8	98.8
6.00	99.7	99.7	99.7	99.7	99.7	99.7	99.7	99.7	99.7	99.7	99.7	99.7	99.7	99.7	99.8

Square root of cumulative variance, that is $\sigma\sqrt{t}$

	Share price divided by present value of exercise price, that is *S/PV(E)*									
	1.20	**1.25**	**1.30**	**1.35**	**1.40**	**1.45**	**1.50**	**1.75**	**2.00**	**2.50**
0.05	16.7	20.0	23.1	25.9	28.6	31.0	33.3	42.9	50.0	60.0
0.10	16.8	20.0	23.1	25.9	28.6	31.0	33.3	42.9	50.0	60.0
0.15	17.4	20.4	23.3	26.0	28.6	31.0	33.3	42.9	50.0	60.0
0.20	18.5	21.2	23.9	26.4	28.9	31.2	33.5	42.9	50.0	60.0
0.25	19.8	22.3	24.7	27.1	29.4	31.7	33.8	42.9	50.0	60.0
0.30	21.2	23.5	25.8	28.1	30.2	32.3	34.3	43.1	50.1	60.0
0.35	22.7	24.9	27.1	29.2	31.2	33.2	35.1	43.5	50.2	60.0
0.40	24.3	26.4	28.4	30.4	32.3	34.2	36.0	44.0	50.5	60.1
0.45	25.9	27.9	29.8	31.7	33.5	35.3	37.0	44.6	50.8	60.2
0.50	27.6	29.5	31.3	33.1	34.8	36.4	38.1	45.3	51.3	50.4
0.55	29.2	31.0	32.8	34.5	36.1	37.7	39.2	46.1	51.9	60.7
0.60	30.9	32.6	34.3	35.9	37.5	39.0	40.4	47.0	52.5	61.0
0.65	32.6	34.2	35.8	37.4	38.9	40.3	41.7	48.0	53.3	61.4
0.70	34.2	35.8	37.3	38.8	40.3	41.6	43.0	49.0	54.0	61.9
0.75	35.9	37.4	38.9	40.3	41.7	43.0	44.3	50.0	54.9	62.4
0.80	37.5	39.0	40.4	41.8	43.1	44.4	45.6	51.1	55.8	63.0
0.85	39.2	40.6	41.9	43.3	44.5	45.8	46.9	52.2	56.7	63.6
0.90	40.8	42.1	43.5	44.7	46.0	47.1	48.3	53.3	57.6	64.3
0.95	42.4	43.7	43.5	44.7	46.0	48.5	49.6	54.5	58.6	65.0
1.00	44.0	45.2	46.5	47.6	48.8	49.9	50.9	55.6	59.5	65.7
1.05	45.5	46.8	48.0	49.1	50.2	51.2	52.2	56.7	60.5	66.5
1.10	47.1	48.3	49.4	50.5	51.6	52.6	53.5	57.9	61.5	67.2
1.15	48.6	49.8	50.9	51.9	52.9	53.9	54.9	59.0	62.5	68.0
1.20	50.1	51.3	52.3	53.4	54.3	55.2	56.1	60.2	63.5	68.8
1.25	51.6	52.7	53.7	54.7	55.7	56.6	57.4	61.3	64.5	69.6
1.30	53.1	54.1	55.1	56.1	57.0	57.9	58.7	62.4	65.5	70.4
1.35	54.6	55.6	56.5	57.4	58.3	59.1	59.9	63.5	66.5	71.1
1.40	56.0	56.9	57.9	58.7	59.6	60.4	61.2	64.6	67.5	71.9
1.45	57.4	58.3	59.2	6.00	60.9	61.6	62.4	65.7	68.4	72.7
1.50	58.8	59.7	60.5	61.3	62.1	62.9	63.6	66.8	69.4	73.5
1.55	60.1	61.0	61.8	62.6	63.3	64.1	64.7	67.8	70.3	74.3
1.60	61.4	62.3	63.1	63.8	64.5	65.2	65.9	68.8	71.3	75.1
1.65	62.7	63.5	64.3	65.0	65.7	66.4	67.0	69.9	72.2	72.9
1.70	64.0	64.8	65.5	66.2	66.9	67.5	68.2	70.9	73.1	76.6
1.75	65.3	66.0	66.7	67.4	68.0	68.7	69.2	71.9	74.0	77.4
2.00	71.1	71.7	72.3	72.9	73.4	73.9	74.4	76.5	78.3	81.0
2.25	76.3	76.8	77.2	77.7	78.1	78.5	78.9	80.6	82.1	84.3
2.50	80.7	81.1	81.5	81.9	82.2	82.6	82.9	84.3	85.4	87.2
2.75	84.6	84.9	85.2	85.5	85.8	86.0	86.3	87.4	88.3	89.7
3.00	87.8	88.1	88.3	88.5	88.8	89.0	89.2	90.0	90.7	91.8
3.50	92.7	92.8	93.0	93.1	93.3	93.4	93.5	94.0	94.4	95.1
4.00	95.8	95.9	96.0	96.1	96.2	96.2	96.3	96.6	96.8	97.2
4.50	97.8	97.8	97.9	97.9	97.9	98.0	98.0	98.2	98.3	98.5
5.00	98.9	98.9	98.9	98.9	98.0	99.0	99.0	99.1	99.1	99.2
6.00	99.8	99.8	99.8	99.8	99.8	99.8	99.8	99.8	99.8	99.8

Appendix 5

Present value of \$1 with a continuous discount rate, *r*, for *T* periods. Values of e^{-rt}

Period	Continuous discount rate (*r*)							
(*T*)	1%	2%	3%	4%	5%	6%	7%	8%
1	0.9900	0.9802	0.9704	0.9608	0.9512	0.9418	0.9324	0.9231
2	0.9802	0.9608	0.9418	0.9231	0.9048	0.8869	0.8694	0.8521
3	0.9704	0.9418	0.9139	0.8869	0.8607	0.8353	0.8106	0.7866
4	0.9608	0.9231	0.8869	0.8521	0.8187	0.7866	0.7558	0.7261
5	0.9512	0.9048	0.8607	0.8187	0.7788	0.7408	0.7047	0.6703
6	0.9418	0.8869	0.8353	0.7866	0.7408	0.6977	0.6570	0.6188
7	0.9324	0.8694	0.8106	0.7558	0.7047	0.6570	0.6126	0.5712
8	0.9231	0.8521	0.7866	0.7261	0.6703	0.6188	0.5712	0.5273
9	0.9139	0.8353	0.7634	0.6977	0.6376	0.5827	0.5326	0.4868
10	0.9048	0.8187	0.7408	0.6703	0.6065	0.5488	0.4966	0.4493
11	0.8958	0.8025	0.7189	0.6440	0.5769	0.5169	0.4630	0.4148
12	0.8869	0.7866	0.6977	0.6188	0.5488	0.4868	0.4317	0.3829
13	0.8781	0.7711	0.6771	0.5945	0.5220	0.4584	0.4025	0.3535
14	0.8694	0.7558	0.6570	0.5712	0.4966	0.4317	0.3753	0.3263
15	0.8607	0.7408	0.6376	0.5488	0.4724	0.4066	0.3499	0.3012
16	0.8521	0.7261	0.6188	0.5273	0.4493	0.3829	0.3263	0.2780
17	0.8437	0.7118	0.6005	0.5066	0.4274	0.3606	0.3042	0.2567
18	0.8353	0.6977	0.5827	0.4868	0.4066	0.3396	0.2837	0.2369
19	0.8270	0.6839	0.5655	0.4677	0.3867	0.3198	0.2645	0.2187
20	0.8187	0.6703	0.5488	0.4493	0.3679	0.3012	0.2466	0.2019
21	0.8106	0.6570	0.5326	0.4317	0.3499	0.2837	0.2299	0.1864
22	0.8025	0.6440	0.5169	0.4148	0.3329	0.2671	0.2144	0.1720
23	0.7945	0.6313	0.5016	0.3985	0.3166	0.2516	0.1999	0.1588
24	0.7866	0.6188	0.4868	0.3829	0.3012	0.2369	0.1864	0.1466
25	0.7788	0.6065	0.4724	0.3679	0.2865	0.2231	0.1738	0.1353
30	0.7408	0.5488	0.4066	0.3012	0.2231	0.1653	0.1225	0.0907
35	0.7047	0.4966	0.3499	0.2466	0.1738	0.1225	0.0863	0.0608
40	0.6703	0.4493	0.3012	0.2019	0.1353	0.0907	0.0608	0.0408
45	0.6376	0.4066	0.2592	0.1653	0.1054	0.0672	0.0429	0.0273
50	0.6065	0.3679	0.2231	0.1353	0.0821	0.0498	0.0302	0.0183
55	0.5769	0.3329	0.1920	0.1108	0.0639	0.0369	0.0213	0.0123
60	0.5488	0.3012	0.1653	0.0907	0.0498	0.0273	0.0150	0.0082

Period	Continuous discount rate (r)								
(T)	9%	10%	11%	12%	13%	14%	15%	16%	17%
1	0.9139	0.9048	0.8958	0.8869	0.8781	0.8694	0.8607	0.8521	0.8437
2	0.8353	0.8187	0.8025	0.7866	0.7711	0.7558	0.7408	0.7261	0.7118
3	0.7634	0.7408	0.7189	0.6977	0.6771	0.6570	0.6376	0.6188	0.6005
4	0.6977	0.6703	0.6440	0.6188	0.5945	0.5712	0.5488	0.5273	0.5066
5	0.6376	0.6065	0.5769	0.5488	0.5220	0.4966	0.4724	0.4493	0.4274
6	0.5827	0.5488	0.5169	0.4868	0.4584	0.4317	0.4066	0.3829	0.3606
7	0.5326	0.4966	0.4630	0.4317	0.4025	0.3753	0.3499	0.3263	0.3042
8	0.4868	0.4493	0.4148	0.3829	0.3535	0.3263	0.3012	0.2780	0.2576
9	0.4449	0.4066	0.3716	0.3396	0.3104	0.2837	0.2592	0.2369	0.2165
10	0.4066	0.3679	0.3329	0.3012	0.2725	0.2466	0.2231	0.2019	0.1827
11	0.3716	0.3329	0.2982	0.2671	0.2393	0.2144	0.1920	0.1720	0.1541
12	0.3396	0.3012	0.2671	0.2369	0.2101	0.1864	0.1653	0.1466	0.1300
13	0.3104	0.2725	0.2393	0.2101	0.1845	0.1620	0.1423	0.1249	0.1097
14	0.2837	0.2466	0.2144	0.1864	0.1620	0.1409	0.1225	0.1065	0.0926
15	0.2592	0.2231	0.1920	0.1653	0.1423	0.1225	0.1054	0.0907	0.0781
16	0.2369	0.2019	0.1720	0.1466	0.1249	0.1065	0.0907	0.0773	0.0659
17	0.2165	0.1827	0.1541	0.1300	0.1097	0.0926	0.0781	0.0659	0.0556
18	0.1979	0.1653	0.1381	0.1153	0.0963	0.0805	0.0672	0.0561	0.0469
19	0.1809	0.1496	0.1237	0.1023	0.0846	0.0699	0.0578	0.0478	0.0396
20	0.1653	0.1353	0.1108	0.0907	0.0743	0.0608	0.0498	0.0408	0.0334
21	0.1511	0.1225	0.0993	0.0805	0.0652	0.0529	0.0429	0.0347	0.0282
22	0.1381	0.1108	0.0889	0.0714	0.0573	0.0460	0.0369	0.0296	0.0238
23	0.1262	0.1003	0.0797	0.0633	0.0503	0.0400	0.0317	0.0252	0.0200
24	0.1153	0.0907	0.0714	0.0561	0.0442	0.0347	0.0273	0.0215	0.0169
25	0.1054	0.0821	0.0639	0.0498	0.0388	0.0302	0.0235	0.0183	0.0143
30	0.0672	0.0498	0.0369	0.0273	0.0202	0.0150	0.0111	0.0082	0.0061
35	0.0429	0.0302	0.0213	0.0150	0.0106	0.0074	0.0052	0.0037	0.0026
40	0.0273	0.0183	0.0123	0.0082	0.0055	0.0037	0.0025	0.0017	0.0011
45	0.0174	0.0111	0.0071	0.0045	0.0029	0.0018	0.0012	0.0007	0.0005
50	0.0111	0.0067	0.0041	0.0025	0.0015	0.0009	0.0006	0.0003	0.0002
55	0.0071	0.0041	0.0024	0.0014	0.0008	0.0005	0.0003	0.0002	0.0001
60	0.0045	0.0025	0.0014	0.0007	0.0004	0.0002	0.0001	0.0001	0.0000

Period	Continuous discount rate (r)								
(T)	18%	19%	20%	21%	22%	23%	24%	25%	26%
1	0.8353	0.8270	0.8187	0.8106	0.8025	0.7945	0.7866	0.7788	0.7711
2	0.6977	0.6839	0.6703	0.6570	0.6440	0.6313	0.6188	0.6065	0.5945
3	0.5827	0.5655	0.5488	0.5326	0.5169	0.5016	0.4868	0.4724	0.4584
4	0.4868	0.4677	0.4493	0.4317	0.4148	0.3985	0.3829	0.3679	0.3535
5	0.4066	0.3867	0.3679	0.3499	0.3329	0.3166	0.3012	0.2865	0.2725
6	0.3396	0.3198	0.3012	0.2837	0.2971	0.2516	0.2369	0.2231	0.2101
7	0.2837	0.2645	0.2466	0.2299	0.2144	0.1999	0.1864	0.1738	0.1620
8	0.2369	0.2187	0.2019	0.1864	0.1720	0.1588	0.1466	0.1353	0.1249
9	0.1979	0.1809	0.1653	0.1511	0.1381	0.1262	0.1153	0.1054	0.0963
10	0.1653	0.1496	0.1353	0.1225	0.1108	0.1003	0.0907	0.0821	0.0743
11	0.1381	0.1237	0.1108	0.0993	0.0889	0.0797	0.0714	0.0639	0.0573
12	0.1154	0.1023	0.0907	0.0805	0.0714	0.0633	0.0561	0.0498	0.0442
13	0.0963	0.0846	0.0743	0.0653	0.0573	0.0503	0.0442	0.0388	0.0340
14	0.0805	0.0699	0.0608	0.0529	0.0460	0.0400	0.0347	0.0302	0.0263
15	0.0672	0.0578	0.0498	0.0429	0.0369	0.0317	0.0273	0.0235	0.0202
16	0.0561	0.0478	0.0408	0.0347	0.0296	0.0252	0.0215	0.0183	0.0156
17	0.0469	0.0396	0.0334	0.0282	0.0238	0.0200	0.0169	0.0143	0.0120
18	0.0392	0.0327	0.0273	0.0228	0.0191	0.0159	0.0133	0.0111	0.0093
19	0.0327	0.0271	0.0224	0.0185	0.0153	0.0127	0.0105	0.0087	0.0072
20	0.0273	0.0224	0.0183	0.0150	0.0123	0.0101	0.0082	0.0067	0.0055
21	0.0228	0.0185	0.0150	0.0122	0.0099	0.0080	0.0065	0.0052	0.0043
22	0.0191	0.0153	0.0123	0.0099	0.0079	0.0063	0.0051	0.0041	0.0033
23	0.0159	0.0127	0.0101	0.0080	0.0063	0.0050	0.0040	0.0032	0.0025
24	0.0133	0.0105	0.0082	0.0065	0.0051	0.0040	0.0032	0.0025	0.0019
25	0.0111	0.0087	0.0067	0.0052	0.0041	0.0032	0.0025	0.0019	0.0015
30	0.0045	0.0033	0.0025	0.0018	0.0014	0.0010	0.0007	0.0006	0.0004
35	0.0018	0.0013	0.0009	0.0006	0.0005	0.0003	0.0002	0.0002	0.0001
40	0.0007	0.0005	0.0003	0.0002	0.0002	0.0001	0.0001	0.0000	0.0000
45	0.0003	0.0002	0.0001	0.0001	0.0001	0.0000	0.0000	0.0000	0.0000
50	0.0001	0.0001	0.0000	0.0000	0.0000	0.0000	0.0000	0.0000	0.0000
55	0.0001	0.0000	0.0000	0.0000	0.0000	0.0000	0.0000	0.0000	0.0000
60	0.0000	0.0000	0.0000	0.0000	0.0000	0.0000	0.0000	0.0000	0.0000

Period	Continuous discount rate (*r*)								
(*T*)	27%	28%	29%	30%	31%	32%	33%	34%	35%
1	0.7634	0.7558	0.7483	0.7408	0.7334	0.7261	0.7189	0.7188	0.7047
2	0.5827	0.5712	0.5599	0.5488	0.5379	0.5273	0.5169	0.5066	0.4966
3	0.4449	0.4317	0.4190	0.4066	0.3946	0.3829	0.3716	0.3606	0.3499
4	0.3396	0.3263	0.3135	0.3012	0.2894	0.2780	0.2671	0.2567	0.2466
5	0.2592	0.2466	0.2346	0.2231	0.2122	0.2019	0.1920	0.1827	0.1738
6	0.1979	0.1864	0.1755	0.1653	0.1557	0.1466	0.1381	0.1300	0.1225
7	0.1511	0.1409	0.1313	0.1225	0.1142	0.1065	0.0993	0.0926	0.0863
8	0.1153	0.1065	0.0983	0.0907	0.0837	0.0773	0.0714	0.0659	0.0608
9	0.0880	0.0805	0.0735	0.0672	0.0614	0.0561	0.0513	0.0469	0.0429
10	0.0672	0.0608	0.0550	0.0498	0.0450	0.0408	0.0369	0.0334	0.0302
11	0.0513	0.0460	0.0412	0.0369	0.0330	0.0296	0.0265	0.0238	0.0213
12	0.0392	0.0347	0.0308	0.0273	0.0242	0.0215	0.0191	0.0169	0.0150
13	0.0299	0.0263	0.0231	0.0202	0.0178	0.0156	0.0137	0.0120	0.0106
14	0.0228	0.0198	0.0172	0.0150	0.0130	0.0113	0.0099	0.0086	0.0074
15	0.0174	0.0150	0.0129	0.0111	0.0096	0.0082	0.0071	0.0061	0.0052
16	0.0133	0.0113	0.0097	0.0082	0.0070	0.0060	0.0051	0.0043	0.0037
17	0.0102	0.0086	0.0072	0.0061	0.0051	0.0043	0.0037	0.0031	0.0026
18	0.0078	0.0065	0.0054	0.0045	0.0038	0.0032	0.0026	0.0022	0.0018
19	0.0059	0.0049	0.0040	0.0033	0.0028	0.0023	0.0019	0.0016	0.0013
20	0.0045	0.0037	0.0030	0.0025	0.0020	0.0017	0.0014	0.0011	0.0009
21	0.0034	0.0028	0.0023	0.0018	0.0015	0.0012	0.0010	0.0008	0.0006
22	0.0026	0.0021	0.0017	0.0014	0.0011	0.0009	0.0007	0.0006	0.0005
23	0.0020	0.0016	0.0013	0.0010	0.0008	0.0006	0.0005	0.0004	0.0003
24	0.0015	0.0012	0.0009	0.0007	0.0006	0.0005	0.0004	0.0003	0.0002
25	0.0012	0.0009	0.0007	0.0006	0.0004	0.0003	0.0003	0.0002	0.0002
30	0.0003	0.0002	0.0002	0.0001	0.0001	0.0001	0.0001	0.0000	0.0000
35	0.0001	0.0001	0.0000	0.0000	0.0000	0.0000	0.0000	0.0000	0.0000
40	0.0000	0.0000	0.0000	0.0000	0.0000	0.0000	0.0000	0.0000	0.0000
45	0.0000	0.0000	0.0000	0.0000	0.0000	0.0000	0.0000	0.0000	0.0000
50	0.0000	0.0000	0.0000	0.0000	0.0000	0.0000	0.0000	0.0000	0.0000
55	0.0000	0.0000	0.0000	0.0000	0.0000	0.0000	0.0000	0.0000	0.0000
60	0.0000	0.0000	0.0000	0.0000	0.0000	0.0000	0.0000	0.0000	0.0000

Appendix 6
Selections from ISO* 4217 currency code list, a.k.a. SWIFT codes

Country	Code	Currency	Code
Afghanistan	AF	Afghani	AFA
Albania	AL	Lek	ALL
Algeria	DZ	Algerian Dinar	DZD
Andorra	AD	Euro	EUR
Angola	AO	Kwanza	AOA
Anguilla	AI	East Caribbean Dollar	XCD
Antigua & Barbuda	AG	East Caribbean Dollar	XCD
Argentina	AR	Argentine Peso	ARS
Armenia	AM	Armenian Dram	AMD
Aruba	AW	Aruban Guilder	AWG
Australia	AU	Australian Dollar	AUD
Austria	AT	Euro	EUR
Azerbaijan	AZ	Azebaijan Manat	AZM
Bahamas	BS	Bahamian Dollar	BSD
Bahrain	BH	Bahraini Dinar	BHD
Bangladesh	BD	Taka	BDT
Barbados	BB	Barbados Dollar	BBD
Belarus	BY	Belarussian Ruble	BYR
Belgium	BE	Euro	EUR
Belize	BZ	Belize Dollar	BZD
Benin	BJ	West African CFA Franc	XOF
Bermuda	BM	Bermudian Dollar	BMD
Bhutan	BT	Ngultrum	BTN
		& Indian Rupee	INR
Bolivia	BO	Boliviano	BOB
Bosnia & Herzegovina	BA	Convertible Marks	BAM
Botswana	BW	Pula	BWP
Brazil	BR	Brazilian Real	BRL
Brunei	BN	Brunei Dollar	BND
Bulgaria	BG	Leva	BGN
Burkina Faso	BF	West African CFA Franc	XOF
Burundi	BI	Burundi Franc	BIF

* International Organization for Standardization.

Country	Code	Currency	Code
Cambodia	KH	New Riel	KHR
Cameroon	CM	Central African CFA Franc	XAF
Canada	CA	Canadian Dollar	CAD
Cape Verde	CV	Cape Verde Escudo	CVE
Cayman Islands	KY	Cayman Islands Dollar	KYD
Central African Republic	CF	Central African CFA Franc	XAF
Chad	TD	Central African CFA Franc	XAF
Chile	CL	Chilean Peso	CLP
China	CN	Yuan Renminibi	CNY
Colombia	CO	Colombian Peso	COP
Congo. Republic of	CG	Central African CFA Franc	XAF
Congo, Democ. Republic of	CD	Congolese Franc	CDF
Costa Rica	CR	Costa Rican Colon	CRC
Cote d'Ivoire	CI	West African CFA Franc	XOF
Croatia	HR	Kuna	HRK
Cuba	CU	Cuban Peso	CUP
Cyprus	CY	Euro	EUR
Czech Republic	CZ	Czech Koruna	CZK
Denmark	DK	Danish Krone	DKK
Djibouti	DJ	Djbouti Franc	DJF
Dominica	DM	East Caribbean Dollar	XCD
Dominican Republic	DO	Dominican Peso	DOP
Ecuador	EC	US Dollar	USD
Egypt	EG	Egyptian Pound	EGP
El Salvador	SV	Colon	SVC
		& US Dollar	USD
Equatorial Guinea	GQ	Central African CFA Franc	XAF
Eritrea	ER	Nakfa	ERN
Estonia	EE	Euro	EUR
Ethiopia	ET	Ethiopian Birr	ETB
Faeroe Islands	FO	Danish Krone	DKK
Falkland Islands (Malvinas)	FK	Falkland Islands Pound	FKP
Fiji	FJ	Fiji Dollar	FJD
Finland	FI	Euro	EUR
France	FR	Euro	EUR
French Polynesia	PF	CFP Franc	XPF
Gabon	GA	Central African CFA Franc	XAF
Gambia	GM	Dalasi	GMD
Georgia	GE	Lari	GEL

Country	Code	Currency	Code
Germany	DE	Euro	EUR
Ghana	GH	Cedi	GHS
Gibraltar	GI	Gibraltar Pound	GIP
Greece	GR	Euro	EUR
Greenland	GL	Danish Krone	DKK
Grenada	GD	East Caribbean Dollar	XCD
Guatemala	GT	Quetzal	GTQ
Guinea	GN	Guinea Franc	GNF
Guinea-Bissau	GW	West African CFA Franc	XOF
Guyana	GY	Guyana Dollar	GYD
Haiti	HT	Gourde	HTG
Honduras	HN	Lempira	HNL
Hong Kong	HK	Hong Kong Dollar	HKD
Hungary	HU	Forint	HUF
Iceland	IS	Iceland Krona	ISK
India	IN	Indian Rupee	INR
Indonesia	ID	Rupiah	IDR
Iran	IR	Iranian Rial	IRR
Iraq	IQ	Iraqi Dinar	IQD
Ireland (Republic)	IE	Euro	EUR
Israel	IL	New Israeli Shekel	ILS
Italy	IT	Euro	EUR
Jamaica	JM	Jamaican Dollar	JMD
Japan	JP	Yen	JPY
Jordan	JO	Jordanian Dinar	JOD
Kazakhstan	KZ	Tenge	KZT
Kenya	KE	Kenyan Shilling	KES
Kiribati	KI	Australian Dollar	AUD
Korea, North	KP	North Korean Won	KPW
Korean, South	KR	South Korean Won	KRW
Kuwait	KW	Kuwait Dinar	KWD
Kyrgyzstan	KG	Som	KGS
Laos	LA	Kip	LAK
Latvia	LV	Latvian Lats	LVL
Lebanon	LB	Lebanese Pound	LBP
Lesotho	LS	Loti &	LSL
		South African Rand	ZAR
Liberia	LR	Liberian Dollar	LRD

Country	Code	Currency	Code
Libya	LY	Libyan Dinar	LYD
Liechtenstein	LI	Swiss Franc	CHF
Lithuania	LT	Lithuanian Litas	LTL
Luxembourg	LU	Euro	EUR
Macau	MO	Pataca	MOP
Macedonia, Republic of	MK	Denar	MKD
Malawi	MW	Kwacha	MWK
Malaysia	MY	Malaysian Ringgit	MYR
Maldives	MV	Rufiyaa	MVR
Mali	ML	West African CFA Franc	XOF
Malta	MT	Euro	EUR
Marshall Islands	MH	US Dollar	USD
Mautitania	MR	Ouguiya	MRO
Mauritius	MU	Mauritius Rupee	MUR
Mexico	MX	Mexican Peso	MXN
Moldova	MD	Moldovian Leu	MDL
Monaco	MC	Euro	EUR
Mongolia	MN	Tugrik	MNT
Montserrat	MS	East Caribbean Dollar	XCD
Morocco	MA	Moroccan Dirham	MAD
Mozambique	MZ	Metical	MZM
Myanmar	MM	Kyat	MMK
Namibia	NA	Namibian Dollar &	NAD
		South African Rand	ZAR
Nauru	NR	Australian Dollar	AUD
Nepal	NP	Nepalese Rupee	NPR
Netherlands	NL	Euro	EUR
Netherlands Antilles	AN	NA Guilders (a.k.a. Florins)	ANG
New Caledonia	NC	CFP Franc	XPF
New Zealand	NZ	New Zealand Dollar	NZD
Nicaragua	NI	Cordoba Oro	NIO
Niger	NE	West African CFA Franc	XOF
Nigeria	NG	Naira	NGN
Niue	NU	New Zealand Dollar	NZD
Norfolk Island	NF	Australian Dollar	AUD
Norway	NO	Norwegian Krone	NOK
Oman	OM	Omani Rial	OMR
Pakistan	PK	Pakistan Rupee	PKR
Palestine	PS	New Israeli Shekel	ILS
		& Jordanian Dinar	JOD

Country	Code	Currency	Code
Panama	PA	Balboa &	PAB
		US Dollar	USD
Papua New Guinea	PG	Kina	PGK
Paraguay	PY	Guarani	PYG
Peru	PE	Nuevo Sol	PEN
Philippines	PH	Philippine Peso	PHP
Pitcairn	PN	New Zealand Dollar	NZD
Poland	PL	Zlotych	PLN
Portugal	PT	Euro	EUR
Qatar	QA	Qatari Riyal	QAR
Romania	RO	New Leu	RON
Russia	RU	New Ruble	RUB
Rwanda	RW	Rwanda Franc	RWF
Samoa	WS	Tala	WST
San Marino	SM	Euro	EUR
Sao Tome & Principe	ST	Dobra	STD
Saudi Arabia	SA	Saudi Riyal	SAR
Senegal	SN	West African CFA Franc	XOF
Seychelles	SC	Seychelles Rupee	SCR
Sierra Leone	SL	Leone	SLL
Singapore	SG	Singapore Dollar	SGD
Slovakia	SK	Euro	EUR
Slovenia	SI	Euro	EUR
Solomon Islands	SB	S.I. Dollar	SBD
Somalia	SO	Somali Shilling	SOS
South Africa	ZA	Rand	ZAR
Spain	ES	Euro	EUR
Sri Lanka	LK	Sri Lanka Rupee	LKR
St Kitts & St Nevis	KN	East Caribbean Dollar	XCD
St Lucia	LC	East Caribbean Dollar	XCD
St Vincent & The Grenadines	VC	East Caribbean Dollar	XCD
Sudan	SD	Sudane Dollar	SDD
Suriname	SR	Surinam Guilder	SRG
Swaziland	SZ	Lilangeni	SZL
Sweden	SE	Swedish Krone	SEK
Switzerland	CH	Swiss Franc	CHF
Syria	SY	Syrian Pound	SYP
Taiwan	TW	New Taiwan Dollar	TWD
Tajikistan	TJ	Somoni	TJS

Country	Code	Currency	Code
Tanzania	TZ	Tanzanian Shilling	TZS
Thailand	TH	Baht	THB
Togo	TG	West African CFA Franc	XOF
Tonga	TO	Pa'Anga	TOP
Trinidad & Tobago	TT	T & T Dollar	TTD
Tunisia	TN	Tunisian Dinar	TND
Turkey	TR	Turkish Lira	TRY
Turkmenistan	TM	Manat	TMM
Turks & Caicos Islands	TC	US Dollar	USD
Tuvalu	TV	Australian Dollar	AUD
Uganda	UG	Uganda Shilling	UGX
Ukraine	UA	Hryvnia	UAH
United Arab Emirates	AE	UAE Dirham	AED
United Kingdom	GB	Pound Sterling	GBP
United States	US	US Dollar	USD
Uruguay	UY	Uruguayan Peso	UYU
Uzbekistan	UZ	Uzbekistan Som	UZS
Vanuatu	VU	Vatu	VUV
Vatican City	VA	Euro	EUR
Venezuela	VE	Bolivar	VEB
Vietnam	VN	Dong	VND
Virgin Islands, British	VG	US Dollar	USD
Virgin Islands, US	VI	US Dollar	USD
Wallis & Fatuna Islands	WF	CFP Franc	XPF
Western Sahara	EH	Moroccan Dirham	MAD
Yemen	YE	Yemen Rial	YER
Zambia	ZM	Kwacha	ZMK
Zimbabwe	ZW	Zimbabwe Dollar	ZWD
		& Botswana Pula	BWP
		& British Pound	GBP
		& Euro	EUR
		& South African Rand	ZAR
		& US Dollar	USD

Source: List of countries and codes extracted from: *BS ISO 4217:2008 Codes for the representation of currencies and funds*, copyright © British Standards Institution (BSI – www.bsigroup.com). Reproduced with permission.

Glossary

Absolute purchasing power parity A form of purchasing power parity which claims that under a fully floating exchange rate regime the ratio between domestic and foreign price levels equals the equilibrium rate of exchange between the domestic and foreign currencies.

Acceleration In relation to a loan, the action of a lender in demanding early repayment of principal in the event of default.

Acceptance The signing of a bill of exchange in formal acknowledgement of the obligation to honour the bill.

Acceptance credit A UK money-market term for a bill of exchange drawn by a customer on its bank, which is accepted and then discounted by the bank, the proceeds being paid to the customer.

Accounting exposure Exposure which arises from the process of consolidating items denominated in foreign currency into the group financial accounts denominated in the parent's currency. Sometimes called translation exposure.

Adjustable rate mortgage (ARM) A mortgage whose interest rate adjusts to a new rate based on prevailing market rates at the time of adjustment.

Alt-A mortgage A loan to a home buyer who may be creditworthy but does not meet the standards for a conforming mortgage. For example, the borrower may not be able to provide the required documentation.

Alienation of assets The risk that a borrower may realise some or all of the assets that form the lender's security.

All-current rate method A foreign currency translation method. All items denominated in foreign currency are translated at current exchange rates. Sometimes called the closing rate method or current rate method – but not to be confused with the current/non-current rate method.

American depository receipt (ADR) Certificate of ownership issued by a US bank to investors in place of the underlying corporate shares, which are held in custody.

American option An option which may be exercised on any business day within the option period.

Amortisation The repayment of, or obligation to repay, the principal of a loan in more than one instalment.

Appreciation An increase in the value of a currency.

Arbitrage A purchase of foreign exchange, securities or commodities in one market coupled with immediate resale in another market in order to profit risklessly from price discrepancies. The effect of arbitrageurs' actions is to equate prices in all markets for the same commodity.

Arm's-length price The price at which a willing seller and an unrelated willing buyer will freely agree a transaction.

Ask price The larger price in a foreign exchange quotation. Sometimes called the offer price.

Asset-backed commercial paper (ABCP) This is similar to commercial paper, but it is issued by conduits or structured investment vehicles holding loans, structured credit securities or other credit assets. *See* Commercial paper.

Asset-backed security (ABS) A debt security collateralised by a pool of assets, such as mortgages, credit-card debt, corporate debt or car loans.

Asset-based swap An interest rate or cross-currency interest rate swap entered into by a party to convert the coupon on an asset to another rate or another currency rate basis.

Asymmetry of information Parties to a transaction may possess different amounts and/or different qualities of information about the transaction.

At-the-money An option when the value of its underlying security is equal to the option strike price.

Average life The effective life of a bond issue calculated as the average of the time periods for which funds are made available to the borrower, weighted by the amount available in each such period.

Back-to-back loan One of two loans of the same initial amount made by one party to another in different countries, the loans being denominated in different currencies and each maturing on the same date. Used as a method of borrowing foreign currency and unblocking funds.

Balance of payments A financial statement prepared for a country summarising the flow of goods, services and funds between the residents of that country and the residents of the rest of the world during a particular period.

Balance of trade The net of imports and exports of goods reported in the balance of payments.

Balance sheet exposure Exposure which arises from the process of translating balance sheet items denominated in foreign currency into the group accounts denominated in the parent's currency.

Balloon The principal amount repaid on maturity of a loan that is significantly larger than the annual repayments. For example an issue could have six payments of 10 per cent, followed by a balloon of 40 per cent at maturity.

Basel Accords A set of international agreements adopted by the Basel Committee on Bank Supervision providing guidelines on capital and asset levels in banks.

Basis The difference between cash and futures prices. Also the difference between yields on similar but different financial instruments.

Basis point A hundredth of 1 per cent. Used in relation to interest rates.

Basis risk With respect to futures contracts, the basis represents the difference between the price of the cash commodity and a related futures contract, a difference that widens or narrows as the cash and futures prices fluctuate. Basis risk refers to the possibility that this difference will change during the life of the contract, resulting in an unexpected loss or gain. The basis is the key to hedging: if it remains constant over the life of a position, a perfect hedge (losses exactly equal to gains) results. Basis risk results when a particular futures contract is used to hedge a portfolio that differs from the underlying futures instrument.

Basis swap An interest rate or cross-currency swap in which the payment obligations of each of the parties are determined on the basis of a floating rate index. A US dollar LIBOR/sterling LIBOR swap would be a basis swap, as would a LIBOR/CD swap in which both parties' payment obligations were in US dollars.

Basket An artificial currency based on a mixture of actual currencies. For example, the ECU is an artificial currency based upon a basket of EU currencies.

Bearer bond or bearer security A negotiable security that is presumed in law to be owned by the holder. Title to bearer securities is effected by delivery.

Bearer instrument A negotiable instrument on which title passes by mere delivery without endorsement or registration.

Bells and whistles The additional features of a security intended to attract investors or reduce issue costs or both.

Benchmark security The choice of a security as a standard for the return on a particular class of securities that serves as a guide for other comparable issues.

Beta A measure of the sensitivity of an asset to changes in the market. A beta of 0.5 means that on average a 1 per cent change in the market in the short run implies a 0.5 per cent change in the value of the asset. *See also* Systematic risk.

Bid–ask spread or bid–offer spread The difference between the prices quoted by a dealer for buying and selling a security.

Bid price The smaller price in a foreign exchange quotation.

Big Mac Index An index of foreign exchange rates based upon the prices of Big Mac burgers around the world. Published and updated regularly in *The Economist* magazine. There is also an iPod index. *See* Purchasing power parity.

Billion One thousand million.

Bill of exchange A negotiable instrument, used mainly in international trade, instructing one person, the drawee, to pay a certain sum of money to another named person, the drawer, on demand or at a certain future time. If the drawee, or acceptor, of the bill is a bank, the bill is a bank bill (known as a banker's acceptance); if it is a trader, the bill is a trade bill; if it is the UK or US government, it is a treasury bill.

Such bills are normally issued with 90-day lives, and their marketability depends on the standing of the drawee or acceptor, the nature of the underlying transaction and whether the bill is eligible for rediscounting with the central bank.

Black and Scholes model A model that provides a means by which to value option contracts. It involves using information on the underlying asset, the strike price, volatility, time to expiry and risk-free interest rates. First formulated by Fischer Black and Myron Scholes in 1973.

Blocked currency A currency that is not freely convertible to other currencies due to exchange controls.

Blue chip An equity share that is considered to be of the highest quality.

Bond A promise under seal to pay money. The term is generally used to designate the promise made by a corporation, either public or private, or a government to pay money, and it generally applies to instruments with an initial maturity of one year or more.

Bond basis The method used to compute accrued interest on some bonds and on some short-term money-market instruments. In the Eurobond market the accrued interest calculated on the bond basis is equal to the coupon rate multiplied by the number of lapsed bond days divided by 360 (known as the 360-day year convention). *See also* Money-market basis.

Bonus issue An issue of shares to existing holders, usually in some set proportion to the holding, but requiring no payment. This has the effect of increasing the company's issued capital and is normally made possible by the capitalisation of reserves. Sometimes known as a scrip or capitalisation issue.

Brady bonds Dollar denominated bonds issued mainly by Latin American countries following the sovereign debt crisis of the 1980s. They enabled commercial banks to exchange their claims on developing countries into tradable bonds.

Bretton Woods Conference A meeting of representatives of non-communist countries in Bretton Woods, New Hampshire, USA, in 1944. Representatives agreed on the characteristics of the international monetary system, effectively the fixed exchange rate system, which prevailed until 1971.

Bridge financing A type of loan, usually at fluctuating interest rates, that takes the form of renewable overdrafts or discounting facilities. It is used as a continuing source of funds until the borrower obtains medium- or long-term financing to replace it.

Bulldog bond A sterling-denominated bond issue made in the UK market by a foreign (non-UK) borrower.

Bullet A straight debt issue with repayment in one go at maturity.

Buyer credit One of the two main techniques by which the United Kingdom supports UK companies in winning and financing engineering and construction projects overseas. Under a buyer credit, the customer settles with the supplier on a cash basis, funds for this purpose being provided to the customer directly by a bank under ECGD guarantee.

Callable bond A bond with a call provision giving the issuer the right to redeem the bonds under specified terms prior to the normal maturity date.

Call option The right, but not the obligation, to buy an amount of foreign exchange at a specified price within a specified period.

Cannibalisation effects The impact that a new product or acquisition may have upon existing products or businesses in the firm's portfolio. This impact may be expressed as a turnover effect or in terms of profit or cash flow.

Cap A limit on the upward movement of a coupon or interest rate.

Capital account A balance of payments term meaning the part of the balance of payments which records the changes in financial assets and liabilities. The capital account is divided into long-term flows and short-term flows.

Capital adequacy The minimum amount of capital that bank, non-bank financial intermediaries and other financial market operators must maintain in proportion to the risks that they assume.

Capital asset pricing model (CAPM) A model that promotes a basis for pricing risk associated with holding securities. Its essence is that rates of return are directly related to a single common factor: namely, the return on the market portfolio adjusted for non-diversifiable risk.

Capital mobility The extent to which private capital is free to be invested abroad. Capital mobility is predicated upon well-developed foreign exchange and financial markets, freedom from official restrictions on foreign investment and confidence that future government policies will not obstruct the repatriation of invested funds.

Capital requirements The amount of capital a bank is required to hold, relative to its average assets, to meet its obligations and absorb unanticipated losses.

Capital structure The distribution of a company's issued capital as between bonds, debentures, preferred and ordinary shares, earned surplus and retained income.

Capped FRN An issue with an upper limit on the coupon rate. Under this type of issue, the lender forgoes the possibility of receiving a return above the cap rate should the market interest rate exceed the cap rate.

Cash flow exposure This is concerned with the effect of currency changes on the present value of future cash flows generated by a company's domestic and foreign operations. Sometimes called economic exposure.

Cash market Where delivery and settlement of the deal is immediate, or within a few days, as compared with the future and options markets where delivery and settlement are delayed.

Central bank The institution with the primary responsibility to control the growth of a country's money stock. It also has regulatory powers over commercial banks and over other financial institutions. It usually serves as the monetary agent for the government.

Certificate of deposit (CD) A placement of money for a specified period of time with a bank. The depositor receives a confirmation, the deposit receipt, which is a negotiable instrument. Bankers dealing in CDs make a secondary market where they may be sold and purchased prior to maturity. Investors usually accept a smaller interest rate on CDs than on regular time deposits because the investment has greater liquidity via the secondary market.

CHAPS *See* Clearing house automated payments system.

Chapter 11 bankruptcy protection The section of the US bankruptcy code that allows an indebted firm to obtain protection from its creditors while being reorganised.

Chartism Interpreting foreign exchange (and other) market activity and predicting future movements over the near term from graphic depictions of past prices and volumes. Sometimes called technical analysis or momentum analysis.

CHIPS *See* Clearing house interbank payments system.

Clean float An exchange rate system characterised by the absence of government intervention. Sometimes called a free float.

Cleared balance The true balance of a customer's account with its banker on which its funds' availability depends.

Clearing house An institution through which Eurobond contracts, futures contracts and other financial instruments, including cheques, are cleared.

Clearing house automated payments system (CHAPS) A network of linked computers operated by UK clearing banks which provides for the rapid transfer of large balances.

Clearing house interbank payments system (CHIPS) An automated clearing facility set up in 1970 and operated by the New York Clearing House Association. It processes international money transfers for its membership which includes over a hundred US financial institutions – mostly major US banks and branches of foreign banks.

Clearing system A transaction or depository system set up for efficient physical delivery.

Close out For a futures contract this means taking a second offsetting position in order to remove the delivery obligation.

Closing exchange rate The exchange rate prevailing at a financial reporting date.

Closing price The price, or spread of prices, at which deals are made just before the close of official business in a particular market.

Closing rate method *See* All-current rate method.

Collar A transaction that combines a cap and a floor so as to provide cap or floor protection at a lower cost.

For example, the buyer of a cap might give up some of the benefits of a decline in interest rates by selling a floor to the writer of the cap, thereby reducing the cost of the cap by the value of the floor. Or, the purchaser of the floor might be willing to give up some benefits of a rise in interest rates by selling a cap to reduce the floor purchase price. The cap and floor portions of a collar operate as described in the definitions of those terms if actual interest rates rise above the agreed cap rate or decline below the agreed floor rate, respectively, for any period. Sometimes called a floor/ceiling arrangement.

Collateral Security placed with a lender to assure the performance of the obligation. Assuming that the obligation is satisfied, the collateral is returned by the lender.

Collateralised debt obligation (CDO) A type of asset backed security that is backed by diversified securities such as loans and credit default swaps and it derives its cash flow from these sources. The asset backing is often split into tranches with different rights in terms of interest receipt and redemption.

Comfort letter A formal letter written to a lender, normally by a parent company, indicating its willingness to accept some responsibility to honour the borrowing obligations of a subsidiary or associate company, but without constituting a legal obligation to do so. Such letters may be written in varying degrees of strength. At one extreme, there is the letter of awareness, which does no more than acknowledge the existence of the relevant borrowing, while at the other comes the unenforceable guarantee. In this latter form, the writer would indicate that it undertook to meet the borrower's obligations in the event of its failing to do so, but that the recipient could not use the letter as a means of forcing it to do so. The essential point is that, while such letters constitute a significant moral obligation, they do not constitute a legally binding obligation. For this reason, they have come to be known in the United States as LOMIs, letters of moral intent. They do not have to be treated as contingent liabilities and have no impact on the parent company's balance sheet.

Commercial bank A bank which takes deposits from customers and lends to customers.

Commercial paper An unsecured promissory note issued usually for maturities of 60 days or less.

Commitment fee A percentage per annum rate charged by a lender on the daily undrawn balance of a borrowing facility.

Community Reinvestment Act US Federal law designed to encourage commercial banks and savings associations to meet the borrowing needs of all segments of the community, including low income areas.

Compensating balance A minimum sum of money which, as a condition of a term loan, the borrower undertakes to maintain on current account with the lender, in theory to increase the bank's security by reducing the risk that the account will be overdrawn. The effect of maintaining a non-interest-bearing deposit is to reduce the true sum borrowed: since interest is payable on the gross sum, the effective rate on the net amount is higher than that quoted. This mechanism was common in the United States until the end of the 1970s but has now gone out of general use, maybe because of the growth in professionalism among treasury staff.

Confirmation The written document confirming the oral foreign exchange contract agreed by telephone between either dealer and dealer or dealer and client.

Confirmed irrevocable letter of credit A type of credit issued by the importer's bank and confirmed by a bank in the exporter's country. The importer's bank commits itself irrevocably to pay the exporter's draft, and the confirming bank (the exporter's bank) adds to this commitment by assuming the responsibility to pay the exporter's draft, provided that all conditions contained in the letter of credit are satisfied.

Conservatorship A US term for an arrangement whereby an entity or person is appointed by a court to make legal decisions for a company or for a financial institution.

Convertibility The ability to convert one currency into another without special permission from exchange control authorities.

Convertible bond A fixed interest security that is exchangeable into equity shares under stipulated conditions.

Convertible Eurobond A Eurobond that can be converted into equity under stipulated conditions.

Convertible FRN A floating rate note that can be converted into a fixed rate bond or into another FRN with a different maturity or a different currency denomination.

Copula A way of formulating a distribution with many variables such that relationships can be represented – a multivariate distribution.

Correlation A standardised statistical measure of the dependence of two random variables. It is defined as the covariance divided by the standard deviations of two variables.

Correspondent bank A bank that handles the business of a foreign bank.

Cost of capital The rate of return expected by a party financing the firm.

Cost-plus loan pricing The interest rate on a loan expressed as a function of some publicly available cost-of-funds measure, such as LIBOR.

Counterparty risk In a contract, the risk to each party that the other party, the counterparty, may not honour its contracted obligation.

Countertrade A generic term for a range of commercial mechanisms for reciprocal trade that include barter, counterpurchase, offsets buy-back and switch trading. The common characteristic of these arrangements is that export sales to a particular market are made conditional upon undertakings to accept imports from that market. Latterly, they are used as a way of promoting trade between developed and less developed nations, and are intended to avoid, or mitigate, the problems associated with sovereign debt by allowing settlement in the produce of the buying country. A number of specialist intermediaries have grown up prepared to exchange the output/produce received by the seller for money/currency, and then to place the output/commodities with the ultimate user for a fee, known as disagio, or by discounting the value of the output.

Country risk A wide range of risk, including political as well as economic risk. Corporate goals of multinationals and the national aspirations of host countries may not be congruent; the essential element in country risk is the possibility of some form of government action preventing the fulfilment of a contract.

Coupon The regular payment made to an investor in a bond or similar security.

Coupon or coupon rate The fixed interest rate attached to a loan.

Covariance A statistical measure of the degree to which random variables move together.

Covenant An obligation in writing. There are covenants in term loan agreements, deeds, mortgages and other similar instruments.

Covered interest arbitrage The process of borrowing a currency, converting it to a second currency where it is invested, and selling this second currency forward against the initial currency. Riskless profits are derived from discrepancies between interest differentials and the percentage discount or premium between the currencies involved in the forward transaction. Covered interest arbitrage is based on disequilibrium in interest rate parity.

Covered position A position in a security that is matched by a counter position in another security, thereby neutralising the initial position.

Covering Protecting the cash value of future proceeds usually from an international trade transaction, by buying or selling the proceeds in the forward market. Although used interchangeably with the term 'hedging', covering is, strictly speaking, protecting a future cash flow amount whereas hedging refers to the protection of foreign-denominated accounting assets or liabilities against pure translation losses.

Crawling peg system An exchange rate system in which the exchange rate is adjusted frequently and deliberately, perhaps many times a year, usually to reflect prevailing rates of inflation.

Credit crunch A situation where banks become so fearful that they stop lending. Used in the financial crisis of 2007–8 when banks became so suspicious of the creditworthiness of other banks that they ceased lending to one another.

Credit default swap (CDS) A contract that entitles the protection buyer to a payment if there is a default on a bond or other type of debt obligation. To enable the contract to continue, the protection buyer pays an annual premium to the seller. Rather similar to insurance but there are differences. Both parties to a credit default swap may sell on their rights and obligations in a secondary market. Credit default swaps normally have a finite life. To be technically 100 per cent correct, the definition could be as follows. A credit default swap is an instrument which gives the holder the right to sell a bond for its face value in the event of a default by the issuer.

Credit rating agency An entity that analyses and rates the creditworthiness of debt and bonds issued by companies or countries as well as similar financial products. The main ones are Moody's, Fitch and Standard and Poor's.

Credit risk The likelihood, in lending operations, that a borrower will not be able to repay the principal or pay the interest.

Credit score A quantified estimate of a potential borrower's creditworthiness (see FICO).

Credit spread The difference between the market rate of interest paid on a safe and widely traded bond, such as those issued by the US Treasury or the UK or German governments, and the relatively higher rate of interest paid on a riskier bond of the same maturity. Riskier bonds offering high-credit spread include corporate bonds.

Cross default provision A clause in a loan agreement that allows the lender to declare the loan immediately repayable and to terminate any further extension of credit if the borrower defaults on any other debt.

Cross-rate The exchange rate between currencies A and B based upon the rates between currencies A and C and currencies B and C.

Currency basket A means of expressing the value of a financial asset or currency as a weighted average of more than one foreign exchange rate. The weights in this average are usually defined as specific quantities of currencies, hence the term 'currency basket'.

Currency option A contract conferring the right, but not the obligation, to buy or sell a specified currency against another currency at a specific price on or prior to a specified date.

Currency swap The simultaneous borrowing and lending operation in which parties transfer currencies from one to the other at the spot rate and agree to reverse the exchange at a future date and at an agreed exchange rate.

Current account As used in the balance of payments, it is that section that records the trade in goods and services and the exchange of gifts among countries.

Current/non-current method A foreign currency translation method in which current items in balance sheets denominated in foreign currencies are translated at current exchange rates and long-term items are translated at historical rates.

Current rate method *See* All-current rate method.

Dealer A specialist in a bank or company who is authorised to undertake foreign exchange transactions.

Debenture In the United Kingdom, a fixed interest secured loan which can be for a fixed maturity or irredeemable. There are two main types: mortgage debentures, which are secured against a specific asset of the issuer; and floating debentures, which are secured against the entire asset base of the issuer.

Debt capacity The total amount which a company is capable of borrowing.

Debt–equity swaps A secondary debt market involving the trading of sovereign debt as between the major lending banks. Recognising that large parts of Third World debts will not be readily cleared from their books, banks have sought new ways of trading their positions by swapping and selling debts between one another and to corporations desiring to undertake projects in the Third World countries concerned. The corporation offers the acquired debt to the less-developed country (LDC) in return for local currency: the LDC thereby redeems the debt.

Debt factoring The purchasing, normally with recourse to the seller, of accounts receivable as a mechanism for providing short-term finance on a continuing basis. The practice is common among small companies in the United Kingdom.

Debt service ratio A ratio used to assess a country's creditworthiness. It is the ratio of a country's debt service payments to exports.

Deep discount bond A low- or zero-coupon bond issued at a discount.

Deep market The situation in which it is possible to trade large amounts of securities without significantly affecting the price.

Default The act of breaching a covenant or warranty in a loan agreement.

Delivery risk The risk, on a payment date when each party has an obligation to make a payment, that one party will make its required payment but the other party will fail to do so. In swaps, this risk is often avoided by providing for net payments. In a currency swap, delivery risk is increased because net payments are often not acceptable, since the parties want to receive actual payments in different currencies.

Additional risk results from the fact that the payments may be due in different time zones so they cannot, even in theory be made simultaneously. On the maturity date of a currency swap the notional amounts are usually exchanged, thus further increasing the magnitude of the risk.

Delta The change in the value of an option given a change in the value of the underlying security. The inverse of the delta gives the hedge ratio.

Delta hedge A method of hedging risk exposure for option writers, involving buying or selling the underlying security in proportion to the delta. For example, when a call option writer is committed on an option with a delta of 0.5, it may effect a delta hedge by buying an amount of the underlying security equal to one-half of the amount of the underlying currency that must be delivered on exercise.

Demand deposit Funds in a current account that may be withdrawn at any time without notice. Demand deposits may or may not be interest-bearing deposits.

Department of Housing and Urban Development (HUD) This is a cabinet-level agency in the USA whose mission is to increase homeownership, support community development and increase access to affordable housing.

Depreciation *See* Devaluation.

Deregulation The removal or relaxation of the barriers or rules that have previously restricted the scope of securities trading and the nature of the operations undertaken by financial institutions.

Derivative products A generic term for the range of traded instruments that have grown up around securities and currency and commodity trading.

Devaluation A substantial decline in an exchange rate, usually effected in one go by government decree.

Direct investment Purchase of a foreign financial asset in which substantial involvement in the management of the foreign asset is presumed. In practice, it is any holding that represents more than 10 per cent ownership of the foreign asset. Also termed foreign direct investment.

Direct quote A rate of exchange quoted in terms of x units of home currency to 1 unit of foreign currency.

Dirty float *See* Managed float.

Discount house A UK institution that acts as an intermediary between the Bank of England and the banking system. Discount houses participate in auctions of gilt-edged stock, enjoy lender-of-last-resort facilities with the Bank of England and discount bills.

Discounting Where a sale is to be settled by a bill of exchange, the seller may surrender it to a financial institution in exchange for immediate payment of an amount less than the face value to reflect interest.

Discount market UK institutions and dealers that trade bills of exchange.

Disintermediation The process of bypassing normal financial intermediaries.

Double taxation Taxes paid twice, once abroad where income is earned and a second time in the United Kingdom, if the company is UK owned. A principle of tax law is that double taxation should be avoided. If the UK company has already paid taxes abroad, it should only pay enough taxes in the United Kingdom to bring the overall rate up to the UK rate.

Drawdown When a part of a borrowing facility is used.

Drop-lock bond A bond or similar instrument which initially bears interest at a variable rate as if it were a floating rate obligation, but which will change to bear interest at a predetermined fixed rate in the event that a defined market rate falls to a stated level.

Dual currency bond A security denominated in one currency with interest or principal or both paid in another at a pre-agreed rate.

Duration A measure of a security's 'length' that considers the periodic coupon payments. It is the weighted average maturity of all payments of a security, coupons plus principal, where the weights are the discounted present values of the payments. Therefore, the duration is shorter than the stated term to maturity on all securities except for zero-coupon bonds, for which they are equal.

ECB *See* European Central Bank.

ECGD *See* Export Credit Guarantee Department.

Economic and Monetary Union A plan to create a single European market with a single currency, to be called the 'euro'. The detailed plan for the single currency was first formulated in the 1989 Delors report. It was refined in the Maastricht Treaty which came into effect on 1 November 1993.

Economic exposure The extent to which the value of the firm will change due to an exchange rate change. This arises due to the effect of currency changes upon the parent currency present value of expected future cash flows to be generated by a company's operations.

ECU *See* European currency unit.

Effective exchange rate A rate measuring the overall nominal value of a currency over time in the foreign exchange market. It is calculated via a weighted average of bilateral exchange rates, using a weighting scheme that reflects the importance of each country's trade with the home country.

Efficient market A market in which there is a sufficiently large number of buyers and sellers to eliminate an incentive for arbitrage transactions, and in which the trade-off between return and risk is fully reflected in prices.

Electronic funds transfer at point of sale (EFTPOS) A system that allows funds to be moved automatically from a buyer's account to a seller's, the transfer taking place at the time of the transaction.

EMS *See* European Monetary System.

EMU *See* Economic and Monetary Union.

Equity risk premium The excess of the required rate of return on equities over that required on a risk-free security.

ERM *See* Exchange rate mechanism.

Escrow account Monies held in a separate specified account to pay obligations or potential obligations but not to be used for any other purpose.

EURIBOR European interbank-offered rate sponsored by the European Banking federation, the Association Cambiste Internationale, and the European Savings and Cooperative Organization as a reference rate for the eurozone. EURIBOR is to be set using quotations from a panel of banks from across the eurozone.

Euro The currency unit of 16 European Union nations – *see* Eurozone.

Eurobanks Financial intermediaries that bid for time deposits and make loans in currencies other than that of the country in which they are located.

Eurobond A bond underwritten by an international syndicate of banks and marketed internationally in countries other than the country of the currency in which it is denominated. This issue is thus not subject to national restrictions.

Euroclear One of the Eurobond market's two clearing systems. It is provided by Morgan Guaranty for over 100 banks and is based in Brussels.

Eurocommercial paper A generic term used to describe Euronotes that are issued without being underwritten.

Eurocredit The Eurocredit market is where highly rated borrowers can gain access to medium-term (one to fifteen years) bank lending. The loan can be denominated in one or several Eurocurrencies as can the interest and the principal. The interest rate is normally fixed as a margin over LIBOR.

Eurocurrency A time deposit in a bank account located outside the banking regulations of the country which issues the currency. Also termed offshore currency.

Eurodollars Dollars held in time deposits in banks outside the United States. These banks may be foreign owned or overseas branches of US banks. But see international banking facilities. Also termed offshore dollars.

Euroland The name for the eleven countries as a whole adopting EMU in full.

Euro LIBOR London interbank-offered rate for euro.

Euromarkets A collective term used to describe a series of offshore money and capital markets operated by international banks. They comprise Eurocurrency, Eurocredit and Eurobond markets. The centre of these markets is London, except for the Eurosterling market which is centred in Paris.

Euronote The Euronote market is one in which borrowers raise money by the issue of short-term notes, generally with maturities of three and six months, that are negotiable like certificates of deposit. As one issue of notes matures, the borrower issues some more so that, while the holders of the debt change over time, the total amount outstanding can be maintained in the medium term. A group of commercial banks may ensure that the borrower in a particular issue will be able to place such notes by standing by ready to purchase the paper should the appetite of short-term investors wane.

Euronote facility This allows borrowers to issue short-term notes through a variety of note distribution mechanisms, under the umbrella of a medium-term commitment from banks.

European Central Bank (ECB) The European Central Bank, which determines monetary policy for the participating member states in EMU from 1 January 1999.

European currency unit (ECU) A currency basket composed of specific quantities of the currencies of European Monetary System members. Following EMU, the euro replaced the ECU one for one.

European Monetary System (EMS) A structure of agreements governing the exchange market activities of participating members of the European Union. Agreements require members closely to manage the exchange values of their currencies relative to those of other members.

European option An option that can be exercised on the fixed expiration date only.

Eurozone The area covered by the 16 European Union countries which use the euro as their currency, namely Austria, Belgium, Spain, Finland, France, Germany, Greece, Ireland, Italy, Luxembourg, Malta, the Netherlands, Portugal, Slovakia, Slovenia and Spain.

Exchange controls Restrictions imposed by the central bank or other government authorities on the convertibility of a currency, or on the movement of funds in that currency.

Exchange rate The number of units of one currency expressed in terms of a unit of another currency.

Exchange rate mechanism (ERM) A system of intervention in the foreign exchange markets designed to keep participating EU currencies within a narrow range versus the old ECU.

Exercise To carry out a transaction, usually applied to the options market.

Exercise price The exchange rate at which a foreign exchange option may be exercised.

Expiry or expiration date The date upon which an option or warrant contract terminates.

Exploding ARM A form of adjustable rate mortgage widely offered to subprime borrowers in which the interest rate is set at an adjustable rate for the first two or three years of the mortgage and then switches to a relatively high fixed rate.

Export–Import Bank (Exim Bank) US government agency established in 1934 to stimulate US foreign trade. The Exim Bank supports commercial banks that are financing exports and provides direct financing, loan guarantees and insurance to exporters and foreign buyers of US goods. Similar to the ECGD in the United Kingdom.

Export Credit Guarantee Department (ECGD) A UK agency dedicated to facilitating UK exports primarily through subsidised export financing and offering export credit insurance to UK exporters.

Face value The money value of a security as stated by the issuer. Not to be confused with market value. Interest and dividends are usually payable as a percentage of face value (a.k.a. Nominal value).

Factoring A financing method in which the borrower assigns or sells its receivables as collateral to a firm, called a factor, which normally assumes responsibility for collection.

Fair market value (FMV) An estimate of the amount that would be received if an asset were sold.

Fair Value Accounting (FVA) The use of a market price to establish the balance sheet amount of some assets and liabilities.

Fannie Mae *See* Federal National Mortgage Association (FNMA).

FASB 8 A US accounting standard in force from 1976 to 1981 that required companies to translate their foreign-affiliate financial statements using the temporal method. Foreign currency translation gains and losses were reported in the income statement as ordinary income.

FASB 52 *See* SFAS 52.

Fat tail distribution A distribution in which the tail events are much more likely to occur than those of a normal distribution curve.

Federal funds Money deposited with the Federal Reserve Bank, the central bank of the United States. This money is available on demand. Purchases of US treasury bills and most other money-market instruments in the domestic US money market may only be made with Federal funds.

Federal Home Loan Mortgage Corporation (Freddie Mac) Freddie Mac is a publicly chartered corporation in the USA with a mission to provide liquidity, stability and affordability in housing backed lending. It was set up and privatised in 1968 to provide competition for Fannie Mae.

Federal National Mortgage Association (Fannie Mae) Fannie Mae is a US-government agency set up in 1938 and privatised in 1968 with the same mission as Freddie Mac.

Federal Reserve System (Fed) As the central bank of the USA, the Fed conducts the nation's monetary policy, supervises both state-chartered banks that are Fed members and all bank holding companies, maintains the stability of the financial system, and provides financial services.

Filter rule A rule for buying and selling securities based on the premise that, once a movement in a currency's exchange rate has exceeded a given percentage, it will continue to move in the same direction.

Finance vehicle An operation involving the setting up of an offshore subsidiary for the purpose of issuing debt and lending the borrowings on to the parent or another subsidiary. The parent normally guarantees the debt issues.

Financial Accounting Standards Board (FASB) The organisation responsible for setting accounting standards for company financial statements in the USA.

Financial bubble A prolonged increase in prices of stocks and shares, real estate, or other assets, which is reckoned to be unsustainable since it is not well founded on fundamental factors or fundamental analysis.

Fisher effect The hypothesis that the nominal interest rate differential between two countries should equal the expected inflation differential between those countries. Also called Fisher's closed hypothesis.

Fisher's closed hypothesis *See* Fisher effect.

Fisher's open hypothesis *See* International Fisher effect.

Fixed exchange rate system A system in which the value of a country's currency is tied to a major currency, such as the US dollar, gold or the SDR. The term usually allows for fluctuations within a range of 1 or 2 per cent on either side of the fixed rate.

Fixed rate interest When the interest on a security is calculated as a constant specified percentage of the principal and is paid at the end of stated periods until maturity.

Fixed rate payer A party that makes swap payments calculated on the basis of a fixed rate.

Floating exchange rate system A system in which the value of a currency relative to others is established by the forces of supply and demand in the foreign exchange markets. Strictly speaking, this implies that intervention by the government should be absent.

Floating or variable rate interest Interest on an issue of securities which is not fixed for the life of the issue, but is periodically set according to a predetermined formula. The rate is usually set at a margin or spread in relation to a specified money-market rate, such as LIBOR.

Floating rate note (FRN) A short-term floating interest rate security. The interest rate is pegged to LIBOR, and is adjusted semi-annually. These securities are attractive to investors during periods of rising interest when fixed rate bonds are subject to depreciation.

Floating rate payer A party that makes swap payments calculated on the basis of a floating rate.

Floor A minimum interest rate.

Flowback The sale of shares, originally placed with overseas investors, back into the domestic market by those investors.

Foreign bond A long-term security issued by a borrower in the capital market of a country other than the borrower's. Usually underwritten by a syndicate from one country and sold on that country's capital market, the bond is denominated in the currency of the country in which it is sold.

Foreign Credit Insurance Corporation A private association of leading US insurance companies, affiliated to Exim Bank, that provides short- and medium-term credit insurance to exporters, enabling them to obtain or offer better financing terms.

Foreign currency bond An issue where the coupon is paid in a different currency from that of denomination of principal.

Foreign direct investment *See* Direct investment.

Foreign exchange Currency other than the one used internally in a given country.

Foreign exchange trader One who stands ready to buy and sell currencies out of inventory and expects to earn a profit for the costs and risks incurred.

Foreign tax credit Home country tax credit given against domestic tax in respect of foreign taxes already paid on foreign-source earnings.

FOREX Foreign exchange.

Forfaiting The discounting at a fixed rate of interest of term bills of exchange without recourse to the drawer.

Forward contract An agreement to exchange specified amounts of currencies of different countries at a specified contractual rate (the forward rate) at a specified future date.

Forward exchange market The market involved with forward contracts for exchange of currency at some future date. The usual forward maturities are for one, two, three, six and twelve months, although contracts for other maturities may be negotiated.

Forward/forward swap A pair of forward exchange contracts involving a forward purchase and a forward sale of a currency, simultaneously entered into, but for different maturities. Sometimes called a forward swap.

Forward margin The difference between the forward rate and the spot rate of currency.

Forward option contract *See* Optional date forward contract.

Forward premium (or discount when negative) The difference between the forward and spot rates, expressed either as an annualised percentage of the spot exchange rate or as so many cents or pfennigs. When forward currencies are worth more than the corresponding spot amount, the stronger currency is at a premium; the weaker currency is at a discount.

Forward rate The rate quoted today for delivery at a fixed future date of a specified amount of one currency against another.

Forward swap *See* Forward/forward swap.

FRA Forward rate agreement or future rate agreement. Essentially an over-the-counter version of a short interest rate future.

Franked income Income that has already been subject to corporation tax.

Freddie Mac See The Federal Home Mortgage Corporation (FHMC).

Free cash flow The net figure obtained by deducting from cash generated by operations or by an investment that cash which has been absorbed by operations or by the investment. Free cash flow disregards all cash flows to do with financing.

FRN *See* Floating rate note.

Front-end fee The commission payable at the start of a financial arrangement.

FT-SE100 A real-time weighted arithmetic average of the equity market capitalisations of the 100 largest UK companies on the International Stock Exchange, London.

Functional currency The currency of the main economic environment in which a multinational operates. It is normally the currency of the environment in which the firm primarily generates and expends cash.

Fundamental analysis A branch of security analysis based upon attempts to value securities in accordance with estimated future profits and cash outturns.

Futures contract A standardised foreign exchange or interest rate contract written against the exchange clearing house for a fixed number of foreign currency or interest rate units and for delivery on a fixed date. Because of their standardisation, futures contracts have a deep secondary market.

FX Foreign exchange.

G7 *See* Group of Seven.

G10 *See* Group of Ten.

GAAP *See* Generally accepted accounting principles.

Gamma The rate of change of an option's delta with respect to the underlying price.

Generally accepted accounting principles US GAAP are the rules for company accounting statements applicable to US companies.

Gilt or gilt-edged Fixed interest, sterling-denominated securities issued by the UK government. They derive their name from the gold edge on the original certificates, subsequently replaced by green certificates.

Ginnie Mae *See* Government National Mortgage Association.

Glass-Steagall Act A USA statute, enacted in 1933 and repealed in 1999, that prohibited commercial banks from engaging in investment banking activities and setting certain other regulations.

Globalisation The trend of bringing major financial markets across the world closer together through technological innovations in communications.

Gold standard A monetary agreement under which national currencies are backed by gold and gold is utilised for international payments.

Goodwill The intangible value of an ongoing business over and above the value of its tangible net assets.

Government National Mortgage Association (Ginnie Mae) Ginnie Mae is a US government-backed corporation that guarantees to investors the timely payment of principal and interest on securities of federally insured or guaranteed loans.

Government sponsored enterprises (GSEs) Shareholder-owned corporations, like Fannie Mae and Freddie Mac, or government agencies like Ginnie Mae, chartered by the US Congress to promote stability, liquidity, and affordability.

Gramm-Leach-Bliley Act The US act of 1999 that repealed the Glass-Steagall Act.

Group of Seven Seven major industrial nations whose ministers meet on a periodic basis to discuss and agree on economic and political issues. It comprises Germany, France, Italy, the United Kingdom, Canada, Japan and the United States.

Group of Ten Ten major industrial countries – Germany, France, Belgium, the Netherlands, Italy, the United Kingdom, Sweden, Canada, Japan and the United States – that agreed in 1962 to stand ready to lend their currencies to the IMF under the General Arrangements to Borrow. The Group of Ten has taken the lead in subsequent changes in the international monetary system.

Haircut The difference between the amount of money lent in a repo contract and the true market value of the security sold and then repurchased. This represents the amount of protection offered to the lender of the money. A haircut of 10 per cent means that the lender is safe from financial loss, should the security not be repurchased, as long as the value of the security falls by nor more than 10 per cent.

Hard A market is said to be hard if prices are rising.

Hard currency A strong, freely convertible currency. A strong currency is one that is not expected to devalue within the foreseeable future.

Head and shoulders A chart pattern which approximates to the shape of a person's head and shoulders, implying a fall in share prices.

Hedge fund An investment fund attracting high net worth investors and pension funds where investors hope to make money from the returns, including capital gains, on the fund's high risk investments. Hedge funds charge their investors fees and use leverage, market knowledge, trading skills, mathematical models, near-arbitrage (called risk arbitrage) and other techniques to achieve their returns. It does not have so much to do with hedging nowadays, but the name came from the technique of looking for two almost identical investments and buying the cheaper and selling the more expensive.

Hedging The generation of a position in a given currency in the forward market or in the money market with the purpose of matching it against the net exposure position as evidenced by the balance sheet. The purpose of hedging is to make the net position for a particular currency at a given date equal to zero. The accounts included in the exposed balance sheet items are determined in accordance with accounting rules. *See also* Covering.

Historical exchange rate The foreign currency exchange rate in effect on the date when an asset or liability was acquired.

Historic cost accounting The method of accounting by which assets are valued at their original purchase price less depreciation or a permanent impairment to value.

Holding company A legally constituted company that may not carry on any trade or industry, but has a controlling interest in one or more subsidiary companies.

Hot money Speculative bank deposits that are moved around the international money market to take advantage of interest rate and currency movements.

Hubris Pride or arrogance. In Greek tragedy, an excess of ambition or pride ultimately causing the transgressor's ruin.

IASB *See* International Accounting Standards Board.

IBFs *See* International banking facilities.

ICCH *See* International Commodities Clearing House.

IFRS See International Financial Reporting Standards

Illiquid A security or a market that is lacking activity.

IMF *See* International Monetary Fund.

IMM *See* International Monetary Market.

Income statement exposure Arises as a result of the process of translating income statement items denominated in foreign currency into group income statements denominated in the parent currency.

Inconvertible currency A currency that cannot be converted into other currencies because of exchange control restrictions.

Indexing In some countries the practice of adjusting debt by some measure of inflation to preserve the purchasing power of the debt in constant monetary units. In Brazil, indexing is applied to wages, business accounts and debt.

Indirect quote A rate of exchange quoted in terms of *x* units of foreign currency per 1 unit of home currency.

Initial margin The amount of margin needed to set up a position in a futures market.

Instrument A generic term for securities, ranging from debt to negotiable deposits and bonds.

Insurable interest In insurance, the requirement that the insured must possess an insurable interest. This means that the insured would suffer a loss if the event that is being insured were to occur.

Interbank rate The rate at which banks offer and bid for funds as between each other.

Intercompany trade Trade flows between fellow affiliates of the same group of companies.

Interest arbitrage The international transfer of funds to a foreign centre, or the maintenance of funds in a foreign centre with the intention of benefiting from the higher yield on short-term investment in that centre. *See* Covered interest arbitrage *and* Uncovered interest arbitrage.

Interest rate differential The difference between short-term interest rates prevailing in two money centres at a given moment. Sometimes called interest rate spread.

Interest rate exposure The risk of loss arising from possible interest rate movements.

Interest rate futures Futures contracts which relate wholly to levels of interest rates.

Interest rate guarantee (IRG) An indemnity sold by a bank or other financial institution protecting the purchaser against the effect of future movements in interest rates.

Interest rate parity The condition that the interest differential should equal the forward differential between two currencies.

Interest rate spread *See* Interest rate differential.

Interest rate swap An agreement between two parties in which each agrees to pay to the other an amount calculated by reference to interest that would accrue over a given period on the same notional amount but using a different rate of interest.

Intermediary company A vehicle company used as a conduit for the transfer of funds between fellow affiliate companies.

Intermediation The activity of a bank or similar financial institution in taking a position between the two parties to a transaction in such a way as to accept a credit or other commercial risk.

Internal exposure management technique Tactics related to the business of the multinational which do not use third-party contracts, but are aimed at reducing exposed positions or preventing exposure from arising or exploiting possible future exchange rate movements.

International Accounting Standards Board (IASB) The IASB is an independent standard-setting board whose mission is to develop a set of high quality and understandable financial reporting standards for companies in all countries.

International Banking Act 1978 US legislation designed to remove many of the competitive advantages that forcign banks had over their domestic US counterparts. Thus the Federal Reserve Bank is now authorised to impose reserve requirements on foreign banks and there are restrictions on their ability to take deposits nationwide.

International banking facilities (IBFs) Free monetary zones in the United States that can be established by certain corporations and by US branches and agencies of foreign banks. The IBFs accepting foreign deposits are exempted from reserve requirements and interest rate restrictions and can make loans to foreign borrowers. The impact of their operations is that some dollars deposited in time deposits in the United States effectively become Eurodollars.

International Commodities Clearing House (ICCH) The central guarantee organisation which clears contracts on LIFFE.

International Financial Reporting Standards (IFRS) A set of accounting standards for financial statements that is now used in over 100 countries.

International Fisher effect The hypothesis that the interest differential between two countries should reflect the future change in the spot rate. Also called Fisher's open hypothesis.

International Monetary Fund (IMF) An international organisation created by the Bretton Woods Agreement in 1944 to promote exchange rate stability. The objectives of the fund include supervising exchange market intervention by member countries, providing the finance needed by members to overcome short-term payments imbalances, and encouraging monetary co-operation and international trade among nations.

International Monetary Market (IMM) A centralised market in Chicago where currency and financial futures contracts, among others, are traded.

In-the-money A call option when its strike price is less than the value of the underlying security price. It also applies to a put option when the strike price is higher than the current price of the underlying security.

Intrinsic value The difference between the strike price of an option and the current market price of the underlying security where the option has value.

Investment bank An institution that acts as an underwriter for companies and others, advises on issuing securities, making acquisitions and divestments, offers investment advice and may deal in securities on its own account.

Investment grade A bond rated BAA or above by Moody's or BBB or above by Standard and Poor's.

Issue price The price at which securities are sold on issue.

Issuing bank The bank that issues a letter of credit. It is usually the buyer's bank.

Issuing house An institution or agency that organises the arrangements associated with an issue of securities.

J curve A model of the delayed effect of a devaluation on the balance of trade. Devaluation allows the foreign price of exports to fall (or remain constant) and the domestic price of imports to rise. But time is needed for orders to be obtained and contracts negotiated before the quantity of exports rises and the quantity of imports falls. Thus, an initial worsening of the trade balance can be expected (the downward part of the J) before the trade balance starts to improve (the upward part of the J).

Junk bond A high-yield bond that is deemed to be below investment grade which became popular as a means of financing corporate takeovers and management buyouts.

Lag To defer payment of a debt. A firm with a subsidiary in a country with a hard currency may encourage the subsidiary to lag its payments in order to take advantage of a possible revaluation of the hard currency or devaluation of the subsidiary's currency.

Law of comparative advantage According to this hypothesis, a country will specialise in producing, and will export, those goods that it can produce relatively cheaply compared with foreign countries. It will import those goods that it can produce only at relatively high cost.

Lead To prepay a debt. A company with a subsidiary in a country with a soft currency may encourage the subsidiary to prepay money due to countries with harder currency to avoid the adverse impact on cash flow of devaluation by the country with soft currency.

Lead manager The main organiser of a new issue, such as a bank or broker, responsible for the overall co-ordination and distribution of an issue and the documents associated with it. The lead manager is also likely to appoint co-managers, to determine the initial and final terms of the issue, and to select the underwriters and the selling group.

Lender of last resort A concession given to a select number of financial institutions whereby their central bank agrees to provide them with funds if they should get into difficulties.

Letter of awareness A formal letter written to a lender, normally by a parent company, acknowledging its relationship with another group company and its awareness of a loan being made to that company. It is the weakest form of comfort letter. Such letters do not constitute a guarantee, but may nevertheless involve a significant moral commitment on the part of the writer.

Letter of comfort A document that indicates one party's intention to try to ensure that another party complies with the terms of a financial transaction without guaranteeing performance in the event of default.

Letter of credit A letter issued by a bank, usually at the request of an importer, indicating that the opening bank or another will honour drafts if they are accompanied by specified documents under specified conditions.

Leverage Borrowing, financial gearing, either by individuals, households or by corporations. The leverage ratio represents the proportion of debt in a company's mix of debt and equity. Financial leverage is measured by the ratio of debt to the sum of debt and equity.

Liar loan A loan, based on deliberately or negligently incorrect information, supplied by the borrower or mortgage broker and accepted by lenders in mortgage lending. Usually occurs in the subprime area.

LIBOR *See* London interbank offered rate.

LIFFE *See* London International Financial Futures Exchange.

Liquidity The ability of a business to pay its debts as they fall due.

Liquidity preference A wish to hold near-liquid assets at the cost of a lower return.

Liquidity premium Normally, the degree by which prices are reduced and interest rates raised because a fixed income security is not easily traded.

Liquidity risk The risk that a security or other asset cannot be readily traded hence making meaningful market prices difficult to obtain.

Listed security A security that is quoted and traded on a major stock exchange.

Loan-to-value ratio (LTV) The ratio of the amount of a mortgage to the value of the home securing the mortgage loan.

LOC backed Letter of credit backed. An issue, usually of commercial paper, backed by a bank letter of credit – effectively a bank guarantee.

Lock box system A method of centralised collection of remittances operated by banks in the United States on behalf of their corporate customers in order to reduce the float time on interstate money transfers.

Lombard rate A German term for the rate of interest charged for a loan against the security of a pledged promissory note. Particularly used by the Bundesbank, which normally maintains its Lombard rate at about 0.5 per cent above its discount rate.

London interbank bid rate (LIBID) The rate at which the major banks will bid to take deposits from each other for a given maturity, normally between overnight and five years.

London interbank mean rate (LIMEAN) The average of LIBID and LIBOR.

London interbank offered rate (LIBOR) The interest rate at which prime banks offer deposits to other prime banks in London. This rate is often used as the basis for pricing Eurodollar and other Eurocurrency loans. The lender and the borrower agree to a mark-up over LIBOR: the total of LIBOR plus the mark-up is the effective interest rate for the loan.

London International Financial Futures Exchange (LIFFE) A centralised market in London where standardised currency, currency options and financial futures are traded.

Long In the UK government bond market, a security with a maturity of more than 15 years. In the US treasury bond market, a security with a 30-year maturity.

Long position Having greater inflows than outflows of a given currency, or more assets than liabilities in a given currency.

Long term In bond markets, bonds with initial maturities of more than seven years. In terms of company balance sheets, debts with a maturity of more than one year.

Maintenance margin The amount by which an initial margin for a future position must be topped up.

Managed float A floating exchange rate system in which some government intervention takes place. Also called a dirty float.

Marginal tax rate The rate of tax due on additional amounts of taxable income.

Margin call In futures contracts, a requirement to provide more maintenance margin.

Marker rate A generic term for a base interest rate defined in a loan agreement to which the spread is added in order to establish the interest rate payable on a variable rate loan.

Mark to market Under fair value accounting, the procedure for revaluing a security, swap, commodity, futures contract or other derivative according to current market prices.

Mark-to-model The valuation of an asset based on internal assumptions or estimates based on a financial model rather than current market prices.

Matching A process whereby a firm balances its long positions in a given currency (assets, revenues or cash inflows) with its offsetting short positions (liabilities, expenses or cash outflows). The remaining (unmatched) position is the net exposure in that currency.

Material adverse change The clause in a loan agreement or similar contract under which the loan will become repayable in the event that there should be a serious (or material) deterioration in the borrower's credit standing. The clause is used by banks as a substitute where they are not able to negotiate a stronger covenant such as a borrowings limitation clause or a ratio covenant. The difficulty with such clauses lies in the definition of materiality. The normal wording in the loan agreement gives no indication of how to interpret the clause. Attempts to define materiality are almost certain to have the effect of changing the clause into a ratio covenant.

Maturity or final maturity The date when the principal or nominal value becomes payable to the holder of a loan or bond.

Maturity (or settlement) date The date on which a contract is due to be settled.

Maturity structure The expression used to describe the borrower's repayment obligation. The term may be used either in relation to a specific loan or to describe the composite repayment obligation arising from a company's total portfolio obligations.

Medium term In bond markets, bonds with initial maturities of between three and seven years. In money markets, maturities of more than one year.

Merchant bank An old-fashioned UK term for an investment bank.

Middle price The average of a bid and an offer price.

Mismatch A situation where assets and liabilities in a currency do not balance in either size or maturity.

Momentum analysis *See* Chartism.

Monetary/non-monetary method A foreign currency translation method. Non-monetary assets and liabilities are translated at their historical exchange rates, while monetary items are translated at current exchange rates.

Monetary policy Those instruments, such as interest rates and term controls, at the disposal of government for influencing the timing, availability and cost of money and credit in an economy.

Money market Financial institutions and dealers in money and credit.

Money market basis The method used to compute accrued interest on CDs and FRNs. The rate is multiplied by the number of days elapsed and divided by the number of days in the accounting year.

Moral hazard The situation that arises when a person or institution is totally insulated from risk and, consequently, has no incentive to prevent such a risk.

Moratorium Authorisation of suspension of payments by a debtor for a stated time.

Mortgage-backed securities (MBS) Securities supported by the cash flows from pools of mortgages.

Mortgagee The mortgage lender. That is the party that holds the mortgaged property as security for the mortgage loan.

Mortgagor The mortgage borrower. That is the party that mortgages the property to secure a mortgage loan.

Multilateral netting A process where affiliates within multinationals offset their debtor and creditor positions with the rest of the group as a whole, so that a single net intercompany receipt or payment is made each period to settle indebtedness.

Mutual fund A pooled vehicle, run by investment managers, that invests collected funds from savers into securities such as stocks, bonds, or money market instruments.

National Association of Securities Dealers Automated Quotations (NASDAQ) A US automated securities price collection and dissemination service for over-the-counter securities traders.

Nationalisation When a national government buys out or otherwise eliminates all shareholders of a company and assumes total ownership.

Negative amortisation loan A loan whose monthly payments do not cover the interest due on the loan. The interest shortfall is added to the loan's principal.

Negative equity Where the amount owed under a mortgage or other loan outstanding exceeds the current market value of the property forming the security.

Negatively sloping yield curve A yield curve where interest rates in the shorter dates are above those in the longer. This occurs when interest rates are expected to fall.

Negative pledge The covenant in a loan agreement by which a borrower undertakes that no secured borrowings will be made during the life of the loan, or ensures that the loan is secured equally and rateably with any new secured borrowings.

Negotiable instrument Any financial instrument such as bills of exchange, promissory notes, cheques, bank notes, CDs, share warrants, bearer shares or bearer bonds, the title of which passes by mere delivery, without notice to the party liable on the instrument, and in which the transferee in good faith and for a consideration of value acquires an indefeasible title against the whole world.

Nemesis In Greek mythology, the goddess of retribution and vengeance. Without a capital letter, any agency of retribution and vengeance.

Net position The overall position given by the sum of long and short positions.

Netting A procedure by which affiliates within a multinational group net out intercompany trade or financial flows and only pass the net amount due.

NIMBY Not in my back yard.

NINJA loan A mortgage where the borrower is someone with No Income, No Job, No Assets.

Nominal exchange rate The actual exchange rate.

Non-callable An issue of securities where the holders cannot redeem the security before its stated maturity date.

Non-performing loan A bank loan where the borrower has stopped paying interest and is therefore in default.

Non-recourse loan Loan under which the borrower has no personal liability for unpaid amounts. So, if the loan defaults, the borrower's loss is limited to the equity in the relevant asset, for example a house.

Normal distribution curve A curve in which the first standard deviation includes 68.2 per cent of its area and the first two standard deviations include 95.4 per cent of its area and it has a bell shape (a.k.a. bell curve).

Note *See* Promissory note.

Notional amount The amount (in an interest rate swap, forward rate agreement, cap or floor) or each of the amounts (in a currency swap) to which interest rates are applied in order to calculate periodic payment obligations.

OECD *See* Organization for Economic Co-operation and Development.

Off-balance sheet finance Any form of finance that does not result in a corresponding liability appearing on the company's published balance sheet. Obviously, on double-entry principles the asset being financed cannot appear either. The impact of such financing methods is to show the company's gearing at a lower level than it usually is. Lenders are rarely deceived by such transparent devices.

Offer price *See* Ask price.

Official reserves Holdings of gold and foreign currencies by the official monetary institutions of a country.

Offshore currency *See* Eurocurrency.

Offshore dollars *See* Eurodollars.

Offshore finance subsidiary A subsidiary company incorporated overseas, usually in a tax-haven country, whose function is to issue securities abroad for use in either the parent's domestic or foreign business.

Open contract A futures contract that has been bought or sold without the deal having been completed or offset by subsequent sale, purchase, actual delivery or receipt of the underlying financial instrument.

Open interest Contracts not yet offset by futures contracts or fulfilled by delivery.

Open market operations Process by which central bank buys or sells government securities from or to others (usually banks or financial institutions) in order to affect money supply.

Open outcry A kind of auction system used by futures markets under which all bids and offers are made openly by public, competitive outcry and hand signals.

Open position The difference between the amount of a foreign currency owned or receivable and the total of the same currency payable under definite contracts. If one exceeds the other, there is an open position. If the amount held and receivable exceeds the amount payable, there is said to be a long position; if the amount held or receivable is less than the amount payable, it constitutes a short position.

Opportunity cost The rate of return on the best alternative investment available, or the highest return that will not be earned if funds are invested in a particular project or security.

Option A contract providing the holder with the right but not the obligation either to buy from or sell to the issuer a given number of securities at a fixed price at or over a specified time.

Optional date forward contract A forward exchange contract in which the rate is fixed but the maturity is open, within a specified range of dates. Sometimes called a forward option contract or an option forward contract.

Option forward contract *See* Optional date forward contract.

Option premium The price paid to the seller of a foreign exchange option for the rights involved.

Option swap A right to enter into a swap on or before a particular date. Also called a swaption.

Organization for Economic Co-operation and Development (OECD) An organisation that provides for intergovernmental discussion in the fields of economic and social policy. It collects and publishes data and makes short-term economic forecasts about its member countries.

Originate-to-distribute Issuing or making a mortgage or loan with the intent of selling it on to another party (a.k.a. originate to sell).

Originate-to-hold Issuing or making a mortgage or loan with the intent of holding it to maturity.

Out-of-the-money A call option when its strike price is greater than the current price of the underlying security. It also applies to a put option when its strike price is less than the current price of the underlying security. In other words the option has no intrinsic value.

Outright forward rate The forward rate expressed in pounds or dollars per currency unit, or vice versa.

Overshooting As overvalued but applied to the value of a particular currency.

Par value Under the Bretton Woods fixed exchange rate system, the par value of a currency was that value measured in terms of gold or the US dollar that was maintained at a fixed rate relative to gold or the dollar.

Parent country The country in which the parent company of a multinational group is located.

Parent currency The currency of the parent company of a multinational group.

***Pari passu* clause** The covenant in a loan agreement by which a borrower binds itself to ensure that the loan will rank equally with its other defined debts.

Parity The official rate of exchange between two currencies.

Parity grid The matrix of bilateral par values for the currencies of members of the European Monetary System. This grid establishes the intervention prices between which member governments are obliged to maintain the exchange value of their currency in terms of every other group currency.

Pip The most junior digit in a currency quotation.

Plain vanilla An issue of securities that lacks any special features.

Point and figure chart A type of chart in the form of Xs and 0s which represent price changes independent of time.

Ponzi scheme Fraudulent investment scheme, where apparent returns to early investors are financed, partly or wholly, by new monies subscribed by later investors. Named after US swindler, Carlo Ponzi.

Pooling The transfer of excess affiliate cash into a central account – the pool – usually located in a low-tax country, where all corporate funds are managed by corporate staff.

Portfolio investment The purchase of a foreign financial asset with the purpose of deriving returns from the security without intervening in the management of the foreign operation.

Positively sloping yield curve A yield curve where interest rates in the shorter periods are below those in the longer. This is the normal form of yield curve.

PPP *See* Purchasing power parity.

Premium The amount by which a currency is more expensive in the forward market relative to the spot price.

Prime rate A US banking term to indicate the rate at which banks are prepared to lend to borrowers of the highest standing.

Private placement A type of placement where new securities are sold by the lead manager to a limited number of investors, usually its own clients, rather than being offered to a wide public.

Project finance A term financing arrangement, usually on a limited recourse basis, under which funds are provided for a specified project by banks against the security of the project cash flows.

Promissory note An unconditional promise in writing signed by one party engaging to pay on demand or at a fixed or determinable time a sum certain in money to or to the order of a specified person or to the bearer, but not legally binding until delivered to the payee or bearer.

Prospectus A document that details the nature, price and timing of an issue of securities to be made to a wide public. It is usually prepared by the issuer's adviser or sponsor and contains an historical record of earnings performance and, possibly, some form of future profit.

Purchasing power parity (PPP) The hypothesis that, over time, the difference between the inflation rates in two countries tends to equal the rate of change of the exchange rate between the currencies of the countries concerned.

Put option The right, but not the obligation, to sell an amount of foreign exchange at a specified price within a specified time.

Puttable A security where there is a provision to redeem prior to maturity at the discretion of the lender.

Random walk A term implying that there is no discernible pattern of travel. The last step, or even all the previous steps, cannot be used to predict either the size or the direction of the next step.

Ratio covenant An undertaking given in a loan agreement by the borrower that it will operate its business within a financial constraint specified in the form of balance or other financial ratios.

Rational expectations A concept implying that the market forms expectations in a way that is consistent with the actual economic structure of the market. The prices that result in the market place represent an average of all investors' expectations.

Real effective exchange rate A rate calculated by dividing the home country's nominal effective exchange rate by an index of the ratio of average foreign prices to home prices. If purchasing power parity is holding, the real effective exchange rate should remain constant.

Real exchange rate The value of a currency in terms of real purchasing power. It is calculated by comparing the price of a hypothetical market basket of goods in two different countries, translated into the same currency at the prevailing exchange rate. It is useful in measuring the price competitiveness of domestic goods in international markets.

Real return The rate of return of an asset after adjusting for inflation.

Receivership A type of company bankruptcy in which a third party, the receiver, is appointed by a court or by creditors to run the company and reorganise it for the benefit of creditors.

Recession A fall in real gross domestic product for two successive quarters.

Recourse A source of help should, for example, a bill be dishonoured at maturity. The holder would have the right of recourse against any of the other parties to the bill, unless expressly negated.

Redemption The purchase and cancellation of outstanding securities through a cash payment to the holder.

Registered security A security where ownership is recorded by a registrar in the name of the holder or a nominee. Title can be transferred only with the endorsement of the registered holder.

Regulation Q A US regulation, now phased out, of the Federal Reserve system that established a ceiling on interest rates on time deposits. Banks were forbidden to pay interest on deposits with maturities of less than 30 days. Regulations played a significant role in the original growth of the Eurodollar market.

Reinvoicing vehicle A vehicle company that performs group exposure or liquidity management functions. Goods exported from or imported to an associated company are shipped direct to the third party or to the associate as the case may be, but invoicing is performed via the reinvoicing vehicle. Title to the goods and payment are thus channelled through the vehicle.

Repurchase agreement (repo) A form of short-term borrowing in which institutions sell securities to investors or to one another and buy them back, usually the following day, at predetermined prices basically reflecting prevailing interest rates.

Rescheduling The renegotiation of the terms of an existing debt obligation, often in the area of sovereign debt.

Reserve requirements or reserve asset ratio The percentage of different types of deposit or eligible asset which member banks must hold with their central bank.

Resistance level A chartism term denoting a level of prices at which a movement has historically faltered or stabilised.

Revaluation An increase in the spot value of a currency (UK parlance). A change – either an increase or a decrease – in the spot value of a currency (US parlance).

Revolver *See* Revolving credit facility.

Revolving credit facility A loan that allows the borrower to draw down and repay at its discretion for a specified period. Sometimes called a revolver.

Risk premium Expected additional return for making a risky investment rather than a safe one.

Risk-weighted assets (RWA) A bank's assets weighted according to perceived credit risk. Thus, corporate loans would have a higher risk rating than government securities.

Roll over When a forward exchange contract is about to mature a new forward contract is entered into to extend the original maturity date.

Round tripping An opportunity to undertake arbitrage which arises when a bank's customer can draw from overdraft facilities and deposit the proceeds in the money markets at rates which exceed the cost of the overdraft.

Same-day funds Funds with good value at the end of the business day on which the order to transfer the funds is made.

Samurai bond A yen-denominated bond issue made in the Japanese market by a foreign (non-Japanese) issuer.

Sarbanes-Oxley Act of 2002 (SOX) A statute passed after the Enron and Worldcom failures, which increases standards of corporate governance, in such areas as internal controls and financial statements.

Saving and Loan Association (S&L) A depository institution, also called a thrift, which specialises in taking deposits, making mortgages and real estate loans in the USA.

SDR *See* Special drawing rights.

Second Amendment This amendment to the Articles of Agreement of the International Monetary Fund, ratified in 1978, allows members more flexibility in the management of exchange rates than under the Bretton Woods system. It also increases the supervisory responsibilities of the IMF and makes the special drawing rights more attractive as reserve assets.

Secondary market The market in which securities are traded after issue. Also called the 'after-market'.

Securitisation The process of packaging assets and liabilities such that they can be sold and traded in markets. This allows the financial institution that originates the deal – a mortgage, a car loan, etc. – to sell the asset to other investors, thus freeing its capital for alternative uses. Securitisation takes the asset or liability off the bank's books. See originate-to-hold and originate-to-distribute.

SEC 10-K The 10K report is an annual report which the SEC requires from companies issuing securities in the USA.

Self-financing loan or self-liquidating loan A loan that is to be used to acquire assets that will produce sufficient return to meet the interest obligations and repay the principal.

Settlement date The day upon which payment is effected and securities are delivered.

SFAS 52 A US accounting standard in force from December 1981, concerning translation of foreign currency financial statements. Results must be measured in the functional currency of the foreign entity, except in the case of high-inflation countries. Translation is done using the all-current method, with transaction losses showing up on the group's income statement and translation losses on the group's balance sheet.

Shallow discount bond An expression used for UK tax purposes to refer to a bond issued in the primary market at a price exceeding 90 per cent of its face value.

Short A UK government bond with a maturity of less than five years.

Short dates A dealing term meaning periods up to one week, but sometimes used to refer to periods up to a month.

Short position A situation in which the anticipated outflows of a currency exceed the anticipated inflows of that currency over a period of time. Also refers to a net liability, net expense or net cash outflow position in a currency.

Short term In bond markets, bonds with initial maturities of less than two years. In company balance sheets, debt with a remaining maturity of less than a year.

Sight deposits Current accounts, overnight deposits and money at call. Deposits with longer maturities are term deposits.

Sight draft A bill of exchange that is due when presented.

Sinking fund An amount in cash or securities periodically set aside by a borrower to redeem all or part of its long-term debt issues.

SIV *See* Structured investment vehicle.

Smithsonian Agreement This began the first stage of the multilateral exchange rate realignments that followed the collapse of the Bretton Woods system of international monetary relations.

Snake The European system of exchange rate setting created in April 1972 and superseded in 1979 by the European Monetary System.

Society for Worldwide Inter-bank Financial Transfers (SWIFT) A standardised electronic message transfer service designed to send and confirm instructions concerning funds transfers associated with international payments in the major industrial countries.

Soft A market is said to be soft if prices are declining. A currency may also be described as soft if there is excess supply and an expectation that its value will fall in relation to other currencies.

Soft currency A weak currency whose convertibility is, or is expected to become, restricted.

Sovereign debt The loans outstanding of individual countries, usually negotiated by their respective governments.

Sovereign risk (a) The risk of government default on a loan made or guaranteed by it. (b) The risk that the country of origin of the currency being bought or sold will impose foreign exchange regulations that will reduce the value of the contract.

Special drawing rights (SDRs) A form of international reserve asset created and ratified by the IMF in 1969. SDRs have their value based on a weighted average of five widely used currencies.

Special purpose entity (SPE) A separate legal and accounting entity from the bank or company sponsoring it, usually created for a particular investment purpose, but which is moved off the balance sheet of the bank or company sponsoring it.

Special-purpose vehicle (SPV) A legal entity set up as a device to acquire and hold assets off its balance sheet, usually prior to selling them to third parties. Putting the assets into the SPV takes them off the balance sheet of the selling entity. Used to window dress the accounts – especially by investment banks prior to and during the crisis. Also widely used by Enron.

Specific risk Another name for unsystematic risk.

Spot/forward swaps The simultaneous spot purchase or sale of a currency and a countering sale or purchase of the same currency in the forward market.

Spot market The currency market for immediate delivery, although, in the spot market, delivery is usually two working days after the transaction date.

Spot rate The price at which foreign exchange can be bought or sold for immediate delivery. In practice spot deals are settled two working days after the transaction date.

Spread The difference between bid and ask prices in a price quote. Also the amount of interest, expressed in percentage terms or basis points, over the marker rate which the borrower must pay on a short-term or variable rate loan.

Standard deviation The positive square root of the variance. This is the standard statistical measure of the spread of a sample.

Stop loss An order to sell a financial instrument when its price falls to a specified level.

Straight bond A bond issued in the primary market which carries no equity or other incentive to attract the investor, the only reward being an annual or semi-annual interest coupon.

Strike price The price at which an option may be exercised.

Structured finance A method used to transfer risk through the use of complex techniques, structures and separate entities. Embraces. the securitisation of mortgages and credit cards debt.

Structured investment vehicle (SIV) An off-balance sheet vehicle usually established by a bank, often in a tax haven, to hold and/or have passed through it asset-backed and mortgage-backed securities. Their losses would technically not be borne by the banks setting them up – but in practice, in the crisis, they were for the banks' account.

Subordinated security An issue that ranks below other debt in right of repayment on liquidation.

Subprime mortgage A mortgage made to a borrower who does not qualify as being sufficiently credit-worthy enough to qualify for a prime mortgage and who, consequently, pays a higher interest rate.

Sub-underwriter A member of a new issue syndicate who agrees to buy a certain proportion of the issue from the managers should the issue be undersubscribed. They receive an underwriting fee and a selling concession on the principal amount of the securities for which they may subscribe.

Supplier credit One of the two main techniques by which the ECGD supports UK companies in winning and financing projects overseas, where credit terms form an integral part of the commercial contract between supplier and customer. Under such an arrangement, that part of the contract price for which the supplier is at risk is secured by promissory notes issued by the customer and guaranteed unconditionally by the ECGD.

Support level A term used in chartist analysis to describe when a security or commodity price has repeatedly fallen to a certain price, but has then recovered.

Swap Where a given currency is simultaneously purchased and sold, but the maturity for each of the transactions is different. The term is also used, generically, to cover interest rate swaps and currency swaps.

Swap rate The difference between spot and forward rates expressed in points – that is, in terms of 0.0001 of a currency unit.

Syndicated loan A loan by a group of banks, normally on a floating rate basis, at a predetermined margin over short-term interest rates.

Synthetic position An option or futures position that has the same risk–return characteristics as another position.

Systemic risk Risk posed to the entire financial system by the possible collapse of an interconnected financial institution, or a particular financial product, for example credit default swaps.

Systematic risk The volatility of rates of return on stocks or portfolios in relation to changes in rates of return on the whole market. Also known as market risk, it stems from such non-diversifiable factors as war, inflation, recessions and high interest rates. These factors affect all firms simultaneously; hence this type of risk cannot be eliminated by diversification.

TARGET Trans-European Automated Real-time Gross settlement Express Transfer system, a payment system linking together one real-time gross settlement system in each participating member state in EMU to enable same-day, cross-border transfers throughout the eurozone. TARGET is open 7 a.m.–6 p.m. Central European Time, each TARGET operating day.

Tariffs Taxes imposed by a country on goods imported into it.

Tax break A generic term for specific financial arrangements or instruments that attract an exemption from or reduced liability to different forms of taxation.

Tax haven A country that imposes little or no tax on the profits from transactions carried on or routed through that country, especially income from dividends and interest.

Tax sparing A Euromarket term (mainly) for a debt that is covered by a double exemption from withholding tax, enabling lenders to offer narrow margins over the reference rate.

Teaser rates Low initial rate of interest on a loan, which lasts for a short period, maybe two years, then rises sharply.

Technical analysis A branch of market analysis based upon the study of price movements and the forecasting of future movements from past movements.

Temporal method A foreign currency translation method. The translation rate adopted preserves the accounting principles used to value assets and liabilities in the original financial statements. Thus items stated at historic cost are translated at historic exchange rates: current exchange rates are used for items stated at replacement cost, market value or expected future value.

Tender A method of issuing securities where allotment takes place according to the higher bids received.

Term auction facility (TAF) A USA term for the Fed's auction of term funds to depository institutions with the intention of addressing elevated pressures in short term funding markets.

Term deposits Deposits, including certificates of deposit, for terms longer than sight deposits. *See* Sight deposits.

Term loan or credit A bank advance that is for a specified period of time.

Term structure An explanation of the framework for establishing money-market interest rates based upon cash flows and maturity or holding periods.

Thin A market with low trading volumes and poor liquidity.

Tier I Capital Ratio Requirement for capital adequacy under the Basel Accords. The ratio between a bank's capital and its risk-adjusted assets.

Time value The value of an option taken as the difference between the premium and the intrinsic value. Time value decreases as the expiry date comes nearer.

Tombstone An advertisement placed by banks shortly after a new Eurobond issue to record their part in its management and sale.

Toxic asset The term is best illustrated by an example using a credit default swap. With no default or only a low probability of default, a CDS might have a positive value of, say, 100 based on the expected income stream from insurance-like premiums. But with defaults looming, the worth of the CDS could alter and acquire a negative value as the probability of having to pay out under the CDS exceeds the probability of receiving inflows (the insurance premiums). The asset, previously worth 100 in this example, may become a liability worth minus 500. The description toxic asset, also known as toxic debt, is truly justified.

Traded option An option that is itself tradable on a securities market.

Tranche One of several levels to a security with different risk/reward characteristics for each level.

Transaction date In foreign exchange markets the date on which a foreign exchange contract is agreed.

Transaction exposure The extent to which a given exchange rate change will affect the value of transactions denominated in foreign currency.

Transfer price The price at which one affiliate in a group of companies sells goods or services to another affiliated unit.

Translation exposure *See* Accounting exposure.

Treasury bill or T-bill A UK or US government short-term debt instrument normally issued at a discount.

Treasury note A US government coupon security with a maturity of not less than one year and not more than ten years.

Triangulation When converting from one national currency unit within EMU to another, the conversion must be done via the euro. This method is known as triangulation.

Trillion One thousand billion.

Turn The difference between the bid and offer prices quoted by an individual market-maker.

Uncovered interest arbitrage A process of borrowing a currency and converting it to a second currency where it is invested. The arbitrageur aims to earn profit from the relative interest rates received and paid. Unlike covered interest arbitrage, the currency in which the arbitrageur invests is not sold forward; instead the arbitrageur waits until the maturity of the investment and then sells the second currency spot for the original currency. Also, unlike covered interest arbitrage, the uncovered version is risky.

Undated A security which has no definite maturity date, but may be redeemed at the discretion of the issuer.

Underlying asset The asset on which an option or warrant is based.

Underlying security The security on which an option or futures contract is written.

Undervalued A security, rather than a market, whose price is considered to be lower than that indicated by fundamentals.

Underwater mortgage A mortgage in which the outstanding mortgage balance due exceeds the current market value of the property securing the mortgage.

Underwrite Undertake to buy unsubscribed securities on a given date at a particular price, thus guaranteeing the full proceeds to the borrower.

Underwriting agreement This states the obligations of each of the sub-underwriters to the managers of a security issue.

Underwriting group Bankers who receive a commission for underwriting a new issue.

Unsecured Bonds that entitle the holder to no recourse to specific assets in the case of default.

Unsystematic risk That part of a security's risk associated with random events which do not affect the economy as a whole. Also known as specific risk, this refers to such things as strikes, successful and unsuccessful marketing programmes, fire and other events that are unique to a particular firm. Such unsystematic events can be eliminated by portfolio diversification.

Value at risk (VAR) A single number estimate of how much a company can lose due to the price volatility of the instrument it holds, for example, a fixed rate bond or an unhedged currency payable/receivable. More precisely, it defines the likelihood of potential loss not exceeding a particular level, given certain assumptions.

Value date The date on which payment is made to settle a deal. A spot foreign exchange deal on Wednesday will be settled on Friday, so Friday is the value date.

VAR *See* Value at risk.

Variance of the probability distribution The expected value of squared deviation from the expected return.

Variation margin Generally, the funds required to bring the equity in an account back up to the initial margin level. Used in the futures market where margin trading is permitted.

Vendor placing The sale of equity which has been issued in settlement of the cost of an acquisition of assets, with the objective of ensuring that the vendor of the assets so acquired receives cash instead of paper.

Volatility The variability of movements in a security's price.

Warehousing Entering into a swap without having entered into a matching swap, but with the expectation of hedging either through a matched swap or a portfolio of swaps.

Warrant A negotiable instrument granting the holder an option to subscribe for new equity in the issuing company at a predetermined price.

Window A time during which certain deals can occur because of particular market conditions. For example, it may be possible to issue certain types of security because of ruling investor sentiment that is not expected to last.

Window dressing An accounting device used to make financial ratios look better. For example assume a firm with assets of 100, debt of 60 and equity of 40. Its debt to equity ratio is 60 to 40, that is 1.5. If, just before the year end the firm uses some assets temporarily to repay debt but to reverse the transaction immediately following the year end, its debt to equity ratio at the year-end falls. Assume the amounts involved in the window dressing are 30 of assets and 30 of debt, then the year-end figures are assets amounting to 70 financed by debt of 30 and equity of 40. The debt to equity ratio has now fallen and is 30 to 40, that is 0.75. The ratio has been cut in half. An apparently much more respectable ratio – but really just smoke and mirrors.

Withholding tax A tax collected by the source originating the income as opposed to one paid by the recipient of the income after the funds are received. Thus a withholding tax on interest payments to foreigners means that the tax proceeds are deducted from the interest payment made to the lender and are collected by the borrower on behalf of the tax authorities.

World Trade Organization (WTO) The WTO is an international organisation that sets and enforces rules designed to facilitate cross-border transactions in goods and services.

Yankee bond A US dollar-denominated bond issue made in the US market by a foreign (non-US) borrower.

Yield The amount of interest payments as a percentage of the amount lent or borrowed.

Yield curve A diagrammatic representation of interest rates prevailing on a class of securities that are alike in every respect other than term to maturity. A yield curve may slope upwards or downwards or be flat.

Yield to maturity That discount rate which equates the sum of the present value of the future stream of income payments and the present value of the principal repayment at maturity with the market value of a security.

Zero-coupon bond A bond that bears no annual interest charge but is, instead, sold at such a discount as will result in the rolled-up interest cost being settled by its redemption at par.

Zero-coupon swap A swap in which a fixed rate payer makes a single payment, on the maturity date, and the other party makes payments periodically.

Zero-sum game A game, or market, in which the sum of the gains made by winning players is equal to the sum of the losses of losing players.

Notes

Chapter 1

1 Auger, P., *The Greed Merchants*, Penguin Group, 2005.
2 Kay, J., 'What a Carve Up', *Financial Times*, 1/2 August, 2009.
3 In this book, unless otherwise stated, '$' will always refer to US dollars. One billion means one thousand million. One trillion refers to one thousand billion.
4 According to the Bank of International Settlement Triennial Central Bank Survey published in 2010.
5 The author is in no way quietly suggesting a resurgence of the Ptolemaic view of the heavens in preference to the Copernican theory. He merely feels that the above form of words far better conveys the message than saying 'as the earth moves around the sun'!
6 These data also come from the Bank of International Settlements Triennial Central Bank Survey of 2010.

Chapter 2

1 Triffin, R., *Gold and the Dollar Crisis*, Yale University Press, New Haven, CN, 1960.

Chapter 3

1 'Agio' means the sum payable for the convenience of exchanging one kind of money for another. The term originally derived from Italian money lending in the Middle Ages.
2 Some textbooks state the interest rate parity formula as:

$$\frac{f_0}{s_0} = \frac{1+i_\$}{1+i_£}$$

This is perfectly correct and is merely an adaptation of the formulation used in this book.
3 Like all laws in the social sciences, we should not give this one status of immutability.
4 Williamson, J., 'Estimates of FEERs', in J. Williamson (ed.), *Estimating Equilibrium Exchange Rates*, Institute for International Economics, Washington, DC, 1994.
5 Balassa, B., 'The purchasing power doctrine: a reappraisal', *Journal of Political Economy*, 72, 584–96, 1964.
6 Samuelson, P.A., 'Analytical notes on international real-income measures', *Economic Journal*, 595–608, 1974.
7 Taylor, J.B., 'Discretion versus policy rules in practice', *Carnegie-Rochester Conference Series on Public Policy*, 39, 195–214, 1993.
8 Ong, L.L., *The Big Mac Index: Applications of Purchasing Power Parity*, Palgrave Macmillan, London, 2003.

Chapter 4

1 Always remember that in the real world the exact number of days must be used rather than months. For simplification purposes, we use months throughout this book.

Chapter 6

1 Meese, R., 'Currency fluctuations in the post-Bretton Woods era', *Journal of Economic Perspectives*, 4 (1), 117–34, 1990.
2 Frenkel, J.A. and Froot, K.A., 'Chartists, fundamentalists and trading in the foreign exchange market', *American Economic Review*, 80 (2), 181–5, 1990.
3 Murenbeeld, M., 'Economics for forecasting exchange rate changes', *Columbia Journal of World Business*, Summer, 1975.
4 If one were to use the model, one should study the original Murenbeeld article to obtain the exact definitions of UNEM, M and G.
5 Bilson, J.F.O., 'Leading indicators of currency devaluation', *Columbia Journal of World Business*, 14 (4), 62–76, 1979.
6 The Marshall–Lerner condition states that, if the sum of the elasticities of demand for a country's exports and that for its imports exceeds unity, then a devaluation will have a positive effect upon its trade balance. Alternatively, if the sum of these elasticities is less than 1 then revaluation should improve the trade balance. The Marshall–Lerner model is built upon a number of grossly simplifying assumptions.
7 Mundell, R.A., *International Economics*, Macmillan, London, 1967.
8 Fleming, J.M., 'Domestic financial policies under fixed and flexible rates', *IMF Staff Papers*, November, 1962.
9 Dornbusch, R., 'Expectations and exchange rate dynamics', *Journal of Political Economy*, 84, 1161–76, 1976.

10 Driskill, R.A., 'Exchange rate dynamics: an empirical investigation', *Journal of Political Economy*, 89 (2), 357–71, 1981.
11 Papell, D.H., 'Activist monetary policy, imperfect capital mobility, and the overshooting hypothesis', *Journal of International Economics*, May, 1985.
12 Levin, J.H., 'Trade flow lags, monetary fiscal policy and exchange rate overshooting', *Journal of International Money and Finance*, 5 (4), 485–95, 1986.
13 Almeida, A., Goodhart, C. and Payne, R., 'The effects of macroeconomic news on high frequency exchange rate behaviour', *Journal of Financial and Quantitative Analysis*, 33 (3), 383–408, 1998.
14 Bosner-Neal, C. Roley, V.V. and Sellon, G.H. Jr., 'Monetary policy actions, intervention and exchange rates: a re-examination of the empirical relationships using federal funds rate target data', *Journal of Business*, April, 147–77, 1998.
15 Beckman, R.C., 'Share Price Analysis', *Investors Bulletin*, London, 1969.
16 Triana, P., *Lecturing Birds on Flying*, John Wiley and Sons Inc., 2009.
17 Dimson, E., Marsh, P. and Staunton, M., *Triumph of the Optimists*, Princeton University Press, Princeton, NJ, 2002.
18 Rogoff, K., 'The purchasing power parity puzzle', *Journal of Economic Literature*, June, 34, 647–68, 1996.
19 Taylor, M.P. and Peel, D.A., 'Nonlinear adjustment, long-run equilibrium and exchange rate fundamentals', *Journal of International Money and Finance*, 19 (1), 33–53, 2000.
20 Buckley, A., *Multinational Finance*, 5th edition, FT Prentice Hall, 2004.
21 MacDonald, R., *Exchange Rate Economics: Theories and Evidence*, Routledge, 2007.
22 Copeland, L., *Exchange rates and International Finance*, 5th edition, Pearson Education, 2008.
23 Pilbeam, K., *International Finance*, 3rd edition, Palgrave Macmillan, 2005.
24 Feenstra, R.C. and Taylor, A.M., *International Economics*, Worth Publishers, 2008.
25 Robinson, B. and Warburton, P., 'Managing currency holdings: lessons from the floating period', *London Business School Economic Outlook*, 4 (5), 18–27, 1980.
26 Bell, S. and Kettell, B., *Foreign Exchange Handbook*, Graham & Trotman, London, 1983.
27 Madura, J. and Nosari, E.J., 'Speculative trading in the Eurocurrency market', *Alron Business and Economic Review*, 15 (4), 48–52, 1984.
28 Hodrick, R.J., *The Empirical Evidence of the Efficiency of Forward and Futures Foreign Exchange Markets*, Harwood, Chur, Switzerland, 1987.
29 Taylor, D., 'Official intervention in the foreign exchange market, or, bet against the central bank', *Journal of Political Economy*, 90 (2), 356–68, 1982.

Chapter 8

1 Srinivasula, S.L., 'Classifying foreign exchange exposure', *Financial Executive*, February, 36–44, 1983.
2 Griffin, P., *FASB Statement No. 8:A review of empirical research on its economic consequences*, Graduate School of Business, Stanford University Research Report, No. 482, January, 1979.
3 Makin, J.H., 'Flexible exchange rates, multinational corporations and accounting standards', *Federal Reserve Bank of San Francisco Economic Review*, Fall, 44–5, 1977.
4 Dukes, R.E., *An Empirical Investigation of the Effect of Statement of Financial Accounting Standard No. 8 on Security Return Behaviour*, FASB, 1978.
5 Garlicki, D.T., Fabozzi, F.J. and Fonfeder, R., 'The impact of earnings with FASB 52 on equity returns', *Financial Management*, Autumn, 36–44, 1987.
6 Giddy, I.H., 'What is FAS No. 8's effect on the market valuation of corporate stock prices?', *Business International Money Report*, 26 May, 1978.
7 Aliber, R.Z., *The International Money Game*, 4th edition, Macmillan, London, 1983.

Chapter 9

1 Adler, M., 'Translation methods and operational foreign exchange risk management', in G. Bergendahl (ed.), *International Financial Management*, Norstedts, Stockholm, 1982.
2 Makin, J., 'Discussion', *Journal of Finance*, May, 440–2, 1981.
3 Logue, D.E. and Oldfield, G.S., 'Managing foreign assets when foreign exchange markets are efficient', *Financial Management*, Summer, 16–22, 1977.
4 Adler, M., 'Translation methods and operational foreign exchange risk management', in G. Bergendahl (ed.), *International Financial Management*, Norstedts, Stockholm, 1982.
5 Modigliani, F. and Miller, M.H., 'The cost of capital, corporation finance and the theory of investment', *American Economic Review*, 48, 261–97, 1958.
6 Aliber, R.Z., *Exchange Risk and Corporate International Finance*, Wiley, New York, 1979.
7 Feizer, G. and Jacquillat, B., *International Finance: Text and Cases*, Allyn and Bacon, Boston, MA, 1981.
8 Dufey, G. and Srinivasulu, S.L., 'The case for corporate management of foreign exchange risk', *Financial Management*, Winter, 54–62, 1983.

9 Shapiro, A.C. and Rutenberg, D.P., 'Managing exchange risks in a floating world', *Financial Management*, Summer, 48–58, 1976.

10 Dufey, G. and Srinivasulu, S.L., 'The case for corporate management of foreign exchange risk', *Financial Management*, Winter, 54–62, 1983.

11 Abuaf, N., 'The nature and management of foreign exchange risk', *Midland Corporate Finance Journal*, 4 (3), 1988, in J.M. Stern and D.H. Chew Jr. (eds) (1988), *New Developments in International Finance*, Basil Blackwell, Oxford, 1988.

12 Rawls III, S.W. and Smithson, C.W., 'Strategic risk management', *Journal of Applied Corporate Finance*, 2 (4), 6–18, 1990.

13 Ross, D., Clark, I. and Taiyeb, S., *International Treasury Management*, Woodhead-Faulkner, Cambridge, 1987.

14 McRae, T. and Walker, F., *Foreign Exchange Management*, Prentice Hall, London, 1980.

15 Jenkins, R.L., *Corporate Management of Exchange Rate Misalignment – the Experience of UK Firms 1972–82, 1987–92*, unpublished PhD Thesis, London University, London, 1995.

16 Oxelheim, L. and Wihlborg, C., *Macroeconomic Uncertainty: International Risks and Opportunities for the Corporation*, Wiley, Chichester, 1987. Oxelheim, L. and Wihlborg, C., 'Competitive exposure: taking the global view', *Euromoney Corporate Finance*, February, 1989. Oxelheim, L. and Wihlborg, C., 'Taking the sting out of economic exposure', *Euromoney Corporate Finance*, March, 1989.

17 Oxelheim, L. and Wihlborg, C., *Macroeconomic Uncertainty: International Risks and Opportunities for the Corporation*, Wiley, Chichester, 1987. Oxelheim, L. and Wihlborg, C., 'Competitive exposure: taking the global view', *Euromoney Corporate Finance*, February, 1989. Oxelheim, L. and Wihlborg, C., 'Taking the sting out of economic exposure', *Euromoney Corporate Finance*, March, 1989.

18 Mandelbrot, Benoit B., *The (Mis)Behaviour of Markets*, Profile Books, 2005.

19 Triana, P., *Lecturing Birds on Flying*, John Wiley and Sons Inc., 2009.

20 Lanchester, J., *Whoops*, Penguin Group, 2010.

Chapter 10

1 McRae, T. and Walker, F., *Foreign Exchange Management*, Prentice Hall, London, 1980.

Chapter 14

1 The terms *buyer*, *owner* and *holder* are used interchangeably.

2 Note that the options are both European. An American put must sell for more than €11 (€55 – €44). That is, if the price of an American put is only €7, one would buy the put, buy the share and exercise immediately, generating arbitrage profit of €4 (–€7 – €44 + €55).

3 However, the formula is applicable only when both the put and the call have the same expiration date and the same exercise price.

4 It should be noted that this lower bound is strictly true for an American option, but not for a European one.

5 This relationship need not hold for a European call option. Consider a firm with two otherwise identical European call options, one expiring at the end of May and the other expiring a few months later. Further assume that a *huge* dividend is paid in early June. If the first call is exercised at the end of May, its holder will receive the underlying share. If he or she does not sell the share, he would receive the large dividend shortly thereafter. However, the holder of the second call will receive the share through exercise after the dividend is paid. Because the market knows that the holder of this option will miss the dividend, the value of the second call option could be less than the value of the first.

6 This graph assumes that, for each security, the exercise price is equal to the expected share price. This assumption is employed merely to facilitate the discussion. It is not needed to show the relationship between a call's value and the volatility of the underlying share.

7 Black, F. and Scholes, M., 'The valuation of option contracts and a test of market efficiency', *Journal of Finance*, 27, 399–418, 1972.

8 Black, F. and Scholes, M., 'The pricing of options and corporate liabilities', *Journal of Political Economy*, 81 (3), 637–59, 1973.

9 Taleb, N.N., *The Black Swan*, Penguin Group, 2008.

10 Triana, P., *Lecturing Birds on Flying*, John Wiley and Sons Inc., 2009.

11 Wilmott, P., *Derivatives*, John Wiley, Chichester, 1998.

Chapter 15

1 Lewis, M., *Liar's Poker*, Hodder and Staughton, 1989.

2 Garman, M.B. and Kohlhagen, S.W., 'Foreign currency option values', *Journal of International Money and Finance*, 2, 231–7, 1983.

3 Leland, H.E., *Option Pricing and Replication with Transactions Costs*, Working Papers, No. 144, Institute of Business and Economic Research, University of California, Berkeley, 1984.

4 Cox, J., Ross, S. and Rubinstein, M., 'Option pricing: a simplified approach', *Journal of Financial Economics*, 7, 229–64, 1979.

5 Cox, J.C. and Rubinstein, M., *Options Markets*, Prentice Hall, Englewood Cliffs, NJ, 1985.
6 Barone-Adesi, G. and Whaley, R., 'Efficient analytic approximation of American option values', *Journal of Finance*, June, 301–20, 1987.
7 Tucker, A., Madura, J. and Chiang, T.C., *International Financial Markets*, West Publishing Co., St. Paul, MN, 1991.
8 Buckley, A., *Multinational Finance*, 5th edition, FT Prentice Hall, 2004.
9 Rubinstein, M., 'Implied binomial trees', *Journal of Finance*, 49 (3), 771–818, 1994.
10 Tucker, A. and Pond, L., 'The probability distribution of foreign exchange price changes: tests of candidate processes', *Review of Economics and Statistics*, November, 638–64, 1988.
11 Tucker, A., 'Exchange rate jumps and currency options pricing', in S. Khoury and R. Haugen (eds), *Recent Developments in International Banking and Finance*, Lexington Books, Lexington, MA, 1990.

Chapter 16

1 Hicks, J.R., *Value and Capital: An Enquiry into some Fundamental Principles of Economic Theory*, 2nd edition, Oxford University Press, Oxford, 1946.
2 Modigliani, F. and Sutch, R., 'Innovations in interest rate policy', *American Economic Review*, May, 178–97, 1966.

Chapter 17

1 Smithson, C.W., 'A LEGO approach to financial engineering: an introduction to forwards, futures, swaps and options', *Midland Corporate Finance Journal*, 5 (4), 16–28, 1987.
2 Black, F., 'The pricing of commodity contracts', *Journal of Financial Economics*, 3, 167–79, 1976.
3 Black, F. and Scholes, M., 'The pricing of options and corporate liabilities', *Journal of Political Economy*, 81 (3), 637–59, 1973.
4 Smithson, C.W., 'A LEGO approach to financial engineering: an introduction to forwards, futures, swaps and options', *Midland Corporate Finance Journal*, 5 (4), 16–28, 1987.

Chapter 18

1 Buckley, A., *Financial Crisis*, FT Prentice Hall, 2011.
2 McDonald, L., *A Colossal Failure of Common Sense*, Ebury Press, 2009.
3 Tett, G., *Fool's Gold*, Little Brown, 2009.
4 Salmon, F., 'Recipe for Disaster: The Formula that Killed Wall Street', *Wired Magazine*, 23 February 2009.
5 David X. Li, 'On Default Correlation: A Copula Function Approach', *Journal of Fixed Income*, 9, 43–54, 2000.
6 Johnson, S. and Kwak, J., *13 Bankers*, Pantheon Books, 2010.
7 Partnoy, F., *F.I.A.S.C.O.*, Profile Books, 1997.
8 Mandelbrot, Benoit B., *The (Mis)Behaviour of Markets*, Profile Books, 2005.
9 Taleb, N.N., *The Black Swan*, Penguin Group, 2008.
10 Triana, P., *Lecturing Birds on Flying*, John Wiley and Sons Inc., 2009.
11 Cassidy, J., *How Markets Fail*, Penguin Group, 2009.
12 Lewis, M., *The Big Short*, Penguin Group, 2010.
13 Zuckerman, G., *The Greatest Trade Ever*, Penguin, 2010.
14 US Senate permanent subcommittee on investigations, *Wall Street and the Financial Crisis: Anatomy of a Financial Collapse*, Cosimo Reports, 2011.

Chapter 19

1 Buckley, A., *Financial Crisis*, FT Prentice Hall, 2011.
2 Financial Crisis Inquiry Report, *Public Affairs*, New York, 2011.
3 Acharya, V.V., Richardson, M., van Nieuweburgh, S. and White, L.J., *Guaranteed to Fail*, Princeton University Press, 2011.
4 Buckley, A., *Financial Crisis*, FT Prentice Hall, 2011.
5 Kindleburger, C.P., *Manias, Panics and Crashes*, 3rd edition, John Wiley and Sons Inc., 1996.
6 Carmen M. Reinhart and Kenneth S. Rogoff, *This Time is Different*, Princeton University Press, 2009.
7 Mundell, R.A., 'A Theory of Optimal Currency Areas', *American Economic Review*, 51, 657–65, 1961.
8 Carmen M. Reinhart and Kenneth S. Rogoff, *This Time is Different*, Princeton University Press, 2009.
9 Story, L., Thomas Jr, L. and Schwartz, N.D., 'Wall St. helped to mask debt fueling Europe's crisis', *The New York Times*, 13 February 2010.

Chapter 20

1 Johanson, J. and Vahlne, J., 'The internationalization process of the firm: a model of knowledge development on increasing foreign commitments', *Journal of International Business Studies*, 8 (1), 23–32, 1977.
2 Luostarinen, R., *The Internationalization of the Firm*, Acta Academic Oeconomica Helsingiensis, Helsinki, 1977.
3 Welch, L.S. and Luostarinen, R., 'Internationalization: evolution of a concept', *Journal of General Management*, 14 (2), 34–5, 1988.
4 Hymer, S.H., *The International Operations of National Firms: A Study of Direct Foreign Investment*, MIT Press, Cambridge, MA, 1960.

5 Kindleberger, C.P., *American Business Abroad: Six Lectures on Direct Investment*, Yale University Press, New Haven, CT, 1969.

6 Dunning, J.H., *Multinational Enterprises, Economic Structure and International Competitiveness*, John Wiley, Chichester, 1985.

7 Michalet, C.A. and Chevalier, T., 'France', in J.H. Dunning (ed.), *Multinational Enterprises, Economic Structure and International Competitiveness*, Wiley, Chichester, 1985.

8 Giddy, I.H., 'The demise of the product cycle model in international business theory', *Colombia Journal of World Business*, 13 (1), 90–7, 1978.

9 Hymer, S.H., *The International Operations of National Firms: A Study of Direct Foreign Investment*, MIT Press, Cambridge, MA, 1960.

10 Kindleberger, C.P., *American Business Abroad: Six Lectures on Direct Investment*, Yale University Press, New Haven, CT, 1969.

11 Knickerbocker, F.T., *Oligopolistic Reaction and Multinational Enterprise*, Harvard University Press, Boston, MA, 1973.

12 McClain, D., 'Foreign direct investment in the United States: old currents, new waves, and the theory of direct investment', in C.P. Kindleberger and D.B. Audretsch (eds), *The Multinational Corporation in the 1980s*, MIT Press, Cambridge, MA, pp. 278–333, 1983.

13 Porter, M.E., *Competitive Strategy: Techniques for Analysing Industries and Competitors*, Free Press, New York, 1980. Porter, M.E., *Competitive Advantage: Creating and Sustaining Superior Performance*, Free Press, New York, 1985.

14 Bain, J.S., *Barriers to New Competition*, Harvard University Press, Boston, MA, 1956.

15 Coase, R.H., 'The nature of the firm', *Economica*, 4, 386–405, 1937.

16 Rugman, A.M., *Inside the Multinationals: The Economics of Internal Markets*, Columbia University Press, New York, 1981.

17 Vernon, R., *Storm over the Multinationals*, Harvard University Press, Cambridge, MA, 1977.

18 Hennart, J.F., 'Upstream vertical integration in the aluminium and tin industries', *Journal of Economic Behaviour and Organization*, 9, 281–99, 1988.

19 Buckley, P.J., 'New theories of international business: some unresolved issues', in M.C. Casson (ed.), *The Growth of International Business*, Allen & Unwin, London, 1983.

20 Casson, M.C., 'Transaction costs and the theory of the multinational enterprise', in A.M. Rugman (ed.), *New Theories of the Multinational Enterprise*, St. Martin's Press, New York, 1982.

21 Kay, N.M., 'Multinational enterprises: a review article', *Scottish Journal of Political Economy*, 30 (3), 304–12, 1983.

22 Rugman, A.M., 'New theories of the multinational enterprise: an assessment of internalization theory', *Bulletin of Economic Research*, 39 (2), 101–18, 1986.

23 Coase, R.H., 'The nature of the firm', *Economica*, 4, 386–405, 1937.

24 Buckley, P.J. and Casson, M., *The Future of the Multinational Enterprise*, Macmillan, London, 1976.

25 McManus, J.P., 'The theory of the international firm', in G. Paquet (ed.), *The Multinational Firm & the Nation State*, Collier-Macmillan, Toronto, 1972.

26 Williamson, O.E., *Markets and Hierarchies: Analysis and Antitrust Implications*, Free Press, New York, 1975. Williamson, O.E., 'Transaction cost economics: the governance of contractual relations', *Journal of Law and Economics*, 22 (2), 233–62, 1979.

27 Teece, D.J., *The Multinational Corporation and the Resource Cost of International Technology Transfer*, Bellinger, Cambridge, MA, 1976.

28 Coase, R.H., 'The nature of the firm', *Economica*, 4, 386–405, 1937.

29 Buckley, P.J. and Casson, M., *The Future of the Multinational Enterprise*, Macmillan, London, 1976.

30 Giddy, I.H., 'The demise of the product cycle model in international business theory', *Colombia Journal of World Business*, 13 (1), 90–7, 1978.

31 Magee, S.P., *The Appropriability Theory of Multinational Corporation Behaviour*, University of Reading Discussion Papers in International Investment and Business Studies, No. 51, Reading, 1981.

32 Rugman, A.M., 'Internationalization as a general theory of foreign direct investment', *Weltwirtschaftliches Archiv*, 116, 365–79, 1980.

33 Teece, D.J., 'Transaction cost economics and the multinational enterprise', *Journal of Economic and Business Organization*, 7, 21–45, 1986.

34 Hennart, J.F., 'Upstream vertical integration in the aluminium and tin industries', *Journal of Economic Behaviour and Organization*, 9, 281–99, 1988. Hennart, J.F., 'The transaction cost theory of the multinational enterprise', in C.N. Pitelis and R. Sugden (eds), *The Nature of the Transnational Firm*, Routledge, London, 1991.

35 Hood, N. and Young, S., *The Economics of Multinational Enterprise*, Longman, London, 1979.

36 Ronstadt, R., *Research and Development Abroad by US Multinationals*, Praeger, New York, 1977.

37 Lall, S., 'The international allocation of research activity by US multinationals', *Oxford Bulletin of Economics and Statistics*, 41, 313–32, 1979.

38 Vernon, R., 'International investment and international trade in the product cycle', *Quarterly Journal of Economics*, 80, 190–207, 1966. Vernon, R., *Storm over the Multinationals*, Harvard University Press, Cambridge, MA, 1977.
39 Wells, L.T., Jr. (ed.), *The Product Life Cycle and International Trade*, Harvard University Press, Boston, MA, 1972.
40 Vernon, R., 'International investment and international trade in the product cycle', *Quarterly Journal of Economics*, 80, 190–207, 1966.
41 Vernon, R., *Storm over the Multinationals*, Harvard University Press, Cambridge, MA, 1977.
42 Giddy, I.H., 'The demise of the product cycle model in international business theory', *Colombia Journal of World Business*, 13 (1), 90–7, 1978.
43 Dunning, J.H., 'Trade location of economic activity and the multinational enterprise: a search for an eclectic approach', in B. Ohlin, P.O. Hesselborn and P.M. Wijkman (eds), *The International Allocation of Economic Activity*, Macmillan, London, 1977. Dunning, J.H., *Explaining International Production*, HarperCollins, London, 1988. Dunning, J.H., 'The eclectic paradigm of international production: a restatement and some possible extensions', *Journal of International Business Studies*, 19 (1), 1–31, 1988.
44 Kojima, K., *Direct Foreign Investment: A Japanese Model of Multinational Business Operations*, Croom Helm, London, 1978.
45 Dunning, J.H. and Archer, H., *The Eclectic Paradigm and the Growth of UK Multinational Enterprises 1870–1983*, University of Reading Discussion Papers in International Investment and Business Studies, No. 109, 1987.
46 Hood, N. and Young, S., *The Economics of Multinational Enterprise*, Longman, London, 1979.
47 Casson, M.C., 'Transaction costs and the theory of the multinational enterprise', in A.M. Rugman (ed.), *New Theories of the Multinational Enterprise*, St. Martin's Press, New York, 1982.
48 Porter, M.E., 'Changing patterns of international competition', *California Management Review*, 28 (2), 9–39, 1986; in H. Vemon-Wortzel and L.H. Wortzel (eds), *Global Strategic Management: The Essentials*, 2nd edition, Wiley, New York, 1991.
49 Levitt, T., 'The globalization of markets', *Harvard Business Review*, 61 (3), 92–102, 1983.
50 Stopford, J.M. and Turner, L., *Britain and the Multinationals*, Wiley, Chichester, 1985.
51 Cvar, M.R., 'Case studies in global competition: patterns of success and failure', in M.E. Porter (ed.), *Competition in Global Industries*, Harvard Business School, Boston, MA, 1986.
52 von Neumann, J. and Morgenstern, O., *The Theory of Games and Economic Behaviour*, Princeton University Press, Princeton, NJ, 1944.
53 Oster, S.M., *Modern Competitive Analysis*, Oxford University Press, Oxford, 1990.
54 Knickerbocker, F.T., *Oligopolistic Reaction and Multinational Enterprise*, Harvard University Press, Boston, MA, 1973.
55 Graham, E.M., 'Exchange of threat between multinational firms as an infinitely repeated non-cooperative game', *International Trade Journal*, 4 (3), 259–77, 1990.
56 Porter, M.E., *Competitive Advantage: Creating and Sustaining Superior Performance*, Free Press, New York, 1985.
57 Helpman, E. and Krugman, P., *Market Structure and Foreign Trade*, MIT Press, Cambridge, MA, 1985.
58 Porter, M.E., *The Competitive Advantage of Nations*, Macmillan, London, 1990.
59 Porter, M.E., *The Competitive Advantage of Nations*, Macmillan, London, 1990.
60 Buckley, A., *Multinational Finance*, 5th edition, Prentice Hall, London, 2004.
61 Feenstra, R.C. and Taylor, A.M., *International Economics*, Worth Publishing, 2008.

Chapter 21

1 Buckley, A., *Multinational Finance*, 2nd edition, Prentice Hall, London, 1992.
2 Hodder, J.E. and Senbet, L.W., 'International capital structure equilibrium', *Journal of Finance*, 45 (5), 1495–1516, 1990.

Chapter 22

1 Bonbright, J.C., *The Valuation of Property*, McGraw-Hill, New York, 1937.
2 Modigliani, F. and Miller, M.H., 'The cost of capital, corporation finance and the theory of investment', *American Economic Review*, 48, 261–97, 1958. Modigliani, F. and Miller, M.H., 'Taxes and the cost of capital: a correction', *American Economic Review*, 53, 433–43, 1963.
3 Myers, S.C., 'Interactions of corporate financing and investment decisions – implications for capital budgeting', *Journal of Finance*, 29, 1–25, 1974.
4 Buckley, A., *Multinational Finance*, 5th edition 2004, FT Prentice Hall, 2004.

Chapter 23

1 Shapiro, A.C., 'Capital budgeting for the multinational corporation', *Financial Management*, Spring, 7–16, 1978.

2 Buckley, A., Tse, K., Rijken, H. and Eijgenhuijsen, H., 'Stock market valuation with real options: lessons from Netscape', *European Management Journal*, 20 (5), 512–26, 2002.

3 Buckley, A., *International Capital Budgeting*, Prentice Hall, London, 1996.

Chapter 24

1 Copeland, T., Koller, J. and Murrin, J., *Valuation*, 3rd edition, Wiley, New York, 2000.

2 Fisher, L. and Lorie, J.H., 'Rates of return on investments in common stock: the year by year record, 1926–65', *Journal of Business*, 41 (35), 291–316, 1968.

3 Ritter, L.S. and Urich, T., *The Role of Gold in Consumer Investment Portfolios, Monograph Series in Finance and Economics*, Salomon Brothers Center for the Study of Financial Institutions, Graduate School of Business, New York University, New York, 1984.

4 Dimson, E., Marsh, P., and Staunton, M., *Triumph of the Optimists*, Princeton University Press, Princeton, NJ, 2002.

5 Buckley, A., *Multinational Finance*, 5th edition, FT Prentice Hall, 2004.

6 Thaler, R., 'Giving markets a human dimension', in *Mastering Finance*, FT Pitman Publishing, London, 1998.

7 Fuller, R.J., Huberts, L.C. and Levinson, M.J., 'Returns to E/P strategies higgledy-piggledy growth, analysts' forecast errors and omitted risk factors', *Journal of Portfolio Management*, 19 (2), 13–24, 1993.

8 Severn, A.K., 'Investor evaluation of foreign and domestic risk', *Journal of Finance*, 29, 545–50, 1974.

9 Haegele, M.J., *Exchange Rate Expectations and Security Returns*, PhD Dissertation, University of Pennsylvania, PA, 1974.

10 Agmon, T. and Lessard, D.R., 'Investor recognition of corporate international diversification', *Journal of Finance*, 32, 1049–56, 1977.

11 Aggarwal, R., 'Multinationality and stock market valuation', *Financial Review*, Summer, 45–6, 1977.

12 Hughes, J.S., Logue, D.E. and Sweeney, R.J., 'Corporate international diversification and market assigned measures of risk and diversification', *Journal of Finance and Quantitative Analysis*, 10 (4), 627–37, 1975.

13 Solnik, B., 'Why not diversify internationally rather than domestically?', *Financial Analysts Journal*, 30 (4), 48–54, 1974.

14 Jacquillat, B. and Solnik, B., 'Multinationals are poor tools for international diversification', *Journal of Portfolio Management*, 4 (2), 8–12, 1978.

15 Buckley, A., *Multinational Finance*, 5th edition, FT Prentice Hall, 2004.

16 Roll, R., *Work in Progress Paper*, Whittemore Conference on the International Capital Acquisition Process, May, Amos Tuck School, Dartmouth, 1993.

17 Dimson, E., Marsh, P. and Staunton, M., *Triumph of the Optimists*, Princeton University Press, Princeton, NJ, 2002.

18 Buckley, A., *Multinational Finance*, 5th edition, Prentice Hall, 2004.

19 Lessard, D.R., 'Incorporating country risk in the valuation of offshore projects', *Journal of Applied Corporate Finance*, 9 (3), 52–63, 1996.

20 Godfrey, S. and Espinosa, R., 'A practical approach to calculating costs of equity for investment in emerging markets', *Journal of Applied Corporate Finance*, 9 (3), 80–9, 1996.

21 Erb, C.B., Harvey, C.R. and Viskanta, T.E., 'Country risk and global equity selection', *Journal of Portfolio Management*, 21 (2), 74–83, 1995.

22 Hooke, J.C., *Security Analysis on Wall Street*, John Wiley, New York, NY, 1998.

23 Jacque, L. and Hawawini, G., 'Myths and realities of the global capital market: lessons for financial managers', *Journal of Applied Corporate Finance*, 6 (3), 81–90, 1993.

Chapter 25

1 Nagy, P., *Country Risk*, Euromoney Publications, London, 1984.

2 Haner, F.T., 'Rating investment risks abroad', *Business Horizons*, 22 (2),18–23, 1979.

3 Morgan, J.E., 'A new look at debt rescheduling indicators and models', *Journal of International Business Studies*, Summer, 37–54, 1986.

4 Shapiro, A.C., *Multinational Financial Management*, 7th edition, John Wiley, New York, 2003.

5 Levi, M.D., *International Finance: The Markets and Financial Management of Multinational Business*, 2nd edition, McGraw-Hill, New York, 1990.

Chapter 26

1 Solomon, E., *The Theory of Financial Management*, Columbian University Press, New York, 1963.

2 Modigliani, F. and Miller, M.H., 'The cost of capital, corporation finance and the theory of investment', *American Economic Review*, 48, 261–97, 1958. Modigliani, F. and Miller, M.H., 'Taxes and the cost of capital: a correction', *American Economic Review*, 53, 433–43, 1963.

3 Myers, S.C., 'Interactions of corporate financing and investment decisions – implications for capital budgeting', *Journal of Finance*, 29, 1–25, 1974.

4 Ross, S.A., Westerfield, R.W. and Jaffe, J., *Corporate Finance*, 5th edition, Irwin/McGraw-Hill, New York, NY, 1999.

Chapter 27

1 Lessard, D.R. and Shapiro, A.C., 'Guidelines for global financing choices', *Midland Corporate Finance Journal*, 1 (4), 1983; in J.M. Stern and D.H. Chew Jr. (eds), *New Developments in International Finance*, Basil Blackwell, New York and Oxford, 1988.

2 Adler, M. and Dumas, B., 'The microeconomics of the firm in an open economy', *American Economic Review*, 67 (1), 180–189, 1977. Adler, M. and Dumas, B., 'Default risk and the demand for forward exchange'; in H. Levy and M. Sarnat (eds), *Financial Decision Making under Uncertainty*, Academic Press, London, 1977.

3 Lessard, D.R. and Shapiro, A.C., 'Guidelines for global financing choices', *Midland Corporate Finance Journal*, 1 (4), 1983; in J.M. Stern and D.H. Chew Jr. (eds), *New Developments in International Finance*, Basil Blackwell, New York and Oxford, 1988.

4 Moran, T., *The Politics of Dependence: Copper in Chile*, Princeton University Press, Princeton, NJ, 1974.

5 Buckley, A., *Multinational Finance*, 5th edition, FT Prentice Hall, 2004.

6 Stobaugh, R., 'Financing foreign subsidiaries', *Journal of International Business Studies*, Summer, 1970.

7 Business International, 'Policies or MNCs on debt/equity mix', *Money Report*, 21 September, 319–20, 1979.

8 Stonehill, A.I. and Dullum, K.B., *Internationalising the Cost of Capital*, Wiley, Chichester, 1982.

Chapter 30

1 Lessard, D.R. and Lorange, P., 'Currency changes and management control: resolving the centralization/decentralization dilemma', *Accounting Review*, July, 628–37, 1977.

2 Stewart, G.B., 'A proposal for measuring international performance', *Midland Corporate Finance Journal*, Summer, 56–71, 1983; in J.M. Stern and D.H. Chew Jr. (eds), *New Developments in International Finance*, Basil Blackwell, Oxford, 1988.

3 Lessard, D.R. and Sharp, D., 'Measuring the performance of operations subject to fluctuating exchange rates', *Midland Corporate Finance Journal*, Fall, 18–30, 1984; in J.M. Stern and D.H. Chew Jr. (eds), *New Developments in International Finance*, Basil Blackwell, New York and Oxford, 1988.

4 Carsberg, B., 'FASB 52: Measuring the performance of foreign operations', *Midland Corporate Finance Journal*, 1 (2), 1983; in J.M. Stern and D.H. Chew Jr. (eds), *New Developments in International Finance*, Basil Blackwell, New York and Oxford, 1988.

5 Choi, F. and Czechowicz, J., 'Assessing foreign subsidiary performance: a multinational comparison', *Management International Review*, 4, 14–25, 1983.

6 Persen, W. and Lesig, V., *Evaluating the Performance of Overseas Operations*, Financial Executives Research Foundation, New York, 1980.

7 Meister, I.W., *Managing the International Financial Function*, The Conference Board, New York, 1970.

8 Stobaugh, R.B., 'Financing foreign subsidiaries of US-controlled multinational enterprises', *Journal of International Business Studies*, Summer, 43–64, 1979.

9 Evans, T.G., Folks, W.R. Jr. and Jilling, M., *The Impact of Statement of Financial Accounting Standard No. 8 on the Foreign Exchange Management Practices of American Multinationals: An Economic Impact Study*, FASB, Stamford, CN, 1978.

10 Oxelheim, L., *Foreign Exchange Risk Management in the Modem Company: A Total Perspective*, Scandinavian Institute for Foreign Exchange Research, Stockholm, 1984.

11 Nobes, C. and Parker, R., *Comparative International Accounting*, 11th edition, FT Prentice Hall, 2010.

12 Buckley, A., *Multinational Finance*, 5th edition, FT Prentice Hall, 2004.

13 Buckley, A., *Multinational Finance*, 5th edition, FT Prentice Hall, 2004.

Index

Note: page references in **bold** refer to terms defined in the Glossary.